Ian Tyrrell is senior lecturer in history at the
University of New South Wales. His books include
*Sobering Up: From Temperance to Prohibition in
Antebellum America, 1800–1860.*

Woman's World

Woman's Empire

Woman's World

Woman's Empire

The Woman's

Christian Temperance Union

in International

Perspective, 1880–1930

Ian Tyrrell

The University of North Carolina Press

Chapel Hill and London

© 1991 The University of North Carolina Press

Manufactured in the United States of America

The paper in this book meets the guidelines for permanence
and durability of the Committee on Production Guidelines for
Book Longevity of the Council on Library Resources.

95 94 93 92 91   5 4 3 2 1

Library of Congress Cataloging-in-Publication Data

Tyrrell, Ian R.
    Woman's world/Woman's empire : the Woman's Christian Temperance
Union in international perspective, 1800–1930 / by Ian Tyrrell.
        p.   cm.
    Includes bibliographical references and index.
    ISBN 0-8078-1950-6 (alk. paper)
    1. Woman's Christian Temperance Union—History.   2. Temperance—
United States—Societies, etc.—History.   3. Reformers—United
States—Biography.   4. Feminists—United States—Biography.
I. Title.
HV5227.T97   1991
322.4′4′0973—dc20   90-43246
                                                                      CIP

To Jessica Alice and Ellen Jane Victoria,

women of the twenty-first century

Contents

Illustrations

Preface

More so than in the case of purely national histories, a comparative and international study demands the help of other scholars. I have been especially fortunate. The thanks issued in prefaces often seem ritualistic or clichéd, but this case truly underlines the value and the reality of cooperation in the international academic community. I beg forgiveness from those I have inadvertently failed to mention.

Pride of place goes to a number of Australian libraries, upholding the traditions of higher learning in these times of utilitarian education: Fisher Library at Sydney University; the unsurpassed collections on Australian and Pacific history at the David Scott Mitchell Library, Sydney; and the University of New South Wales Library. In relation to the latter institution, it has been my pleasure to be associated especially with Pam O'Brien and the staff of the Social Sciences and Humanities Library, who obtained so much material by purchase and on interlibrary loan.

Other libraries provided valuable and often indispensable collections. The University of Toronto Library assisted in the microfilming of important periodical sources on the Canadian WCTU. No historian of the international women's movement can afford to neglect the holdings of the Fawcett Library, City of London Polytechnic. Invaluable in my case were the papers of Josephine Butler. Material drawn from the Castle Howard Archives, Yorkshire, England, with the courteous and knowledgeable assistance of Archivist Eeyan Hartley, is used with kind permission of the Honorable Simon Howard. Martin Ridge and the Huntington Library made possible investigations into the history of the nineteenth-century women's movement on a sojourn there during my sabbatical leave in 1982. For New Zealand, thanks to Massey University for collecting the published WCTU sources in a single microfiche collection. Other valuable collections used were at the Schlesinger Library; Widener Library, Harvard University; the Bancroft Library, University of California; the University of California, Los Angeles; the New York Public Library; Boston Public Library; Smith College; the Swarthmore College Peace Collection; National Archives, Washington, D.C.; and the Lilly Library, Indiana University. No librarians, however, provided more generous assistance than those at the Sherrod Library, East Tennessee State University, Johnson City, Tennessee, where the literary remains of Jessie Ackermann are stored. Without the resources of the

British Museum's newspaper and periodical collections at Colindale, the comparative material contained in this book would have been much the poorer. Equally valuable in the final research work was the Library of Congress, whose stacks contain an embarrassment of riches on most aspects of temperance, prohibition, and women's history.

Professor Robin Room, of the University of California, Berkeley, and the Alcohol Research Group, contributed to this project in unforeseen ways. Not only did he track down an important piece of information on a key character, Jessie Ackermann, but by organizing with Susanna Barrows the Social History of Alcohol Conference in Berkeley in 1984, he indirectly provided a forum for my ideas and encouraged me to pursue the theme of internationalism in temperance and alcohol studies. His example of the interaction of historical and sociological study is a fine one for us all. I am also indebted to the commentary upon my paper at that conference by Barbara Epstein. Contacts made there among researchers from Finland (Irma Sulkunen) and Sweden (Per Frånberg) have been particularly valuable; they have patiently answered my inquiries and put up with my ignorance of Scandinavian languages. Another participant, the Canadian scholar Wallace Mills, also generously supplied me with a copy of a paper on African temperance movements that has given me confidence to push further the argument in chapter 7.

The network of historians associated with the *Social History of Alcohol Review* has been of critical importance. Thanks especially to David Fahey of Miami University of Ohio, who provided bibliographical knowledge and generously gave me access to his study of a figure whose career was similar to that of my temperance missionaries, Jessie Forsyth, while that study was still in manuscript form. Like David, Lilian Shiman is a mine of information on the British temperance women, particularly for the period before the 1890s. Most of all, Jack Blocker's fastidious scrutiny of my manuscript was, as always, much appreciated.

Many other scholars answered my inquiries from the blue. Especially generous were two researchers into British women's history: Sandra Holton of Adelaide, South Australia, on the British women's suffrage movement; and Olwen Niessen of the University of Waterloo on the BWTA. Also helpful were Steven Hause (on continental temperance connections and the lack thereof), Charles Debeneditti (whose advice on the peace aspects of this book were appreciated), Calvin Davis (on the same subject), Ruth Bordin, Barbara Strachey, and Patricia Grimshaw.

Craig Simpson and Jack Blocker made valuable comments on a version of chapter 3, delivered at Huron College, London, Ontario, in 1981. At a Latrobe University Department of History seminar in Melbourne in 1985, Anthea Hyslop and others commented on a report of the general themes, to my benefit. Without assistance from Robert Weibe at the inception of this project, I might never have experienced firsthand the delights of WCTU headquarters, especially that marvelous relic, Rest Cottage, nor sampled the excellent library at Northwestern University.

The cooperation of WCTU officials around the world (and that of other temperance organizations) has been essential, since many of the most valuable manuscript records are still in their possession and are not always microfilmed. Millicent Harry of Tasmania, former World's WCTU president, kindly supplied me with counsel on Jessie Ackermann and gave me a sense of the continuity in the World's WCTU work. Staff at the WCTU headquarters made my research trip to Evanston valuable and gave me access to both microfilm and nonmicrofilm sources. Thanks especially to Rosalita Leonard, who endured an untidy scholar and was gracious also in her friendship and hospitality in introducing me to members of the WCTU sorority and to scholars interested in Methodist women's history. Similarly, the Canadian WCTU, through office secretary Mary Smith, gave me open access to their records in Toronto. Both the Southern California WCTU in Los Angeles and the California WCTU in Oakland (the division is a legacy of the Willard period) generously opened their fine collections to a stranger and helped in my appeals for information on the later lives of WCTU missionaries. In Australia, the Victorian WCTU and the Queensland WCTUs provided rich collections to supplement the Mitchell Library holdings. Staff of the United Kingdom Alliance, London, gave me unfettered use of their manuscript and printed sources, including much on the WCTU and its British affiliates. I also wish to thank Lewis Bateman and the editorial staff at the University of North Carolina Press for their patience and their faith in this project.

The University of New South Wales School of History is the source of much of my intellectual inspiration—in this regard I wish especially to thank Max Harcourt, who is as brilliant as ever, and Beverley Kingston for her reading of two chapters and for her general encouragement. But my major intellectual indebtedness is owed to Diane Collins. From her, too, I take the personal sustenance required to labor on (as I also do from my energetic daughters, Jessica Alice and Ellen Jane Victoria, who as yet know nothing about the WCTU). My wife's parents, Ken and Gwenda Payne, provided much needed child care at a number of crucial points; my own mother, Doris Tyrrell, remains a source of pride in demonstrating what women can achieve on their own. In my dedication, I look back, also, to seek inspiration from the women's movement of Frances Willard's century, and forward to that of a vastly different and, I hope, better time to come for women, and for humanity.

Marrickville, N.S.W.
February 6, 1990

Abbreviations

The following abbreviations are used in the text. For additional abbreviations used in the notes, see page 295.

ABCFM	American Board of Commissioners for Foreign Missions
ASL	Anti-Saloon League
BWTA	British Women's Temperance Association
NUWSS	National Union of Women's Suffrage Societies
NWCTU, National WCTU	National Woman's Christian Temperance Union
WCTU	Woman's Christian Temperance Union
WLAA	World League against Alcoholism
WLF	Women's Liberal Federation
WSPU	Women's Social and Political Union
WWCTU, World's WCTU	World's Woman's Christian Temperance Union
YMCA	Young Men's Christian Association
YWCA	Young Women's Christian Association

Woman's World

Woman's Empire

1

Introduction

On the fifteenth of November, 1884, a woman sailed from the city of San Francisco, bound for Honolulu and beyond on board the steamship *Alameda*. Nothing in her demeanor or her departure hinted at the significance of her undertaking. The event itself was inauspicious, marked only by the well-wishes of a few close friends. Yet this woman's journey would touch off one of the most unusual and intriguing episodes in the history of women, in the history of evangelical reform, and in the history of American relations with the rest of the world. Mary Clement Leavitt, a former Boston schoolteacher and the mother of three, had embarked on a mission of reconnaissance on behalf of Frances Willard, the American president of the Woman's Christian Temperance Union. Leavitt left in the knowledge that her voyage was the vital first step toward the creation of an international women's temperance organization.

What she did not know at the time were the epic proportions of the journey she would complete and the extent of the organizing work she would set in motion. The trip across the Pacific to join the hemispheres in battle against all "brain poisons" would eventually take her around the world and involve eight years away from home, much of the time in the company of men alone, rarely in the presence of anyone who spoke the Queen's English, or even the American variety. Women had certainly embarked before on long international trips, and as missionaries had voyaged to exotic lands unprotected by male companions. Some may have gone around the world. But none had, so far as can be ascertained, undertaken so solitary and protracted a journey through so many countries. When Leavitt returned triumphant to Boston and an appointment as honorary World's president of the WCTU in 1891, she was sixty-two and, allegedly, the heroine of a half-million temperance women in five continents. She was, Frances Willard said, "our white ribbon Stanley."[1]

This story is not Leavitt's alone, but that of many women who contributed to the missionary impulse of the WCTU from the 1870s to the 1930s. Only one of these women individually rivaled Leavitt's prodigious feat, but together their efforts made the WCTU an international force in the temperance and women's movements. The World's WCTU had spread to more than forty national affiliates and many more countries by the 1920s, and at its peak in 1927 the organization had 766,000 dues-paying members and claimed a following of more than a million women. Certainly no organization made a more persistent claim to pursue the international aspects of temperance reform. But the WCTU's work also rivaled the achievements of the suffrage movement in the dissemination on an international level of the principles of women's emancipation.[2]

The WCTU was not the largest organization of women in the United States over the period from the 1870s to the 1930s. Nor was it the only women's group operating on an international plane. In their combined impact, the missionary efforts of the various women's boards of the American evangelical churches exceeded the WCTU in financial commitments and in numerical support for international action, certainly after the turn of the century, and probably before as well.[3] The WCTU's missionary work was clearly an outgrowth of this larger social movement and must be seen in the context of missionary developments. Yet the WCTU's emphasis was different and deserves separate treatment.

As the first mass organization among women devoted to social reform, the WCTU's program was more overtly political in its aims and in its effects on women. The WCTU linked the religious and the secular through concerted and far-reaching reform strategies based on applied Christianity. Its focus could never be upon purely gospel work or soul saving, though these remained the foundation of women's temperance. The leavening influence of the White Ribbon movement, exerted through its connections to both church-based evangelism and the more explicitly feminist groups such as the women's suffrage societies and the National Council of Women, made the organization of critical importance in both religion and women's emancipation. Caught between those differing interests, the WCTU exposed on both the national and international levels the inconsistencies and weaknesses of the women's movement as well as its many strengths and achievements.

This influence was often exerted in unexpected ways that have typically been missed by historians because the WCTU has not been put into an intelligible context of religion and reform. The WCTU's international campaigns were not unique. They were, in fact, part of a much larger outreach of American power and culture. A large part of American expansion took the form not of political or even economic penetration but of the spread of institutions and cultural values. The most obvious examples of cultural penetration were the missionary groups but the role of others such as the YMCA and the United Society for Christian Endeavor must never be underestimated.[4] The WWCTU was an integral part of this process and indeed maintained strong ties with these bodies. The Christian Endeavor movement, begun by the Reverend Francis Clark and devoted to revitaliza-

Introduction

tion of the Protestant churches through interdenominational social gospel work, was remarkably similar to the WCTU in its international ambitions, its emphasis on Christian and family values, its elevation of women to a position of equality, and its willingness to tackle all manner of social reforms. This should not be surprising, since Frances Willard addressed Christian Endeavor conferences, and the movement in fact took from her the Do-Everything policy and so extended the WWCTU's influence beyond its own ranks to include many other church people, including many men. This was how the WCTU operated on an international level as part of an interlocking elite of organizations and personnel that created the constituency of Anglo-American internationalism.[5]

The only part of that context of reform that has received much recent attention is "first-wave feminism." Historians have studied the turn-of-the-century women's movement, including the International Woman Suffrage Alliance organized by Carrie Chapman Catt and the various peace initiatives that culminated in the Women's International League for Peace and Freedom after World War I. Ironically, this rehabilitation has ignored the international efforts of the WCTU, even though these were far more extensive and more indicative of the scope and limits of internationalism than any other part of the women's movement except the vast foreign missionary endeavors. Indeed, the various international organizations sponsored principally by the leaders of the American women's movement were often mere letterhead organizations of interest to only a small minority of activists. This criticism was much less true in the case of women's international temperance activity, though the limits to internationalism in the WCTU must still be acknowledged.[6]

One women's group that did take the principles of internationalism very seriously was the YWCA. Because this organization was formally separatist like the WCTU, sent out its own emissaries as did the WCTU, organized a World's YWCA, and promoted international sisterhood, comparisons with the work of temperance women are inevitable. As an expression of the social gospel in action, the YWCAs ultimately proved by the 1920s to be formidable competitors for the energies of young Christian women. Yet it must be remembered that the WWCTU began in the 1880s. The World's YWCA held its first convention in 1898, but the YWCA's international heyday was much later. The overwhelming proportion of its overseas missionary appointments came in the 1920s and beyond, as a recent study shows. The World's WCTU was a pioneer in work later taken up by the YWCA and other social gospel groups.[7]

Feminism's international aspirations were by no means unusual. Temperance, too, had its share of similar ideas. The most grandiosely conceived scheme was undoubtedly that of the WLAA, started after World War I and dedicated to worldwide prohibition. That organization's most recent chronicler finds the WLAA American-dominated and not genuinely international in its scope. But the league did at least illustrate the global ambitions of the American prohibitionist movement and showed that these sentiments went well beyond the WCTU. What has not been noticed, however, is the role of the World's WCTU in providing a model for international activity. Ernest Cherrington, who inspired and directed the league's work, candidly admitted that it was the temperance women who had carried the burden of international organizing in the period from 1876 to 1920. This work his organization hoped to emulate in the 1920s.[8]

Earlier and more formidable competition for the WWCTU among temperance groups came not from the WLAA but from the Good Templars, whose networks of lodges extended over many countries by the 1880s. Through the activities of women like Jessie Forsyth, British-born but a longtime American resident who ended her organizing days in Australia, the Templars provided illustration of persistent internationalist sentiment in temperance circles that supplemented the WWCTU's work. I say supplemented because the Templars and the WWCTU were not antagonistic and mutually exclusive organizations. It can be easily demonstrated that the Templars provided recruits for the WCTU and that through the Templars the influence of the World's WCTU was once again extended beyond its own ranks.[9]

All of these organizations made the WCTU more than an important part of the nineteenth-century international women's temperance movement. The WCTU became, like the Christian Endeavor societies and the YMCA and YWCA, a critical instrument for spreading the American dream. More prosaically and accurately put, the WWCTU constituted an important vehicle for the assertion of the values associated with one kind of American dream at a time of broader economic, political, and cultural expansion of Western societies with which the WCTU could only partly sympathize. The dreams of temperance women that the gospel might soon triumph in heathen lands were endangered by the dreams of merchants who hoped to gain by exporting alcohol to indigenous peoples. Military expansionism also made many in the WCTU uncomfortable. But hostility to aspects of Western cultural penetration could only be discharged by reliance on the extension of European and, specifically, Anglo-American power and by insistence on the values that were deemed to represent the best or truest elements of that culture. The efforts of temperance women to emancipate their sisters from subordination to prevailing customs ironically became enmeshed in the extension of European values and in the domination of large portions of the globe by the imperial powers. The dialectic of internationalism as a concept and the Anglo-American roots of the WCTU's power cannot be escaped in any analysis of the World's work.[10]

Here the WCTU forged its own version of a cultural imperialism. Wil-

5

Introduction

liam T. Stead, the English journalist, gave expression to these aspirations for the creation of an Anglo-American cultural aegis in his *The Americanization of the World* in 1902. Stead, who looked favorably on the women's temperance movement, understood that the WCTU was part of this Americanizing and westernizing process. Enthused Stead: "[The World's WCTU's] indirect influence in compelling women at once to . . . recognize their capacity to serve the State in the promotion of all that tends to preserve the purity and sanctity of the home, has been by no means one of the least contributions which America [has] made to the betterment of the world."[11] To the extent that this process involved the extension of Anglo-American colonial authority or de facto political and military domination over other peoples, the World's WCTU became, from one point of view, culturally imperialistic. But behind that simple and somewhat glib phrase are layers of meaning that must be probed in all of their complexity through the experience of temperance women. As a missionary endeavor, the WCTU could hardly avoid the currents of cultural imperialism that have been analyzed by a variety of historians of the women's missionary movements. The WCTU did seek to assert Western value systems in much the same way as more orthodox missionaries did. That has been the subject of frequent and ironic comment. Some have even suggested that women missionaries were "more culturally imperialistic" than their male counterparts.[12]

History is replete with such ironies in which the dominated become agents of domination. No exception, the history of women's temperance is rooted in the ambiguous implications of the struggle of women to be free. This is not to deny the reality of the physical or economic oppression these temperance women sought to overcome, nor is it to reduce their vast and complex experience to the simplistic formula of personal advantage. The women of the WCTU, in the course of building their movement, constructed a web of institutions and values that purported to unite women in a worldwide sisterhood. The world of women they created did exist in all the richness of its culture, but that very world circumscribed their freedom of action and limited their ability to comprehend the complexities of that other world, with its other cultures and other classes of women. The confrontation of the reformer's conception of how the larger world ought to operate with the tough experience of its material realities and alternative cultural meanings constitutes an important concern in this book.

If cultural imperialism is a predictable theme in the writing on American missionary endeavors, in the case of the WCTU the export of values and institutions was vastly more complicated. Unlike Anglo-American missions, the WCTU proselytized as extensively in Britain and the British empire as in non-Christian lands. Since drinking and associated "vices" were as much if not more commonly associated with European peoples, the notion of the cultural superiority of whites and the Christian religion could not be assumed. WCTU campaigns abroad involved not only hierarchical relations between Europeans and their colonial dependents but also similar relations of power among European nations.

The WCTU enterprise was also complicated, if one wishes to stress the evidence for cultural imperialism, by its assimilationist and universalistic emphasis. Provided one accepted the values of the WCTU, there was nothing to prevent a non-American member from rising to positions of power within the organization. Australian women, at many points the unwitting and uncomprehending victims of cultural penetration that could only truthfully be described as cultural imperialism, became at other times missionaries in the reexport trade, taking the message of abstinence and purity back to the United States and Britain as well as to the nonwhite world. This reciprocity of metropolitan and colonial reform would be manifest in the issue of women's suffrage as well, in which colonies like New Zealand and South Australia outstripped Britain and almost all of the American states.

Nor should the insistence on the dimension of cultural imperialism be taken to mean that the WCTU simply forced its own conception of a superior morality on less fortunate peoples. Collaboration and solicitation always played their parts as the WCTU confronted the non-Anglo-Saxon world. Often it was the non-American and even the non-Western clients who sought to extend the WWCTU's domain, and the leaders of the movement in America were as much the victims of misleading assessments of power and potential at the periphery as they were the instigators of their own illusions. These international relationships the WCTU preferred to describe as evidence of sisterly solidarity, but the WWCTU's genuine egalitarianism was inevitably encased in hierarchical conceptions of evangelical reform. The processes of benevolence created constituencies of givers and receivers locked in reciprocal and unmistakably maternal relations that sat uneasily alongside the commitment to sisterhood.

Although non-Americans and nonwhites became linked in a dependence on American moral power and material largesse, the penetration of WCTU values outside the United States hardly proceeded without obstruction. Quite the contrary. The resilience of different cultures appears as a recurrent theme; so too does the interaction of American women with women and men of markedly different expectations on the liquor question and on the issue of women's emancipation. The lives of these WCTU women were irrevocably altered in the process. They saw much that was honorable and instructive in the lands they hoped to conquer in the name of Christ and sobriety, and they forged bonds of sympathy with their sisters based on a common awareness of their sex's oppression.

But contradictions remained as gigantic fissures in the substance of their enterprise. Any endeavor of a missionary kind faced this stubborn difficulty. Christianity provided the energizing force for the WCTU crusade, and

Introduction

Christianity provided the materials for an antiimperialist critique that surfaced at times in the WCTU and threw up contentious issues that tended to disrupt the worldwide sisterhood. Nonetheless, Christian temperance women could not quite escape the logic of their religious faith. Even those who made the effort faced the equally compelling logic of their peculiar brand of feminism. In their experience, of all nations it was the United States that allowed women greatest latitude in the development of their talents and promised the kind of women's emancipation WCTU women earnestly desired. Thus even the empathetic impulse of a worldwide sorority rooted in a common sense of gender oppression had to contest the unmistakable assault on tradition and patriarchy implicit in the movement's egalitarianism. Ironically, the most progressive elements in the WCTU—who battled against parochialism and held out the hand of friendship to those of other religions in international solidarity—were themselves blind to the political implications of their evangelism. What looked from one point of view to be an unproblematic internationalism became from another angle the extension of Anglo-American cultural hegemony.

The World's WCTU cannot be called anything but a failure if its ultimate goals of a sober and pure world are accepted at face value. The study of failure is, however, not taken seriously enough by professional historians. The worlds of these women were no less interesting because these objectives remained ultimately unrealized. The struggles of Leavitt and those who followed her highlight the importance of internationalism in temperance reform and yet demand that simplistic and uncritical accounts of international temperance efforts offered by participants be closely interrogated. While American historiography boasts a flourishing school of comparative method, the genre of international history, involving larger units than the nation state, remains underdeveloped. The ebb and flow of ideas, institutions, and personnel across national boundaries in the women's international temperance movement promises ground to test approaches that transcend the boundaries of national historiography and qualifies the traditional emphasis on national units, even in comparative analysis.[13]

At the same time, the checkered career of the World's WCTU indicates that the survival of national and local peculiarities must be recognized. For this reason, it is necessary to combine the study of international influences with the comparative history of the WCTU in its different national contexts. Much valuable yet obscure research has been done on the impact of the WCTU in such places as Canada, New Zealand, and Australia. Equally important work on the impact in Britain is well under way, and there are tantalizing hints of the missionary endeavors of temperance women in exciting new studies emerging on American women missionaries abroad.[14] Nothing has been done, however, to integrate these projects and to show the interconnections of the women's temperance movement. Where the issue has been most forcefully addressed, it has been suggested only that temperance was conducted upon an Anglo-American terrain.[15] This Atlantic perspective should not neglect the broader scope of the WCTU's influence and frame of reference, particularly in the colonial outposts of Britain and America and wherever Anglo-American Protestant missionaries penetrated.

Not only does an international and comparative outlook help to reorganize our insights and give new meaning to existing research. In the international work of the WCTU there occurs abundant and rich evidence of the interaction of feminism and culturally imperialistic themes. This exercise entails, among other things, analysis of the commentary on the women's movement and drink questions in the often perceptive accounts of WCTU travelers. Cut loose from their national moorings, these women frequently provided more penetrating insights on the civilizations they visited than on their own. No less interesting was how this information was absorbed by the participants into existing cultural frameworks and their adaptation to diverse experience inhibited.[16]

That these women failed to overcome insuperable obstacles and failed to transcend the limits of their culture in so many instances does not denigrate their effort or deny the irrepressible energy with which they worked out their own version of women's emancipation. If in the process the weight of tradition prevented, in Marx's terms, a revolutionary breakthrough, this testified largely to the circumstances in which all revolutions in human affairs must be wrought. No attempt to create a new order—not even Marx's proletarian revolution—can do so without resort to the language and hence the culture within which the revolution in question takes shape. The dead hand of the past, understood as the cultural tradition and other material circumstances, certainly constrained, therefore, the movements for women's emancipation as much as it continues to shape all egalitarian movements today. The issue of abstract equality was typically situated in the context of the struggle against concrete evils, perceived or real. The struggle against such evils could not but deeply affect the quest for equality. This was the circumstance of the WCTU's appeal and also the source of its failures.

BEFORE PROCEEDING to unravel the story of the WCTU's international endeavors, it is necessary to codify the main organizing principles that govern the themes of this study and that apply as much to the national WCTU's history as to its international manifestations. Recent scholarship has understandably emphasized the role of Frances Willard, the period from 1879 to 1898 that she dominated, and the feminist or quasi-feminist content of the movement. This book could hardly deny Willard's influence, stature, or charisma, but it is important to recognize that the WCTU was a vast and complex organization and that the role of Willard can be overestimated. This study will give Willard her important place, but it also seeks to recognize the contributions of many other able figures, both in the United States and abroad.[17]

Second, this study covers a much broader timespan than most studies of the WCTU. By looking beyond the period of Willard's death, we can see more clearly her strategic role and also view the ways in which policies she and her co-workers set in motion were changed over time. In some previous accounts, this change appears so sudden or complete that only the removal of Willard's influence can fully explain it. Yet the gulf between the pre- and post-1898 periods must not be exaggerated. The WCTU did not suddenly abandon broad social reforms at home, and still less evidence of a sharp break at 1898 can be found in the international work. A narrowing of the WCTU's social vision did gradually occur, but even in the 1920s both the American and the World's WCTUs espoused social welfare policies and other reforms that went way beyond the issue of prohibition.[18]

A third caveat upon existing scholarship concerns the role of religion. Though the WCTU was undeniably important as a vehicle for women's aspirations as women, not nearly enough attention has been given to the connection of the WCTU with evangelical religion and to its context of domestic values that linked women and men together. When the WCTU is portrayed as an extension of women's culture, or as a brand of liberal feminism, much of critical importance in the WCTU's Christian commitment is missed. This generalization applies as much to Willard as anybody else, since Willard derived her power from her roots in mainstream evangelicalism, with all of its strengths and limitations. In this study, therefore, I make the religious drive and rhetoric of the WCTU critical and argue that the WCTU's feminism only makes sense in this context.[19]

Nonetheless, I still think that it is appropriate enough to call these women feminists, provided the reader accepts that the feminism described in this book is not the same as that of today. The women's temperance reformers of Willard's generation were attempting to expand the area of opportunities for women, however complicated and compromised that process might have been. It should therefore be understood that I have treated feminism as a *historical* phenomenon whose meaning has been shaped and reshaped by differing generations, not as an abstract set of legal or—still less—*philosophical* positions.[20]

SINCE MY ACCOUNT is largely topical rather than chronological, a note on the format of this book is in order. Chapter 2 explains the roots of temperance internationalism and argues that the World's WCTU was not an aberration but the culmination of a tradition of missionary work, international organization, and millennial thinking among Anglo-American Protestants. Chapter 3 explains the organizational structure of the World's WCTU, chapter 4 documents the reception of WCTU work outside the United States, and chapter 5 highlights the cultural travail of the missionaries who carried out that organizing work. Chapter 6 explains the contradictions of the WCTU's motivating ideology of sisterhood and motherhood. It links these concepts to religion and family values through the WCTU's espousal of harmonious relations between men and women in a system of companionate marriage. The remaining chapters treat the complex of issues that the WCTU's international temperance agitation involved: the export of alcohol and opium to colonial peoples, peace, antiprostitution (purity) work, women's suffrage, socialism, and prohibition. Each of these enables us to explore the contradictory relationship between gender and cultural imperialism. No one issue expressed the essence of the WCTU's campaign; rather, the WCTU's work was overdetermined in a set of interlocking contradictions expressed in the various issues the WCTU championed. Each episode allowed the WCTU to push aspects of its message of human liberation; at each turn the WCTU also confronted in new ways the contradictions of its enterprise. The world of women could never be separated from the world of empire.

Yet the outcome of these issues was not predetermined, and the journey did not end where it began. The controversy over the export of alcohol to colonies, the social purity issue, and worldwide campaigns for prohibition demonstrate the shift of agitation from an Anglo-American political hegemony in the 1890s to a new kind of cultural hegemony based on American moral leadership in the 1920s. That is the subject of the epilogue.

2

Origins of Temperance Internationalism

Leavitt's journey merged abrupt shifts in the rhythms of her own life with slow, almost imperceptible changes in the larger world of missions and women's reform. Superficially, the cycle of marriage, domesticity, childbirth, and childrearing did not distinguish her from thousands of other cultured and middle-class women in the mid-nineteenth century. Leavitt was, however, unusual. Her marriage in 1857 to a wealthy Boston landbroker had quickly gone sour in scandal and personal unhappiness. Thomas H. Leavitt was, by all accounts, "a spendthrift," and it is likely that this was not the greatest of his sins.[1] When the mismatch ended in divorce in a Nebraska court in 1878, Leavitt had already returned to the classroom and had developed, by 1877, an interest in temperance fueled by a meeting with the then corresponding secretary of the National WCTU, Frances Willard. In 1881 Leavitt gave up teaching to take on temperance and suffrage work full time in Massachusetts. As early as 1882, Willard had tried to get Leavitt to undertake an international assignment, but until the death of her aged father in June 1883, she had refused. Then she abandoned her labors in the eastern states to become superintendent of work on the Pacific Coast.

The liberation from familial restraints provided the opportunity for a new career. But Leavitt left little information to explain her precise motivation in undertaking her unprecedented journey. Buried in the WCTU's *Our Union* for October 1881 is the most helpful clue. There Leavitt reported a Tremont Temple meeting at which Mary A. Livermore, the suffragist and WCTU worker, had spoken upon her return from a European tour. Leavitt was most impressed with the call that Livermore made for temperance workers to internationalize their movement. After reviewing the prevalence of "alcoholism" in other nations, Livermore stressed the superiority of Americans in the matter of drinking patterns. "America should see that she is the Messiah of the nations; that she is to give other nations better than they ever dreamed of," reported Leavitt. Along with this encomium went the implied threat that failure to extend the example would bring down the wrath of God and so undermine American civilization itself. Not only would other nations benefit through the example of American abstinence; "a glorious future" would be thereby "assured" for the United States.[2]

Many layers of meaning and experience underpinned Leavitt's cryptic report. Livermore's address did not demand American political expansion abroad. The thrust of her remarks concerned the familiar notion of the United States as a "beacon of liberty" to the corrupt and aristocratic societies of Europe. But underlying Livermore's Boston address was an assertion of American cultural superiority. There were "no men like her men"; the nation had only to "recognize her powers" located in the resources of an upright people. The concept of an export of American moral power tied Livermore and Leavitt to messianic and millennialist currents in American reform movements. The impulse to send American women abroad and to colonize the institutions of the WCTU is inconceivable without this experience.[3]

Three specific components of this intellectual inheritance demand attention if the sources of the international women's temperance movement are to be understood. These are the long and intensive American involvement with temperance reform, which spilled over national boundaries long before the time of Willard and encouraged ideas of American moral superiority; the specific experience of women within the temperance movement; and the extensive deployment of American missionaries in foreign lands from the 1820s onward, as a network for the use of reformers, as an example of what could be done, and as a source of religious and emotional inspiration.

Americans began sending Protestant missionaries to the nether regions of the globe in 1811 through the ABCFM. Temperance reformers in the 1820s and 1830s strongly supported this organization, and indeed of the sixteen men who founded the American Temperance Society in 1826, fourteen were ABCFM members. Though women were not initially sent as missionaries in their own right, they did go as the wives of evangelists, and their role steadily increased during the nineteenth century. By the time that Leavitt departed, the efforts of American women in fund raising, and as missionaries themselves, made the entire missionary enterprise unthinkable without their substantial contribution.

The gospel command and the institutional connections ensured that temperance reformers would value international work. Since they conceived of intemperance as a heinous sin and an obstacle to gospel work, they took it as axiomatic that temperance must triumph everywhere if the ABCFM was to succeed. "The word of the Lord" would "run swiftly" in a sober world and usher in the fruits of "millennial glory," said the founders of the American Temperance Society.[4]

But such rhetorical exhortations did not mean that the early temperance workers regarded international and American work as of equal importance in the immediate matters of organization and tactics. The foreign references of Justin Edwards, American Temperance Society corresponding secretary, contained a large element of self-flagellation. They were designed in part to spur Americans at home to action by creating the impression that other countries were looking to the United States for leadership. If a sober republic were not quickly created, concluded the *Journal of Humanity* in 1831, the opportunity for a moral ascendancy on a global scale would be lost. A sober America would be ideally placed to carry "the blessings of Christianity and civilization to the remotest and most degraded nations." Freed of the "abomination" of intemperance, Americans could also perpetuate "free institutions" and "spread the light and glory of *that* freedom round the globe."[5] These shrill appeals tapped ideological and political convictions as well as religious zeal. From this very early period, religion was mobilized in the context of a republican patriotism that buttressed the would-be missionary reformer's sense of national superiority.[6]

This millennial vision became, by the time of Mary C. Leavitt and Frances Willard, the staple of temperance missionary thought and justification. But the burden of the argument subtly altered. The progress of temperance in the American republic by mid-century enhanced the implicit identification of American values and world interests by temperance reformers. On the other hand, the movement of women into missionary and temperance work abroad would continue to draw on thinly veiled criticisms of western moral standards in the "civilized" world. Thus the contradictory elements contained in the drive to export American reform remained and were in many ways exaggerated by experience. Willard's grand tour of Europe and the Middle East from 1868 to 1870 elicited the conventional patriotic response: "Oh! native land—the world's hope, the Gospel's triumph, the Millenium's [*sic*] dawn 'are all with thee, are all with thee!'"[7] Willard's gushy endorsement came prior to her involvement in the women's temperance movement. Under its impact, Willard was driven toward a critique of American institutions and values that sent her searching, along with Leavitt and others, for a culture that transcended the nation state and represented the interests and aspirations of women in every land. In the course of this service, the sense of cultural superiority would be questioned. The missionary element in the World's WCTU would become less patriotic and would help turn the image of Frances Willard into that of an international stateswoman whose allegiance was to sex more than to nation. Therein lay the source of deep conflicts for the American women's temperance movement that neither Willard nor the World's organization could resolve.

More than religion underpinned the expansionist mentality of women temperance reformers. The experience of Americans with the drink issue reinforced Livermore's suggestion that "there were no men" (or women) like those of the United States. When Mary Leavitt set out on her journey from San Francisco, the American temperance movement was just completing what Willard and others called the first temperance century.[8] Though the century had begun inauspiciously in 1784 with the publication of Benjamin Rush's *Inquiry into the Effects of Ardent Spirits on the Human Body and Mind*, by the time temperance reformers celebrated their centennial, the temperance movement could point to huge changes in patterns of American drinking and cultural expectations concerning the use of alcohol. Historians continue to argue about the extent of the decline in liquor consumption, but the best available evidence suggests that per capita consumption dropped sharply from the early nineteenth century. According to W. J. Rorabaugh, American consumption, which had been much greater than Britain's in 1800, was by 1880 less than half the British and Danish figures in terms of absolute volume of alcohol consumed and only a third of the French or Italian. The United States could no longer be called the alcoholic republic.[9]

Not only had Americans become more sober, but significant changes had occurred in the composition of the drinking population. The rise of immigrant drinking and the decline of the native-born use of liquor is common knowledge, but little attention has been given to the important shifts occurring in the drinking of women. Impressionistic evidence from the early Republican era, reported by Rorabaugh, indicates that women drank from one-eighth to one-quarter of the total liquor bill and that drinking, though not "tippling" in taverns, was customary among many women.[10] By the 1880s, a perceptible change had occurred. When Mary Livermore toured continental Europe and Britain in 1881, she was shocked at the much greater amount of drinking among English women. Other observers also cited the greater "soberness of the women of America" as evidence for the very different degrees of political success achieved by the temperance movement in the two countries. Rates of death for cirrhosis of the liver, which in the late nineteenth-century United States can be held as a fair indication of alcohol damage, verify the popular perception of an absence of habitual drunkenness among native-born American women. Only among the Irish immigrants and first generation Irish-Americans did the rates of death for women approximate those for men.[11]

More important, the use of alcohol by respectable women was much less pronounced in the United States than in Britain. In both countries the social elite of women continued to drink, but in an aristocratic society like Britain, the example of the elite was more important. The WCTU strove, with success in the case of the wives of Hayes, Garfield, and Cleveland, for evidence of abstinence. But in no way was the example of the first lady so important as that of Queen Victoria, who continued to take and give wine at her table and thus illustrated the persistence of an etiquette among the

British upper classes that was hostile to the WCTU's goals and values. Much to the embarrassment of WCTU leaders in America, the queen violated the very Victorian morality to which she gave her name.[12]

At the other end of the social scale, prostitutes and "common drunkards" made up the vast proportion of the arrests for drunkenness among women in both countries. What troubled American WCTU women looking at British drinking practices was that the line dividing the working-class woman and the prostitute was not clearly drawn, for the sign of immorality was contained in the decision to drink in public. The behavior of women in public houses in Britain and the employment of women as barmaids therefore drew the most extended opposition and comment, since it offered apparent evidence of sin and impurity and displayed a bad example for the society to follow. No wonder, then, that Livermore was shocked by the extent of casual drinking and association between the sexes in France and Germany as well as dismayed that an Anglo-Saxon country like Britain could diverge so much in its standards for women from American behavior. What most shocked her was the "women standing with bloated faces and bleared eyes, swallowing gin at the bar of the 'public house.'" The difference in the "moral condition" of the peoples that the temperance reform had itself helped to create fed the conviction that the United States was indeed the last, best hope for man, and for woman.[13]

If American women were, as Livermore argued, more sober than their British counterparts, this must in some measure be grounded in the vitality of the American women's temperance movement. Women comprised as much as 60 percent of the membership of some male-led temperance societies there as early as the 1830s, and women's temperance societies had also appeared. In the New York Washingtonians in the 1840s, the advocacy of temperance by women became quite open and, at times, militant in its defense of the rights of women against the "cruel wrongs" of alcoholic indulgence by men. To be sure, women's temperance societies existed prior to the coming of the WCTU in both Britain and some of its colonies. Elizabeth Windschuttle has shown this to be the case for New South Wales prior to 1850, where the parallels with the American Washingtonians were remarkable. A women's temperance paper had been published, women spoke on the temperance platform, and in a modest way the issue of women's rights had been raised, as it was in the American case.[14]

For all that, nothing in Britain or its colonies paralleled the Woman's Crusade of 1873–74 in the United States. When women took to the streets in defense of the home and prayed in the saloons, they displayed a level of militance and direct action that British admirers could not copy. "It is hardly likely," said Margaret Bright Lucas, later president of the BWTA, that "we can go through the streets and kneel at the doors of the gin palaces." Lucas did not say why, but Mary White, recalling the occasion of the Wom-

Woman's World/Woman's Empire

an's Crusade nearly twenty years later, echoed the many observations of WCTU travelers in Britain. "At that time it was the rarest thing for any woman to speak in public." This in turn reflected the more formalized class divisions of English society. Middle-class women shrank from doing anything as indecorous as public agitation. Class and gender combined to make American women seem different and, to their British counterparts, almost Amazonian in their assertiveness. Whether Britons were for or against women's involvement in temperance, it was unquestioned that Americans provided the leadership and innovations.[15]

By the time the WCTU began organizing internationally, the moral ascendancy of American women on the temperance question seemed assured. But for the temperance movement as a whole, any convictions of moral superiority came only slowly, and the underlying insecurity grounded in evangelical self-criticism remained for both sexes. Thus driven, American temperance reformers did not wait for Americans to sober up before they began international campaigns. Armed with a millennial vision, they made no clear distinction between the American and the international audience. Zealous converts plied their trade in temperance pledges to anyone who would listen. Neither nativist prejudice nor national xenophobia barred the immediate extension of the pledge to other nations. As early as 1829, Massachusetts ship captains were winning applause from the American Temperance Society for introducing the pledge to Liverpool and promoting the formation of a temperance society in that British port.[16] Nathaniel Hewitt, first agent of the American Temperance Society, visited France and England in 1831 and had helped form in the latter country the British and Foreign Temperance Society. It was Hewitt who urged British sympathizers not to rest content with a purely English organization but to extend the movement's "blessings throughout the kingdom and throughout the world."[17] This lively interest in European countries persisted after prohibition replaced total abstinence as the central goal of the American temperance movement. When the prohibitionist forces assembled in New York to publicize the Maine Law in 1853, they followed antislavery practice by calling their meeting a World's Temperance Convention and invited delegates from Canada and Britain.[18]

The transatlantic connection in reform movements has been extensively studied, and the World's Temperance Convention was an important part of the exchange of ideas and institutions. By no means was this commerce in morality one way. The English reformers had, for example, first and most effectively publicized the pledge against all alcoholic stimulants, and they gave the name *teetotal* to the world. British and Irish immigrants brought their Rechabite and Father Mathew temperance societies to American shores in the 1830s and 1840s. Father Mathew himself made an extensive tour of Canada and the United States in 1849, where Protestant reformers hailed him despite the presence of anti-Catholicism in the native-born population.[19]

The British and Irish contribution to American temperance ideas hardly reversed the balance of the trade in reform, however. The social and ideological climate for temperance was more favorable in the United States, and it was from there that reformers elsewhere in the Anglo-Saxon world principally looked, whether to be informed, shocked, or horrified. This was true not only for the English temperance reformers but also for a bemused European aristocrat like Alexis de Tocqueville, who, puzzled at the formation of societies to promote temperance by voluntary abstinence, took the American Temperance Society as the model for his study of the voluntary organization as a distinctive phenomenon of "American democracy."[20]

When the introduction of prohibition in the state of Maine made Neal Dow a hero on both sides of the Anglo-American reform community, American dominance of the international temperance movement was further enhanced. Stimulated by a visit from the silver-tongued orator John B. Gough, the United Kingdom Alliance made prohibition its policy in 1853, despite the fact that the long preparatory skirmishes that produced the prohibitionist solution in New England had no parallel in Britain. A complementary export of American solutions occurred in Canada, where the New Brunswick legislature passed its own Maine Law in 1852 and imitated Maine again by strengthening the law in 1855 before a fatal clash with the royal governor precipitated the prohibitionist law's demise.[21]

The American preference for reform by a nation's shining example did not survive this shift to prohibitionism. A form of organizational imperialism began to supplement the process of exhortation. The spread of temperance values through American institutions did not begin with the World's WCTU. The Sons of Temperance, a fraternal lodge based on temperance principles founded in New York in 1842, had reached New Brunswick in 1847, where it provided the leadership of the controversial Maine Law campaign in that colony. By 1849, lodges appeared in both Ontario and England. Like some later American trade unions, the Sons of Temperance envisioned itself as an international organization, and squabbles erupted in the 1870s over the control of the affiliates in the British colonies, which both British and American lodges claimed. If this schism undermined the organization's international unity, the failure of the Sons of Temperance to provide adequately for the role of women in the temperance movement contributed more to its declining effectiveness in the years after the Civil War. As early as the 1850s, it was no longer possible to regard the role of women in the temperance movement as purely subordinate. Women had responded to the temperance pledge in greater numbers and with more enthusiasm than men, and for this reason the establishment of the Good Templars in 1852 assumed first-rate importance.[22]

Whereas the Sons of Temperance had treated with great suspicion the desire of women to be admitted as full members, the Templars rested their appeal on equality between the sexes. Women could join, hold office, and speak from the Templar platforms. In most cases, however, the leadership positions continued to be held by men, and the organization maintained existing stereotypes of women as shy, domestic creatures whose best work was still done in the home or through the traditionally sanctioned female weapon of moral suasion. The St. Louis *Good Templar* noted in 1872 that men had no "right to deprive woman of the ballot" but asked "why should she want it?" The position of women in society could be improved by sympathetic men through the strengthening of the conjugal family "without necessitating woman to step forth from her own beautiful and necessary sphere."[23]

Though fairly conventional purveyors of the separate spheres, the Templars remain significant as the principal vehicle for involvement of women in temperance outside the United States prior to the inception of the World's WCTU. Everywhere the WCTU missionaries went, they built upon the work already done by the Templars, who had spread to England, South Africa, New Zealand, and the Australian colonies by the early 1870s. By the time the WCTU reached Australian shores in the mid-1880s, the Templars were entrenched with 29,000 members, in comparison with 9,000 in the Sons of Temperance and 25,000 in the Independent Order of Rechabites. In comparison, the WCTU in Australia could manage only 4,000 by 1887. It was the Templars who hired the halls, paid the traveling bills, did the advertising, and provided the audiences for Leavitt and for her successor, Jessie Ackermann, in New Zealand and Australia.[24]

The Templars also made possible the very rapid spread of the WCTU to Britain only two years after the meeting in Cleveland that turned the Woman's Crusade into the WCTU. Margaret Parker, a Good Templar living in Dundee, Scotland, had come with her husband to the United States in 1875 as an international delegate to conferences of the Good Templars in Illinois. There she had met Eliza Stewart, one of the heroines of the Woman's Crusade and popularly known in the matriarchical ideology of the WCTU as Mother Stewart. Much impressed by the stories of women taking the temperance issue into their own hands through the power of prayer, Parker had invited the celebrated motherly agitator to Britain to disseminate her novel approach to reform. Stewart arrived early in 1876 where she was "warmly welcomed" by the Good Templars. A Templar herself, Stewart took quick advantage of the organization's annual meeting at Newcastle-on-Tyne in April 1876 to found the BWTA, with Parker as first president.[25]

Though the WCTU and the Good Templars worked in harmony at first, the rather conservative opinions of the latter on the position of women as vessels of domestic admiration did not sit well with the bolder elements in the WCTU. Led by Frances Willard, these began as early as 1879 to shift the organization's focus from temperance alone to a broader emphasis on women's emancipation. Moreover, the WCTU differed fundamentally from the Templars in its principles of organization. A society run by women offered different emotional appeals and career attractions to one which lumped women and men together. Charlotte Gray, a WCTU worker assigned to proselytize on the European continent in 1885, was, like many other temperance women, a Templar before she became a member of Willard's society. The attraction of the Templars was, she explained, that "we meet as men and women on a perfect equality." Yet Gray also conceded that the WCTU promised much that the Templars could never do. "There is very much that belongs especially to women to do, and that can best be accomplished when they plan and act alone."[26] The WCTU could, like women missionaries, reach women in their own homes quietly and prudently while at the same time sustaining the emotional commitment of women one to another. The WCTU's more effective appeal to women is illustrated by contrasting two temperance meetings held in Australia. The International Temperance Convention organized in Melbourne, Victoria, in 1880 contains in its voluminous papers no mention of women and no women delegates despite the fact that it was organized by the Good Templars. When the next international convention met there in 1888, after Leavitt's trip, women's issues and the role of the WCTU received much publicity.[27]

Still, international temperance clearly did not begin with Leavitt, nor was it a peripheral question in the thought and practice of temperance reformers prior to the 1880s. For that matter, nor was the WCTU the first organization to involve women on an international level. What remains to be demonstrated is how deeply the WCTU itself was implicated in international strategies prior to the departure of Leavitt. Historians from the time of Mary Earhart on have followed Frances Willard's own claim that her conversion to internationalism was a sudden one in 1883. On a tour of the Pacific states she had, as the WCTU president reported, looked "into the mystic face of the Orient" and, according to Earhart, "overnight" became an "internationalist." Exposed to "the opium curse in San Francisco," Willard instantaneously appreciated "the outreaching of other nations toward our society and their need of us." From this spiritual and strategic assessment, Willard proposed the establishment of a World's WCTU.[28]

Willard did not become an internationalist overnight, nor was her conversion a product of a mystical experience. She had in fact shown an interest in international temperance work as early as 1875 and had been involved in planning the Woman's International Temperance Convention, which the WCTU sponsored in April 1876 to coincide with the Centennial Exposition held in Philadelphia. As president of the Chicago WCTU, she asked temperance reformer and suffragist Elizabeth Harbert for suggestions as to "how our temperance cause can be most vividly presented to the *eyes ears* and hearts of the World's assembled representatives" at the exposition.[29] Willard's first presidential address in 1880 began with a resume of international, not American, achievements and went on to predict that another international women's temperance convention would soon be held.[30] While on route to California in 1883, before she had seen the opium dens of San Francisco, Willard issued a call to the British and Canadian women for a campaign "throughout the English-speaking world" to mark the decennial of the foundation of the WCTU.[31]

Willard's attempts to guide the WCTU in the direction of internationalism had their emotional roots in the Methodist culture, with its growing emphasis on foreign missionary work by women and its injunction to save souls everywhere. WCTU women took very seriously and literally the injunction of John Wesley that the world was their parish. This enthusiasm for the broader field was not uncommon among the women she led after 1879. The WCTU itself had, from its very beginnings, pushed internationalism. Just two years after its founding in 1874, the American WCTU had sponsored the international conference that Willard's letter to Harbert promoted. Annie Wittenmyer, the then national president, went so far as to boast that this meeting was "the first . . . international convention . . . for women the world has ever known."[32] At that convention, an International Woman's Christian Temperance Union was formed under the leadership of Margaret Parker. Wittenmyer was probably correct in her claims for novelty, since an International Council of Women did not meet until 1888 and the International Woman Suffrage Alliance did not convene its first conference until 1904. Nonetheless, the 1876 meeting testified more to the pious sentiment of internationalism than to the strength of commitment to international organization. Only four countries, Canada, the United States, Britain, and Japan, were represented (and the latter by a self-appointed delegate in the form of an American missionary on furlough). Of those elected to office-bearing positions, very little was ever heard again. Moreover, the International Woman's Christian Temperance Union remained hamstrung by its "entire lack of funds" and by the inactivity of its members.[33]

Willard knew the International Woman's Christian Temperance Union had been crippled from the start, but that correct judgment should not obscure the scope of international activity by the WCTU between 1876 and 1884. Even before the 1876 convention, Stewart had begun her campaign in England that produced the BWTA. Her considerable platform efforts were augmented by Mary Coffin Johnson, recording secretary of the National WCTU, who carried on in 1876 her extensive and innovative series of drawing-room meetings among the women of the British upper classes. Both Johnson and Stewart had found that the tactics of the American temperance movement did not necessarily work in the different culture and

Origins of Internationalism

Frances Willard, 1894 (Anna A. Gordon, *The Life of Frances E. Willard* [Evanston, Ill.: National Woman's Temperance Publishing Association, 1914])

class structure of British society. The strength of the Church of England among the upper classes made it difficult for American Methodist women to reach many women of influence. Johnson, a pious and retiring evangelical woman, was the perfect vehicle for this unpublicized and often unnoticed work. Believing her work "a call from God to save souls," Johnson went back in 1878–79 to take the message of total abstinence to the Protestant women in the north of Ireland and to resume her efforts with the British upper classes. Though she soon left the WCTU, Johnson had established an important line of work that was thereafter carried on by the WCTU among the elite women of the eastern seaboard of the United States as well.[34] These pioneering forays were soon supplemented by a steady trickle of WCTU visitors that included Mary Bannister Willard (Frances's sister-in-law), Amelia Quinton, who reported on British conditions in 1878, and Livermore. Livermore, along with Maria Treadwell, Mary B. Willard, and Charlotte Gray, carried the WCTU's principles to France, Belgium, Sweden, and Germany as well from 1885 to 1887.[35]

European initiatives were only part of the rapid dissemination of WCTU ideas and institutions. From 1876 to 1883, the International Camp Meetings organized by Professor George Foster, a Canadian prohibitionist, held each summer at such places as Hamilton, Ontario, and Old Orchard Beach, Maine, featured temperance programs sponsored by the WCTU in the United States and brought together Canadian and American workers. Although the emphasis was heavily religious and the meetings geographically restricted, a degree of international exchange did occur. It was at one such Old Orchard meeting, "in the great grove of pines, with blue sky overhead and flashing sea waves near," that Willard claimed to have devised the Home Protection strategy of advocating votes for women, after listening to Ontario's Letitia Youmans call for home protection to match the tariff protection for Canadian industry.[36]

The involvement of Canadian reformers demonstrates that international work among women was no more a one-way process than among men. The internationalist impetus did not come from American sources alone. Between 1875 and 1880, a spontaneous expansion of WCTU activities occurred in a number of countries. Youmans had turned up uninvited at the WCTU's national convention in 1875 and formed the Ontario WCTU the following year "to make common cause with our sisters of the United States."[37] The Woman's Crusade spread rapidly through the activities of British and American missionaries. A letter from Britain's Margaret Parker produced a union in Port Elizabeth, South Africa, in 1878, and heartened by "cheery accounts" of its work, she urged as early as 1881 a "mission" to India to instruct "that far-off land in the blessed cause of Temperance, as a part of religion." Even before Parker's injunction, a Bengal Temperance League was copying the Ohio crusaders by praying outside Calcutta's liquor

shops and handing out gospel tracts. Led by an American Baptist missionary's wife, the league opened a coffee shop in 1878 to entertain the many
foreign sailors who frequented the port.[38] Also worthy of note is the fact
that the women of Sydney, Australia, already had a WCTU when Leavitt
arrived. The organization was brought there in 1882 without the sponsor-
ship of the American WCTU by Eli T. Johnson, husband of the same Mary
C. Johnson who had labored in Britain.[39] Willard's decision to proceed with
a World's organization at the end of 1883 was taken in the full knowledge of
these groups and was partly spurred by their efforts.

Behind these diverse initiatives could be detected two related strands of
the evangelical heritage: millennialism and holiness. As developed by the
preeminent Methodist woman evangelist Phoebe Palmer, holiness involved
the "entire sanctification" or "perfection" of individuals. Palmer asserted
that justification by faith absolved believers of their sin; sanctification was a
second stage in the conversion process in which the sinful nature of the
sinner was transformed and the holy life begun after consecration on the
altar of Christ.[40]

Palmer and her husband, Walter, were prominent among evangelical re-
vivalists who took the message of Christian perfectionism to Britain and
Canada in the 1850s and 1860s. Though Palmer died in 1874, before the
World's WCTU was founded, she undoubtedly influenced many temperance women in the Anglo-American reform community. Not an overt feminist, she nonetheless showed women the influence they could exert in religion and moral reform. Some of her key techniques, notably summer camp
meetings and her drawing-room scripture readings, were also employed by
the women's international temperance movement just a few years later.
Palmer's specific theological contribution, too, influenced a number of key
WCTU officials, notably Frances Willard, Mary Woodbridge, and Hannah
Whitall Smith.[41]

Holiness doctrine gave women on both sides of the Atlantic a shared set
of assumptions concerning Christian service and sacrifice. At the same
time, holiness gave women a sense of spiritual power. It was also significant
that this doctrine was interdenominational and attracted into a broader
reform coalition such Quaker women as Smith and Woodbridge. The former wrote with her husband, Robert, *The Christian's Secret of a Happy Life*
(1875), a key holiness text, and toured England in aid of the perfectionist
"higher life movement" that swept that country from 1873 to 1875.[42]

Yet nothing in the doctrine of holiness specifically impressed upon wom-
en the need for *international* action. The influence of holiness was strengthened by combination with another set of doctrines that Palmer's theology
did not stress. This was the millennial tradition. The concept of a perfect
moral order that represented God's plan for human salvation realized in
earthly form inspired not just Mary Leavitt but many others within the

American WCTU as well. The vision of a Christian millennium gave the United States a special role within the providential destiny, since the working out of those plans clearly required a global campaign of the forces of good against those of evil. Internationalism was indeed at a premium in religiously inspired temperance campaigns.[43]

Nineteenth-century Protestant evangelicalism had long encouraged this millennialist streak. Preachers depicted the world as a battleground in the contest for human souls centered upon the revival meeting and the conversion experience. This spiritual struggle engendered conflict within the evangelical mind, however, because sensitivity to sin was heightened by the process of conversion, yet "evil" remained abstract. The attempted resolution to this problem in psychological terms was to externalize the source of evil in concretely conceived moral practices, to demonstrate, in effect, faith through its external manifestations in right behavior. Of the moral issues evangelicals focused upon, drinking and its abuse were ideal for the discharge of evangelical tension because they involved personal control and helped define the boundaries of order and disorder required if sin, afoot everywhere in the world, were to be kept at bay. The concern with symbols of moral pollution, common to the search for social cohesion in all cultures, took the specific form in American society of purity in individual moral conduct.[44]

The WCTU's Do-Everything policy can be interpreted along these lines as a comprehensive evangelical assault on possible sources of polluting customs. These were all linked in some way to the central agent of evil, that is, alcohol and its capacity to loosen inhibitions and to encourage "immoral" behavior. So too, the international campaign was a natural extension in a spatial dimension of this principle of moral contagion. Good and evil knew no geographic boundaries, and pollutants anywhere threatened evangelical integrity everywhere. Willard drew on this logic when she quaintly remarked that "the thistles of one country" would surely "crop up in another" if moral action were not internationally coordinated. A group of Scottish women made much the same point more pithily when they said, "Wherever there is drink there is danger."[45]

A morally regenerate world was linked in this Protestant eschatology with the coming of Christ's kingdom on earth, the rule of a thousand years as biblically foretold. But millennialism divided on this score, between those who argued that the coming of Christ would itself produce the world's purification and those who saw earthly purification as a sign of regeneration already in process that would culminate in the Second Advent. Christian temperance women tended markedly to the latter postmillennial interpretation, which encouraged social action toward reform as a positive sign of Christ's coming. Willard charged the various national affiliates of the WCTU set up in the 1880s and 1890s to take on a comprehensive war against slavery, drunkenness, lust, gambling, ignorance, pauperism, Mormonism, and war. After that gigantic set of tasks had been completed, "We shall not have much difficulty in settling all our theological and ecclesiastical differences, and the glory of God, who is the happiness of men, will fill the whole earth."[46]

When Willard framed these aims, she could draw, therefore, upon an established tradition of evangelical action. Among missionary groups, global evangelism had already been embraced, and the role of women as agents of the missionary enterprise was increasingly accepted. But the WCTU's campaign had its own distinctive elements. Postmillennialism's search for moral and socially regenerative causes tended to secularize in an uneasy and never complete way the evangelical impulse. A persistent tension appeared between the pietistic reliance on evangelism and the more concretely conceived programs of social reform. Louise Purlington, a close friend of Frances Willard and World's missionary superintendent of the WCTU in 1909, expressed the tension when she combined an advocacy of westernization of subject peoples through missionary activity with the suggestion that such secular efforts must be linked to and rationalized by the Christian millennial purpose. "God is in the world, and His mighty steppings are felt throughout the earth," she felt sure as she witnessed the beginnings of the colonial world's material transformation. Nationalism and egalitarianism were not the only reforming impulses in these domains, Purlington assured the WCTU flock in the *Union Signal*. The catch cries of liberty, equality, and fraternity must continually be coupled with the "faith, love and unity" that were "world-wide tokens of a conquering Christ."[47] Though Purlington claimed to be representing the world as it really was, she expressed an unmistakable anxiety that the secular aspects of reform might overwhelm reform's underlying religious purpose.

The WCTU's version of millennialism was further complicated by links with the fate of American reform. The millennium had already become married in American minds with the national purpose, as the examples of Justin Edwards, Leavitt, and Livermore indicated. But the identification of the millennial worldview with the extension of a specifically American experience was not limited to American expression alone. England's Isabel Somerset (Lady Henry), as World's vice-president of the WCTU in the 1890s, would equate, just as surely, the United States and the millennial theme. "The whole of that great [new] world pulsates," she enthused after her first American visit in 1891, "with the larger hope, and that optimistic spirit seems breathed into its philanthropy, for the air is filled with the presence of regeneration and reform."[48]

Millennial enthusiasm should not be confused, however, with an uncompromisingly ideological viewpoint and a blind disregard of practical problems of organization. The millennialist vision in the international extension of Do-Everything was harnessed to the national organizing drive of 1883. In this period, Willard and her closest confidante, Anna Gordon, criss-crossed the country in a bid for a dramatic increase in membership to mark the tenth anniversary, in 1884, of the WCTU's inception. The famous visit to the opium dens of San Francisco and the pronouncements in favor of international efforts came during that trip and were specifically linked by Willard to the decennial drive for membership.[49] The dispatching of Lea-vitt was intended to signal the completion of basic organizational work with-in the continental United States and to rededicate the membership to a further ten years' effort in the solemn belief that in that time women's temperance could gird the globe.

Pragmatism was also found in the way the WCTU treated in its interna-tional work the application of its religious principles. In the Communion issue especially, the ideological rigidities of the WCTU's millennial vision were avoided. The logical extension of the pollution hysteria was the attack on Communion wine, which clearly breached the boundaries between good (Communion) and evil (wine) and so created an anomalous category that threatened to corrupt the moral and set a bad example for others. Yet the Communion wine issue never became one of central importance in the World's WCTU. In Britain, the WCTU would get significant support from within the Church of England, which opposed interference with the tradi-tional interpretation of the sacraments, and sections of the BWTA tried with some success to keep resolutions on the issue out in the cold. When the BWTA's organ, the *White Ribbon*, reviewed the issue in 1915, its editors concluded that little had been done because the BWTA was "interdenomi-national" and "some of its most devoted members are in communion with the Church [of England]."[50] Because of the strength of this opposition and the positioning of British officials in key roles in the World's WCTU, that organization never made the Communion issue a test of membership or a matter of its program, though departments for the use of unfermented wine flourished in some other auxiliaries like Scotland and New Zealand, where the heritage of evangelical dissent was particularly strong.[51]

The failure of the BWTA to endorse the perfect moral order expressed in such issues brought conflict rather than cohesion within the World's WCTU affiliates, as the history of the WCTU's involvement in purity and prohibition will show.[52] But these and other controversies did not result in the imposition of a uniform moral vision on the World's WCTU or its affili-ates. What the Communion issue actually demonstrated was the tension that a culturally aggressive campaign of moral purification could engender when confronted with a world replete with complex parochial loyalties and diverse religious and moral beliefs. Even within the Christian millennial tradition there was room for such divergent interpretation of the meaning of purity and reform. The tendency was for the WCTU's experience of

Origins of Internationalism

these realities to push the organization toward a more secular and gradual-ist conception of moral change, but the tension could not be resolved with-out abandoning the movement's raison d'être.

As part of the nexus between the millennial temper and secular social reform, nothing was more important than what might be called the imperi-al connections of the WCTU. From the moment in 1886 that Frances Wil-lard grasped the hands of Margaret Bright Lucas, BWTA and first World's president, on the stage of the WCTU national convention in Minneapolis, the American leader steadily pursued the goal of an Anglo-American re-form coalition. Announcing that Britain had joined the World's union, Wil-lard prophesied the imminent coming of "that blessed morning when home shall rule the world, and the fiends of alcohol and lust slink to their native hell, crying *'Galilean, thou hast conquered.'* "[53] Here Willard tied the ascendan-cy of Anglo-American culture to her spiritual vision of a global regenera-tion. The medium of this triumph would be imperialism and colonialism.

Willard recognized that the age was marked by the geographic expansion of Western political influence and technological innovation. She under-stood that these two forces were in the process of creating one world, not as a sentimental cliché, but as an economic reality. When she notes the possi-bilities of the "aerial car," from which she hoped to dispense her temper-ance message around the globe, her position is easy to satirize, but Willard also pointed to the spread of the telegraph and telephone as instances of the communications revolution. "[How] incalculably swift their progress and diffusion" would be "when time and space are practically annihilated," she enthused.[54] A communications revolution tended, but only tended, to strengthen the hands of those who simultaneously fastened their economic and political hold on parts of the non-Western world, though there was no necessary connection between Western technological expansion and the quickening of territorial aggrandizement by European imperialists.

Willard pushed for more than technological change. She hoped to exploit the political changes of the imperial age. With the extension of British po-litical control over vast territories hitherto independent, the chances of the WCTU exerting its influence would be enhanced by "strengthening the white-ribbon movement in the central country of the English-speaking race, with its mighty outreach of power to its great colonies."[55] It was with this aim in mind that Willard installed Margaret Lucas as World's president in 1885 by executive fiat, so that she could "press the Temperance question" upon those who attended the 1885 Colonial and India Exposition in Lon-don.[56] If the WCTU could influence British drinking habits, in turn the British influence would serve to extend WCTU power around the world.

The pro-British strategy predated Willard's own personal reasons for re-treating to the refuge of aristocratic patronage in England in the 1890s. The strategy was well under way by the time of the 1886 Minneapolis national convention, when Hannah Smith, a close friend of Willard's and by then a permanent resident in London, was appointed as World's WCTU representative in Britain. The same 1886 convention testified with all of the florid ritual that Willard could deploy the importance she attached to the British link. Judging by the audience's emotional response, they too accepted the racial and cultural solidarity of the Anglo-American reform community and were prepared to endorse the rhetoric that justified Willard's plans. As the British and American delegates held hands on the platform, the convention sang "God Save the Queen," and Willard vowed that the daughter colony had rejoined the mother country in the battle against the evils of drink. "For the first time in history the imperial mother and the dauntless daughter of the Anglo-Saxon race clasp hands in a union never to be broken."[57] By the 1890s, this theme of Anglo-American unity would be tied to the notion of Anglo-Saxon cultural, economic, and political dominance. Differences between the two countries were fading, it was argued, and those that remained were being settled by arbitration. Willard and others in the WCTU looked forward to the era of projected world federalism and depicted the WCTU as both a sign and a cause of a coming political millennium.[58] Willard now proposed to use this Anglo-Saxon hegemony in a new age of imperialism to further the twin and for her inseparable goals of women's emancipation and social reform.

As an integral part of this process of political evolution, the World's WCTU would serve as an agency of communication; it would reveal to women in every corner of the globe the methods of work that were most successful in raising the position of women anywhere and would enhance the study of the proposed and implemented laws governing women. These were modest goals on the surface, but in an era when women lacked political rights to enter the national sphere on a basis of legal equality with men, international association provided important emotional sustenance as well as ammunition in the struggle for women's emancipation. Furthermore, Willard envisaged the World's WCTU as focusing on "international questions affecting social and temperance reforms." In particular, pressure would be brought to bear by the concerted efforts of a united society upon the "awful curse of the liquor traffic" carried on between the West and the colonial and quasi-colonial world. As the grab for territorial empire and spheres of influence proceeded apace, "this [was] exactly the time when prompt and uniform action ought to be taken to force every government to protect these helpless people."[59]

Willard's strategy was not unreasonable. The struggle to keep alcohol and opium out of Africa and Asia was, necessarily, an international one that involved lobbying of governments and the monitoring of international treaties. The social purity campaign, too, involved as one of its aspects the attack on an international trade in women for prostitution. That offensive

would require extradition treaties if it were to succeed. Later feminist reformers in the interwar years found that Willard's commitment to an international campaign against these social problems offered the only hope of
success. Laws affecting the legal status of women varied greatly from one
country to another, and in the absence of international treaties, the position
of women in an age of great international migration was constantly being
threatened or eroded. If a woman moved with her husband from one country to another, for example, she followed the nationality of her husband.
Because this could entail loss of cherished legal and civil rights, the whole
issue was later taken up by the League of Nations. Willard in the 1880s had
correctly anticipated these later international feminist concerns.[60]

Theoretically, her plans involved all imperial powers, but the spread of
the temperance message was largely confined to the Anglo-Saxon of these
nations. Reaching the other European colonial powers would involve Anglo-
American influence. If necessity prompted such a course, Willard and other WCTU leaders were nevertheless intellectually and emotionally attuned
to the Anglo-American leadership theme. *Woman and Temperance*, Willard's
major literary and biographical compendium of the 1880s, emphasized in
sketches of her own and her colleagues' backgrounds their Anglo-Saxon
heritage.[61] Willard embraced the Social Darwinist doctrines that suggested
connections between racial stock and political as well as intellectual capacity.
If this led temperance women on the national level to propose educational
tests for voting, internationally the intellectual and moral leadership of the
Anglo-Saxon race seemed equally indisputable. Willard was prepared to
exploit the economic and political dominance that underpinned moral
leadership, but she also saw her own contribution and that of the WCTU as
factors strengthening the projected English-speaking hegemony.

Behind the pro-British strategy one could also detect the logical implications of the matriarchal ideology of the WCTU. The role of motherhood
was emphasized in WCTU ritual and symbol, and it made some sense for
an organization devoted to mothers to pay homage to the "mother" of the
Anglo-Saxon race. Given Willard's devotion to her own mother, it is not
surprising, either, to see her associate the two emotions. "God bless the
great old mother-nation of which I learned from my own blessed mother
when she taught me hymns and songs from your poets as I sat upon her
knee," said Willard in an emotional endorsement of her hosts during her
stay in England in 1894.[62]

Willard's original commitment of the WCTU to an Anglo-American reform alliance in the 1880s did not meet opposition within the American
WCTU, and it certainly strengthened her position in developing temperance sentiments among women in Britain and its colonies. In Australia, for
example, women could reconcile their concepts of a "Greater Britain," of
which they were part, with an American domination of international tem-

perance. Sara Nolan, WCTU president in New South Wales in 1899, looked forward to the creation of an Anglo-American diplomatic alliance that would one day "rule the world."[63]

At this juncture, Willard's personal career intervened, for better or for worse, in the WCTU's strategy. What had in the 1880s been a generalized endorsement of the British became, under political and personal changes, a dogged and very thorny question of material commitment. Willard's own mother had died in 1892. Almost immediately she had discovered in Lady Somerset a friend and companion capable of relieving her of the great grief she felt upon that loss. Willard's trip to England and her stay there on and off for most of the time until 1896 flowed from this change in her personal position.[64]

But more than personal grief was involved. In the 1880s, Willard had hopes of great influence in American political life through the alliance she was developing within a coalition of labor, social, and agrarian reformers. Despite her interest in the World's work, her physical commitment remained focused on the national political level. With the defeat of her attempts to bring the Prohibition and People's parties together in a reform alliance in 1892 and the demise of political prohibitionism for a time in the United States, Willard began to turn more and more to Britain as a source of influence. Disillusioned with the pace of reform in her own country, Willard became impressed with the potential power of a section of the British women's movement symbolized and to some extent embodied in the character of Lady Henry. In an 1894 speech, she noted the advantages the British reformers had. The area they covered was "so restricted," in comparison with the geographic and political dispersal of the American population in "fifty separate state or territorial legislatures." "You are going to get there first" she told her BWTA colleagues, because "you can turn out a Government any day if it does not represent the aroused enthusiasms and expectations of the commonweal." While it was inconceivable for an American woman to become a member of the president's cabinet within twenty-five years, Willard predicted that the British, through someone like Lady Henry, would quickly achieve the parallel honor through the parliamentary system.[65]

Willard wrote these lines at a time when great hopes were held for temperance reform through the Liberal government. As members of the WLF, figures like Somerset and other BWTA members seemed to possess a direct channel of influence with the government. As it turned out, Willard's assessment was shortsighted and reflected ignorance of the British political system. The period after 1895 would be a time of waning political influence on the part of the English temperance movement, just as the drive for national prohibition in the United States would soon dispel the disillusionment of the early 1890s. But this judgment is a retrospective one. When

Origins of Internationalism

Willard's pro-British strategy reached its apotheosis, circumstances did seem to favor the British women's movement over the American, bogged down as the latter was in a seemingly interminable and unprofitable struggle for the suffrage. Willard yearned for the power and wealth of the English aristocrats, resources that might relieve her American frustrations.[66]

Central in this campaign for wider social influence would be her close emotional and even closer political relationship with Somerset. Particularly impressive was the amount of financial aid the latter could provide for the temperance cause. The aristocratic Lady Henry was one of the wealthiest women in the realm. Her Eastnor Castle, a Norman baronial structure in Hertfordshire, was "one of the showplaces" of the county, while Somerset also owned extensive property in three other counties. She was in 1895 said to have 100,000 tenants, of whom most lived, despite her reputation as a benevolent reformer, in her vast slum properties in East London. Ironically for a "world-famous temperance reformer," these included a number of licensed premises in the poor district of Somers Town. Even though, as BWTA president, Somerset attempted to close the premises and turn the property over to other uses, only to be defeated in the courts, from these and other rents she was able to provide the BWTA with ample financial resources. In 1893 alone, Somerset herself gave an amount equivalent to the entire American WCTU dues commitment to the World's WCTU.[67]

Somerset had more than money. She possessed an influence with people Willard believed could help her cause. Especially valuable would be her close links with William Booth of the Salvation Army. These good offices would be effectively exploited in petitioning campaigns and in efforts to deal with unemployment and the problem of international refugees, which taxed the WCTU conscience in the 1890s. Somerset's friendship with high officials of the British armed forces, notably Lord Roberts, the commander-in-chief of the Indian army, was expected to help extend the WCTU campaign to many more millions in the British possessions. As the fifth-ranking member of the WLF, she was, in the early 1890s, soundly placed to influence that body as it attempted to put pressure on the Liberal government and the parliament on such issues as implementation of the suffrage for women and the measure of local prohibition known as the Direct Veto Bill.[68]

It is no wonder then, that Willard proclaimed that Somerset would be a cabinet minister one day and hailed her as "our [Temperance] Shaftesbury."[69] From Somerset, Willard could obtain bounteous secretarial assistance and elegant accommodations, something which, as national president, she had long denied herself so that precious funds could be focused on organization. When Willard faced criticism at home for the time she spent in England under Lady Henry's tutelage, she replied that with double the secretarial staff and the rest that her generally poor health made necessary,

Lady Henry Somerset, 1890 (Anna A. Gordon, *The Beautiful Life of Frances Willard* [Evanston, Ill.: Woman's Temperance Publishing Association, 1898])

she had been able to accomplish more at the cost of much less effort than at home.[70]

Lady Henry's own ideology reinforced Willard's emotional and practical Anglophilia. Somerset shared Willard's commitment to Anglo-American moral leadership. The "Anglo-Saxon mission" was to seek moral reforms that would put the race in "the van of progress." While her tour of the United States in 1891 had convinced Somerset that "our American kins-folk" were doing their part, she wished to assert a distinctively British place in the new trans-Atlantic movement for women's temperance and women's emancipation. The British had in particular an obligation to the colonies to seek international moral reform and so lift moral standards in the rapidly expanding British dependencies. Without moral reform, the colonial populations might be corrupted, and empire's foundations undermined.[71] "To the Colonies we send our sons," she warned her followers in a classic expression of the logic of moral contagion, "and it is a poor consolation to know that while we are working to mitigate the temptations at home, they are rife in those places where a more scanty population makes public opinion even more lax."[72] From certain of these colonies the sons returned too often, to corrupt and vitiate the good work done in England. The same logic meant that temperance in Britain (and other European powers) was a sensible thing to support in the United States. As Willard asserted in 1892, the "best women" from these places ended up as emigrants to the United States, so the WCTU was "but protecting American women from the same awful level of practice and opinion."[73] With the progress of immigration, it made sense to attempt reform at the source of the trouble. Somerset advanced part of this explanation in 1902, but as early as 1892–93, she sought to goad British women into self-reform in order to assume with Americans the leadership of a coalition of the virtuous. The essential unity of the Anglo-Saxon race, so "rudely and violently broken by the narrow and prejudiced views of a British king," was in her opinion being repaired by the WCTU.[74]

If the logic governing this extension of Anglo-Saxon cultural imperialism seemed faultless to Willard and Somerset, the meaning of this powerful rhetoric remained unclear. To what extent did the case for a World's WCTU reflect the hopes of ordinary temperance women in both the United States and other lands? To what extent was the strategy designed to spur a commitment that was lacking on the part of the rank and file? To be sure, temperance women were prepared in the early 1890s to endorse the instincts of their leaders. Nonetheless, the World's WCTU would create tensions in the women's temperance movement in both England and North America. The lofty preoccupations of a small coterie of internationally oriented leaders would at times threaten to erode their support within their own national constituencies. On a practical level, rhetorical commitment to

Anglo-Saxon moral power would not necessarily be matched by financial contributions from the WCTU's base of support.

This clash of parochial and internationalist visions cannot be denied, but its impact must not be exaggerated nor its effects confused with other conflicting tendencies in the World's WCTU. More important were those controversies in the international women's temperance movement that reflected and shaped the meaning of the international vision itself. Should the WCTU be an agency for the extension of power and cultural values on behalf of a segment of the Anglo-American reform elite or a movement of genuine emancipatory consequences for women, not only in the United States or Britain, but around the world as well?

3

The World's WCTU

Testing the Limits
of Internationalism

Are women more inclined toward internationalism than men? This is a question that many interested in the issue of nuclear disarmament ask today, yet the question is not a new one. During the era of first-wave feminism, visionaries in the women's movement eyed the parochial national rivalries of their time and hoped for a better future. In certain respects, these dreams drew upon a common climate of opinion shared with men. The hopes for an international brotherhood of man were strongly voiced by sections of the trade union and socialist movements. But the position of women was, according to the feminist exponents of internationalism, quite different. They surmised that women would not repeat the mistakes of the past because their loyalties had been forged in a different social context. The granting of male suffrage had coincided with the rise of the modern nation state and had wedded the male population to irrational nationalist loyalties. But women had been excluded from the developing political society of the nineteenth century and had forged different loyalties that reflected their own political experience.

Katharine Anthony, the feminist and novelist, put the point succinctly in her *Feminism in Germany and Scandinavia* in 1915. "The disfranchisement of a whole sex, a condition which has existed throughout the civilized world until a comparatively recent date, has bred in half the population an unconscious internationalism," she asserted. Anthony felt confident, moreover, that the subsequent integration of women into their respective national political communities would come too late "to inculcate in them the narrow views of citizenship" that had commonly accompanied the granting of suffrage to men. Women would, Anthony predicted, soon turn from their "unconscious internationalism of the past" to "the conscious internationalism of the future."[1]

Possibly because twentieth-century history has defied Anthony's sanguine expectations, her interpretation of the women's movement up to 1915 has fallen on deaf ears. Even as she wrote, internationalist sentiment faced in the Great War a devastating blow. The decades that followed would, in their emphasis upon the power of nationalism, consign her hopes to the oblivion that the women's movement itself seemed to face. Her predictions went astray, yet Anthony did at least draw attention to a prominent theme in the history of both women and reform. Modern history has been largely written in terms of the nation state, and the manifold evidence of internationalist sentiment among women ignored.

But Anthony was only half right, even in her survey of past achievements. Internationalism was not an activity restricted to women, nor was that activity unconscious in the era of first-wave feminism. What is most striking is the proliferation of organizations expressing international sentiments, both among women and among men. Of these, none was more prominent than the WCTU. This chapter examines the internationalism of the WCTU by looking at the development of its tangible organization, the World's WCTU. At the same time, however, the professions of internationalism that Anthony uncritically accepted must not be taken at face value. Internationalism cannot be measured with the precision of voting returns or legislative roll calls, but the assertions of feminist leaders concerning the strength of international sentiment must nevertheless be scrutinized as constituent parts of feminist ideology and practice.[2]

Evidence of interest in international work among American women is manifest in the temperance press. (An American reader on the windswept plains of Nebraska could, to take just one example, pick up a copy of the *Union Signal* and read detailed reports of the Australasian WCTU's conventions thousands of miles away and glance at photographs of WCTU picnics and tea parties held on the shores of the Australian continent's most beautiful harbor, Port Jackson.)[3] Throughout the life of the *Union Signal* an uneven if surprising amount of such material was printed. A five-year sample between 1885 and 1925 shows that a median figure of approximately 12.5 percent of all *Union Signal* copy was given over to reporting international events, places, and personnel. This ranged from a low of 2 percent in 1885 to a high of 18.84 percent in 1925. But the volume of material fluctuated markedly, with years of World's conventions surveyed showing a higher level of treatment.[4] The effort of the leadership to promote the World's conventions, and the printing of material associated with those conventions, partly account for such fluctuations.

Nor does content analysis measure the appeal of these issues for the readers. Here evidence must be inferential. Editorials frequently discussed World's WCTU issues, and lively debates among correspondents also denoted the importance the editorial staff and, by their willingness to buy the paper, some readers attached to the international dimension of temperance work. The best evidence for an (at least episodic) interest in international

The World's WCTU

work that can be derived from the content of WCTU news concerns the special World's WCTU issue that appeared on 14 May 1891. Demand was so great that 200,000 copies of the *Union Signal* were ordered, twice the average circulation.[5]

Another way of measuring international interest is the anatomy of giving. "What we translate into money is what we love," Louise Purlington, World's superintendent of cooperation with missions, so succinctly put the issue in 1913.[6] Though the quantitative analysis of giving is not the only measure of international sentiment, it is an important one for gauging the relative shifts in levels of commitment. Here an unpredictable oscillation in patterns of interest is clearly seen. When Mary Leavitt journeyed abroad in 1884–85, the local WCTU unions responded enthusiastically to Willard's pleas for financial support. In ten months, temperance women had freely given over $3,000, an amount almost half the total routinely exacted from the state branches for the running of the National WCTU. But once the euphoria had subsided, regular contributions dwindled, and by 1888, only twenty-six state and territory affiliates were contributing any money at all, and total contributions amounted to only 4 percent of national dues.[7] Willard tried as early as the 1886 national convention to institutionalize the high level of giving to the Leavitt fund by proposing, unsuccessfully, that a 5-cent-per-member contribution be made to the World's WCTU. The suggestion was utopian, since at that same convention, national dues had just been raised from 5 to 10 cents a member. Willard's proposal told more about her own commitment to the World's WCTU than about the level of interest in her schemes for a dry world in 1886.[8]

The paradox of upsurges of interest amid resistance to systematic giving was to persist. With the World's WCTU dependent on handouts from the National WCTU executive committee and a few wealthy contributors, organized missionary activity was stymied. But in the spring of 1891 Willard resolved to end the financial stringency. She made her "first personal appeal" to aid the WWCTU in the leadup to the proposed first World's convention in Boston in November, and donations poured in. This time over $3,800 was raised, all in a matter of a few weeks. Again, as in the case of Leavitt's fund, the money came in small scattered offerings from many parts of the country.[9] Yet when dues paying was finally instituted later in 1891, the World's and National WCTU convention set them at a paltry rate of half a cent per member.[10] Two years later the World's and National WCTUs did heed Willard's pleas and doubled per capita contributions, but the financial obligations of the affiliates languished there not only for the rest of Willard's life but into the 1920s as well. This did not mean that evangelical women spurned the international commitment. They were already contributing heavily to the many women's foreign missionary societies; for ordinary members, this imposition of an extra regular contribution to temperance missionaries was too much. As a result, the World's WCTU was forced to rely heavily over the next twenty-five years on donations, financial support in the host countries, and indirect assistance through the missions themselves.[11]

The problems of financial contributions intersected with those of organization. The WCTU was, historian K. Austin Kerr reminds us, a pioneer in the development of a more complex and bureaucratic organization among temperance reformers at a time when such organizational forms were sweeping through the business communities of America. Norman Clark goes further and sees the WCTU as part of a process of "moral 'bureaucratization.'" Yet as Kerr points out, the WCTU mixed bureaucratic and democratic forms, and it was this mixture that provides a key to the paradox of the ordinary supporter's allegiance to, and at times indifference toward, the World's WCTU.[12]

The complexity of international campaigns required a high level of coordination and specialization that implied an intensification of bureaucratic tendencies in the WCTU. To succeed as an international movement, the WCTU required a strong organization that could combat male power structures, transcend the vast cultural differences and language difficulties, and overcome the sheer distance and isolation that often threatened to bury attempts at international cooperation.

Just as clearly, this elitist structure demanded an effective appeal to WCTU members and sympathizers at the local level if the international enterprise was to conform to evangelical expectations. This religious ideology exposed further contradictions in the idea of a moral bureaucracy. Evangelical religion's importance for the international temperance movement lay, in the foreign mission field, in its ability to galvanize supporters through a personal sense of commitment to people not of any immediate relevance to the everyday lives of temperance women. That commitment would be as much spiritual and moral as material and would involve the continual dedication of lives to a common movement across national boundaries.

In this instance, the problem of bureaucratic control of an evangelical temperance impulse was similar to that of the larger Protestant missionary work, when those organizations tried to systematize giving. As Patricia Hill points out in her study of the women's foreign missionary movement in America, the foreign missionary societies around the turn of the century shifted their approach from praying to paying and from the use of enthusiastic amateur helpers to paid organizers whose worth depended not on religious commitment but on (essentially secular) knowledge of the foreign mission field. An important step had been taken toward the secularization of missions and, Hill believes, toward their ultimate demise as a source of inspiration to American middle-class evangelical womanhood.[13] The World's WCTU expressed such a contradiction insofar as it contained strong elitist tendencies that sought to concentrate WCTU power far from the local communities around the world where the prayers and the money were sought and provided. But World's missionaries and organizers distant from the local unions and parochial problems faced severe difficulties in sustaining vital financial and emotional endorsement at the local level.

These anomalies made necessary a process of personal appeals for funds to keep the incipient bureaucracy going, but these funds could only be elicited through the development of special rituals that would express religious convictions and channel the evangelical energy into saving others far away. The whole organizational history of the WCTU is the tale of attempts through the Polyglot Petition, the rituals of membership, the colorful and much-publicized conventions, and inspirational literature and symbolism to routinize and rationalize the democratic and religious forces that the WCTU in the United States already tapped and that a World's WCTU initiative needed. In its organization, the World's WCTU indeed expressed elitist tendencies, but legitimated by the mechanisms of popular will.

Each aspect of the WCTU's organization as it developed in practice involved this fundamental tension. It was the strange and exotic Polyglot that Willard first attempted to use to tap the residual interest in World's work revealed by the Leavitt trip. Faced with evidence of lethargy, it was Willard's genius to perceive the importance of a concrete objective around which to organize such a latent sentiment as internationalism. Drawing explicitly on her Home Protection petition campaign in Illinois in 1879—and on the long tradition of women's petitioning that went back to antislavery days— Willard concluded that the World's organization needed its own petition as a focus of endeavor. After all, the Illinois effort had been followed by a dramatic rise in prohibitionist activity in that state, and Willard reasoned that the same could easily occur internationally. And so began one of the more quixotic of Willard's many ambitious plans for a worldwide influence.[14]

The Polyglot Petition idea first occurred to Willard in 1885. After learning of the British involvement in the opium trade in India and China, Willard conceived of a petition to the governments of the world as a way of dramatizing the impact of drugs on the lives of women everywhere. "The *women of the whole world*," so "immeasurably cursed" by a "two-fold traffic" in alcohol and opium, would through their petition, "unitedly appeal to the men of the world."[15] In its commitment to attack "the poison habits of all lands," the petition signaled an international shift in the treatment of social issues away from the narrow base of mere temperance activity as decisively as the Home Protection campaign did on the national level. Willard already displayed in the framing and promotion of the Polyglot a flexibility that would lead her to promote many innovative strategies within the World's WCTU.[16]

Today the Polyglot Petition sits, faintly ridiculous in its monstrous bulk, amid other relics of the Willard period at Rest Cottage in the pleasant Chicago suburb of Evanston, Illinois. In 1886, the petition lay at the heart of Willard's plans to turn the WCTU into an international organization. Above all, the petition gave women something concrete to achieve and so afforded "a nucleus around which women may rally."[17] As Willard stated in 1885, "Every signature sets several thoughts in motion and helps to educate the brain behind the hand that writes."[18]

Critics charged that the Polyglot was useless because women were not accepted, even in the most advanced democracies, as full citizens. This point did not bother Willard or her beloved co-worker Anna Gordon, and the latter suggested that one consequence of the petition would be its demonstration of women's inferior status. The petitioners were outside the barriers of the individual governments concerned, and their petition had no legal validity. Nor could their signatures command a direct political response.[19] Nonetheless, the petition could have an effect on both legislation and temperance organization, as prior American experience suggested.[20]

The gathering of signatures at first proceeded mainly outside the United States. Missionaries in Burma and Ceylon were the quickest to respond, and Margaret W. Leitch, an ABCFM missionary in Jaffna, Ceylon, translated the petition into Tamil and "many [other] languages in India."[21] Ruth Ranney, an American Baptist missionary in Burma, claimed that Burmese women were receptive. "There was roused in these poor hearts a spark of the true *esprit de corps* of womanhood," reported Ranney.[22] Through these tireless efforts, sources outside the United States still provided the majority of names as late as September 1891. It was only in preparation for the first World's WCTU convention later that year that the American WCTUs began to catch up through a state organizing drive. By 1895 Americans accounted for 57 percent of the 1.12 million signatures given by women, a figure that corresponded closely with the dues paid by the American unions in the 1890–95 period. The Americans had caught up, but the initially slow response to the Polyglot within the United States indicated once more that Willard's ambitions exceeded the will of her followers.[23]

The petition was, nonetheless, a novel and sometimes effective means for mobilizing support. Thus Agnes Bray, who organized in Ebbw Vale, Wales, went house to house and obtained over two thousand signatures in 1891. She found the Polyglot to be a potent device to enable "Temperance and Gospel words to be spoken where perhaps they were never heard before."[24] Even in the United States, the *Union Signal* reported that recruitment had been given a spur in 1895 by the most sustained petitioning ever.[25] More important, in absolute numbers the petition had been signed by three times as many women as were actually enrolled in the World's WCTU in the mid-1890s. The Polyglot did, in this sense, help provide Willard support in the form of a mass endorsement that went well beyond the capacity of her organization, or any other, to incorporate women who could make financial contributions and attend regular temperance meetings.[26]

The organizing potential of the Polyglot was by no means its only function, therefore. Willard repeatedly used it for symbolic and propagandistic purposes. Each World's convention, as well as many other international temperance conferences from 1885 to 1898, saw the petition produced. The early signatures were hastily displayed at the first International Congress against Alcoholism in 1885 in Antwerp, and delegates were encouraged to sign. On the occasion of the Boston meetings of the WWCTU in 1891, the "monster," as it was called, was "used to festoon Faneuil Hall and Tremont Temple as a mighty object lesson of protesting womanhood." Photographs and descriptions of the petition emphasizing its bulk as evidence of women's protests were included in WCTU handbooks and commemorative publications.[27]

Authors who discuss the Polyglot follow Willard and talk of 7 million signatures gained, or even of 7 million women who signed.[28] Far fewer actually did sign. The image of a massive, democratic upsurge implied in these figures must be severely qualified. Willard had surmised in 1885 that perhaps five years or more would be required to complete the petition. She could not have known that ten would be the minimum before a satisfactory number of signatures would be gathered. Only in 1895 did she feel the numbers adequate for a presentation, dutifully made, to a bemused and taciturn President Grover Cleveland in Washington.[29] Even the 7 million signatures presented did not reveal the whole story. Originally the petition was to be signed by women alone, but as the difficulties of organizing women became more apparent, Willard resorted to the signatures of men as well as organizations signing on behalf of men and women. In 1891, for example, the Salvation Army in Britain came good, through Willard's friendship with Lady Henry Somerset, with a quarter of a million signatures. By no means all of these Salvationist petitioners were women. Thus of the 7 million "signatures," in fact less than 1.2 million women actually signed. In any case, compared with the 16 million signatures and attestations of American sabbatarians to the Sunday Rest petition in the late 1880s, the Polyglot pales somewhat in significance.[30]

The shift in emphasis produced opposition within the WCTU because it seemed to contravene the very thrust of the petition. Gwenllian Morgan of Brecon, Wales, the petition's organizer in Britain, opposed both men's signatures and the garnering of attestations by the leaders of societies. The reference in the petition to the "physically weaker sex" now made no sense. Formerly "unique," the petition no longer "seemed to [her] so expressive as

The Polyglot Petition (Anna A. Gordon, *The Beautiful Life of Frances Willard*
[Evanston, Ill.: Woman's Temperance Publishing Association, 1898])

being the voice of the voiceless." Men, concluded Morgan, "have already
the remedy in their own hands" and did not need the pleadings of a petition.[31] The size of the petition also provoked humor and a certain skepti-
cism. When preparing it for the Columbian Exposition in Chicago in 1893,
Alice Briggs of the *Union Signal* office staff complained that it was becoming "a veritable white elephant. . . .You can have no idea of the bulk of the
'creature' unless you see it," she told Willard.[32]

More serious opposition came from those who noted the absence of
many critical elements of the WCTU's national and even international program. When first formulated, the twin targets of alcohol and opium pointed to an expansion of the WCTU's brief for moral reform. By 1895, the
petition caused embarrassment because it did not specifically endorse, for
the benefit of women outside the United States, the wide variety of reforms
that the World's WCTU already pushed, from peace campaigns to antiprostitution to the right to vote. If Willard thought, as she later said, that these
issues would have seemed extravagant outside the United States in 1885,
the sentiment in the international movement had shifted considerably under the impact of WCTU agitation itself and rendered the original Polyglot
an anachronism.[33]

The World's WCTU

Neither the growing ridicule nor the criticism deterred Willard. She earnestly pushed a plan, conceived first in 1890, to proceed around the world, perhaps by air transport, depending on the time that elapsed before the journey was to be undertaken.[34] By 1894, Willard was restraining her public observations to the hope that she and likeminded reformers might circumnavigate the globe by the less visionary means of a chartered steamship, with Somerset. As late as June 1895 an enterprising Methodist missionary turned journalist and travel entrepreneur, Dr. Henry S. Lunn, advertised cruises around the Baltic and Mediterranean as part of the international "progress of the Polyglot petition."[35] Though Willard and Somerset's plans never materialized beyond that summer's trip to Europe, Willard retained her stubborn faith in the Polyglot. Even on her deathbed in 1898, her last ramblings included an injunction to resurrect its glories and secure more signatures.[36]

Later WCTU leaders did indeed remember the Polyglot, perhaps in the process demonstrating too literal a commitment to the paraphernalia of the Willard years. What Willard had chiefly had in mind was the publicity value of the petition, which served at first to highlight the inadequacy of laws concerning the position of women in many different societies, and so implicitly raised the issue of the gender subordination of women. When, in the 1920s, Anna Gordon attempted to revive the tactic, the memory had overtaken the substance. In part, the sheer replication of an old strategy in a vastly transformed era, marked by the expansion of powerful new technologies of persuasion and exploitation, pointed toward the intellectual ossification of the WCTU in the 1920s. Partly, too, the position of women had been transformed so that they no longer, at least in the Anglo-American democracies, lay beyond the political pale. But prohibition in the United States also profoundly influenced the nature of the WCTU's agitation, irrevocably altering the demands of the WCTU in the international arena. The Polyglot had ceased to be an active instrument of policy and had become instead an artifact.[37]

If the Polyglot depicted a popular and international upsurge among women, the organization of the World's WCTU between 1885 and the petition's presentation to Grover Cleveland in 1895 remained fundamentally elitist. From 1886 to 1891, the work was carried on by a committee of the general officers of the American WCTU, without interference from the national convention, which heard reports but did nothing else except delegate its power to Willard and her friends. The constitution and bylaws had been "drafted by a few leaders," as Willard freely admitted, and only "tacitly accepted by the Society as a whole."[38] Beyond this vague endorsement, which connoted as much a lack of vital interest among many as it did a consensus of support, the rank-and-file contribution was in these years practically nonexistent. Frances Willard best expressed the elitist character of the organization but also revealed the compromise between hierarchical impulses and the need for democratic legitimation. "In all new movements it is necessary that a few who grasp the situation should exercise whatever power is needed in order to set the wheels of such [a] new movement in motion." Alongside this frank expression of the elitism of the World's WCTU went the recognition that "power" ultimately still rested, by necessity, in the hands of "the majority." "Delegated authority" was, Willard acknowledged, "the surest basis of a successful and long-enduring effort."[39]

Willard wrote these lines late in 1890, after the National WCTU had endorsed her plan for a World's convention to coincide with the 1891 national convention in Boston. In keeping with the elitist cast of her schemes, the decision seems to have been closely connected to the power politics of the WCTU. In June 1890, Judith Ellen Foster, the organizer of the Non-Partisan WCTU, the breakaway group of Republican women who objected to Willard's interest in third-party politics, had gone to Britain and participated in the BWTA's annual meetings. Though the evidence is circumstantial, the decision to hold a World's convention to cement links with the BWTA was probably related to this event. Foster campaigned on her British tour against the majority WCTU strategy on the politics of prohibition and received support from sections of the BWTA. Foster also claimed that Somerset, who had just been elected BWTA president, was disloyal to Willard. Somerset denied the charge but suggested to the American leader that interest in international work in Britain would languish until a World's convention was held.[40] Whether Willard was motivated, in response to this suggestion, by a desire to check Foster is unclear, but the fact remains that the World's convention in November 1891 marked a new stage in the development of the World's WCTU. A constitution was agreed upon, superintendents of departments elected, dues set, and Willard was formally elected as World's president to succeed Lucas, with Lady Henry as her deputy.[41]

But these formal matters were not at the heart of the convention process. The 1891 meeting was a success in precisely the manner Willard had intended. That body did not make policy but merely endorsed the decisions of the executive committee, which met before the convention opened. (The committee consisted, by Willard's own design, of the WCTU's general officers and the presidents of the various national WCTUs established in Canada, Britain, South Africa, and elsewhere.) Rather, the convention acted as a showplace for the values of the World's WCTU and as evidence of its impressive spread. The prize exhibit was Mary Leavitt who, to thunderous applause, returned to her home city fresh from her magnificent temperance witness to the world.[42]

Meeting in Faneuil Hall, Boston, with all of its revolutionary and patriotic symbolism, the WCTU sought to match the achievements of men on the national stage with "woman's work for humanity." Mingling with the portraits of Washington, Lincoln, and two Adamses, and other famous sons of Massachusetts and the nation was the Polyglot, that testimony to worldwide desires for home protection. The hall was gaily decorated with a profusion of flowers, the flags of all the WCTU's far-flung "possessions," and banners to the WWCTU's original motto, "For God, Home and Humanity." Beside Leavitt "sat representatives from every continent save South America" as delegates listened to the speeches of Willard, Somerset, and other temperance luminaries. As the audience rose to sing "God Save the Queen" and "Coronation" while Somerset and a Canadian representative escorted Willard to the dais, it was unclear whether they did so out of deference to the British delegates or in honor of the woman so many regarded as their own queen—the "uncrowned Queen of America"—Frances Willard.[43]

All the conventions would become vehicles for the expression of the WCTU's international scope and womanly solidarity. Conventions were held once every two years from 1891 to 1897, then in 1900, 1903, 1906, 1910, and 1913. The outbreak of World War I intervened, but regular meetings resumed in 1920 and continued in 1922, 1925, and so on until long after national prohibition collapsed.

Obvious difficulties of communication and travel plagued the planning and execution of these conventions. Though the vast majority of delegates were Anglo-Saxons or Anglicized colonials, the presence of Scandinavian, German, Swiss, Italian, French, Icelandic, and other diverse delegates made communication difficult at times. Some delegates spoke only briefly, like Tel Sono of Japan at the 1891 Boston convention, not because their words of wisdom were unwanted but because "her command of English is not sufficient." Tel Sono had, however, developed the quaint habit of adding an "Amen" to any word in English that she recognized, much to the amusement of the assemblage.[44] In 1900, at Geneva, the *Scottish Women's Temperance News* reported the problem of language with sympathy and illustrated how much it was the mere appearance of a diversity of delegates that produced an emotional solidarity: "Of all the presentations the most interesting were of those who spoke in broken English. It was remarkable, however, how well they spoke, and when words failed, gestures expressive and inimitable came to their aid, and delighted the assembly."[45]

Travel to the conventions usually took the form of chartered steamers for the large English, American, Canadian, and Scottish delegations, but for those from the antipodes, conventions often needed to be combined with never-to-be-repeated, round-the-world tours or a visit, in the case of Sara Nolan of New South Wales in 1910, to her ancestral home in Britain. Sometimes attendance was a payment, too, for work well done at home. Elizabeth Nicholls attended the 1900 Edinburgh conference "which was needed as a rest and change after the arduous toils of office for the preceding years," but only because "some friends" in the South Australian WCTU "collected

Woman's World/Woman's Empire

A group of delegates at the fourth convention of the World's WCTU, Toronto, 1897. *Front row, left to right*: Layyah Barakat (Syria), Rebecca Krikorian (Armenia), Olifia Johannsdottir (Iceland), Marie Kirk (Victoria), Mrs.
Tomo Inoyue (Japan), Ruth Shaffner (United States, representing China),
and Jennie Ericson (Finland). *Back row, left to right*: Miss Janie Ware (Victoria, World's Anti-Gambling Superintendent), Emily Cummins (Australia),
Elizabeth Vincent (England/Australia), Lillian M. N. Stevens (Maine), Agnes Slack (Britain), and Mrs. Bruun (Norway). (collection of the Dominion
WCTU, Toronto, Canada)

the funds for the trip."[46] For delegations from Japan, India, and China, the
WCTU frequently relied on missionaries returning on furlough, women
who had previously lived in those countries, or the visiting World's WCTU
missionaries. Though the cost of travel theoretically prevented all but the
well-off from attending, the experience of Nicholls was not uncommon.
Many local affiliates pooled their resources to send delegates. Thus the
contributions of ordinary WCTU housewives were being used to, in their
terms, give glory to the World's WCTU.[47]

Visiting delegates from afar paid much in time and money to attend but
were invested with expertise that reinforced their positions as leaders in
their own communities. A return from a World's convention, whether the
delegate came from California, Cape Town, or Queensland, meant a round

of meetings explaining the World's work and retelling incidents from the convention. If this was one important means for spreading internationally knowledge of the issues that the WCTU championed, equally important was the information disseminated concerning the leaders of the WCTU themselves. The conventions exposed delegates to the famous women whom they had worshiped from afar. When Emilie Solomon of South Africa met Willard, Somerset, and Hannah Whitall Smith at the London meetings of 1895, she did not "know whom to admire more of those three lovely and gifted women."[48] Susan Sagar of Queensland came with her husband 12,000 miles to the same London convention to speak for just two minutes on the platform. Beyond demonstrating the loyalty of women in such a far-flung colony of the WCTU, Sagar was able to return to wax lyrical on the power and impressiveness of the leading American (and British) women. As much as nine years after the event, Sagar was still in demand in Queensland because of her personal knowledge of the World's leaders.[49]

The conventions involved more than meetings. Hannah Smith described the first in 1891 as an exhausting "whirl" that took in committee assignments, rallies, and social visits.[50] Since up to 3,000 delegates and visitors reportedly attended these meetings,[51] the chances to meet workers from all around the world were considerable, but the occasion was hectic. This was a time to sound out the various national leaders on the appointment of missionaries and to check up on those who had returned or were on furlough.[52] In relation to the 1893 meetings at Chicago, Willard had made a special point of asking Anna Gordon to speak to the peripatetic missionary Jessie Ackermann. Ackermann's long absence abroad had not been punctuated with many personal letters to Willard. Willard's hope that the convention would bridge the gap proved illusory. There was "so much going on" in connection with the convention and the Congress of Religions associated with the world's fair that "it was simply impossible to get hold of . . . Ackerman [sic] long enough to ask her one single blessed question."[53]

The inspirational function of the World's conventions repeatedly surfaced in the speeches and correspondence of delegates. Typical was the claim of a South African delegate to the 1910 convention in Glasgow, Ethel MacKenzie, who returned to Cape Town to tell her own Cape Colony women that the "great World's Conference exceeded all my thoughts of what it would be." She had been inspired with "a greater outlook, a wider horizon, and," Mackenzie emphasized, "as we work for our own country we must foster a missionary spirit, and work for those around us, and reach out into the great world."[54] World's conventions were almost invariably described in this light, so much so that it assumed the proportions of a cliché to call them a time of inspiration, as Sara Nolan put it.[55]

Long after attendance at the conventions, members and friends returned to this inspirational appeal. Men as well as women were so affected. Edward

H. Todd, vice-president of Willamette University, recalled to a WCTU member in 1912: "I was present in Boston over twenty years ago when the International Convention was held there. It was a meeting which I never can forget and the personages present at that time made a great impression on my mind."[56] Other sympathetic Americans as well as foreigners gratuitously professed to be similarly affected. One was Mrs. J. H. Edwards of Dansville, New York, who reported being "overwhelmed" by the "wonderful" World's convention of 1897.[57]

A sizable part of the "overwhelming" impression in the early conventions was made by Willard herself. Much has been said about her charismatic appeal to her followers, and a large proportion of this turned on her platform presence and oratorical abilities. Willard could, said Emilie Solomon, "play upon the emotions of her audience as a musician plays upon an organ."[58] So commanding a figure was Willard on the public stage that many women confessed, like Mrs. J. H. More of Connecticut, that they sat through the World's conventions "primarily to see Miss Willard, & secondarily to benefit by the meetings."[59] This attraction was especially noticeable among women from other WCTUs around the world, who marveled, like Susan Sagar, at the "sweetness and power" of "our dear leader Miss Willard" and her "very impressive" speeches.[60] When illness kept Willard from attending the meetings held in connection with the Congress of Reforms in Chicago in 1893, it was not only Americans who were dismayed. Margaret Suddath of the *Union Signal* office staff reported that "the foreign women, particularly, were so disappointed" that had they known of Willard's absence, they "would not have left their distant lands."[61]

Such women, whether American or foreign, had little opportunity to shape the grand strategies of the World's WCTU work but could vicariously experience the broad vision through emotional identification with a president they self-consciously proclaimed a world figure. Mrs. More inquired if Willard could come and speak to her Winstead, Connecticut, union but held out little hope. "The *world* calls for & listens to Miss Willard, and our small communities must catch the echoes." Though More could not get Willard to come, she used the experience of the World's convention to coax Olifia Johannsdottir, of the Iceland WCTU, to visit her local to convey some of the flavor of the World's work to her fellow members.[62]

Despite this element of personal attraction evident in responses to the World's WCTU president, Willard's magnetic appeal cannot account for the awe with which World's conventions were endorsed, since the pattern of praise for World's WCTU leaders and their performances included the other figures.[63] Rather it was the visible attestation of strength that impressed, and the experience was reinforced by the ideas and styles of the leaders of the movement, which lowly and obscure delegates sought to emulate. As the New South Wales WCTU secretary noted, "We feel proud to stand identified with such an army."[64]

Though the conventions had an inspirational effect, they also illustrated the unequal power relationships within the World's WCTU, women's temperance, and the international women's movement. All conventions were held in the Northern Hemisphere, despite offers from the Australians and South Africans. This reflected the reality of travel costs and the domination of the organization numerically by the Anglo-American groups. But an inevitable effect flowed from the very real and positive achievements of these more successful women. Distant travelers came and were "conquered" by Willard and her fellow leaders. They were bound to be impressed by the accomplishments of the American and British women. Even the Anglo-Saxon sisters from the antipodes felt this unequal relationship, though they did not disapprove. Sara Nolan returned from the 1910 convention especially impressed by the "very large" American delegation. The Australian "numbers seemed small" in this company, but Nolan took comfort from the fact that the then World's president, Rosalind Howard, Countess of Carlisle, "praised Australia very highly."[65]

These feelings of worth bestowed hierarchically on colonial women were reinforced by the selection of women from the lesser affiliates as members of the executive committee. Thus every nationality was integrated into the work. When five Australians were chosen as World's superintendents of departments at the 1897 convention, Amelia Pemmell of Sydney rejoiced. She reported the return of delegate Marie Kirk from the meetings with "five Australian strings to her bow" and noted Kirk's "great joy" that Willard was "proving Australians worthy."[66]

The purpose of meeting internationally was to focus world attention on the temperance and women's questions. Cleverly, Willard timed the early conventions to coincide with other important events. This reduced the cost of travel and inconvenience on some occasions and gave maximum publicity on all. Boston's inaugural convention highlighted the introduction of no-license in Cambridge, Massachusetts. The 1893 meeting coincided with the Chicago World's Fair, and indeed the women delegates met in the Lakeside Palace where many of the other representative congresses associated with the fair had convened. In 1895, the London meeting was designed to focus attention on the British general election and the Liberal party's plans for a measure of prohibition. The Dominion plebiscite on the liquor question provided the context for the 1897 convention in Toronto.[67]

The convention was but part of the attention of the WCTU to an intricate system of ritual and symbol that had its international aspects. The notion of the women of the world united in temperance activity was strengthened by the provision of hymns, emblems, slogans, badges, flags, and banners.

Woman's World/Woman's Empire

When women in Melbourne, Cape Town, Edinburgh, Tokyo, Rangoon, Vancouver, and Chicago sang, "There are Bands of Ribbon White, Around the World, Around the World," a sense of solidarity was undoubtedly achieved. The repetitive effects of such ritual would reinforce a commitment and give emotional sustenance. At the same time every day, the women of the WCTU everywhere were supposed to be engrossed in prayer. On the same days of each year, offerings were to be taken up for the cause of international temperance, and the same speeches and slogans repeated. Unions dutifully observed most elements of this ritual.[68] As Phillida Bunkle notes perceptively in her study of the New Zealand WCTU, the affirmation of the international connection was the "staple," the "highpoint" of national and district conventions or local meetings in such a distant outpost.[69]

Though the WCTU realized the importance of public ceremony and display, its approach always involved the expansion of a literary and educational culture as well. Frances Willard and her friends are correctly known as reformers, but what exactly was a woman reformer at the century's turning? It is often forgotten that Willard and her fellow activists were first and foremost journalists who earned their livings by the exploitation of the generous literary culture of the Victorian middle classes. Like other temperance organizations, the WCTU sought to tap the expansion of libraries and the development of new and more intense styles of reading. This was not simply a matter of what lay on the printed page. The WCTU was closely aligned with the development of a public literary culture in the Chautauqua movement, and the WCTU's local branches should always be seen not simply as talking shops but also as reading rooms and as vehicles for the expression of the same values of self-improvement as the Chautauquas. Jane Stewart, a Toledo journalist, put the point succinctly in describing the meaning of her five-year association with Willard in the 1890s. "I had finished my 'five years' course at the World's and National W.C.T.U. University."[70]

As part of this cultural offensive on an international level, the development of the World's WCTU organization entailed a quest for standardized sources of information. Not only did the *Union Signal* strive to include international news. The paper's editors promoted it as the major journalistic organ of the World's WCTU and a repository of information suitable to be disseminated among various national affiliates. In the euphoric atmosphere of world prohibition anticipated in 1919, the American WCTU even sponsored an international monthly edition.[71]

But just as the *Union Signal* had to compete against state papers, so too in the 1890s did the various national affiliates establish their own. By 1900, Canada had its *Canadian White Ribbon Tidings*, New South Wales and Victoria both produced *White Ribbon Signals*, South Africa sported its *White Ribbon and Y's and Otherwise*, and Scotland its *Scottish Women's Temperance News*.

The World's WCTU

England's *White Ribbon* was the most successful of these papers with a circulation of 23,000 a month in 1910, while others like India's *Temperance Record and White Ribbon* struggled with a circulation of 500. To coordinate this material the World's WCTU supported from 1896 onward a *World's White Ribbon Bulletin*, begun by Lodie Reed of Indianapolis and edited by Britain's Agnes Slack after 1897. This monthly, four-page publication collated information from all parts of the WCTU's far-flung empire. That the material was carefully selected and presented in brief form to enable its reproduction as a separate page of the papers of the national affiliates undoubtedly aided the dissemination of WCTU literature and propaganda.[72] In many countries this process was also aided by the establishment of Demorest Medal contests in which young children competed against one another in the recitation of temperance material. A model for this and related work among the young was the WCTU *National Educator*, a manual of stories and other temperance information designed for the young.[73]

The WCTU also pushed strongly for the passage of scientific temperance instruction (STI) laws on the American model promoted by Mary H. Hunt of Boston. Hunt outlined her approach in the United States to the International Congress against Alcoholism held in Brussels in 1897 and at the meeting in Berlin in 1903. First had come the legislative work, which involved the passage of laws requiring the teaching of health risks associated with the use of alcohol; then, the composition and promotion of suitable texts embracing total abstinence themes and "temperance physiology"; finally Hunt urged, through political lobbying, the enforcement of STI laws. At the time of Hunt's international mission to Europe in 1897, said Willard in a personal endorsement, "her text books are in use throughout the United States, and have been translated into many languages. Sixteen million of children . . . are now under Scientific Temperance Instruction as a result of her grand leadership."[74]

Hunt had been made World's superintendent of this department, and scientific temperance instruction work was prominent not only in the Anglo-Saxon affiliates but in places like Japan, Germany, China, Chile, and Mexico as well. In Japan, temperance missionary Kara Smart had an enthusiastic response in attempting to spread Hunt's ideas. Japanese reformers translated several of Hunt's pamphlets and prepared another of their own entitled "Sake Is a Poison." In the latter part of 1903, Smart addressed thirty-seven government schools and many mission schools and civic audiences in northern Japan. As a result, she reported "a wonderful awakening" among school officials. Although Hunt's dream of a standardized treatment of alcohol education worldwide remained utopian, in many countries like Japan, school boards and education departments did draw to an impressive degree on the American example.[75]

The standardization of literature, ritual, hierarchy, and rules was intended to duplicate on an international level the success of the WCTU national-ly. Together with the development of a quasi-bureaucratic structure, these features did propel the World's WCTU toward the model of a moral bu-reaucracy suggested by Norman Clark.[76] Organization was indeed at the center of Willard's strategy for the WCTU and, in particular, for its global expansion. It was her insight that the collective division of labor would enable largely powerless women to exert a degree of political influence. No doubt, part of the international attraction was affiliation with an efficient, worldwide organization and knowledge that strength came from combina-tion. Because of the appealing principle of specialization that was part of the moral bureaucracy, "ordinary women" with little experience or time could utilize "one talent" in a particular branch of the WCTU's work. As Sara Nolan noted, this form of specialization meant that colonial women had "learned that it is not needed to be great and clever in order to be useful."[77] This point of view, popular in the antipodes, was drawn exten-sively from the American WCTU's own propaganda and represented an expansion of American conceptions of organized moral reform abroad. The South Australian WCTU proclaimed a local union "comparatively in-significant" but "recognizing itself as part of the colonial, Australasian, and World's Union it becomes a mighty force." And where was this praise for an interlocking and hierarchical network drawn from? From the pen of Ester Pugh, national treasurer of the American WCTU.[78]

Internationally the translation of WCTU organizational principles did not always work as smoothly as this. Specialization into departments of work made sense only where the movement was strongest. Visitors to the field soon became persuaded that departmentalization only retarded temper-ance work in the mission stations. Leavitt felt, as did later observers like Katharine Lent Stevenson, that "the simplicity" of evangelization rather than the complex pattern of American specialization must be the sole pri-ority there.[79] Japan, for example, had to struggle to maintain fifteen de-partments in 1896, and all were concerned with temperance, purity, and evangelism.[80] Even in the more receptive fields, like Australia, department-al development fell short of the American model.[81] The energies of WCTU women in many affiliates should not be too thinly spread.

Geography compounded the problems of applying a consistent bureau-cratic formula for international success. Organizationally, the WWCTU was not on as firm a foundation as the national units because distance made executive meetings of members drawn from all over the world difficult, if not impossible, to arrange; because the conventions could not be held an-nually, for the same reasons; and because workers could not be found to do all lines of work in many of the countries that the WCTU penetrated. In the World's WCTU, control of policies remained concentrated in a small band of leaders: the superintendents of departments, the vice-presidents, the national WCTU executives and, occasionally, the WWCTU missionaries. These constituted the core of the WWCTU, and the executive committee was drawn from these sources, though its particular structure varied over the half-century that this book treats. Within that framework, much latitude was given by default to particular individuals who ran, largely as their own bailiwicks, the special causes that the World's WCTU championed.

Hunt's scientific temperance instruction department illustrates the problem. Hunt became estranged from sections of the American WCTU leadership in the mid-1890s; she felt that not enough financial support or prestige was given to her important work and became involved in several petty disputes over funding. Hunt continued to take seriously the international dimensions of her labors, since she regularly attended international conferences as World's WCTU representative and carried on, up to her death, an impressive correspondence with world leaders of the scientific temperance instruction department within the WCTU. Yet by the turn of the century, Hunt ran this department almost entirely independently of National or World's WCTU influence and moved closer to the ASL in her own political affiliations. After her death in 1906, a messy dispute erupted between her chosen successor, Cora Stoddard, and National WCTU officials; this led to a formal split and the formation of the Scientific Temperance Federation under Stoddard. Not until 1918 were the two organizations reconciled.[82]

These sometimes quarreling officials presided over a rank and file whose commitment was more uneven and conditional than the public professions and private hopes of the leadership usually suggested. Exposure to the World's WCTU was episodic at best for most WCTU members in the United States and in other countries, and at times calls were made to abandon the organization. When Frances Willard died in 1898, the WWCTU seemed even to Somerset as Willard's special creation, and she wondered just how it would survive without her.[83] Several years later, new World's president Rosalind Carlisle professed her own despair. She complained of the "hole & corner" management of the World's work, within Britain in particular. As a result "the W.W.C.T.U. is never properly kept in view as there is no machinery for this purpose and the Brit. Women I am convinced care not one whit for it." Carlisle's indictment was too sweeping, and also self-serving, since she wanted to erase sources of authority alternative to her own. Especially did she object to the "autocratic, isolated, single handed" power exercised since Willard's death by World's and BWTA secretary Slack. Though Carlisle claimed to be a "Committee woman through and through," like Slack her personality tended strongly toward the domineering, and the two clashed repeatedly during the early years of Carlisle's presidency.[84] This self-serving aside, Carlisle's indictment did reinforce the many invocations calling upon the rank and file in both Britain and America to support the World's work and demonstrated a gap between the elite's commitment on behalf of temperance women and the depth of feeling on international issues in particular communities.[85]

No one should be surprised that local and national loyalties usually took precedence. Yet sometimes local issues reinforced loyalty to the World's WCTU rather than to national bodies. The parochial allegiances of the various Australian colonies, in particular, made them distrustful of one another, and this conspired to keep the Australasian WCTU weak in the 1890s. Even when political federation came in 1901 with the creation of the Commonwealth of Australia, some temperance women opposed payment of affiliation dues to the national Australian WCTU and, through it, to the World's WCTU. Victoria preferred direct representation and very reluctantly submitted to national authority after 1903. More successful were the New Zealanders, who resisted a federation with the WCTUs in Australia in the 1890s on the grounds that the Australians were both distant and different. Emma Packe of Christchurch invoked internationalism to justify the New Zealand stance. "We are complete with our local, national, and worldwide Unions, owing allegiance to one world-wide President, subscribing to one World's Fund, with liberty and local self-government."[86] This was not the only case in which, ironically, localism found a strange bedfellow in internationalism. Local issues that made the Scottish WCTU's needs quite distinct from the BWTA's led in 1904 to secession and affiliation directly with the WWCTU. In Canada, a bitter dispute over seemingly trivial issues of organization between Quebec and Ontario in 1913–14 meant that both sides had more cordial relations with their World's WCTU sisters than with each other.[87]

Local loyalties were not firm foundations for internationalist sentiment, however. They provided only temporary conditions for the flowering of the World's WCTU. By the 1920s, national loyalties would be a potent force cutting across the rationale for a World's WCTU. As Katharine Anthony correctly pointed out, it was the exclusion of women from the political process on the national level that bred "unconscious internationalism." The Polyglot Petition played on this theme of unrepresented and wronged womanhood, but the evidence suggests that when the franchise was given, internationalist sentiment altered in character though it did not flicker out. Even before enfranchisement, the extent and depth of women's internationalism was open to serious question, if the history of the World's WCTU offers any guide.

This qualified character of its support did not diminish the WWCTU's importance. A widespread sentiment of international feminism among the leaders of the women's temperance movement persisted alongside a residual level of support in the larger WCTU constituency, in which notions of internationalism competed uneasily with more concrete manifestations of an Anglo-American cultural imperialism. Within this context of feminist dreams and aspirations the significance of the World's WCTU as organization and symbol must be sought.

Lady Carlisle's gloomy assessment notwithstanding, the World's WCTU was not abandoned; in fact it grew in importance within the international women's temperance movement into the era of national American prohibition. Nor should skeptical assessments of the international movement's popular support be taken as evidence of the WWCTU's irrelevance to international women's temperance, or to women's emancipation more generally. But in order to assess the international movement's worth, it is necessary to ask, Who benefited from the WWCTU? Not in a crass sense of personal material interest is this question to be posed; rather we must gauge the WWCTU's importance in the politics of that elite of feminists who did take a very serious interest in the organization's well being.

Financial arrangements told clearly how power functioned in a hierarchical fashion. Instead of attempting to raise formal affiliation fees, the WWCTU executive committee actually appeared to prefer a resort to private philanthropy, even after the death of Willard. To fund its grandiose aspirations on the world stage, the organization relied quite heavily throughout its existence on unsolicited donations from a minority of women deeply committed to the international cause. This process reinforced the bureaucratic tendencies of the organization and its leaders' aspirations. Especially valuable was the assistance of rich women like Somerset and Carlisle. In 1914, Carlisle gave $4,000 to subsidize the missionary work, and between 1913 and 1921 she contributed enough to sustain all the existing WCTU missionary commitments.[88] It is small wonder then that Anna Gordon, as national president of the WCTU in America, was always solicitous of Carlisle's views in the missionary field. When Carlisle refused to continue the policy of sending missionaries to Anglo-Saxon countries and pushed heavily for missions for India, China, and Japan, the American WCTU did not object and neither did anybody else. The British strategy of Willard's was similarly based on the strong support given to the WCTU by Lady Henry.[89] That Lady Henry exerted an inordinate influence between 1893 and 1906 over the World's WCTU flowed in part from her personal financial involvement.[90]

Within the American WCTU, the same pattern applied, with heavy donations to international work coming from a few key sources. Willard herself very generously gave the $3,000 that the National WCTU had raised as a special fiftieth birthday gift.[91] Annie Kennedy Bidwell, a noted humanitarian and Indian reformer from California, was one of a number who gave disproportionately, and Bidwell was also one who in 1883 urged upon Willard a global strategy. All in all, donors (narrowly) provided more in the 1890s than the total commitment of dues paid by members to the World's WCTU.[92]

The reliance on donors was one issue in the great controversy of the late 1890s concerning Lady Henry's influence over Frances Willard. The British woman was said by discontented Americans to have virtually hijacked Willard by payment of an "annuity."[93] Willard denied the charges, and the furor over British financial domination of the World's WCTU died down, but the need to reform the structure of the organization had been exposed. Willard had always said that eventually the WWCTU would become democratic and fully responsible to conventions, the way that the NWCTU was. Elitist tutelage would only persist during the period of growth, while international sentiment remained weak. But Willard never did anything about reforming the decision-making process. She was quite content to maintain the hierarchical structure. Ironically, she could see that democratic control conflicted with her aspirations for the WWCTU to be a truly international society. Since the National American WCTU held a majority of dues-paying members at the end of the century, representation at conventions was correspondingly slanted. If the convention controlled all decisions, other countries would conceivably get little representation on the executive committee and policies would be decided by the American group. In the interests of a broader international representation, Willard appointed all superintendents and gave disproportionate representation to the non-American affiliates, particularly those in the British empire. "The idea was," she explained in 1895, to make each Auxiliary National WCTU "feel included, however weak that society, or however distant."[94] But after her death, the issue was revived. Against British opposition, World's appointments were made subject in 1903 to convention approval for the first time, and resolutions ceased to be rubber-stamped by the delegates.[95]

The hierarchical nature of the giving process was not eliminated by this constitutional revolution, but only changed. Since conventions met only once every three years, by necessity power still gravitated toward the executive committee. Moreover, the assertion of democratic principles ironically reinforced the tendency toward colonialist relations within the WCTU between its largest (American) affiliate and other constituent unions. After 1903, many of the smaller national affiliates did lose, as Willard had feared they would, some of their influence within the World's WCTU, despite the fact that they were disproportionately good contributors to the World's coffers. This circumstance arose because the Americans were better dues payers, but poorer donors, than some other key affiliates. Over the period 1899–1906, when this controversy was fought out, the American WCTU provided a median 55.9 percent of dues (and hence seats at World's conventions) but only 43.5 percent of direct financial contributions to the World's body.[96] Canada, Australia, and Britain were much better sources of donations. This pattern was not simply the result of major contributions from rich British aristocrats, as the example of the British dominions indicates. Marie Kirk, Australian World's Missionary Fund superintendent, was despondent at the decline of Australian contributions between 1910 and 1913, but the amounts raised were still impressive when compared with the American contributions. With 20 times the Australian population, the United States provided 28 times the Australian dues contribution, but only 15 times the total financial contribution, and a paltry 3.8 times the level of Australian donations.[97]

Though the World's WCTU was controlled by an Anglo-American elite, in fact the sources of most generous per capita financial support lay outside the empire's nerve center. Many countries gave beyond the proportion of their memberships. Indeed, the level of financial contributions outside the Anglo-American unions was much higher than the official figures indicated. Mary Leavitt was funded by the National WCTU initially, but only 14.5 percent of her total expenses between 1883 and 1891 were met by the national union.[98] Temperance supporters in the countries visited largely funded her epic trip. The picture was even clearer in the case of the second round-the-world missionary, Jessie Ackermann, who received no funding at all from the NWCTU and yet by 1895 had eclipsed Leavitt's achievements in miles traveled, countries visited, and unions established. In all, Ackermann raised for her temperance work over $12,000 in her first five years abroad, much of it in the British colonies. Leavitt recognized early that the English-speaking countries would be strong contributors to an international movement, and she was right.

Colonial unions gave to the grandly conceived if ill-fated Woman's Temple in Chicago, a Chicago office block planned as headquarters of the WCTU and the Woman's Temperance Publishing Association. South Africans and Australians also freely aided the Duxhurst colony that Lady Henry established in the Surrey countryside for reformed women alcoholics, even though neither union had any direct stake in the venture. Contributions to both the temple and Duxhurst simply reflected a commitment to international solidarity between women.[99] South Australia gave to the temple because it was a symbol of women's achievements and because unions that donated would have their names emblazoned on special commemorative bricks in the temple precinct. Elizabeth Nicholls took great comfort from this fact because thereby "visitors [to the temple] may see that we are a part of the [World's] organisation."[100]

The pattern was maintained for every missionary who went to the Anglo-Saxon colonies and dominions. The Americans (and the World's WCTU) did have to pay heavily in the non-European countries, but even here attempts were made to get the local unions self-funding, and touching and generous amounts were donated to the temple and other projects in the WCTU's heartland.[101] But such efforts were invariably swamped in the global picture. The view from the center was very different from that at the periphery. No small country could possibly compete with the United States and Britain in terms of gross financial support. British and American sources contributed around three-quarters of the total funding from 1899 to 1906.[102]

The uses to which the money was put illustrate, like the Woman's Temple and other financial projects, the hierarchical and promotional aims of the World's WCTU. Willard's aim was to use the international temperance movement to raise women's consciousness by elevating the authority and prestige of the movement's leaders. She and her coterie were to be "representative women" in the manner familiar to the late nineteenth-century biographical directories. Willard herself coauthored one such compilation, *A Woman of the Century*, in which the heroines of the WCTU figured prominently.[103]

Willard never sought fortune, and indeed she died a relatively poor woman, but fame was sanctioned so long as she and her friends thereby represented the achievements and virtues of womanhood. As far back as Willard's 1869 European tour, the splendors of European royalty had prompted "dreams, dim and momentary," of "such a destiny" as "to be great, to be powerful." But these ambitions were instantaneously sublimated by the greater desire "*to be good*—that one's single will might be the good angel of millions." It was no accident, therefore, that at a time of imperial expansion and enhanced international travel, Willard sponsored the journeys of intrepid women around the globe and publicized their heroic endeavors. Nor was this desire to use the World's WCTU to publicize Willard's brand of women's emancipation limited to travel. Temperance women's use of the analogue of international power politics and the solicitation of the trappings of its ceremonial roles is striking. Much was made of the fact that Jessie Ackermann had met the king of Siam and, indeed, claimed to be on speaking terms with all of the rulers of world worth knowing, that Mary Hunt had been summoned to meet the German empress, that Germany's Ottilie Hoffmann had been honored by the kaiser, that Leavitt had obtained an audience with King Leopold of Belgium to discuss the export of alcohol to native peoples, and so on.[104]

Willard was a master at the art of soliciting fame. At an international meeting held in London in January 1893, miffed that the American WCTU had not sent her a telegram in support of her efforts in Britain, Willard herself arranged to have the telegram saluting her international stature sent.[105] Temperance and general newspapers sympathetic to her cause described her as the "world famous" temperance lecturer, while others more royally inclined were content to describe her as the "Queen of temperance." She had, so World's WCTU secretary Slack claimed, achieved more good between Britain and the United States than "any living statesman," and her work was compared with the punier efforts at political arbitration then being undertaken by the two great Anglo-Saxon powers.[106]

These images did not escape the irreverent observations of those mordantly disposed toward either the temperance movement or women's emancipation. The practice of World's conventions, which involved the publication of a vast array of material on the achievements of the "world honoured names" of the most "famous" delegates, incurred the amusement of these unsympathetic types. The *London Evening Dispatch* attacked in 1895 the "self-advertising coterie of Anglo-American ladies" whose "routine" consisted of "writing each other's biographies, telling beautiful stories of one another, and publishing each other's photograph[s]."[107]

Like the Polyglot Petition, Willard's dreams for a World's WCTU seem visionary in retrospect. If the augustly named World's union never fully matched substance with promise, the goals underlying Willard's commitment were shrewd, nonetheless. Willard seized the opportunity to present herself as an international figure; the stateswoman, the diplomat, the head of state, all converged in the image she projected.

But it was not just Willard who projected a farsighted cosmopolitanism. For the 1897 convention, the *Chicago Inter-Ocean* published a "composite picture" of WWCTU leaders that included Somerset and Gordon. These three were said with hyperbole to have done "more than all the rest of the universe for the temperance cause,"[108] but other officials could easily have been included. In the 1880s and 1890s the Quaker Mary Woodbridge, Mary Sanderson and Ella Williams of Canada, and Hannah Smith were candidates for the first rank of leaders. After Willard's death in 1898, there was added to the group a number of others. Most notable was the strong-minded Carlisle, who with her four daughters, aristocratic connections, and great wealth became indispensable to the World's WCTU prior to her death in 1921. Also influential was Agnes Slack, who remained secretary of the organization for nearly fifty years until just before she died in 1946. These officials bore no marks of a common personality type. Anna Gordon was self-effacing and much loved by all; Slack was said, privately by many in the organization, to be obtuse, but her positions as editor of the *World's White Ribbon Bulletin* and World's secretary made her an influential, if at times controversial, figure. Many women in the organization disliked her, and even her biographer and friend, Aelfrida Tillyard, provides a most unflattering portrait of this key official. Slack was typically described as "in her element dominating and inspiring a vast audience."[109]

This group constituted the core of a WWCTU sorority that expanded and contracted with changes in personnel and historical circumstances. Mary Leavitt was never part of this intimate circle, though she did hold the office of honorary president for a number of years. Her (functional) exclu-

General Officers of the World's WCTU, c. 1896. *Left to right*: Anna A. Gordon, assistant secretary; Agnes E. Slack, secretary; Frances Willard, president; Lady Henry Somerset, vice-president-at-large; and Mary E. Sanderson, treasurer. (Anna A. Gordon, *The Beautiful Life of Frances Willard* [Evanston, Ill.: Woman's Temperance Publishing Association, 1898])

sion from the inner circle may explain her disillusionment, apparent after 1895, with the policies of the World's WCTU. The movement's leaders may, in the language of the social scientist, be seen as bureaucrats of a kind, though in the late 1890s the high-handed and close-knit band of World's officials appeared to Leavitt and some outside observers as "the junta," a dictatorial group that ignored the wishes of the rank and file.[110]

These officials had personal reasons for seeking power and promoting the international glory of the World's WCTU, but they did believe earnestly in the efficacy of women's temperance as a means for uplifting their sex and transforming the hierarchical relations of gender apparent across a wide range of cultures. Since they pursued simultaneously their personal goals for power and the extension of women's sphere, theirs was not a simple case of false consciousness, nor was their internationalist ideology a Machiavellian screen for less honorable motives. Ideology, personal ambition, and the dynamic patterns of organizational development combined to ensure that international issues would never be far from the center of controversies within the women's temperance movement.

It was this elite group that claimed to speak for up to two million temperance women at the turn of the century.[111] Publicly they stood at the head of a mighty phalanx, but privately they questioned the efficacy of their global ambitions. But the picture had a brighter side, since support could be measured in two ways. If one was the contentious commitment to a specifically international organization, the other was a modestly successful diffusion of women's temperance ideology and organizational forms between the 1880s and the 1920s. The WCTU and its principles did spread to more than forty countries and the international work of the organization became in this era the preeminent vehicle for the global dissemination of American temperance principles.

Beyond the issue of support, with all of its local and national variations, lay the impact of the actual policies the WCTU pursued. Here the World's WCTU work went further than the ranks of the union itself and intersected with the wider realm of reform and feminist politics. More important still was the largely unacknowledged battle in which the WCTU became engaged as both agent and critic of Western expansionism, contributed to cultural upheaval in the underdeveloped world, and even stimulated, unwittingly, the terms of the nationalist reaction. As the leadership and the rank and file worked out these issues, they confronted a world vastly different from the environment that gave women's temperance its American reputation and power. Their success abroad would be measured by their ability to transcend the environment that, ironically, gave them the impulse to internationalize their crusade.

4

Bands of Ribbon White around the World

Patterns of International Support

T he sun never sets on the World's Woman's Christian Temperance Union," pronounced Basil Wilber-force, friend of Lady Henry and Anglican canon at the first and special British conference of the organization in May 1892. That remark deeply touched Willard as well as Somerset because it gave recognition to the movement's international achievements and conveyed an impression that the WCTU was a moral empire as extensive as Britain's imperial posses-sions.[1] The Anglican temperance reformer was literally correct, since the WWCTU's nominal coverage included every continent, except Antarctica, and many of the islands that dotted the seas in between. Willard's creation did achieve an impressive international representation that partially real-ized the ambitions of the founder to gird the globe with a white ribbon. The movement's stationery proudly emphasized this symbol of internation-alism and united purpose; so too did the noontide hour of prayer. With affiliated national unions in more than forty countries and representatives in many more all stopping to pray for a sober world at midday, the WCTU could take comfort that at any time of the day or night, women were work-ing for temperance somewhere.

Though the American WCTU was the largest and routinely had be-tween 50 and 60 percent of the paid-up memberships during most of the period in question, in both proportional terms and in absolute numbers the WCTU was very active in several other countries. This point is easily ob-scured if relative population size and stages of development are not taken into account. In the early 1890s, for example, the Australian affiliates had enrolled proportionately almost as many members as the American, while in Natal, per capita membership among white settlers had reached, after four years, the level attained in the United States after twenty years' orga-nizing.[2] In the 1890s, it was not the American affiliates but the Japanese that could claim the largest increase in membership and so win in 1897 the World's WCTU banner. (The Japanese, anxious to imitate American ways, enrolled a respectable 4,000 members by 1910, and 10,000 in the 1930s.)[3]

Though not as impressive in terms of proportional increases as the Japanese, the British contribution was, in numerical terms, of vital importance. By 1910 the paid-up membership of the British unions amounted to 157,000 members, compared to the Americans' 235,000.[4] This made the BWTA far and away the largest women's temperance society outside the United States. Without its support, the American WCTU could hardly maintain its international ambitions. Not only was the British the largest affiliate. It was, curiously, more successful in numerical terms than its much vaunted cousin across the ocean. Though the total American population was 2.2 times the British in 1910, its WCTU membership was only 1.4 times that of the BWTA.[5] In addition to these major sources of strength, it must also be noted that the WCTU had unions in such unlikely places as Germany, Denmark, France, Austria, Belgium, Bulgaria, Russia, Chile, Palestine, Egypt, Uruguay, Argentina, Syria, and many more locations.[6]

If the sun never did set upon this empire, its rays shone more brightly on some areas than others. Mary Leavitt told Ruth Stephens, a Queenslander, in 1907 that "the results" of her work had "been large wherever I reached English speaking communities."[7] She did not state the corollary, that elsewhere the WCTU failed dismally. For all of its global pretensions, the WCTU remained tied to its Anglo-Saxon base and the spread of that civilization to the far corners of the earth in an age of imperialism. Only in Britain, Scandinavia, Canada, Australia, New Zealand, South Africa, Hawaii, and the missionary outposts of the Anglo-American empires in Japan, China, and India did the WCTU achieve more than cursory local significance. Both here and elsewhere, the union relied on Anglo-American and, especially, American influence.

Among the unpromising fields that the sowers of the WCTU gospel surveyed, none presented such an inhospitable prospect as France. When Ida M. Tarbell, temperance supporter and muckraking journalist, visited Paris in 1891, she inquired of her French music teacher where the WCTU was located. His reply was both humorous and instructive of the WCTU's international pretensions. "Ah, Mademoiselle," he said, "maybe there is such a thing in Paris, the foreigners have brought in many odd things, but I do not know; you will have to ask your English friends."[8] The position had not changed much by 1897, when the *Chicago Inter-Ocean* reported that "visitors are unable to find the headquarters [of the French WCTU]. The only place where the name W.C.T.U. is displayed is in a restaurant which is eminently secular."[9] WCTU work was largely restricted to the French capital and to that city's English-speaking enclave. Throughout the 1890s, WCTU organizers focused on an alliance with the Blue Cross organization, which in fact did not practice total abstinence itself and concentrated on the provision of temperance restaurants where alcohol was not sold. This approach produced few results and convinced World's officials that the French White Ribboners cared more for purity work than they did for an antialcohol crusade. Even though the World's WCTU struggled hard in its attempts to get a foothold in France after the turn of the century by reshuffling the French leadership, by 1910 the organization could claim only ninety-seven members.[10] As Steven Hause and Anne Kenney remark in the course of their study of French suffragism, "a French WCTU, with tens of thousands of women seeking to prohibit the consumption of all forms of alcoholic beverages, is scarcely conceivable."[11]

The position in Germany was a little different. Fifteen hundred members had been enrolled in the Deutscher Bund Abstinenter Frauen by 1910, 52 unions had 2,600 members by 1912, and the founder, Ottilie Hoffmann, was active in the moderate wing of the German women's movement.[12] The kaiser was apparently impressed. He awarded her the Royal Prussian Order Frauen Vereinskreuz for social work in 1909, and the commanding general of the German army ordered twenty officers to attend, in full uniform, a meeting of the women's association.[13] But it is undoubtedly of some significance that Hoffmann was a leading Anglophile and had in fact been a governess in the home of World's and BWTA president Rosalind Carlisle. Hoffmann retained this and other contacts with the Anglo-American temperance movement in later years.[14]

No one factor can explain the inability of the WCTU to transcend its Anglo-American roots, but the issue of abstinence is a logical place to start. European support was extremely difficult to come by because of the Anglo-American temperance movement's insistence on teetotalism. As a product of cultures in which the experience of drinking had been shaped by the rising consumption of spirits in the late eighteenth and early nineteenth centuries—gin and whiskey in the British case and rum and whiskey in the American—the Anglo-American temperance reformer found the use of wine as a part of the daily diet difficult to accept. This ambiguity was well illustrated in the observations of WCTU travelers in Europe. Isabella Irish, a Wisconsin WCTU woman resident in France, was particularly perceptive in her grudging comments written back to the *Union Signal* in 1885. "Intoxication is less frequent here than in America," she reluctantly conceded, because wine, not spirits, was taken and often diluted with water as well. Moreover, in comparison with the American habit of consuming alcohol in a saloon, the French tended to drink with their meals, a practice that inhibited gross displays of alcoholic excess.[15] Almost all the active temperance societies in France, Germany, and Switzerland adopted the formula of moderation that Americans had discarded in the 1830s.[16] The WWCTU recognized this problem to the extent that in 1910 Agnes Slack promoted, quite openly, associate membership in women's "clubs" that permitted the taking of light wines, and she vowed to use this strategy to educate women in the wine-drinking countries to abstain from all alcohol.[17]

But the different attitudes of the wine-drinking cultures cannot alone explain the limits to the WCTU's appeal. The wine-drinking clubs made only a marginal impact in France, Germany, and Switzerland, for example. Wine drinking cannot be the whole answer in any case because even in those countries where the use of spirits predominated, like Finland, the WCTU never made a major impact on the temperance movement.[18] The use of the English language may have provoked resistance among those in Europe who valued their cultural independence. Isabella Irish certainly mentioned the language problems faced by Anglo-American temperance reformers.[19]

But the WCTU also had difficulty in penetrating anywhere in Scandinavia, despite the fact that representatives of other strands of the Anglo-American temperance movement had considerable impact there and despite the long and partially successful agitation of Finns, Norwegians, and Icelanders for antialcohol legislation. Sweden's 6,000 members in 1913 made that union the most important non-English-speaking affiliate, but the WCTU in Sweden was dwarfed by the Good Templars, which had by 1913 a quarter of a million members.[20] The presence of the Good Templars, which like the White Ribboners had originated in the United States, casts doubt on the explanation that resistance to Anglo-American language and culture lay behind the WCTU's relative weakness. In Norway, the position was similar, with 3,604 White Ribbon (WCTU) members in 1910, and over 80,000 in the Norwegian Total Abstinence Society.[21] In Finland, the membership of the White Ribbon peaked at 3,960 in 1906, but over six times this number of women were enrolled in the main temperance society that catered to both men and women.[22] Thus even where temperance sentiment was stronger and conditions for an Anglo-American influence propitious, the WCTU largely failed to play more than a secondary role at best. Something more than the language barrier or hostility to Anglo-American influence must have been at work.

The most obvious strengths of the WCTU were also its greatest weaknesses outside the Anglo-American world. Protestant evangelical religion's role should not be neglected in this regard. Nowhere did the WCTU succeed where the descendants of John Calvin and Wesley were not in evidence. Frances Willard might appear at Irish-American temperance society meetings and praise the Catholic total abstinence effort in America, and Slack organized specifically Catholic auxiliaries in Dublin in 1896, but no amount of ecumenism could shift the attitudes of lesser mortals on both sides. Few Catholics and still fewer Jews patronized the WCTU in America, and one could hardly expect these groups, or Moslems, Buddhists, and

Woman's World/Woman's Empire

Hindus, to rush to the defense of the white ribbon, even though the last three had a pronounced cultural and religious preference for abstinence.

But in wine-drinking countries, as Irish pointed out in 1885, the Protestants as well as the Catholics tended to drink. Longtime English Protestant residents joined locals in accepting the wine-drinking customs of those societies. Even more to the point, in Scandinavian countries the Protestant groups were dominant and yet they too were only modestly attracted to the WCTU, which stood for total abstinence. In Norway and Denmark, major temperance groups allowed the use of low-alcohol (2.5 percent) beer.[23] In part, the source of this resistance would have been familiar to Willard, just as it is to the student of comparative temperance movements today. In Scandinavia, the established churches were Lutheran, and those churches perpetuated a more ritualistic approach to worship and church doctrine that contrasted with the emphasis on personal conduct in the inheritors of Calvin's legacy, or that of Wesley.[24] Lutherans everywhere and not just in Scandinavia were less likely to accept teetotalism than the Wesleyans. Actually, though, the position was more complex than the sociological typology of liturgical versus pietistic approaches suggests. The Lutheran churches themselves were split over the drink issue. The temperance movement appears to have prospered in Scandinavia where Protestant revivalism was conducted, as in Sweden, on an Anglo-American model that stressed the conversion process and measured spiritual progress by personal conduct and religious benevolence. These conditions were not met nearly so well in Denmark, where the revivals were more inward-turning and pietistic. This stymied the development of a strong temperance movement concerned with public conduct, despite the high consumption of alcohol in Danish society.[25]

Yet the progress and content of evangelical religion on its own cannot explain the poor showing of the WCTU in Scandinavia, relative to other temperance groups. Among the revivalistic Swedes, the WCTU's support was not strong, and, moreover, WCTU observers and allies cited additional forces retarding the women's temperance movement in those Protestant countries. What appears to have been especially damaging to the WCTU in northern Europe was resistance to women joining single-sex temperance organizations, a resistance that was manifest among both men and women. Historian Irma Sulkunen finds this to be the case for Finland around the turn of the century, just as in the 1880s, WCTU representatives noted the differing impact of feminism and movements for women's emancipation in northern Europe in comparison with Anglo-American countries. Charlotte Gray, WWCTU representative in Europe, told one international temperance convention in 1888 that despite the strength of temperance in Scandinavia, "women have as yet done but little." She felt certain that "in these old conservative nations woman has not the same freedom as in new countries,

and it is much more difficult for her to take any prominent part in anything outside her home."[26]

Corroborating evidence of conservatism in Scandinavian temperance
came from a Good Templar official, Jessie Forsyth, who also participated in
international missionary work and organizing for the WCTU. Forsyth was
surprised when she attended a Good Templar convention in Sweden in
1885 that she was relegated to the back of the speakers' platform. Unde-
terred, she told the audience that she had come from "a country [the United States] in which it was not the custom to put the women in the back
seats."[27] The Danish representative of the WWCTU, Elizabet Selmer, who
also served in the 1890s as organizer for the whole of Scandinavia, felt the
same. "It is nearly impossible," she warned the American WCTU, "for you
English-speaking women to understand how small the influence of women
is here."[28] Though Selmer did mention the hindering influence of Christian husbands on their wives, Selmer emphasized in most of her reports
that Danish women were themselves "our great antagonists."[29] They were
reluctant to join because their conception of women's influence was the
indirect influence of the woman behind the throne. Both Sulkunen and
Swedish historian Per Frånberg corroborate this evidence for Finland and
Sweden respectively and emphasize that few outright feminists joined the
movement.[30]

The WCTU was largely unable to capture the loyalties of the more advanced sections of the women's movement in Scandinavia. Indeed, the organization appears to have been more conservative on women's questions
than its American equivalent. The White Ribbon societies—as the WCTU
was known there—enrolled but few feminists in Sweden and espoused the
cult of domesticity largely unrelieved by themes of women's emancipation.[31] (Even such a feminist as Ellen Key, who proposed a revival of the
role of motherhood as a central tenet of the emancipation of women, did
not, we shall see in a later chapter, become allied with the WCTU because
Key did not accept the conventional conception of sexual morality that underlay the theme of purity in the temperance movement.)[32] The position in
Finland was similar, judging from the available evidence. Only a minority of
temperance women favored separatist organizations, and even these wom-
en "were not 'feminist' but very strongly domestic and moralistic" in
approach.[33]

The reluctance of feminists to join the WCTU in Scandinavia is striking,
given the much closer links between temperance and women's emancipation in England and America in the late nineteenth century. Selmer did
establish certain rather formal connections with the more active feminists
by speaking at feminist meetings, but she also reported that in her own
country the Danish Union for the Emancipation of Women "feels but very
little interest in this work."[34] Those of professional status dominated the

Woman's World/Woman's Empire

emancipationist movement, and in Denmark these were mainly doctors who tended rather to "adopt the customs of men," which meant that they were likely to equate women's emancipation with such personal freedoms as the right to drink.[35] This explains, at least in part, why few of the more outspoken feminists—themselves a small minority in Scandinavian societies—cooperated with the WCTU, in comparison with the interconnections of these groups in the Anglo-Saxon world.

Reinforcing this divergent understanding of emancipation were issues of personal morality and anticlericalism. In many European countries, the most advanced sections of the women's movement tended to spurn the consolations of organized religion, to dabble in free thought, and to question conventional bourgeois morality. The literary radicalism of Norwegian writers in the 1880s, most notably Henrik Ibsen, polarized thinking on sexual and feminist issues, so "disturbing" was its development "to the conservative ruling groups in Scandinavia," says historian Ross Evans Paulson.[36] The gulf was much more pronounced in Catholic Europe to the south. In France, for example, Catholicism was strongly identified with right-wing attitudes among the women of the French bourgeoisie. Advanced positions in the women's movement tended to be taken by socialists and anticlerical republicans. Among both groups, religion was identified with reactionary policies. Ede Marrin, a supporter of the Congrès des oeuvres et institutions feminines (a moderate French Protestant reform group of feminist sympathies) wrote to Willard in 1891 expressing the dilemma: "The great difficulty for us is that the group of the more advanced women is entirely materialist and atheist and with them, after deep consideration, I renounced to work. The emancipation of woman if not based on religious principles and feeling is doomed to hell."[37]

The WCTU was thus caught in the middle between the poles of a conservative domestic conception of women and a radical emancipationist one. In America this gulf could be bridged, at least partially, by a Frances Willard, but not in Catholic Europe and only to a small extent in Protestant European countries. The dialectic of domesticity and feminism could prove, as Harry Levine says, to be the source of the WCTU's huge appeal, yet the ambiguity of the WCTU's stance on the public and private roles of women proved costly in other cultural contexts.[38]

The class question must also be considered. Several studies have documented the class basis of the American WCTU, and the conclusions, though hampered by inadequate histories of the American class structure, are always the same. While the WCTU made efforts to appeal to working-class women and achieved some successes in the Protestant artisan and skilled worker strata, the movement's strength lay among the white middle-class propertied people. These analyses stress occupational categories, but the message is also reinforced by the movement's ideology, which is said to reflect, in large part, conventional American middle-class religion and morality common among professionals, shopkeepers, merchants, and other business people.[39] Parallel studies of the Victorian, New Zealand, and Canadian WCTUs come to the same conclusion. Despite the rural emphasis of settlement in western Canada, the WCTU prospered in smaller towns and took, in the case of Saskatchewan, its leadership from the small-town business community. Farmers' wives may have sympathized with the WCTU, but they were less visible in the movement's ranks and its public agitation. In the New South Wales case, too, the movement was strongest in the country towns and in the well-to-do Sydney suburbs of the late nineteenth century, like Petersham, Burwood, and Stanmore, where the movement's strength in active auxiliaries was among the wives of ministers of religion, doctors, and small businessmen.[40]

In England, as in parts of the United States, the movement reached out to working-class women and factory girls, but the alliance was never really consummated. As a group of working-class women in Manchester explained during an affiliation dispute with the BWTA in 1893, "There is too little real sympathy between these good women [of the Manchester BWTA] and us girls for them and us to get on well in the [affiliation] relation proposed." The working-class group wanted knowledge about "the general condition of women who have to labour for their own living." This they did not get from Manchester's BWTA women, whose focus was "almost exclusively religious." Besides, the Manchester working women wanted "to do their own work in their own way and did not want to be managed" by others.[41]

The middle-class basis of the WCTU was a further liability in Europe. There, especially in Scandinavia, the temperance movement won powerful support among the working class and the peasants, who formed their own temperance societies, and in the case of Finland, these organizations were major forces in the push for prohibition before World War I.[42] Though this emphasis in the Finnish movement stemmed in part from a nationalist desire to break Russian domination, elsewhere in Scandinavia the same connection can be observed. In Denmark, the temperance movement was "recruited chiefly from the masses of the people—in the country among farmers and day laborers, in the cities among artisans and the middle class."[43] Per Frånberg's case study of temperance in Umeå, Sweden, is largely compatible with this contemporary analysis. The "petty-bourgeoisie, artisans and workers" became, at the turn of the century, organized "in temperance societies for self-protection" against capitalists who promoted the use of alcohol in saloons, and they rallied to the "populistic branch of the Liberal Party," which was "social-liberal in outlook and pledged to the principle of egalitarian democracy."[44]

Given Willard's interest in gaining labor and Populist support for temperance in the United States, the WCTU might have been expected to exploit this working-class sentiment in the interests of interclass solidarity on the temperance question. But the workers dominated their own temperance associations in Scandinavia and tended to favor political action in support of prohibition and other restrictive legislation through established working-class political parties and trade unions. The class divisions and the particular historical development of the temperance movement denied to the WCTU or other Anglo-American temperance groups the chance of attaining an ideological hegemony.[45]

Given these manifold handicaps of gender, ideology, religion, culture, and class, the wonder is that the WCTU extended its influence so far and enrolled so many diverse supporters in so many countries. This it achieved precisely because its Anglo-American origins gave the movement sources of core support that enabled its "white ribbon bands" to encircle the globe. Since the late nineteenth century saw the expansion of American and English cultural influence, the World's WCTU stood to benefit. The WCTU's crusade was therefore strengthened as well as limited by being tied organically to the larger penetration of Anglo-American missionaries, travelers, government officials, and traders abroad.

Ironically, the clientele to be saved as well as the savers themselves were, in non-Anglo-Saxon countries, often British or American. Sara Crafts, World's WCTU superintendent of Sunday schools, reported during her European tour of 1901–2 that "a drunken person" was "rarely seen" in Barcelona "and if seen, is probably not a Spaniard." For the same reason Josephine Butler scoffed at the effects of a temperance crusade in Italy.[46] But Butler missed the point. When Jessie Ackermann started on her around-the-world mission in 1889, she carried "fifty letters from American mothers, who had sons wandering somewhere over the earth, God alone knew where."[47] Several observers noted that the WWCTU's major work in China, as far as drinking went, was among the foreign-born population of sailors, consuls, business people, and their entourage. A Shanghai missionary told Anna Gordon as late as 1914 that "the [intemperate] women with whom we have to deal . . . are almost entirely English and American."[48] Very early work done in Calcutta in 1878 in emulation of the Woman's Crusade was similarly focused on the transient foreign population. "We take tracts in sixteen different languages," proclaimed the American Methodists who started the service for sailors, "as sailors from every land are to be found in Calcutta."[49]

Those who responded to the problem of foreign drinking were first and foremost Anglo-American missionaries, though occasionally they were backed up by American businessmen and their wives abroad who, along with teachers in missionary schools, comprised the respectable American expatriates. In Latin America, the help of these expatriates was particularly sought by WCTU missionaries, but with mixed results. In Mexico City, for example, the work was centered in "the American colony" where, as in other parts of Mexico, American women saw temperance as a means of protecting their children from what they described as hostile Catholic influences and degrading moral standards among the peasants.[50] In Uruguay, the same reliance on expatriate influence and Anglo-American culture was attempted. The WCTU missionary Hardynia Norville began her work in 1917 among the English-speaking community that sent its children to the Methodist school at Lomas.[51] Reliance on American business people, however, weakened the work in Mexico and elsewhere in Latin America even while it provided the WCTU with essential support because the expatriate business community was said to be "continually changing."[52]

The contradictory impact of American business was never clearer than in the case of consular activities. Elizabeth Wheeler Andrew and Dr. Katharine Bushnell had been met and supported by the American consul at Cape Town, Capt. George F. Hollis, in 1891 during their missionary tour,[53] and the prominent WTCU suffrage worker in Melbourne in the 1880s, Catharine P. Wallace, was the wife of George Wallace of St. Louis, the American consul-general there. But he was said to have introduced the novel principle—novel, that is, for the expatriate business community in Australia—of a dry Fourth of July. The majority of American consuls in the antipodes were said in the nineteenth century to be "a disgrace to the United States government."[54] The writer of these words, Mary Love of Virginia, believed that these men had succumbed to "the drinking customs of the colonies," but it is likely that long residences in places where the temperance movement was in less sparkling condition made the consuls even more besotted elsewhere. Alvine Muriel Ayres's encounter with this group in South America was typical. "Some of the American men" resident in Uruguay, including the consul and other government officials, were "hard drinkers, and . . . far from being representative Americans," she wrote in 1920.[55] This was also the opinion much earlier of Mary Leavitt, whose exposure to consuls was, by the very nature of her trip, almost unrivaled. Indeed, Leavitt went even further and berated the consuls for pushing, as part of their commercial duties, the international trade in spirits, especially that of American rum and whiskey to West Africa.[56]

More sympathetic were other Americans not closely identified with the business community, particularly teachers and missionaries. Sometimes these colonies of American influence appeared in less likely places than Latin America, too. In South Africa, the major initial impetus to the WCTU was provided by the women who ran the Huguenot seminaries for young women in Wellington and Paarl in the Cape Colony. When Bushnell and Andrew arrived at the Cape in 1891, they found at Wellington "nearly a score of American teachers" who were "noble, grand women, enthusiastic in

W.C.T.U. work." Virginia Pride, principal of the Paarl seminary, was also president of the Cape Colony WCTU, and Abbie Ferguson of the Wellington Seminary carried on the tradition of Mt. Holyoke, Mary Lyon's famous evangelical college for women of the antebellum period.[57] While the Cape provided the outstanding example of American influence in South Africa, Natal had its ABCFM, where Laura Bridgman fostered the WCTU, and in Transvaal resided yet another bearer of American culture. The founder of the WCTU there, and a World's departmental superintendent as well, was Mary Tyler Gray, a missionary's daughter who was both American-born and -educated. She had been a student in the United States at the time of the Woman's Crusade, and, she recalled, her teachers had "interested us all in the movement and showed us its great importance and value."[58]

Among the English settlers, too, an American influence was indirectly felt in South Africa. Closely linked to the American temperance movement was Emilie Jane Solomon, "the earthly pivot round which the W.C.T.U. had revolved" from about 1900 to 1930.[59] This characterization was only fitting for a woman who served as Cape president from 1911 to 1919, South African national president from 1919 to 1925, and World's vice-president from 1925 to 1931. Though a member of one of South Africa's most prominent Anglo–South African families (her three brothers all received knighthoods and one became chief justice of South Africa), Solomon found the opportunities for women in the Cape Colony in the 1880s "limited."[60] She became discontented that her education had been, in spite of her social prominence, "comparatively elementary," but her dissatisfaction was intensified by exposure to the American women who organized the Cape WCTU, and she became a member of that group by receiving further training at the Wellington Seminary when in her mid-twenties.[61] The teachers there in turn convinced Solomon to go to the United States for advanced teacher training at the Cook County Normal School in Chicago and Bible study at the Moody Institute. While traveling abroad she met both Willard and Somerset and became thoroughly committed to the international temperance work by the time she returned in 1896.[62] Solomon was clearly a bearer of important aspects of American reform and religious culture, despite her South African origins and loyalties.

Such examples should not produce the false conclusion that the reform influence was purely American in the British colonies. It could not have been, because Americans and those who traveled from the United States were always a tiny minority, even of the leaders. In Australasia, Canada, and South Africa, there were large contingents of British immigrants, and in the Australian case, at least, the leadership of the WCTU tended to come, with the exception of prominent American examples like Jessie Ackermann, from the British-born rather than either the Americans or the native-born colonials. The leadership of the New South Wales WCTU, for example, was between the 1880s and 1914 largely English and Scotch at a time when 70 percent of the Australian population were native-born.[63]

I have speculated elsewhere that the international orientation of Australian WCTU leaders may have reflected their experience of temperance in the BWTA and emotional ties to the homeland. Many colonials identified with Britain at a time when the empire stood at the apex of its power. One such prominent official was Marie Kirk, who came to Australia from London in 1886, where she had been "a devoted mission worker with the Society of Friends" and a BWTA official. Kirk served for many years as president of the Victorian WCTU, and, claimed the writer of her obituary, "the international character of [WCTU] work formed a responding echo in her wide, sympathetic and understanding heart."[64] This did not mean a purely American influence, since Kirk maintained close links with her London BWTA colleagues and, in the 1890s, sided with World's purity superintendent Josephine Butler in her conflict with Lady Henry over the future of prostitution in British India.[65] More important, she displayed considerable coldness toward the American Ackermann's plans to federate the colonial WCTUs in 1891 and opposed Ackermann's (successful) bid to win the Australasian presidency.[66]

In Canada, too, there was an especially strong English and Scotch influence in the WCTU in the Maritimes, in parts of Quebec, and in Ontario. Mary Sanderson of Danville, Quebec, World's treasurer and a long-serving Quebec WCTU official, was one Scot who carried a strong conviction of empire loyalty into the WCTU and depicted the World's organization as an Anglo-American, not just an American, creation.[67] Temperance in the Maritimes drew upon the support of similar women. On her trip to Canada's eastern provinces in 1891, Willard found vast differences in temperance sentiment, with enthusiastic support among the Scotch communities in Cape Breton and Nova Scotia but nothing among the Quebecois.[68] This should not surprise, as Wendy Mitchinson's study confirms the domination of English-speaking evangelical Protestantism in the organization in Canada.[69]

The Cape Colony WCTU also had essential non-American support, but this was almost entirely composed of English-speaking women like Solomon and purity worker Julia Solly.[70] Few inroads were made into the Dutch burgher community in the Cape where the wine industry flourished, but the Anglo-South African groups partly expressed their ethnic hostility to the Boers through identification with such causes as the WCTU.[71] Not until well after the South African war could a temperance worker like Mrs. K. H. R. Stuart travel to the Transvaal and report in 1919 that the Dutch churches were now prepared to cooperate with the English in the drive for prohibition. Indeed, the WCTU obtained more support from the native population than from the Dutch burghers of the Cape. The WCTU's non-

Anglo-American support was heavily concentrated in the "Coloured" unions organized separately but with white leadership.[72]

As an example of the nonwhite unions indicates, the WCTU did attract a degree of non-Anglo-Saxon support in South Africa and in many other places. The Japanese, Chinese, and Indian faces photographed at World's WCTU conventions provided symbolic testimony to the fact. When Helen Stoddard visited Mexico in 1897 to organize unions, she, too, stressed that in non-Anglo-Saxon countries, the WCTU had to and could get the support of non-English-speaking people. In the eleven unions she left behind, the converts were "mostly Spanish-speaking" people. Only in Monterey was she convinced that work was well-established in the English-speaking community, a finding corroborated by the Mexican WCTU's president, Addie M. Sperry.[73]

The WWCTU crossed racial and cultural barriers most notably in the missionary communities of China, India, and Japan. In India, the work was mainly among the Anglo-Indians suspended between the imported and the indigenous civilizations and in the native population from the lowest castes, the same people drawn to evangelical missionary activities.[74] "Our membership is almost wholly among missionaries, Eurasians, and poor native Christians," said Margaret Denning, World's organizer for India, in corroborating testimony written in 1910.[75] Though the Indian WCTU was dwarfed by the massive size of the native population, the union was able to inaugurate national conventions by 1893, and its membership rose steadily from 620 to 2,537 by 1913.[76]

China was another case where the problem of excessive drinking was mainly among foreigners, but the WCTU's success was heavily concentrated in the native-born population. Ruth Shaffner, a World's WCTU missionary, pointed out in 1893 that "the unions thus far organized are entirely among the natives, save one in Shanghai, among the foreign community; those secured to the work are mainly from the classes associated in some way with Christian missionaries. Some are from among the native helpers in the hospitals or dispensaries, others are women or girls in the [Christian] schools."[77]

But the pull of American influences was strong even among those not of Anglo-Saxon heritage in such widely divergent countries as Uruguay, Japan, and Italy. The chief indigenous Uruguayan contacts were, for example, Professor and Mrs. Eduardo Monteverde. The professor taught mathematics at the University of Montevideo, participated in American scientific and professional conferences, and, significantly, was a Methodist.[78] In Japan, the temperance reformers displayed, as Kiyoshi Sugiura, an enthusiastic supporter, put it, a particularly "strong desire to further any plan that will increase our knowledge of American institutions." They wished, said another strong Japanese ally, "true liberty through temperance and [the] American system of local self-government."[79]

This theme of receptivity to aspects of American culture also underlay the relatively successful efforts, documented in a previous chapter, to spread the message of scientific temperance instruction. The National Education Association of Chile, for example, was run by men like Professor Monteverde. Its statutes were modeled after those of the American NEA, and "its principal mission" was to "devise and implant a system of education" that would seek "to develope [sic] the energies of our race by forming the individuality of the child," by "habituating him by means of moral and civic education to govern himself." Whereas previously Chileans had looked to Hispanic culture for their models, the Chilean NEA identified with the moral and material progress of "advanced nations" in general and the "sister republic" of the United States in particular. Here the message of economic and social development became intertwined with that of temperance reform through programs of scientific temperance instruction.[80] Through such organizations and aims, the WCTU spread its influence beyond women and beyond the ranks of those who actually joined the World's WCTU.

Nonetheless, the forms of American liberty encased in the WCTU's message were especially apparent to the women of non-Anglo-Saxon countries and to Protestant women in particular. Italy's Arabella Angelini, that country's representative at the first World's WCTU convention, had a deceptive name. She was in fact American-born and married to an Italian who had converted to Protestantism. Although she had lived in Italy since her early childhood, Angelini displayed markedly pro-American attitudes. She told the World's convention in Boston that a "Catholic girlhood meant" that Italian women were "secluded [and] sheltered" until they reached "maturity," when they were "kept hedged in and ignorant" by their early educational deficiencies. This she contrasted with the freedom typically allowed to young American women and the strong emphasis on self-reliance in American women's education.[81]

If Angelini's denunciation of women's role in Italy reminds us of the importance of the Protestant religion in the WCTU's support, the diatribe also emphasized the issue of women's emancipation, as interpreted by American temperance women. The American ideal of women's influence in both home life and reform was a positive model that Angelini stressed.[82] For many women outside the United States, the WCTU women did present attractive role models. To Australian women, the WWCTU's leaders, especially, were larger-than-life figures, and in recognition of this estimate, many WCTUs measured their own achievements by the extent to which they lived up to the standards of their heroines.[83] This process of emulation led Sara Nolan to be known as Australia's own Frances Willard, just as

Kaji Yajima was accorded the same honor in Japan.[84] The same element of worship meted out to women who had achieved much to open new avenues for their sex was also evident when the South African WCTU activist Emilie Solomon depicted Willard, Somerset, and their friend Hannah Whitall Smith as "lovely and gifted women."[85] Solomon's testimony demonstrates that the WCTU's appeal to women in far-flung places went way beyond the temperance question itself. For at least some members, the issue of women's opportunities for personal advancement transcended any particular appeal to Christian temperance.

IT MUST ALSO BE conceded that beyond the specifically feminist connections lay the appeal of "Americanization." A huge part of this attraction for women was the models the WCTU women presented in the organization of housework and in the application of technology to the home. Margaret Parker was one of a number of non-American temperance women who displayed this attraction. Parker scoffed at the argument often heard in British political circles that "Yankee notions" should be avoided. She boastfully told the Boston *Woman's Journal* that "I have an American cook stove in my kitchen, an American sewing-machine in my sitting room, and all the American books I can get in my library."[86]

Though Parker's statement showed that American domestic technology was valued by other temperance women, the attraction was deeper than to technology itself.[87] (Nor did Parker find American homes blessed with an abundance of immigrant labor.)[88] What struck Parker as the American advantage was the "know-how" of Americans, a concept always at the center of controversies in the English-speaking world over Yankee notions. Parker's account of her American travels, *Six Happy Weeks among the Americans*, noted very early the dearth of domestic help. "It is no uncommon thing to see elegant, refined houses . . . with no domestic—the lady and her daughters quietly doing all with the greatest ease."[89] Labor-saving devices they did have, but, she stressed, "Knowledge alone can make these available." "Domestic economy" she found amply emphasized in the schools she visited, and the better levels of education for women, in comparison with Britain's, were especially praiseworthy because a woman with knowledge of the best in domestic science and correct moral conduct would, according to Parker, make the best mother. American homes were better organized, with rooms more efficiently set out to reduce unnecessary walking or wear and tear, and while the scarcity of servants presented a problem, the daughters of the reform-minded families she visited tended to be well trained to rise early, clean their own rooms, and help their mothers.[90]

Perhaps this is a rosy, even glossy picture. Travelers' accounts are always suspect, and there is no doubt that Parker mixed in middle-class circles during her stay. But that reservation is not important, because it was precisely these groups that were most attracted to the WCTU. Parker's account is eloquent testimony to the impact of Catharine Beecher's *Treatise on Domestic Economy* among the American middle-class Protestants who joined the WCTU. It was she who, more than any other author, faced the issue of servant inadequacy and proposed the "democratic" alternative of domestic self-help through reorganization of the nature of work in the home. Beecher's book is strikingly like a blueprint for the behavior that Parker observed.[91] Moreover, Parker's observations are confirmed by others who knew the American scene more intimately. Hints of a superior domestic economy located in middle-class domesticity appeared in the *Union Signal* and in private correspondence among temperance leaders. Mary Hunt, for example, received the praise of Willard for the "systematic working" of her home. Willard especially appreciated her "methods of utilizing space and keeping everything classified and shipshape" and hoped to publicize abroad this example of what a domestic outlook shaped by women's temperance could achieve.[92]

There can be little doubt that women abroad found this domestic version of the American work ethic a model worth emulating, especially where servants were in short supply. The pages of the *Canadian Woman's Journal* for the 1890s provide ample evidence of the popularity of domestic advice, much of it drawn from American sources. Strong emphasis was placed on efficiency, cleanliness, daughterly duties, and morality. "Self-respect, self-denial and *thoroughness* in small things" was the recipe for bringing up a daughter, so the advice for mothers went on.[93] This advice built upon the practice of Canadian women temperance leaders. Letitia Youmans, the founder of the WCTU in Ontario, was, like Parker, attracted to American know-how. As a young mother she elicited both the curiosity and criticism of neighbors in Picton, Ontario, because "the new mother used books to assist her in her domestic management."[94]

These pro-American sentiments never went uncontested, however. Parker's support of American technology, it must be reiterated, was couched in terms of the Victorian debate over newfangled Yankee innovation.[95] Anti-American sentiment was also persistent in conservative circles in Australia, but being so far away from the United States, their anxieties did not match those of some Canadians. In a Canada that was already sensitive to the problem of American cultural penetration, objections were bound to be raised to the use of American temperance materials as a surreptitious way, as one WCTU woman reported it, to "disseminate disloyalty."[96] Britain was equally sensitive to the cultural penetration of "Brother Jonathan," and enthusiastic acceptance of Americanization by some BWTA women severely limited the World's WCTU appeal among others. Pro-American attitudes were not uniformly diffused but were concentrated in the more liberal and democratic elements of society and, in particular, within the Anglo-American reform community analyzed long ago by Frank Thistlethwaite. It was no coincidence that the first World's president was the sister of John Bright, a friend of American democracy. Margaret Bright Lucas found in visits to relatives to the United States in the 1870s that "the advanced views and institutions of a less trammelled social system were so many congenial influences to her own mind" and praised the "temperance women and those connected with the Women's Suffrage question who took her up with kind eagerness as John Bright's sister."[97] But even within reform circles, an American-instigated society like the World's WCTU was sure to strike opposition.

The whole issue of Americanization was raised most centrally in the debates over the affiliation of the BWTA to the WCTU in 1893–94, but the charge continued to be made through the 1890s.[98] When Lady Henry returned from North America in April 1892, she found, according to Ruth Bordin, "that an anti-American conservative majority on her [BWTA] executive committee violently opposed the prosuffrage resolution she supported, did not favor a World WCTU, and generally distrusted the innovations she imported from the United States." At the 1893 annual council meeting, "a strong minority" fought against her and against Willard's influence and left the BWTA after they were defeated "only by a majority of 69 in a total vote of 455." (Another author has gone further and erroneously claimed that British conservatism actually prevailed over Somerset and Willard in these battles of 1893–94 and implied that this represented a decisive defeat for Americanization in the temperance movement.)[99]

Without further amplification, a false impression of a disastrous and major split in the BWTA may be given by these interpretations. In the affiliated unions under BWTA control, only one-sixth actually seceded, and though membership figures are not complete, it is likely that less than one-sixth of the membership actually left. The *Scottish Reformer* claimed that 103 affiliates had pulled out and that 69 of these had a membership of 5,840, while the BWTA's membership figures for 1894 (also incomplete) put the organization at over 50,000 strong. (If the other seceding affiliates had roughly comparable numbers, a total of approximately 8,700 members must have followed the old executive committee out of the organization.)[100] Other sources confirm these estimates, since the seceding societies formed a British Women's Total Abstinence Union that had a recorded maximum membership of 21,000 in 1903. Meanwhile, the BWTA had grown from 50,000 in 1894 to 90,000 in 1897 and to 114,000 in 1904.[101]

One of the reasons for the difference in interpretation is that previous estimates have relied on the executive committee numbers, yet it was clearly understood in the debates in 1893–94 that London was overrepresented in the committee.[102] Somerset's base of support lay in Wales, Scotland, and the north of England, the traditional strongholds of both temperance and dissenting religion in Britain. Somerset had at that time given up her membership in the Church of England to worship in a Methodist chapel. She was for this reason extremely well placed to elicit the devotion of outsiders in church politics and the hierarchical structure of English society even though, ironically, her aristocratic pedigree compared favorably to that of several members of the "conservative" and so-called anti-American minority.[103]

The performance of the two societies after the split shows that affiliation with the World's WCTU was no liability. Indeed, the more evangelical and millennialist elements in Scotland were particularly fervent in their devotion to international principles and participated more actively than the English in the World's WCTU's missionary campaigns. The WWCTU's affiliates in Britain increased their membership from approximately 30–40,000 immediately after the split to 220,000 members during World War I. Meanwhile, the total abstinence union languished at less than one-sixth the size of the parent organization.[104]

The WWCTU's opponents were an insignificant minority in the 1890s in British women's temperance, but it must also be noted that the issue was never a clear-cut one of American influence versus British nationalism. The opponents of Lady Henry in the BWTA were also solicitous of American support. They attempted to develop an alliance with the Non-Partisan WCTU; welcomed to the BWTA convention in 1890 that thorn in Willard's side, Judith Ellen Foster; and sent their own delegates to Non-Partisan WCTU conventions. Moreover, it is ironic that the chief strategist of the total abstinence union was none other than Jessie Fowler, the American businesswoman daughter of hydropathist Lydia Fowler. The British Women's Total Abstinence Union, like the BWTA, explicitly recognized the importance of international links with the powerful American women's temperance movement and testified to the large degree of American penetration of British women's temperance.[105]

The real basis of disagreement in the BWTA was the Do-Everything policy, which the conservatives feared would deflect the organization from its original purpose—temperance reform—and involve it in sectarian and political difficulties. Lady Henry's identification with the WLF was so strong that it antagonized some aristocratic temperance supporters in the Church of England who belonged to the Conservative party's equivalent, the Primrose League. In this respect, the British action did resemble the split in the United States between Willard and Foster's Non-Partisan WCTU and demonstrated that philosophical and political disagreements rather than cultural and nationalist prejudices lay at the root of the contest over the role of the World's WCTU.[106] The conservative elements in the BWTA had indeed stopped paying dues to the World's WCTU. Yet it was not affiliation as such, but the establishment of a special British World's WCTU Committee under Somerset's control as a rival source of authority that agitated the conservatives. The minority showed that they saw this issue of financial affiliation through the British World's WCTU Committee as a threat to the independence of British action, but only a small fraction of British temperance women agreed with them, and the debate was liberating rather than stultifying for the BWTA. Never was that organization to be so successful as it was after Somerset took charge.[107]

The British case takes the whole argument back to the issues of evangelical Christianity and women's emancipation. The split in the BWTA showed that the movement was strongest where Methodists, Presbyterians, Congregationalists, and Baptists predominated. Also apparent was the extent to which the dispute with Lady Henry involved not just the issue of a suffrage resolution for the BWTA, which was technically not part of the Somerset platform, but the whole strategy of opening up new avenues to women through the Do-Everything policy. The "programme of work" of the progressive elements for 1893–94 did not include "the Labour Question, Woman's Suffrage, Peace and Arbitration, the Opium Question, and Social Purity" and was in fact quite pedestrian and pragmatic in its emphasis on temperance matters; but as editor of the *Woman's Herald*, Somerset had become identified as the champion of "terminating the legislative injustices from which women suffer." She had vowed not to rest until "every statutory or customary disability now imposed upon woman because of her sex" had "been swept away" by the "Forward Movements of our time." These statements were not lost upon her opponents nor upon her supporters in the succeeding five years in which she dominated British women's temperance.[108]

Neither the evangelical nor the emancipationist pillar of the WCTU's faith was repudiated by the international movement's leaders. To them it was self-evident that the WCTU stood for both. Possible contradictions between these twin aims of Christian temperance and women's uplift were not admitted, nor was the obstinate opposition to these themes in many countries among many classes of women directly acknowledged. Whilst the potential of the WCTU was enhanced by adherence to this creed, at the same time it set limits to the WCTU's success. This irony would be manifest in the efforts of the missionary temperance women and in the sentiment of sisterhood that partly inspired them.

5

In Dark Lands

Temperance Missionaries
and Cultural Imperialism

I leave now for dark lands; again my woman's heart almost fails me sometimes, but your prayers are back of me, and back of all is our Father, with all his promises. . . . My health holds out; but I have grown very old, and my hair is quite white, but it is all in His service." So wrote the WCTU's second round-the-world missionary, Jessie Ackermann, to her colleagues in California as she prepared to leave Australia for Burma in the latter part of 1892, midway through an odyssey that in many respects eclipsed that of Leavitt.[1] When she returned to the United States in 1895, Ackermann had been traveling for seven years and had circumnavigated the world twice. Her statements to reporters summed up a vast if apparently bleak experience of peoples and cultures: "I shall never take up work in heathen lands again. I have no message to the heathen; if I have a mission or a message it is to the voters of Christian lands."[2]

With that enigmatic statement, a woman who had been hailed by John G. Woolley as "the second greatest woman in America" behind Frances Willard quickly faded into obscurity. Her exploits, comparable to those of Leavitt, did not warrant a place in modern scholarly biographical dictionaries, either of her native land or of countries like Australia where she did so much to stimulate temperance reform. When she finally died in a Los Angeles nursing home in 1951 at the age of 94, Ackermann's passing was barely noted even by the World's WCTU on behalf of which she had undertaken such arduous labors. Not until 1962 did the Australian WCTU, which she had served as first president in 1891, nominate her for a memorial membership to honor her vivid but forgotten contribution.[3]

Ackermann's gloomy epitaph hardly reveals the pleasure with which she consumed experience. She boasted, for example, that when traveling by sea she adopted the practice of scaling the mastheads of ships to hail other vessels; on one occasion she had been washed overboard during a storm in the Indian Ocean and had to be rescued by a passing ship. She claimed she had been the first European woman, traveling amid the pearling fleets between India and Australia, to don a diving suit to see for herself "the wonders of the deep." She had climbed in the Himalayas and had trekked across the deserts of the Kalahari and the Nullarbor Plain. She claimed to have spent one Fourth of July on an iceberg inside the Arctic circle and traveled widely in Iceland, Alaska, and Russia. In China she had lived six weeks in the interior without seeing a single European and had dressed in Chinese costume, with nothing to eat but boiled rice. She boasted of interviewing the king of Siam and knowing most of "the potentates of the East," and she proudly announced that she had slept, by 1895 alone, in 2,003 "beds in houses, tents, steamers, hammocks, etc." in the aid of the WCTU.[4]

Ackermann does not qualify as the typical WCTU missionary, if there ever was such a person. Her career was more extravagant and her character more eccentric than most. But her relish for travel certainly was common among these women, and in her response to the meaning of her missionary work Ackermann pointed toward the central dynamic of the missionary impulse, with all of its limitations and ambiguities. The hyperbole of the Christian martyr aside, the experience of foreign service—whether in lands that were literally in "heathen darkness" or not—seared the hearts of temperance missionaries. When they emerged from their work, it was obvious that a toll had been taken in the service of the Lord. Though the biographies, obituaries, editorials, and sermons spoke only of victory and Christian service, a large part of the temperance missionaries' careers concerned the reality of loneliness, doubt, and failure in the face of monumental obstacles. At the core of Jessie Ackermann's testimony, amid the copious amount of detail on the quantity of her missionary effort, there remained silences about this experience that this chapter seeks to explore. What was it like to be a round-the-world missionary in the era of Mary Leavitt? What drove temperance women amid such privations as Ackermann detailed? How did the missionary crusade in its practical operation both reflect and in turn influence hopes for women's emancipation and assumptions of a culturally imperialistic kind? Of these questions, the last lies close to the heart of the international work of the WCTU.

The travail of Jessie Ackermann highlighted the confrontation of an Anglo-American, evangelical woman's culture, backed by a simple conviction of moral righteousness, with the variety and complexity of experience in those "dark lands" beyond the sea. The WCTU's round-the-world missionaries demonstrated contradictions between the appeal to a universalist morality and its emissaries' inability to transcend fully the cultural and political context in which the message was conveyed. That alone did not make them distinctive or worthy of special attention, since every evangelical missionary faced dilemmas of this kind. WCTU women also evidenced a trend in late nineteenth-century evangelical church life toward a greater reliance

Missionaries and Cultural Imperialism

on women missionaries who both implicitly challenged and yet also championed a culture and a religion in which they remained subordinates. That irony clearly made the WCTU missionaries intriguing but hardly rendered their experience unique either.[5]

What did make the WCTU different was the fact that their own missionaries were above both nationality and church denomination and that their message of temperance and female emancipation was explicitly critical of Western churches and European missionaries. As Christian critics of Christianity, their cooperation with regular missionaries was fraught with difficulties. But for the same reasons, these temperance women could plausibly make larger claims to universality and a cross-national appeal than the regular evangelical missionaries could.

The difference was also institutionally rooted. Frances Willard had adopted the novel idea that her appointees should be international in their mode of operation and in their origins. "As a rule," she told the 1893 World's convention, the WWCTU believed that their "missionaries should be migratory rather than stationary, in order that fresh enthusiasm may be constantly brought to the work, and that the danger of yielding to prejudice and habit by long association . . . may be avoided."[6] This notion of a peripatetic missionary force was probably derived from Willard's exposure to the Methodist circuit riders of her youth, but it did enable her to project not merely a universalist message of reform but one that was grounded in the experience of evangelical temperance women. Though Willard conceded in 1893 that the danger of this plan was its superficiality and sanctioned missionaries who worked in only one country as well, the WCTU missionaries retained this distinctive emphasis on their international allegiance.

The exploits of Mary Clement Leavitt, at least, have been documented by scholars, but it has been wrongly assumed that her "herculean effort" was "never matched" by later emissaries who are said to have "labored briefly in Australia and Africa."[7] This was not true of Jessie Ackermann nor of many of the others who carried the WWCTU banner to more than forty countries prior to World War I. The extent of WCTU operations was in fact far greater than any previous account has conceded. Leavitt was part of a vast if ultimately thankless outreach on the part of the WCTU that involved dozens of workers. The official lists of missionaries showed that thirty-four women were commissioned after Leavitt, between 1888 and 1925, as round-the-world missionaries—the title was changed to World's WCTU organizer in 1920—but at least another thirty-four traveled from the United States and other sponsoring countries to undertake ad hoc assignments as missionaries or organizers from 1876 to 1928.

This was still a small group in comparison with the many women who went as evangelists with the regular missionary boards, and the WWCTU's cause would surely have achieved little of value if the round-the-world missionaries had not been able to tap the ranks of the regular missionaries for support. Sometimes these women were formally engaged for service. Over the period from 1891 to 1919, the World's treasurer's reports and other publications such as the *Union Signal* reveal that the World's WCTU harnessed volunteers from this larger body of workers to supplement the efforts of its temperance organizers. More than thirty women, mostly regular missionaries, were engaged in this way, and the financial records indicate numerous other cases where small amounts of funding were supplied to missionary groups and WCTUs, though individuals were not always specifically named. In all, the cadre of World's missionaries and ancillary workers in the years of this study totaled at least 108. This does not include all the missionaries who served as WCTU office bearers in their host countries or the many women who, like Canada's Sara Wright, did missionary organizing or international lecturing on route to World's WCTU conventions.[8]

The women studied here are drawn from over a long period of time and had varying levels of service. The groups concerned are all quite small, and the conclusions that can be reached from analysis of their collective biography are best considered as illustrative of their experience and thought. For this reason, I shall place emphasis not on quantitative data but on case histories of their unusual endeavors, so as to reconstruct the mental world of these spirited women as they set out to shape that larger world and were in turn shaped by it. Theirs is not the experience of the WCTU as a whole but highlights the intellectual and moral trajectory of some of its most hallowed heroines. For the sake of clarity, only those officially appointed—the thirty-five—are called World's organizers or round-the-world missionaries in what follows.

How were these women chosen? In the early period, Willard saw the international work as a simple extension of the pattern of national organizing, which now focused on the Pacific states and led on to the "mystic Orient." Round-the-world missionaries may have been distinctive in their exploits and perhaps eccentric in character, but the most striking aspect of their recruitment in the 1880s and 1890s was the way in which national organizing work easily extended into international missionary endeavors. Mary Leavitt had been organizing on the Pacific Coast, and both she and Willard regarded the trip to Hawaii and beyond as a natural elaboration of that work. Ackermann's case was similar, since she also traveled in California and did work in Alaska before accepting her position as round-the-world missionary.[9]

Later missionaries were chosen as part of a more deliberate strategy. No longer would it simply be a question of taking advantage of those whose private travel plans already put them halfway toward where Willard wished the WCTU to go. But all of the women chosen in the 1890s were either national organizers with plenty of experience in regions of WCTU weakness or were personal friends of Willard's. In 1891 Katharine Bushnell and Elizabeth Wheeler Andrew, both Evanston residents, went to Britain and from there to India, South Africa, and Australia. In 1892 Alice Palmer, another WCTU national organizer, was sent to South Africa, and in the same year, Mary Allen West, a former editor of the *Union Signal*, went to Japan. Not until 1897 did the pattern change with the appointment of the first non-American missionaries. Elizabeth (Lizzie) Vincent and her companion Emily Cummins had been Australasian WCTU organizers, though Vincent was English by birth and upbringing. Joining them were an American who had served as a missionary in China, Ruth Shaffner of Pennsylvania; Helen Bullock, another American national organizer; Jennie Ericson of Finland; Clara Parrish of Paris, Illinois; and Rhode Island's Susan H. Barney, national superintendent of prison work. After 1900, England's Ethel Beedham, Olifia Johannsdottir of Iceland, and Australia's Bessie Harrison Lee were recruited. Altogether, by 1925, four in every ten official round-the-world missionaries had come from non-American sources.[10]

The early pattern of activity stressed the Anglo-American connection. Though Leavitt went to all continents save Antarctica, her work and that of the early missionaries was concentrated on Australia, New Zealand, Britain, South Africa, and Canada. This was true not only of the official round-the-world group but also of the larger selection that undertook international organizing, beginning with the exploits of Eliza Stewart and Mary C. Johnson in Britain after 1876. Only with Parrish's appointment in 1897 to Japan did this emphasis significantly alter. Thereafter, with the WCTU well and truly established in the Anglo-American world, attention shifted, along with American commercial and foreign policy, to Asia and, after the Spanish-American War, to the Hispanic-speaking peoples south of the Rio Grande. Missionaries were sent to Cuba, Puerto Rico, and the Philippines in the wake of 1898, and considerable attention was devoted from 1900 onward to the provision of organizers for Mexico, whence Addie Northam Fields went as a round-the-world missionary in 1900. By 1914, the WCTU was also establishing a beachhead for what it hoped would be an invasion of South America through the labors in Argentina and Uruguay of two other round-the-world missionaries, Hardynia Norville and Elma Grace Gowen.

The WCTU closely followed or anticipated lines of imperial advancement in other cases as well. After early labors by Andrew, Bushnell, Ackermann, and Leavitt, India was largely left to the English and Scottish WCTUs who sent a number of women there between 1903 and 1915, though both Ella Hoover Thatcher and Katharine Lent Stevenson also evangelized there before World War I.[11] In China and Japan as well as in India, the WCTU increasingly relied on resident Britons, Americans, or Canadians for its supply of missionaries—women like Eliza Spencer Large, a Canadian missionary in Japan—and especially in the case of Japan and China, began to

Woman's World/Woman's Empire

The first six WCTU round-the-world missionaries. Mary C. Leavitt, *top*; Alice Palmer, *bottom*; Mary Allen West, *left*; Jessie A. Ackermann, *right*; Elizabeth Wheeler Andrew, *center left*; Dr. Katharine C. Bushnell, *center right*. (Frances Willard, *Do Everything: A Handbook for the World's White Ribboners* [Chicago: Ruby I. Gilbert, 1905])

appoint indigenous women from the native Christian churches in the second and third decades of the new century. These, like Frances Willard Wang and Mrs. Ren Yin Mei, had usually received higher education or missionary training in the United States.[12] Wang, for example, had gone to Northwestern University and lived in Willard's home, Rest Cottage. Finally, in the 1920s a new and more specialized type of missionary (or rather, organizer) was sent. Lydia Johnson, Deborah Livingston, Mary Harris Armor, and Eva C. Wheeler went to Sweden, South Africa, Australia, and New Zealand, respectively, for the express purpose of promoting prohibition. Julia Deane and Anna Gordon also undertook major forays into Europe and South America for the same purposes.[13] Thus did the main lines of WCTU missionary activity unfold in the world arena of colonial expansionism.

Somewhat different from the majority were the European appointees, who do not quite fit the pattern of activity in the colonial world, though their social backgrounds were similar to their Anglo-American allies. At

Missionaries and Cultural Imperialism

first Willard used friends or acquaintances who went to Europe for travel or business, such as Maria C. Treadwell. Willard's own sister-in-law Mary Bannister Willard was announced in 1886 as the WWCTU's press representative in Europe when she went to Berlin to set up a finishing school for girls. Specific missionary appointments began with an English resident in Europe, Charlotte Gray, in 1887, who organized in Switzerland, Germany, and Norway.[14] By the 1890s Johannsdottir and Finland's Ericson were at work, and the Dane Elizabet Selmer was employed as World's organizer for Scandinavia. Unlike many of their Anglo-American colleagues, these women did not actually go around the world at all. Mostly they worked in Scandinavia. Johannsdottir toured North America, however, and Ericson accompanied Ruth Shaffner to Puerto Rico. On the other hand, the Anglo-American appointees toured extensively in northern Europe. Britain's Agnes Slack made several forays into Scandinavia; Leavitt campaigned in France, Holland, and Sweden; and women like Ackermann and Shaffner went to Iceland and actually helped found the WCTU there.[15]

Nothing held such a diverse group together other than a commitment to temperance, Christianity, and the will to travel. Of this trinity of values, evangelical commitment was the most overtly professed and acted out in the missionary field. Jessie Ackermann was typical in her conviction that the Lord had led her into the temperance missionary field. "Only seven years ago," she reminisced in 1895, "I stood on the deck of a westward bound steamer" heading out of San Francisco, her only resource "a profound conviction that the Voice had said to me, 'Thou art the woman!' "[16] Like many others, she operated in the context of a thriving evangelical women's culture that revitalized the American foreign missionary effort in the late nineteenth century.[17] Several of these women had strong connections with the foreign mission movement prior to becoming round-the-world missionaries. In fact, apart from WCTU work, experience in a foreign missionary society was the most common form of voluntary activity undertaken by women who subsequently became temperance missionaries. Alvine Muriel Ayres of New York state, who went straight into WWCTU missionary work as a young single woman, was fairly typical. Ayres came from a family in which the tradition of sending men and women to the mission field was strong. "My first definite incentive for missionary service came through the reading of missionary papers in our home," she explained in 1919 as she prepared to embark for South America.[18] Others, like Shaffner and Bushnell, had actually been missionaries in China before returning to the United States only to take up World's WCTU appointments.

Even those who turned down the chance to be round-the-world missionaries testified to the importance of the evangelical impulse. Belle Kearney reacted to her appointment in 1895 with trepidation. Every day since receiving the call, she had "been in an agony of unrest, and waited constantly on God in prayer for guidance. My desire was strong to *go*, but the divine leanings not to go were at last very definite and infinitely stronger." (Kearney did in fact later do WWCTU missionary work, but not until her 1904–5 tour of Europe and the Middle East.)[19]

But religious zeal was clearly not the only thing that motivated these women, and it did not operate independently of the everyday circumstances of their lives. Spiritual enthusiasm could be restrained by family conditions, though indirectly religion could also be seen as crystallizing and shaping discontents with conventional restrictions on women's uplift. In some cases, there were hints that the foreign mission field had long attracted these women and that marriage or unfortunate material circumstances had repressed their desires until Willard extended a very special opportunity. The "early proclivity" of Susan Barney, for example, was "for the work of foreign missions," but "in those days," in the 1850s, "very few women were sent out." Barney became active in the Woman's Foreign Missionary Society of the Methodist church and "made her first attempts at public speaking in its interests" long before she became identified as a popular prison reformer. She spent the 1850s to 1870s raising a family; by the 1890s, her family grown, Barney was able to indulge her early passion for foreign missions. In all, between 1895 and 1922 she made five overseas tours for the WCTU and circumnavigated the world in 1897–98.[20] Another of this type was Carrie C. Faxon of Michigan, who went to the Philippines in 1901. She had been "connected for twenty-five years" with the Woman's Foreign Missionary Society, which was her "first field of public work." Her sister, another WCTU member, was already in Manila as a regular Methodist missionary, so Faxon went to stay with her.[21]

Like Barney, Faxon was one of many American women denied a missionary career until well past menopause. But like Addie Northam Fields, Leavitt, Parrish, and many others, Faxon was not without experience of work outside the home. The typical WWCTU missionary had in fact been a schoolteacher, though a significant minority that included Ackermann, Elizabeth Andrew, and Mary Allen West had adopted journalism as their profession. As can be gathered from these career backgrounds, World's WCTU organizers tended to be of above average education, with almost all of the American women who participated possessing high school education at a time when only a minority of Americans stayed in school beyond the onset of adolescence. A quarter had gone to college, and at least one, Bushnell, was a doctor specializing in women's medicine.[22]

Apart from education, marital status most distinguished these women from the general population. None had significant childrearing responsibilities; all were either single women who never married, single women who later married and abandoned the temperance missionary calling, widows, divorcees, or women beyond menopause with tolerant or supportive hus-

Missionaries and Cultural Imperialism

bands. Thus for every woman like Leavitt, Faxon, or Barney, for whom temperance missionary service came as a career late in life, for as many others, such service did not have to be deferred. When England's Ethel Beedham married a Baptist missionary bound for the Congo, the wedding "opened a way for the fulfillment of her [childhood] desire to work in the foreign mission field." When her husband died there in 1901, she grabbed the opportunity to channel her grief and her convictions into a World's WCTU appointment to Burma. She was only twenty-seven at the time.[23] Clara Parrish, Kara Smart, and Ruth Shaffner all served abroad as young women in the 1890s before retiring to apparently contented domesticity. Others, like Australia's Bessie Cowie, New Zealand's Anderson Hughes-Drew, and Katharine Stevenson lived largely independently of their husbands. Cowie, one of the most indefatigable of all of the missionaries, married twice but never let marriage interfere with her missionary career. She left her first husband in Melbourne on several occasions to undertake missionary work during his long periods of illness and, in her autobiography, made only a passing reference to his death in 1908. In the person of Andrew Cowie, she found a more suitable substitute. A wealthy New Zealander, he was a man who, she said, "helps me in every phase of Christian work," a man who was prepared to subsidize her travels and support all her missionary endeavors.[24]

Round-the-world missionary activity opened new careers for women otherwise bound by the conventions of nineteenth-century Anglo-American marriage. But religion was also linked to another theme in the missionary experience. What stood out in the careers and correspondence of so many of the temperance missionaries, and many of the other international organizers, was a pronounced interest in adventure. Travel was a theme in the missionary experience long before the WCTU. Ann Judson, wife of the famous Baptist missionary Adoniram Judson, had between 1814 and 1822 "plied the American Christian reading audience" with what amounted to "a rudimentary form of cultural anthropology." Judson's published letters were "filled with information about the social and economic life of Burma."[25] Literature of this type soon became commonplace in missionary publications and shaped the hopes and dreams of young evangelical women. To women raised in a stultifying domestic environment, the job of round-the-world missionary provided a chance to pursue these latent interests. The very nature of the global adventure encouraged such motives and enhanced expectations of excitement, and the more secular character of the temperance crusade worked in the same direction. If the travel theme was still linked in some way with the presentation of exotic information, the temperance missionary felt even less inhibition than the authors of the genre of missionary hagiography about dwelling on the cultures visited.

It is difficult to avoid the conclusion that these were women who reveled in the travel as much as in the saving of souls. The pages of the *Union Signal* were filled with details of the customs and geographical peculiarities of the many countries the World's WCTU missionaries visited. Katharine Stevenson's long tour around the world in 1909–10 was marked by an equally long series of articles in the WCTU papers entitled "Leaves from a Traveler's Notebook." Another who matched Stevenson's capacity to consume the cultures of the countries visited was Flora Strout, who worked for the WWCTU from 1910 to 1942 in foreign lands as an official round-the-world missionary. In Ceylon, Strout enthused about her good fortune: "How I love Ceylon! The Singalese and Tamil people are charming, the blue, blue sea is bluer, I am sure, than any other sea, and the soft moon shining through the tall, straight broom-top coconut palms brings to the oldest heads dreams of romantic days long since dead."[26]

On many occasions, travel was rhetorically justified in spiritual terms. Leavitt's response to the great crater in Hilo during her stay in the Hawaiian Islands was typical. "Wonderful are thy works, O Lord; in wisdom hast Thou made them all."[27] Even Stevenson's "Traveler's Notebook," written in a later and more secular spirit, turned dutifully in each issue from the gushy evocation of places visited to the serious discussion of temperance and religious issues and thereby reminded her audiences that her visits did indeed have a deeper spiritual purpose after all. For the Yorkshire-born Christine Tinling, seeing Niagara was wonderful, but more so in the company of other WCTU workers. If, in the old cliché, travel broadened the mind, for WCTU missionary women its pleasures were legitimated by spiritual enlightenment.[28]

Adventure's fascinations went far beyond the ranks of those women who actually experienced the joys of international travel. Travelers' tales were very much in demand among Anglo-American evangelical women, as their prominence in the *Union Signal* revealed. For every woman like Agnes Slack who was able to marvel at the ruins of Pompeii or like Belle Kearney to journey to the Pyramids and organize WCTUs in places so entrancingly named as Damascus and Cairo, there must have been thousands transported weekly to these exotic worlds through the printed page and the lantern slide lecture. This was probably even more true in outposts of the WWCTU such as Australia and New Zealand, where the thirst for knowledge of the world was in direct proportion to the isolation. Jessie Ackermann raised funds for her temperance campaigns by combining pledge taking with firsthand reports of her trips through Asia. She and the English/American missionary Tinling each wrote several books on their round-the-world experiences, in which spiritual endeavor often seemed subordinate to the satisfactions of travel itself.[29]

The life of adventure alone partly explains this fascination for exotic places in an era of the increasing routinization of life. Even church missionary enthusiasm was now being subordinated to the imperatives of boards and committees and to a vogue for systematic study of mission methods. The yearning for mystery repressed in routine life could live on in vicarious identification with the unfamiliar, but more than yearnings for the unknown were involved. This attraction for the trappings of antique civilizations paralleled, perhaps, the antimodernist theme revealed by T. Jackson Lears in elite American culture at the turn of the century and may have reflected a genuine ambivalence toward modern American industrial capitalist civilization. Stevenson was one missionary who epitomized the European fascination with the ancient monuments of South and Southeast Asia, while it was also Stevenson who expressed a vaguely unfocused discontent at the warring individualism of American society with its corporations and its "survival of the fittest." Significant it surely was that missionaries enthused not so much over foreign cultures per se but upon the ruins of temples, such as Agnes Slack visited in Italy in 1914, or "every semblance of age," all the "silent monuments to a nation's great past," that moved Stevenson in Ceylon. Such women were not uncomprehending of the values of those civilizations their own religion sought to eclipse. They were willing to concede that the places they visited had heritages of spiritual value from which the modern world could learn.[30]

In addition, the travel mania revealed in yet another form one of the manifestations of women's emancipation. Though the life of a woman missionary has sometimes been described as one of freedom unobtainable within the confines of American domestic culture, more careful and considered evidence suggests that the patterns of sexual domination and subordination were at least to some extent reproduced in the missionary population. This is the conclusion of an exemplary analysis of women missionaries in turn-of-the-century China, where single women who became career missionaries were not treated as the equals of men, and where tension existed between the single and married women in the mission stations because of the latter's higher status.[31] Missionaries under the banner of the WCTU were different to some degree, however. They were sent out by a separatist society and were not under the control of male missionaries at all. In the zestful careers of many of the more intrepid temperance missionaries are hints that service in the World's WCTU appealed to the adventurous as more exciting than a conventional missionary calling.[32] Dr. Katharine Bushnell's first missionary call had been at twenty-four years to China in 1879 under the Woman's Mission Board of the Methodist Episcopal church. "This was not quite to my liking," she later recalled, "but I yielded to their wishes." Within three years a dissatisfied Bushnell returned to do postgraduate work, determined to seek a more intellectually challenging post in the medical field. Only with the creation of the WCTU's purity department and the campaign against medical inspection of prostitutes did she find satisfactory work that enabled her to combine her medical career with her desire to uplift women. Within the churches, Bushnell felt, women were too "cribbed, confined, bound down by the traditional view of the duties of women."[33]

Bushnell's evidence suggests that some of the round-the-world missionaries rejected the domestic isolation and subordination that the more settled missionary environment often reproduced. More plentiful is the testimony that many were attracted to a calling more adventurous than those that beckoned at home, whether home be the United States, Britain, or Australasia. Clara Parrish was said to be a conscientious young schoolteacher in Paris, Illinois, "but soon became dissatisfied with her school-room work; the four walls of her little school home seemed to her a prison."[34] She turned to full-time organizing for the WCTU and soon took the opportunity to serve Willard in Japan and to visit most of the Far East. The lure of a more exciting life in places far away was especially strong for Australian WCTU missionaries, who readily testified, like Ada Murcutt, to the enticements of a much larger world. Writing from Pennsylvania in 1903, Murcutt found her extensive temperance work in Canada, the United States, and Japan crowded with the excitement "of one who travels to the uttermost ends of the earth" in search of "increased responsibilities" and an "enlarged sphere of usefulness."[35] Bessie Cowie had the same experience. Her first trip to England from her native Australia "opened up to [her] astonished gaze" a "new world of opportunity" in which "scores of the greatest souls" made her feel she had won "a place in the first rank" of moral reform.[36]

Though women's emancipation was being daily demonstrated in practice through herculean exploits, other more conscious and ideological aspects of women's emancipation were also present. Jessie Ackermann epitomized this sterner face of the World's WCTU in the campaign against women's subordination. In any conservative colony of the British empire where "a woman had never spoken before," "to those places . . . she always made a point of going." Especially did she go if there was any hint that "she was not wanted."[37] Ackermann may have been unusually contrary, but from the very beginning the World's WCTU espoused emancipationist themes in its missionary work. Biographical sketches of Ackermann, for example, made a point of referring to the number of male conventions that she had defied and the list of "firsts" she had achieved for women. This theme of liberation was often expressed in terms of women's sheer physical activity. Indeed, for another missionary, Alice Palmer, that "dauntless energy" outweighed the issue of "the effects of drink" in the psychology of her commitment. It was the strength of the temperance women themselves that attracted Palmer.[38]

In still other ways did emancipationist themes surface in the lives of the WCTU missionaries. Some, like Ackermann and Bushnell, noted, as other regular missionaries did, the need for the women of Asia to be freed from the restraints of law and custom and preached against the survival of foot-binding and other physically restrictive practices. Bushnell identified such practices as deliberately designed to keep women physically subordinate to men.[39] Kara Smart had gone to Japan to do temperance work but found young Japanese women besieging her for lectures on dress reform. Smart soon became an expert on this subject and its relation to "physical culture." She was, so she said, introducing "The New Woman" to Japan.[40]

Against these motives pulling women into missionary work there were, of course, equally strong conditions discouraging the less intrepid from going, and shaping in unexpected ways the experience of being a missionary. Health problems bedeviled the missionaries. Mary Allen West died only a few months after arriving in Japan in 1892, and F. E. Stroud Smith was quickly taken in India by "black measles" in 1914. Muriel Ayres lasted only two years in South America in the early 1920s, while Elma Gowen succumbed without warning in Peru in 1912 after returning from a furlough. Both Leavitt and Ackermann suffered repeatedly and severely from fevers that threatened in places like China, India, and the Congo to take their lives. "Any one going to those Eastern countries," lamented one WCTU missionary supporter from India, put herself "in touch with constant possibilities of fatal diseases." It was a wonder, she remarked, that more were not taken.[41]

The dangers were not always from the climate. Leavitt was attacked by what she described as a "Romish" mob in Pernambuco, Brazil, in 1891, while Ellen Stone, a regular missionary in Bulgaria who lectured for the WCTU, and Christine Tinling, in China, were both captured by bandits.[42] These were, however, unusual cases. More often injury was sustained through the primitive means of transport. Vincent, Cummins, Leavitt, Palmer, and Ackermann all complained about rough roads and still rougher transport, but none suffered the fate of Kara Smart. The South Dakota-born missionary returned from Japan in 1906 "seriously ill on account of constant labor and the unaccustomed climate and customs." The turning point in Smart's career came in 1904 when in a rickshaw accident she was "tipped" into "one of the sea canals" and "practically every part of her body was twisted or dislocated or broken."[43]

Not only the methods but also the terms of travel took a toll on these women. It was the combination of distance, isolation, loneliness, and the responses of an often uncomprehending population that wore many of these women down. The exploits of the Anglo-Australian pair, Cummins and Vincent, in the outback of Australia give a vivid picture of the tribulations of temperance missionaries sent to Western Australia to minister to the miners. After a coach journey of 100 miles "without even a drink of water," the two missionaries reached the settlement of Mt. Margaret, "blis-

Jessie Ackermann on the gospel trail, in outback Australia (Jessie Ackermann, *Australia: From a Woman's Point of View* [London: Cassell, 1913]).

tered with the heat of the sun" in their faces. The population of Mt. Margaret was hostile. The postmaster did not at first offer to help them alight
from the coach because no rooms were said to be available in the town. A
room was eventually found at the local pub, but the licensee declined to put
them up when he found they represented the WCTU. The two young
women refused, however, to budge and proceeded in crusade style to hold a
"Gospel temperance meeting" singing hymns on the post-office veranda
until they had raised enough money to go on. Though they presented this
incident as a triumph of the Lord, another six years of such trials in North
America, South Africa, England, and Australasia left them with no emotional energy. "A long cart journey over the rough veldt" in the Cape Colony and "sleeping in a tent" during a cold and windy Natal winter ruined
Vincent's health in 1903. They retired to more sedate work in the slums of
Birmingham, England.[44]
   Some would-be missionaries balked at emulating such strenuous labor.
The case of Belle Kearney has already been cited because she claimed the
"divine leanings" persuaded her not to go, but the reasoning behind this
decision involved "the arduous labors" which round-the-world missionary
work entailed. Her health was already depleted, though she did not have
the excuse of age that served well for some others.[45] Eliza Stewart and
Leavitt had established the precedent of the postmenopausal temperance

missionary, but few had their strong constitutions. Helen Bullock was sixty-one when appointed in 1897, but ill health soon forced her to postpone a prolonged stay overseas, and she limited her World's service to a brief trip to Europe in 1903. Susan Barney did proceed around the world in her sixties in 1897, but on Willard's instructions she stayed away from the tropics, which had taken such a toll on some missionaries.[46]

The rigors of climate and transportation provided only physical obstacles. The barriers of culture had also to be breeched. Language stood as the most obvious of these impediments, though Leavitt did not think so. She claimed to have found English and a little French sufficient, but this testimony itself reveals that Leavitt's work failed to penetrate beyond the Anglo-American communities wherever she went. Clara Parrish more perceptively noted in 1903 that in Japan ignorance of the language was a distinct liability.[47] Interpreters could, of course, be helpful—Ackermann used 175 to communicate in thirty-seven tongues on her trip—though these removed the intimacy from the meeting of speaker and potential converts.[48] A tour of Egypt and Ceylon in 1911 by the Australasian WCTU president, Sara Nolan, while on her way home from the 1910 World's convention, was marked at first by the awkwardness an interpreter introduced, but by the time she had reached Ceylon, "I had become accustomed to speaking through an interpreter, and an audience of a darker skin than my own seemed quite natural."[49] Still, the language problem remained and necessitated a greater reliance on regular missionaries not only as intermediaries but also as potential White Ribbon functionaries as the organization strove to spread beyond its Anglo-Saxon constituency. Long-term residents knew the languages and the cultures much better than any round-the-world missionary could. The spate of appointments to Hispanic-speaking countries typified the shift after the turn of the century, with women like Elma Gowen and Hardynia Norville, both of whom had already taught in Hispanic countries, readily sought for appointment.[50] In contrast, Addie Northam Fields of Indiana, one of the first WWCTU missionaries to go to a Latin American country, wasted months trying to learn elementary Spanish.[51]

Neither interpreters nor command of the language could overcome the loneliness of women severed from their own culture and yet prevented by their assignments and their beliefs from an immersion in the host culture that might have brought a greater wisdom. Language in this sense was only a symbol of what divided the roving missionary from her audience. Not simply linguistic but personal isolation as well was the message of Charlotte Gray in Europe in the early 1890s: "The work here is very hard," she wrote Frances Willard during a trip to Germany. "I often feel the need . . . of some friend to whom I can speak in my own language."[52] To this was added in the non-Western world the equally observable difference of race. Nolan's

Woman's World/Woman's Empire

account of the itinerant and inexperienced white woman lecturing a sea of black and brown faces captured it all, since behind the problem of communication was the gulf of race and culture of which both sides could only be keenly aware.[53]

If the experience of the temperance missionaries was arduous, it was also exhilarating, and most missionaries would have agreed with Jessie Ackermann's conviction that her initial impulse to go had been vindicated. And yet the women who returned were plainly altered by their time abroad. Ackermann's grey hair upon one still so young represented the spirit of self-sacrifice, but the transformation in the lives of the missionaries, at least those who undertook round-the-world assignments, was more profound.[54] Women who went out to shape the world in the image of Christian temperance were in turn affected by that world, intellectually, culturally, and spiritually. Some even returned prepared to question Western ways and to doubt the efficacy of a World's WCTU crusade.

The case of Mary Leavitt, who after her missionary days became an outspoken critic of Lady Henry Somerset, raises the question of whether missionary service affected these women and changed their personalities. Willard certainly thought it had when she discussed the foibles of some of her most famous appointments in an analysis that involved Andrew, Bushnell, and Ackermann as well as Leavitt. These women constituted, in Willard's mind and the minds of some of her closest advisors, the core opposition to the Willard/Somerset axis in the World's WCTU.[55] Willard raised the issue in correspondence concerning the proposed round-the-world trip by Susan Barney in 1897. The WCTU chieftain cautioned Barney on the issue of proceeding beyond Australia, but the letter is mysteriously cut off at precisely the point where she was about to explain why she was offering this advice.[56] However, the point is made clearer in comparison with correspondence between Willard and Mary Whitney, president of the Honolulu WCTU. "I grieve as you do," wrote Willard, "over the great change in some of our best women, who, as I think, and doubtless you share the opinion, were gone too long to the hot countries." The letter to which this was a reply makes clear that Willard was referring specifically to Leavitt and Ackermann.[57] Oral evidence indicates that the missing part of Willard's letter to Barney may have referred in part to allegations that Ackermann had become unbalanced in her attitude toward Willard after falling sick while in China in 1895. An opiate had allegedly been prescribed, and the World's superintendent of the antiopium department was now accused of being an addict herself.[58]

It certainly is true that Ackermann fell sick with malaria and that she spent several years recuperating, punctuating bursts of journalistic and lecturing work with unexplained absences. Moreover, Ackermann had fallen afoul of the World's WCTU leadership. When, much later in 1907, the

Scottish Christian Union proposed sponsoring Ackermann for another WWCTU round-the-world missionary tour, Agnes Slack and Rosalind Carlisle vetoed the appointment and claimed to have "abundant evidence" questioning Ackermann's "fitness" for the job.[59] While something devastating had indeed happened to Ackermann, neither her private correspondence nor that of other WCTU officials gives any firm clues as to the source of her malaise. Nor was there any trace of the alleged condition at the end of Ackermann's long life.[60]

All that is known for certain is that the health of Ackermann, like that of most of the missionaries, did deteriorate and that this experience left her and others in a self-righteous temper, and scornful of the failings of lesser mortals. Leavitt's hostility to Somerset was fueled by memory of the sacrifices she had made, which she contrasted with the pocketbook evangelism of Lady Henry.[61] Andrew and Bushnell also suffered greatly in health during and after missionary service and resigned, charging that the "high standards" of the World's WCTU were no longer "being maintained."[62] Others did not openly break with the WCTU but plainly displayed disillusionment with the scope of their success. Among these was Alice Palmer, who returned to Indiana from South Africa disgruntled and critical of international temperance work. Like Ackermann, Palmer believed that the "English speaking and Christian countries" were the major impediment to the triumph of the World's WCTU, and she became convinced that the real missionary work needed to be done at home.[63] This disillusionment was rarely so clearly articulated, however. If some of the early missionaries became outright enemies of the World's WCTU, more simply dropped out, like Clara Parrish, Ruth Davis, and Kara Smart. Though these women remained nominally connected with the World's WCTU, they either expressed a feeling as Vincent and Cummins did that the financial returns of missionary work did not justify its physical privations, or they turned like Ackermann to other reforms at home and demonstrated a pattern of gradual spiritual declension.[64]

The intellectual and moral change in these women was in fact as marked as the physical deterioration. Did such critical insights as these women developed on their travels contribute to a more comprehensive understanding of the social and political context of their endeavors? Did experience of diverse cultures enable them to transcend their own cultural origins and forge genuinely international perspectives? Ironically, the evidence is strong that the round-the-world formula, designed to liberate the WCTU from hidebound modes of thinking, actually made it more difficult for these women to appreciate what other cultures could offer in the way of experience for temperance or women's emancipation. At the same time, their universal mission made WWCTU appointees suspicious of Western imperial adventures and critical of any temporizing toward moral corruption in imperial systems. The temperance missionaries thus became stranded between the polarities of a universalist mission that transcended cultural boundaries and the hard fact that any such universal message necessarily offended the particular cultural heritage of those the WCTU came to save.

Other missionaries faced the same paradoxes but often became so familiar with the peculiarities of the peoples they served over many years that they found ways to tap particular sources of discontent in indigenous societies. Some even became "multicultural" in approach and, perhaps, in philosophy.[65] Though touched by similar experiences, the WCTU's universalistic approach deprived the temperance missionary of this avenue of influence. But at the same time, the WCTU's commitment to "every land" heightened an awareness of the limitations of Anglo-American Christianity and its cultural blind spots. Whereas the missionary combined knowledge of the particulars with a certainty of faith, the WCTU experience cast doubt on the faith without creating any social roots from which to construct in the missionary countries an alternative cultural perspective.

A certain sensitivity to other cultures was necessary to the work, and even cultural imperialists recognized this. Leavitt urged those who followed in her footsteps "to study the country in which [they were] to work, its history, religion, customs, prejudices, superstitions, so as not unwittingly or unnecessarily to antagonize the people upon subjects not connected with the work."[66] Willard followed this remark with admonishments to her rank and file to pursue what she called the "modern missionary effort." She went much further than Leavitt in her willingness to contemplate tactical adaptation of temperance work. "The study of oriental religions by occidental scholars, and the dissemination of their practical ideas of life by means of the press, has shown how much good there is in the teachings of all the great religious leaders of the past," she told her national WCTU convention in 1893.[67] Under her influence, the *Union Signal* sponsored publication of the proceedings of the Parliament of Religions held in conjunction with the Chicago World's Exposition and called the deliberations "the most important event of the century." An advertisement in that paper showed Buddhism, Hinduism, and other faiths as links in the great chain of "one supreme being."[68]

This remarkable concession to a world religion was the subject of much ridicule among regular missionaries, some of whom were connected to the WCTU. These women were under no illusion that non-Christian faiths could hold the key to spiritual and moral uplift, let alone the life everlasting. Adelaide Daughaday, an eleven-year resident of Japan, felt betrayed by the WCTU's apparent endorsement of "dense superstition and ignorance," while another woman of missionary experience, Mrs. C. W. Scott, deplored the evidence that temperance women were turning from the faith of their

Missionaries and Cultural Imperialism

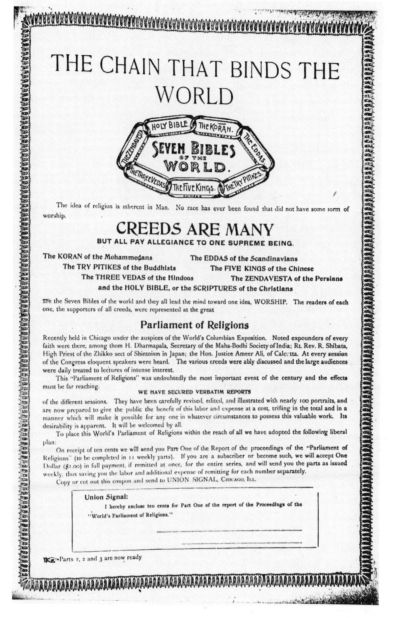

Ecumenicism of the World's WCTU as illustrated in an advertisement for
the reports of the Parliament of Religions in the *Union Signal*
(*Union Signal*, 9 Nov. 1893)

fathers to "the vapory, vague, but cultured-oh, so cultured! 'isms,'" so "flabby" had they "grown in their . . . religious texture."[69]

Given this atmosphere of declension, it is significant that among the round-the-world temperance missionaries a more ecumenical disposition surfaced in their responses to the Parliament of Religions and in their reports of alien cultures and faiths. Jessie Ackermann learned something of value from her exposure to other cultures that affected her Christian and temperance faith. She told the Australasian WCTU convention in her last annual report as president in 1894 that the Parliament of Religions had indeed been valuable as an exchange of "various opinions, with a due and just regard for the opinions of others." Brushing aside the criticisms of those who allowed their "prejudices" against "the needs of the Eastern world" to cloud their vision, she concluded: "It [the parliament] has taught our own hearts to respond to the heartbeats of a great world."[70] Others were even more ecumenical. While Stevenson found Buddhism in Burma and Ceylon "sadly perverted and distorted" by accretions to its "fundamental principles," these—"mercy and compassion"—seemed "not to have been impaired and their effect [had] been to develop a people of great gentleness and of high courtesy."[71]

This same awareness of value in other cultures was also implicit in the thinking of all missionaries who damned European Christians for bringing liquor to non-Christian people. This was the burden of the messages to "the voters of Christian lands" from returning missionaries like Palmer. Round-the-world missionaries did realize that principles of temperance were already present in the Eastern religions, particularly in Islamic countries and among Brahmins and Buddhists, and noted the temperate behavior of these peoples. "The one great virtue of the Mohammedan religion is prohibition," concluded Sara Crafts, World's WCTU Sunday school superintendent, after a tour of Europe in 1901. Wherever in southern Europe the Islamic influence had been strong, she found "a habit of abstemiousness" that centuries of subsequent Christian dominance had not entirely erased.[72] Other workers, like Flora Strout in Burma and Ceylon, fostered and promoted temperance societies for Buddhists and set aside the question of Christianity. In 1919 Strout spoke, for example, "in a Buddhist hall in connection with a temple" in Ceylon and had in attendance "a good many priests, one of whom made me a long speech of thanks."[73]

Under the impact of this cultural exchange, these WWCTU missionaries certainly did what they could to provide Anglo-American women with more reliable information on the complexities of the cultures and regions they had traversed. Quickly they were made aware of the astonishing ignorance of large sections of the literate American population concerning events and people outside the continental United States. Alice Palmer found "comical and provoking" the "blunders about countries and peoples" in southern

Africa among "the women of the United States" after her return in 1895 and, like Ackermann, spent time lecturing on her experiences at least in part to reduce the ignorance.[74]

But even in the case of thoroughly ecumenical women—Stevenson was the outstanding example after Willard—it was the people rather than the religion or the culture that won the missionary's heart. "I have come to love the Great Empire. I have come to love the Chinese people," Stevenson wistfully concluded at the end of her stay as she stood gazing at Hong Kong harbor as her ship steamed out, bound for Australia.[75] Mary Campbell in India in the 1920s professed the same respect for the people and civilization of her "beloved India" that had entranced Stevenson in China in 1909. Asked to send a message back from furlough in America, the only greeting she could convey was, "Tell the people that we love them."[76] Yet another China missionary, Ruth Shaffner, best expressed the thinking of these women on the essential humanity of all the peoples of the world. Divided from Europeans by religion and culture, the Chinese were, nevertheless, worthy of great respect. "They are so strangely like ourselves" in their needs and emotions, she concluded. "Mother-love" they expressed just like any WCTU woman, and despite technological backwardness, showed evidence that they were "industrious, frugal, polite and capable." Shaffner especially denounced "the high-handed treatment" they had experienced from westerners and included in this bill of particulars not only the opium wars but also "the disgraceful exclusion enactments of the Americans" that kept Chinese out of the United States.[77]

In an era of Jim Crow segregation, Shaffner stood out against racism in the name of Christianity, and her attitudes did reflect the wider experience of the World's WCTU missionaries. Leavitt announced to the first World's convention that the WCTU would treat all peoples equally and repeated what another temperance woman had told her: "God must love the dark races as He had made a great many more" of them.[78] Even after the warm glow of her witnessing to the peoples of every culture receded, Leavitt held out in 1895 the hope of a universalistic morality that would transcend racial divisions. "I have conversed with persons of every colored race on earth who were as well fitted by native ability, by education, by manners, by elevation of character and purity of life to take the title of gentleman or lady as any white person in the United States."[79] Bushnell and Andrew, too, stressed the equality of humanity and showed a disregard for caste and racial barriers in dealing with Chinese and Indian prostitutes.[80]

It was understandable that black missionaries like Amanda Smith and Fanny Coppin, both of whom did WCTU work in Africa in the course of regular missionary duties, should express such sentiments more clearly still and make connections between the imperialism of European powers and the oppression of race. Coppin, whose husband served at the turn of the century as a Methodist Episcopal church bishop in South Africa, directed much of her time toward "organizing black South African women into Woman's Christian Temperance Union Societies and Woman's Mite Missionary Societies" between 1902 and 1904. Like other black missionaries, she "questioned the benefits of European rule" and scathingly noted that "black South Africans remained uneducated, lived in dilapidated homes, and were exposed to all kinds of disease because of the unsanitary living conditions."[81]

The missionary experience, and the desire to be seen in a favorable light by non-Western peoples, had some effect on WCTU policies and pronouncements. At the 1892 National WCTU convention, delegates debated a resolution on the World's WCTU missionary activity that originally included a derogatory reference to lands "that sit in heathen darkness." This was strenuously and successfully opposed by Marion H. Dunham of Iowa because "other nations have their religions." Willard and Anna Gordon supported Dunham and noted how hurt their Indian WCTU lecturer and friend Pandita Ramabai was when she heard WCTU women singing the words of the Reginald Heber hymn, "From Greenland's Icy Mountains." When Christian women contrasted the pleasant "prospects" of every clime with the essential "vileness" of the inhabitants of "heathen lands," Ramabai did not recognize her own non-Christian but holy father and resented the slur on her people.[82]

The cultural imperialism implicit in the Christian temperance formula was also blunted by the experience of temperance reformers in Christian Europe. The fact that European soil generally proved so barren to the cause of temperance was not lost upon the missionaries, who drove home the implication that Europeans were not necessarily superior in their morality to other people.[83] The language used by Edith Smith Davis to describe Italian society was little different from that used by Ackermann in her tours of Southeast Asia or by Nellie Burger in her denunciations of the drinking habits of Mexican peasants. Indeed, because Christian Europeans should have known better than the peasants in the colonial outposts of civilization, the European was if anything treated more harshly by visiting temperance missionaries. "All Italians drink the native wines," Davis observed with disgust during a tour in 1909, "and the degradation, the filth, the squalor of the people is simply indescribable."[84]

Not all European nations were described as equally debilitated. Alice Gordon Gulick, Anna Gordon's sister, claimed that "during thirty years of life and work in Spain I have seen only one prostrate drunkard." But the WCTU's conclusion was to indict Spain because its merchants allegedly exported their wines and hence their alcoholism to other countries. The implication was still clear, as in other WWCTU pronouncements, that there was no necessary connection between moral worth and racial mix.[85]

None of this chastisement of Christian and "civilized" peoples changed the impact of the cultural messages of superiority imbedded in the WCTU's version of the Christian commitment. The WCTU's evangelical commitment prevented "good" Indians and other "temperate [but colored] races" similarly viewed from being officially included in the ranks of the WCTU and barred their acceptance as fully human. Clara Parrish put the point bluntly in the light of six years' labor in the East. "Japan is not a civilized country yet, although it may have put on some of the outward forms of civilization. . . . Only Christianity and Christian Temperance can ever make it such."[86]

It would be comforting to think that Willard herself escaped the harsher judgments of this aspect of the missionary culture. It may also be tempting to see Willard's acceptance that the Lord spoke to different peoples in different ways as evidence of "sympathetic tolerance" toward Islam and perhaps other "Oriental" faiths.[87] When seen in the full context of World's WCTU activity and Willard's commitment to women's emancipation, such sentiments cannot be sustained. She, no more than any WCTU women, wished to abandon the basic tenets of Christianity as the vital impulse of the temperance movement. Rare indeed were the women temperance missionaries, like Isobel Gibson Scott of Paris, who embraced the syncretic alternative of theosophy. Willard did meet Annie Besant, thus suggesting a certain questioning of the narrow faith of her upbringing, but one thing above all kept Willard in the conventional camp—her conviction of the connection between Christianity and the emancipation of women.[88]

Willard's own grand tour of Europe and the Middle East with Kate Jackson in 1869–70 prompted the temperance leader to conclude that "only Christian countries treat women kindly."[89] Crossing the Danube from Islamic Turkey into a Christian village in Bulgaria brought the message home to her. The Turks shunned their womenfolk, dressed them poorly, and made them wear veils. Across the river a group of men and women danced merrily together under a maypole in a Christian Orthodox community. "Even in the degenerate form in which the Greek Church dispenses Christianity," she later remembered, "it has thus made women the comrades of men, and made men the brothers of girls." Willard never shifted from this position and, in a prospectus for the World's WCTU written in 1891, pleaded "for the word Christian in the name of every . . . auxiliary." But for the gospel, "we should to day be slaves, and the question among leaders in mosque and temple would not be whether we should be admitted to the highest ecclesiastical councils . . . but whether or not we had any souls to save or immortality to gain!"[90]

This belief put Willard squarely in the middle of her following. Ruth Ranney, who served for a time as WWCTU president in Burma, expressed the missionary opinion that Jesus was "the true Emancipator of women."

"If any one doubts" what the Christian religion did for women, exclaimed Jessie Ackermann while in China, "let him witness the condition of our sisters of Asia."[91] Leavitt agreed, and her tolerance of racial differences did not involve a concession that other religions were equal in any way. "Colored people" were as worthy as whites but worthless unless "saved." Ruth Shaffner hoped to use temperance to help bring China into the twentieth century free from the foreigner's immoral yoke, but this could only be achieved by sloughing off "superstition" and "idolatory."[92] These things stood as the barriers between the races and made humans seem so different. The solution was, it is true in the cases of Willard, Leavitt, Shaffner, and Parrish, universalistic in pretension, but that claim in turn was based on the notion of Christian superiority, no matter what the sins of Christian nations.

The WWCTU thus erected, in the question of religion, a hierarchy that linked the worth of a civilization to its efficacy for women's emancipation. Culturally imperialistic attitudes were integral to this hierarchy. Non-Western nations stood at the bottom; the Orthodox, with their "debased" form of Christianity, were in the middle; and the Protestant nations above these. At the pinnacle were those countries that practiced evangelical Christianity. "Only where the Bible is an every day home book, has Christianity shown its full possibilities of uplift for the gentler and more spiritual half of humanity."[93] In turn, identification of moral worth with evangelical Christianity linked the WCTU's view with late nineteenth-century Anglo-American superiority, notwithstanding all the kind words said about the native races. The "English-speaking race" Mary Leavitt charged with the potential and hence the responsibility for temperance reform because "we . . . have had the Bible open, and have interpreted it for ourselves."[94]

None of this was exceptional in the context of late nineteenth-century Anglo-American attitudes of race and power. What the WCTU could contribute was experience of the "reality" of these generalizations. The finding of the early missionaries on this point was clear: non-Christian nations systematically oppressed women. The contradictions within the evangelical temperance impulse, so far as it affected the issue of women's emancipation, were thus exposed. On the one hand, evangelicalism proved to be a potent ideology for engendering bonds of "solidarity of sentiment among women everywhere" by identifying manifestations of women's oppression.[95]

On the other hand the very tool of analysis used to explain the identified sources of oppression undermined the notion of a systematic cross-cultural basis to gender subordination. If Leavitt sought to achieve through her missionary endeavors the "ecclesiastical emancipation of woman," her experience as she went about this task tended to contradict her discontent with restrictions upon the activity of women in the Christian churches of

America. Her epic trip led her to announce quite early that "while there is much to be gained in America," the women of the United States were "more favored than in any other country."[96] It was easy to conclude, as Mrs. R. Jay Greene, an American missionary resident in Hawaii, did after a return visit to the United States, that the strength of the evangelical churches and women's commitment to Christian temperance underpinned this contrast with other nations. Only in the United States could women work for temperance "and receive full wages."[97] Even temperance women in Australasia, where the formal signs of women's emancipation were marked, conceded this point.[98]

Occasionally the WCTU appeared to deviate from rock-bottom faith in Christian supremacy in moral reform. In Bulgaria the White Ribboners were part of a larger Bulgarian Temperance Union in which the word *Christian* was conspicuously missing. Said Mrs. Elleuka Nikolora: "The work is not only for Christians, but for all humanity regardless of sect."[99] But this pragmatism that local conditions sometimes prompted did not affect the ideology of the broader movement. "We shall have to discuss . . . the question as to whether Buddhists are eligible as W.C.T.U. members," pleaded England's Ethel Beedham in 1903, during her stint in Burma.[100] The answer was always, as far as most WCTU missionaries and the movement's leaders were concerned, in the negative. The wrath of World's president Carlisle fell upon the Indian WCTU in 1920 over precisely this issue. How could the Indian executive "keep Mahometans, with their uncivilized views about women, in harmony with the attitude of the W.W.C.T.U. on these moral points?" She advised strongly, therefore, that all those who practiced "the humiliation of women in the harem" be kept out of the unions in India.[101]

Even had the issue of women not arisen, the White Ribbon movement had for both Carlisle and Willard been "born and cradled and matured as a Christian movement." When Carlisle called Islam "an alien and aggressively propagandist religion," the redoubtable British temperance worker may have expressed her private consternation at the antics of a brother, a convert to Islam, but she also reiterated a view heard often in WCTU circles drawn from decades of missionary experience and centuries of cultural antipathy.[102] Willard damned as early as 1870 "the fanatic stupidity of its [Islam's] adherents," and though she appeared at times to make concessions at odds with this view, she always returned to its comforting illusions.[103] The WWCTU therefore kept the letter *C* in its official title. It had to because if Christianity limited the movement's appeal, evangelicalism was also the movement's vital source of willpower and spiritual comfort. As late as 1962, the WWCTU was still willing to debate earnestly but negatively the question of whether to drop the *Christian* from WWCTU and bring in those of non-Christian faith.[104] The organization remained long after prohibition's demise in the United States, impaled on the contradiction of its energizing force of gospel faith.

These limits to tolerance and acceptance of religious diversity should not surprise, because the WCTU was part of the larger missionary endeavor even while it criticized missionary lethargy. In the pages of the *Union Signal*, reports from regular missionaries commented on the "essential rottenness" of the Hindu religion, for example, at the very time the WWCTU was preparing to send missionaries for temperance to India.[105]

But behind the religious judgment was the larger issue, so ably demonstrated by Edward Said, of the Western discourse on the people of Asia as homogeneous in culture and "Oriental." The Orient was for Willard, as for Western scholars and missionaries alike, full of mystery that beckoned, but on the other hand it was a realm of repulsive and essentially unchanging tradition. The East was passive and slumbering, to be awakened only by the modernizing forces of the West. Among these, bringing knowledge and power, was the message of Christian temperance. What both demonstrated the backwardness of the vast Orient and held the key to its uplift was, for the WCTU, its treatment of women. Louise Purlington was one WCTU missionary supporter who made the place of women central and so expands upon our understanding of the discourse of Orientalism. There had been, said Purlington, "no greater obstacle in [woman's] path than the Oriental conception of herself; from her long subjection and enforced ignorance." The Orient's awakening, concluded Purlington, was woman's.[106] This judgment even won the backing of indigenous Indian temperance workers who conjured up images of an ancient and pure Oriental civilization that had since succumbed to vice and that must make the most of the moral stimulus of the women of the "Occident."[107]

Trapped in this discourse, the women of the WCTU tended to reject particular experiences that might have prompted them to overturn their worldview. The temperance missionaries could not really help, though they did supply much information that belied existing stereotypes. Jessie Ackermann noted that Japan and China were often merged in the minds of many Americans, though on the issues that interested the WCTU, she found them to be poles apart to the credit of Japan. In her own round-the-world missionary reports, Mary Leavitt emphasized not a homogeneous Orient but diversity in customs, peoples, and geography. "It would be as wise to say a certain custom prevails all over Europe," she cautioned, "because it exists in Sweden or Italy, as to say it of India, because the custom mentioned exists in some part of the country."[108] But this did not make Leavitt tolerant of those diverse customs, and she still linked them all inconsistently in the overarching and totalizing concept of "eastern depravity." Why?

Being cut off from regular missionary ties was supposed to allow more

Missionaries and Cultural Imperialism

enlightened attitudes to prevail among WCTU emissaries. Yet when these women confronted other cultures at odds with "progressive" values, the result was not a new cultural synthesis. In practice a round-the-world missionary was likely, through the superficiality of her contact with various cultures, to have her prejudices reinforced. These women saw exotic temples that both attracted and repelled their sensibilities, animals sacrificed, men with several wives, women with veils, peasants who were impossibly poor by Western standards of technological advancement, and homes that lacked the amenities and standards of cleanliness and domesticity accepted in the United States. Their responses rarely went beyond the register of shock and a mixture of sympathy and revulsion.[109]

The isolation of the temperance missionary often meant that the core beliefs became a source of refuge and withdrawal from serious contact with the cultures experienced. Ackermann wrote to Willard of her loneliness and explained how the experience opened up her heart to Christ. "It is hard to give up home and loved ones, and be always among strangers, . . . but . . . in removing me so far from earthly friends He [God] has been more than all of them to me."[110] If Ackermann relied on the Lord, Flora Strout placed additional emphasis on "the brave leaders who [stood] back of this work." In that light, Strout felt "that I should never falter, that my faith should never fail."[111] Either way, the missionary did not to any significant extent confront the "Other"; she failed to become a multicultural woman. Neither was a cross-cultural exchange made more likely by the practice of traveling in pairs that many of these women adopted to combat loneliness. Bushnell and Andrew, and Vincent and Cummins, were inseparable pairings; Ackermann went to Iceland with Shaffner and then to Japan with Ada Murcutt; Ericson teamed up with Shaffner; Bessie Cowie with Mabel Beddow; and so on. The "added help and inspiration of each other's companionship"—to use the phrase of that exemplary team, Vincent and Cummins—may have encouraged the perpetuation of received opinion, as it is intended to do with present-day Mormon missionaries.[112]

This is not to say that the missionary experience did nothing to alter the cluster of attitudes within the WCTU's cultural imperialism. The intensification of their evangelical commitment that came with suffering and isolation made some of these women more deeply committed to the internationalist and universalistic aspects of the crusade. As such, they became bitter critics of any compromise with power, and at the expense of morality. While the details must be taken up in later chapters that deal with the specific issues of peace, purity, and prohibition, the central point can be quickly made. The early round-the-world missionaries did not simply end their careers as physically exhausted malcontents. From their experience came the focus for opposition to the policies of the World's executive committee, where these policies seemed to compromise the original purposes and moral integrity of the World's WCTU. They also became simultaneously critical of Anglo-American political and even economic imperialism and of women in the World's WCTU who seemed to them apologetic of empire. The round-the-world missionary women felt that because they had sacrificed so much for the cause, everyone else should do the same. Disillusioned by the dominance of organizational imperatives over their own conception of self-sacrifice and commitment to absolute truth, these women renounced the work. They were not replaced with women quite so distinctive or eccentric, because the whole nature of the World's WCTU's relationship with the mission movement was gradually changing.[113]

The pioneers of the 1880s and 1890s, especially, were the heroic individuals of the World's WCTU. But more and more the work became routinized, and vocal criticisms of imperial power and missionary insufficiency became muted. This gradual shift was associated with the convergence of WCTU objectives with those of the (evolving) mission organizations themselves. By the early twentieth century the emphasis in the Protestant home missions was shifting. Spiritual commitment did not lessen, but in organizations like the Student Volunteers for Foreign Missions, greater emphasis was placed on organizational skills, formal training, systematic financial contributions, and ecumenicism among the mainstream churches.[114]

This girding of effort affected the WWCTU. Around the time of Willard's death, the WCTU began to take more seriously the question of missionary temperance finances and began the payment of round-the-world and other missionaries on a regular, salaried basis.[115] Leavitt had received over $3,000 from the National WCTU, but she returned more than half of this and financed most of her trip by private contributions along the way. Ackermann, Bushnell, and Andrew similarly went unpaid.[116] Of the early missionaries, only Palmer was given a passage. It really was a case of believing that "the Lord will provide."

Reliance on the Lord's financial help meant that cooperation with missionaries was always regarded as essential to success, not just after 1900. Do not offend missionaries, Leavitt told the World's WCTU assembled for its inaugural convention in Boston in 1891. "One who antagonizes missionaries would always do more harm than good."[117] Nonetheless, antagonize missionaries the WWCTU itinerants sometimes did. Ackermann's attendance at an 1890 China missionary conference in Shanghai caused controversy. "Some dear old missionaries, who had been buried in their work for forty years in the midst of a heathen nation, had not realised that the world moved." Opposition to Ackermann speaking from the platform was, however, confined to a section of the convention, and a special evening was set aside outside the formal proceedings to allow organization of a WCTU of China. In India three years later, an English missionary went further. Many people had not invited Ackermann to speak or grumbled when she did, but this Church of England chaplain refused outright.[118] Much later in 1912, Ella Hoover Thatcher found Congregational missionaries in Hong Kong who similarly declined to help her.[119] Clara Parrish was, like other women, disturbed and hurt by such responses. "If I could have realised," she wrote, "how much prejudice there was against women 'preaching,' as well as against the W.C.T.U., even among the missionaries, I should have made fewer mistakes."[120]

This ambivalent and sometimes hostile relationship with regular missions would not have astonished Leavitt, who despite her admonition to cultivate the missionaries was happy to disclose and criticize their drinking practices. Leavitt noted that hostile missionaries were mostly among the non-Americans, and for this reason she preferred contacts with Americans as resident representatives of the temperance cause.[121]

Such contacts were inevitable and essential if the work of the World's WCTU was to be anything other than superficial. The round-the-world organizing tour had advantages for WWCTU propagandists in demonstrating the determination of its leaders to be truly international, but it also provoked persistent criticism of the ephemeral nature of much of their work. Leavitt organized sixteen WCTUs in India during her eight months there in 1887–88, but by 1891, only three were found by Jerome H. Raymond to be "active."[122] This assessment was contested by WCTU workers in Burma, where Ruth Ranney replied that a good many of Leavitt's creations had survived, but the essential point would not have been denied by Leavitt herself. She readily conceded the obvious; eight months on the subcontinent and two in Ceylon were a sizable part of her seven years abroad, but necessarily a superficial visit for all that.[123] Even in more receptive countries such as Australia where language was no obstacle, complaints were heard that the visits of both Stevenson and Barney were hampered by whirlwind itineraries. Said the Australasian convention report in relation to Stevenson's visit: "The time devoted to each State [was] wholly inadequate to accomplish the work which is so sorely needed."[124]

Superficiality could not be so easily charged against the accounts of the women the WCTU sent to reside in one country, like the missionaries appointed to China, Japan, Burma, India, Argentina, and Uruguay between 1903 and 1920. But no one person could possibly cover even these more limited fields. India needed a dozen such women, claimed Leavitt, to be situated in a variety of regions. The stupendous nature of this task made reliance on "local talent" inevitable.[125] For this reason resident missionaries were increasingly used either as official appointees or were given funds for particular periods and projects. In China, much use was made of the American Congregational missionary Sarah B. Goodrich, the Presbyterian Mary Jane Farnham, and a Methodist, Mrs. Ren Yin Mei, an American-educated associate of Dr. Mary Stone. In India, the union had the services

of Pandita Ramabai as national lecturer and Helen E. Dunhill, a "consecrated young woman" of Eurasian extraction, who ministered to her Indian
audiences in a native sari. The World's WCTU also generously supported
through salaries and travel allowances the succession of missionaries in India who served as National presidents from 1893 to 1923.[126]

Temperance work done by resident missionary women was varied but
usually included petitioning against opium and alcohol, pledge gathering,
rescue work among prostitutes, revivalistic gospel temperance meetings,
and school visiting. Some missionaries had special projects, such as Goodrich's attacks on the use of tobacco in China after 1910, the Japanese
WCTU's successful campaign in 1909 to close the geisha district of Osaka,
the victorious assault in Calcutta in 1902 on the use of English barmaids,
and in many places the translation of temperance and purity literature.[127]

The use of women who had been regular missionaries, or part-time reliance on women who still were, strengthened the missionary connection that
was present from the beginning. After 1908, the establishment by the National WCTU in the United States of a Department for Cooperation with
Missionary Societies represented a decisive reinforcement of the direction
of change. The shift was both a product of the larger transformation of
missionary strategy toward systematic education and an attempt to take advantage of that change of policy. Henceforth the American and other
World affiliates concentrated on attempts to instill in regular missionaries a
pro-temperance attitude. Joint meetings with mission society auxiliaries
would raise funds to send literature on the temperance issue to mission
stations. Temperance secretaries within the mission societies in the United
States would contribute to a growing awareness of the importance of the
temperance movement to the success of missions. Thus would the WCTU
influence potential missionaries on the need for temperance work before
they embarked for duty abroad. This work was one of the most strenuously
pursued of all the causes in the Do-Everything galaxy. Renamed the temperance and missions department during World War I, the section had, by
1919, affiliates in forty-two states, more than either the peace, the labor, or
the purity departments. In 1910, the World's WCTU culminated the drift
toward integration with missionary work by creating a new World's Department for Co-Operation with Missionaries, under the direction of Louise
Purlington.[128]

The new cooperation movement, with its stress not upon an emotion-
charged change of heart but upon the provision of reliable and "enlightening" information, dovetailed with the shift in WCTU mission thinking.
Women sent out during the First World War and in the 1920s stressed
preparatory educational goals. It was assumed that the strength of prohibitionist sentiment reflected the long-term influence of the WCTU in the
United States through scientific temperance instruction laws. Christine

Missionaries and Cultural Imperialism

Tinling and Frances Willard Wang, who went to China in 1921 for the World's WCTU, were specifically charged with working for the STI laws and for the inculcation of temperance principles in the schools through the Loyal Temperance Legion and the Young People's Bureau.[129]

Increased reliance on missionary organizations strengthened the scope of the World's work, particularly that emanating directly from the United States. But there were political consequences, since mission domination muted the often independent and critical tone of WCTU pronouncements on Christian missionary failings. Criticism of missionaries, heard frequently in the 1890s, disappeared, but the impact was more disturbing still. WCTU knowledge of the non-Western world, and of the impact of great power policies on alcohol, opium, and prostitution in their colonies, was increasingly drawn directly from regular missionaries and the mission boards.[130]

This does not mean that the WCTU's missionary effort was running out of steam. The women's missionary movement in America, it has been suggested, lost impetus in the 1920s as secularization proceeded. The very process of bureaucratization and routinization of mission work (implicit in the WCTU program of cooperation with mission societies) deprived the women's missionary movement of its vitality and removed the rationale for a gender-specific mission movement. If dollars and cents rather than sentiment held the key to success in foreign fields, no appeal to conceptions of separate spheres would be effective.[131]

Traces of a similar process can be found in the World's WCTU in the twenties. The name *organizer* was chosen to replace the term *missionary* in a move that hinted at secularization. So too did the greater focus in the 1920s on prohibition rather than individual spiritual conversion, seen in the dispatching of Deborah Livingston to South Africa and Eva C. Wheeler to Australia. On the other hand, clear evidence that secularization spelled decay for the WCTU is lacking. The WCTU itself was always an uneasily constructed bridge toward secular social reform, and this ambiguous experience persisted in the 1920s. The focus on reform did not erode the WCTU's Christian commitment, though it may unnecessarily have tied the faith to a panacea of controversial status on the international stage. This point, however, directs attention away from the internal dynamics of social organizations to the larger context of cultural and political struggle.[132]

Prohibition did not have the same impact on the international missionary vision of the WCTU as secularization did on missions. National victory in 1919 allowed the WCTU to pour more sentiment and effort on the heathen than ever before. The World's missionary campaign did not gradually succumb to these larger social changes by the 1920s. Befitting the decade of remarkable cultural ferment that it was, the twenties would be in a purely quantitative sense the halcyon period of World's WCTU missionary activity as the United States WCTU tried to extend the "blessings" of the Eighteenth Amendment around the globe. American financial support for missionary work peaked in these years, and unprecedented propaganda efforts littered the record of the decade. Temperance missionary work in India, Burma, Japan, the Philippines, and especially China intensified, and new work was sponsored by Australia in Egypt under WCTU auspices as well. The pretensions to worldwide evangelism of the WCTU would end in 1933 not with a whimper, but with a bang.[133]

Some of the missionaries who began their labors in this last great decade of the World's WCTU's history traveled as widely as their predecessors, and their levels of energy were also comparable. Mary Campbell was still active in the late 1940s at the age of eighty-four after eight world trips, twenty years' White Ribbon service, and thirty-three years as a regular missionary before that in India. But the later missionaries lacked an independent vision. Exuding piety and spirituality rather than a commitment to women's emancipation, they had in fact become cogs in the much larger wheel of American international prohibitionism spearheaded by the ASL. They were also indistinguishable from the vast array of regular missionaries whose evangelical work they wholeheartedly reinforced. The newer recruits avoided controversies over the power and morality of empire to a degree that would have been foreign to their predecessors of the 1890s.[134]

And yet there were still crucial links with the dynamic processes of temperance evangelism. Not openly critical of imperial rule, the newer missionaries sought nevertheless like their predecessors to exploit the incipient forces of popular nationalism by mobilizing indigenous temperance societies. Indirectly, their emphasis on democratic participation in temperance agitation in colonial societies actually went further than that of the earlier appointees, because in the 1920s temperance missionaries could not operate according to an assumed Anglo-American hegemony. Instead, their actions anticipated a new era in which European authority would be overthrown, though they themselves rarely expressed an opinion on this subject.

Intriguing indeed it would be to enter the minds of Ackermann, Leavitt, Cummins, Vincent, Andrew, Bushnell, or Palmer in this later period of more routinized missionary endeavors and to determine what the earliest missionaries thought of these later developments. Any such quest is, however, bound to be frustrated, since their lives ended in embittered isolation and, with the exception of Leavitt, almost total obscurity. The silence that settled over most of the early missionaries after their epic labors were over remains unbroken. As far as can be ascertained, they seem to have remained faithful to the causes of Christian evangelism and women's emancipation long after their names and labors were forgotten by the World's WCTU and, in some cases, even after prohibition itself was a distant memory.

Missionaries and Cultural Imperialism

Compared with the mountains of information on her travels compiled in the 1890s, relatively little is known of Jessie Ackermann's later life. The records that have survived fail to shed any additional light on the central driving forces of her character. She remains, perhaps intentionally, a mysterious figure. But the restless and rootless pattern of her personal career persisted, and her values stood consistent with the spirit of the WCTU's early endeavors. In 1937 she was still described during a visit to Los Angeles as "an ardent feminist" who "radiates pride in women and their achievements." On her death certificate is the information that she herself supplied. Her occupation was lecturer, her "business" was "religion."[135]

6

Sisters, Mothers,
and Brother-Hearted Men

The Family Ideology
of the World's WCTU

Nothing is more calculated to bring out a latent spirit of humanitarianism than the problem of the refugee, yet nothing is equally likely to expose the contradictions of such benevolent impulses. In the Ottoman Empire, the Turkish forces had unleashed after 1894 a regime of barbarous atrocities against the subject Armenian people. Thereby they had created new opportunities for the conscience of women's emancipation. Alongside the wholesale slaughter of thousands went the destruction of farm crops, the burning and looting of villages, and the creation of a large refugee population. In the late summer of 1896, Willard and Somerset found themselves drawn irresistibly away from the pleasant prospect of a bicycling holiday in France toward these matters of more serious moment. Alarmed by the reports of the refugees' plight, they hastened to the port of Marseilles to see what they could do to help those Armenians arriving from the trouble spot.

In addition to ministering personally to the escaped victims, Willard launched an appeal "To the Christian Women of America" that encapsulated the terms of her endeavor and that gives us insights into the ideology of the WCTU's international work. Prominent in the rhetoric was the call to help wronged sisters, the helpless female victims of the Turks. The WCTU's response to the Armenian crisis was indeed generous, and both the terms of Willard's appeal and the strength of support for international relief among temperance women have prompted suggestions that in the Armenian refugee problem the essence of the WCTU's ideology of sisterhood was revealed.[1]

In the recent flowering of women's history, no issue has had so much written about it as this theme of sisterhood. Not only are the bonds of sisterhood said to be strong among nineteenth-century American women, but the international dimension of this sentiment has also been asserted. Historians have been quick to note that the WCTU shared in this sisterly concern for other women beyond the national boundaries of the United States. The "privileged position of protection and respect" that WCTU women felt in their own lives led them, according to recent interpretations, "to save their oppressed sisters" in other lands.[2]

Unquestionably, Frances Willard and many others in the WCTU used the language not merely of sisters, but of sisterhood, and an international sisterhood at that. This impulse toward sisterly solidarity as an underpinning of the World's WCTU requires closer scrutiny, however. The existence of a sisterhood among turn-of-the-century feminists has been too freely assumed. Professions of sisterly concern have been accepted at face value as evidence of cross-class and cross-national solidarity, and little attention has been given to how the language of sisterhood was employed at that time. Most important of all, the relationship of sisterhood to other concepts of critical importance in the culture of temperance women must be examined. The WCTU's ideology must be set in the wider context of its attitudes toward men and the ascendant ideology of motherhood in the latter part of the nineteenth century.[3]

The international aspects of this ideology of sisterhood deserve the most serious and critical scrutiny of all, for there both the potential and the pitfalls of such a worldview are exposed most clearly. The concept of sisterhood implied an identity of (unconscious) interests among all women. National boundaries and state parochialism had no place in this feminist consciousness, which genuinely sought to emancipate women not only in the United States but in other countries as well. But national and cultural differences were transparently obvious on the international arena, and the notion of sisterhood had to face not only the obstinate refusal of many women to accept a communal interest, but also the emergence of different and conflicting interpretations of sisterly consciousness. Within the World's WCTU were illustrated internecine conflicts that can be part of any family, but which sisterhood's interpreters neglect at their peril.

The discovery of "firsts" is a precarious pastime among historians, but the use of the term *sisterhood* to refer to a women's reform movement went back at least to Mary Bannister Willard's description of the women's suffrage associations in 1882.[4] Her fellow WCTU workers soon joined in the adoption of a sisterhood ideology in the mid-1880s, even before the International Council of Women was formed. When that organization first met in Washington, D.C., in 1888, it was Frances Willard who hailed it as yet another expression of international solidarity among women and used the precise language of sisterhood to describe the scope of feeling between feminists.[5] This usage by Willard and her sister-in-law went beyond the tendency of antebellum temperance women and evangelical reformers to describe themselves and those they wished to reform as "sisters." Willard did not denote the World's WCTU a sisterhood until 1889, though the American WCTU had been so described as early as 1884. In taking up the concept of sisterhood Willard implied that more than a vague feeling of sorority was required. A sisterhood for her involved a more tangible set of relations based on a demonstration of mutual effort and organization.[6]

What gave particular strength to the notion of sisterhood in the WCTU was the way that ideology became intertwined with the actual lives of the women who forged the women's consciousness. WCTU women did not merely profess sisterhood. Many of them lived it. Emotional connections and networks of female friends were common, at least among the upper-middle-class and middle-class women of native-born, Protestant stock in the mid- to late nineteenth century first studied by Carroll Smith-Rosenberg. Many women inhabited, so it seems, a predominantly female world shaped by the separation of the spheres. As women of the middle classes moved out of the home into paid employment after the Civil War, they both extended the boundaries of domesticity and carried the emotional networks of their youth, and of an earlier generation, into the public sphere. They adapted these networks to political purposes, and the women's culture became a powerful contributor to women's emancipation.[7]

The WCTU's guiding light in the 1890s was clearly part of this process. Willard lived with and professed love for a variety of women, from the time of Kate Jackson in the 1860s to Anna Gordon, her "loved and *last*."[8] Her many relationships with women had an intensity that belies the image of the passionless woman. What is one to make of her planned meeting with the literary figure Lilian Whiting in Tremont Temple in 1892? She admitted in the course of her private praise: "I have long desired you," and signed the letter, "Thy sister."[9] In a series of passionate letters to Anna Gordon, whom she described as her "love bird," written during a short separation in 1891, Willard exclaimed: "You seem to me the sweetest and sacredest of darlings. Every fibre of you is like the red shroud the Brahmin wears to indicate his holy caste. You grow upon me all the time. You seem to be a favorite of heaven. I believe you will be a tall Angel to God. *I Love you*."[10] In the case of Willard and Gordon, "love" meant not simply living under the same roof with other women but a physical intimacy as well. The two slept together and wrote forlornly of each other's absence from "our bed" when parted by the pair's extensive travel and speaking engagements.[11]

Willard's relationship with Gordon was not an aberration in the WCTU's ranks but rather a widely admired example. Gordon's companion role, including her well-publicized self-sacrifice to Willard and the needs of the WCTU, was taken by some as a great expression of love to be eagerly emulated. Mary Wood-Allen, the World's purity department superintendent, was one prominent WCTU activist who had her own little "Anna Gordon," her "companion, hands, eyes and feet." Many other women acquired similar companions, among them the missionaries Bessie Cowie and Katharine Bushnell, and Gordon herself in her later years.[12]

These women frequently recognized in their correspondence and their actions the variety of services a close woman companion provided. Lizzie Vincent found in Emily Cummins a lifelong helper: "Miss Cummins is so devoted, being as she has been for years now, Mother, Sister & Friend to me."[13] Other women experienced such relationships in a serial form. After the death of her "dear co-laborer" Elizabeth Andrew, Katharine Bushnell did not live alone but acquired a series of live-in friends as substitutes. When one of these—her "dear house-mate and secretary" of many years standing—died in 1943, Bushnell was "shaken with grief" and "crave[d] and covete[d]" a new "personal acquaintance" to replace her.[14] Some relationships were more episodic but nonetheless real in their emotional and even physical dimensions. Jessie Ackermann's several admirers were forced by her peripatetic lifestyle to take consolation in her letters, though they looked forward eagerly and "lovingly," like Amelia Truesdale of San Francisco, to her visits.[15] More than one relationship blossomed at international meetings and World's conventions. Perhaps the most celebrated of such close friendships was that of Agnes Slack and Anna Gordon, long after Willard's death. Said Slack's biographer: "Miss Gordon and Miss Slack expect that when they attend conferences that they will always be given rooms near each other in the same hotel. 'I feel lost without Anna,' says Miss Slack, 'and I believe she feels lost without me.'"[16]

Companionship between women in which mutual love and respect were integral parts could easily be justified in terms of a common religious purpose. Two women active in the support of temperance missionary work illustrate the intersection of love and religious devotion that stimulated many of the World's WCTU's endeavors. Ella Gilbert Ives and Louise Purlington were typical female friends within the WCTU. They had been students together and for more than twenty years conducted a school for girls in Dorchester, Massachusetts. All the while, they worked together in the WCTU, serving as national and World's superintendents of the Department of Co-Operation with Missionary Societies. Only Ives's death in 1913 separated them. Wrote Purlington: "With Miss Ives I have lived, worked, and prayed almost since our schooldays at Mt. Holyoke, and life's aims and purposes are the same."[17]

Sometimes women like these exhibited a certain defiance toward the conventions of marriage. When the Toledo-based WCTU journalist Jane Stewart was asked, "Why did you never marry?" she quipped in return, "Because I have never felt able to support a husband."[18] Stewart openly espoused the superiority of relationships between single women, though her close friend, the South African and World's WCTU official Emilie Solomon, offered a slightly different but equally defiant explanation of her own deviation from the conventions of marriage: "I never saw the man I would wish to live with, and only one or two ever gave any signs of wanting to marry me, when I discouraged them immediately." From her college days she had formed a "bosom friendship with a colleague, Miss Fisk," and forty years later it was Fisk who was made the beneficiary of her will.[19]

Companionship could and did mean many things to these women. What these friendships shared, despite such variations, was an emotional proximity best revealed in the practice of the women who surrounded Willard. These women certainly did regard the "loves of women" seriously and sympathetically. Rest Cottage, where Willard and her entourage lived or visited when in Evanston, exuded an intimacy inherent in the rituals of communication that she and her friends adopted. Willard's habit of referring to members of her immediate circle in terms of familiarity and endearment rubbed off on close and sometimes not so close associates and established a tradition that Lillian Stevens and Gordon perpetuated. Thus Willard was "Frank" or "Beloved Chieftain"; Helen Hood was "Hoodie"; Stevens, "Stevie"; Somerset, "Cossie"; Julia Ames, "Yolande"; Frances Beauchamp, "Little Beechie"; almost any friend, "Dearie"; and so on. Just as contemporary sporting teams create bizarre nicknames as badges of masculine solidarity, so too did Willard's circle use these little rituals to create the WCTU's distinctive culture.[20]

This jovial intimacy sometimes fell flat or even offended those who did not wish to be assimilated to the sisterhood. Georgia M. Jobson of Richmond, Virginia, told how after a single meeting with Lillian Stevens she was showered with praise and received many tedious letters headed always "Dearest Jobbie," though Jobson felt she hardly knew the woman. Emotional closeness, whether solicited or unwanted, lasted only so long as women like Jobson followed WCTU policies and remained loyal to the organization. When Jobson shifted her allegiance to Cora Stoddard's rival Scientific Temperance Federation, Stevens dropped the Virginia reformer "like a hot potato."[21] The intimacy that surrounded WCTU women's relations with each other was an all or nothing affair; in such cases as Jobson's, love could quickly turn to distrust or even hatred when the terms of the intimate circle were broken. This theme was illustrated in spectacular fashion in the National WCTU in the case of Judith Ellen Foster when the latter adopted the Non-Partisan strategy of prohibitionism, but within the World's WCTU the same theme was repeated many times, most notably in the falling out of Willard and Mary Leavitt.[22]

It is impossible to say with any accuracy how far other, less prominent women associated with the WCTU took the concept of female companionship. Evidence of such feelings documented among nineteenth-century women is usually restricted to an elite.[23] Yet for the WCTU, the strength of emotional feeling between women can be more broadly gauged in the voluminous and adulatory correspondence that Willard elicited from co-workers and the rank and file. Willard was not simply admired by her followers. That adoration touched profound emotional needs for female companionship in many women attracted to the temperance movement. The element of physical and moral attraction the rank and file found in her public performance must not be ignored. Here too, love served as a special force binding members together in solidarity. This emotional force has to be reckoned with, whether or not women lived in intimate circles with other women. Nor did it cease to be a factor when Willard died, since the mythical Willard, the WCTU's "promoted" saint, lived on in the memory of her "beautiful life."[24]

It is undeniable that love for Frances Willard was an element in the emotional networks WCTU women created. Said Canada's Letitia Youmans, who knew Willard from the earliest international contacts in the 1870s: "She was youthful, attractive and possessed of great magnetic power. I was irresistibly drawn to her."[25] Even after twenty years' battling for temperance and women's emancipation, Willard retained this strong physical and emotional appeal for other women. South Africa's Emilie Solomon said of her in 1895: "How can I describe her? Her beautiful face alight with intelligence and love, her bright little eyes and wavy auburn hair. She was gowned in silver-grey satin, with creamy lace at her throat, and I was fascinated by her grace and friendliness."[26] Others expressed the desire to see and touch this woman whom they regarded as the epitome of beauty and truth. Mrs. J. H. More of Connecticut wrote not directly to Willard but to Anna Gordon to express her "love and admiration for Miss Willard." More had kept "Miss Willard's picture . . . hung in my room for several years, and I admired it, but one must look upon Miss Willard, in order to get that spiritual, Christlike sweetness of expression." When she did meet her heroine in 1897, she said, "I just feasted on her beautiful face," but "I could not find the opportunity to take her by the hand."[27] Another American, Emma Taylor, echoed these comments when "coming face to face" with her leader. Like More, Taylor could not fulfill her desire to "reach her" and had to be content with worship from afar.[28]

Some married women confessed that they found Willard's attentions uncomfortable as they strove to reconcile the love they felt for their husbands with the emotions Willard elicited. One correspondent, "Christiana" (Mary Woolley, wife of the well-known prohibitionist John G. Woolley) felt torn between the love and loyalty she felt for Woolley and the feelings her blossoming friendship with Willard brought forth. Her attraction to Willard (and Somerset) deepened during a tour of England with her husband in 1893. "I *loved* my husband [as] I could do no other man," she reminisced as

she looked back at her married life. But the praise and affection of the
World's president brought forth new and stronger emotions. "I sing in my
heart all day for your kind words of me, and I am loving you and Lady
Henry very much these days."[29]

Too much must not be made of such professions of love as these. As
Zerelda Wallace of Indiana wrote to Willard of the latter's great emotional
attractions for her: "How I long to pour out my soul to you this morning
but cannot with the freedom I would because I fear that some other eye
than yours may see and not understand."[30] In the first instance, one must
distinguish between the relationships of WCTU women who lived in intimate networks of female companionship and the more generalized profession of love for women that drew on the literary conventions of the Victorian period and the unself-consciously effusive language of the nineteenth-
century women's culture. In the special case of the WCTU, the religious
ideology also has to be taken into account. Women schooled in evangelical
language and concepts were familiar with the different meanings of the
word *love*. It was commonly said in evangelical circles that the words translated as *love* in the English Bible had seven different meanings in the He-
brew original. Protestant women were particularly familiar with the notion
of the love of Jesus that was not all sexually threatening to them, though
Freudian psychologists claim wonders of illumination with the underlying
psychological and sexual dynamics of this missionary culture.[31]

On a more diffuse plane, the WCTU shared and expressed expectations
of Victorian culture concerning relations between women. Mary Ryan has
pointed out that "the presumption of female purity . . . allowed women to
live celibately or even in sexual intimacy with other women without inviting
suspicion, scorn, or stigma."[32] As Ruth Bordin notes, Willard and her circle
fitted easily into the pattern of "homosocial" relations common enough
among women of her social background, and their physical and moral
proximity did not imply any commitment to genital sex between women.[33]
Willard, like Mary Livermore, was hostile to homosexual relations. Both
abhorred Oscar Wilde and Walt Whitman as purveyors of obscenity, though
in commenting on Wilde's conviction on a morals charge, the World's
WCTU convention, under Willard's direction, in 1895 expressed horror
that similar outrages on the purity of young womanhood went unpunished.
Here, as in other cases, Willard's primary stance was taken against all forms
of the double standard in public or private life.[34]

What is most important is not the issue of a supposed lesbian culture but
the uses to which women put their complex and diverse range of feelings
for other women. For the WCTU, emotional solidarity constituted the cement for the international temperance organization and provided the impulse to save women in other lands. Purlington and Ives, for example,
shared the work of integrating temperance and missionary activity in the

United States. When Ives died in 1913, her long-term companion was galvanized for renewed missionary temperance activity. "I cannot convey to you my heart in this matter," wrote Purlington, "only I long to have you eager, with me, to build a beautiful memorial of work in her name and for Christ's sake."[35] Helen Hood, corresponding secretary of the Illinois WCTU, was shattered in a similar way by the death of her companion Julia Ames late in 1891; Hood was "constantly with her throughout her illness and brought her remains back to Rest Cottage" for burial. Later Hood submerged her grief in tireless organizing for the BWTA and as Willard's private secretary in Britain.[36]

Sometimes the international aspects of sisterhood within the WCTU reflected, as on the national American scene, actual family relations between women, which became a model for the creation of larger kin networks that were artificially constructed. The WCTU in Spain was led, for example, by Anna Gordon's sister Alice Gordon Gulick, and another sister, Elizabeth, was also active in the organization. The WCTU's first representative in Berlin was Mary Bannister Willard, sister-in-law of Frances. The first president of the WCTU in Victoria was the Virginian Mary Love, who came to Melbourne to live with her sister, another WCTU member, after the death of her husband. Similarly, Carrie C. Faxon went to the Philippines as a WCTU missionary because she wished to join her sister Cornelia Moots, and the Scot Margaret Leitch served for a time as a missionary in the West Indies with her own sister, Mary. Most striking of all was the whole Hannah Whitall Smith family, whose efforts for religion and temperance on both sides of the Atlantic bore testimony to the importance of family relations in the Anglo-American reform movements. Two of Smith's daughters, Alys and Mary, also served in the BWTA and contributed to World's WCTU work.[37]

But familial relations provided only the core around which WCTU women constructed their conception of a larger sisterhood. These sentiments took in women who were only temporary companions or even women who had never met. The desire for sisterhood was not directly proportional to the availability of single or widowed women who could establish a separate culture. The sororital aspect of the WCTU was strongest in the most isolated parts of the WCTU's far-flung empire. The tendency of women in colonial outposts to describe the World's WCTU as a sisterhood may have reflected this actual isolation from strong networks of female friends. The lament of Annie Carvosso of Brisbane was typical, when she mournfully told Anna Gordon: "It does make us feel a long way off from everywhere when it takes such a long time for news to reach us."[38] The WCTU round-the-world missionaries made similar complaints of isolation, and perhaps with even more justice. It was they, among WCTU officials, who were most likely to take a close female companion, and the nature of their travels served as a powerful inducement to do so. It was also these women, particularly Mary Leavitt and Jessie Ackermann, who left strong bonds of sisterhood behind in the communities they visited, as evidenced in their sustained correspondence with old contacts in the British colonies.[39]

Distance did not seem to matter. In fact, it made the connections more intense. Anderson Hughes-Drew, the New Zealand missionary, had Anna Gordon's "dear photo framed in [her] drawing room" when she wrote to express her "sisterly" love.[40] Margaret C. Millar of Gympie, Queensland, had never met Gordon but felt "I know you and have known you for over twenty-five years that I have been a member of Gympie W.C.T.U." Neither had she met Lillian Stevens, but this did not stop her from writing, "I admire her and love her" as much as Frances Willard.[41] Mary C. Leavitt continued a friendship with her "able and beloved" fellow worker Elizabeth Brentnall of Brisbane that began in 1886, when the American missionary toured Queensland, and continued for nearly two decades, despite the fact that they never saw one another again.[42] Katharine Stevenson did not even need to meet New Zealand WCTU president Frances Cole in order to "love Mrs. Cole. I do love her and I expect to love her forever."[43]

The sheer difficulties of distance were compounded by feelings of social isolation. When Wilhelmina Bain, a New Zealand writer and feminist on the fringes of the WCTU agitation in her home country, returned there in 1908 after four years abroad, she displayed strong signs of restiveness. During a long stay in Los Angeles, she had met and befriended Caroline Severance, the California women's rights advocate, and hoped to find for herself a similar "companion" back in New Zealand; "no one," however, could be found "who shares my convictions and anticipations." Nor was there any agitation, other than that of the WCTU, to channel Bain's emotional interests since the National Council of Women had, she said, become moribund when Kate Sheppard, the temperance and suffrage advocate, left for England.[44] Circumstances of isolation, coupled with the WCTU's international affiliation, made the organization the best and often the only reform vehicle for such women, since it linked them securely to a larger movement that could provide a sense of emotional solidarity.[45]

These appeals to sisterly solidarity were never exclusive of other claims upon temperance women. After all, the World's WCTU represented "God, Home, and Every Land." The Scottish WCTU lecturer Helen Barton, who toured Australia in 1926 to explain the benefits of American prohibition, fleshed out the eclectic meaning of the WCTU's motto. It was necessary to acknowledge "the Fatherhood of God, and the brotherhood of man. [The] great sisterhood [of the World's WCTU was] really a band of organized mother love." Though the WCTU was indeed a sisterhood, the emotional strength of its women's networks was to be marshaled to larger, and ultimately self-denying, ends and did not preclude strong familial bonds of another kind.[46]

These ends cannot be understood without reference to the WCTU's religious roots. When Letitia Youmans sojourned in Britain as one of several Canadian delegates to the BWTA annual meeting in 1885, she described the love they felt for their English colleagues as that of "sisters in the Lord."[47] Temperance missionaries felt the same, as Leavitt evidenced when she described herself to the women she had met around the world as "your sister in Christ."[48] No innovation in religious ideology was necessary for WCTU women when they identified such emotions with an organized sisterhood. Religious orders in the Anglican and Catholic churches in England and the United States in the early and mid-nineteenth century were so described and, according to a recent study, formed an important element in the assertion of a style of life for "spinster" women in Britain that was "independent" of men.[49] Willard drew on this tradition of religious sisterhoods when she called for the creation of a cadre of spinster women like herself to be paid functionaries of the organization and labeled such women "protestant nuns."[50]

The religious ideology was indeed very important in the sisterhood concept, but it is necessary to dissociate the meaning of that concept for women of the nineteenth century from contemporary notions. Sisterhood in the religious sense involved, above all, service. WCTU women even called their organization, as the BWTA did in 1898, "a grand sisterhood of service that stretche[d] its White Ribbon band all over our land, and not our own land alone, but over many other lands as well."[51] In a much applauded speech in 1891, Lady Henry Somerset described the "highest privilege" of the WCTU as being "to share the burden of the world's sin, which nailed Him to the cross of Calvary."[52] That concept involved a subordination of individual wills to the good of humanity, not an assertion of independence or autonomy.

The biographies of prominent WCTU women may not represent the average WCTU member nor reflect even the minority of WCTU women they do treat, yet for the purposes of understanding the ideology and culture of women's temperance, the constant reference to the selflessness of WCTU women is worthy of attention. "There is no lasting beauty or enjoyment that does not come as a result of service; the desire to live and the living for others, the living outside one's self," explained Clara Parrish in summing up her experience in Japan.[53] Willard aide Helen Hood "had no self while with us," remembered Gweneth Vaughan, a Welsh organizer. "Self had been absorbed in the cause to which her life was devoted." Similarly selfless was Elizabeth Andrew, who described herself as merely a "weak" vessel "to carry His message," before her departure on missionary work to South Africa.[54] If this was familiar language among the missionary women of the WCTU, the same ideology pervaded the thought of those who watched them go. Mary Woodbridge, a Quaker and a World's WCTU secretary, praised Andrew and her companion Kate Bushnell because "their bodies, and spirits [were] wholly given to Him."[55]

Service meant so much subordination of individual will in some cases that WCTU women were extraordinarily reluctant to provide even the barest amount of information for official biographies. Among those "too modest to furnish the data for a complimentary sketch" for the *Union Signal* were Christine Robertson of Ayr, Scotland, the leader of the Native Races work, and Caroline McDowell of Pittsburgh, Pennsylvania, a major financial and organizational contributor to missionary work.[56] Others, like Jessie Ackermann and Andrew, earned fame within the WCTU for their globetrotting exploits but remained strangely inaccessible individuals about whose private lives little is or was then known. Still others, like Zerelda Wallace, were said to be equally self-effacing though their achievements were much better publicized. Wallace was by all accounts reluctant "to talk of herself and never relates her reminiscences unless almost forced to do so."[57]

It is possible that reticence in these latter cases was designed to reassure potential followers. Shy heroines demonstrated that prominence in the WCTU did not entail the sloughing off of womanly modesty in favor of an Amazonian aggressiveness. Yet in their private conversations as in their public professions, these women counted themselves for little and drew their power from other sources: from God, from their friends and companions, and from the collective work and tradition of WCTU women that encompassed both motherhood and sisterhood.[58]

Whatever the personalities of WCTU women on this score, a self-effacing ideology pervaded the organization's ranks and inhabited the recesses of its ritual. The Frances Ridley Havergal hymn, "Take My Life and Let It Be, Consecrated, Lord, to Thee," was the favorite of women as diverse as peace advocate Hannah Clark Bailey and Jessie Ackermann and formed a Sunday staple at Rest Cottage, where the circle of Willard's own "sisters in Christ," such as Ames and Hood, had gathered to internalize the service ethic. For the 1897 World's WCTU convention, evangelistic superintendent Elizabeth Greenwood even prepared as the central theme of the religious observances a "new consecration" in which the assembled women—and those in "our Unions all around the world"—waited in "silent prayer" for their "surrender to the Holy Spirit, and fresh anointing for service."[59]

This theme of consecrated service stemmed in part from the holiness tradition of trans-Atlantic revivalism. Phoebe Palmer's concept of "altar theology" involved surrender of self upon the altar of Christ. Yet in turn, self-sacrifice provided, through the process of sanctification, the spiritual power of the Holy Spirit that, according to Palmer, invested women with untold strength to serve others.[60]

The sense of power temperance women experienced in their religious lives explains the other, seemingly contradictory side of the service concept.

Matching the self-denial of service was an air of confidence and assertiveness. To be in the service of the Lord together provided the emotional energy for campaigns that were, like the efforts to make a World's WCTU a reality racked with doubt on the inside and subject to ridicule on the outside. Service gave a conviction of certitude and rectitude and fed the development of the more assertive side of the WCTU woman's character. WCTU women were nothing on their own, but everything in Christ. On her deathbed, Willard shored up her faith and discharged her bitterness at the thought of ultimate failure with the exaggeration of the service ethic. "There never were such women as our white ribboners—so large hearted, so generous, such patriots, such Christians."[61]

Occasionally, the service theme became linked explicitly to the question of emotional relations between WCTU women. These kept each other's company not simply because of their Christian feelings but because "single women"—those without family ties—"make the most appreciated and unselfish friends."[62] Others lived this ethic without expressing such sentiments quite so openly, but more commonly, Christian service among temperance sisters was effectively channeled into the fulfillment of wider maternal and social obligations.[63]

INTERNATIONAL SERVICE was tied to another hierarchical conceptualization of the world that vied with sisterhood and threatened to undermine its egalitarian assumptions. WCTU women described other women as their sisters who deserved saving from their sins, but WCTU service was also rationalized as an expression of the ideology of motherhood. It was Hannah Whitall Smith who coined the notion that the World's WCTU was "organized mother-love," and Willard claimed that the organization was engaged in the uplift of the "mother-half of the race."[64] Motherhood as an ideology was deeply rooted in the thinking of the rank and file, too. The WCTU, a study of the Boulder, Colorado, union notes, involved "an expansion of woman's mothering role in the family to a maternalism that encompassed the whole society."[65] Clara Parrish expressed an at least partial truth about the WCTU when she wrote in the *Japanese Evangelist* that her organization was "not an organized protest against the marriage relation. . . . Instead of being organized to make women dissatisfied with the home, it is calculated to make them far better mothers."[66]

Ruth Bordin has suggested that Willard used the nineteenth-century ideology of motherhood and domesticity to advance women's rights—"her whole attitude was to push women forward in new ways."[67] Yet Willard's veneration of her own "Mother Willard"—*A Great Mother* in the book of that title—is an inescapable and rock-bottom reality of Willard's psychology that drove her to personal greatness. Willard felt the loss of her mother in 1892

Mary Willard, Frances Willard, and Anna Gordon (*left to right*): sisterhood and motherhood epitomized (Anna A. Gordon, *The Beautiful Life of Frances Willard* [Evanston, Ill.: Woman's Temperance Publishing Association, 1898])

so intensely that the grief was only discharged by a renewed commitment to work and a shift of focus in her personal life from Evanston to Lady Henry's Surrey estates.[68]

The worship of their mothers in life and in death is a theme that pervades the literature describing the lives of prominent temperance women. Deeply venerated campaigners were commonly described in terms of a maternal role shifted to the public arena: as Mother Stewart, Mother Willard, or Mother Thompson. Every state had its own "Mother" heroines, usually dating back to the days of the Woman's Crusade in 1873–74.[69] The practice extended to other WCTU strongholds, such as Australia. There, World's flower mission superintendent Amelia Pemmell labeled Euphemia Bowes (first colonial president) her "temperance mother" because of her role in introducing Pemmell to temperance work.[70] To be greeted as a mother in the WCTU sisterhood was as natural as the label *comrade* in the international socialist movement.

"Mothering" was not simply a rhetorical flourish but a fundamental part of everyday life for these women. Biological mothering was valued highly, but more important was the use of the model of a "great mother" in personal relationships with other women and as a practical program for wider social action. Willard's relationship with Gordon took on this tone, as at times did Hannah Smith's affection for Willard.[71] Smith described herself as one of those "Hens" who "are never so happy as when their wings are outspread over something or somebody they love."[72] Hannah Bailey even wrote a long and turgid speech describing the critical role of the great mother in the ranks of WCTU heroines, beginning with her own mother and that of Frances Willard.[73] Special targets for such mothering were visiting lecturers on the international temperance circuit. Agnes Slack found a mother in Lillian Stevens, and the Armenian worker Elizabeth Dombourajian was mothered in a similar way by Frances Beauchamp during a 1913 tour of Kentucky.[74]

Quite naturally, the death of a mother profoundly affected these women, as any loss of a parent should, but in their autobiographical memoirs, WCTU women harked back to their mothers' death more often than to their fathers' and made it clear that separation by death often precipitated women into temperance work, so intense was the loss.[75] The death of Charlotte Gray's mother when Charlotte was fourteen was "a terrible blow" that she claimed "has influenced my whole life."[76] If a common theme in the private correspondence of WCTU women was the death and illness of their own mothers, characteristically, the fate of fathers did not rate a mention. This contrasting coldness was especially clear in Willard's autobiography.[77]

Occasionally these women appeared to suffer from overprotective relationships with their mothers. On the day of her wedding, when the time came to leave with her husband, Isabel Somerset "clung to her mother as if she was afraid to leave her."[78] Slack "found herself somewhat in conflict with her mother's Victorian ideals of sheltered womanhood" when she chose to travel the world as a temperance lecturer, but the "affection on both sides was so intense and so reasonable, that there was never any real disagreement."[79] The private record bears out these comments by Slack's biographer, since Slack's mother, Mary, selected Stevens as Agnes's "mother" for her American tours, and Slack identified emotionally with her mother's choice.[80] Belle Kearney noted the instant affection that Stevens provided when the WCTU vice-president took the younger temperance woman under her wing and proclaimed that both she and Slack would be prepared, were they men, to marry Stevens, so much did they appreciate her motherly affection.[81]

Whether overprotective relationships were any more common in the WCTU than in the general population is impossible to say from the fragmentary private records. Certainly childrearing practices encouraged strong relationships between daughters and mothers in Victorian America and did nothing to promote psychological rebellion against mothers as part of the process of asserting personal autonomy. In this sense the WCTU was merely an expression of larger cultural patterns.[82] But a more important point shifts the emphasis away from the psychological dynamics of women's temperance. It matters little whether these much-worshiped women really were "great mothers" or whether daughterly devotion supplied the psychological basis of their own temperance commitment. The key point was that the WCTU printed no evidence of unsatisfactory mothers and gave no hints of conflict in mother-daughter relations. Quite the reverse. The WCTU was promoted and understood by outsiders as embodying the maternal virtues, and the WCTU's relationship to the world was one of motherly concern expressed in Hannah Smith's inimitable phrase.

To argue that the WCTU pursued maternalist policies and so touched the experience of ordinary women hardly involves denigrating their achievements. Today sections of the women's movement question the rejection of women's maternal roles and suggest that women should be compensated and rewarded for performing crucial tasks of biological and social reproduction. The assertion of individual rights, rights to compete with men in the arena of the career open to talent, while not repudiated, seems to fail to get to the roots of women's oppression. This contemporary self-searching draws the modern women's movement back to the nineteenth century for inspiration and to those "material feminists" who in the nineteenth century identified women's biological and social experience of mothering as crucial to women's subordination and emancipation.[83]

But the search for historical analogues for the politics of social and biological reproduction is often misplaced. To be sure, the assertion of motherhood ideologies was an integral part of that first-wave feminism, and not just in the United States. Karen Offen has pointed to the parallel importance of "republican motherhood" in France, and in Sweden, the motherhood feminist Ellen Key won considerable support for her critique of the individualism and the self-defeating qualities of the Anglo-American women's movement. Her philosophy stimulated the Bund fuer Mutterschutz in Germany and the provision of maternal and child welfare payments in the states of western Europe before and during World War I. Since Willard was among those Ellen Key regarded as principal representatives of the triumphs and weaknesses of the Anglo-American feminist tradition, it is fitting to consider the links and gaps between the thinking of Key and American temperance women on the motherhood issue.[84]

In different circumstances, one could imagine an alliance between Key and Willard, or at least between the kind of feminism each represented. Key, after all, was also a temperance advocate who admired Willard as one of the world's "great women agitators" who "set thousands of women into action . . . against intemperance."[85] Key's assertion that the new century would be "the century of the child" won support among progressive and child-saving circles in the United States, and the WCTU actually used this phrase to promote its goal of an alcohol-free environment in which children could be raised.[86] If the WCTU could have tapped this international movement for the reform of the conditions of motherhood, its place as a successful international reform organization would perhaps have been assured. The WCTU might have moved beyond its Anglo-American center to take in the women of that most reluctant of temperance targets, continental Europe.

Closer inspection of the evidence indicates that this was never a possibility. Glorification of motherhood was an international phenomenon, but the meaning of the motherhood ideology was very different in Sweden, Germany, and France. Though the WCTU echoed some of Key's phrases, Willard and the Swedish feminist were poles apart on the issue of sexual morality and its relationship to motherhood. Willard's purity platform—the "white life for two"—attempted to raise men to the higher moral plane established by sexually pure temperance women. In contrast, Key championed full expression of women's heterosexual drives as the path to true equality through acceptance of sexual difference and linked motherhood to this concept. Women and men were not just different in culture and training, as Willard suggested; they were, according to Key, fundamentally different in their biological drives. Whereas the WCTU was ambivalent on the issue of gender equality, Key claimed that woman's true fulfillment was sex-specific and "intrinsically bound to the nurturance expressed in maternity."[87]

As a matter of practical policy, she also advocated state support for single mothers, whose right to bear children must take precedence over any moral censure. True, this maternity policy was founded on the realities of Swedish demography, wherein women of childbearing age outnumbered males and illegitimacy rates were high. But the stance was also a matter of philosophical conviction, an outgrowth of her comprehensive ideology that far transcended the Victorian pieties of the WCTU's approach. For this reason, Key found no American allies in the WCTU. Her vision was more congenial to the newer type of feminist represented by Marie Stopes in Britain or Margaret Sanger in the United States, who rejected any suggestions that women should not have the choice of full sexual fulfillment within heterosexual relationships.[88]

Not only did the newer feminism allow women a sexual freedom the WCTU could not accept; Key's philosophy involved a commitment to state interference in the politics of reproduction that went beyond Willard's reformism. The WCTU was critical of laissez-faire, and temperance women were prepared to sanction social welfare as a form of state intervention in family life. But state-sponsored progressivism in the Anglo-Saxon world was envisaged as piecemeal reform. In the case of Key, and later in Helene Stöcker's Bund fuer Mutterschutz in Germany, state control was a holistic program that entailed "a radical transformation of society and sexual ethics."[89] The specific proposals for maternal and child welfare that Key favored eventually made their way to the United States during and after World War I and contributed to the Sheppard-Towner Act in the 1920s. The WCTU supported this initiative and noted with embarrassment as early as 1917 that "European countries" led the United States in the provision of "maternity insurance." But the major champions of such schemes were academics and professional welfare workers.[90]

Perhaps if the American WCTU had faced the same demographic problems that shaped Swedish and German feminism, more flexibility would have been demonstrated by temperance women. Yet such an outcome would have been most unlikely, since the whole experience of these Anglo-American women contained their maternalism within the confines of a third concept that needed to be reconciled with those of motherhood and sisterhood. This was the notion of a correct relation with men mediated through a system of companionate marriage.

ATTITUDES TOWARD MEN, as both marriage partners and fellow reformers, have not been probed with the same regularity as the notions of sisterhood or even motherhood. Study of this issue has been vitiated by an ahistoric quest for analogues of contemporary feminist concerns in the area of sexuality. These attitudes, and other aspects of the WCTU's familial ideology, can be better understood if members' experiences of marriage and family can first be considered in their structural and demographic aspects.

Family Ideology of the World's WCTU

Sisterhood had its cultural possibilities created and confined by the changing demographic structure. As is only too well known, the second half of the nineteenth century was the era in which a culture of single and highly educated reformers and professional women was created in the United States and Britain.[91] The percentage of single women among WCTU leaders, as identified in several collective biographies, was quite striking. Ruth Bordin has noted in her own study of "prominent" temperance leaders—that is, those for whom biographical information is available—that 20 percent of leaders were single in the late nineteenth century, whereas more than 90 percent of all adult American women at this time married. In Norton Mezvinsky's sample, Bordin reports, 24 percent were single, and in Janet Giele's, 23 percent. This evidence is consistent with the trend among late nineteenth-century women with professional aspirations and college education to choose a career rather than marriage. Willard was a representative of this social type.[92]

The figures for lower-ranking officials of the WCTU—national and top state officers—suggest much lower participation by nonmarried women of from 3 to 7 percent within the United States, but these figures, too, need further scrutiny and comparison. Titular leadership positions, as opposed to paid positions in the national organization, were likely to be taken by older, married women, but the American data may not, in any case, represent the cadre of lower level officials on the international level. Outside the United States, the percentage of single women in the lower ranks of the WCTU was quite high and consistent with the assumption that the WCTU did attract, disproportionately, single women. Especially interesting is the British case, where the WCTU had, as in the United States, an articulate and substantial class of spinster women on which it could draw. Twenty-five percent of WCTU officials in the London area, for example, were single women in 1904, and 30 percent in 1894. Among the young women's groups—the Ys—where one would expect the percentage of WCTU single women to be higher, 63 percent were single in 1904, and among the White Ribbon bands for factory workers, 23 percent were single.[93] In the case of Quebec, we have figures not only for leaders but also for the entire rank and file as well. There, fully 26 percent of WCTU women were single in the mid-1880s.[94] Even in Australia, where the opportunities to marry were higher for women in the period 1860–90 than in the United States, the organization attracted substantial percentages of single women (34 percent single in 1893 in New South Wales among local officials). This is also apparent in the collective profile of prominent officials (29 percent never married, 1882–1926).[95]

Interpreting this data is very difficult and, ultimately, just short of fruitless in its application to problems of ideology and consciousness. Take the case of the Australian colonies. The depression of the 1890s meant many marriages were deferred in some colonies, and the First World War had the same effect in shutting off marriage opportunities. By the time of the 1921 census, the proportions ultimately never marrying in Australia "were remarkably high" by world standards, according to the thorough demographic study done by Peter McDonald.[96] Can it be argued that interest in the WCTU in these years (1891–1921) represented an alternative to blocked marriage opportunities for single women destined to become spinsters? The minority of single women who did not fulfill the society's notions of early marriage may have clustered in the WCTU in search of a spinster culture and identified with British and American women who did develop such an alternative culture. But the marriage rate in Australia fluctuated markedly, thus making such simplistic correlations difficult to identify. Those who staffed the WCTU in the 1890s were predominantly women whose experience of marriage had been shaped not in the depression but in the optimistic years before, when the standards of bourgeois domesticity had been set in the urban centers.[97]

As the Australian data indicate, the category of "single women" should not be seen in isolation. Rather, fluctuations in the marriage and life cycles must be taken into account. Widowhood was a common experience for nineteenth-century women, as it is, along with divorce, for women today, and it is pertinent to consider single and widowed women together. If the number of widows is added to Bordin's total for prominent single women in the American WCTU, then the percentage without husbands becomes 38, "far larger than previous studies have indicated."[98]

This demographic construction explains much about the WCTU culture. WCTU women included a core of prominent leaders, who would never marry; many others were or would be widowed; still others had husbands; and others were awaiting marriage. Marriage was still the fundamental goal of most nineteenth-century American women in the absence of alternative and realistic means of economic support, as it was in France, Britain, and the Australasian colonies. The variations in percent single in the general population between these countries were relatively slight.[99] Whether single, married, or widowed, these WCTU women lived primarily in a world of women, but one would hardly expect this particular group of women to repudiate marriage; they did not erect a culture of "independent women" but combined elements of a separate women's culture with one that emphasized companionate marriage.

This is one reason why it is necessary to reconceptualize the significance of the WCTU as a manifestation of female separatism, or an autonomous women's culture. Despite the rhetoric of sisterhood and the commitment to close emotional relationships between women, the WCTU defies the label of an anti-male organization. From a tactical point of view, the WCTU tried to work with male groups, such as the Populists and the Prohibitionist party in America and the Liberals and the United Kingdom Alliance in England, and though these experiences involved frustration at male backsliding and inadequacy, the WCTU never repudiated but always sought to build upon male support.

The attitudes of WCTU women toward men reflected their contradictory experiences as members of a separatist society, but one in which close relations with men in marriage and reform were both practiced and preached. Temperance missionaries occasionally declared men "deficient in backbone," as Ackermann did during her tour of Australasia in 1890, but other WCTU activists in the colonies were highly critical of this outburst. Mrs. M. A. Alway of the Malvern, Victoria, WCTU leapt to the defense of men and pointed out that in Australia, as elsewhere, men were able to join the WCTU as honorary members and that this support was highly valued by the WCTU in Victoria. While some were deficient in backbone, others had "quite enough for two."[100] Though it was the WCTU's "special aim to unite the Christian womanhood of all denominations in [their] work," she said, "our honorary membership enables us to take in a much wider field, and to become a veritable Christian Temperance Union."[101] Looking back from her retirement in California in 1939, an elderly Katharine Bushnell liked to remember Frances Willard as agreeing with her own point of view that the WCTU women could represent "the cause they [were] working for in a better way than any of the men could represent them."[102] But female separatism was only one strain in WCTU thinking.

Willard herself emphasized the important cooperation of sympathetic men, like Neal Dow and Terence Powderly in the United States and William T. Stead in Britain, within the Anglo-American reform movements.[103] Mary Livermore voiced the common belief that Dow was the epitome of the best in men. Not only was he a prohibitionist, but he was "all the while living a beautiful and immaculate life as husband, father, and private citizen."[104] So worshiped was Dow that his birthday was a red-letter day on the WCTU calendar, which emphasized the WCTU's commitment not only to the emancipation of women but to the larger prohibitionist movement as well. The case of Stead was similar. A great friend of Lady Henry's and an advocate of purity reform in alliance with the WCTU, the British journalist and moral reformer died in the sinking of the Titanic in 1911. The *Union Signal* ran as an obituary Agnes Slack's mournful lament upon "this devastation" to the "two branches of the great Anglo-Saxon race."[105] Thus was Stead's cooperation with the Anglo-American women's movement valued.

WCTU propaganda went beyond praise of particular male heroes to emphasize their role in marriage. The positive side of marriages within a framework of temperance and purity received special attention. The marriage of American WCTU official Emily Huntington Miller and John Miller was one of those alliances "happily increasing in these later days, in which the blending of two lives to form the beacon-light of home dims no ray of native brilliance in the gentler of the two."[106] When death brought an end to such happy marriages, the WCTU duly noted the grief experienced by female partners. Hannah Bailey had grieved so much that she wrote *Reminiscences of a Christian Life*, a "laudatory biography" of her husband, to wring out her sorrow.[107]

As part of this emphasis on relations with men, the WCTU cooperated with (mixed sex) organizations that promoted the values of companionate marriage. At the Cleveland national convention of Christian Endeavor in 1894, Willard endorsed the organization as the exact expression of her own family values. That is to say, "cooperation" rather than "competition" between the sexes striving together to create Christ's kingdom was her goal, not sisterhood alone.[108] Christian Endeavor's founder, Francis Clark, cited the WCTU as the model for his own organization's emphasis on the "ideal family" that contained "both brothers and sisters."[109]

Willard coined an expression to describe the character of ideal males such as Dow or Clark. They were "Knights of the New Chivalry." So important was this theme in her thinking that it formed the substance and the title of her first public lecture in 1871.[110] This assessment became a benchmark against which WCTU women measured their husbands and other males around them. Thus Clara Parrish wrote from China describing the Reverend Dr. J. M. W. Farnham as "the good husband" of Mary J. Farnham, president of the WCTU of China. He was, said Parrish, "the kingliest 'Knight of the new chivalry' you ever did see."[111] Similarly, Mrs. K. H. R. Stuart, white South African liberal and president of the South African Coloured WCTU, described her uncle, Theo Schreiner, as "a true Knight of Chivalry" who "ever stood up for the women of all races."[112] The editors of the *Union Signal* concurred with such judgments, calling male colleagues "brother knight[s]."[113]

A chivalrous knight treated his wife as an equal in all matters of morals and finance within the marriage bond. He was to be both temperate and pure. In another of Willard's felicitous phrases, he was to be a "brotherhearted" man.[114] This formulation captured the essence of the WCTU's ideal of manhood. Rather than a father or a husband who might dominate, the husband was expected to be essentially on a par with his sisterly wife, intimate and yet not sexually threatening. Behind these much-lauded qualities lay a fear—well founded in the context of the economic and legal subordination of women—of unequal sexual relations, since reproductive responsibility was not fairly shared in the larger society. Above all, the WCTU repudiated sexually threatening men as part of a rejection of male domination. Willard was not alone in expecting these standards to be upheld. Thus when the WCTU solicited letters on the subject of "My Ideal Man," the replies printed in the *Union Signal* emphasized gentleness, Christian profession, and purity in men, even though the tone of the testimonies varied in other ways.[115]

This emphasis upon companionate marriage gained strength from contemporary social changes, mirroring developments in the suburban middle-class communities of the eastern seaboard. The WCTU was closer to the new image of what Margaret Marsh calls "family togetherness" and a "masculine domesticity" than to Victorian standards of male and female separation and masculine dominance. Yet the WCTU emphasized also that these images, drawn from ladies' magazines and the lifestyles of the upper middle classes, did not correspond to the reality of social life for many women.[116] Willard agreed with those feminists who found contemporary patriarchal marriage relations as little different from prostitution. She endorsed the argument of American statistician Carroll D. Wright, that a woman in a "conventional and loveless marriage" did more than the prostitute did; the latter bestowed "the possession of herself for a brief period upon him who [would] . . . supply immediate wants," but the subordinated wife made "this exchange, not for an hour, but for a lifetime."[117] Willard did not use the words "legal prostitution," but the implication was plain that a "conventional and loveless marriage" turned a woman into a "bond-slave after she [was] married."[118]

Willard was painfully aware that many men did not reach the benchmark of the ideal man, and she strove to create the environment in which men and women could live and work together in harmony without coercion or the subordination of women. Not only was this Willard's sophisticated program for the reform of relations between the sexes, outlined in her *Glimpses of Fifty Years*. The whole strategy of the WCTU, which was predicated on an elemental battle between the home and the saloon, pointed in the same direction. In its attempts to suppress saloons and brothels as threats to the family, the WCTU acknowledged that the home had a powerful competitor for the affections of men, including husbands. Implicitly, temperance women admitted that their crusades for purity and sobriety were necessary because the knight of the new chivalry was not the dominant social type in the Anglo-American democracies, let alone elsewhere.[119]

Within the experience of WCTU members there was ample evidence for the fragility of the companionate marriage type. If many WCTU women did have tolerable or happy marriages based on mutual emotional support, such happiness was conditional in each case on survival of the cooperating and enlightened male, since death could deprive a woman of her buffer against a society in which male domination was still well enshrined in law. Plenty of examples existed, moreover, within the ranks of the WCTU, of marriages that had gone wrong and of men who did not fit the prescriptions for a brotherly companion. Divorce rates were rising in the late nineteenth-century United States and provoked much comment nationally and internationally concerning the likely effects on marriage. Despite evidence of hostility to divorce within the WCTU that is easily documented, divorce was not unknown in the WCTU's ranks. Leavitt's husband, it must be recalled, was a ne'er-do-well, and other temperance women could identify with her unhappy experience. Somerset is certainly the most celebrated example; her marriage ended when she discovered that her husband was homosexual, and she never remarried, preferring to retreat into religious seclusion from which she emerged only to lead the BWTA.[120] Judith Ellen Foster, on the other hand, was a divorcee who did remarry and lived happily with her new husband, who encouraged her reform activities and her struggles to become a lawyer.

Still other marriages did not end but were clearly unhappy. One such was that of Hannah Smith, whose husband maintained a "polished female friend" in London in the 1890s. Though she "could hardly bear the sight of him," Smith's commitment to family, motherhood, and Victorian decorum condemned her to a long unhappiness and quiet fury. Perhaps, like other WCTU women so afflicted, she found refuge in her matriarchal position— it was, after all, she who coined the phrase "organized mother-love" to describe the WCTU. Ironically, her daughter Alys, who also figured prominently in the BWTA at the turn of the century and accompanied her mother to World's WCTU conventions, also suffered a long and unhappy marriage to the philosopher Bertrand Russell; that union ended in divorce in 1921.[121] Yet another corroborating case was that of Rosalind Carlisle, whose marriage did not end in divorce, but who was virtually not on speaking terms with her husband. The Carlisles' differences on the issue of Home Rule in Ireland were publicly aired in the 1880s, but the extent of the breakdown in their marriage was not widely known and certainly not publicized in the ranks of the World's WCTU. The two lived apart during the last twenty years of their marriage, and some of the animosity between them stemmed, according to Carlisle's daughter, Lady Dorothy Howard, not from political differences alone but from the additional "offence" the BWTA president took at "her husband's preference for the company of pretty young women." Like Smith, Carlisle erected a matriarchy around her relationship with her daughters, who also served as BWTA officials.[122]

Beneath the surface of Victorian platitudes, bourgeois marriage had its anxieties. Willard was perfectly aware of these, and it was in this connection that the WCTU's attitude toward relationships between women must be cast. Alongside her "belief so orthodox" in companionate marriage, Willard publicly noted and sanctioned the existence of networks of female companionship of which her relationship with Anna Gordon was an outstanding example. "The loves of women for each other grow more numerous each day," she wrote in 1889. Far from merely endorsing the conventional Victorian morality with its built-in assumptions of male dominance, the WCTU gave women the alternative of a female sorority alongside its advocacy of a new and equal relation between the sexes in companionate marriage.[123] The problem for Willard and the WCTU as a whole was how to reconcile this practice of female friendships and the organization's equally deep commitment to bourgeois domesticity in the ideal.

The context of evolutionary thought helps provide the answer on the intellectual level. For Willard, at least, the customs of society, including marriage, were in a state of constant flux. While she conceded that the "present marriage system" was "the greatest triumph of Christianity," Willard knew its weaknesses and looked forward to vast improvement under the impetus of reform. Women like the "Maids of Llangollen," who "spent their happy days in each other's calm companionship" were in this scheme of history "tokens of a transition age."[124] Because women had evolved moral sensibilities in the course of their subjection in the home, they showed, so Willard surmised, increasing evidence of refusal to submit to males who had not embraced the new spirit of equality within marriage. It was better for such women to remain single until the moral reform movements had raised all men to the same high plane. In this way did the WCTU square its support for women's sororal relations with its defense of companionate marriage.

To be candid, this resolution was a theoretical and intellectual one alone. The Social Darwinist panacea did not fully satisfy the contemporary needs and dreams of women; the tension between women's emancipation and companionate marriage remained to trouble feminists in the WCTU. Companionate marriage itself encouraged notions of autonomy, but the ideology and practice of women's autonomy put strains on domesticity by holding up the alternative of a world of independent women in which men hardly mattered. This tension was present everywhere that the WCTU functioned as an element in the women's movement, but especially does it help explain the peculiar attractions of the American-inspired organization for particular groups of women outside the United States.

Though the standards of a companionate marriage were not fully achieved even in the United States, American women seemed, to outside observers from WCTUs elsewhere and temperance missionaries who toured the world, to have much more freedom of movement within marriage and outside of it. These observers attributed the greater strength of the American WCTU to this factor. Sara Nolan noted, in the course of her visit to the World's convention in 1910, that the American delegation was most impressive in two ways: the American women seemed "most capable," and a large part of this impression stemmed from the fact that "some had husband and children with them too."[125] Temperance missionaries to Scandinavia concurred and contrasted the greater freedom within marriage that American women experienced and demonstrated through their prominence in the temperance movement with the patriarchal attitudes and practices dominant in countries like Sweden and Denmark. The rural and "traditional" aspects of the Swedish social structure, for example, made peasant and working-class women of greater economic importance, but this rough equality did not translate into social equality in the public sphere. It was the irony there, as in the Anglo-American democracies, that women barred from the "productive sphere" of trade and industry developed the ideologies of reform, women's culture, and feminism in the late nineteenth century.[126]

The tensions between companionate marriage and autonomy were easily resolved in the Swedish case. The absence of the marriage type preferred by Willard and her colleagues meant that the WCTU found relatively marginal appeal for its invocations of sisterhood and emancipation. A contrary case that strengthens this line of argument was that of the Australasian colonies, where the WCTU and the ideology of companionate marriage were both stronger. There the supportive role of husbands and wives in the women's temperance movement found its clearest manifestations, and there too, the contradictions between the goal of companionate marriage and the reality of women's subordinate status were most pronounced.[127] It was an Australian, Ada Murcutt, who lectured the British temperance women on this point very effectively. She told the annual council of the BWTA in 1900 that women "were not competitors with men" in their "great movement" for temperance reform. But women "could help them, and they believed that men and women working together, side by side, would hasten the glorious day" of prohibitionist victory.[128]

Australasia did prove a more favorable environment than Europe for expressions of this companionate ideology for a number of reasons. None was more important than the fact that men were more likely than anywhere else to be supportive of women's assertiveness within the temperance movement. In the early organization of the WCTU in Australia, the role of temperance men was prominent in encouraging women. But the emphasis in the attitudes of those male temperance reformers was on the functions of women within domestic life as wives and mothers, not on the fulfillment of their separate and independent destinies as individuals. Male cooperation in the early organization of the women's temperance movement was especially noticeable in Queensland, where Mary Leavitt found women accepted more as equals in the temperance movement than in any other place that she visited outside the United States. That equality however, was framed within the context of an ideology of companionship between wives and husbands, brothers and sisters, and fathers and daughters. The Reverend James Williams told the Queensland WCTU at its inaugural meeting that the WCTU would serve to uplift the home and so provide an alternative for men to the solace of "the public house."[129]

This readiness to acknowledge the separate role of women may be interpreted as part of the spirit of "sexual egalitarianism" in nineteenth-century

Australian family life. But it must always be kept in mind that the position of women within the family was not, truly speaking, an egalitarian one in the colonies. In 1913, Jessie Ackermann noted this tension in her important book, *Australia: From a Woman's Point of View*. Ackermann pointed out that while there was consultation on important matters of morality and family business, Australian women were manifestly inferior in legal status. Within the family the husband occupied an "assured position as head of the home." The absence of "independence" among Australian women—who would not take leadership positions in the WCTU without consulting their husbands —she found "entirely out of keeping with what the position of wives and daughters should be in a country of boasted equality."[130] The attractions of the WCTU to those Australian women were closely tied up, as they were for their South African and New Zealand equivalents, with the models of womanly independence they found in traveling lecturers like Ackermann. These colonials also tried to use the WCTU as a practical "university" to develop their own leadership skills and knowledge of the wider world. The WCTU supplied these women with a channel for self-development and raised their consciousness as women.[131]

In this way, the WCTU's appeal to women as individuals and its rein-forcement of their roles as mothers were different parts of the same ideo-logical field. Women who were given encouragement by either their hus-bands or their ministers to take an active role in reform were also those most likely to experience the contradictions between women's moral au-thority and their public subservience. They were the ones to emphasize, too, conflict between the ideology of women as equal partners in bourgeois companionate marriage and women's tenuous and halting steps toward emancipation in the political and economic fields. These women undoubt-edly found in the sisterhood concept a practical model to admire and emu-late, but this advocacy of a sisterhood was combined with, and had its roots in, the WCTU's espousal of motherhood and family values.[132]

Only in the United States and Britain did a separate spinster culture actually give WCTU women practical alternatives outside marriage. This meant that internationally motherhood and relations with men inevitably took precedence, though sisterhood expressed the contradictions women's inferior position engendered. But even in the United States, advocates of women's emancipation within the WCTU realized that the independent women's culture operated on the margins of power and wealth, and they simultaneously affirmed the importance of women's role within the family alongside concepts of womanly solidarity. Despite the reputation these women achieved elsewhere in the World's WCTU, the tensions within WCTU ideology remained for Americans, too, unresolved because women did not have the luxury of a purely theoretical solution to the problems of women's status. Arguing from a position of weakness, they combined the contradictory elements of sexual egalitarianism and the familial ideology of the Victorian middle classes because they had no other alternative. Women, like men, did not make history as they chose.

THE COMPARATIVE STUDY of the WCTU's ideology of sisterhood sheds light on some of the more sweeping interpretations of women's internationalism and humanitarianism cited at the start of this chapter. The ambiguities of the WCTU's version of a women's culture place us in a better position to evaluate the claims that WCTU women, like other missionary women, were propelled into international work by a strong sisterly identification with the wrongs of women elsewhere. Were temperance women in America inspired by the assumption that their own condition was superior? Did they have a desire to save others they identified as their more oppressed sisters? Did this dynamic impulse that flowed from their own cultural position lead them away from a critique of patriarchal relations in the home society?

Underlying the notion of superiority was the nagging suspicion that the condition of women in other lands expressed the essence of gender subordination that American women felt they shared. When in 1910 Katharine Stevenson observed Japanese prostitutes being imported into Burma, she noted that the United States could hardly condemn the Japanese or British governments, given "the fearful revelations" of a similar "slave traffic" in the United States.[133] Despite the intellectual inheritance of cultural imperialism, Anglo-American temperance women were wary of identifying their status as superior. Rather, these women expressed contradictory attitudes that reflected the very real tensions generated by their own precarious and often anomalous social situation. Americans might have felt privileged in relation to those sisters unlucky enough to live elsewhere, but there were always enough points of similarity to make American WCTU women wonder whether their own conditions really were secure.

This is the only way to make sense of the rhetorical style of the WCTU's campaign against polygamy. One of the WCTU's more persistent commitments, extending from the 1890s to the 1920s, was the attack on Mormon marriage practices. By 1913, the organization had persuaded thirty states to adopt antipolygamy resolutions calling for a constitutional amendment. Not only did the American WCTU attack polygamy at home with ferocity equal to that dealt the institution abroad, but temperance women also used the same language to describe Mormon practices that they devised for "heathens" abroad. A pamphlet entitled "An American Harem" was widely circulated to make just this point, that the practices of Turkey and other backward and barbaric nations were still sanctioned within the United

Family Ideology of the World's WCTU

States.[134] Mormonism was, stated a tract approved by the WCTU, "The Islam of America." Nor was it simply a matter of rhetoric. The WCTU's commitment to companionate marriage appeared threatened by an "actual increase" in plural marriages from the late nineties until the time of the congressional investigations of Mormonism in 1903. The WCTU's campaign against polygamy at home was thus not irrational in the terms of its own ideology, nor did that campaign reflect different concerns to the assault on the institution abroad.[135] Polygamy was denounced as a threat to sexual morality that underscored the essential fragility of bourgeois domesticity. In order to defend women and the American family, it was necessary to obliterate its opponents anywhere.

More than the polygamy case can be adduced as evidence of the interlocking of foreign and domestic fears of the erosion of family and women's values. Another case involved child sexuality and exploitation. At precisely the time when Willard urged American temperance women to aid the child widows of India, through the work of the Indian WCTU's Pandita Ramabai, Willard and her fellow purity workers were busy trying to raise the age of consent from its very low levels and to eliminate child pornography.[136] The temperance missionary's urge to save less-privileged sisters did not serve, therefore, as a testing ground for the shaping of domestic policies of morality that would later inform the Progressive era drive against child marriage in the United States. The missionary impulse in the WCTU, at least, coexisted with domestic sexual reform and came from the same source as the campaigns against immorality and female subordination in American society in the late nineteenth century.

Whenever the WCTU joined campaigns to "save" the inhabitants of "every land," in keeping with the WCTU's ideological and cultural matrix, this process involved saving men as well as women. The WCTU's attacks in 1896 on the Turkish massacre of the Armenians did more than protest the "outrages" perpetrated on women. The WCTU did point in a later appeal to the horror worse than death that personal violation of women entailed, but the original document attacked in broader humanitarian terms "the agony and outrage inflicted by Moslem savages upon our brother and sister Christians."[137] It was not simply one gender that the World's WCTU sought to serve, but "Humanity," as Leavitt framed the issue in the WWCTU's original motto.

Saving humanity prevented the WCTU from organizing an international sisterhood in the terms of contemporary debates. The WCTU's work was of women and by women, but not for women alone. Instead of focusing purely on the economic and sociological problems that women shared in their gender subordination, the WCTU espoused a larger moral program that was maternalist and implicitly less egalitarian in thrust. On this score, WCTU

Pandita Ramabai, national WCTU lecturer for India, friend of Frances
Willard, and crusader for the child widows, with her daughter Manorama
(Pandita Ramabai, *The High Caste Hindu Woman*, ed. Rachel Bodley, rev. ed.
[New York: Fleming H. Revell, 1901])

women were not simply confused, since their contradictory consciousness of family and feminist values was deeply rooted in group and personal experience and represented a rational response to their social situation.

Equally limiting were the terms of the WCTU's understanding of sisterhood, squarely based as they were on notions of Anglo-Saxon cultural hegemony. When the WCTU under Willard denounced Turkish atrocities and sought in the 1890s to save the oppressed and high-caste Hindu widows of India, the humanitarian campaigns raised thousands of dollars of aid in the name of sisterhood, but the egalitarian implication that all women were equal applied only if they embraced the tenets of evangelical Christianity and the WCTU.

The attack on "the Turk" for his lechery, polygamy, and violence toward Armenian women homogenized the enemy as a subhuman "Other." The manipulation of intra-ethnic rivalries in the Turkish empire by the authorities was ignored, as was the Armenian revolutionary movement in the 1890s itself.[138] Conversely, WCTU attitudes toward the persecuted community were strongly sympathetic, but in keeping with the ethos of the WCTU's cultural imperialism, patronizing as well. The Armenians were taken up as a cause célèbre not just because they were so cruelly treated but also because they were said to have committed no crime other than to display their devotion to Christianity and "their loyalty to a pure home."[139] Willard defended the Armenians as representatives of "the home against the harem"; they were standard-bearers for the type of companionate marriage that she envisaged as the ideal for the United States. Willard ignored the sociological probability that the Armenian men she helped were not brother-hearted but patriarchal in their attitudes and practices. Armenia was in danger of becoming an abstraction slotted into the WCTU's discourse on marriage and the family.[140]

Within this context, concepts of motherhood rather than sisterhood better expressed the nature of the relationship between Armenians and their WCTU patrons, since that relationship was indelibly hierarchical. Armenian temperance women like Rebecca Krikorian and Elizabeth Dombourajian illustrated this dependence financially in their reliance on American consciences for funds, but the American side also revealed hierarchical assumptions in the treatment of Armenians.[141] Belle Kearney discussed the Armenian refugees as helpless objects, not as subjects in their own right, when she asked to be supplied with a "young Armenian" to "make her home with mother on the old plantation in Mississippi." "How can I get one?" she asked Lillian Stevens. Her main concern was with the provision of a suitable object of mothering for her own mother.[142] Anna Gordon hoped that Willard and Somerset would be able to do much, so she said, "in the way of helping exploit [sic] these Armenians to America," and WCTU

"Our Armenians," 1896 (Anna A. Gordon, *The Beautiful Life of Frances Willard* [Evanston, Ill.: Woman's Temperance Publishing Association, 1898])

correspondents became preoccupied with the logistics of shipping refugees to and fro.[143]

The response to Willard's special humanitarian appeal was impressive; the WCTU raised in 1897 through its own separate canvas over $7,300, the equivalent of more than half of the dues paid to the National WCTU.[144] The WCTU contributed more than any other single organization, helped stimulate the more general campaigns of the Armenian Relief Association, and contributed $10,000 to relief work. The model of generosity established in this case was to be repeated during the First World War and in the attempts to relieve the devastation of families after the end of that terrible conflict.

Willard was careful to point to the humanitarian need, but she also reminded *Union Signal* readers that gifts to Armenian funds must not take precedence over regular giving to that paper. It was necessary above all to preserve and extend the institutions of the WCTU as "an engine of power for God and human Brotherhood & Sisterhood."[145] Willard went further toward putting humanitarian relief in perspective, however. She asserted the role of the Armenian tragedy in demonstrating the capacity of women for alleviating human suffering and, in so doing, bringing credit to themselves. She was especially proud of the way women's "business capacity [had] been attested on a large scale by the administration of funds and the reorganization of human chaos into Christian society." Heroine philanthropists had had their names "burned into the memory of their proud countrymen and forever enshrined in the hearts of Armenia's hapless daughters."[146] Humanitarianism exacted its price, even if that price was the progress of women's emancipation.

7

Alcohol and Empire

Amuch-neglected theme in the history of European expansionism is the connection between imperial power and alcohol. Western liberal historians have expended disproportionate energy refuting the shadowy thesis of a purely economic imperialism concerned with the export of capital or the search for markets. At the same time, the context of both power and morality within which the late nineteenth-century antiimperialist debate took shape has been given inadequate attention. Unlike present-day ideologues in the debate over imperialism, late nineteenth-century liberals and social reformers dwelt not on economics per se but on how economics was intertwined with the extension of imperial power, with all of its connotations of class and racial hierarchy. Despite British pretensions to free trade and an open market, the foundations of Western imperialism rested, even in the case of Britain, upon an assertion of governmental and military strength that underpinned the safety and prosperity of traders and missionaries and that both expressed and reinforced class distinctions of domestic origin by providing suitable careers for the sons of the upper middle class.[1]

The neglect of power and morality is curious and inexcusable, since, at least in the much-discussed case of John Hobson's *Imperialism*, an unmistakable moral dimension is present. For Hobson, imperialism was a parasitic accretion upon the political economy that depended upon the extension of malevolent influences for its special favors. Empirical analysis of the economic interests involved should not lose sight of this spirit of moral distaste and of Hobson's deeper awareness that the interests of trade and finance that imperialism served to advance were interconnected with the sociological and political aspects of imperial rule. In this respect, at least, Hobson was correct, even if his analysis was flawed in many other ways.[2] The European impact was much more complex than an economic one, and the cultural, religious, social, and psychological aspects of Western domination of less fortunate peoples must be addressed in any competent historiography. Among issues of concern to those critical of imperialism was the involvement of Western governments and traders in the sale of opium and alcohol. Because the trade in these commodities provided valuable governmental revenues and supplemented the profits of private enterprise as well, the issues of power, morality, and economics became intertwined through the medium of drugs.

The WCTU was intimately connected to this moral debate. From the headquarters of Western expansion, in England in the early 1890s, Frances Willard penned a document that set out the potential virtues of a World's WCTU. Pressure could, through such an organization, be brought to bear "against the forcing of alcoholics and other narcotics upon savages and uncivilized communities." The World's WCTU would be especially concerned, she said, with this trade "by the so-called civilized merchants of all nationalities" at a time when "the uncivilized portion of the world" was "being rapidly divided under the nominal sovereignty of the various great Powers." These governments should assert their newfound authority and take prompt action to protect those deemed too weak to protect themselves.[3]

Willard's plea highlighted a major part of the raison d'être of the World's WCTU. Yet temperance women were not first into the field. Missionary organizations provided the critical impulse, and the role of the WWCTU was, it must be stressed, an auxiliary one, but one that illustrates the profound connections of the WCTU's international campaigns with cultural imperialism. When Willard made this plea for an attack on the alcohol problem among "uncivilized" people, the Protestant crusade against the importation and manufacture of alcohol in the colonial sphere was well under way. What the campaign against the intoxication of the "natives" did do for the WWCTU was considerable, nevertheless. It forged closer bonds with the missionary organizations and reinforced conceptions of trusteeship and maternalism toward their darker sisters (and brothers) at the same time that the attack on colonial liquor policies hinted at a powerful critique of Western materialism and economic penetration.

The export of alcohol to Africa, India, and the islands of the Pacific was indeed growing, as Willard alleged, in the latter part of the nineteenth century, at precisely the same time that European powers were asserting their own territorial ambitions in those regions. In addition to the commercial penetration of traders, there was developing in the case of the world's largest and most influential empire a potent connection between the sale of alcohol and the state of government revenues. Without the funds generated from this source (and from the opium excise in the critical case of India), the cost of empire to the British taxpayer may well have been prohibitively higher, and the many benefits of imperial possessions may have looked more like liabilities. When temperance advocates harped upon this theme, they implicitly brought into question both the practical operation and the moral authority of empire.

Sadly, from the point of view of the World's WCTU and its illusions of a worldwide influence, this potentially antiimperialist theme in the campaign on behalf of the native races was nearly always circumscribed by the terms of its own critique. Because the WCTU and other likeminded organizations sought to assert reform through Western, imperial structures and the morally ambiguous principle of trusteeship to little brown brothers and sisters, the implication was always that a just imperial authority would remove the source of friction and establish the legitimacy of colonial rule. This prevented temperance critics of imperialism from winning potential converts among the educated indigenous peoples who, instead, inclined toward nationalism. These nationalist groups were delighted to take up the terms of the European reformers' moral critique of imperial authority but without the delusion that imperial power could, disinterestedly, transform itself into an expression of the true will of the people. In this way, the missionary expansionism of the WCTU, like the larger missionary endeavor of the Anglo-American world, stimulated the attack on Western imperialism without reaping the benefits or even understanding in full the processes its actions had helped stimulate.

Concern with the international impact of drugs went further than the case of alcohol. The contest over alcohol, which reached its apogee between 1890 and 1925, was shaped not only by the realities of Western trade in alcoholic substances but also by the prior moral perception that Britain's imperial power depended on its role as merchant of all drugs of addiction. If by 1893 Willard was prepared to take on the European empires over the export of alcohol to the underdeveloped world, in 1883 opium was more on her mind than alcohol when she surveyed the potential international conquests for the WCTU. Part of the appeal of a worldwide WCTU for Willard was the splendid opportunity this crusade provided to enlarge the WCTU's sphere of operation to include, as she put it in her 1884 address, "all stimulants and narcotics." As a result of her efforts, the attack on opium was incorporated into the Polyglot Petition in 1885 and became a definite item of World's work in 1886. Willard thereby defined the WCTU not simply as an antialcohol organization. The international wing of her movement was to be used to make the WCTU into an all-purpose reform coalition by committing temperance women to a Do-Everything policy.[4]

Opiate addiction was increasing in postbellum American society. Middle-class white women provided the chief market for addictive drugs prescribed mainly by their doctors for the relief of pain during menstruation or available in patent medicines. This unease over the domestic use of opium and morphine may have stimulated WCTU involvement, and in a subterranean way sensitized the WCTU constituency, though the medical addiction of housewives was not the most visible part of the opium "problem."[5] Instead Willard focused on the opium dens of San Francisco, brought by immigrant Chinese. It was against this threat that Willard's antiopium campaign was explicitly directed, as a revolution in the morals of Chinese abroad would dry up the opium epidemic at its source. Willard's "sudden" revelations in San Francisco were also undoubtedly spurred by the knowledge that reformers in Britain were beginning to organize against opium and to identify the Chinese opium addiction as a cultural curse that might spread to the British population through its imperial contacts. The possibility is quite strong, nonetheless, that support for the WWCTU's worldwide opium campaign was fueled within the United States by women who themselves knew of the addiction of friends, or perhaps knew firsthand of the problem of medical addiction.

Willard's call for an international campaign does seem to have stimulated antinarcotic agitation within the American WCTU. Previously limited to tenuous jibes at tobacco, the antinarcotic thrust took its principal late nineteenth-century shape after Willard alerted her co-workers to the foreign danger. Mrs. James Haven of Indiana, first national superintendent of the narcotics department, provided some substance for the idea of a connection between international action and women's own parochial concerns in her first annual report in 1886. She had found in her own personal experience "white-souled women of exquisite culture and natural mental qualities who have gradually fallen victims to this fatal habit until they have become mental and physical wrecks."[6]

Armed with this support, Willard was able to mount an attack in tandem with the churches on the international trade in opium, and inevitably, this attack became linked with a critique of the policies of European powers. Especially open to condemnation was the fact that the British exported opium from India to China and, through trade treaties, forced the acceptance of this commerce by the Chinese government. With the revenue derived from this source and the supply of opium to the Indian population through licensed outlets, the opium industry was used to underpin imperial operations in India. In the early 1880s, at about the time when the British antiopium agitation and its American WCTU counterpart took shape, 15 percent of Indian government revenues were derived from this tainted source. The volume of drug exports from India reached its peak in 1879–80, and net revenues to the Indian government did the same the following year. Opium revenue declined to 7 percent in 1905, but most of this decrease occurred after 1893. In the five years ending in 1893–94, opium still accounted for 14 percent of total revenue.[7]

The antiopium offensive began with the inclusion of all narcotics in the Polyglot Petition and peaked with the appointment of Jessie Ackermann as a World's superintendent in 1893. The WCTU kept this department active into the 1920s and continued to attack the imperial drug trade. "Alcohol and opium" were "deathly agents and ministers to vice," Ackermann argued, "yet the government sanctions both." She found her attempts to spread Christian temperance principles in China were constantly met by the educated with the retort, "You have sent us opium, and what has it done for us?" "Don't," advised Ackermann, "talk to an intelligent Chinese about Christianity and its advantages."[8]

Yet the antiopium agitation failed to compete effectively with the attack on the trade in alcohol. In part this possibly reflected the WCTU's origins and objectives. These remained fundamentally concerned with the relationship between issues of women and those of temperance. The antiopium crusade never quite penetrated to the inner core of these concerns. More likely, the WCTU's emphasis after 1895 on alcohol rather than opium reflected the realities of imperial power and the patterns of trade and revenue. The opium traffic with China and within India was already in decline in the 1890s, while the trade in alcohol was steadily expanding in these years in which the WCTU built its World's organization. And finally, the antiopium agitation was largely a British operation, given the overwhelming British control of the international trade. The opium issue was heavily focused, despite attempts to extend its relevance to include Chinese immigration in both Australia and the United States, on Britain's relations with China. The alcohol traffic was much more widely dispersed, with almost every major European nation contributing, and the United States as well. Much to the despair of reformers, the British Royal Commission of 1895 had reaffirmed the opium traffic as relatively harmless, and the dominance of Conservative governments determined to defend the integrity of imperial revenue for more than another decade constituted a major obstacle to the hopes of the antiopium forces. Conservatives in Britain created a dilemma for reformers by asserting that the structure of imperial revenue was such that if opium were banned, the government of India would be forced to rely even more heavily on the alcohol excise. The *Times* of London posed this dilemma when it quoted a former governor of Bengal, Sir George Campbell: "I have no doubt whatever that, so far as the population of India is concerned, there is very much more danger from the drink traffic than from opium."[9] Opium, some imperial apologists claimed, was essentially benign, and moreover, the government believed that if Britain gave up its lucrative China market, local producers would simply take over. The matter of morality was continually deferred until the Chinese displayed a resolute opposition to the traffic themselves.

These arguments were never totally acceptable to temperance women who would not concede gradations of evil, yet the WCTU's antiopium efforts did slacken noticeably after 1895. Indeed, a general, if temporary, decline in the whole antiopium movement occurred. Though the BWTA had formed a department in 1896, there had "been great difficulty in arousing any interest" because of the findings of the royal commission. In 1904, the department was actually discontinued.[10] Where American jurisdiction was involved, as in the case of the Philippines, the WCTU and its

church allies had more success, for there in 1906 the U.S. government
turned away from a proposal to license the use after a congressional prohibition was imposed.[11] The WCTU had lobbied for this prohibition but
played only a minor role in the victory, and the eventual destruction of the
British opium trade owed, we shall later see, little to WCTU agitation. Even
within the United States, the most influential church-based reformer was
Bishop Charles Henry Brent, an Episcopalian who had the ear of President
Roosevelt and good connections with the Archbishop of Canterbury. The
WCTU, with its roots in Methodism and English dissent, was of tangential
importance in this diplomatic struggle. The World's WCTU could hardly
do more on the international front than tack its objections against opiates
onto its outrage against the supply of alcohol to non-Western peoples. It
was this latter struggle that the WCTU principally used to define the relation of temperance women, and their cultural imperialism, to the currents
of colonialism and nationalism.[12]

The first to sound the alarm were the bearers of that preeminent gift of
Western civilization, the alleged blessings of Christianity. Protestant missionaries contested the use of alcohol virtually from the beginnings of their
struggle to bring the Bible to the non-Christian world. Certainly by the time
the ABCFM was sending emissaries to the Sandwich Islands in the 1820s,
alcohol was already a contentious issue between the advocates of Western
civilization and the indigenous peoples in Polynesia and Micronesia.[13] If the
missionaries had gained some kind of cultural dominance in this region by
the 1870s, alcohol did not cease to be conceived as a serious problem, either
there or in the wider context of imperial expansion that took in large parts
of Africa and Asia as well. By the 1880s the organized humanitarian and
Christian movements in the metropolitan countries, particularly in Britain
and America, were set on a course of confrontation with the demon liquor
in all of its alcoholic varieties. The critics of imperial expansion in the 1880s
noted that one doleful accompaniment of the territorial aggrandizement
was the increasing availability of alcohol of Western origins. To the deep
chagrin of these missionaries, along with the Bibles went the bottles. Missionary groups especially liked to use the testimony of the indigenous people themselves. "The country," claimed a group of young Christians in West
Africa in a typical jeremiad, "is inundated with rum and gin; the inhabitants are dying; there is no longer any order; anarchy reigns everywhere;
kings and officers abuse their position; parents and children do not acknowledge their mutual duties; and, what is more deplorable, infants are
brought up on these poisonous drinks."[14]

Joining these churchmen and -women and Christian converts in condemnation of European mischief were the highly publicized travelers and journalists. In 1885, Henry Morton Stanley "vividly described" in his *The Congo*
the "suicidal habit of indulgence in drinking alcoholic liquors in hot cli-

mates," but perhaps the most effective journalistic stimulus came from W. T. Hornaday's *Free Rum on the Congo* in 1887. Hornaday, the American naturalist who later became head of the Washington Zoo, had no particular affiliation with the temperance movement but was shocked by what he saw happening in Africa. He damned the European powers for their failure at the Congress of Berlin in 1884. They had ignored the alcohol problem in their deliberations upon the exploited Congo region. In the demand that trade in the region be absolutely free, Hornaday located the subordination of European policy to the spirit of "gain, pecuniary advantage and international greed."[15]

The attacks of Hornaday and the exposés by missionaries were taken up by mission societies and humanitarians on both sides of the Atlantic and led to the formation in Britain of the Native Races and Liquor Traffic United Committee, in league with which the World's WCTU would eventually act after 1907. Lord Salisbury, secretary of state for foreign affairs in the British government, was persuaded by the committee to pursue the issue at the forthcoming International Slave Congress in Brussels, and this in turn spurred representatives of seventeen nations assembled there to sign the General Act of the Brussels Conference, 1889–1890. This restricted for the first time the importation of spirits into parts of Africa.[16]

The WCTU joined the chorus of opposition to British and European policy around this time. *Free Rum on the Congo* touched off the ambivalent responses of American temperance women on the subject of economic modernization, particularly as it applied in colonial forms, when Hornaday wrote: "The idea that civilization is an unmitigated blessing to be sought after by every savage, is one of the dearest delusions of this age." With the addition of a sympathetic foreword written by Hannah Whitall Smith, World's WCTU secretary, Hornaday's book was published and marketed through the Woman's Temperance Publishing Association.[17]

In addition, temperance women also provided their own invaluable evidence for the missionary indictment. Mary Leavitt was at least as well qualified as Stanley to comment on the woes of alcohol-soaked Africa, but she had further advantages as a propagandist. As a round-the-world traveler without par, she could make comparisons and show the interconnections of policy in Africa, India, and the Pacific. As a woman she could highlight the poignant and sentimental aspects of family disorganization and could focus Victorian moral outrage by directly counterposing the moral authority of the domestic ideology with the harsh realities of life for less-privileged women. Leavitt's reports of her travels in Asia and Africa between 1887 and 1890, published regularly in the *Union Signal*, drew the attention of WCTU women in America to the penetration of European alcohol in the non-Western world. At the Third International Congress against the Abuse of Spiritous Drinks, in Christiana, Norway, in 1890, Leavitt documented what she saw as the enormity of the problem with statistics designed to stun the audience: "At Madeira, where many, but by no means all, of the ships going to Africa touch, the following amounts were declared in *one week*: 960,000 cases of gin, 24,000 butts of rum, 30,000 cases of brandy, 28,000 cases of Irish whiskey, 800,000 demijohns of rum, 36,000 barrels of rum, 30,000 cases of 'Old Tom,' 15,000 cases of *absinthe*, 40,000 cases of *vermouth* all costing $5,230,000."[18]

Leavitt was the principal WCTU contributor to the barrage of evidence, but she was joined by others like Ackermann who, during her tour of China, noted the passengers on a steamer traveling between Hong Kong and Shanghai. "They all drank freely, and the Japanese took brandy in their coffee. . . . I thought," she added tellingly, "it is no use to look for a spot free from *civilized vices*; I do not think it could be found." Katharine Bushnell added to the growing criticism during her visit to southern Africa. She especially condemned the owners of gold mines who sold liquor to their black workers. "Those who are interested in money-making inside the gold and diamond mines are often interested in debauching the natives with bad brandy and whisky. In some places men, women, children and even babies will be seen lying along the road drunk."[19]

Central to the antialcohol critique was the suggestion that an alcoholic stupor was being forced upon "helpless" indigenous peoples.[20] Leavitt related how on her travels she had met the queen of the Hovas in Madagascar, who bitterly complained because France and Britain had forced commercial treaties on the island state that prevented the queen from prohibiting the importation of alcohol. The *Cyclopedia of Temperance* made particular use of Leavitt's evidence as a key example of Western perfidy and to demonstrate the overwhelming European responsibility.[21] "Treaties made by Western nations with weak and dependent peoples," charged Leavitt, "force the trade upon them" through the medium of "despotic" European merchants.[22] In a similar fashion, a correspondent of the *Canadian Woman's Journal* in 1890 drew the sweeping conclusion that "all the intoxicating liquors used in Africa come from so-called christian nations."[23]

This was a gross exaggeration. The suggestion that a taste for drink was foisted on passive recipients by rapacious westerners will not stand up to scrutiny. The relationship between alcohol consumption and Western commercial penetration was exceedingly complex. The Europeans did not always introduce alcohol to indigenous peoples in Africa, Asia, or the Pacific. In fact, virtually no society, however "primitive" or pristine, lacked intoxicating substances or drugs, though some did not have alcoholic beverages.[24] The reports of temperance missionaries frequently told of "native drinks." John G. Paton, the WCTU ally, Scottish Presbyterian missionary, and foe of all intoxicants, told of how his native charges in the New Hebrides consumed kava—"a highly intoxicating drink. . . .This they freely drink; it does not make them violent, but stupefies them and induces sleep like opium." In Mexico, reported Missouri's Nellie Burger, the peasants drank pulque, the fermented sap of the cactus. "The people there use this liquor almost universally, not drinking water." Like kava in the New Hebrides, pulque was said to be "a narcotic" with "a stupefying effect." In West Africa, a "native beer" was made from corn, rice, or millet, while in Kenya, sugar was used for the same purpose. Perhaps the best known of all was the toddy produced from palm sap in Madras (Tamilnad). An entire caste, the nadars, made their living from this production in the early nineteenth century.[25]

As these reports indicate, the WCTU and its missionary allies were prepared to admit in more candid moments that the use of alcohol involved a two-way relationship. The *Union Signal* conceded that though shipments of New England rum and other liquors to Africa had fallen between 1885 and 1889, "the shrewd natives are themselves making an intoxicating liquor which, at much less cost than Boston rum, does the same deadly work." In Hawaii, too, "awa" was "in its effects upon the human system even more disastrous than the imported liquors," reported WCTU official and missionary Mrs. R. Jay Greene.[26]

According to anthropologists Mac and Leslie Marshall, missionaries in the Pacific Islands especially condemned the native liquors because of their use in non-Christian religious ceremonies. Since missionaries quickly substituted a concern with tobacco on those islands where they did not find liquor usage as part of indigenous cultural practice, the Marshalls conclude that one element in the missionary crusade was a symbolic contest for power with the indigenous peoples. Renouncing alcohol became a symbol of Christian commitment in the struggle with the heathen. The Marshalls have further contended that this struggle encompassed parts of the European "beach" communities, which were also depicted as obstacles to a spiritual transformation. In effect, the missionaries of Micronesia in the mid-nineteenth century are interpreted as fighting for moral authority and social ascendancy over the rough and rowdy communities of traders, beachcombers, whalers, and other Europeans in those islands whose lives were caught up with the consumption of alcohol and who were seen by missionaries as a contaminating influence on the native peoples.[27]

But the thesis of a purely symbolic crusade for social control must be measured against the changing moral perceptions of the custodians of imperial morality. Certainly the well-orchestrated international campaign of the 1890s to 1920s cannot be explained in terms of the missionary-beach community struggles of the 1850s. The Marshalls are convinced that the missionaries in Micronesia had established their authority by the 1880s, but it was at precisely this time that men like John G. Paton began to spread their agitation from the island communities of Melanesia and Polynesia to

Alcohol and Empire

influence opinion in the metropolitan powers. The campaign of the 1890s must be examined in the context of the extension of European political power in that decade, and in the American case, this involved the assumption of territorial empire at the end of the century with all of its moral anxieties and opportunities for benevolent reform. The international networks of temperance and missionary societies devoted to the prohibition of alcohol among the indigenous peoples reflected and helped shape this changing imperial sensibility. If the WCTU and other similar organizations sought control of recalcitrant peoples through identifying drinking as sin, temperance reformers also voiced in their central indictment of Western policy and inactivity a commitment to religious benevolence and displayed a feeling of guilt that Western penetration was destroying formerly sober peoples. To the extent that drink did become a powerful symbol for political mobilization, it did so by focusing that sense of unease at the process of Western domination on a substance and a set of practices within the nominal political control of the European powers, not on the natives to be controlled. Christian temperance mobilized the conscience of expansionist European peoples to resolve the contradictory impact of the international market economy on "backward" peoples.

The lobbying in 1907 over the American ratification of another Brussels conference showed how temperance and church groups sought to resolve this conflict. A group of twenty-six American Presbyterian missionaries in the Cameroons argued typically in their remonstrances to the American secretary of state: the "rum traffic" was "not only not a profit but a hindrance to lawful trade, as testified to by the traders themselves." Drunkards were not, in their opinion or that of the WCTU, good buyers and sellers. The sale of intoxicants was, said Marie Brehm and Minnie Horning in a telegram to Theodore Roosevelt on behalf of the Illinois WCTU, "destructive both to the trade and morals of nations." By attacking unprincipled traders who dumped alcohol on unsuspecting natives or used alcohol as an adjunct to the manipulation and coercion of native tribes, the missionary simultaneously sanctioned the extension of the rule of Western administrations that must police prohibition of alcohol and opium and endorsed "legitimate trade," orderly economic progress, and the spread of literacy and modern communications—indeed the entire infrastructure upon which colonialism depended.[28]

Equally to the point, the use of alcohol as a symbol of native/white cultural struggle must be carefully gauged against the possibility that alcohol consumption did rise dramatically under the European impact. A critical issue that the thesis of a symbolic crusade underrates is the scope and substance of drinking under imperial expansion and westernization. This would include quantitative trends in consumption of alcoholic beverages and the social problems associated with that consumption. Studies of temperance reform organizations in the United States no longer neglect the issues of alcohol consumption and damage,[29] and neither should those questions be ignored when the expansion of the American temperance movement elsewhere is analyzed. Issues of drinking and public drunkenness must be integrated with changing perceptions of the "alcohol problem" if the character of antiliquor movements is to be fully understood.

Though alcoholic beverages often preceded the European arrival, that is not to say that European penetration had no social effects related to the consumption of alcohol. When the fabric of indigenous society was rent, the effects were bound to spread through all areas of life. European influences, both economic and cultural, gradually brought, in many cases, a serious disruption of patterns of culture and in the rituals that expressed authority. Drinking practices were therefore certain to be affected. Though alcohol had been used for several centuries in many of these societies, it must be remembered that the ways liquor was used often differed from those of more highly commercialized and industrializing societies. The important role of alcohol in religious ritual ensured that its use would not breach community solidarity and controls. The religious significance of alcohol was noted by Paton in his observations of New Hebrideans: "A portion is always poured out to their Gods; and the dregs in every mouth after drinking are always spit out with the exclamation, 'That's for you, Kumesan!' "[30] Whenever evangelical Christianity was adopted, the renunciation of animistic religions involved a turning away from this religious use; the symbolic renunciation of association with evil in these cases proceeded in a fine analogy with the process of temperance conversion in the Anglo-American world. The antialcohol message among the missionaries was, in this and other similar cases, undeniably and inextricably connected to the struggle for religious and cultural authority among these people.[31]

But the abandonment of such circumscribed usages was accompanied by more disruptive applications of alcohol. Commentators frequently observed, in the testimony on native drinks discussed above, that these had a narcotic or stupefying effect, quite unlike the behavior patterns associated with drunkenness in the United States. Such reports may lend credence to the hypothesis of Craig MacAndrew and Robert B. Edgerton that the ways in which drinking influences behavior are conditioned by cultural norms. Yet it is also very likely, as the WCTU believed, that the drinks themselves, with their different alcohol contents and chemical structures, conditioned the different behavioral impact.[32] Whatever the true explanation, the breakdown of cultural controls and sanctions against disruptive behavior can be charted as part of the Western impact.

The pervasive and intricate effects of European rule have been perceptively and sensitively analyzed by Charles Ambler in a case study of drinking in colonial Kenya. Ambler's study makes clear that the impact of European rule on drinking practices between 1900 and 1939 went far beyond the quantity of alcohol imported. Kenyans had long brewed their own native beer from sugar, but this was only available seasonally. The introduction and spread of a colonial political economic structure with modern transport, ports, and international commercial connections enabled sugar to be imported at any time, along with crushing equipment for more efficient milling. The development of a colonial political economy also meant the introduction of a wage economy that made available the money to purchase liquor. In consequence the seasonal nature and ritual significance of drinking was greatly affected, and "the stability of established drinking practices" was "rapidly undermined." Ambler detected, in particular, that drinking was more a symptom of the declining tribal authority and tribal economy of colonial Kenya at the turn of the century than the root cause of social disorganization, though no doubt the greater availability of alcohol interacted with other social changes to compound the difficulties. Especially important, youths were liberated from economic dependence on fathers for wives, and hence the elders' control of youthful drinking practices was eroded.[33]

The Kenyan data cannot be readily applied to all colonial contexts, since the structure of the preexisting cultures varied, and the extent of the European impact was equally diverse. Even in Africa, some tribes like the Akan of Ghana were fortunate enough, partly because of low levels of contact with whites and the selective impact of economic development, to be able to incorporate much of the increased usage within traditional patterns of consumption, at least prior to 1910. But cultural variability was most noticeable in the East, as reformers themselves sometimes conceded. In China and Japan, for example, the WCTU admitted that drunkenness among the indigenous populations was not as severe a problem as in parts of Africa, the Pacific Islands, or in industrial Europe. "Drunkenness is far less common in China than in so-called Christian lands," reported Ruth Shaffner to her superiors in Chicago in 1893. In India, where temperance reformers railed against the government excise on liquor, it was clear, reading between the lines, that most Indians were still relatively abstemious. The strength of Indian institutions and symbols impressed WCTU missionaries profoundly, and reformers concentrated mainly on the question of prevention but accompanied this tactic with admissions of shame that it was the Europeans in India who did much of the heavy drinking. It was the irresponsible example of this group that, according to the WCTU, threatened to lead India astray.[34]

Parts of Africa south of the Sahara did indeed present more visible signs of the social disruption attendant upon economic penetration than India, and these the World's WCTU propagandists seized upon for their own purposes. Thus Leavitt drove home the perceived connection between economic change and alcohol abuse when she reported that in the Congo, liquor was "very largely the currency of the place in trade with the natives." This was a judgment WCTU observers held to be true in the case of some South African mine workers as well who, paid in cheap alcohol, "return to their kraals drunken and irredeemably depraved." More commonly, indigenous peoples' propensity for drinking increased precisely because of their incorporation into the cash economy. Both historian Charles Van Onselen and sociologist G. P. Hunt have noted the supply of cheap alcohol available at company stores as a means used by mine owners in southern Africa to tie the native wage-labor force to longer periods of employment, and Hunt has also emphasized the role of alcohol among traders seeking to dispossess indigenous people of their lands.[35]

WCTU reports not only corroborate the use of alcohol as a tactic by mining companies; instances of land alienation connected to the abuse of alcohol also abound. The *Union Signal* publicized, for example, the appeal of King Khama of Bechuanaland against the establishment of liquor shops within that protectorate, because the move was, allegedly, aimed at the alienation of native land in the interests of the chartered company. Kate Bushnell also reported cases of "whites" who "talk unblushingly of the day when they [the natives] will all be killed off by rum and they can have the land."[36]

Not only was alcohol, whether imported from abroad or internally produced, socially disruptive under the new conditions of colonial political economy. It was also likely that, as missionary observers suggested, the absolute volume imported was on the rise under the impact of free or preferential trading agreements instigated through European coercion. This was certainly the case in British India, where the statistical records are especially good. Between 1875–76 and 1901, the great era of liquor imperialism, imports of potable spirits into India rose 85 percent while the total population increased only 42 percent. Liquor imports were also on the increase in West Africa in the period of greatest alarm in that region just before the First World War. Between 1901 and 1910, for example, the quantities of alcohol imported into present-day Nigeria rose 33 percent to 4 million gallons. On the Gold Coast, imports of spirits doubled from 1890 to 1912, in which year they reached an all-time peak. Nigerian historian E. A. Ayandele concludes, "That [the] trade in liquor increased in proportion to the establishment and extension of British administration . . . is beyond dispute."[37]

An increase also occurred in southern and eastern Africa during the 1870s and 1880s and particularly in the 1890s as sugar producers in Portuguese-administered Mozambique struggled to compensate for declining sugar prices by entering into extensive distilling and marketed cheap spirits to the Transvaal. When that market collapsed in 1897 after British intervention to stop the "natives" from drinking such heavily alcoholic drinks,

sugar producers turned to their own local customers in Portuguese territory, again with devastating effects on tribal morale.[38]

This evidence suggests that missionaries were probably accurate in their
depiction of an emerging problem of alcohol damage in parts of the colonial world, even if they exaggerated its extent and often homogenized its
character. Reformers, including those in the World's WCTU, were inclined
to gloss over such complexities. For them it was enough to know that the
spirits trade was increasing and that dependent peoples needed help. How
to help people patronizingly defined as victims was the problem that
loomed largest for the Anglo-American reform coalition. A crucial dilemma was how to influence events that occurred so far away and that inter-
fered with the normal processes of trade in a market society. The WCTU,
because its roots were in the United States, was inclined to stress American
responsibility for the African liquor trade, especially that on the West Coast.
This Leavitt linked to the memory of slavery. The celebrated traveler drove
home the point that the trade in spirits went back to the infamous triangu-
lar trade, and as a result, "America's guilt" was far-reaching. For the next
twenty-five years, the World's and American unions pushed this same
theme that the "drink traffic [made] darker the dark continent." This was a
late nineteenth-century precursor of the powerful nationalist charge that
the West had "underdeveloped" Africa through colonialist exploitation.[39]

The assumption of American responsibility deepened in 1890 after the
Brussels conference recommended the prohibition of imports of spirits into
a vast region of central Africa. The United States initially failed to ratify the
agreement, thus provoking a lobbying campaign in which WCTU activity
on this issue went for the first time beyond the mere gathering of information. Willard delivered a thunderous denunciation of American policy at
the 1891 national WCTU convention and appealed for petitions. Thousands flowed in and testified to the concern of evangelical churchwomen
who, like Emiline Hicks of Lansingburg, Ohio, "hasten[ed] to obey" Willard's appeal in order to aid the "wiping out" of "that 'burning shame' that
rests on our beloved country." This program was closely coordinated with
the foreign mission societies of the Baptist and Methodist churches and
gathered under the WCTU banner the signatures of thousands of men as
well as women. Other WCTU women, already stirred up by Hornaday's
exposé of liquor imperialism in the Congo, helped to distribute copies of
that book.[40]

The petitions and the letters accompanying them displayed the depth of
feeling over the issue. It was not difficult to mobilize Christian women for
such a crusade. Temperance supporters were already familiar with feelings
of guilt toward black people through the slavery issue, and the impact of
alcohol on their own "native race" was a matter of shame to Protestant
churchgoers in the United States, as in Canada and Australia.[41]

Under such pressures, the American government fell into line in 1892, and central Africa became a zone of at least partial prohibition. Upon this foundation, succeeding Brussels conferences in 1899, 1906, and 1912 sought to build. The duties on imported spirits were gradually raised, and prohibitions were placed on the importation of spirits into areas deemed to have been "dry" on grounds of religious (largely Islamic) principles prior to the European impact. Emboldened by this success, the WCTU and its allies broadened the campaign and shifted the geographic focus. After 1891 attention turned from the "rape" of central Africa to West Africa, whence the European powers continued to pour their seemingly endless supplies of surplus spirits, and in particular to the British possessions there and in India, where the export of alcohol was threatening to reach the same alarming proportions. Though it was fully recognized that "feelings of shame and wonder and righteous indignation" ought to be addressed to the "French and German Colonies" as well as the British, the WCTU's way of influencing continental imperialists remained through British and American sources because there the WCTU had its strength.[42]

The details changed after 1891, but the modus operandi of the WCTU remained essentially the same. Temperance women could not vote to change the policies of the American government or of any other imperial power in the 1890s. Even American women, with their reputation for political advancement, depended on their good connections within the broader ranks of American social reformers and evangelical activists. The exertion of this influence was in the "native races" issue always connected to the missionary societies. But the role of the WCTU was enhanced after 1895 when Margaret Dye Ellis went to Washington to become a formal lobbyist for the National WCTU, and she was well placed to deepen the WCTU's connections with the evangelical reform coalition.[43]

The controversy over the export of liquor to the Pacific islands at the turn of the century illustrated the WCTU's place within the larger missionary lobbying process. In December 1901, a group of reformers met Secretary of State John Hay to persuade the American government to reenter negotiations with the British government over the prohibition of the international trade in intoxicating liquor in the New Hebrides. Behind this well-publicized campaign was Paton, whose exploits as a missionary in the western Pacific were already legendary. The WCTU promoted the Scot's case for exclusion of alcohol from the region and joined other church-based reform groups to exert pressure on American policy. At the meeting were representatives of the ASL, the Methodist Episcopal Missionary Society, Christian Endeavor, and Wilbur Crafts of the International Reform Bureau, a Washington-based group concerned with purity, sabbatarianism, and related questions. Representing women was the WCTU's Margaret Ellis.[44]

Alcohol and Empire

The mere presence of Ellis demonstrated the WCTU's excellent network of influence, which extended internationally and through a host of related organizations. The WCTU credentials were also emphasized by the presence of Crafts, who worked closely with the temperance women and whose wife, Sara, was World's superintendent of Sunday schools for the WCTU. But not only was the WCTU well-connected in church circles; the organization could claim, as could no other evangelical reform body, to speak "for the women of the world" and also on behalf of Paton, who was a personal friend of Ellis. No secretary of state could avoid the harsh realities of international and domestic economic pressures, but neither could Hay afford to oppose such moral arguments. Their view was his, he assured them, and Hay did persuade the administration to negotiate with Britain and to support the Gillett bill, which forbade the sale of intoxicants to any "uncivilized" people by Americans.[45]

In succeeding years, the WCTU continued this lobbying role. The international arm of the organization was especially active. Crafts's International Reform Bureau felt sure that the World's WCTU's cable of support helped to secure at the 1906 Brussels convention "the raising of the prohibitory tax on alcohol" for importation into Africa "from 70 to 100 franks."[46] The 1912 international conference broke up without agreement, but the World's WCTU continued to push the Liberal administration in Britain for unilateral action. The World's WCTU superintendent responsible for this subject, Christine Robertson of Scotland, rejoiced at the responsiveness of colonial secretary William Harcourt to representations from the BWTA and other temperance and church groups in extending "the zone of prohibition in the Nigerias over more than 3,000 square miles in Southern Nigeria" and in prohibiting "the importation of distilling apparatus for potable spirits into Britain's West African Colonies" in 1913.[47]

The Americans, too, had a complementary role in shoring up the actions of the British in West Africa at this time. The American WCTU worked hard in 1913 along with the General Convention of Baptists of North America to get Secretary of State William Jennings Bryan to pressure the Liberian government to refuse a German company permission to open a distillery in that country. Bryan, whose wife was a WCTU official, was sympathetic and complied, though it undoubtedly helped that the United States government opposed all special commercial concessions in Liberia as part of general American economic foreign policy. The American intervention arrested the German plan, which would have threatened the effectiveness of the British efforts to exclude spirits from their own West African territories.[48]

Liberia was a special case, however. Nowhere else in Africa did the United States have a comparable interest, so from the point of view of the American government, the WCTU, Crafts, and others like them were moralistic gadflies who misunderstood the delicate character of international politics. Though Secretary of State Elihu Root acknowledged at the time of the Brussels Conference of 1906 the "wide interest of the American people" demonstrated in the WCTU's efforts, his own departmental officials complained that temperance advocates wanted the United States to "butt in" to business that only indirectly concerned them. Since the United States was not a signatory but only an adherent to the 1899 treaty, it had not been invited to Brussels in 1906 and could only offer its moral support to the negotiations through a strongly worded message from President Theodore Roosevelt.[49]

These circumstances pointed to the need for American reformers to cooperate internationally and, through the BWTA, to interest the British government in this work. This was also the symbolic message of the various international antialcohol congresses in which the WCTU took part in the first decade of the twentieth century.[50] Accordingly, the WCTU had appointed Scotland's Robertson as World's superintendent of the Department of Native Races in 1903, and it was she who devoted the next ten years to the international and imperialist contexts of this question. As the Nigerian case indicates, Robertson was indeed active in drawing attention to the ramifications of this problem in the British empire. Though the BWTA had shown little appreciation of Britain's "guilt" prior to 1900, under Robertson's leadership both it and the World's WCTU focused on the case of British India. Agnes Slack and Florence Balgarnie both paid extensive visits to India in the first decade of the new century and indicted British policy. The World's WCTU also sent Katharine Stevenson and Ella Hoover Thatcher, and the BWTA sponsored a number of minor visitors as well.[51]

In the Indian example, the WCTU seized upon the central elements in the moral critique of imperial rule. Especially important was the growing reliance of the Indian government on alcohol excise for revenue. Land tax still remained the staple of imperial finances in India, but as early as the 1890s 14 percent of the revenues of the Ceylon presidency were derived from the liquor excise. Robertson tirelessly criticized the tendency for these duties to grow. In 1874 the revenue from this source was £1,561,000, and in 1908, £6,717,000.[52] This massive increase of some 430 percent vastly outstripped the population increase of under 50 percent. By the early 1920s, 27 percent of the total government revenue came from the excise on alcohol. This compared with 2 percent in 1874, 7 percent in the early 1890s, and 10 percent by 1905.[53] Equally important, liquor revenues had exceeded the politically and morally sensitive opium excise in absolute terms by 1900. Government officials argued that the increase represented largely a more efficient collection of excise, but the number of liquor outlets was also sharply up, and the charge was duly issued that westerners were corrupting a formerly temperate people. According to Katharine Stevenson, "revenue" had obviously taken precedence over "righteousness."[54]

The attack on the excise struck at the heart of British rule in India, which involved making the Indians pay for their own domination. Repeatedly the WCTU's representatives in India, Britain, and America rammed home the point that an empire that promised to rule in the interests of its subjects in fact exploited them morally and economically. Florence Balgarnie carried the indictment about as far as anyone in the WCTU was willing to go. Balgarnie referred to "the fettered condition of India in being governed by aliens, and said that while [British] rule was good in many respects, the price paid for it by India [was] far too heavy." The nuggety English reformer called the level of taxation "a national crime" and singled out for harsh treatment the keeping of a standing army and the nefarious taxation "connected with the liquor traffic." Indians, she told British audiences upon her return from the subcontinent, "complain that we are forcing the drink traffic upon them" and that "the sale of licenses by public auction [was] a great iniquity" because it encouraged more intensive commercial exploitation of the market.[55]

Even Slack, who took a much more pro-imperial line, was forced to admit that the excise on opium and alcohol was the "weakest spot in British rule in India."[56] But apart from her conviction that the source of revenue was morally tainted, Slack stressed a different point. She feared the loosening of caste barriers that would surely accompany increased violation of traditional prohibitions against drinking: "Unless . . . vigorous action is taken[,] the horrors of drink amongst the teeming easily-led native races will surpass anything we have ever heard of, and then indeed India will become seditious."[57]

Balgarnie's position, though probably not Slack's, was compatible with a moderate nationalism, and the acts and statements of the temperance critics of empire did stimulate nationalism of a kind.[58] By providing a platform on which the different national and racial groupings could focus, the antiliquor, antiexcise agitation was a point of potential unity. Sometimes WWCTU workers deliberately sought to strengthen such intercaste and interracial cooperation. Christine Tinling, Flora Strout, Katharine Stevenson, and other WCTU missionaries took this position. Stevenson, for example, "tried to put the temperance reform in the light of a race problem, requiring a unity of effort on the part of all peoples."[59] At Slack's meetings in Lucknow, the World's WCTU secretary rejoiced: "One could but notice that while Hindus, Mahomedans and Christians are separated by social and religious difference, here was a great common ground on which all [could] unite."[60] None of these women restricted their pleas to the purely Christian element but worked to establish societies among the non-Christian community as well. Stevenson went so far as to sanction the vast, indigenous temperance movement that had arisen in Ceylon as a kind of nativist revival among the Buddhist Singalese and contrasted their protests against the source of British revenue with the steadfast opposition of the imperial government to the nativistic boycotts of the liquor outlets during 1905.[61]

The critique even included, as Stevenson's analysis suggested, the depiction of the Western imperial power as corrupt and decadent. The English missionary Frances Hallowes, then president of the WCTU of India, published in 1908 *The Enemy: A Study in Heredity*, which sought to root home the dangers of self-destruction said to be inherent in the misguided imperial policy. Not only did the free availability of liquor demoralize the Indians and corrupt the revenues. The entire racial and class hierarchy was at risk. The book told the story of the "ruin" and eventual death of a deputy commissioner's young wife when "ruthlessly exposed to the seductive influences of the 'smart set.'" Her "nauseating picture" of "English society in India" conveyed to antiliquor activists righteous indignation and a sense of alarm. Said the editor of the Anglo-Indian temperance journal, *Abkari*: "For the sake of our [the British] good name one hopes that this aspect of the official world is not too much exposed to the gaze of the millions we are supposed to be governing for their moral and material benefit."[62]

The WCTU was by no means the only temperance organization in India that worked toward the stimulation of native pride, the rejection of Western immoral practices, and the creation of an intercommunal solidarity. The WCTU worked in cooperation with the Anglo-Indian Temperance Association, founded in 1888 by the Reverend W. S. Caine.[63] Tours of India by Slack and others were conducted as much under the Anglo-Indian temperance organization's auspices as those of the WCTU itself. But the role of the WCTU remains an almost totally neglected aspect of the historical development of Indian cultural nationalism. The WCTU was, unlike most Indian temperance associations, organized throughout India, and its non-denominational stance encouraged the bridging of social and racial barriers. American missionaries in Burma testified to the important role of the WCTU, and the same was true of parts of the Punjab where Jeanette Hauser, an American missionary and Indian WCTU president in the early 1890s, had been especially active. There, and in the United Provinces, an impressive network of societies had been established by 1919, and not only involving women. Throughout India, the WCTU realized that it must appeal to men as well as women and consequently organized Bands of Hope, student temperance associations, and men's temperance societies in many towns penetrated by Christian missionaries.[64]

Indian nationalists took up elements of the WCTU's antiimperialist critique as a means to revitalize traditional culture. The nationalist themes of unity and moral regeneration were articulated by the indigenous supporters of the temperance movement in India. Men like Sir Bhalchandra Krishna, president of the Bombay Temperance Council, made this point that "the temperance movement [was] the only common platform" for the diverse castes and religions represented in the presidency, when he spoke at a rally in support of Slack late in 1907.[65] Soon, in the aftermath of World War I, the theme of nationalism would be explicitly fused in the Gandhian movement with that of religious purification. To Gandhi and his followers, drink was "Western" in origin, just as the missionaries and the WCTU had insisted. Before the coming of Europeans, so the nationalist propaganda of the interwar period went, few Indians had been prepared morally to defend the custom of drinking. Like the missionaries, too, Gandhi deliberately understated the importance of "native drinks."[66]

But the nationalist attack on drink differed from that of the missionaries in its attention to the cultural roots of an indigenous antialcohol movement. The denial of drink involved a renunciation of the West, not just the most obvious examples of immoral practices identified by Indians with European colonialism. Prohibition was "not merely an economic or moral question. It [was] a question of deep religious and cultural significance." Indian nationalists wanted "to be true" to their "Indian culture which has always forsworn drink."[67]

The response of the WCTU to this turn of events was mixed. Some of the older missionaries and World's WCTU officials matched their delight at the promise of a genuine moral uplift with fear of the possible collapse of British authority. Margaret Denning, Indian WCTU president during the First World War, spoke uneasily at the time of the riots in Amritsar of the possible threat to British rule if the use of alcohol among Indians spread. "The handful of Europeans would melt as snow before the hordes. Of course we are sure that in the end the British forces would triumph, but in the meantime how much of a setback would be given to culture, to education, to Christianity itself[?]"[68] Like many others, including Slack, Denning found it difficult to foresee that the moral uplift of the Indian people could occur without permanent British tutelage. It was only gradually recognized in the WCTU, therefore, that the "unrest" might stem in large part from a movement of *indigenous* moral regeneration.

This void in the moral perceptions of some WCTU women had its roots in the historic dilemma of the missionary under the raj. Caught between the imperial authority on which they depended to spread their moral message and the rejection of that authority by sections of the Indian masses, they tended to oscillate uneasily. Criticism of the imperial policies, which undermined the moral probity of Western and hence, implicitly, Christian action, gave way at times of crises to recognition that only through a Western paternal domination could their message get through at all. Since the liquor problem had been defined as a case of Western exploitation of inferior races, only strong Western guidance could save the easterner and humanity as a whole. This stance meant a rock-bottom reliance on the strength of imperial authority, even though Christian reformers provided Indians with insights into aspects of the West's moral weakness.[69]

The World's WCTU had not been helped in this dilemma by its prewar reliance on British support to make a worldwide temperance movement even a plausible fiction. Thus the American WCTU women, who tended to be those most critical of British deviousness on the subject of the international trade in drugs, had to contend with the opinions of colonials. New South Wales's Sara Nolan told her rank and file in 1912 that "British rule has ever aimed at the protection of the weaker races, and we know that no other country can rule over the weaker peoples with as much leniency and justice."[70] Nolan was especially concerned to make clear the need for an assertion of imperial power as an answer to the "unrest" already evident in India in 1911. This was also the position of Slack, and even the more radical Balgarnie held out the possibility that if the Indian government ceased to rely on the excise revenue and applied its taxation to "good ends" like education, the Indian people would cease complaining.[71] The onus was still on the West to lead the moral reformation.

These prewar illusions ought to have been shattered by postwar events. In a sense they were, for the tenor of observations changed with Emma S. Price's appointment as Indian WCTU president in 1920. This American Methodist missionary was well aware of the potential of a nationalist movement that effected a cultural revitalization. She noted the "growing self-consciousness and aspiration toward nationalism" that was producing "a social conscience such as she [India] has never had before." Price found in the antialcohol movement, which united "many different communities," the basis of "the uplift of India" and recognized that this sentiment drew on the religious inheritance of the Islamic, Hindu, and Sikh peoples.[72]

While this statement echoed prewar observations, Price and her new executive went further. Jane Clemes, another Methodist missionary and secretary of the Indian WCTU, proclaimed starkly, "It is a recognized fact that Europeans in India will never bring about prohibition. Indians must do it."[73] Price agreed, and linked India's rejuvenation with the coming of democracy and attendant social upheaval of a progressive kind. "India's progress in temperance," she assured Indian temperance women in 1922, "is quite in harmony with that in other parts of the world, only more rapid than in some other lands." This perception linked the emergence of prohibitionism as a mass force in India with the notion of an international "new democratic age" that would "not unprotestingly suffer longer at the hands of big business and vested interests; the sovereign people [were] coming to the throne, and to realise that what should be done can be done; and institutions, old or new, must prove their right to stand, or they must go down."[74]

This linking of the prohibition cause with democratic themes of American progressivism was implicitly corrosive of British rule, a fact reinforced by the WCTU's publication of temperance and nationalist propaganda by Indian activists like Taraknath Das. American temperance women learned in 1921 from the pages of the *Union Signal* that the prohibition movement in India was one of "National Purification" designed "to make the people more capable of carrying on their struggle for independence." Das was later jailed for sedition, and with the declaration of martial law by the British in 1922, reports from India assumed a more cautious and apolitical tone. To have openly endorsed the actions of Indian nationalists, or even to have printed their now outlawed propaganda, would have been to set the women's temperance societies in India in direct defiance of British policy, which by no means accepted the notion of democracy for India at this time.[75]

If the WCTU appeared at this point to throw off its patronizing cast of thought, the desire to exploit the Indian prohibition movement for other purposes remained supreme. The Indian WCTU's postwar effort to encourage indigenous temperance received a stern rebuff from Slack and Rosalind Carlisle, who considered that Price and missionary Mary Campbell were dabbling too much in non-Christian work.[76] This position was reinforced by the whole thrust of the WCTU's propaganda and policies on an international level, which sought increasingly in the 1920s to assimilate the Indian movement to a universalistic theme under an American ideological leadership. To be sure, Gandhi's attacks on alcohol appeared in highlighted form in the *Union Signal*, and his name graced the World's WCTU conventions. For his part, Gandhi was mildly interested in the fate of American prohibition, but it was too late to build an alliance, if ever it had been possible, with his own brand of nationalism. Gandhi's message to the World's convention in 1928, solicited by the World's organization, emphasized the "study [of] the facts about every country in which a temperance movement is being carried on by them and then and not till then may they expect a proper solution." For Gandhi this empirical study would have a nationalist, not an internationalist, implication since he emphasized that "total prohibition in India is impeded not by the people but by the policy of the existing Government."[77]

Given the knowledge of popular opposition to prohibition in the United States, Gandhi's advice contained a none too subtle message that reversed the question of moral leadership. In America, it was the people who impeded prohibition; in India, a foreign government. The WCTU had little option but to ignore his pointed counsel to them that "many movements of reform lack" the "simple foundation of facts" concerning the country to be studied, since such advice highlighted cultural variation rather than the universalistic theme of an American moral hegemony. The *Union Signal*'s correspondents who visited Gandhi in India and reported back to Evanston dwelt upon the solidarity of Indian nationalism with the worldwide prohibitionist struggle led by the United States.[78] By the early 1930s, the WCTU was merely interested, as its depiction of Gandhi's statements on American prohibition indicated, in using the mahatma's testimony to shore up prohibition in the United States. That is to say, these two manifestations of prohibition in the international arena were so vastly different that their representatives could only talk at one another.

Did all this mean that the efforts of Price and those who had gone before her had been in vain? Women's temperance reformers in India had failed to make the WCTU or any other vehicle of Western temperance principles the representative of colonial opinion but had, with their male counterparts, stimulated social currents in indigenous society and so contributed to the emergence of the very nationalism they had only partly comprehended. The various British administrations professed desires for reform, but their policies were fundamentally conservative ones that sought power and profits through support for the status quo. As Kenneth Ballhatchet points out, the position of the missionaries was different because they needed to overthrow traditions and breach the social and racial barriers to reap converts among the indigenous populations. They, not the British administration, proved to be the most effective agents for the introduction of modernizing and revitalizing impulses despite their ambiguous relationship with imperial rule. This was especially true of American missionaries. American women "often find it easier," concluded William T. Stead perceptively in his 1902 publication, *The Americanization of the World*, "to win the confidence of the people among whom they labour" because they were not regarded as representatives of the British government.[79]

The temperance missionary's message, however, only had this positive effect in those cultural and social contexts that were conducive to the themes of purity and bodily control. Though the WCTU raged more loudly at the undoubtedly more socially disruptive effects of alcohol in Africa than in the Indian case, and though Wallace Mills shows temperance to be a source of proto-nationalist sentiment in southern Africa as well, only in India did WCTU concerns effectively touch the power of cultural tradition. All of the rhetoric and institutional manipulation in the world did not allow the WCTU to win its goal of a dry Africa or even to witness the emergence of a nationalist movement deeply committed to prohibition. The trade in spirits frequently provided a much larger proportion of revenues in West Africa than in the Indian Empire. In southern Nigeria, the alcohol excise provided between 53 and 61 percent of government finances before World War I, more than double the Indian maximum. But the role of liquor did

Alcohol and Empire

not become an important part of the nationalist movement's ideology in Nigeria, where fear of alternative taxes overwhelmed, for the middle classes that led the early nationalist agitation, any purely moral scruples.[80]

Instead, the WCTU had been forced to rely there and in the Pacific on a more elitist policy of international manipulation. Measured in international treaties, this strategy had been partially successful. Some representatives of temperance opinion pointed to falling consumption in areas where treaties had been introduced. In both East and West Africa, noted Ernest Cherrington's *Standard Encyclopedia of the Alcohol Problem*, 1923 imports were well below prewar levels, but the conclusion that the Native Races and Liquor Traffic United Committee and its members should be credited with this change is dubious. As the committee's own statistician, Alexander Blackburn, explained, the decline in consumption was almost entirely a result of the wartime disruptions to European trade. Postwar academic studies pointed to evasion of duties and increased consumption as economic conditions returned to "normal."[81]

The international temperance movement's inability to effect any long-term reduction in the European liquor trade in Africa illustrated the need for strong nationalist allies. Even the convention agreed to at Saint Germain in 1919, which capped a thirty-year consideration of the problem of imported European spirits, merely "eliminated"—and then, in reality, only partially—the cheapest types of imported spirits amid immense wrangling and jockeying for the advantages of trade. The WCTU rejoiced that most of formerly "wet" Africa was now dry, but Africa was never really dry, only partly damp. The agreement of 1919 had so many exceptions in its text that international commerce could still negotiate the gaping holes.[82] The same denouement had already occurred in the opium issue. Though the WCTU railed against opium for almost thirty years, only the Chinese revolution of 1911 produced a concerted and committed effort on the part of the British government to end the opium monopoly.[83] Imperial administrators did not listen seriously to women reformers, or even to their male counterparts, when these well-intentioned people spoke on behalf of the colonized; they did listen when the subject peoples spoke for themselves.

8

Peace as a Way of Life

Of all the diverse crusades the WCTU embraced in the 1880s, none had such immediate international relevance as peace. Peace between nations entailed a commitment to international cooperation and understanding. Peace could, under these circumstances, be a powerful vehicle for criticism of the nation state and its operation. In an era of imperial expansion, the need for arbitration between nations was a pressing one, but to advocate the peaceful settlement of international difficulties risked identification in the minds of more simplistic patriots with the nation's enemies. By the same token, to advocate peace involved, under certain circumstances, a critique of imperialism itself, where national aggrandizement depended, as it usually did, on the military subjugation of colonial peoples. Inexorably, the WCTU found itself drawn by its peace commitments into these controversies and faced the charge of unpatriotic behavior. The irony was that the WCTU's own definition of peace depended on and actually advanced notions of cultural imperialism.

C. Roland Marchand makes the generally valid point that "the participation in and support of the peace movement by many . . . women's organizations" was "often merely pro forma and lacking in commitment."[1] If this were true of the WCTU's efforts in the international arena, then studying the contribution of women's temperance reformers to the peace movement would make little sense. There was indeed no need for grass-roots financial support for the peace movement, since a handful of wealthy and committed activists were willing to take so much of the work upon themselves. But these peace reformers in the WCTU did succeed in organizing peace departments in a large number of states and were able to use the organizational clout and numerical strength of the WCTU to push the cause of peace in ways far from nominal in their levels of commitment. By 1894, just seven years after inception of the work, twenty-four states and the District of Columbia had been organized, though only seventeen of these reported to national superintendent Hannah Clark Bailey that year. By 1916, thirty-three states were organized with twenty-two reporting, and by 1921, thirty-five states were involved. This must be contrasted and compared with other departments. Temperance and labor, which has received much more attention from historians, could rarely manage more than fifteen or sixteen states reporting, and even the incontestably more important purity departments only had between twenty-five and thirty-two states reporting over the same period.

Though no other country matched the size of the American women's effort, peace work was undertaken in some twenty-seven countries under WCTU auspices by 1907. As in other aspects of the women's temperance crusade, the strongest response to the peace department, outside the United States, came from Australasia, Canada, Britain, and Scandinavia. In the missionary arena, too, peace was preached, and especially in Japan did WCTU women demonstrate the abhorrence of non-Western women for war. But non-American work in this field was overshadowed through most of the World's WCTU's history to an extent rare in other aspects of the Do-Everything policy. The strength of the American personnel involved, the complications of empire for Japanese, British, and colonial women, and the power of the ideology of domesticity made American developments of unusual importance.[2]

Peace work was not only of respectable size; it was also growing from the 1880s to the First World War. Pro-peace resolutions were persistently passed by National WCTU conventions, and petitions were gathered containing many thousands of signatures. There was no decline in peace activity by these measurements after Willard's departure. Indeed, the reality of war with Spain in 1898 gave an emotional intensity to the work that was only broken by the failure of Wilson to keep the republic out of the European conflict in 1917. Though peace was clearly not embraced with enthusiasm by every WCTU member, a majority of WCTU women seem to have found its values fairly central to WCTU ideology. Frank L. Byrne can claim with some justice that, for the pre-World War I period, Hannah Bailey orchestrated what was "the greatest women's peace movement of the nineteenth and early twentieth centuries."[3]

To understand the depth of the WCTU's commitment to the peace crusade, one must realize that for temperance women, peace was an extension of the culture they had created from evangelicalism and domesticity. Peace meant more than an absence of war. In contrast to the more specialized groups devoted today to stopping the spread of nuclear weapons, or the activities of bureaucratic organizations specifically constructed to manage tensions from above, the WCTU envisaged peace as a way of life.

The WCTU's peace crusade began not in the mind of Frances Willard but among the rank and file, with the creation of a state superintendency in Ohio in 1885. Two years later, the Ohio WCTU persuaded Willard to organize peace nationally, using as her superintendent Hannah Bailey.[4] Though many others contributed to the development of peace programs in the

WCTU, Bailey served as national superintendent for thirty years and also directed the World's WCTU branch from its inception in 1889 until 1920. A forty-eight-year-old former schoolteacher from Winthrop Center, Maine, Bailey was ideally suited to the new job.[5] Not only was she a Quaker with excellent connections to the Friends' own peace agitation, but her husband, a prominent manufacturer, had died in 1882 leaving her as probably the wealthiest woman in Maine. (Her brother-in-law, who had been in partnership with Moses Bailey, her husband, was said to be worth $10 million, and Maine's richest citizen.) Independently wealthy as few WCTU women were, and without dependent children, Bailey was thus able to devote considerable personal resources to her chosen cause. Nor was she a retiring housewife. She managed her late husband's business affairs aggressively and successfully and, in addition to peace work, was also active in a variety of other reform efforts, including suffrage, foreign missions, and penal reform.[6]

Peace for Bailey had roots in the Quaker tradition, and at first her movement represented an application of the Do-Everything policy to the issue that mattered most to many Quaker women in the WCTU organization, not just to Bailey. Mary Woodbridge, who had started the movement in Ohio, was that state's most prominent WCTU figure of Quaker persuasion. Quakers like Bailey and Woodbridge preached "the Golden Rule" and rejected all violence, not merely state-imposed warfare.[7] "To voluntarily take human life" was, said Bailey, "over-stepping the bounds of human authority."[8] Men and women should be allowed to live out their appointed days without the outrageous intervention of human will. Bailey stressed the role of Jesus as peacemaker and linked, in Quaker fashion, the inner peace of a spiritual and pure life with the abolition of wars on an international scale. In place of the Old Testament notion of an eye for an eye, Jesus had enjoined a religion of humility and benevolence. "Warfare" was "a sin forbidden under the New Testament teachings," she always insisted.[9] The surest way to achieve peace was, therefore, to accept the truth of Christ's teachings. To those who said pragmatism and national interests derived from the past made war inevitable, Bailey looked to a Christian future. "If Christians will adhere to the peace principles which are inseparable from the Christian religion, warfare will cease." As part of this confident prediction, Bailey spoke in millenarian terms of the time when "the joyful notes of the peacemakers who shall inherit the earth shall be heard, and over all shall be the smile of God."[10]

This millenarianism tied her ideology to that of the WCTU, but Bailey did not put the attainment of a Christian religion before the struggle for peace. Both should go on simultaneously. Bailey conceded that many "professing Christians" did not always obey the "divine plan for righteous living." This point was brought home with painful detail in the First World War, though Christian shortcomings were also apparent long before.[11] It was necessary to reform the churches and Christians as well as to convert others, and much of Bailey's struggle was taken up with obtaining what she regarded as a proper interest in peace within the WCTU and the churches.

Bailey's Quaker sincerity and religiosity were only one-half of the WCTU's peace ideology. The other and connected part concerned the role of women. Women were, peace advocates repeated in the proportions of an immense cliché, especially suited to the work of peace. Men were the makers of war, and women the sufferers. This timeless message, still heard on Greenham Common, had a powerful appeal to WCTU women, schooled as they were in the moral superiority of women, and the ideology of domesticity. Women were said to be more peacelike for several reasons. The religious example in which the women were "last at the cross and earliest at the grave" of Jesus linked the role of women in peace with evangelical religion.[12] But much more than religious training was involved. According to some recent historians of the women's movement, peace activists in the late nineteenth and early twentieth centuries believed that peace and women went together for biological reasons. At times the WCTU did give substance to the idea that women were biologically programmed for peace. In the aftermath of the Great War, the role of women as producers of sons and, therefore, as natural opponents of war drew support, for example, from the National WCTU's new peace superintendent Lella Dillard.[13]

The major emphasis was different, however. Women were seen more realistically by temperance women as both purveyors of war and promoters of peace. Bailey noted how women rulers and schemers in history had been directly responsible for many wars or had cheered on the males who started them. History was, insisted Bailey, "teeming with instances, where woman has been a prime factor in inciting wars." Bailey reached back into antiquity, citing the examples of Cleopatra, that "queen of battles," and Helen of Troy, "the direct cause of the long Trojan War." Nor was the murderous instinct found only in "women of nobility," since "the sisters, wives and mothers of common soldiers" had "considered it an honor to send their dear ones to the cannon's mouth."[14] Indeed, the women of contemporary times still exerted grievous influence by instilling in their children an unthinking patriotism that was "synonomous" with "military glory."[15]

For these reasons, woman's nature was never sufficient. The molding power of environment and correct teaching could make women a force for good or for evil. These influences were, however, not interpreted in an arbitrary way isolated from larger issues of power and ideology; the role of women in the peace movement was slotted into and made intelligible by a reading of the sweep of human history common in late Victorian society. Willard, in particular, propounded an evolutionist view in which the concepts of civilization and savagery were linked to the emancipation of women. In an analysis obviously dependent on widely disseminated Victorian concepts of progress, Willard described the course of human history as an evolution from force to reason. Men had, in primitive times, seized control of production and monopolized force. They had restricted women to the castle or the fortified town because this was the best place for women to be in an era of brute force. But within the home, women, deprived of the use of force by their inferior strength and by sexual politics, had evolved into peacemaking creatures. If in the era "of force, of war, and pioneering," violence had been necessary to the subjugation of nature, the development of material prosperity and a more complex civilization had rendered coercion no longer functional.[16]

Indeed, the expansion of the means of force had ensured that violence would be, in future, counterproductive to increasingly "peaceful, homelike communities."[17] In the new stage of a more creative evolution, Willard proclaimed, women would use their skills as peacemakers to pacify the world and to change the natures of men. This was already happening, Willard believed. In her exposition of the "new chivalry," she emphasized the benefits of changing notions of masculinity for peace as well as for gender relations. When she sang the praises of the new social type of "homely men" with their "delicacy" and "brotherly considerateness" that was "the outcome of their nurture," Willard anticipated a new cultural force. Such enlightened men (and women) would through reform agitation and international conciliation eradicate all war.[18]

The environmental influence that conditioned women's superior sense of peace in the modern age was, above all, the experience of domesticity. Against the militaristic values they saw all around them, temperance women pitted the peaceful influence of "the Home." The importance attached to domesticity indicated that peace was not simply an absence of war, nor was war simply an unfortunate extension of diplomacy or politics. Rather, the prevalence of war could be traced deeply to the conditions of everyday life; if peace were to prevail, then these patterns of human conditioning, and not just the superficial causes of wars, must be confronted. Women were, according to Bailey, those best equipped to tackle militarism at its sources in the human character, because domestic training had given the female of the species special conciliatory skills. She told the Lake Mohonk Peace Conference in 1895 that it was "part of the duty of a mother" to "make peace in her family where contentions exist, or, better still, to prevent them by timely care."[19] This was not an original idea. Frances Willard had told the National WCTU convention the previous year that women had "the finest qualities of diplomacy." For "unnumbered centuries," women had "been the chief member of a board of conciliation in the home, hearing complaints, adjusting differences, forming treaties of peace, administering justice, and ointing the machinery with patience and goodwill."[20] This view did not, like those of some other advocates of women's special moral role, depict the home simply as an arena of natural harmony. Bailey and Willard both recognized the existence of conflicting interests within the family and presented a more realistic picture of managed and conciliated strife.[21]

But women were expected not merely to manage strife within the home; they were also expected to use the domestic arena to produce changes in human character. Since evolution, not biology, had made women moral, the same evolutionary forces could be seized by feminists to forge a higher and more pacific human future in which women would lead men to peace by example, motherly training, education, and political influence.

The role of women in the peace crusade therefore began at the cradle. They alone could at this evolutionary stage make peace not simply a reform movement, but a way of life. Hannah Bailey emphasized in her work the importance of an early peace education. In line with the WCTU's motherly ideology, she focused on the training of small children in the ways of peace. Militaristic toys were condemned because they etched warlike sentiments deep in the psyche. "One of the first steps towards bringing about a cessation of warfare is to keep the children from a love of military pursuits and this can never be accomplished so long as they are supplied with military toys." Bailey wrote to toy manufacturers to try to persuade them they could make a sizable contribution to world progress by encouraging pacifistic toys. To the argument that this would bring financial ruin, Bailey urged substitution of "representations of the life saving services," such as "fire brigades."[22]

In schools, Bailey campaigned against military drills for the same reason, because these legitimized warlike activity as part of national patriotism. She was particularly active in protesting against the use of militaristic procedures in boys brigades that had sprung up as adjuncts of some of the Protestant churches. This deeply offended her Quaker religious convictions. From 1889 to 1901 Bailey edited for young people a special publication called *The Acorn*, in which the ways of peace were taught through children's stories. In addition the WCTU tried to create, as in other areas of policy, an alternative culture through the creation of the rituals of peace in everyday life. Observation of Hague Day, commemorating the international arbitration conferences, was promoted in schools, while Peace Day was also instituted in WCTU locals, and prizes were given for essays on subjects such as disarmament and arbitration.[23] In addition, the WCTU sponsored its own lecturers, beginning with leading WCTU official Mary Woodbridge, and the organization had ten in the field in the early 1890s, pushing the message of peace in the churches and communities.[24]

Because peace was envisaged as a holistic strategy, the department's work embraced the issues of labor conflict, antilynching, boxing, and arbitration as well as the more conventional aspects of the peace issue, though the related subject of cruelty toward animals was not only agitated in the peace department but also in a specialized Department of Mercy. Mercy superintendent Mary F. Lovell of Philadelphia made a point of attacking blood sports and prize fights for promoting the brutalization of humanity. Her work had an interesting and enlightening international twist, since it both reflected and helped promote American attitudes that were tinged with cultural imperialism. In 1896, Lovell put together a petition to the pope, protesting the failure of the Catholic church to oppose the gore of bull-fights in Spain. Lovell did not conceive this as purely an isolated issue of individual conscience. To the mind of a WCTU woman schooled in the principles of a gentle "homelike" influence, the coarseness inherent in the spectacle of bullfighting bore its final fruit in the inhumanity of Spain's army in Cuba. "If they [the Spaniards] had been trained in their youth to be gentle and merciful instead of being amused by witnessing the torture of bulls," the world would probably not be witnessing "its legitimate results" in the "horrors" committed "under the command of General Weyler," Lovell righteously concluded.[25]

Peace and mercy agitation was aimed not so much at suppressing immoral behavior as at promoting a more positive and productive morality. As mothers of the sons who went to war, temperance women did not dwell upon the "cruelties" or "horrors" of war. They did not attempt, in the manner of contemporary antinuclear activists, to shock the electorate into supporting peace by presenting alternatives too terrifying to contemplate. Instead they looked to longer-term strategies and stressed that "women can do much in training their children." With antimilitaristic influences ascendant in the home, "in the next generation the world will be at peace."[26]

This grass-roots approach necessarily involved the WCTU with other antiwar organizations that could disseminate peace principles and mobilize public opinion. In this way, the WCTU's efforts went beyond the temperance movement itself. Bailey used her Quaker connection to lobby other peace groups for support and to work with them to influence government policy. Bailey was on good terms with Lucia Ames Mead, the foremost women's peace activist of the pre–World War I period. Mead lectured, with Bailey's support, before local WCTUs, and her addresses were regularly reprinted in the *Union Signal*.[27] Bailey was also a founding member of the Woman's Peace party in 1915 and supported the Women's International League for Peace and Freedom after World War I.[28] This cooperative strategy was far from new and in fact went back to the beginnings of the WCTU peace crusade in 1889 when Anna Braithwaite Thomas, a leading Quaker activist in Maryland, was chosen as a WCTU representative at the First Universal Peace Congress held in Paris, and the WCTU was represented again in 1890 in London and in 1893 in Chicago.[29] In 1893, a committee of peace society delegates was chosen to lobby the American government "for a permanent treaty of arbitration" with Britain. Bailey was one of three women among the eleven delegates.[30] Bailey also wrote letters to senators, congressmen, and even, in 1916, President Wilson concerning issues of war and peace, lobbying for WCTU support, for example, of the Hague Peace Conference in 1899 and against United States military preparedness during and after World War I.[31] In doing so, she cooperated with other participants in the women's and peace movements, such as Caroline Severance of Los Angeles and May Wright Sewell.[32]

This lobbying activity was often unsuccessful; congressmen like Frederick Hale of Maine in 1919 displayed obvious irritation that Bailey could not understand how warlike and heavily armed other nations were and argued, therefore, that "we [the United States] cannot have too much preparedness." The American delegation to the first Hague conference in 1899 also displayed annoyance in private concerning what they believed was the naive lobbying of the pacifist groups, but the organizational help of the WCTU was useful in getting the Hague convention ratified by the United States Senate.[33]

The Achilles' heel in this peace program was the absence of suffrage. Women could petition, but they could not actually affect the size of military budgets. That in no way vitiated their campaigns, from Bailey's viewpoint, but merely demonstrated the many disabilities women suffered. Thus did the peace crusade link up with the WCTU's emphasis on equality of status for women in the public sphere. Bailey spent much of whatever spare time she had lecturing on "How Woman's Ballot Can Help the Peace Department."[34] With the vote, there would be "no need of [peace] petitions. A few women in our legislative halls would find a better use of our money than to invest it in instruments of destruction," she felt sure. Bailey also made the point that with the ballot, women would take more interest in the cause of peace than they currently did. In so doing, she implicitly admitted that women were not as strongly identified with the peace movement as its ideology sometimes has suggested.[35] Bailey also put her ideas into practice by leading, for a time, the suffrage fight in her home state as president of the Maine Woman Suffrage Association from 1891 to 1897. When women in the United States did finally get the vote, Bailey's successor superintendents Alice Kercher and Lella Dillard threatened that women now had "the ballot in our hands," which they would use "to avert war" and "bring in the reign of reason."[36]

In assessing the impact—and the limitations—of this WCTU peace ideology, comparisons with the larger peace movement are inevitable. The WCTU's own antiwar agitation tended at times to reflect the arguments commonly used in the American peace crusade of the period 1890–1914. Bailey and her cohorts were not ordinary women, but within the ranks of peace activists, much of their stock ideology was the epitome of ordinariness. Like their colleagues so ably portrayed by David Patterson in *Toward a Warless World*, WCTU peace workers were often confused, sometimes contradictory, and ineffectual. They filtered and fostered the predominantly Waspish, middle-class, and morally conservative attitudes of late nineteenth-century opponents of war in the United States.[37]

But some elements did distinguish the temperance contribution, if only in matters of emphasis. Their advocacy of women's role and the social gospel enabled the WCTU to transcend the label of social conservatism at times and to offer some novel and potentially radical solutions to international problems. Their emphasis as early as the 1890s on arbitration was by no means unique, but effective and important. There the connection of peace with their own cultural attitudes and class experience shone forth and enabled women of the WCTU to offer realistic tactics in support of peace that have since become divorced from the moral and evangelical context within which they were initially promoted. "Arbitration" was not something only or even especially designed for international conflict as far as temperance women were concerned. Rather, its advocacy grew out of their daily experience and their temperance ideology. WCTU resolutions on the peace issue always coupled international conciliation of disputes between nations with the settlement of labor problems—the class war at home—by means of boards of arbitration. Again, Willard foresaw a special role for women in this process of conciliation. At the 1894 National WCTU Convention, she urged the appointment of women to all boards of labor arbitration, because of the practical skills women had in the management of tensions in family life.[38]

Bailey was a classic advocate of arbitration systems, not only because they enforced peace, but also because her class experience conveyed to her a sense of the irrationality of labor conflict. She expressed the American middle-class distrust of monopolies with their "greed of gain." She advocated enlightened cooperation between employer and employee. As an employer of labor herself, she witnessed and indeed aided the implementation of an arbitration system in her own state of Maine and saw such boards of conciliation as means of settling the class war and hence preventing the advent of socialism.[39] Bailey took from her husband's business the attitude toward labor relations best described as an enlightened paternalism. The Baileys' oilcloth making business did not tolerate tardy or intemperate employees, but the Baileys also had a reputation for paying their workers well, and for making those little concessions that could sometimes smooth over the troubled waters of industrial disputation. For example, her brother-in-law and business associate, Charles M. Bailey, had the custom of presenting to each employee at Thanksgiving "a large, fat turkey for his family," and he always paid his employees overtime for the Saturday shifts he insisted upon. Self-made entrepreneurs like the Baileys, who still managed their businesses themselves, could, from their parochial and regional standpoints, abhor the incessant battle of capital and labor and condemn both trade unions and the vast corporations that waged such dire struggles in the national arena.[40]

This connection of labor with peace reflected a basically conservative hostility to social conflict, though it embodied criticism of rapacious capitalists at home and abroad and acknowledged the rights of labor. The notion that it was greed on the part of either capital or labor that stood in the way of interclass harmony could be taken into the international realm, and it was by Bailey and her co-workers. Mae Whitman, superintendent of the Department of Temperance and Labor in 1909, argued that "commerce and competition have furnished the incentive for the larger part of the world's war for conquest."[41] Labor sympathizers in the WCTU could go further than this and look toward the internationalism of the labor movement as a countervailing pressure. Whitman imagined, as did many socialists at the time, a potentially progressive outcome to this struggle, for "as brotherhoods increase among organized workmen in all lands, world-wide peace will be established by their refusal to fight one another." "Wage-workers" were among those, she frankly admitted, most deeply interested in peace because they had "furnished the victims of war."[42] In this way the contradictory elements she correctly depicted in the international economic system would ultimately be resolved in a natural process of evolution.

This quasi-socialist analysis derived from the golden rule fed the WCTU's peace crusade, but only as one of a number of conflicting sentiments. Christian socialism of the WCTU variety was inclined to depict the solution to strife between the classes, and the nations, as involving a change of heart. The existence of irreconcilable differences was hardly understood, and the lion and the lamb were expected to lie down together. Collectivist attitudes derived from a reading of Edward Bellamy or other socialist writers were grafted onto a tradition of pacifism derived from nineteenth-century liberal-individualism.

For this reason, WCTU attitudes toward economic expansionism were ambiguous. Mae Whitman's sympathies for labor did not prevent her from depicting the global expansion of industry as "links in the chain" of international organization "binding civilization with common interests." Certainly, the unholy spectacle of conquest for booty was condemned, implicitly, along with militaristic imperialism and war profiteering. Mary Garbutt, peace superintendent in California during the First World War, carried this theme even further and linked the European conflagration, as did other American socialists and radicals, with economic gain. Garbutt persuaded the Southern California WCTU to condemn in 1914 "certain great industrial corporations [which] for the sake of financial gain may at any time seek to imbroil our country in this war" and pushed through a resolution against the shipment of goods, especially arms, to the belligerents.[43]

For a radical like Garbutt, whose connections were with the American Socialist party and who had numbered Jack London among her friends, economic imperialism was still defined in narrow if evocative terms as the offspring of speculation. Economic expansionism, notwithstanding its connection at times with a degree of political coercion that was unmistakable, did not receive anything other than praise. The Panama Canal she endorsed as "that wonderful piece of constructive work" that would bring "the ends of the earth together in closer bonds of brotherhood." The circumstances under which the canal was built brought no comment. Garbutt remained true to her convictions that commerce was naturally pacific, but she was mindful, too, that militaristic motives could pervert its benign promise. Thus for her, the role of the peace crusade in the WCTU was not simply to celebrate the positive benefits of commerce but to ensure through moral pressure and mass action that commerce was kept on its productive course. The redoubtable California agitator led a vocal campaign against the fortification of the canal and in favor of the erection of a peace statue at its entrance.[44] With tireless work from Garbutt's friends in the Socialist party, women's clubs, and peace movement, and with WCTU and church support, over 2 million American women had (unsuccessfully) endorsed this proposal in petitions to Congress by the time the United States entered the world war.[45]

Garbutt and Whitman represented the leftist, pro-socialist element in the WCTU, and they carried the critique of greed much further than Bailey did in her initial formulation of WCTU peace ideology in the 1890s. Like them, Bailey had made a crucial distinction between militarism and peaceful economic expansionism, but unlike her younger colleagues whose views took shape in the era of corporate consolidation and global military conflict, Bailey did not conceive of commerce as anything other than pacific. In this way she was a truer representative of the nineteenth-century peace tradition and closer to the mainstream of WCTU thinking. War was seen purely as an obstacle to economic prosperity by Bailey and not as its adjunct or its cause. Rather, she stressed the atavistic impulses of militarism: the product of "the dark and bloody ages of the past," as she told the World's WCTU's first convention in Boston in 1891. War she depicted, as did many other nineteenth-century peace advocates, as entirely inappropriate to the new "twentieth century civilization" of "internationalism" and "the brotherhood of man" about to dawn.[46]

Under her leadership, the WCTU peace departments waxed lyrical at the improvement of international communications and technology, without appreciating the extent to which the very same technology allowed a more frightening military aggrandizement and a more systematic commercial penetration that could itself encourage military adventures. The Boer War was influenced by bold imperialists with their eyes firmly set upon the promise of gold and diamonds, Bailey conceded in condemning its bloodletting, but at the same time she found the root cause to be, as in the case of all wars, "mutual dislike and ignorance among nations."[47] Bailey condemned the Boxer Rebellion as an outrage upon civilization, without taking into account the relationship of its nativistic impulse to the penetration of Western capital and missionary influence. The Western military response she endorsed as evidence of increased "internationalism" because it represented the cooperation of the great powers on behalf of "the entire civilized world."[48] This was little different from the *Union Signal*'s own rationalization of the Boer War as an unpleasant and gory but nevertheless necessary response to Boer failure to civilize the land they claimed. "It is too late in the day," claimed the *Union Signal*, "for any people to appropriate any portion of the earth unless they are capable of setting up a government in accordance with nineteenth century ideas of right and justice."[49]

Nor did Bailey's assumption of steady moral progress to accompany pacific commercial expansion take into account the conflicts of interest that arose between European expansionism and indigenous peoples. With remarkable insensitivity, she endorsed around 1910 the view of William G. Hubbard, president of the American Peace Society, that the United States in the nineteenth century had achieved great material prosperity because it had experienced "a hundred years of almost unbroken peace." Not a word was uttered in this account of the wars of continental conquest or the very different interests of Mexicans or American Indians who suffered from American material progress and geographic expansionism.[50] Bailey seemed momentarily to have forgotten the broken treaties, which elsewhere offended her commitment to arbitration. In 1891, she had declared in the aftermath of Wounded Knee that "the quarrels and battles with the Indians in the United States" were "a disgrace to the civilization of this age."[51] But the WCTU's commitment to Indian reform, though not inconsiderable, was inconsistently divorced from its peace work, and Indian reformers of WCTU affiliation concentrated, like most others did, on themes of benevolent assimilation.[52] This left open the way for a peace reformer like Bailey to regard the treatment of the Indians as an unfortunate aberration in the progress of an increasingly benign American civilization.

As this case reveals, the peace policy of the WCTU was vulnerable to criticism because it was so transparently conditioned by culture and ideology. The WCTU championed the values of the home against those of militarism, but the home in question, Frances Willard made clear in 1887, was "the American home," which she felt was steadily beating back the "harem philosophies of Turkey" and other antiwoman cultures.[53] The home symbolized for Willard a cluster of interdependent values that tied the WCTU to the extension of Anglo-American power. The entire position of women was seen as indicative of a country's state of civilization, and in turn, civilization was said to be dependent on the overthrow of premodern and "barbaric" values of force and on their replacement by the values of commerce, which allowed women, the weaker sex, to prosper.[54] Evidence was found for this circular set of propositions. The ideology of domesticity had been more influential in the United States than anywhere else; the position of women was better; material progress compared favorably with aged Europe; and it was in America that the opposition to war was most pronounced. While warmongering by any nation deprived it, even the United States, of the title *civilized* in WCTU eyes, the whole idea of civilization as understood by the WCTU was a Western and particularly an American conception. Bailey saw the American WCTU's mission in 1891 as the export of peace to "the European countries, bound as they are by despotic militarism." In contrast, America was not one of the "military lands" but a democracy in which the "common people" could take up moral reforms and therefore implement peace.[55]

This affirmation of American uniqueness was tempered only by the suggestion that Britain, as another commercial nation, could slough off its militaristic atavism and, together with the great republic, lead the way to peace and to, in the cliché that neither Willard nor Bailey ever tired of, the "Parliament of Man, the Federation of the World."[56] Willard had already identified the WCTU abroad with success in Britain and its colonies, and Bailey built upon this assumption of an underlying coincidence of cultures and obligations. The Maine Quaker was, along with Willard and British colleagues like Agnes Slack, particularly anxious to achieve in the realm of practical policy arbitration between Britain and the United States in the 1890s. This emphasis was tied to a much larger and more complex cultural and political rapprochement between the elites of the two nations. The sentiments of Anglo-Saxon racial identity and cultural superiority among WCTU members were constituent parts of this process. Bailey wished to "lift the Anglo-Saxon race . . . to arbitration . . . and brotherly living" and by so doing, bring "all other races" to a level "worthy of a nineteenth-century civilization."[57] The *Union Signal* agreed that war between the United States and Britain would be "a disaster to humanity" because they were "the great missionary nations" whose "institutions offer the only visible hope for the solving of the social and economic problems of the age."[58]

The Anglo-American link compromised the WCTU's peace commitment even further. To the British and colonial WCTUs, peace was equated with a pax Britannia based firmly on British military superiority. In particular, the greater implication of British subjects in notions of formal empire confounded their opposition to militaristic expansion and so threatened the integrity of Bailey's worldwide crusade. The collision of international and British imperial objectives in the WCTU was most apparent in the case of the Australian colonies, where WCTU peace sentiment had a tone slightly different from that in the United States. Colonial women stressed the role of Britain's navy, in effect its military preparedness, in keeping the peace. "As a British nation we have been saved from any great war," said Sara Nolan in her presidential address to the Australian WCTU in 1912.[59] Despite her Quaker upbringing, these sentiments also affected World's WCTU official Hannah Smith when she moved to England. Both she and her daughter Mary Smith Costelloe had become, in Smith's words, "great jingoes" who cheered on "the victories of the English army in Egypt" in the 1890s. "It seems a dreadful thing for the English to go on continually conquering and subduing these wild tribes," she admitted, "but when one realizes how infinitely superior English rule is to the best of their own, one begins to think there may after all be a Divine plan in it."[60]

As Smith's astounding admission makes clear, the British and colonial connection implicated American women reformers in a world imperial strategy. Manifestly, the WCTU's deeply felt tradition of peace was severely tested in the process. Smith, Nolan, and a host of others came uncomfortably close to equating peace with an Anglo-American cultural hegemony backed by British military might. The New York WCTU could call upon "Queen Victoria . . . to use all honorable means to stop the War in South Africa," but in Canada, the war "roused [WCTU members] to fresh consciousness of the love and duties we owe to our Queen and country."[61] In southern Africa itself, the strongly pro-British WCTU saw the war as a means of bringing the wine-loving Dutch burghers to heel.[62] The Cape Colony's most prominent temperance woman, Emilie Solomon, even saw the extension of British power in South Africa as a means of extending prohibition of alcohol to the native races neglected by Afrikaners. Little wonder that the World's convention in Edinburgh in 1900 conspicuously failed to mention the peace issue among its resolutions, even though peace was a staple of international meetings.[63]

This cluster of values and experience ill-prepared the WCTU for the American republic's own adventures in militaristic imperialism. The circumstances of the war with Spain made opposition initially well-nigh impossible. The WCTU did not side with the more extreme pacifists but, through the *Union Signal*, joined in the widespread public praise of American heroism and moral motives. Drawing upon the rhetoric of mercy superintendent Mary Lovell, the *Signal* denounced Spain as a barbaric nation that deserved to be punished by a more civilized society for "unspeakable" outrages.[64] The military triumph also brought to the WCTU a temporary rush of patriotic blood. Dewey's achievement in defeating the Spanish navy in the Philippines the WCTU hailed as demonstrating "the qualities which go to make up the strength of the American character." These were "mechanical genius" and such virtues as "wisdom, courage . . . , faithfulness [and] patriotism."[65]

By 1900, as the effects of war lingered on, the WCTU joined the growing chorus of opposition to American military involvement. Bailey and her peace department were, to their credit, in the forefront of the peace groups opposing continuation of the military conflict in the Philippines. The WCTU's state peace departments circulated petitions condemning the "killing and destroying" of "the inhabitants of those islands, in order to bring them under subjection," as "unworthy of a Christian nation." Under the influence of state president Luella McWhirter, the Indiana WCTU petitioned President McKinley "in the name of Home and Humanity" to end "such anger and hatred and pitiless destruction."[66] This was an antiimperialism based on the pacifist strain in the WCTU's culture of domesticity. The *Union Signal*, in an editorial possibly written by Bailey and certainly reflecting her views, denounced the administration's talk of "civilized warfare" as a contradiction in terms, just as Andrew Carnegie did.[67] The American policy in the islands was, the WCTU in Colorado claimed, inconsistent with American policies of fair play and respect for the "equality of nations."[68]

With Panglossian assurance, Bailey concluded that the war had actually strengthened American pacifism by stimulating antiwar feeling, but within the WCTU these sentiments were complicated by other issues of policy. As the issue of social purity would demonstrate, antivice sentiments both gave sustenance to antiwar agitation and yet limited the longer-term, critical analysis of peace and war. Opposition to the war in the Philippines was complicated by the news that the American military presence was accompanied by all of the sinful practices the WCTU sought to stamp out in the continental United States. Thus opposition to war did not present a case of clear-cut pacifism, and antiimperialism after 1900 continued to be fed, for most temperance women, not by a critique of the economic and social order but by a revulsion against the moral excrescence of colonialism. In the hands of nationalist groups in various parts of the world, this Protestant critique derived from missionary analysis of imperialism was indeed an important component in the ultimate rejection of colonial rule.[69] But for antiimperialists in the metropolitan powers, such an analysis was vulnerable to reform of the imperial system and to calls for patriotism in time of war.

This is not to deny the power of a moral critique of imperialism for temperance women; indeed, it can be argued that only by identifying international questions with the progress of temperance and moral reform at home could the WCTU hope to make the internationalism of its elite a living commitment for ordinary members. In an ingenious analysis, the WCTU focused much of its ire on the military canteen in the Philippines. If the pun may be pardoned, this they conceived as a dry run for prohibition in the United States. Just as slavery extension in the 1850s had proven to be the cutting edge of the antislavery controversy, so too did the WCTU self-consciously hone policies for national consumption in the international arena and in the name of international sentiments of brotherly and sisterly love.[70]

Bailey's antiimperialism after 1900 was also fed by the sentiments of racial superiority implicit in her endorsement of Anglo-Saxon cooperation. The people of the Philippines were, she insisted, members of an inferior race, and in the possibility that they would become permanent American dependents or, worse still, citizens, she saw the full fruit of a pursuit of militaristic policies against the wishes of colonial peoples. "The social plane of the people . . . is at the lowest [level]. Their only wants realized by themselves consist of shelter, food, and enough clothing to partially cover themselves, and perhaps ornamental decorations for their almost nude bodies. Their moral status is unmistakable when we remember that the custom of cannibalism still prevails in many of the islands."[71] If this was an antiimperialist streak, Bailey's opposition to an empire in the Philippines was not of an attractive kind.

Nor were these views unusual in turn-of-the-century America, since historians have identified with great ease a racist tone in much of the antiimperialist movement.[72] But it is perhaps significant that Bailey kept these racial views, at least the more extreme version of them, to her own draft reports and private correspondence and focused her public criticism on the inhumanity of the imperialist policy and its denial of self-determination. The WCTU did not wish, because of its international aspirations and connections, to be identified as a racist organization. This much had been demonstrated in the 1890s when Willard had abandoned, with embarrassment, a weak antilynching resolution originally passed in 1894 at the National WCTU convention. She subsequently enforced a strong antilynching stance within the organization in response to pressure coming from the BWTA.[73] Moreover, the campaigning against lynching that Bailey and her Maine colleague Alice Douglas carried out as part of the peace work did attest to these aspirations for international brotherhood and sisterhood across racial boundaries.[74] Probably for this reason, Bailey kept to herself denunciations of "the cheap labor of the Philippines" and "the folly of sentimentality" involved in the idea of the assimilation of "an alien race."[75]

With the settlement of military conflict in the Philippines in 1902, the contradictions in the WCTU's peace policy gradually receded from view. Bailey could emphasize the positive gains in peace agitation, such as the number of states organized and the pages of literature circulated. But underlying difficulties remained. Few in the WCTU had objected to the annexation of Hawaii or Puerto Rico, and the banning of the military canteen and legalized vice in the Philippines removed even the moral basis of the critique that had dominated WCTU thinking in the first few years of the new century. The fulfillment of the commitment to give Cuba at least its nominal independence in 1902 reinforced the sense that right (that is, democratic) thinking had prevailed in government circles. Despite the Platt amendment, which compromised Cuban national status, the United States had completed, said the *Union Signal*, "a splendid bit of humane work."[76]

Would Frances Willard have acted differently? Would the gradual if subtle endorsement of pro-imperial policies have been avoided had the "great chieftain" survived beyond February 1898? Certainly it has been suggested that Willard would have been less "conservative."[77] But the entire context of the WCTU's peace ideology and the specific evidence as well refutes any such claim. Willard, it must always be remembered, was an enthusiastic supporter of imperial expansion in the 1890s. In 1893 she endorsed, through a *Union Signal* editorial, the view that in Hawaii as in India "the Caucasian race" must "dominate," and in 1897 she announced her attitudes toward the annexation of the Hawaiian Islands to Mary Whitney. "How greatly I hope that they will soon be annexed. It cannot be that our Government has so little common sense as to permit itself to lose a prize like that."[78] Nor would it be true to argue that the WCTU's concern with the by-products of imperial expansion *after 1900* was limited to trivial or narrow moral issues. The WCTU's concerns with imperial policy were always broad enough to encompass the moral legitimacy and efficacy of colonial rule, as the response between 1900 and 1902 indicates. For this reason, military expansion and the morality of imperial rule were indeed issues for the WCTU in relation to the Philippines, just as they were in other military conflicts that confronted the WCTU elsewhere in the world. Only the end of the Philippine war, and the assumption that American rule would be progressive and civilizing in its functions, allowed the evangelical consciences of peace advocates to be assuaged.

Once the military embarrassments had been resolved, American peace activists in the WCTU could, like other products of the era of late Victorian liberalism, wax lyrical at the progress of civilization once more. At the 1913 Brooklyn convention of the World's WCTU, Bailey reported to the assembled delegates that the outlook for peace had never been brighter. Peace societies had "of late been rapidly multiplying." Because the cost of armaments had become so cripplingly expensive, nations would soon see their folly. The world was "never so near as now to the glad day when the nations shall beat their swords into ploughshares." Her report was greeted with great rejoicing.[79]

Hardly had the rejoicing subsided when the outbreak of war in 1914 shattered the illusions of peace activists like Bailey and devastated hopes for a new internationalism in the WCTU. It was not simply that contact with other nations in the WCTU sisterhood such as Germany and Austria was disrupted, because these members still were, said Alice Blow of New South Wales, "our sisters in enemy lands."[80] Since Britain and the United States were conceived as the very center of civilization, the BWTA inevitably endorsed the war because the German invasion of Belgium represented an assertion of the barbarism the WCTU identified as the opposite of its own endorsement of "the values of civilized nations."[81] The ex-colonies of the settlement empire, such as Australia and New Zealand, joined in, though like the BWTA, the New Zealand WCTU did not rejoice at the possibilities for a national catharsis. Bessie Cowie wrote Hannah Bailey that her New Zealand sisters felt "sick and sad, to see our fine young men going away," but "what can they do," she asked, "when honor is involved?"[82] Moral ambivalence on the subject of legalized murder was stronger still in the United States, where the identification of American moral superiority with peace remained unshaken.

For the United States, the rationalizations were slightly different, therefore, from these sentiments of pragmatic resignation. The American WCTU had continually defended itself against charges of unpatriotic behavior in its peace campaigns. Bailey had argued the case for a "higher" form of patriotism in which unthinking loyalty to the nation gave way to a self-critical love of country. This "new patriotism" was, the *Union Signal* had proclaimed in a hallmark editorial in 1902, rooted in neither geographical context nor historical traditions; the "highest type" of patriotism was, rather, an "ethical" and "prophetic love." The WCTU attached itself here to the concept of America as "a redeemer nation" whose purpose was to realize "the great trend of the Divine purpose for a universal humanity."[83] This approach sanctioned military interference in the affairs of other nations and identified progress with the assertion of American values. Not surprisingly, the *Union Signal* endorsed as "remarkable" W. T. Stead's *Americanization of the World* and equated American material expansion with the "revolutionary pacific influences" of American institutions and technology. According to the WCTU's editorial chiefs, Stead identified a "tremendous responsibility" for the nation to lead the world along a moral and ethical pathway.[84]

A higher love of country could mean many things, but in the context of the First World War, the concept tied the WCTU at least temporarily to patriotic service in support of the war effort. When war came, it was hardly shocking to find Anna Gordon, national president, admitting that the WCTU's "educational work for peace" must give way to patriotism because "we are loyal daughters of our country."[85] After all, it was Frances Willard who proclaimed on her deathbed that the world had "never" seen "such women, . . . such patriots."[86] If this recourse to the temperance women's saint hinted at a certain guilt that true sisterhood was being violated, the WCTU's position was little different from that of many other high-minded advocates of international cooperation in the pre–World War I United

States. And it must be remembered that those advocates of another internationalism, the German Social Democrats, voted, almost to a man, for war credits in 1914.

This does not mean that the war vanquished internationalism in the WCTU, nor specifically that the peace crusade was terminally paralyzed, though it was for the duration of the war stymied in the ranks of the World's WCTU.[87] Indeed, internationalism in the WCTU quickly became identified with Wilson's peace program. In May 1917, the Southern California WCTU demanded "universal peace at the very earliest possible moment, with such an international reorganization as will require adjudication of disputes among nations, disarmament, freedom of the seas, and protection of small nations."[88] After the war, the National WCTU called for the United States to join the League of Nations, but when that appeal failed, attention shifted to the issue of the World Court, which the United States eventually did join. The American WCTU had to console itself with President Ella Boole's suggestion that the World's WCTU was a "little League of Nations" of its own.[89]

The changing emphases in the peace issue in the postwar world created new possibilities for agitation on the part of the WCTU, but new obstacles as well. While temperance women could see the creation of legalistic mechanisms for adjudication of disputes as fulfilling their nineteenth-century dreams, the creation of the League of Nations accentuated a trend already evident in the prewar years toward a focus on expertise in the prevention of war seen most clearly in the quasi-scientific and empirical approach of the Carnegie Endowment for International Peace. For the WCTU, this shift of focus made its own moral agitation of declining importance within the new coalition of internationalist forces. The old maternal ideology's concern with childhood preparation for peace persisted but became less fashionable in an era in which the technical aspects of peace and disarmament issues won increasing attention.[90]

The postwar stress on institutions rather than sentiment also complicated the pursuit of women's peace agitation, by raising the difficult question of women's representation. True, women could now threaten to vote for peace, as the WCTU did consistently argue in all countries of the Anglo-Saxon world in the 1920s. But few lawyers or other "experts" were women, and it was necessary for the WCTU to begin again with a new campaign, in alliance with such organizations as the Women's International League for Peace and Freedom and the National Council of Women, to introduce women representatives in the League of Nations. For American WCTU women, this last was an impossibility, and in Britain the declining influence, both numerical and political, of the BWTA made its ideas on the subject less and less important. But in those countries like Australia and New Zealand, which were represented in the league and possessed strong and vocal

WCTUs, the peace departments were prominent in the feminist agitation to have women appointed as delegates to the various commissions and sections established as part of the league's multifarious activities.[91]

The prewar version of the peace movement was well and truly transformed by the failures of 1914–18, and with the new interests and new complexities of war and peace, the WCTU's involvement changed, though peace reform remained an important objective of temperance women, particularly in the early 1920s. In 1921, Kaji Yajima, veteran president of the WCTU of Japan, came to the United States to present to President Harding "a petition for World Peace and to pray with the women of America for a successful outcome of the Washington Conference" on disarmament. Ten thousand Japanese women either affiliated with the WCTU or sympathetic to its aims had signed.[92] The American WCTU made much of this show of international solidarity, and Anna Gordon and other officials accompanied Yajima to the White House for the ceremony of acceptance. The American union itself had been instrumental in gathering 199,000 signatures and 2½ million attestations to a much larger "Women's Peace petition" presented to Secretary of State Charles Evans Hughes and had participated in the National Council for the Limitation of Armaments.[93] During the 1920s, however, the WCTU's commitment to peace became increasingly rhetorical and was concentrated on support for Carrie Chapman Catt's Committee on the Cause and Cure of War, which met annually from 1925. Organizations like the Women's International League for Peace and Freedom had emerged as much more vital organs of international peace agitation than those of a multipurpose body such as the World's WCTU, and the union was no longer the most important or the most radical source of peace activism among American women. Moreover, Bailey had resigned as American superintendent in 1916 and as World's superintendent in 1920, in a gesture symbolic of the WCTU's change of emphasis. She would die a relic of a superseded era in 1923.

But the narrowing of the American WCTU's peace agitation owed more to the political context than to changes in personnel. It had "seemed wise," said national president Ella Boole in 1932, in looking over the previous decade's peace work, "to limit the activities . . . for Peace" in the national union "to the work of the [Catt] Committee" because "there are so many Peace organizations doing effective work." If the WCTU "were to open up our local unions to the activities of all of them, or even half of them," argued Boole, "there would be little time left for our major issues—total abstinence and prohibition."[94] World War I may have been an unmitigated disaster for turn-of-the-century peace activists, but out of its carnage a great blessing had emerged for those peace reformers who linked war and the issue of intemperance. South Australian president Elizabeth Nicholls raised the issue clearly as early as 1916, when she noted with some enthusiasm that "the horrors of the war" had produced a heightened understanding of prohibition's "necessity in many lands."[95] In prohibition there was a chance to redeem the blood spilled in battle through moral regeneration. The end of war and the new internationalism of the 1920s brought new challenges for the WCTU in the form of agitation for prohibition in many lands, but unlike peace, prohibition required above all a prior commitment to national action and legislation before international cooperation. By the time Ella Boole explained, ex post facto, the WCTU's new postwar peace strategy in 1932, the legal suppression of the liquor traffic in the United States had so drained WCTU resources that little energy remained to fulfill the nineteenth-century dreams of Hannah Clark Bailey. If peace was part of a way of life, the foundation of that life now faced in national prohibition its greatest opportunity, and its sternest test.

9

A Fatal Mistake?

The Contest for Social Purity

In October of 1897, two former missionaries published a sensational document addressed to the membership of the World's and American WCTUs. The authors were Elizabeth Wheeler Andrew and Dr. Katharine Bushnell, both personal friends of Willard, and among the most controversial and able organizers the World's WCTU ever employed. "We believe," the two earnest Christian campaigners announced at the outset of their *A Fatal Mistake*, "that a crisis has come in the history of the W.C.T.U., and that God is weighing the organization in the balance." Temperance women faced "a great conflict of moral principles," in a battle "being waged the world over." "God" was "waiting to see" what the "foremost organization of women in the world are willing to do in behalf of their own sex." Though the WCTU was ostensibly a temperance organization, the "fatal mistake" was, for Bushnell, Andrew, and many who rallied to their cause, not temperance nor women's suffrage nor peace. The issue that threatened to split the World's and American WCTUs involved the allegation that none other than the vice-president of the World's WCTU had advocated licensed prostitution. Moreover, the WCTU had refused to condemn her. Thereby the WCTU was said to have brought upon itself the moral shame that only the issue of social purity could evoke among Victorian women.[1]

A strong case can be made on the basis of this and other evidence that, despite the implication inherent in the name that the WCTU was primarily a temperance society, in practice no campaign assumed more importance than that of social purity. This was especially true in international perspective. The fate of "fallen women" far away in India and the ramifications of regulationist practices there and in Europe deeply stirred WCTU supporters in several countries in the 1890s, and the white slavery scare of the first decade of the twentieth century also included an unmistakable emphasis on the problem of foreign contagion.

In actuality, the continuity of concern with the purity issue is misleading because the discourse over illicit sexuality itself was not static. The debate in reform circles over prostitution turned in part upon the meaning of purity reform itself, and upon the emphases to be given to various aspects of that agitation. A wide range of interests clustered together under the purity banner, and these changed over time. Rescue and refuge work with poor prostitutes in the 1880s fed in the 1890s a widespread opposition in the WCTU to regulation of prostitution. But these impulses competed with other and sometimes more coercive campaigns: the provision of alternative "pure" influences to combat sexual temptation, legislation to raise the age of consent, censorship of "obscene" literature, and crusades to suppress red light districts. So too did the character of the international campaigns vary, since an effort to "save" the fallen women of India under British imperial rule had different connotations from the eventual denouement of social purity in the paranoia over "white slavery."

The quantity of propaganda turned out hinted at how central these issues were to temperance women. Of specialist literature produced by the Woman's Temperance Publishing Association around 1890, purity was said to account for half the total. This interest did not slacken but rather grew after the turn of the century. In California, for example, it was the WCTU that outstripped all other organizations in its campaigns against prostitution between 1910 and 1913.[2]

For workers in the WCTU's purity department, like Edith S. Davis, any form of illicit sexual activity went "hand in hand" with the drink issue. Prostitution was commonly associated in the minds of reformers with the proliferation of drinking places. Liquor consumption was also routinely and correctly connected with the loss of self-control that broke down inhibitions, including sexual taboos. In her inimitable and infectious style, Willard captured the fears of temperance women on this point when she depicted "intemperance and impurity" as "iniquity's Siamese Twins."[3] The rhetoric of seduction was central in this comparison, as was a conception of the use of liquor as a solace for shame. Willard's language at the 1893 national convention was typical: "When a man would rob a woman of her virtue or a woman is about to sell herself in the most degraded bargain that the mind can contemplate, what does he give her, and what does she take? STRONG DRINK!"[4]

Behind the concern over purity was a more important issue than the connection of drink and prostitution. There was in the tenacity of purity campaigns in the WCTU a deep concern with personal violation, with the preservation of bodily integrity against external assault. The evangelical inheritance of the WCTU stressed the danger of sin and the omnipresence of evil. This concern with moral contagion encouraged the development of a set of pollution beliefs in which certain practices were prohibited because they obscured the clarity of the division between evil and good. Among these was sex outside of marriage and not for the purpose of procreation, long a matter of concern in Christian morality.

As Phillida Bunkle points out, this symbolic structure of pollution beliefs came to be of special significance to the WCTU because the emergence of industrial capitalism and the decline of household production were gradually undermining the productive role of middle-class women. "It was not that women had nothing to do; they were busy enough; it was that their labor had no exchange value. When the family ceased to be a productive unit, it was in fact threatened by male economic and sexual freedom." In asserting control over their own bodies by a purity reform that excluded illicit sexual contact, women were resisting "objectification" as items of consumption. Purity thus became for WCTU reformers an important source for transforming their own powerlessness into a "positive identity" by "taming the male's destructive force."[5]

If this argument has both brilliance and validity as a coherent intellectual system, it must be remembered that the achievements of WCTU women did not take the form of an essential contradiction from which all else flowed. Rather, their activities represented an ensemble of interacting social relations and contradictions in which these considerations were often central, but never overbearing. After all, purity beliefs were shaped in a cooperative endeavor by men as well as women and by women who breached the boundaries of the domestic economy by working and living as single career women. Moreover, the WCTU's purity campaign took the form of a gradually constructed program in which pragmatic political objectives and external cultural influences also had impacts in ways that defy the categorizations of systematic belief; both the timing and the precise content of these beliefs thus reflected the WCTU's position in a broader cultural context.

The ferocious pursuit of the goals of the purity crusade becomes intelligible in the light of these practical and ritualistic dimensions of purity beliefs. What is not nearly so well understood is the international dimension of these struggles. WCTU purity ideology was shaped in many ways by images of women in other lands and by experiences of trying to "save" them. Within the United States, such work had begun as early as 1877, and the histories of the national union have sketched the character and evolution of these important campaigns on the national level to the end of the nineteenth century with ample detail. Nowhere, however, do the historians of temperance and women acknowledge the startling degree to which the style and the timing of the program were produced by international as much as by domestic American influences. For this it is necessary to turn, for even remotely adequate accounts, to the historians of the purity movement.[6] The WCTU efforts are also in the standard versions largely segregated from the complex and diverse purity crusade, of which the WCTU was only one constituent agency. These contextual questions occupy the central place in

Woman's World/Woman's Empire

the first part of this chapter. The WCTU's campaign, with its shifting composition and emphases, only makes sense in terms of the larger world of reform that the WCTU inhabited.

Though the evidence has been ignored, the WCTU freely admitted at the time that, as Willard put it, the "silence" on the issue of purity had been broken largely in England. The purity campaigns were more advanced there, and the American WCTU did not hesitate to imitate the British movement. W. T. Stead's exposé of child prostitution in the *Pall Mall Gazette*, his 1885 article, "The Maiden Tribute to Modern Babylon," electrified moral reformers on both sides of the Atlantic.[7] It was this incident that provoked, at the 1885 national WCTU convention, the formation of the Department of Social Purity and the expansion of a tentative campaign, begun in 1883 against the "social evil." Just a year later, during the visit of Margaret Lucas to the United States and her participation in the NWCTU convention in Minneapolis, the World's WCTU constitution was proclaimed, and purity reform was conspicuously present. The plan of work for the organization, written by Hannah Smith's daughter Mary Smith Costelloe, made purity equal in importance to temperance as the "twin causes" of WWCTU reform.[8]

A powerful underlying stimulus to this campaign came from efforts in England to abolish the contagious diseases acts of 1864, 1866, and 1869. These draconian examples of Victorian class legislation had enshrined the regulation of prostitution in British law and required the incarceration in "lock hospitals" of "common prostitutes" found by periodic police inspection to be infected with venereal disease. Needless to say, the laws expressed sexist standards, since male clients were not subject to inspection, and in practice it was working-class women whose morality came under scrutiny. In the 1870s, a formidable opposition to these incursions on civil liberties arose under the leadership of Josephine Butler, the wife of an Anglican clergyman, and the issues Butler agitated attracted Willard's attention across the Atlantic.[9] Perhaps the tension between Butler's abolitionist campaign and a women's temperance society based on enforcement of morality through law ought to have been immediately apparent, but it was not. Temperance women were not systematic thinkers, and they responded to the needs and opportunities of the moment, as Butler did too.

Butler's influence was indirectly felt in the Minneapolis convention. The prominence of purity in the new World's organization undoubtedly reflected the presence of British delegates inspired by the anti–contagious diseases acts campaign. But underlying the platform change was Willard's shrewd suspicion that if the WCTU were to make headway in Europe, it must take advantage of moral issues most prominently agitated in those countries. Willard made this pragmatism explicit much later, in 1893. The

WCTU had found it almost impossible "to gain a foothold" among European women, Willard admitted. Through an alliance with the British, Continental, and General Federation for the Abolition of the State Regulation of Vice, the WCTU would first "involve their sympathies as women."[10] Thus did international ambition encourage Willard to court Butler and concern the WCTU as much with "vice" in Europe and Asia as in America.

The British impact manifested itself still further the following year when the WCTU in Michigan emulated Stead's daring exposé in what the *Union Signal* called "Another Maiden Tribute."[11] Just as Stead had sought firsthand knowledge of the conditions of prostitution in London, so too in the WCTU did a comparably intrepid figure emerge to put propriety aside and rub shoulders with vice. That figure was none other than one of the two authors of *A Fatal Mistake*. Kate Bushnell had first been influenced by Willard as a medical student in the 1870s at Northwestern University, where Willard had served as president of the Ladies College affiliated with the university. Later, as evangelist with the newly formed social purity department of the National WCTU, the young doctor ransacked the lumber camps of Wisconsin during the latter part of 1888 to interview "degraded women in the northern pinery dens." There she found evidence of some sixty "stockades" in which women were forced to remain in prostitution, "abused and often murdered," restrained by "fines, threats, arrests [by abetting officials], high board fences, lock and key, and, in one instance at least, a ball and chain."[12] Willard attributed quite rightly to Stead the instigation of this brand of reform journalism, but the WCTU made such sensational moral outrage backed by "facts" its trademark. The exposé continued thereafter to be a standard part of the organization's procedure, with intrepid women journalists seeking out similar stories of unwilling women in bondage to lascivious and money-hungry men in California, Wisconsin, Hawaii, India, Hong Kong, and the Philippines.[13]

The international connections involved were more than a formal borrowing of British styles of journalistic exposé. American WCTU women were worried lest foreign vices be imported into the United States. Bushnell characteristically found that the dens in which women were kept in the midwest were run by foreigners "or men of foreign extraction."[14] Such perceived effects of immigration heightened the WWCTU's more general concern about moral contagion.[15]

Yet more significant than the issue of immigration itself was the importation of ideas and customs. The United States purity campaign differed from those in Europe and the British empire, in that the regulation of prostitution by the state hardly existed in the American case. This absence was not the fault of the forces supporting regulation. They, principally medical doctors, made repeated efforts to get the licensing of prostitution accepted. The most notorious experiment had been effected in St. Louis under municipal regulations delegated by the state legislature in 1870. Though repulsed with indignation by purity supporters, the regulationists demonstrated a persistence that both amazed and horrified purity reformers; the specter of regulation hung over many American cities in the following thirty years, including those, like Minneapolis in 1902, that tried police regulations rather than overt medical controls.[16]

All of these schemes were turned back with righteous anger, but the intellectual issue of regulation remained alive. Debates for and against medical inspection continued to rage, as the publication in 1914 of Abraham Flexner's survey, *Prostitution in Europe*, shows. The appearance of that now classic study demonstrated this point at the same time that it affirmed, in Flexner's mind, the importance of maintaining unsullied American opposition to "European" regulation. This affirmation of American uniqueness is not unfamiliar to students of progressive American thought, but American uniqueness must not be exaggerated. The fear of importation of these schemes was a very real one, precisely because such persistent efforts were made to apply them to American conditions. Willard understood this. It was certainly her interpretation that prostitution "deliberately planned and sanctioned by the state" had its origins in France at the beginning of the nineteenth century. For Willard, the contagious diseases acts were nothing other than an attempt to apply this "Parisian" system to the Anglo-Saxon race.[17]

The threat of contamination from abroad entailed more than the matter of prostitution itself. There was, for many feminists, the fear that venereal disease could be communicated to the innocent through husbands who frequented prostitutes. Christabel Pankhurst was not alone in claiming wildly that a large proportion, possibly 75 percent of the adult male population, was infected with venereal disease. But this fear did not make social purity advocates focus on medical prophylaxis, since they were fundamentally concerned with the avoidance of pollution. Not until after the turn of the century when medical authorities, particularly Prince Morrow and his American Society for Medical and Moral Prophylaxis, turned medical opinion away from pro-regulation policies did the WCTU and other similar social purity organizations effect a reconciliation with medical opinion.[18]

Social purity advocates were, above all, determined to prevent immoral behavior, and removal of the specter of contracting venereal disease would not have advanced their cause. For this reason, the issue of contagion in the 1890s for the social purity department of the WCTU was essentially a question of male morals and female subordination. "The moral contamination of the future husbands and fathers," wrote Willard in a denunciation of the contagious diseases acts, "is a calamity immeasurably greater than their physical deterioration." Willard took heart at the knowledge that the regulationist forces had been defeated in Britain itself in 1885, but the acts remained in force in the British empire. Here was a great work for the WCTU. Its roving missionaries were perfectly placed to comment on, and to expose, the existence of state-regulated vice throughout the world.[19]

Just as moral issues took precedence over physical, it followed that the cultural impact on attitudes toward women was central in this concern with sexual impurity. Wherever women were "degraded," the process put "the stamp of deterioration upon all women."[20] This is why Willard came to believe that the purity issue in the United States and Britain could not be divorced from the regulation of prostitution in those "distant lands." Regulated prostitution in imperial India for the benefit of the British army would be central to this debate. "What it must mean to England," exclaimed Elizabeth Wheeler Andrew, speaking of British soldiers in the Indian army, "to have these young men going down in the ways of death, and then returning after a short service, to bring these degraded ideas and practices home."[21] Men would return from the colonies with those attitudes, and on the basis of cultural prejudices acquired or reinforced abroad, would degrade womanhood in the European countries, especially Britain. Since Willard's strategy for world influence depended on reform in Britain and its empire, the international crusade against sexual immorality assumed special importance for the leadership of the World's WCTU.

This sentiment projected the WCTU purity campaign quickly onto the world stage. Willard was not content to remain the recipient of reform; she saw that the World's WCTU could be used to strengthen both the temperance and purity causes internationally, and so bolster the position of the World's WCTU in the international women's movement that she envisaged as the product of the new feminism. Just as Willard perceived opium's inclusion in the WWCTU pledge as likely to enhance the organization's appeal in countries where alcohol was not widely used, so too did she regard purity campaigns as giving her movement "a world-wide basis."[22]

Willard therefore encouraged Bushnell to embark in 1890 on a round-the-world tour as a WCTU missionary specially charged with social purity responsibilities. Bushnell was ideally placed for Willard's purpose. As a medical practitioner with an interest in women's medicine, she was well qualified to take issue with the body of medical opinion that endorsed regulation. As an evangelist and purity worker, she had already demonstrated her capacity to generate publicity on the issue and to defy the usual inhibitions against women working with prostitutes. As a feminist, she had distinct claims to speak on a women's issue, and as a veteran of two and a half years as a missionary in China, she knew the dangers that faced her. When she embarked on her temperance assignment she was thirty-five and in the full vigor of her mission in life.[23]

After a brief sojourn in Germany doing medical research, Bushnell proceeded to Britain, where she enlisted the support of Andrew, another member of Willard's Evanston circle. A forty-five-year-old widow of a Methodist minister, Andrew was a former teacher and journalist with the Woman's Temperance Publishing Association.[24] Together they would tour the world several times and make the purity issue their own long before they authored *A Fatal Mistake*. In a common cause their lives would become entwined. They would not be separated again until Andrew's death in 1917. Andrew and Bushnell quickly won the endorsement of Butler, who was then at the height of her prestige. When the Americans informed her of their intention to go to India to investigate the perpetuation of state-licensed prostitution there, Butler was overjoyed. "They are gentle and quiet, and I think have deep & strong convictions. . . . I cannot help seeing the hand of God in this circumstance." It was, at least initially, a bonus that they represented "the Social Purity branch of the Great Women's Temperance Society of America, of which Miss Willard is the President."[25] Later, Butler would regret her connection with Willard, but in 1891 the impression Andrew and Bushnell made convinced Butler to become World's superintendent of the purity department of the WCTU. Thus were the two causes linked, and Willard's objective of enhanced power and prestige for the WCTU was at least temporarily achieved.

Butler undoubtedly hoped to get something of value in return from these two impressive American women. She had always recognized what Willard now acted upon: that regulation was an international question. The contagious diseases acts were not, despite the focus in historiography on the English campaigns, designed for England alone. They were, fundamentally, imperial laws erected for the benefit of England's army and navy. After removal of the acts from the statute books in 1886, attention turned to these crucial imperial connections. Alfred Dyer, the Quaker purity reformer, had gone to India to investigate their operation for himself in 1887; his revelations that inspection lived on in India led to abolition there in 1888; but the Indian army was determined to check the spread of venereal disease, and cantonment acts restricting the movement of prostitutes had, for this purpose, been passed as a replacement by the Indian government.[26]

These acts provided for hospitalization of people (sex unspecified) suspected of contracting venereal disease. Those who would not accept the regulation were liable to be expelled from the cantonment. This was a contagious diseases act by another name.[27] The stage was now set for Bushnell and Andrew. Though Dyer and other purity reformers continued to fulminate in the early 1890s against the surreptitious regulation of prostitution through the cantonment provisions, little notice taken in England of their outrage, in marked contrast to Dyer's earlier revelations. As Kenneth Ballhatchet observes in his exemplary study of this subject, it was clear that new tactics were required. The distinctive contributions that Andrew and

Bushnell could make were obvious. They were Americans; they were women; and they had impeccable missionary connections. As American missionaries they could more easily develop a rapport with their informers in the cantonments who could help describe the workings of the prostitution system there than British missionaries who were sometimes distrusted by Indians. Their position as women was, however, more important because it dramatized contradictions in contemporary Victorian ideology. Comments Ballhatchet: "The thought that two respectable ladies had seen indelicate things [in India] sanctioned by the military authorities was bound to excite Victorian public opinion."[28]

The pair left England in July 1891 and worked first in South Africa lecturing on both temperance and purity before proceeding to India in December upon the onset of cooler weather on the subcontinent. Their four-month tour of military stations included inspections of lock hospitals, interviews with army officials, and forays into the brothels themselves. With ease they were able to demonstrate that the Indian government erected the facilities in which prostitutes lived, that the prostitutes were paid by the cantonment magistrates, and that watchmen wearing government uniforms guarded the entrances and exits of the cantonments.[29] Their accounts were particularly effective because they expressed the empathy and intimacy of women helping women. The language was not simply that of journalistic shock and horror. Rather, it was the "consecrated" language of religious identification. Though at first "distracted" by the "barbaric appearance" of the "degraded women," the impulse of "sacred work" soon overwhelmed them as they became immersed in the suffering; so "intensely absorbed" in the "thoughts and feelings of these poor enslaved creatures" were they that, said the two missionaries, "we moved as freely and unconsciously among them as if in our own native land."[30]

The American women raised more than the issue of sex. Their religious and feminist sympathies brought to the surface the embarrassing issue of racial contact between Europeans and Indians, and as part of this process, Bushnell and Andrew openly highlighted the fate of the Eurasians, despised and rejected in both cultures.[31] This "harvest of woe" was the point upon which most sympathy could be found for the purity workers from within the Indian government and in European society in India, since the preservation of racial distance was important to the preservation of imperial power.[32] The WCTU women, however, attacked this issue in ways vastly different from the official Indian government viewpoint or that of the resident white communities, except that of important sections of missionary opinion. Bushnell and Andrew bridged the social distance between the races and identified with both Eurasian and native women. This identification was subversive of British rule not only because it attacked the actual practices of the imperial regime but also because the missionaries challenged the underlying cultural rationale of the authorities. While interracial sex was officially discouraged within the upper echelons of government, for the uneducated rank and file of the British army, regulated sex was considered necessary to prevent discontent and unlimited fraternizing with native women. This was essentially a class position, in which the preservation of the raj was central.

The two intrepid Americans were unprepared to accept such hypocrisy; as missionaries they pressed forward the egalitarian point of view whenever they could by associating openly with these degraded women and by identifying their oppression as a corrupt imperial bargain. Like other purity workers in England, they hit at the organization of the Indian empire when they demanded an increase in the proportion of married troops among the British soldiers sent out. Evidence that native soldiers, who were more often married, had much lower rates of venereal disease undermined the economic basis of imperial rule. The proportion of married European troops with wives in residence had been reduced progressively from one-third to 6 percent in the period of the contagious diseases acts as a money-saving device. Clearly the empire could not or would not be allowed to carry the expense of married troops.[33]

With the completion of their investigations, Bushnell and Andrew prepared a report for Fanny Forsaith, secretary of the British committee of the General Federation for the Abolition of the State Regulation of Vice. But they did not return directly to England. Nor did they make their charges known in India. Instead they fled the hot Indian summer for further work in the Southern Hemisphere, while waiting for their evidence to reach the corridors of power through Forsaith's machinations. They may have been anticipating that the victory of the Liberals in the British general election in the summer of 1892 would soon produce a more favorable hearing for their case than any Conservative administration would offer. In the meantime, they demonstrated the concern of both Butler and the WCTU for international work by following the imperial vice connection to the Australasian colonies. There they conveyed information on the operation of the cantonment acts and the duplicity of imperial authority. Their visits were extremely important in galvanizing the purity workers in those colonies, as they had been in South Africa. The Indian specter was of immediate relevance to the Cape Colony, for example, "for it was always the military doctors, often fresh from India, who were most pressing in their demands for the regulation of prostitutes."[34] But the Australasian colonies were also part of the empire and were subjected to the same kinds of arguments. Contagious diseases acts modeled on the now outlawed British system were still on the statute books in several of those colonies. Bushnell and Andrew were able to tell audiences in Queensland and New Zealand that in India women were kept under inspection against their will, that they were sometimes

The Contest for Social Purity

tricked or sold into the cantonments, that soldiers could beat them with impunity, and that they were afraid to talk lest they be victimized.[35]

Especially effective was the suggestion that the cantonments exaggerated "vice" by regularizing its operations. "Fallen" women were identified publicly and could never return to native society as anything other than "social pariahs." To Bushnell and Andrew this represented a grave injustice, since the missionaries believed these women were not personally responsible for their position but rather were victims of misfortune, ignorance, poverty, and not infrequently, male violence. What might be a temporary fall from grace was turned by the imperial system into a permanent condition of inferiority.[36] These were powerful arguments against regulation in the colonies and for British audiences, though not necessarily for Indian audiences, many of whom felt that British troops would rape respectable women if prostitution was not controlled by the authorities. Equally disturbing for colonial and domestic British audiences was the allegation that the new regulations were merely perpetuating a prior commitment to inspection for the benefit of empire. This suggested that the system, once established, was very difficult to shake. "They were in the power of a relentless system," said Andrew in an appeal to purity workers for a worldwide campaign against legalized prostitution.[37]

Andrew's clarion call did have its expected effect. The two intrepid missionaries returned from Australia and New Zealand to England via India, where they made further investigations and then made public their sensational charges in April 1893. At first the military authorities attempted to question the truth of their testimony. Lord Roberts, the retiring commander-in-chief of the Indian army, gave an unfortunate interview on arriving back in England, in which he denied the evidence completely. Roberts must have been poorly appraised of the political situation, and certainly he appeared to play into the hands of the reformers. The new Liberal government had established a committee to investigate the charges that prostitution was continuing under imperial authority in defiance of the House of Commons resolution of 1888. Bushnell and Andrew testified before this committee, and corroborating material came from John Hyslop-Bell, a British journalist who had retraced some of their steps. In the light of this and other evidence, Roberts appeared as either a liar or an incompetent. Neither image was attractive to British public opinion. At last the Indian government and the Indian army had to beat a strategic retreat. Roberts apologized to the American women and confirmed that their charges were largely true. New legislation outlawing inspection in any form was introduced.[38]

The impact of the campaign on the prestige of the WCTU was mixed. Within the American WCTU, the exploits in India both enhanced the importance of purity work in the temperance organizations and made the two

American women heroines. Moreover, Andrew and Bushnell had at least temporarily established Willard's credentials as a world leader of the women's movement within the ranks of purity reformers. British purity workers through the British committee of the General Federation for the Abolition of the State Regulation of Vice warmly thanked the two and claimed, "a better piece of public work has [never] been done."[39] Yet Willard was chagrined that the "secular press" did not readily admit the WCTU contribution. When the names of Andrew and Bushnell were mentioned in the English and American newspapers, these items "overlooked the fact that they were sent out by the general officers of the World's W.C.T.U." Nor did papers note that Josephine Butler was not only connected with English purity reform but was "World's W.C.T.U. superintendent of Social Purity work" as well.[40]

In these seemingly innocent comments lay the origins of a conflict with Butler that would by 1897 almost split the women's temperance movement. By that time, Butler was sure that there was something "hollow and vainglorious" in the World's WCTU.[41] The "self-glorifying" about which she had complained two years earlier was illustrated in the behavior of the two American missionaries. Bushnell objected to the low representation of American workers on the executive committee of the Ladies National Association in 1895.[42] When Butler retorted that the Americans did not deserve larger representation because they were latecomers to the movement, Bushnell resigned, though she continued to work in alliance with Butler. Butler was undoubtedly correct in her assessment that Willard and Somerset sought to claim credit for purity work worldwide. Though she professed no animosity, Butler transparently resented, in private correspondence to her sister in Italy, the intervention of Willard in a cause the English reformer had pioneered.[43]

Behind this struggle over personalities and self-promotion lay further sources of animosity. The power contest exposed a conflict of priorities. Butler came to regret the alliance with the WWCTU because she felt other reforms in the Do-Everything policy harmed the purity movement. Butler's concern was manifest in her response to the issue that was the very rationale for the WCTU's existence. According to one biographer, Butler was not even "a teetotaler by conviction," and certainly she did not accept an inevitable link between impurity and drinking. It was "the abuse—not the use, of God's gifts against which we make war," she told fellow purity worker Fanny Forsaith.[44] These attitudes surfaced at the time when Somerset and Willard were planning their round-the-world tour with the Polyglot Petition. One of the first stops was reported to be Italy, which, Butler felt, was not ripe for a temperance movement because "the only person not sober whom I have ever seen in Italy was a foreign sailor." In contrast,

Butler felt that Italians, like the rest of her "Continental friends," desperately needed purity reform because prostitution did thrive there.[45]

Butler's instincts that her own movement would be swallowed up in a chimerical quest for a teetotal Europe were compounded by her doubts that the WWCTU had displayed sufficient commitment to her own crusade. It was not that she questioned Willard's sincerity, and she certainly applauded the work of the two American women missionaries and utilized WWCTU funding. Rather, the very character of the American purity crusade made its emissaries suspect. As Butler repeatedly pointed out, Americans had never known a state-regulated system of prostitution on the vast scale of some European countries. Butler portrayed herself as an abolitionist; that is, she professed a classic nineteenth-century liberal opposition to "the seal of legal sanction and State approval" of "depravity." This was similar to the stand taken by William Lloyd Garrison against the sanction of chattel slavery in the American constitution, and Butler was fond of making the connection in her propaganda pieces written, ironically, for the World's WCTU. Butler rightly saw Willard and Somerset as advocates of a more positive state interventionism aimed at the repression of prostitution. Butler feared that any such intervention would be administered by men and would in practice not abolish prostitution but institutionalize it in a way that would give the police wide powers over prostitutes and hence bring back de facto regulation.[46]

The impact of this different political and philosophical style was clear to Butler by 1895. "Ignorance of the abolitionist question" in purity matters had, according to Butler, already led the World's WCTU in a "sadly wrong" direction. Butler claimed to have a letter from the Danish and Norwegian WCTU women, signed by Countess Jarlsberg, Elizabet Selmer, and others, favoring "compulsory examinations of women to be continued while professing to wish to abolish the *old* regulation system." Even worse, she fumed, these women had spurned Butler's authority and appealed to Willard and Somerset to decide "whether they or I am right!" Butler's suspicions were confirmed when Willard refused to condemn WCTU women who favored some form of regulation, preferring "to consider both sides of the question."[47] This response outraged Butler, for whom only the harshest condemnation was in order for anyone who flinched from an uncompromising abolitionist position. From this time on, Butler's relations with the World's WCTU became largely formal, although not until 1897 did their disagreement split the alliance in a public and permanent way.

Again, India provided the context for the shaping of Anglo-American attitudes. Even after the public exposure of state regulation on the subcontinent had forced pro-repeal legislation on the Indian government, the British army in India remained resolutely opposed to the goals and tactics of purity reform. By 1896, a concerted campaign had emerged to reverse the decision, based on rising venereal disease rates measured since the abandonment of regulation. It did not matter to the imperial lobby in London, to army officials in India, or to medical groups alarmed at the rising rates of venereal disease that the latter phenomenon was part of a more general increase in syphilis that transcended the shifts in imperial policy pursued by the British government through the 1880s and 1890s.[48]

The WCTU was drawn back into this controversy when in April 1897 Lord George Hamilton, the secretary of state for India in the new Conservative government, wrote Somerset a letter asking her to comment on the proposed new rules for "checking the spread of Venereal Disease among the British Troops."[49] As a sop to the social purity forces, the regulations included instructions to the army both to provide alternative forms of recreation and to do nothing to encourage "immoral" behavior. That the regulations were sent to Somerset for comment implied that Hamilton knew or believed already that he could get support from the World's WCTU vice-president and so split the purity movement. If he were successful, Hamilton would neutralize much of the opposition to the de facto reintroduction of an inspection system. Somerset took the bait and replied in an open letter published in the London *Times* on 21 April.[50]

Somerset used the occasion not only to express general approval of the new policy but also to urge that inspection be carried further. Apparently her contacts within the British aristocracy, in whose ranks regulationist sentiment was concentrated, had led her to believe that regulation could not be avoided, and she had concluded that it was best to get a system that operated upon both sexes. Hence the striking novelty of her proposal was the compulsory inspection of male soldiers who frequented the brothels. A quarter of each cantonment should be reserved for women permitted to remain in camp; these would be "compelled to remain in houses or rooms specifically reserved to each by a registered number," and the admission of men to these rooms should be "strictly supervised." All (of either sex) who were found upon inspection to have venereal disease were to be quarantined.[51] Somerset went on to endorse the proposal of the British government "to improve the moral and physical condition of the British troops in India, and enlarge the means of their instruction, occupation and recreation."[52]

The impact of this letter was extraordinary. Here was a leading official of the World's WCTU and BWTA president publicly sanctioning the state regulation of prostitution. Bushnell and Andrew were as appalled by this alarming development as was Butler with the general thrust of World's WCTU thinking. Though Somerset had clearly sought to avoid the powerful feminist argument that inspection entailed a double standard, she did not succeed. As Bushnell pointed out, even under Somerset's supposedly

The Contest for Social Purity

evenhanded treatment, "the woman shall be the prisoner, while the man goes free."[53] Moreover, Somerset's plan implied that the biological imperatives of sex were located within only the male of the species. For modern feminists, this would entail a denial of woman's sexuality; for Bushnell and Andrew, who had thoroughly imbibed the sexual morality of the Victorian women's movement, these proposals made an unnecessary concession to vice. They took particular exception to Somerset's rationale that without regulation "the soldiers are literally forced into the wildest forms of debauchery" by their passions. Herein lay "the very heart of the claim that men cannot be held to the same standard of morality as women, namely, the assumption that men are 'literally forced' to sin if temptation be sufficiently strong." Andrew and Bushnell used their actual experience of regulation in India and Bushnell's medical knowledge to good effect. They pointed out the "anatomical difficulties" entailed in the supposition that men could not help themselves. Tellingly they concluded that these gaffes could "perhaps . . . be pardoned in the statements of a non-professional woman who attempts to pronounce opinion upon medical matters."[54] What they could never forgive was the perpetuation of the double standard and its concession that evil could not be eradicated.

Somerset's action brought swift and predictable retribution within the purity sorority. Bushnell and Andrew had already resigned from the World's WCTU in June 1896 over disagreement on a broad range of issues that included prohibition as well as purity. But after the publication of Lady Henry's letter, they felt they could no longer "refrain from open opposition" and instigated a campaign to remove Somerset from her office.[55] In this they had the support of Butler, who was already threatening to resign as World's superintendent of purity unless a sufficient retraction came from the World's vice-president herself.[56] Equally important, they had an ally in Mary Leavitt, whose long-standing opposition to Somerset now came to the fore. In an "Open Letter" to the WCTU published in September 1897, Leavitt called for Somerset's resignation lest "the odium which now rests upon her will cover and smirch the W.C.T.U. everywhere."[57] Leavitt had come to despise Somerset as early as 1891, when, as a World's missionary, she had tried to get the English aristocrat to go to India to stimulate WCTU work.[58] In an unmistakably ironic tone, Leavitt recounted that when she had implored Somerset to go, she had "failed to comprehend all the obligations that rest upon her Ladyship to *live* in England."[59] From her own position of righteous self-sacrifice, Somerset appeared to Leavitt as a superficial friend of temperance whose commitment did not approach her desire to preserve her aristocratic style of life. This opinion accorded with that of Butler, who had a jaundiced view of the English aristocracy as rife with sexual corruption, and with Bushnell and Andrew's American-derived distrust of formal class pretension.[60]

This was a formidable coalition of women, because their international contacts were impeccable. Leavitt commanded considerable loyalty within the unions she had helped establish in many countries; Butler was as well known as Willard; and the two American missionaries were nothing if not zealous in their support for the eradication of any taint of evil. These women were together able to internationalize the regulation controversy in ways deeply embarrassing to Willard and potentially damaging to fulfillment of her dreams for the World's WCTU.

The gravest concerns arose from the fact that the American and World's WCTUs seemed to sanction Somerset's controversial stand by refusing to repudiate her openly. Willard did not exactly endorse the opinions of her friend, but she used her still-dominant position in the American WCTU to resist pressure to have Somerset resign. Moreover, Willard sought to explain Somerset's views in a way that seemed to opponents to excuse them. She noted, for example, Somerset's own argument that it was all very well for purity reformers to castigate English attempts at controlling the social evil, but it was necessary to understand the vast differences between social conditions in Britain and America. "We in America have practically no standing army; we have no 'oriental difficulties,'" whereas "the British Government must deal with 'a condition and not a theory.'"[61] This was not an argument likely to sway Butler. From her perspective, it was precisely because the United States had no regulationist system that the WCTU's best workers were "not wholly alive" to the abolitionist critique of regulation.[62]

With Willard now drawn into the conflict, international issues threatened even the stability of the American WCTU. That the principal histories of the American WCTU have not emphasized this point is understandable, since opposition to Lady Henry's stand did not surface at the national convention of the WCTU in Buffalo in November 1897.[63] There it was the financial quagmire of the Woman's Temple that dominated proceedings. Historians might conclude from this that the American WCTU cared little for the fate of the purity issue abroad, but at the World's convention in Toronto held in October, before the national convention, purity and Somerset took center stage. This was the correct forum for opposition to Lady Henry, since she was vice-president of the World's WCTU. Though Willard and her supporters controlled the convention, much discontent was expressed by both American and non-American delegates at the reelection of Lady Henry by the executive committee. Since the convention had no say in this choice made by the committee, delegates for the first time openly voiced criticism of the leadership and its domination of the constitution and the convention. As Clara Hoffman, a Willard loyalist, pointed out, the question of representation and procedure would "never have come up . . . if there had not been an uneasy feeling among the delegates that the executive was not coming out fairly and squarely for the cause of . . . social purity."[64] Under the impact of this opposition, the World's WCTU executive committee was forced to clarify its position and passed a strong resolution against licensing of prostitution.[65]

Though Americans were also prominent in the debate, the most lurid and critical attack came from Amelia Yeomans of Manitoba. The siting of the 1897 World's convention in Toronto helped give a platform for Canadian opponents, and the Winnipeg doctor, suffragist, and social purity advocate took full advantage on the floor of the convention. Her stirring if somewhat melodramatic speech raised the specter of alcohol and moral impurity once more.

> I see as I speak a mental picture, a vast circle. In the centre the legalized liquor traffic, staunch and sturdy; by it united by a fleshy bond its twin, fed by alcohol, . . . the monster, social impurity, the despair of the civilized world. . . .[T]he circle is bounded by great guns, which represent the departments of work of the W.C.T.U., and the mouth of every gun is turned upon these monsters. . . . One of these guns is our department of social purity. Oh, let it not be spiked or charged with nourishment for the monster impurity through any unfaithfulness on our part with regard to our chosen officers, for it is by our actions, not our resolutions, that we shall be judged.[66]

Pious resolutions disavowing regulationist sentiment were not enough for Yeomans and many other delegates. They wished to see Somerset retract or be dismissed. In subsequent weeks, Yeomans therefore organized a revolt in the Canadian WCTU that greatly concerned Willard because it threatened Canada's alignment with the American and World's affiliates.

On top of the potentially damaging Canadian revolt came the decision by Bushnell and Andrew to take the fight directly to the BWTA after the Toronto World's convention. This was not in itself enough to shift Somerset, however, since she still commanded majority support in a society very dependent on her personal charisma and her ample finances. Loyalty was intense toward the woman who had effected the Do-Everything policy in the BWTA in just four years of leadership and brought the organization to its peak numerical strength, so much so that neither the executive committee nor the annual council was prepared to accept her own bold bluff to her opponents when she offered to tender her resignation.[67] Influential BWTA member Hannah Whitall Smith went so far as to say that Somerset had been "misunderstood" and that the BWTA executive committee conceded she must not be dismissed for what, "after all" was not *our* main line of work, but only one of our side issues."[68] This was an insensitive viewpoint, and truly it did not accord with opinion within the World's WCTU, when the attitudes of those WCTU supporters outside the Anglo-American leadership are taken seriously.

The control Willard and Somerset still exerted in the Anglo-American temperance axis was not reproduced in the outposts of the WCTU empire. There, loyalty was as much to Leavitt or Bushnell and Andrew as to Willard. Remember, WCTU women in the British colonies and in the missionary stations had actually met these figures, but few knew Willard or Somerset. More important, the opposition to Somerset was centered in those places that either had contagious diseases acts in operation or had recent experience of attempts to introduce them. Strong letters of support, not to Willard, but to Butler, came from WCTU women in Australia, India, New Zealand, South Africa, and Canada.[69] Tasmania's Jessie Rooke (later to be Australasian WCTU president) swiftly backed Butler and expressed alarm that after so long a labor to "suppress & eradicate these abominable C. D. Acts . . . [,] there should be the faintest shadow" of their "[re]appearing."[70] Especially active and influential was Marie Kirk, president of the Victorian WCTU, who later wrote Butler to express her "hearty support" on behalf of "the women of Australia." They were, she said, "true to the core of this great question."[71] Kirk was not boasting in vain. The WCTU of Australasia executive committee had already acted decisively in its opposition to Somerset and the WWCTU's support of her in a letter of September 1897. State regulation in India the Australian WCTU women opposed lest, "emboldened by the action of the British Government," supporters of regulation should "endeavour to follow the precedent, and bring these scandalous laws into operation all over the colonies." This severe protest to the WWCTU was signed by 170 officers and superintendents of departments in the Australian colonies and broadcast through the purity platform of the British empire, *The Shield.* Australasian WCTU leaders had also been in touch with their friends Bushnell and Andrew to orchestrate the anti-Somerset campaign.[72]

More disturbing still for the World's WCTU leadership, the union lost leaders in countries where it was ill equipped to cope. Defections occurred particularly in France, Denmark, and Sweden. Danish purity workers were aghast to hear that "any English ladies ask for the further degradation . . . of their wretched fallen sisters," but the Swedish threat was even more serious. The White Ribboners of that country, regarded as vital to European proselytization by the Americans, voted in January 1898 "to have no connection whatever with the World's W.C.T.U. until Lady Henry Somerset resigns."[73]

This pressure from outside the Anglo-American leadership was vital. Despite the rumblings of opposition to Lady Henry led by Mary Leavitt within the American WCTU, Willard was able through loyal assistants like Clara Hoffman and Lillian Stevens to fend off opposition. Since this auxiliary contained the largest share of the World's WCTU membership, the American leaders and their English allies could be expected to contain any convention battle. It was the position of the Americans, in particular, that loyalty to Willard and her friend should prevail. "The Tail of the W.C.T.U.," Hoffman said with a "considerable show of feeling," should not be able to "wag the dog." After all, she said, it was the Americans who provided the bulk of the funds for the worldwide missionary work.[74] Hoffman's outburst was partly correct, for the WCTU refused to abandon Somerset as World's vice-president, but Willard *had* been forced at the World's convention in Toronto to repudiate Somerset's plan. In this sense, and in the events that followed the 1897 convention, the tail had already begun to wag the dog. The episode illustrated not the objective position, as measured in terms of numbers within the opposing ranks of the WCTU, but rather the impact of international divisions on the worldwide aspirations of Willard and her entourage.

The pressure on Somerset to recant did not ease after the Toronto convention but rather began to mount further. Two factors influenced the British leader. By January 1898, Willard lay gravely ill in New York, suffering from pernicious anemia. She would not recover, and with her beloved Frances failing fast, on 27 January 1898 Somerset retracted publicly. Lady Henry's biographer, Kathleen Fitzpatrick, who had the luxury of access to her now unavailable papers, attributed Somerset's change of heart to Willard's illness.[75] But correspondence between the World's WCTU officials on the purity issue written in the last weeks of the crisis focused not on Willard's health but on the disruptions being wrought in the World's WCTU by Somerset's stand. Whereas in October 1897 Willard and other officials had been prepared to stand by Somerset despite her policy, by mid-January 1898 their tone had changed to one imploring Somerset to retract for Willard's sake and for the sake of the international union's survival. The words that Somerset used in her recantation of 27 January had in fact been suggested to her by Suzannah Fry, an American WCTU official. Fry emphasized in correspondence with Willard the damage to the cause being done in England, where the BWTA was now more deeply divided over Somerset's stand than ever, and with Willard's concurrence, Fry had written to Somerset to implore her to end the divisive stand over purity taken by the British leader.[76] So too had Katharine Lent Stevenson in another epistle to Somerset written on Willard's orders, which focused on the infighting in the WWCTU inspired, so she said, by Leavitt.[77]

Stevenson's letter pointed to the broad context of international concern, since in her mind the issue involved was the "World's society" and who was to run it. Sweden had already pulled out, and several important letters, including one from World's treasurer Mary Sanderson, stressed the dangers of further contention in Canada where another secession from the World's WCTU seemed more likely every day.[78] One Montreal correspondent to Suzannah Fry actually suggested dissolution of the World's WCTU as the only answer.[79] While Willard's mortal illness may well have inspired the recantation, behind the pressure placed on Somerset by WCTU officials was Willard's deathbed fear that the World's WCTU would disintegrate if the English aristocrat maintained her unorthodox views.[80]

Somerset's reversal did not satisfy Butler and the two American missionaries. They would only be satiated by the English aristocrat's dismissal from office. Butler was particularly upset because Somerset had stated that her hopes that the military authorities would institute a "higher standard [of morality] in the Army" had proven to be false. This left open the possibility that had the army instituted satisfactory "moral efforts" then regulation could be accepted as an "auxiliary" to this system.[81] This face-saving device continued to produce discontent in the WCTU, but with Willard's death, and the recantation, anger could not be so easily focused or maintained as it was in 1897 and early in 1898. Soon new issues in the purity campaign would restore confidence in the WCTU, especially in the United States, and dramatically reaffirm the antiregulationist credentials of the Americans.

In the meantime, Somerset's defeat illustrated the immense importance of the purity question, and its international aspects, for WCTU thinking and practice. The episode made clear that WCTU women in many countries vitally cared what the movement's policy was on this issue and that these women regarded the outcome of the regulation controversy in India as directly affecting their interests and status. This attack on Lady Henry and her sentiments crossed national boundaries and became in effect an oppositional movement within the WCTU that brought the very existence of the World's WCTU into question.

For Butler, Somerset's position confirmed her fears that the WCTU was not sound on the abolition issue. Aided no doubt by the munificence of Butler's surviving papers, historians have followed her judgment on the decline of abolitionist sentiment in the purity movement. Even the exemplary analysis by Judith Walkowitz maintains that Butler's crusade against regulation gave way after 1885 to a sexually repressive campaign against illicit sex in the name of social purity. Butler's sympathy for women was, it is said, replaced after the defeat of the contagious diseases acts in England by the repression not only of prostitution but also of other forms of illicit sexual activity. Other historians have identified the WCTU with this new phase of the antiprostitution movement, which was much more sexually and class repressive than the repeal campaign.[82]

The tangled narrative of Butler's conflict with Somerset in the 1890s does not support the straightforward polarization of abolitionist and social purity sentiment that Butler sought to convey. The defeat of Somerset represented the work of a coalition of social purity and antiregulation forces that persisted well beyond 1885. When the focus of analysis is widened beyond the national sphere to consider the imperial operation of the conta-

The Contest for Social Purity

gious diseases laws, a more complicated and sometimes contradictory picture emerges. Butler's early alliance with the WCTU alone suggests the complexity of the relations between social purity and abolitionism after 1885. Though the Anglo-American leadership of the WCTU supported Somerset, the balance of opinion among WCTU women consistently favored Butler despite the fact that they also supported, simultaneously, preventive moral education and, in some cases, vigilance activity against prostitution. Rather than demonstrating a shift away from an egalitarian feminist orientation dominant prior to the mid-1880s, the World's WCTU involvement in the movement against prostitution in the 1890s illustrates the contradictory nature of purity thought and practice. Repressive and liberationist themes coexisted in feminist attitudes at the turn of the century and could not be separated at least as long as the contagious diseases acts remained a highly visible obstacle to women's emancipation. Only after the turn of the century did this shift occur on the international level, and even then, opposition to regulation remained a potent force among temperance women until the First World War.

The organizational impact of the conflict is less controversial than its historiographical meaning. The episode had been immensely damaging to the WCTU and to the purity cause as well. The advocates of regulation in England took particular satisfaction at the division in the opinion of the hitherto united purity forces. In the London *Times*, which epitomized in its editorials British imperial ruling-class concern with the condition of the empire, the account of the World's WCTU convention controversy was confused and factually inaccurate, but a distinct impression was given that its outcome involved "a decisive victory for the Lady Henry Somerset party."[83] An American journalist and minor literary figure, Harold Frederic, went further and applauded the WCTU for refusing in 1897 to abandon Somerset. He took this action (as many Butlerites also did), as a backhand endorsement of what she had advocated. Frederic applauded Somerset's "common-sense, patriotism, and wise humanity" against Butler's "fanaticism" and proclaimed "the triumph of the sensible intelligent element of the World's Woman's Christian Temperance Union Convocation" in its Toronto deliberations.[84] Writers like Frederic—who according to *The Shield* was "connected with some of the leading London daily journals"—used the WCTU's failure to dissociate itself from Somerset to justify continuance of the new regulations of inspection even after Somerset retracted. And not only did Somerset please journalists. Kenneth Ballhatchet, the episode's preeminent chronicler, concludes that the disagreement among the purity forces was "comforting to the authorities."[85]

The political position of the India agitation had now been transformed, as the two American missionaries soon discovered when they returned in 1899 to the scenes of their sensational labors to reexamine conditions under the raj. They found the inspection system fully entrenched, but without political support from the WCTU and in the face of the indifference of a Conservative government in Britain, their attempt to rekindle the fires of indignation fell uncharacteristically flat. Regulation would continue there and in some other places in the British empire, like South Africa, until the end of the First World War. In the long run, improved tests for venereal infection and new drugs such as Salvarsan to combat its incidence changed the dimensions of the problem and made a system of inspection of prostitutes less necessary from a public health perspective. It was disillusioning in the extreme for women like Andrew and Bushnell to know that science and bureaucratic change had altered the purity debate where moral reform had failed, and had rendered the notion of sexual continence increasingly unfashionable for several generations.[86]

THIS STORY has been difficult to tell without reference to those committed and intense figures like Bushnell and Butler who did battle for Christ and personal authority at the same time. But the purity issue must not be trivialized as the fetishist concern of a few prominent women reformers. The defeat of the purity forces hardly depended on the particular moral stances or agitation of individuals within the purity movement. The issue was very much determined by larger considerations of imperial power. Butler had been able to win a decisive domestic victory because the contagious diseases acts affected only certain regions of England. Removal there was much easier than in the case of the empire itself. Beyond Britain's national boundaries, the need to keep the British troops contented took precedence over the wishes of feminists. Only during the short period of Liberal government from 1892 to 1895 did the purity forces have the politicians even remotely on their side. After that, the Conservatives were much more inclined to favor empire over the status of women.

This decisive defeat remained a constant thorn in the side of the opponents of prostitution, especially in the WCTU. One response was to bring to the surface an underlying moral objection to imperialism, at least as conducted by militaristic and politically expansionist powers. But this torrent of womanly indignation also revealed a potential contradiction in the ranks of the WCTU, because the organization and its members remained in many ways committed to an assertion of Western influence as both inevitable and morally necessary to the purity cause.

The severe reversal to abolitionist work in India altered the attitudes of some WCTU women to larger issues of power and contributed to the underlying critique of empire contained in the WCTU's commitment to women's emancipation. Vice and empire went together, the advocates of social purity announced. Women were not alone in drawing this conclusion. A

The Contest for Social Purity

contributor to W. T. Stead's *Pall Mall Gazette* had analyzed as early as 1887 the use of prostitution as an adjunct of imperial domination.[87] Women reformers, and especially women steeped in the culture of the WCTU, were, however, strategically situated to build upon this analysis since they were the principal architects of a social purity feminism and because women were always the chief victims of regulated prostitution. Further, the WCTU was already, and for independent reasons, critical of militarism as well.

Among those who took a jaundiced view of empire were Bushnell and Andrew. As early as 1893 they had taken exception to a *Union Signal* editorial advocating acquisition of Hawaii. Especially distressing was the editorial's suggestion that the United States could do as much for the progress of civilization in the Pacific as Britain did in India. Andrew wrote to Willard in scathing criticism and pointed out that the legitimacy of British rule was negated by its sanction of vice.[88] As late as 1900 the two Americans were convinced from their earlier experience that "the expansionist policy" in both Britain and America signaled the onset of "evil times."[89] They were not alone in the WCTU's ranks as antiimperialists, though Willard herself favored the acquisition of a territorial empire. She did not live long enough to see its consequences, but her lack of inhibitions provides more evidence that the "great chieftain" was prepared, along with Somerset, to ignore the moral perils of empire and the growth of state power inherent in military expansion in order to extend Anglo-American influence internationally. For Bushnell and Andrew, these were immoral means to moral ends.[90]

It was left to another important WCTU figure, Mary Livermore, to take up Andrew's argument and make the antiimperialist case within the American WCTU. Territorial empire required a standing army and navy, and, concluded Livermore, these always went alongside a decline in morality. "Wherever there is an army encampment," she told *The Coming Age* in 1899, "intemperance and gross sensuality prevail."[91] Soldiers in occupied countries required entertainment, so the British army generals had chorused. This military pressure made it necessary for the WCTU to accelerate its peace campaigns to prevent wars and the seizure of territories, but ironically the acquisition of empire gave the purity movement, especially its international wing, a further lease on life. Purity advocates within the WCTU were hardly surprised when the acquisition of an island empire that had to be policed militarily by the United States after 1898 brought to the republic problems similar to those Britain had already experienced. Armed with the Indian example, the American WCTU was now determined to keep the regulation of prostitution out of the new American possessions, particularly in the Philippines and Hawaii.[92]

Prior experience, selectively interpreted, played a central role in the attempts to keep America's new empire clean. When missionaries of the

Protestant churches in the Philippines after 1898 began to complain that brothels were springing up to "service" American occupation forces, the missionary and reform press in the United States exploded with anger. What especially concerned the WCTU was the allegation that these houses of prostitution were being "inspected" by "the consent of the army authorities."[93] The general officers of the WCTU in October 1900 petitioned the president and the secretary of war and emphasized the experience of the British empire, which was so recently in their minds. "We are unwilling to believe," they wrote, that "our Government will allow . . . that infamous system which brought such just contempt upon England." Though the "Stigma" of "the condition of affairs in India" played heavily upon the WCTU's thinking, it clearly did not among the army authorities. A reply from the secretary of war promised an investigation, but the details, revealed in a letter from the commander of the army in the Philippines, Gen. Arthur MacArthur, brought little satisfaction. According to WCTU officials, the American army had virtually admitted that "the system of regulation . . . did exist," but scandalously provided no remedy.[94]

When the WCTU again petitioned, this time to the new civil commission under Governor William H. Taft, they again referred to international experience. In response to administration rationalizations for the need to maintain military inspections, Lillian Stevens and her executive committee now emphasized not only the moral aspects of the evil but also the dangers to public health. Regulation in the Indian army had not lessened the spread of venereal disease, an argument supported, up to a point, by modern authorities. As Ballhatchet notes, "It was in the context of rising statistics [of infection] that systems of control were successively established and abolished in the nineteenth century."[95] Until 1900, neither regulation nor abolition seemed to have a significant effect. This was not quite Lillian Stevens's point, since she emphasized only that repeal of the contagious diseases acts for England represented an admission that they were a "complete sanitary failure." The WCTU did not mention that venereal disease rates had begun to fall in India after the introduction of the new inspection system in 1897, though, to be fair, these regulations had not been in force long enough to produce more than fragmentary statistics.[96]

Once more, in her 1901 presidential address, Stevens raised the international theme, but this time she returned squarely to the moral arguments. Regulation was "contrary to the principle of righteousness, justice, purity, and [was in the Indian Empire] a most fruitful source of demoralization and degradation." Again Stevens's use of evidence was selective. No reference to the reintroduction of inspection in India was made, only mention of its failure there and in other countries. The address, for all its omissions, or possibly because of them, pleased the WCTU, which voted to send Michigan's Carrie C. Faxon to the new island possessions to work against American government support for prostitution and other immoral practices.[97]

No such effect was wrought upon the American administration, which made little effort to face the charges of its critics. Governor Taft's commission did not deal resolutely with the issue, despite promises, and it was at this stage that the special skills of the union's Washington lobbyist became useful. In the spring of 1902, Margaret Ellis obtained a copy of an actual inspection book used by the military medical authorities in Manila. The book documented the "official records" of a "child prostitute" and provided details of "her regular examinations by a government surgeon."[98] Armed with explosive evidence not only of prostitution itself but also of its association with the exploitation of children, Ellis showed the book to congressmen and government officials and circularized thousands of WCTU members and church supporters with the details of the case, urging them to petition the War Department. Ellis's appeal to WCTU women took particular issue with Taft's suggestion that Manila was "as orderly and moral a city as any in this country [the United States]." This explanation Ellis did not deny, but from her perspective it was a "humiliating confession" to suggest a parallel level of "immorality" in the continental United States. The only comfort Ellis could find was her knowledge that vice was illegal and subject to continual efforts at suppression at home, whereas in the Philippines impurity appeared under government encouragement. What Ellis and the WCTU were determined to prevent was the introduction into the United States of this same system of regulation. Taft's claims merely made the suppression of this system abroad more urgent, lest it be imported to the American mainland.[99]

The public campaign initiated by Ellis proved to be what the purity forces desperately needed. Claims of forcible exploitation, condoned and abetted by the United States government, seemed undeniably valid. Ten War Department clerks had to be employed to answer the mail generated by the circular. Enormous political pressure had been placed upon the administration, which as a result issued an order "discontinuing the periodical examination of prostitutes and suspected women and the charges connected with [them]." Another order stressed "the responsibility" of the commanding officers for the "moral as well as the physical welfare of the enlisted men."[100]

Ellis won credit for this episode not only from the WCTU but also from purity forces abroad. *The Shield*, organ of the British antiprostitution forces, quoted the Boston *Woman's Journal*, which praised the role of Ellis. The National American Woman Suffrage Association had been lobbying Congress on this subject for two years without effect. But, noted *The Shield*, "through its wide organization and friendly relations with clergymen of many denominations," the WCTU had "been able to do most effective work in stirring up public opinion." The *Union Signal* was also happy to accept such praise since, it boasted, "no other philanthropic society in the world" had "such facilities for quickly reaching the people and reaching so many of them."[101]

As this piece of self-promotion makes clear, it was not Ellis's evidence itself that made the difference, since the substance of her charges, if not the sensational detail, was already public knowledge. What the WCTU provided was organizational skills and political contacts. Just as she had done in the case of the export of alcohol to the Pacific islands in support of Wilbur Crafts and John G. Paton, Ellis worked behind the scenes with Crafts to influence the Republican political elite at the highest levels. She even lobbied Theodore Roosevelt himself. In a letter to Col. Clarence Edwards, chief of the Division of Insular Affairs in the War Department, Ellis pointedly remarked, in the course of explaining her "Social Evil" circular and the concurrent WCTU purity campaign, that "with the exception of the southern states, seven-eighths of our women have husbands and sons in the Republican party."[102]

If the administration's records reveal that President Roosevelt and Secretary Root were extraordinarily attentive to the moral concerns of these mostly Republican women, the concession was gained at a price.[103] Ellis's husband, J. T. Ellis, had obtained a personal interview with Edwards in which Edwards informed him that "examinations" of "pronounced prostitutes" would continue.[104] But Mr. Ellis nevertheless gave an undertaking that his wife would provide favorable publicity for the administration in return for a promise of strict enforcement of the orders banning official inspection and encouraging the provision of alternative physical recreation to drinking and prostitution for the troops. As he confided: "Mrs. Ellis . . . will be glad to make public the favorable showing you have so kindly given me regarding this whole Philippine business[.] By public I mean through the W.C.T.U. organ & by circularizing to her state superintendends [*sic*]."[105]

In this action, Mrs. Ellis appeared less a critic of government policy than an agent for it. That policy involved as much an attempt to obscure the persistence of de facto regulation as an effort to remove it. This was clear enough from the reasoning behind the executive order that discontinued inspection. Secretary Root secretly spelled out to the War Department officials in the Philippines that the essential change would be the elimination of fees for inspection and the issuing of certificates of examination. "The medical officers" could still "keep their own records," and public "protection against disease" could be secured "without . . . the charge that we are maintaining a system of licensing prostitution."[106] Not only did prostitution continue in the Philippines. The WCTU executive committee, at least, knew that its victory against regulation was largely symbolic, and the organization was prepared, in the new climate of American colonialism, to exploit that victory pragmatically for propagandistic purposes not strictly in line with the WCTU's earlier antiregulationist principles. This was unknown to *The Shield* when it praised the WCTU's stance.

This is not to deny the importance of the concessions gained or their implications for prostitution policy both in the American island possessions and on the mainland. In India, the authorities had officially encouraged a system of inspections after 1898 as a matter of central government policy, and brothels flourished openly in the army cantonments. In contrast, the existence of prostitution in specific, red-light areas in the Philippines was merely tolerated, and definite and strenuous efforts were indeed made by the Bureau of Insular Affairs to separate the American government from direct implication.[107]

The WCTU would not have achieved even this partial success without the presence of a social framework vastly different from that applying in the British case. Symbolic antiregulationism was more successful for the WCTU in the American possessions than in British India because the American empire was much more limited in extent. Contributing, too, was the absence of licensed prostitution on the mainland, which continued to make fear of imported regulation more intense and which reduced the vested interests supporting more tolerant approaches.[108] The impulse within the WCTU toward emancipation of women from the "stigma" attached to their sex by government-supported prostitution thus received a renewed boost. Though inspired in part by Ellis's "indignation" that "these half civilized girls of the Orient" were not under the Stars and Stripes "as well protected . . . as our own dear girls," the practical outcome favored a more insular sentiment. American WCTU women after 1900 could take pride in the fact that they had at least stemmed what they perceived as a tide of legalized immorality in areas under American control.[109]

This result no doubt reinforced a certain parochial attitude that was foreign to the aims of Bushnell and Andrew. In the 1890s, the American WCTU had fought its most controversial and critical battles on the purity front abroad. WCTU missionaries continued to carry on the tradition established in the 1890s and made rescue campaigns on behalf of Chinese, Japanese, Indian, Ceylonese, and Filipino prostitutes an important part of their work well into the twentieth century. But for the American WCTU, the Philippines episode proved to be both the last major attempt to fight "the social evil" on an international plane, and, because the Philippines was under American tutelage, the first round of a new temperance campaign to consolidate the purity forces in America itself.

After the Filipino "success" in 1902, attention turned much more to matters at home. American women still sympathized with the plight of their foreign sisters, but their rhetoric and actions clearly subordinated international to American purity concerns. When Frances Hallowes, president of the Indian WCTU, wrote in 1909 to seek help from the American WCTU in a new petition against the "traffic in women" on the subcontinent, the response of the American leadership was much less friendly than it would have been in the era of Bushnell and Andrew. Said the *Union Signal*: "We can and will give our prayers to India, but in the meantime let us not forget America, to which we can give not only our prayers but our work."[110] It would appear that both the failures and embarrassments of the foray into India and the more favorable experience in the Philippines had reinforced an inward turning in the leadership's ranks, or at least a reluctance to enter the controversies generated by unwinnable foreign purity wars. This more isolationist sentiment entailed, in turn, a shift of emphasis in purity programs.

Curiosity about the international dimensions of purity work did not as a result evaporate, but as in the case of alcohol prohibition, interest in foreign experiments declined in favor of an emphasis upon the export of American solutions. As early as the 1890s, the American WCTU had begun to stress both preventive moral education and the legal suppression of prostitution, and after 1900, these concerns gradually eclipsed reformatory work.[111] In the councils of the World's WCTU, the American leaders, notably Mary Wood-Allen and her daughter, Rose Wood-Allen Chapman, encouraged other countries to emulate their own program of a dissemination of literature aimed at the young. This effort accelerated between 1906 and 1910. Education programs using American literature written by Chapman, such as *The Moral Problem of the Children*, were pushed strenuously in Australia, and works by Chapman and others in the American purity department of the WCTU were translated into Norwegian, Chinese, Japanese, and Spanish. Under American influence, the World's WCTU endorsed in 1910 a "thorough and far-reaching moral education" program as "the only sure method" for the "extermination" of "the menace of immorality."[112]

If the plans of Wood-Allen Chapman made the United States the moral center of the universe, and so reinforced a kind of cultural imperialism, success in the Philippines also undermined the antiimperialist critique that stemmed from the association of vice and empire. Claims that these two were inextricably linked did not develop into a thorough denunciation of imperialism. Rather, by seeking to reform the imperial structure, the WCTU undermined the potential of a moral antiimperialism. Once the regulation of prostitution had been officially removed from the Philippines, and temperance missionaries like Carrie Faxon and Annie Darley had worked there, the WCTU became more sympathetic toward retention of that territory as well as that of other island possessions like Hawaii and Puerto Rico. Temperance women saw the opportunity for saving souls and also for testing reforms that could later be applied to the mainland United States. Katharine Stevenson could not in 1898 hide her anguish over the

Spanish-American War and the acquisition of the island territories.[113] But in 1909, as Stevenson's ship steamed past Zamboanga on her way from Hong Kong to Australia, "old glory" came into view on the island's shore: "I need not tell you that I saw it through tear-dimmed eyes, nor that my earnest prayer was that it might stand in the Far East as the symbol of righteousness." This experience, though so fleeting, gave her a "new respect for our island possessions."[114] Faced with the tangible evidence of imperial grandeur, and the chance for moral influence, women of the WCTU succumbed, like other missionaries, to patriotism.

AT THE HIGH POINT of its purity preoccupations, the WCTU had pushed its feminist concerns with sexual bondage toward a sentiment of racial solidarity with nonwhite peoples. This policy had been strongly invoked in the condemnation of regulated prostitution involving European imperial powers and their dominion over native peoples. When the stance of Bushnell and Andrew was vindicated within the World's WCTU in 1898, the solidarity of the organization with the bondage of women across cultural, social, and racial boundaries was emphasized, and the feminist and antiimperialist aspects of the World's work were highlighted. Even after 1900, when most purity workers in the United States spoke of "white slavery" and succumbed to a racial hysteria, the World's WCTU continued to emphasize the "slavery" of *all* women involved in prostitution. After all, said the World's convention in 1910, "the coloured races" did "furnish a very large proportion of the victims of vice." Thus Lillian Stevens reminded the national American WCTU convention that they fought not a white slave traffic but a "women's slave traffic." In this sense their international experience to some extent insulated temperance women in the Anglo-Saxon world against the more extreme and hysterical tendencies in purity thought after the turn of the century that grossly exploited fears of the possible racial suicide of European civilization.[115]

Yet this insulation was always incomplete and vitiated by the WCTU's position on issues of women's emancipation. WCTU purity workers abroad rarely understood that some prostitutes did not want to be rescued, and the same reformers were quite naturally unsympathetic toward the cultural traditions that limited women's choices in such places as China and Japan. Here the case of Japan provides even clearer evidence of cultural difference than the Indian because the issue was not complicated by the involvement of a European colonial power. Eliza Spencer Large, Flora Strout, and other WCTU missionaries in Japan who fought against the geisha system before World War I always emphasized the symbolism of women's oppression contained in the caging of women. Could the smiling faces and the sounds of laughter that Large heard when she toured the geisha districts of

Tokyo be evidence of consent and even happiness? Large did at least pose the question for her own supporters in the WCTU at home in Canada but dismissed the possibility in favor of an analysis that emphasized the "cages full of my sisters."[116]

Quite apart from the purity movement's reliance on the exaggerated image of women as sexual victims, the egalitarian content of this invocation of bondage had always been double-edged. Its implicit reliance on an extension of European cultural influence exposed this form of feminist thought in the women's temperance movement to the themes of cultural and patriotic chauvinism. As Frances Willard put it to the World's WCTU convention in 1897 before she died, "in oriental countries women are helpless in the hands of men, as they have been through the dark centuries."[117] European and Anglo-American women who, like Large, Strout, and Stevenson, carried the mantle of the WCTU's purity policies into the twentieth century were convinced that they alone could, through their message of one sexual standard, bring enlightenment on sexual practice to all other peoples. Such women were bound to be tempted by the prospects of a new kind of empire, shaped by a universalistic and egalitarian morality, that beckoned in American relations with the island territories. Devoted to peace, purity, and prohibition, the WCTU now found itself not a critic but an agent of this newly emerging American domain of moral and cultural power.

10

Women, Suffrage, and Equality

The experiences of temperance women in peace and purity campaigns underlined the necessity of voting rights. Women could, through the Polyglot Petition, attempt to shame men into action on moral issues, but the reality was that women lacked political power. So familiar is this point that most historians readily concede the significant role played by the WCTU in the training of converts to the cause of suffrage. Just as surely, a consensus exists over the meaning of the WCTU's support for voting rights. The impact of the WCTU's experience was, so the argument goes, inherently conservative. Temperance women wanted the ballot not for its own sake but to advance the women's culture of evangelical domesticity.[1] In this view, the American WCTU's endorsement of the vote reflected the dissemination of the doctrines of expediency in the larger Anglo-American suffrage movement. In place of the arguments of justice based on John Stuart Mill's liberal creed, British and American suffragists came increasingly in the late nineteenth century to argue for the ballot on instrumental grounds.[2]

This contrast between justice and expediency must not be overdrawn, as it frequently is. Suffrage supporters used both sets of arguments after the turn of the century, though literature emphasizing the instrumental value of suffrage was more common. Consider the case of the WCTU. For an organization routinely placed in the expediency category, a surprising amount of its propaganda involved justice arguments, which revealed a deep ambivalence over the instrumentalist case for voting rights. This eclecticism has been overlooked precisely because the WCTU/suffrage connection has not seemed problematic. Researchers interested in emphasizing the radical character of the quest for suffrage have naturally looked to other groups whose feminist credentials seem less open to challenge.[3]

Comparative perspectives can illuminate these issues. In the same era that the WCTU was organizing its international movement for women's emancipation, suffrage workers were stepping up their own campaigns. The formation of the International Woman Suffrage Alliance in 1902 testifies to the interest American feminists took in the international dimensions of their struggle. Reformers could not fail to notice that the assumed superiority of the American women's movement over its counterparts in other countries was compromised by the continuing failure of the American political system to secure for women the privileges of full voting rights and citizenship. As Californian suffragist Ellen Sargent exclaimed in 1910, "Who that realises the situation can be patriotic?"[4] Feminists became, at least for a time, rhetorically inclined toward internationalism and followed the WCTU's example in promoting feminist agitation on an international level.

Nor could feminists ignore the "triumphs" of suffrage in other countries, particularly in the antipodes. If the ideas of suffrage were first conceived in metropolitan powers like Britain, France, and the United States, these ideas were quick to take root in settlement colonies like New Zealand and South Australia and in frontier communities like Wyoming. As in many other aspects of the struggle for women's equality, that struggle was an indivisible and international one in which examples, institutions, and personnel passed back and forth across national boundaries. The suffrage movement was, in part, exported abroad as part of the cultural imperialism of the Anglo-American women's movement. Yet reciprocal effects were felt in the United States and Britain as the impact of suffrage spread worldwide.

Superficially, the campaign for suffrage in other countries where women's temperance was strong has seemed to confirm the summary judgment derived originally from American evidence. WCTU women were champions of expediency par excellence. According to Carl Degler, the same "conservative purpose, deriving from woman's traditional role in the family" allowed women to get the vote without much opposition in Australia at the end of the nineteenth century.[5] This, too, was the conclusion of Richard Evans in his path-breaking comparative study, *The Feminists*. Women's enfranchisement in both Australia and the American midwest he judged "a peculiarly narrow movement with limited objectives." Central to this interpretation was his contention that the WCTU dominated the suffrage struggle in Australia, except in Sydney.[6]

While many historians accept the role of the WCTU in the suffrage movements of the settlement colonies, they have not used the evidence from the antipodes to reexamine the timing and character of the temperance/suffrage connection. Did the WCTU have such limited objectives there that it demanded the vote only for a few specific moral reforms? Did its successes in these distant outposts of the Anglo-Saxon world have any impact on the strategies, tactics and ideologies of the larger suffrage movement in Britain and the United States? And exactly how important was the WCTU in the dissemination of the ideas of the Anglo-American suffrage agitation on an international level?[7]

Women, Suffrage, and Equality

ABSTRACT ARGUMENTS about expediency and justice flow easily from the pens of historians, yet most striking in the work of the WCTU is the difficulty of separating these concepts. For the WCTU's Clara Hoffman, who toured California in support of the suffrage referendum of 1897, expediency was pretending that women would not use the vote to oppose the sale of liquor. California suffragists had requested her not to wear the white ribbon while speaking in the campaign and to refrain from using temperance arguments. That the referendum failed merely reinforced Hoffman's conviction that "the only people deceived were the suffragists themselves."[8] Hoffman's complaint highlights the tension between competing visions of women's equality, not the WCTU's inability to measure up to an ahistorical standard of women's emancipation. For Hoffman and the WCTU, equality necessarily involved practice, not merely abstract rights. It was unjust to prevent women from preserving the sanctity of their homes just as it was inexpedient. Coming out of an evangelical culture that emphasized the subordination of women's individualism to the values of family and state, it was difficult for many WCTU women to think in terms of abstract equality.

But the WCTU did not therefore argue that women should be given the vote simply because to do so would enhance the progress of morality in society. Temperance women tended to combine arguments of natural rights indiscriminately with those of expediency and to see both as necessary to justice, in much the same way as other suffragists did between 1900 and 1920. The precise relation between these arguments employed by the WCTU varied considerably and did not always follow the typology of a retreat to conservatism implicit in a good deal of the critical commentary on the American suffrage movement. What is most striking is the variability of circumstances in which suffrage was connected to the temperance issue, even in the narrow perspective of the Anglo-American world.[9]

There was very good reason for the WCTU to combine both sets of arguments. In many parts of the United States and in the white settlement colonies of the British Empire, the WCTU was indeed prominent in the suffrage fight. In South Africa, New Zealand, and South Australia, it was the WCTU that began the organized push for voting rights among women. Others outside the WCTU's ranks soon formed their own organizations, but even the formation of the various franchise leagues was originally dependent on the WCTU's initiatives. This was the case in South Africa, where the WCTU began work in earnest in 1892, and where the first suffrage organization, the Cape Town Women's Enfranchisement League, was not formed until 1907, and then under WCTU guidance. The first president of the Women's Enfranchisement Association of the Union of South Africa, formed in 1911, was WCTU official Mrs. E. MacIntosh, and as late as 1926, when South African women still struggled for the vote under the peculiar conditions posed by the racial composition of the population, the

WCTU was one of six women's organizations that gave evidence before a parliamentary select committee on enfranchisement and supported women's suffrage through the arguments of World's WCTU official Emilie Solomon.[10]

The prominence of the WCTU in the suffrage struggle in South Africa and elsewhere in the British colonies did not mean that all women who sported the white ribbon put temperance first on their own list of priorities. Because of its strength within the women's movement in those places, the WCTU attracted some of the more advanced advocates of feminism. This was particularly true in New Zealand where temperance women under Kate Sheppard's energetic advocacy in the 1890s assumed a hegemonic position in the women's movement of that country. Little independent suffrage agitation existed, and WCTU-trained women also dominated the National Council of Women.[11]

Kate Sheppard did not ignore the liberal-individualist arguments, concludes the New Zealand suffrage movement's most prominent historian, Patricia Grimshaw. In 1888, Sheppard published an important pamphlet, *Ten Reasons Why the Women of New Zealand Should Vote*. Sheppard drew "especially," according to Grimshaw, on the arguments of John Stuart Mill.[12] Later, in 1891, she expanded this appeal to justice and equality in a larger propaganda piece that listed not ten but *Sixteen Reasons Why Women Should Vote*. Versions of this pamphlet were circulated in Victoria, South Australia, and Western Australia and became integral parts of the Australasian suffrage movement's intellectual rationale. *Sixteen Reasons* indiscriminately mixed issues of rights and expediency but argued that moral, social, and individual considerations all pointed toward the justice of giving women the vote, no matter what they did with it.[13] Because of the pioneer suffrage victories in New Zealand and South Australia, Sheppard's views were widely disseminated among temperance women and transcended their antipodean origins. In Britain, both the *Woman's Herald* and the *Woman's Signal* lauded Sheppard's achievement and utilized her arguments. In 1894, the latter paper published several articles that drew upon the structure of her case. In "Why Women Want the Vote," Mrs. M. Walters of Leeds offered only nine, not sixteen reasons, but she matched Sheppard's eclectic mixture while emphasizing like the New Zealander those arguments derived from principles of justice and equality.[14]

The widespread currency afforded to Sheppard's writings cannot therefore be considered an aberration, nor can New Zealand itself be regarded as a special case of deviation from WCTU values in the 1890s. The point of all this is not to muddy the waters of historiographical controversies. Rather, it is important to understand why the WCTU in Australasia, in particular, seemed to be willing to combine these allegedly incompatible arguments. Where the WCTU assumed an energetic role in the suffrage campaigns, it tended to include the justice arguments partly because under the WCTU umbrella were women of diverse aspirations. All work done under the WCTU banner was not, for example, the product of WCTU women as such but simply reflected the organizational advantages of the union and its ability to exercise a wider influence. Kate Sheppard herself conceded the large element of ecumenical cooperation within the New Zealand women's movement. "At least one-third of the women who collected the signatures" for the WCTU's final suffrage petition "were not members of any Temperance body."[15] Women's enfranchisement leagues devoted only to suffrage had done effective work in New Zealand, she noted in 1894, "although most of the principal workers in those leagues [were also] members of the W.C.T.U."[16] Cooperation was also considerable in Queensland, where the WCTU "assisted in forming Suffrage Societies among women outside [their] own ranks, and helped to educate them upon the methods of voting."[17]

The importance of the WCTU was facilitated in these places, as well as illustrated, by the fact that branches of the National Council of Women did not appear until the WCTU's suffrage agitation was well under way. In the New Zealand case, the Council did not emerge as a center of women's public activity until 1896, three years after the vote had been granted. When Sheppard went to England in 1907, the Council became moribund, and only the WCTU remained active in politics. In this (relative) institutional vacuum of colonial life, the temperance issue attracted women like Sheppard, South Africa's equally impressive Julia Solly, and South Australia's stalwart Elizabeth Nicholls, all of whom took a broad view of the issue of women's emancipation. Had these same women lived in Britain, they might have been attracted to the suffrage associations rather than the temperance movement as a focus of activity.[18]

The WCTU was strong in these British colonies for the same reasons that it was indispensable to the suffrage movement in the American west and south.[19] The WCTU had the broadest spread of local organizations, which meant that it could reach so many more women than the suffrage workers, who were usually restricted to the larger towns. This critical grass-roots role of the WCTU has been copiously documented by Catherine Cleverdon in her yet to be surpassed study of the Canadian suffrage agitation. As Cleverdon noted in the case of New Brunswick, the "province-wide scope of the W.C.T.U., as compared with the purely local character of the Enfranchisement Association, often carried greater weight with the lawmakers at Fredericton."[20] In South Australia, too, historian Helen Jones has emphasized the "part which the Woman's Christian Temperance Union played" as "very important in view of its large membership and geographical spread."[21] As a result, of 11,000 petition signatures collected on behalf of the Women's Suffrage League in 1893, 8,268 were secured by the WCTU through their forty-one auxiliary branches.[22]

These patterns of cooperation between the WCTU and the suffrage leagues in South Australia, South Africa, Canada, New Zealand, and elsewhere did not mean that the relationship between these groups was utterly harmonious. While the suffrage associations wished to use the WCTU organizational apparatus, as a general rule they did not want to become entangled in the claims of temperance women for prohibition nor tied to the Union's perceived sectarian limitations. As Maybanke Anderson, a leading suffragist in New South Wales, later recalled, "Our league demanded no qualification for membership, except a desire to help the enfranchisement of the woman."[23] Some Australian suffragists feared, as Mary Lee did in South Australia, that the WCTU women were lukewarm allies. In her view they had to be constantly cultivated and coaxed toward full acceptance of the suffrage cause.[24] This was not, however, a fair assessment of the leaders of the WCTU in South Australia, who associated with the suffrage elite and helped shape its ideology and tactics. Nor does Lee's judgment take sufficient account of the political impact of the WCTU's critical petitioning role in that colony.

But her critique did contain more than a little truth, especially when applied to the case of the more conservative colony of New South Wales. There, the Union lacked the strong commitment to doctrines of equal rights apparent in both New Zealand and South Australia. The tradition of religious dissent was broader and deeper in both those colonies, with their heritage of radical liberalism, middle-class ideals, and the absence of a strong Catholic element.

It was, rather, in New South Wales that the tension between the franchise leagues and the WCTU was most apparent, though even in this case cooperation was considerable and the WCTU's role should not be underestimated. Through its numerous auxiliaries and sheer numbers, the union there was a useful vehicle for financial help and a source of petitions. Yet at times a glaring gap separated the leadership from elements of the rank and file in their consciousness of the need for suffrage. Although the New South Wales WCTU had, in 1890, been the first organization to attempt to form an independent franchise league, the leadership's commitment encountered early opposition. The suffrage report of the colonial WCTU for 1894 made a significant admission in this respect: "The work has been a difficult one, as many of our own members have been, and some still are, adverse to it." The colonial superintendent, Elizabeth Ward, found that her members occasionally objected that to agitate for the right to vote was to ask for something unusual in the lives of women. Ward did not regard this objection as a valid one but was forced to make biblical analogies with women like

Women, Suffrage, and Equality

Deborah, Mary, the women of Samaria, and other role models of the Protestant evangelical churchwoman to connect her own concern with equality
to the experience of others.[25]

Arguments derived from the rights of women were for these tactical reasons rarely seen in isolation in the WCTU's ideological arsenal, and when
they were pushed most heavily, the emphasis often did reflect the leavening
example of and interaction with the suffrage societies. In South Australia, it
was Mary Lee who first urged upon temperance women the argument of
natural justice when she spoke at their meetings in 1889.[26] This leavening
effect meant that the colonial WCTU moved from a position emphasizing
expediency to one favoring justice as well, as its appeal broadened and the
campaign drew to a climax in 1893. This shift was almost the opposite of
what was allegedly happening in the larger suffrage movement in the United States. Whereas the American women's rights reformers of the 1850s
had staked the claims of justice before the emergence of the WCTU in the
United States in 1874, in South Australia the expediency arguments tended
to appear simultaneously with those based on egalitarian principles, or even
before the latter were articulated.[27]

Different again from South Australia was the process in New South
Wales, where the franchise league resisted WCTU initiatives for a joint
organization. As a result the arguments for natural justice were less often
stated in the New South Wales WCTU literature. The WCTU remained
everywhere fundamentally committed to the notion of the suffrage's utility
for moral reform, but White Ribboners displayed subtle tactical variations
in their arguments, which reflected the composition of WCTU support and
alliances in various regions and colonies.[28]

The preference of the WCTU for arguments of moral utility did not
mean that the struggle for women's enfranchisement was rendered peculiarly narrow in the colonial context. In reference to the Victorian case,
Richard Evans has argued that "the WCTU never really desired votes for
women as anything more than a means to the end of liquor [production]."[29]
It is true that the Victorian union specifically excluded the demand that
women should be able to stand for parliament and claimed they only wanted the opportunity to elect "good men." This was not an uncommon stand.
Euphemia Bowes, first colonial president of the WCTU in New South
Wales, championed this position when she argued that "it was not the right
to enter Parliament they wanted. They would not go in if asked to do so.
There were plenty of good men in New South Wales to make the laws."[30] If
this and similar statements exposed the conservatism of many WCTU wom-
en—and the pragmatism of others unwilling to offend male legislators before suffrage had been granted—too much should not be made of the
point, which played a very minor role in the WCTU suffrage agitation.

Statements of this kind were part of the WCTU's cultural inheritance but should not be interpreted as an indication of an ideological essence hostile to women's equality. WCTU policy in Australia varied on this issue and depended on political circumstances. Elizabeth Nicholls, who edited *Our Federation*, the organ of the Australasian WCTU at the turn of the century, expressly opposed the exclusion of women from parliamentary careers. Nicholls wrote the New South Wales WCTU in protest against Bowes's speech: legislation "must, inevitably, come" to full equality, "for justice demands completely equal political rights and opportunities." The Queensland WCTU took the same position, cooperated on this issue with leading non-WCTU feminist Rose Scott of Sydney, and called any such ban on women in parliament a "sex stigma" in the legislation.[31]

There is scant evidence that these women were self-satisfied with their successful agitation; nor did they feel that the struggle had been easily won. The commonplace observation that Australasian women had been handed the suffrage on a platter was largely the patronizing creation of the New Zealand politician William Pember Reeves in a comment contained in his *State Experiments in Australia and New Zealand*. "One fine morning of September, 1893, the women of New Zealand woke up and found themselves enfranchised. The privilege was theirs," wrote Reeves, "given freely and spontaneously in the easiest and most unexpected manner in the world by male politicians."[32] This statement was made in 1902, but in 1893–94, the women (and male supporters) of the suffrage movement harbored no such illusions. Sir John Hall, ex-premier of New Zealand, told a London audience in 1894, with Kate Sheppard's concurrence, that women's suffrage was "not won suddenly or easily" but "after a struggle of fourteen years."[33] It would be another eight before New South Wales president Sara Nolan could claim victory "after long years of working and waiting" that went back at least to 1888, so far as the New South Wales WCTU agitation was concerned. Had these women been forced to wait until 1919, they may have felt especially privileged, but they did not greet the franchise with such a false perception.[34]

Nor did these women suggest that the quick granting of the vote signified that feminist goals, so bitterly contested in other countries, had already been achieved. The struggle for equality went on despite the symbol of equality attained in the suffrage victories. Nolan turned in 1902 immediately to the education of the newly enfranchised women and stated that "our work for the franchise is but begun." Nolan was one of a number of WCTU workers who engaged in citizenship education and voter registration work and who saw the disabilities women faced as vastly more complicated than disenfranchisement. To her the critical issue was "political economy," which for Nolan meant the way the state exercised and distributed resources between different groups and, especially, between men and women.[35] Eleanor Trundle, Queensland franchise superintendent, had similar views. She em-

Women, Suffrage, and Equality

Elizabeth Nicholls, prominent suffrage activist in South Australia, Austral-asian WCTU president, 1894–1903, and delegate to the 1900 and 1920 World's conventions (Isabel McCorkindale, *Torch-Bearers* [Adelaide: WCTU of South Australia, 1949]; reprinted by permission of the Woman's Christian Temperance Union of South Australia)

phasized, with her colleagues Susan Sagar and Agnes Williams, the legal
disabilities women faced, and she argued that the position of working wom-
en needed amelioration under conditions of women's enfranchisement.[36]
The Victorian WCTU also adopted this broader view of the meaning of
women's political power and pointed out, simultaneously with their own
very protracted struggle for voting rights, that the educational position of
women in Victoria was noticeably inferior to that of women in both the
United States and Great Britain.[37]

"Even enfranchisement itself is no finality," said a New Zealand friend of
Kate Sheppard's in a letter to noted California clubwoman Caroline Severance. It was, rather, "a poor and frequently blundering means to . . . a
spiritual rebirth of the whole globe."[38] Such dissatisfaction with the symbolism of the vote was widespread among antipodean feminists, but never
were such sentiments more clearly articulated than in the writings of the
American observer Jessie Ackermann on her last visit to Australia in 1911.
Her conversations with the leading feminists of the new Commonwealth of
Australia produced a pessimistic assessment: "There is a widespread feeling
among thoughtful women in Australia that the boasted 'equality' of the
sexes is more or less a farce. As a matter of fact that equality extends scarcely beyond the privilege of casting a vote."[39] The identification of the Australian WCTU leaders with the international movement was strong precisely because of this recognition of practical inequality. As Elizabeth Nicholls
and Sara Nolan perceived when they voyaged to World's WCTU conferences in 1900 and 1910 respectively, antipodean women still lagged beyond
their American and British sisters in practical status.[40]

Apart from the dimension of an emotional solidarity with a larger wom-
en's movement, the international connection was also of obvious value to
the women who joined because it presented them with readily accessible
information on the suffrage and related issues. Kate Sheppard began her
suffrage crusade in Christchurch, New Zealand, in 1885, with the help of
American WCTU literature on women's voting rights in Wyoming territory.[41] Australian WCTU women followed suit, and their publications in the
1890s carried reports of any success achieved abroad.[42] Ackermann was
sedulous in circulating WCTU literature on her missionary trips and was
active in the colonies in "pressing home the just claims of women to the
ballot."[43] Nor should it be forgotten that Mary Leavitt had been a franchise
superintendent for the WCTU in Massachusetts before becoming a temperance missionary, and she, too, stimulated interest in this subject through
her public lectures as early as 1885 in New Zealand and 1886 in Australia.[44]

Arguments derived from American WCTU propaganda naturally stressed
the issue of home protection, which had recently been accepted through
Willard's efforts in the United States. This same strategy seemed appropriate to Australasian circumstances, particularly at the beginning of the agita-

tion in the late 1880s. But this utilitarian theme was usually linked to the issues of citizenship and human rights at the same time. Though Mrs. E. J. Ward of the New South Wales franchise department used home protection arguments, Ward told the colonial convention of 1899 that she followed Frances Willard's example. The latter had "no sooner addressed herself to grapple with the evils of intemperance, than she discovered that the key to success lay in the extension of full citizenship to women."[45] Home protection had led Ward to desire citizenship as part of women's emancipation. In addition to the familiar arguments that are expected as a matter of course among WCTU supporters, other propaganda was derived from the wider context of the suffrage struggle in America. The South Australian WCTU noted in 1894 that the suffrage congress at the Chicago World's Fair was "a triumph" for Susan B. Anthony, and colonial president Elizabeth Nicholls proudly claimed that "this intrepid woman has comrades like-minded in South Australia." Among these she numbered herself as well as her colleagues on the council of the Women's Suffrage League.[46]

The American influence went well beyond the emulation of arguments to include the impact of American personnel as well. Suffrage work was stimulated not only by the transitory presence of Leavitt and Ackermann but also by the residence in Australia of a number of expatriate Americans. One of these, Mary M. Love of Virginia, was the first colonial WCTU president in Victoria, and another, Catharine P. Wallace, wife of George Wallace of St. Louis, the American consul-general in Melbourne, was first superintendent of the colonial WCTU franchise department.[47]

The propaganda stimulus was reciprocal. Wallace, for instance, returned to the United States in late 1893 after her husband was replaced as consul-general, and she talked freely of her experiences, and not only to WCTU women. Wallace's articles on the Australasian suffrage agitation had already appeared in the *Union Signal* before she returned, but she also spoke in the United States before the Mississippi Valley Women's Congress and the Missouri state suffrage association on "voting in South Australia" and reported the audience's "interest and enthusiasm."[48] A good deal of Australasian material appeared in the various international WCTU publications, including Britain's *Woman's Signal* and the *White Ribbon*. Such material was used by American and British temperance women to reinforce their claims to the ballot. What was good for the women of South Australia and New Zealand was surely suitable for women in more sophisticated societies.[49]

Since the use of Australasian examples to spur suffrage workers in Britain and America peaked in the 1890s and shortly after, it is pertinent to ask what impact these antipodean examples had on the development of suffrage ideology. The triumphs in the Southern Hemisphere from 1893 to 1902 overlapped with the stagnation in the American suffrage movement after 1896. It was at this time that the American WCTU and the suffrage societies began to take greater heed of victories abroad and to point to American deficiencies. The use of Australasian material thus coincided with the push for arguments of expediency within the suffrage movement in the United States itself. Suffragists were able to point to the successful alliance between feminism and temperance in Australia and New Zealand to bolster the argument that the crusade for the ballot would, as Clara Hoffman had contended on her tour of California in 1897, be strengthened by acknowledging what women could do with the vote.[50]

In this context, the broader range of arguments for granting the suffrage, and the nature of the colonial circumstances that promoted the alliance of temperance and suffrage, tended to be obscured. The American WCTU assimilated the Australasian evidence to its own purposes, which required an emphasis on the temperance contribution. Moreover, since the vote had been achieved more rapidly in Australasia than in the major centers of Anglo-American suffrage activity, it seemed natural to temperance women that these victories must have reflected the greater prominence of the WCTU in the colonial struggles. For these reasons, the WCTU's propaganda concentrated on explaining that women's suffrage in Australia had "been instrumental in bringing many reform measures before the federal and state parliaments." The Australian example was "hastening the day when, in all Christian nations, women as well as men, shall be voting citizens."[51]

This was not a stance taken only by the WCTU. The wider coalition of women's suffrage groups was susceptible to the same tactical and ideological pressures. In fact, suffragists in the United States who used Australasian examples were more inclined than temperance workers in the antipodes to stress expedient rather than egalitarian arguments for granting the vote, and American suffragists were also more inclined to emphasize the conservative results of the ballot in Australasia. Alice Stone Blackwell, editor of the Boston *Woman's Journal*, used Kate Sheppard's material but stressed much more than Sheppard the arguments of "purity, sobriety, and honor" in promoting votes for women rather than the fact that such a reform would be "fair and right." Blackwell's own *Twelve Reasons Why Women Want to Vote* borrowed the structure and rhetorical style of the New Zealander's *Sixteen Reasons* but emphasized women's duty to clean up American politics and "increase women's influence."[52] Similarly, Ida Husted Harper, the biographer and friend of Susan B. Anthony, wrote several pertinent articles on the suffrage issue in Australasia, and she too emphasized "temperance and morality." Harper cited the testimony of New Zealand's male politicians like Richard Seddon that "drink shops [had] been closed on election day, [and] the tone of politics [improved]."[53]

Partly this shift in ideology resulted from the emergence of a new generation of reformers who took charge of the American suffrage movement

Women, Suffrage, and Equality

The Union Signal

OFFICIAL ORGAN
NATIONAL WOMAN'S CHRISTIAN TEMPERANCE UNION

Published Weekly

Subscription Price, $1.50 a Year in Advance

Entered as second class matter at the Postoffice at Evanston, Illinois

| Vol. XLVII | EVANSTON, ILLINOIS, MARCH 17, 1921 | No. 11 |

A Strong Sweep and a Long Sweep Will Do It!

To Make the Whole World Safe for Future Generations the Women Voters of All Nations, With Their Ballots, Must Sweep Away the Traffic in Alcoholic Beverages.

INTERNATIONAL EDITION

The vote as an extension of domesticity as illustrated in the *Union Signal*'s expectation of what women's suffrage would bring
(*Union Signal*, 17 Mar. 1921)

when Elizabeth Cady Stanton and Anthony passed from the scene. The new leaders were women like Anna Howard Shaw and Carrie Chapman Catt, both of whom had been members of the WCTU and were still sympathetic to its aims. Both were aware of the importance of the WCTU to any successful suffrage agitation. Catt addressed the 1913 World's convention and told the assembled delegates that the temperance pledge was "the first vow I took in this world." Said Catt: "I have learned that the greatest enemy today to the enfranchisement of women is not ignorance, is not stubbornness, is not prejudice, but the legalized government-protected saloon system. And so after all we are not so very far apart. . . . The aim of all [of us] is to make this old world better."[54] Shaw, an honorary lecturer for the National WCTU, maintained friendly relations after her election to the National American Woman Suffrage Association presidency in 1904 and canceled her lecturing engagements to appear at the 1904 NWCTU convention. Like Catt would do seven years later, she spoke at the Boston World's convention in 1906 "not only as a Woman Suffragist but as an old Crusader and a member of the W.C.T.U."[55]

The impact of this temperance connection is difficult to assess. The American suffrage forces had decided to woo the temperance elements at the cost of ideological purity because their votes were desperately needed. Yet the suffragist Abigail Scott Duniway has confused historians on this point. Duniway claimed that temperance women were backward on the suffrage issue and charged that many "never lifted voice or finger to secure their right to vote." But this testimony must be used with caution.[56] Clara Colby of Portland, Oregon, secretary of the Woman's Federal Equality Association, gave Caroline Severance a different view. "We had great hopes in Oregon but our affairs are very much complicated here now. Mrs. Duniway has antagonized the W.C.T.U. who were our best helpers by saying they killed the [suffrage] amendment—and now they are not taking hold of the petition work which is progressing but slowly."[57] Shaw and Catt did not share Duniway's prejudices, but the question remains whether the tactical alliance between temperance and suffrage that they favored influenced the suffrage ideology.

To the extent that the suffrage/temperance alliance entailed expression of support for prohibition on the part of committed suffragists like Shaw and Catt, the emphasis on expediency was indeed partly secured by WCTU examples. But did the evidence the WCTU presented of the link between moral reform and votes for women abroad influence this ideology? These two leading suffragists did, it must be reiterated, address World's WCTU meetings, and Catt was particularly active in promoting international support for suffrage. It was she who was the "prime moving force" behind the formation and growth of the International Woman Suffrage Alliance between 1902 and 1923.[58] The alliance's declaration of sentiments did not, as was to be expected in a body focused purely on the issue of votes for women, have anything specific to say about temperance but did argue that only a "noble and fully developed womanhood" would allow a "noble and fully developed humanity." WCTU propagandists in turn hailed Catt's alliance as evidence of the potential for moral uplift inherent in the suffrage cause and as evidence of a growing sense of internationalism in the women's movement.[59]

The antipodean influence in this convergence must not be exaggerated, however. What is striking in the suffrage agitation after 1902 is not the extent of antipodean references but their dearth. Despite Catt's heightened awareness of the importance of the international suffrage movement, she placed relatively little importance on the particular achievements in Australia and New Zealand. In fact, on her much-publicized world trip of 1912, she did not even go near those British dominions, preferring instead to concentrate on Africa and Asia. These were areas where women's suffrage was not victorious and where the oppression of women assumed particularly stark forms. This does not mean that the fruits of the WCTU's labors went entirely unnoticed. Catt visited Japan, for example, where the Japanese WCTU under Kaji Yajima had fostered a close connection between the antiprostitution movement and the local campaign for women's suffrage.[60]

But so far as the suffrage experiments in the South Pacific were concerned, the enthusiasm of the 1890s was largely lost in a global agitation. American congressional hearings saw Catt and other suffragists failing to do more than catalog antipodean triumphs among others designed to shame Congress into passing a suffrage amendment. It is significant indeed that the American exception to this generalization was Alice Stone Blackwell. Alone among those who testified in 1913 before a special congressional committee on women's suffrage, Blackwell drew upon the WCTU's record in Australasia. Possibly because of her contacts as editor of the *Woman's Journal* and almost certainly because of her own longtime membership in the WCTU, Blackwell did drive home the connection between temperance and suffrage in those places. Blackwell made telling reference to the role of the women's vote in humanitarian reform and the expansion of a maternalist ideology in the broader sphere of public life. Experience contradicted the arguments of the antisuffragists, she testified. Suffrage had produced "many benefits, including the improved care for child life which has made New Zealand's death rate the lowest in the world."[61]

The absence of significant reference to Australia and New Zealand can be partly explained by the fact that the very granting of suffrage meant that these examples were no longer controversial or topical after 1902. Attention was focused elsewhere, since the suffrage struggle had itself shifted geographically. Suffragists may not have wished to draw attention to the unpalatable truth that women did not vote in Australia as often as men did.

Though Jessie Ackermann made this connection, suffragists emphasized other aspects of women's enfranchisement in Australia and New Zealand.[62]

Particularly important was the fact that not one of the Australasian cases involved a truly independent country, and all were comparatively insignificant in the world of international politics. Ida Harper explained the contrast between success in Australasia and failure in the United States in simple yet effective terms designed in practice to draw attention from the lessons of the antipodes. Though relevant as a laboratory of moral and social reform, and "the most important event in the history of the movement toward woman suffrage" up to 1904, the Australian example offered, in Harper's view, few tactical lessons for Americans, except in very negative terms. Suffrage could "be extended by legislative action" in Australia, while in the United States, "it must be granted by the existing voters." Beyond the difficult process of amending the American constitution by referenda, "no further explanation" was in her view "needed." For Harper, the United States was too democratic to make suffrage victories easy since the "ignorant" and "vicious" male immigrants could vote suffrage down. In contrast, the emphasis on parliamentary initiative ironically allowed colonial liberalism to take its natural course without fear of a backlash from conservative male voters.[63]

Even the WCTU succumbed to the logic of this argument, which treated Australia as a special and irrelevant case after 1902. Thus the *Union Signal* followed the lead of the *New York World* in 1909 in hailing the importance of the Swedish suffrage victory. While Australia and New Zealand had been pioneers in the movement, so this argument went, New Zealand was small and Australia "lives under colonial conditions which largely exclude international problems from consideration." But Sweden was "a factor in world politics quite out of proportion to its five million [inhabitants]. . . . She [was] wholly independent, highly educated, [and] perplexed by all the problems of modern industrial life."[64]

As the suffrage struggle moved back from the periphery of the Anglo-American world to its metropolitan centers, therefore, the links with temperance declined in relevance, despite the prominence of former temperance workers among the leaders of the mainstream suffrage societies in the United States. Yet the connection was never entirely lost, not even in the spectacular case of Britain, where militant suffragism became a divisive issue after 1906. The role of temperance was different in Britain, to be sure, because the political, legal, and institutional context was different. Yet the British story still contains a variation on the same theme: a complex interplay between suffrage and the moral reform programs of temperance women.

The unitary system of government, the hostile House of Lords, the rise of militancy, the class structure, and the peculiar relationship between the

Liberal party and the temperance movement pushed suffrage and temperance into more antagonistic channels in Britain. The WSPU under the Pankhursts was founded in 1903 in response to frustration over the efficacy of moderate political tactics. A complementary contextual and organizational influence on the WSPU came also from the growing strength and vitality of working-class politics. The WSPU was inclined to argue that drink was not the cause of working-class emiseration and that economic and political reform was essential to the solution of capital/labor conflict. BWTA secretary Agnes Slack and the WSPU's Emmeline Pankhurst clashed "angrily" over the issue at a series of public meetings in 1910. Declared Pankhurst: "Women would not be drunken at all if they had healthy homes and decent food."[65] This was typical of the WSPU and contemporary British suffragettes. The Women's Co-Operative Guild in London investigated in 1916 the social and moral effects of economic emiseration and reported as final testimony that "while they allow such slums to be they must expect dirt and drink. Before they start reforming women, let them reform the slums."[66]

The BWTA and other moderate suffrage organizations in Britain were also at odds with the increasingly militant tactics of the WSPU and its allies. This was not a dilemma faced by the WCTU in the United States, at least prior to the formation of the Congressional Union in 1915. The American suffrage movement's attachment to the liberal and bourgeois notions of constitutional procedures was much more uniform and more deeply engrained than in Britain. Militancy had to be imported to the United States movement from Britain, but even in England, many suffrage workers were not party to the more extreme tactics of the radicals. This was especially true in the case of the BWTA, which expressed shrill opposition to the various parliamentary demonstrations and the resort to violent tactics. Slack assured Anna Gordon in the midst of the most controversial conflict in 1913 that the BWTA was "*heart & soul against militancy.*" At the 1913 BWTA conference Lady Dorothy Howard's successful motion had deplored "the lawless methods of the militants," and she refused to accept an amendment that would have conceded that those methods were the result "of gross provocation" by insensitive and unresponsive politicians.[67]

Though the BWTA stood firm, the significance of this stand must not be misunderstood. Historians of the British suffrage movement have been attracted to the colorful tactics of the radicals, which are as impossible to ignore now as they were in 1914. Yet the main part of the British women's suffrage movement remained opposed to the WSPU, and the role of the BWTA within this broader if more moderate coalition has not yet been adequately studied.[68] Because of its links with the WLF, the BWTA was influential in behind-the-scenes lobbying of parliamentary candidates and in suffrage education work at the local level. As WLF president, Rosalind

Carlisle was said to have "been worth at least 20 votes" in the parliamentary roll calls.[69]

The rift with militant suffrage did not exactly coincide with the expediency/justice controversy. Militants in both the United States and Britain were prepared to use instrumental arguments at times, and some firmly hoped that suffrage would enable women to push such causes as socialism and peace.[70] Rather, militance was offensive primarily because its style violated stereotypes of womanly behavior and because that style conflicted with the BWTA's conception of its own forms of influence. Carlisle occupied a particularly delicate position in relation to the suffrage issue. She believed, like most BWTA members, that the most effective course would be the quiet lobbying of members of parliament backed by resolutions in the WLF conferences. Any hint of militancy would have severed her connections to the Liberal government and threatened BWTA influence in the WLF. A joint parliamentary deputation of suffrage organizations, including a BWTA representative, arranged for 19 May 1906, had been broken off after "the [radicals'] disorderly interruptions" in the House of Commons on 25 April during Keir Hardie's suffrage speech. Carlisle fully endorsed this move by the suffrage moderates, and the BWTA refused to cooperate further with the WSPU because "if they did, Parliamentarians would use it against them, and would class British Women with those who pursue unruly methods."[71] As WLF president, Carlisle sponsored a long series of antimilitant resolutions, and these same resolutions were publicized in the United States by WLF member Agnes Slack to assure the Americans that their British co-workers were free of the militant taint.[72]

This antimilitant stance was not uniformly adopted in other WCTU affiliates, and when Slack raised the issue in international forums, controversy dogged her trail. On a trip to Canada in 1913, she first clashed angrily on the hustings with those she called "violent" militants, then tried to get the Canadian WCTU at its Dominion convention to adopt an antimilitant resolution similar to that put forward by the BWTA. Finally, Slack sternly lectured the organization for its publishing what she regarded as pro-militant propaganda in the *Canadian White Ribbon Tidings*. But the Dominion WCTU did not succumb to Slack's blustering tactics for fear of splitting the WCTU in Canada. Even in the United States, where the executive committee had welcomed the British stance in 1913, Slack's pursuit of militants provoked a mixed reaction. When she attacked the WSPU at the World's convention in Brooklyn, some American delegates dissented from Slack's reelection to the position of World's secretary by supporting a write-in candidate from New Zealand, Anderson Hughes-Drew. While controversy was not unusual at World's conventions, the opposition to Slack, as demonstrated in private correspondence as well as public acts, was bitter indeed.[73]

The reasons for this opposition were most clearly set out in a frank personal rebuke written by South Africa's Emilie Solomon. She told Slack in 1913 that the BWTA's assault on the militants was unfair because it did not take account of the immense provocation produced by the Asquith cabinet's failure to display any genuine interest in the women's cause. Asquith had "insulted and tried to ignore the women ever since he came into power." Slack had nailed her colors to the Liberal cause, but the Liberal cabinet had "shown how prejudiced and illiberal Liberals can be." Solomon agonized over what she regarded as the regrettable (that is, violent) aspects of the militant tactics but pointed out plainly the political truth that Slack sought to avoid. It was the militants, not the moderates, who had stirred public opinion in South Africa by 1913. "I have no hesitation in saying that nothing has aroused attention in the Colonies like the action of the Militants. Hundreds of people who have never heard of any other Suffrage Societies watch their every movement with interest, and whether they approve or not they cannot lose sight of the question." Whereas Slack felt that change could come peaceably, for Solomon every important democratic innovation had in the past been conditioned by the need for the people to resort "to disorder & acts of violence" to "show their desire for reform."[74]

Solomon's indictment should not be allowed to exaggerate the importance of militant arguments in the ranks of the World's WCTU nor to diminish the significance of work done by Slack, Carlisle, and other temperance Liberals. Among WCTU supporters, the militant case won some sympathy in Canada, South Africa, and Britain, where suffrage had not been attained, but in Australia, where women had had the vote in federal elections since 1902, the new national president, Lady J. W. Holder, poured scorn on the radical cause in 1913. She claimed that women could achieve more by "acting wisely," that is, moderately. Always a minority sentiment within the World's WCTU, sympathy for militant suffragism nevertheless demonstrated the variability of the connection between women's enfranchisement and temperance and emphasized the diversity of opinion within and between the national affiliates.[75]

Solomon correctly understood that the connection with the Liberals made it impossible for the BWTA to lead the suffrage fight or to shape innovative tactics. The public attention passed to others, but the BWTA remained an important part of the constitutional suffrage struggle. The BWTA took part in the great Parliamentary Suffrage Procession and Demonstration in February 1907, and again they participated in 1910 under the general banner of the National Union of Women's Suffrage Societies.[76] The BWTA included on its roster twenty special "suffrage lecturers" who stumped the country in the last ten years before the European war demanding equal franchise. Such important BWTA activists as Florence Balgarnie, Laura Ormiston Chant, Agnes Slack, Jennie Clarkson, and Annie M. Lile participated in this concerted campaign.[77]

Woman's World/Woman's Empire

The tactics of Millicent Fawcett's NUWSS were more moderate and hence less newsworthy than those of the WSPU, but that is not to say that the moderates were without political influence. Within that coalition, the BWTA was of much greater importance, particularly from 1893 to 1909, than its almost complete neglect in the secondary literature on the subject would indicate. The BWTA could, for example, claim to speak on behalf of 145,000 members as early as 1906 and argue that support for women's suffrage was, on the basis of annual council debates, practically unanimous. The BWTA's petitioning skills were valued by NUWSS affiliates, which benefited from a drive in 1903–4 netting over 10,000 signatures from BWTA locals in London.[78]

Within the coalition of moderates, the BWTA was particularly active in promoting women's suffrage at the local level, where links between the NUWSS affiliates and the BWTA have been documented by historian Sandra Holton. These links were more noticeable in the north, where evangelicalism and dissent made the BWTA and temperance important social forces. The Glasgow Women's Enfranchisement Society, for example, forged close bonds with temperance M.P.s and the local BWTA affiliate. Similarly, speakers from the North of England Society for Woman Suffrage addressed BWTA meetings in that region in the 1890s.[79]

Yet another indication of the local impact of the BWTA was the organization's role in the promotion of voting at the county and borough levels. Though the parliamentary franchise was denied all women in the United Kingdom prior to 1918, quite extensive enfranchisement of women at the nonparliamentary level had existed since 1888. In 1898, for example, there were over 100,000 women voters at the municipal level in London alone.[80] The skills and resources of the BWTA's broadly based and well-organized society were employed in the period 1890–1910 to maximize the effectiveness of this vote and to compensate for some of the obvious obstacles ordinary women faced in exercising their limited franchise rights. "If some voters had 'no time,'" a BWTA worker "minded the shop, nursed the baby, or cooked the dinner, while the voters went to the polling station."[81]

Superintendent of Woman Voters' Work, Bertha Mason, another WLF member, was especially active in pushing the rights of women to vote and also to serve at the municipal and county levels as a demonstration of their fitness for the full parliamentary franchise. As Lancashire County president of the BWTA, treasurer of the NUWSS, and author of *The Story of Suffrage*, Mason brought together the causes of moderate suffragism, temperance, and the Liberal party. Under her leadership, the BWTA conducted between 1904 and 1907 a strenuous lobbying and petitioning campaign to gain women the right to be elected and to act on the borough and county councils. (Similar but more limited rights had existed prior to 1903; the eligibility of women to serve on school boards had been removed when the functions of the boards were transferred to the borough councils.)[82] After these rights were granted in 1907, Mason concentrated on getting women to vote for women and to publicize their achievements. Voting at this level was compatible with the arguments of expediency because county councils were responsible for the housing of the poor, the administration of education, the supervision of public health, the regulation of the "purity" of amusements, and other social welfare and moral "housekeeping" functions.[83] But the BWTA also argued that behind the local voting drive was the desire to "demonstrate that [British women] wanted the vote."[84] Mason was keen to publicize the election of women because it demonstrated their ability to take part in politics and highlighted the achievements of BWTA franchise work. Her *Story of Suffrage*, in line with these interests, concentrated on the liberal-individualist side of the suffrage issue, stressing legal inequalities faced by women and the organizational and parliamentary battles required to win full citizenship.[85]

There is some evidence that this and other BWTA work was of declining significance in the suffrage movement after 1910, as Solomon claimed from afar.[86] The emergence of militance itself was not the cause of the ebb of BWTA influence, but the fact that the Liberals now held the Treasury benches was. As a consequence, the NUWSS adopted a more critical attitude toward the Liberal program during the immediate prewar years. With the effort of Millicent Fawcett in 1912 to court Labour party support in retaliation for Liberal prevarication, the position of many temperance women in Britain on the suffrage question was compromised. Because of the tight WLF/BWTA link, the role of women like Bertha Mason in the NUWSS agitation diminished thereafter. Yet the temperance contribution was never entirely lost, nor should such links between moral reform and suffrage be neglected in any comparative survey of the WCTU's role in the struggle for equality.

The suffrage/temperance nexus in the British case differed from that of other World's WCTU affiliates, but even where a sophisticated and diverse suffrage movement existed, and even where the WCTU did not assume critical importance in the struggle, temperance women developed their own deep commitment to women's enfranchisement. They did so *both* because they believed that voting alone could give women power to further social and moral causes *and* because they actively promoted—in many circumstances—the ideals of justice enshrined in the concept of legal equality. The luxury of choosing between these two poles of suffrage thought was, in the context of their organizational battles and intellectual heritage, not theirs to make. Equality for them, as for many other suffrage workers, could only be given meaning in its practice.

11

Women and Equality

The Socialist Alternative

The arguments for suffrage made clear that equality always entailed something more than a badge of political freedom to the WCTU. But what exactly was that something more? Equality for many women outside the Anglo-Saxon world did not mean voting and embraced instead a wide variety of social and national aspirations. As an organization with international pretensions, the WCTU could not help but be touched by these themes of social justice and women's emancipation, which the WCTU also championed at home. Moreover, because one source of its political sentiments lay in the moral and religious heritage of evangelical Protestantism, the WCTU was not totally oblivious to the critique of liberal-individualism coming from the left. The WCTU demonstrated an awareness of other sides of the issue of equality that involved the actual conditions of life in which many millions of women around the world lived.

Until recently, it would have seemed strange to associate the name *WCTU* with anything so ostensibly un-American as socialism. Yet historians today think otherwise, and research on the WCTU has directed considerable attention to the meaning of equality by focusing on the relationship between temperance women on the one hand and labor and socialism on the other. In the 1880s and early 1890s, particularly, Frances Willard forged an alliance with the Knights of Labor, then moved steadily in the direction of advocacy of socialism as the solution to the problems of humanity in general and of women in particular.[1]

Willard's socialist phase coincided with her involvement in the international women's movement through the World's WCTU and her friendship with Isabel Somerset. A close connection existed, so it appears, between internationalist and socialist sentiment in the World's WCTU. Yet this connection has never been investigated. Did the BWTA reflect the allegedly "more radical nature" of the British temperance movement? Did the British women evidence closer links than their American counterparts with "working-class and socialist elements"?[2] How far did the socialist tinge in the American and World's WCTUs derive from these international sources?

The case for an international influence on the socialist element in the WCTU rests mainly on Willard's association with Lady Henry. It was during the period of her friendship with Somerset that "Socialism . . . moved to the center of Willard's interests."[3] It is true that the BWTA worked in an environment in which socialism, at least in the form of trade union and labor politics, was on the rise in the 1890s, and Lady Henry was among the vanguard of those who embraced the cause of labor in the British women's movement. Along with Willard and Hannah Whitall Smith, the BWTA's controversial president was one who sympathized in 1893 with the plight of the striking English coal miners in their fight for what Smith bluntly called "a living wage." Rosalind Carlisle was also a prominent Christian socialist, and the BWTA supplied other socialist sympathizers of note in trade unionist Amy Hicks of London and Margaret Parker, the wealthy manufacturer's wife who led the WWCTU's precursor, the International WCTU, in the late 1870s.[4]

These were certainly active and colorful figures, but all the evidence indicates that socialist sympathies were stronger in the American WCTU than elsewhere. Only the American WCTU established a specific department to deal with working-class issues, and this operated effectively under a variety of titles from the 1880s to the end of World War I. Willard herself had first become interested in socialism from her reading of the work of the American Edward Bellamy, whose *Looking Backward* helped popularize a Christian socialist vision in the late 1880s. The WCTU's socialism was not derived from Marxism's predominantly economistic approach to the problems of social reconstruction in the period of the Second International after 1889. Rather, it was deeply rooted in the Protestant evangelical temper, with its critique of excessive materialism.[5] That commitment on Willard's part was strengthened by her sojourns in Britain and her friendship with Lady Henry, but the indigenous influences remained strongest and continued to shape participation in the temperance and labor department by other WCTU workers who had never been outside the United States.

For most socialist sympathizers in the WCTU, it was the blend of their beloved chieftain's personal vision of social justice, the evangelical heritage of social reform, and the environment of labor unrest and Populist protest in the late 1880s and early 1890s that proved crucial to their commitment. But socialism in the WCTU was indirectly linked to internationalism. Those women in the WCTU most inclined to stress worldwide evangelism were also those attracted to notions of an international brotherhood as a solution to the world's economic and social problems.

Willard expressed the nature of the socialist strain of WCTU thinking in her 1893 address to the NWCTU on "Gospel Socialism." "In every Christian there exists a socialist; and in every socialist a Christian," she proclaimed as she invoked the vision of a gradually triumphant golden rule to chart the future course of human evolution away from selfish individualism to "a corporate conscience."[6] It was this appeal to a Christian morality and the demand for the alleviation of suffering that won a degree of acceptance in the WCTU for socialistic criticisms of the existing economic system. As labor and temperance superintendent Mae Whitman of California pointed out in 1909, the WCTU looked at "the ethics of labor from a Bible standpoint." Scouring biblical texts, Whitman had no difficulty concluding that "the [Old Testament] conception of justice in matters of economics was in advance of our own" because "speculation was forbidden by law" and every man had "a right to the product of his toil."[7]

Hostility to a grasping materialism was widespread in the WCTU and fed the demands for economic justice that the temperance and labor department espoused. Lillian Stevens may have been "no socialist" when she succeeded Willard as NWCTU president in 1898, but though Stevens's husband was a wealthy manufacturer, she displayed in her presidential addresses the same hostility to excessive accumulation of wealth that informed Willard's more educated and cosmopolitan critique. Stevens affirmed in 1910 the WCTU's support for a ten-hour day and a "living wage" for labor and insisted that, as much as Frances Willard, she sought to "uphold justice and kindness as opposed to greed of gain."[8] This was not an isolated or purely apologetic statement. In a *Union Signal* editorial in 1904, she had already more explicitly attacked "faulty competition" that "made possible the extremes of wealth and poverty" in America and produced "the abuses of the wage system."[9]

These anticommercial sentiments combined with hostility to the growing power of large corporations and Willard's personal prestige to give impetus to work for labor. Branches of the temperance and labor department were established in seventeen different states by the turn of the century. Though at one stage this department was charged with "relations between capital and labor," its solutions to the labor "problem" put great emphasis on moral reform within the working class. Susan Emery, national superintendent at the height of Willard's flirtation with socialism, concentrated in this period on the distribution of temperance pledges to workers. In a technical sense, Willard was undoubtedly more consistent in her socialist advocacy than her underlings between 1889 and 1897. Yet even Willard conceded in 1892 that "three-fourths of the whole labor question" could be explained in terms of the evil effects of the saloons in creating want and encouraging anarchism. An ideology of individual restraint and moral uplift persisted in the thinking of the socialist visionaries within the WCTU even while they championed state intervention to achieve the new moral order.[10]

The Socialist Alternative

Unlike Marxist socialism, this approach did not treat economic and class conflict as central to socialist analysis. The aim was rather to bring the classes together in cooperation. Willard and other exponents of Christian socialism despised and feared equally the greedy robber barons who ignored the common interest and the radical socialist agitators whose threats to social stability and appeals to violence mimicked, in Willard's view, the selfishness of their polar opposites. For their part, male radicals and Marxists in the United States frequently espoused patriarchal attitudes toward women in general and women in the socialist movement in particular. Given the ethnic conflicts and sexual discrimination within American socialism in the 1890s, it would have been difficult for even sympathetic WCTU women to cooperate with such types. Rather, the WCTU's socialism was that of a middle class sandwiched between the power of capital and the threat of labor and anarchism. Only the middle class could be, as Nellie Burger of Missouri, a World's organizer, put it, "regardful of others" because they had "higher ideals than those who have not had the advantages of . . . education."[11]

This form of socialism, with its roots firmly in the chapel and the Victorian drawing room, did enable the WCTU to criticize many forms of economic and social exploitation. As part of its criticism of "faulty competition" the WCTU was able to combine socialism's moral vision with dreams of women's emancipation. The plight of women workers—so much more poorly paid than male counterparts, and compelled to eke out a living while trying to raise children—especially appealed to the socialist element in the WCTU. As World's superintendent of the labor department in the mid-1890s, Amy Hicks demonstrated this sympathy. Secretary of the Rope-makers' Union in East London, Hicks attacked the "starvation wages" paid to women and their "unhealthy" conditions of labor. She worked tirelessly for women factory inspectors as a partial solution, as did BWTA lecturer and temperance missionary Florence Balgarnie. This position won much sympathy within the WCTU, and the *Woman's Signal* followed up Hicks's campaign with a series of articles on "Working Women," including one on "The Influence of Occupations on Health."[12]

But the terms of the socialist appeal to the WCTU combined contradictory elements that inhibited the critique of the economic and social order. Mary Garbutt of Los Angeles warned fellow members less responsive than she to the needs of working women that "we cannot separate ourselves from our working sisters in the east. We are partners in the great industrial scheme of things."[13] Garbutt noted that overworked women could not resist temptation, and the resulting moral and physical deterioration would leave female factory operatives less able to bear children. Garbutt worshiped Willard and constantly invoked her reputation as a socialist. Moreover, Garbutt herself was active in the wider socialist movement, and her work for peace and improved industrial conditions caught the essence of all that was best in the WCTU's antimaterialism. Although as radical as any in the WCTU, Garbutt's justification for socialist work in the WCTU made much of the issues of moral reform and the protection of women. She advocated, therefore, a shorter (ten-hour) day for women in California factories as part of the Progressive era push for special protective legislation for women.[14]

Willard's own position was really no different, as an exchange with an English working woman in the early 1890s had made clear. Inspired by an account of the American WCTU chieftain's life published in the *Woman's Herald*, a young dressmaker had written for advice as to how she could help the temperance cause, which appealed so very much to her. She would have liked "to give my life to the Temperance cause, but I see no way of being able to do this because I am poor, and, unfortunately, in this country, if a girl is poor she must remain so. . . . I am often tantalised by reading of great men who have risen through their own efforts from poor boys to a high place in life, but I have never read of such a thing happening to a girl. She has not the advantages her brothers have, and this is most unfair, for she is in every respect as clever as they are, and, in my opinion, should occupy an equal position." The writer went on to detail what would today be called the effects of the gender division of labor, that "weary, hum-drum existence" experienced by the working girl who had "no prospect of any change or improvement in [her] condition."[15]

So struck by the force of this appeal was Willard that her reply was published as a World's WCTU pamphlet under the title, *A New Calling for Women*. The prominence given to this document was fully justified because the exchange did raise the issue of occupational discrimination against women and differences in the meaning of class and gender in England and the United States. Willard's recipe for advancement lay firmly in the realm of intellectual and moral self-culture. By reading reform literature and by participating in a small way in local reform efforts, the confidence of the seamstress and others like her could be strengthened, and moral reputations enhanced. "First of all, I should start my seam by a good firm stitch set in the fabric of my own habits, and go on from that a stitch at a time." Women who had followed her advice not infrequently had, she claimed, been able to develop the material support within the moral reform movements to devote their lives full time to "philanthropy and reform." She urged young women to become involved in moral agitation and to make "the Temperance reform" their "basis, for the reason that it is self-evident that no adequate progress can be made in any reform unless the workers are at the top of their condition mentally, with clear brains, steady pulse, and those normal physical conditions throughout, from which alone clear thinking comes."[16]

What was most striking about this set of recommendations was the absence of any practical advice on the material conditions of life. To be sure, Willard acknowledged the existence of a huge group of so-called superfluous women. The labor market was "over-stocked with women workers, and the marriage market is so vastly over-stocked that we have in England three million more women than men." But Willard presented no answer to this problem except in terms of individual restraint and moral improvement "under the present system of things."[17] The latter phrase alluded to Willard's firm conviction that collectivism would eventually overturn the exploitation of which she wrote, but Willard's conception of the collectivist solution contained its own insoluble burdens for any interpretation that seeks to emphasize the socialist dimension of the WCTU.

Willard did have an answer, derived from her international experience, to the great questions of economic and social organization, though her contribution owed nothing to feminism and little to the intellectual stimulant of socialism. Rather, her suggestions drew upon the rapidly growing complex of ideas in the 1890s that we may call "social imperialism." Willard was "profoundly interested" in the plans of the Salvation Army's William Booth to solve the problems of inner-city poverty through a complex web of "farm colonies" that would train the urban unemployables for a future in the colonies of the British Empire. Booth's ideas were first published in 1890 in his *In Darkest England and the Way Out* and popularized in America by the army's commander there, Frederick Booth-Tucker.[18] In her 1897 presidential address before the World's WCTU, Willard praised these plans for the establishment of colonies in the American west as "the key to collectivism."[19]

But these colonization schemes principally affected Willard through the intermediary of Lady Henry. It was Somerset who gave the clearest articulation of Booth's ideas among the international elite of temperance women. Her Duxhurst Colony for Alcoholic Women, founded in Surrey in 1896, was conceived along the lines proposed in *Darkest England*, and Somerset saw the British Empire as an integral part of her strategy for moral and material progress.[20] Building on a theme she had first essayed in 1893, the English aristocrat told the 1902 BWTA conference that as part of "the Anglo-Saxon mission," responsible reformers should promote Anglo-Saxon unity through international moral reform. The mere acquisition of land in the colonies was not enough; "the moral and material condition of the people" there must be attended to, because morally regenerate colonies, full of temperate and pure people, were needed to become the centers for the reception of the United Kingdom's surplus population.[21]

Neither the BWTA nor the World's WCTU responded directly to these suggestions, though in both South Africa and Australia affiliates praised the Duxhurst plan and contributed to it.[22] Earlier, Scottish BWTA official Margaret Parker had anticipated such concerns with moral demographics when she proposed in 1888 a scheme to sponsor the emigration of poor but respectable servant girls from the British Isles to California. This would, she hoped, relieve the severe shortage of domestic labor on the Pacific Coast.[23] After 1900, the link between social imperialism and WCTU-inspired temperance reform was unmistakable. The idea of using motherhood to strengthen the bonds of empire became a highly developed theme. Somerset and Alys Smith Russell (daughter of Hannah Smith) connected "national deterioration" with "infant mortality." They joined a widespread movement in Britain and its colonies to improve scientifically the conditions of motherhood as part of the program of social imperialism and the cult of national efficiency. In the United States and Canada, too, the alleged increase of drinking among women was seen as contributing in an alarming way to racial deterioration.[24] In the 1890s, this specifically eugenic current had not yet developed in WCTU circles. The earlier formulations of social imperialism in the time of Willard were vaguer, but still influential in shaping the content of the WCTU's socialism.

Willard's own interest in the relation of colonizationist schemes and labor problems surfaced first in England in 1894. Asked by American Federation of Labor president Samuel Gompers to write an article for the *American Federationist* based on her observations of the British coal strike, Willard sent in a piece stressing England's overpopulation as the root cause of Britain's labor troubles. Much to the annoyance of both Gompers and reformer Henry Demarest Lloyd, Willard ignored economic conflicts, insisting instead that Britons lacked the "elbow room" of the American west.[25]

Underlying Willard's preference for a demographic rather than an economic solution to the class problem of the 1890s was her own experience as an American confronting the hierarchical ranking of European societies. Class, Willard acknowledged, structured social relations in Britain, but like many white, middle-class Americans, she believed that these rigid hierarchies did not operate with anything like the same force in the United States. Though this was an unexceptional viewpoint, Willard's special position as an internationally renowned interpreter of issues of women's emancipation is relevant here, since her view of class relations was heavily influenced by her experience of women and moral reform in America.

An incident in Portsmouth involving the return of Lady Henry Somerset and Willard from a European holiday in the summer of 1893 encapsulated for Willard the differences in the class and gender systems in the Anglo-American community. She noted angrily a "sycophant[ic] man . . . lugging Lady Henry's light bags and letting me lug my own." Willard's moral is instructive. "To be a woman in America is to be a queen, that is all anybody needs to know, and a cultivated man would help a washer-woman quicker than one elegantly dressed because he saw she needed it more."[26] In egalitarian America, class did not take precedence over gender, but rather, she felt, socially constructed gender relations mitigated the divisive effects of class. Given this romantic view of American realities—which said nothing of race or ethnic prejudice and discrimination in employment against minority women, nor the very real differences of wealth and power—it was impossible for Willard to use her brand of feminism, or her deeply felt and experienced hostility to human exploitation, to make any significant contribution to the analysis of economic problems troubling Anglo-American society in the 1890s.

If the limits of Willard's socialism were exposed in her British experience, the thinking of other WCTU women who ventured abroad reinforces the view that the WCTU's socialism could not transcend the American evangelical culture that produced it. Barbara Epstein has made the point that under Frances Willard, temperance women avoided in their support for labor the narrow view that might otherwise have restricted the WCTU to a purely middle-class constituency. Without Willard's advocacy of socialism, the WCTU might have translated its "concern for respectability into a support for the status quo and into a view of labor organizations as troublemakers."[27] This was the position of elements of the American WCTU's leadership, but case studies indicate that grass-roots commitment to labor reform among White Ribboners had definite limits.[28]

More important, WCTU women who at home were supporters of labor against the depredations of big capital narrowed their vision when they faced the reality of socialist practice abroad. Katharine Stevenson was an illuminating case, since she made no secret of her hostility toward the "war . . . being waged by commerce and business circles every day."[29] In the United States, Stevenson was a determined supporter of the progressive elements in the WCTU and championed the rights of labor against the great corporations. But as a World's WCTU missionary in New Zealand, Stevenson came face to face with moderate, Fabian socialism as a political force. Stevenson praised New Zealand's progressive social policies on the one hand but gave greater emphasis on the other to the criticisms of antipodean experiments. "It is pointed out," she reminded her American readers, "that a government monopoly may be quite as irresponsible and quite as exacting as a monopoly of the type with which we are more familiar." Stevenson concluded: "Laws of a strong socialistic tendency have not quite brought in the millennium, even in New Zealand." No such reservations surfaced in her accounts of moral progress and temperance reform legislation.[30]

Jessie Ackermann went further and expressed her grave discomfort at the thought of laboring men actually taking charge of governments and directing the affairs of nations. Certainly, the moral conscience that fed socialist sympathies was evident in her comments on the economic problems of Australia. "I feel there must be something wrong, very wrong, when willing hands lack work. . . . Nothing stirs my heart like the awful cry for bread." Though Ackermann saw the critique of poverty in depression Australia in the 1890s as evidence of the "clamor for a new social order, with a broader and more thoroughly Christian basis, founded upon the equality and brotherhood of man," she matched her sympathies with denunciations of the union leaders of the colonies. These seemed "to be men of little or no principle, urging the men on to riot and lawlessness."[31] Of these two seemingly contradictory sentiments, it was the latter that ultimately triumphed in Ackermann's practice. On a subsequent visit to Australia in 1911, the former world missionary spent time organizing women voters in Western Australia for the fledgling Liberal party, formed as a conservative alliance to defeat the already powerful trade union movement and its political wing, the Labour party.[32]

The dichotomy of progressive views at home and more conservative ones abroad is easily understood. Though labor violence and class conflict were endemic in American society in the late nineteenth century, the political lines were not so clearly drawn between pro- and antilabor positions as they became in Australia increasingly after 1900, as the political representation of the labor movement grew in the antipodes. In New South Wales, for example, the "class composition of the main body of the temperance movement gave it an inherent bias against [the] Labour [party]" as early as 1904. By 1914, state politics in New South Wales had become polarized between labor and conservative forces and, as in New Zealand, the WCTU and other proponents of prohibition strongly favored the conservative side.[33] Anderson Hughes-Drew, the New Zealander, wrote Rosalind Carlisle from the Brisbane Australasian convention with these corroborating observations in 1912: "The Labour party is very strong out here and in the main is opposed to our work. You will be surprised to learn this because in the old [land] the Labour Party is not unsympathetic."[34] These antipodean sentiments and pressures tended to influence to an even greater extent American visitors who saw things through the eyes of local temperance reformers and shared fundamentally similar class positions and fears. In the United States, however, party politics did not take the same class forms, and so the alignment of temperance, labor, and middle-class reform could go deeper and last longer.

The position in Britain, on the other hand, was not as different as Hughes-Drew's comments suggested. Relations between the BWTA and the Labour movement were cordial enough so long as Labour did not threaten Liberal dominance of the BWTA and of social reform. But during the First World War, BWTA members, like the prominent Liberal Bertha Mason, objected to an invitation that Ramsay MacDonald speak at the 1915 annual meeting because his support of Britain's war effort was less than wholehearted. An exaggeratedly agitated Agnes Slack worried whether the BWTA would "remain a strictly working Temperance Ass[ociation]" or become "an appendage of the Labour Party."[35]

As the British case suggests, the domestic politics of temperance in these leading WCTU nations began to converge during the First World War. The United States must be included in this judgment. Just as the social divide between liberal reformers and labor politics appeared between 1900 and 1914 in the antipodes, so too did the relationship between progressive elements in the WCTU in the United States and the socialists become strained a few years later as class relations deteriorated during the European conflagration. Anna Gordon's 1915 presidential address was a bellwether of this shift in the perceptions of the middle-class reformer. She noted that "the recent report of the Federal Industrial Relations Commission shows the difficulty of agreement on any specific remedies for industrial discontent." What was the WCTU's answer to this evidence of intractable class conflict? "Annihilate the liquor traffic and much of the discontent will disappear. The sober workingman and his family will be well housed, well fed, and well clothed." The WCTU's program of social reform was being curtailed in favor of the panacea of prohibition not because the WCTU had become a "narrow" organization but because American society's cultural and social polarization had made the earlier and broader vision of the WCTU increasingly irrelevant.[36]

WHAT ARE THE IMPLICATIONS of this comparative survey of the WCTU and the labor issue for the WCTU's internationalism? Because the WCTU's socialism was a product of American conditions and flourished best in American circumstances, temperance women paid little attention to the internationalist perspectives of the wider socialist movement, particularly that in continental Europe. Frances Willard's view of the industrial system was indeed similar to that advanced by socialist thinkers in her understanding that collective ownership of the means of production would have to be achieved if socialism was to be effected, but nowhere did Willard, or any other WCTU advocate of socialism, articulate a socialist vision of the international aspects of the economic order. Since the WCTU was concerned with and inescapably shaped by imperialism's late nineteenth-century expansion, it is striking that the organization's understanding of that phenomenon remained, even more than their knowledge of domestic capitalist economics, restricted to purely moral criticisms.[37] Rarely did the women's temperance movement go so far as to question the need for overseas markets that was used to justify imperial aggression.

The BWTA's *White Ribbon* did report, approvingly, on Henry J. Wilson, a Liberal M.P. and a purity and temperance reformer, when he questioned the "need to go to the ends of the earth conquering black men in order to get markets." Through temperance reform at home, prosperity could be achieved, Wilson asserted boldly, and Britons would "find the markets for our products in the back slums and courts" of England's cities.[38] Such sentiments could be seen as part of the Hobsonian radical-liberal critique of imperialism. They point up the turmoil in the consciences of elements in the BWTA over the burden of political imperialism shouldered by Britain in the Boer War. Yet the opposition to colonial acquisitions did not proceed beyond such expressions of ill ease because the temperance forces were so deeply divided over the righteousness of empire. Among the leading officials in the BWTA, none was more influential than World's secretary Slack, who consistently sided with the imperialists in the Liberal party, published pro-imperial propaganda in the *World's White Ribbon Bulletin*, and used her influence against contrary sentiment in the BWTA.[39]

Not only were explicitly antiimperialist sentiments rarely pursued into policies of antiimperial agitation in WCTU circles either in England or America. The preference of both Willard and Somerset for farm colonies and emigration schemes as the means of handling Europe's surplus population indirectly implicated these leading WCTU thinkers in the economics of imperial administration.[40] These sentiments were no doubt innocent of the darker drives of empire, but to achieve their dreams of a slum-free Britain, a territorially expansive policy and an expensive imperial navy were both required. There was no escaping that the WCTU's moral critique of empire remained limited by its association with statist conceptions of social reform and by its belief in an Anglo-Saxon moral and political superiority. But this approach drew as much from its American sources in Bellamy's nationalism as from British experience. Willard correctly depicted herself as one of those high-minded individuals whom Bellamy hoped would stand above class rivalries and promote social peace through technological improvement and rational bureaucratic reorganization.[41]

The limitations of the WCTU's form of socialism hardly detracted from the organization's practical efforts to improve the position of women in the labor market, however. The WCTU advocated breaking down the gender barriers that prevented women from earning their own living and favored equal remuneration for women. According to historian Jack Blocker, the WCTU was probably responsible for having a plank demanding equal pay for equal work by men and women placed in the Prohibition party platform of 1892. This was the first such platform adopted by any national American political party. But the contribution went beyond words and symbols. The WCTU's own officials, and not just Willard, were put forward as role models for working women everywhere.[42] Wherever the WCTU spread, its missionaries took their own example and the evidence from United States experience indicating that women could and ought to have the right to labor untrammeled by sexual distinction. Jessie Ackermann made this point as plainly as any when she stressed to Australian audiences the advances made by women in the United States. "The true dignity of labor is being taught to girls, and the world is beginning to look with discredit upon women who hang helplessly on men, instead of doing their own work, and, if necessary, earning their own living."[43] Willard was even more explicit in her commitment to make women, through open access to careers and equal legal and property rights, financially independent of men.[44]

Despite such farsighted commitments, WCTU endorsements of women's economic freedom remained ambiguous. Willard's own imperfect intellectual synthesis was symptomatic of the ambiguity. Alongside advocacy of opening careers to women went the conviction that women's ultimate destiny was to serve others, not to seek individual advancement. The emancipation of women in employment was for Willard only a stage in their evolution. "It is my firm conviction," she told the young English dressmaker in *A New Calling for Women*, "that in the new adjustment of society, after having conquered a firm foothold in the trades and professions, women will gradually withdraw from mechanical work and devote themselves to the noblest vocations that life affords—namely, motherhood, reform work, and philanthropy."[45] It was not simply that the WCTU's commitment to equality in the public sphere was compromised by its devotion to domesticity and the bourgeois family in the private sphere. The WCTU's advocacy of women's equality in the public sphere was itself ambivalent, the product of a contradictory consciousness.[46]

The domesticity ideology made it possible for the WCTU to advance a moral, if not socialist, critique of modern capitalist society, but that same ideology inhibited the understanding of the relations of class society that undoubtedly disturbed temperance women. If the WCTU's notion of equality went further than a purely political or legalistic conception, its specific policies on women's labor were deeply flawed. Special protective legislation aided certain classes of women but encouraged the perpetuation of the gender division of labor by establishing sexually specific conditions of employment that employers and male employees could manipulate to their own advantage. If the WCTU's thinking on equality for women contained such unmistakable contradictions, this fact reflected not so much the weakness of the WCTU as the uncertain position of women in modern capitalist society. No theorist or practical politician grasped adequately the interconnection of women's legal and economic position in society with their role in biological and domestic reproduction. The task of combining these elements in a more comprehensive theory that might liberate women from prejudices and restraints all too familiar to Frances Willard—but without doing violence to the aspirations of women themselves—confronts us still today.

Woman's World/Woman's Empire

In that task, the WCTU offered moments of illumination that went beyond socialism. Temperance women advanced, implicitly, a critique of society that recognized the profound impact of gender in the structuring of women's lives. This cannot be assessed simply by truncating the WCTU's Do-Everything policy according to conventional classifications of issues and policies. In its understanding of the interrelation of the problems of peace, purity, prohibition, and women's emancipation, to mention only a few issues of substance, the WCTU demonstrated that women were oppressed not simply by laws but by culture and custom. The recognition of the weight of these underlying material restraints imposed by tradition and experience on women's equality offered something socialists might well have sought to incorporate into their own quest for human freedom.

12

Prohibition and the Perils of Cultural Adaptation

The coming of national prohibition in 1919 was for the WCTU the beginning, not the end, of its campaigns. Of course the Eighteenth Amendment in the United States would have to be safeguarded, but above all in the hour of victory, thoughts turned to the spread of prohibition around the globe. The WCTU announced as its goal "To Make the World All White," through the triumph of the White Ribbon, and promised the annihilation of the liquor traffic internationally by the end of the decade. A map published in the *Union Signal* indicated how much had been achieved and yet how far there was to go. The "'Wet' and 'Dry' Map of the World" divided up the globe into areas that were already under prohibition, those that had local option, those in which religious sentiments or customs made them practically dry, and those that were thoroughly wet. Finland and Iceland were on a par with the United States, and Canada was said to be "a near-prohibition country," while Russia and Norway were listed, dubiously and vaguely, as dry too.[1] In its propaganda, the WCTU also drew attention to the "large extent of territory in Asia and Africa under so-called prohibition as a result of one of the teachings of Mahomet."[2] What matters is not the accuracy of these claims but the evidence they reveal of the international aspirations of the WCTU. The 1920s witnessed the apogee of all attempts to make the world dry in the American image.

This export of American institutions embodied several impulses. Wartime enthusiasm for moral intervention in the affairs of Europe contributed. Andrew Sinclair puts the point nicely: "The mentality of war and the fantastic hopes of a millennial peace encouraged the drys' sense of international mission." If Woodrow Wilson had sought to make the world safe for democracy, the president of the ASL hoped to make "a democracy that is safe for the world, by making it intelligent and sober everywhere."[3] Such enthusiasms featured heavily in the pronouncements of the WCTU as well. Postwar strategists like Anna Gordon and *Union Signal* editor Julia Deane believed that their new struggle called for "a grandeur of consecration that

Woman's World/Woman's Empire

links us [American temperance women] with the heroic men and women who in the world-war patriotically answered the call to colors."[4] In Gordon's view the American mission to save the world rested plainly on the principle of moral and disinterested benevolence. "It would be criminally selfish in us as Christian temperance women to content ourselves with ridding our own land of the greatest enemy of the home and childhood."[5]

Notions of benevolence easily mixed with themes of a more mundane kind. Coexisting with the urge for expressions of stewardship toward others were the organizational imperatives of American prohibitionism. The search for new frontiers expressed the needs of an organization that had achieved its primary goal to reformulate its strategies in order to ensure its continued prosperity. This organizational drive was clearly connected to the World's WCTU work. Anna Gordon gave priority to the union's worldwide responsibilities when she explained "Why the Woman's Christian Temperance Union Must Carry On."[6] In this context, it is telling that Gordon also linked the achievement of global prohibition to the 1924 jubilee campaign target of a million members and an endowment of a million dollars.

Making other nations conform to American liquor controls was not, however, a product of prohibition's American triumph alone nor an ad hoc response to wartime developments. The 1920s experiment with global evangelism was for temperance women neither an aberration nor an afterthought. It was rather the culmination of a persistent internationalist concern dating back to the 1880s. Nor was the enthusiasm of the twenties a purely American imposition. Prohibitionist sentiment extended to many countries, and partisans of the dry cause in those places had no hesitation in encouraging American dreams of a sober world.

But the international theme is more important still. American concern with liquor laws abroad was inextricably tied to the shaping of prohibitionist sentiment in the United States. In addition to the export of prohibitionist ideas, there was a lively debate in the American context, going back to the 1890s, over foreign alternatives to the total exclusion of alcohol. Defeat of these alternatives was essential to the progress of American prohibition. In a very real sense, prohibition as ideology and practice was forged in contest with these rival systems of liquor control. As an organization of worldwide scope, the WCTU could not avoid this controversy.

These underlying themes persisted from the 1880s to the 1930s, though the patterns of international concern ebbed and flowed. From the 1880s to around 1910, the principal focus involved defining American prohibition and repelling foreign conceptions of drinking and its control. After 1910, interest in international questions temporarily declined while American reformers pushed for national prohibition. After 1920, internationalist ambitions were revived, but in a different form. Now WCTU supporters elsewhere became the ones most desirous of importing models of liquor con-

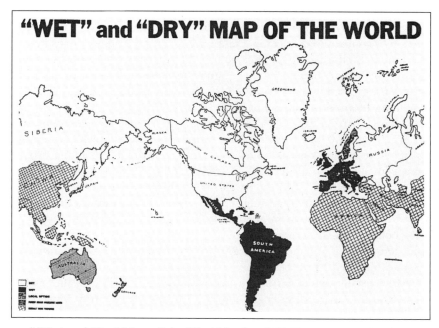

"'Wet' and 'Dry' Map of the World," a key WCTU propaganda piece, which interprets selectively the state of global liquor reform. Countries depicted as dry, among them the United States, Canada, and Russia, are shown in white, and wet countries—all those in Latin America plus Ireland, England, Portugal, Spain, Belgium, the Netherlands, Germany, Austria-Hungary, and Greece in Europe—are shown in black. The diagonally-striped areas permitted local option (Sweden, Switzerland, and Scotland as well as Australia and New Zealand). In the widely crosshatched areas in Africa and Asia alcohol was practically prohibited, either by religion or by international agreement, and in the narrowly crosshatched European countries of Denmark, Italy, and France certain intoxicating liquors were, according to the WCTU, prohibited. (*Union Signal*, 20 May 1920)

trol, and the model most favored was American prohibition. This interest in American models combined with the millennialist theme of completing worldwide prohibition to produce an intense program of global agitation, which only waned when prohibition in the United States itself collapsed.

The wet and dry map showed that the key to world prohibition lay in Europe. That was the continent most thoroughly resistant to the dry forces and was the chief source of rival schemes of liquor control. Among those alternatives none produced more controversy in the Anglo-Saxon world than the Gothenburg system, so named because it originated in the Swedish city of that name in 1865. The principle behind the scheme was simple. Private profiteering should be removed from the liquor trade by the introduction of companies possessing a monopoly over the supply of hard liquor and bound by the law to pursue policies of "disinterested management." Licenses were sharply reduced; beer and wine consumption was, since these were not regulated, to be substituted for the more alcoholic spirits; and the remaining licensed premises put in the hands of the *bolags*, or commercial companies. Great emphasis was placed upon improving the conditions under which alcohol was consumed by introducing "light, pleasant restaurants, where the worker could buy food" to accompany his drinking. Apart from a small interest of 5 percent on the capital invested, the city and state were paid the remainder of the profit for use in the reduction of rates and other taxes. For the city this amounted to a fivefold increase on the return from the previous system of auctioning licenses. In later modifications of the scheme, the central government also offered the Swedish WCTU and other temperance organizations grants for their educational work from the revenues received from the *bolags*.[7]

A superficially similar but more restrictive scheme known as the *samlag* was introduced in Norway beginning in 1871 and extended in 1894. But the Norwegian profits were to be appropriated for "benevolent," that is, charitable, purposes. Profits available to the municipalities were severely restricted to reduce the temptation to promote the sale of spirits, and by 1903 beer and wine were added to the liquors controlled by company management.[8] The Norwegian system also retained a measure of local option, which allowed rural areas and, after 1896, towns, to prohibit the sale of spirits.

Discussion of the Scandinavian models was intense in the Anglo-Saxon temperance world in a way that only the history of American prohibitionism can explain. Long experience had combined with the heritage of Protestant evangelical convictions and a political economy averse to governmental regulation to make large sections of the American temperance movement favor prohibition rather than regulation. But the dominance of prohibitionist sentiments was never complete. Because of the political failures of the temperance movement in the 1880s and early 1890s, and partly to overcome the potentially disruptive political impact of prohibitionism, the method of government or local monopoly over the liquor business appeared as a contentious issue. Municipalization was favored by elite groups like the proper Bostonians who backed the attempts of some members of the Massachusetts legislature to introduce such a system in that state in 1893–94. Edward Bellamy had come out in favor of governmental control in 1891, and so did a report written for the American commissioner of labor by a Canadian-American scholar and elite reformer, Dr. Elgin R. L. Gould of Johns Hopkins University.[9]

Prohibition and Cultural Adaptation

Support for state control of the liquor traffic was not limited to a social or intellectual elite such as these figures represented; both the Prohibition party and the Populists had advocates of municipalization in their ranks. The "broad-gauged" faction of the Prohibitionists sought alliance with the People's party by adoption of the principle of governmental control, which some state Populist parties also favored.[10] Prohibition ultimately triumphed within the temperance movement as the dominant solution when the Prohibition party split in 1896 between narrow-gauged Prohibitionists and advocates of a radical reform coalition. But liquor regulation continued to be advanced by the elitist Committee of Fifty, whose reports stressing the success of regulation in Sweden appeared in such publications as Raymond Calkins's *Substitutes for the Saloon*. Though the committee's deliberations assumed a decidedly theoretical air after reformers began, around 1907, to push successfully for prohibition once more, the controversy of the 1890s had helped shape the character of American prohibitionism for a generation.[11]

The ASL was, it is generally agreed, a product of the failure of the Prohibition party to make any impact on the two-party system. The new organization signaled the beginning in 1893 of a vigorous and clearly focused strategy to suppress public consumption of alcohol. But the emergence of the Anti-Saloon League was more than an innovative tactical response to a domestic political failure of the prohibition movement. Its growth cannot be divorced from the crisis within the prohibitionist ranks over the efficacy of prohibition itself and the emergence of practical political alternatives to prohibition. In turn, the threat posed by a loss of internal direction in the prohibition movement in the early 1890s possessed an international dimension that has been all but ignored. The appeal of imported solutions to the liquor problem was intimately connected to the perceived decline in the political prospects of prohibition. The Scandinavian schemes were important, as the contemporary debates in prohibitionist publications reveal, precisely because their potential appeal to a broad cross section of the American population threatened the evangelical prohibitionists' domination of the wider "temperance" movement in the United States in the 1890s.[12]

One source of concern with the importation of allegedly foreign schemes of regulation involved the introduction in 1893 of the dispensary system in South Carolina. There the supply of hard liquor was put under the monopoly control of state stores run by salaried officials. No liquor could be consumed on the premises. This scheme was anathema to orthodox prohibitionists for many reasons, but in looking back at the beginnings of the ASL, it is intriguing to note that Ernest Cherrington, the key ASL official and author of several histories of the movement, stressed foreign influences. The dispensary was, said Cherrington in 1920, "the Americanized form of the Gothenburg system." According to Cherrington, all prohibitionists saw the dispensary as a threat to prohibition because by eliminating "the element of private gain," South Carolina threatened "to clothe the traffic with a garment of respectability." He called this "the most insidious and dangerous aspect of the liquor problem in America at that date."[13] Suddenly it was necessary to look more closely at temperance in Europe, and no little effort was exerted to identify Gothenburg with South Carolina and to condemn both systems as malevolent. This upsurge of concern among American prohibitionists about the impact of liquor policies in other nations signified more than a humanitarian concern with the fate of others. American interests demanded a "correct" interpretation of the European scene.[14]

As the contemporary record reveals, Cherrington's interpretation contained a large degree of hindsight. The ASL in 1893–95 displayed little or no interest in matters beyond its immediate and parochial tactical concerns. In Ohio and in the District of Columbia, where the ASL began in 1893, local matters overwhelmed any concern for the broader picture, even a few hundred miles away in South Carolina.[15] Nonetheless, if we shift our analysis to the larger prohibitionist movement and take in the whole of the 1890s, it is clear that the ASL could not avoid the issue of the Scandinavian alternatives because of their importance within the larger prohibitionist debate. By the end of the 1890s, prohibitionism had indeed become orthodox in its opposition to foreign liquor schemes. The *National Temperance Almanac and Teetotaler's Year-Book* began singling out the Gothenburg system for specific denunciation in 1896, and in 1899, W. E. "Pussyfoot" Johnson went to Scandinavia to study its effects, only to report in most unfavorable tones to Chicago's *New Voice*. The *American Prohibition Year Book* after the turn of the century added its own weight to the new orthodoxy, which was also reflected in a variety of other monographs and pamphlets.[16]

Prohibitionists like Johnson in the United States and James Whyte, secretary of the United Kingdom Alliance, pronounced the Gothenburg system a failure and cited evidence of an increase in the consumption of beer to match the decreasing consumption of spirits. They argued that absolute consumption of alcohol had only temporarily decreased and that after 1890 the incidence of public drunkenness had increased alarmingly.[17] Moreover, rates of pauperism were said to be both rising and much higher than the figures for the United Kingdom, where licensing was in force.[18] While disputes over the statistics raged back and forth, another and more insidious line of argument appeared. From the perspective of the advocates of liquor regulation, prohibitionists seemed to gloss over the differences between the Norwegian and Swedish schemes. The journalism of Sara Crafts, World's WCTU Sunday school superintendent, exemplifies typical prohibitionist reasoning. The Norwegian *samlag* was "the same thing" as the *bolag* "under another name," she reported in the *Union Signal*.[19] This statement would

Prohibition and Cultural Adaptation

have been misleading even prior to 1896, but when Crafts toured Europe in 1902, it was manifestly unfair to equate the two. Denying any real diversity in the European schemes, as Crafts did, was essential to the purpose of painting a set of only two diametrically opposed alternatives for the American population to contemplate.

Because of its strong roots in the American prohibition movement, the WCTU might have been expected to have set itself steadfastly against liquor regulation in the 1890s when the question was first raised by the dispensary. If Cherrington's retrospective comments had been accurate, the WCTU would have taken such a stance. In reality, any homogeneous discourse on liquor regulation, with all of its complicated mechanisms for screening out unpalatable information and producing positive knowledge of the alleged facts of prohibition, would have to be patiently constructed.

Especially within the ranks of the WCTU in the 1890s did turmoil over this issue prevail. The organization desperately needed to settle its own policies before it could contribute to the new strategy of the ASL in the United States and help export prohibition overseas. This search for a rapprochement with orthodox prohibitionism had domestic roots but conflicted with the WCTU's internationalist ambitions and commitments. Support for liquor regulation obviously made sense in Europe, where the WCTU wished to extend its influence. But the matter was further complicated by the presence of important figures within the World's WCTU who espoused various forms of regulation. The Scandinavian experiments were actively championed within the WCTU by none other than the World's president from 1898 to 1906, Lady Henry Somerset, and there is ample evidence that Frances Willard also flirted with the possibilities of a regulatory system. Moreover, her international connections pushed the great chieftain further in the direction of regulation than she probably would have gone had she remained fixed purely within the context of a parochial American debate.

Willard's initial reaction to the South Carolina dispensary was one of cautious indecision. Her 1893 NWCTU presidential address, delivered in her absence by Lady Henry, advocated a wait-and-see attitude. Too far away in Britain to judge, she promised to support the decision of local prohibitionists.[20] In reality, the WCTU's stand was a pragmatic one dictated by the fact that the state commissioner appointed by Governor Tillman to run the dispensaries, D. H. Traxler, was married to an official of the South Carolina WCTU and was an abstainer himself. Caught in the midst of this turmoil in the ranks of the South Carolina WCTU, the *Union Signal* merely called for enforcement of the law and hoped it would, as promised, help to reduce consumption and liquor outlets and prove to be a measure on the road to prohibition.[21] WCTU opinion did not shift until another local controversy within the United States intervened.

In 1894 an attempt was made to introduce the Norwegian model into

Woman's World/Woman's Empire

Massachusetts based on the recommendations of a report prepared for the state legislature by John Lowell, Henry P. Bowditch, and John Graham Brooks. Brooks, a social reformer and former Boston Unitarian minister had been to Scandinavia, but the report also drew upon the research of Gould and that of John Koren, later to be associated with the Committee of Fifty.[22] Though some WCTU members such as Mary Livermore wrote in support of the legislation on the grounds that it would allow local option, the state WCTU was strongly opposed to any compromise with "evil," and the *Union Signal* began to print much anti-Gothenburg material from its own and other prohibitionist sources.[23] Simultaneously, editorial policy hardened against the dispensary scheme, which was denounced as just another way of implicating the state and the people in the "greed" of the liquor traffic.[24]

Thus far, local issues had dominated WCTU practice and policy. But if prohibitionists thought the WCTU's orthodoxy had been reestablished by the editorial of 1894, they did not reckon on the international complications in the WCTU's position. Implicit in the World's WCTU program from the start was the principle of cultural adaptation. In her 1884 presidential address, Willard hoped that her women would "carefully study the adaptation of methods to varying climates and nationalities, no less than to prevailing habits of brain poison."[25] While Willard predicted that one result of this endeavor would be the broadening of the pledge to include all intoxicants and narcotics, another possibility could entail "varying" conditions dictating a retreat from either total abstinence or prohibition.[26]

Conditions on the European continent illustrated the necessity for some form of cultural adaptation of the WCTU's American-inspired program. This hostile environment was long-standing and largely a function of the general indifference to total abstinence principles. When Mary Leavitt toured there in 1889 and 1890, she noted that "we Americans overrate the strength and solidity of the temperance movement in Europe, because we always understand temperance to mean total abstinence, while it is not the case here."[27] Leavitt believed that the WCTU in Europe should concentrate on creating the groundwork for legal coercion and should not expect successfully to force prohibition on an unprepared and uncomprehending population. The problem for the WCTU was, however, that prohibition was indeed advocated in Europe by some and in a number of cases posed a serious threat to schemes of regulation. Thus the World's work always found allies for American-style prohibitionism abroad whose chief role was to serve as architects of illusion for the World's WCTU campaigns.

As if the failure of most Europeans to appreciate the virtues of prohibition were not enough, some WCTU women in the continental affiliates were indirectly involved in the sanctioning of the regulatory system. The

Norwegian White Ribboners had joined the main body of temperance forces in endorsing the act that modified the *samlag* system in 1894. Suitable facilities for the promotion of moderate patterns of consumption—such as pleasant restaurants run on "disinterested management" principles—would still be provided, but only where local voters continued to approve the sale.[28] This Norwegian position was depicted in sections of the Anglo-Saxon temperance movement as a bargain with the devil, since the state remained implicated in the trade's evil effects.

But the White Ribboners saw the matter differently, as Elizabet Espenak, a Norwegian WCTU official, explained. She told an inquisitive Australian co-worker, Sara Nolan, that "total abstainers and temperance workers in Norway believe that whatever limits the sale of intoxicants also limits their consumption." Far from accepting a permanent liquor trade, the Norwegian temperance workers still regarded as "their programme" the "final prohibition of the liquor traffic." They supported the regulatory system as modified in 1894 because it included local option provisions that allowed local prohibition and, furthermore, curtailed the worst excesses of alcoholism through the *samlags'* restrictions on the sale of hard liquor. "Temperance reformers here agree," Espenak assured her correspondent, that the system had been "of value, for the right to manufacture and sell brandy was more widespread and general in Norway before its adoption than it has ever been in any other country."[29]

Willard, perhaps speaking with the spirit of cultural adaptation in mind, announced that the WCTU was tolerant of such divergence within its ranks and gave "the widest space to honest differences of thought and purpose."[30] But Willard did more than tolerate such views among sections of her rank and file. She actively encouraged them by her own favorable comments on the Norwegian example. Though Willard focused on the local option provisions of the 1894 Act of the Norwegian Parliament and saw the *samlag* system as an agent for abolishing the trade, her methods would hardly please the staunchest prohibitionists. After announcing in April 1896 that the Norwegian law had resulted in the abolition of licensed sale in a number of towns, she professed a desire to go there "and study up the causes which have led to that glorious state of things."[31] For American prohibitionists ignorant of circumstances both political and social in Norway, this was not the step toward prohibition that the Norwegian White Ribboners and Willard depicted. Evidence on the motivation of the Norwegians was not widely disseminated in temperance circles since it would call orthodox American antiliquor strategies into question, and Willard's deviation from the narrow-gauged prohibitionism was therefore bound to upset some within the WCTU in the United States.[32]

The unease went further, however, for Willard spoke at the same time in favor of the New York Liquor Tax Law of 1896 (the so-called Raines Law), a stringent excise system that trebled fees on saloons and was correctly interpreted in temperance circles as a form of high license.[33] Whatever Willard advocated for Norway was one thing in the matter of prohibition, but to suggest the same thing for the United States was, for Kate Bushnell and Elizabeth Andrew, unthinkable. In June 1896, the two resigned from their positions as round-the-world missionaries, not because of the contagious diseases controversy, which did not erupt until the following April, but because they believed the WCTU's total opposition to liquor, forged in "the early days," was "not being maintained."[34]

High license involved imposing very heavy taxes on liquor outlets in an attempt to reduce the number and eliminate the poorer classes of saloons, but it was anathema to many prohibitionists because it gave the state or local authority a larger financial interest in the liquor business. Willard was not deterred, however. She was "of course . . . a prohibitionist" but "willing to take anything that is better than the old legislation."[35] In explaining her stand, Willard stated that she had really only meant to endorse the prohibition of Sunday trading under the law, but in fact the law's restrictive features were quickly and widely evaded through legal loopholes. So preoccupied in 1896 with international issues was Willard that she did not and could not exert sufficient effort to examine the fine detail of the scheme. Indeed, Willard's mind was clearly elsewhere, since she introduced the evidence of the success of the Norwegian scheme to justify support for the Raines Law. Willard's position was in fact very similar to that of the Norwegian WCTU. She was in favor of any restrictive law that could be construed as contributing to prohibitionist sentiment through the exertion of state power. When the defects of the Raines Law became apparent, Willard drew back in response to criticism and professed to be "puzzle[d]" and undecided over the law, but the damage had been done. Willard had been branded in the press as soft on prohibition and had been forced onto the defensive in a way that diminished her prestige. Even within her own organization, the rumblings of discontent with her leadership were further fed by this incident, as the resignation of Bushnell and Andrew indicated.[36]

The unholy specter of liquor regulation was further encouraged by Willard's close association with Lady Henry. Not only was Lady Henry under attack for advocacy of licensed prostitution. She was already, in 1896, airing suspect views on the liquor question. At the BWTA annual council meeting the Scottish delegates had protested Somerset's support for a parliamentary bill that would tax liquor outlets and use the funds to reduce the number of licensed premises. Willard sat through the discussion on the same platform as Somerset without raising a breath in opposition. The silence did not go unnoticed. It appeared that the two leaders of the World's movement were pushing the organization toward high license and away from unsullied prohibitionism.[37]

For Somerset's opponents, these unorthodox positions on prohibition were tied to other deviations on the temperance issue that revealed an alarming penchant for cultural adaptation in the English aristocrat. Bushnell and Andrew alleged, though the charge was denied, that Somerset had asked Anna Gordon's sister, Alice Gordon Gulick, to use her influence in Europe to canvass the subject of a "modified pledge" for European members.[38] Very soon Leavitt was adding to the charges. The subject was Lady Henry's testimony before the British Royal Commission on the Liquor Licensing Laws in 1897. Somerset had admitted that until comparatively recently she had served wine to house guests because "she does not think it necessary for all persons to become abstainers" and "she does not wish all public houses (the exact equivalent of saloons in the United States) to be closed."[39]

Somerset's position on wine was in fact common among members of the British aristocracy who supported the temperance movement. Her successor as BWTA president, Carlisle, did the same for many years, though she accompanied each serving of wine to her son-in-law, Professor Gilbert Murray, with tongue-lashings on the evil effects of even moderate drinking.[40] But Somerset was less circumspect than Carlisle and tended to carry her flexible personal convictions into the public arena and into areas of policy. What Somerset did say on prohibition was that she "should certainly not be in favour of prohibition by Act of Parliament." She was, however, "in favour of such education that it would lead to an inanition of the trade."[41] Such was not good enough for Leavitt. Somerset was, the World's missionary said, "utterly unfit to be the leader of the W.C.T.U."[42]

More disturbing still to Leavitt and her anti-Somerset allies was the extent to which the American WCTU was prepared to defend the British leader. This alarming trend clearly did not end with Willard's death. The new charges by Leavitt brought forth a defense of Somerset's conduct from both the BWTA and the American WCTU. The *Union Signal* rebuked Leavitt because she "judges one people by the standards of another, and attempts to foist upon Great Britain America's ideas as to the best methods for obtaining the desired end of all Temperance legislation [prohibition]." In an invocation of Social Darwinism, Leavitt was denounced because "she [had] fallen into the utterly unscientific method of disregarding environment and present conditions as necessary factors in the working out of any permanent reform."[43] Here again, the principle of cultural adaptability was being asserted. And as if the authority of the *Union Signal* were not enough, the World's WCTU completed the process of providing sanction to Somerset's view by formally confirming her as World's president in 1900.

The crux of the dispute was the political context of temperance reform in Britain. The *Union Signal* backed Somerset not simply because she had been Willard's friend or because she contributed so much financially to the international cause. The WCTU's flirtation with Somerset and with regulatory schemes continued for several years because of the political circumstances within the BWTA in particular and the British temperance movement in general after 1895. The roots of the controversies with Somerset went much deeper than personal factors and concerned the profound defeat administered to British prohibitionism by the Unionists (Conservatives) in the general election of 1895.

British prohibitionists had gone into the election of 1895 backing the Liberal party and its promise of local veto—that is, a measure of local control over the issue of licenses that would enable prohibition to be established in regions where the temperance movement was strongest. Willard and Somerset, both resident in England at the time, lent their financial and organizational support to that campaign. The alliance of temperance forces and the Liberal party strengthened the already visible links between the Conservatives and what temperance forces derisively referred to as "the Trade." For this reason alone, the heavy defeat of the Liberals was a disaster for the temperance forces, which, according to many accounts, never recovered their mid- and late-Victorian vitality.[44]

The political impotence of the prohibitionists was indeed underlined by the 1895 defeat, and even when the Liberals returned to power in 1906, they faced a hostile House of Lords. By that time, prohibition was considered by hardened political realists, including more than a few within the temperance movement, to be dead and buried in the English case at least, but controversies over the future course of liquor legislation were only enhanced by the retreat from power. The turmoil in the World's WCTU over high license and the Gothenburg system was in part a product of the search for an alternative to prohibition that could be realized within the constraints of British political circumstances.

The appointment by the Conservatives of the liquor license law royal commission in 1896 fortuitously gave the temperance movement a (lesser) cause around which to regroup. Despite the fact that the forces for and against local veto were evenly balanced among the appointees, the chairman, Lord Peel, underwent something of a "drastic conversion to temperance reform" during the course of the hearings.[45] The commission broke up without reaching a unanimous agreement, and both majority and minority reports were written. Though the majority favored the liquor interests by providing extensive compensation for loss of license and proposed reduction of liquor outlets only at the existing slow rate, the minority or Peel report was more favorable to the temperance viewpoint. The Peel recommendations proposed fairly rapid reduction in the number of licenses with compensation paid only for seven years from a fund provided by taxation of the remaining licenses. On the negative side, any form of compensation was anathema to many prohibitionists, and the Peel report also involved delaying the introduction of local veto for a stated period in Scotland and Wales and indefinitely in England. The temperance forces were, in the words of historian David Fahey, being asked to "swallow" the delay of veto and a "diluted version of compensation in order to get drastic reduction in the number of licenses and the elimination of any claim to a permanent vested interest" in the holding of licenses.[46]

The Peel proposals did not receive uniform backing from temperance forces. But a significant group, including a number of executive committee members of the United Kingdom Alliance, signed a Temperance Manifesto, which backed the proposals when they were taken up in amplified form by the opposition Liberal leader Sir Henry Campbell-Bannerman in a speech at Manchester in November 1899.[47] The BWTA was among the groups that got behind Peel. A resolution of the executive committee in October 1899 welcomed the Peel report but asked for local veto as well.[48] The significant omission was any trace of opposition to compensation. As the Peel proposals developed in the debate within the Liberal party, it became clear that temperance support could be found for raising license fees and using the revenue to buy out licenses considered excessive. As the debate progressed, the BWTA became one of the strongest backers of this aspect of the proposed reforms.

By the middle of 1900, the BWTA had gone further and was prepared to drop its criticisms of the delay of local veto legislation in order to defeat the majority proposal. Agnes Slack, then BWTA secretary, told the annual conference that the British women should, with their "utmost energy, oppose the Majority's scheme; and this," it appeared, could "only be successfully done, in the present condition of opinion in the country, by securing the adoption of the scheme of Lord Peel." A resolution was passed to this effect. The BWTA adopted the spirit of "compromise" which was "everywhere inevitable."[49] From the perspective of the more extreme prohibitionists, especially those in the United States, this was an implicit capitulation to a form of high license similar to the Raines Law for which Willard had been roundly condemned after her Rochester speech in 1896.

It could be argued that the BWTA's high license policy was a product of Lady Henry's extraordinary hold over her membership. After all, Somerset had been advocating high license as early as 1896, before the Peel report had been presented.[50] Josephine Butler was not the only one of Somerset's opponents who lamented "her title and winning manners" and hurled abuse at those "foolish ones who follow her anywhere."[51] But the BWTA's policy was much more deeply based because the organization continued to support high license long after Somerset resigned the BWTA presidency in 1903.

If anything, circumstances conspired to force even more pragmatism on the BWTA after the passage of the Licensing Act of 1904 by the Conservative government, which enshrined the principle of monetary compensation that was at the heart of the majority report. The BWTA's angry response included as its centerpiece the demand for taxation of licenses to prevent their monopoly value from accruing any longer to the trade.[52] So long as the 1904 act remained law, the BWTA proposed to work within it to demand "a higher standard of conduct" from licensees and urged BWTA members to attend license renewal hearings.[53] BWTA lecturer Florence Balgarnie explained the new policy to an appreciative WCTU and United Kingdom Alliance audience in Lancashire. "She would like to see the Act absolutely repealed, but the final power . . . would be in the House of Lords, and she had no hope of the Lords in regard to such a course as that. She urged that they should go in for increased taxation of the monopoly value of licenses."[54]

This high license stance was tied to the Liberals' election strategies. Because the Liberal party opposed the act and promised temperance reform based on the Peel proposals, the already strong link between the BWTA and the Liberals was sealed indefinitely.[55] After 1904, the BWTA solidly backed the Liberal party's temperance legislation, including its attempts to get increased license duties introduced as part of the ill-fated 1909 budget. "The trade," editorialized the *White Ribbon* in a firm endorsement of high license, "owes to the state for the evils it entails upon the community." The BWTA hoped that as a result of the new duties on beer, the drink bill for the nation would be "markedly reduced" and "licensed premises . . . diminished."[56] The budget was of course rejected by the House of Lords in the great constitutional struggle, and even this small piece of practical legislation was consigned to the dustbin of history.

The shift to high license in the BWTA ought to have been embarrassing for the American WCTU and the World's WCTU, since both were committed to seeking prohibition. But in an important editorial of March 1900, Lady Henry was anointed by the *Union Signal* as "our World's leader," and nothing was said of her heretical views on the liquor question. In fact, her address before the royal commission was disingenuously hailed as "a most powerful prohibition argument which had wide influence." No mention was made of the divisions within British politics or the temperance movement over the responses to the Peel report.[57] The American WCTU was no longer prepared to defend Somerset and advocate diversity, as the *Union Signal* had done in 1898, but implicitly accepted the existence of that diversity within the World's WCTU. It seems likely that the editorial leadership was determined to avoid the controversies that followed in the wake of Lady Henry's every utterance and hoped to keep American WCTU members ignorant of different policies now being pursued across the seas. Nonetheless, the symbolic importance of Somerset holding the office of World's president remained to rankle women like Andrew, Bushnell, and Leavitt and continued to present the possibility of cultural adaptation of the WCTU's strict morality.

But the issue was not merely one of symbols. The World's WCTU itself appeared to lower the standard of absolute prohibitionism in order to accommodate the shift in British policy. The belligerent stand against "compromise with the evil" insisted upon at the 1897 convention was progressively if subtly watered down so that in 1903, the equivalent resolution emphasized prohibition as only an "ultimate goal."[58] This erosion of the prohibitionist stance corresponded strongly with the shift of the BWTA toward a high license position. It also corresponded with the siting of the 1900 and 1903 conventions in Edinburgh and Geneva, respectively. American delegates displayed discretion in their failure to push for a stronger platform that would have pleased prohibitionists in the United States. While the prohibitionist stance of the American WCTU remained unaltered, the element of compromise and adaptability inherent in the WWCTU's striving for an international application of temperance principles continued to operate after the demise of the Willard/Somerset axis in the Anglo-American women's temperance movement.

Flexibility and pragmatism did not stop at high license. More important was the continuing flirtation with antiprohibitionist positions within the BWTA. At this juncture the systems of liquor regulation prevalent in Scandinavia became of vital concern to the British temperance movement and to Somerset in particular. While she had already pioneered enough innovative tactics to last most reformers a lifetime, Somerset appeared, after Willard's death, to have been cut loose from any restraint imposed upon her unconventional approaches to prohibition. The turning point was the publication in 1899 by two British temperance workers, Arthur Sherwell and Joseph Rowntree, of *The Temperance Problem and Social Reform*.[59] This book, which was highly critical of American prohibition laws, favored local option as more practical for strongly prohibitionist areas and advocated disinterested public management for the rest. Somerset called the book "remarkable" and proclaimed it "the most valuable addition to the literature of the Temperance cause that to my mind has yet been given."[60]

As was the case in other aspects of her unorthodox career, Somerset found allies in the World's WCTU. The *Canadian Woman's Journal* followed Somerset's position almost exactly, wished the advocates of disinterested management success, and called the Rowntree/Sherwell volume a "priceless work."[61] This stand supplemented the Norwegian White Ribboners' own advocacy of the *samlag*, a position Willard had already stated as acceptable to the World's WCTU.

Three years later, Somerset, still World's and BWTA president, journeyed to the United States to see for herself the evidence Rowntree and Sherwell claimed to have unearthed and to examine liquor regulation controversies more generally. She returned convinced more than ever that moral customs and political conditions on each side of the Atlantic were vastly different and that American solutions were not suitable in British circumstances. "No matter what trials beset them," she told the 1903 BWTA conference, "their problem is less intricate than the one that meets us here."[62] Here again, Somerset was pushing the argument for cultural adaptability that she had jointly explored with Willard in the 1890s. Its limits and the tolerance of the American WCTU for such diversity had not yet been fully tested.

Now those limits would be explored for the last time. Disinterested management went too far for the bulk of WCTU supporters in Britain, let alone the United States. When Arthur Whittaker, the author of the Temperance Manifesto in support of the Peel proposals, advocated a system of company management on the lines of Scandinavian policies and joined Rowntree and Sherwell in 1903 in forming a Temperance Legislation League to advocate such policies, the BWTA threatened to split apart. Somerset resigned the presidency to campaign for the league and sought support for the new scheme through her allies remaining in the BWTA.[63] As unofficial leader of the antiprohibitionist opposition in the BWTA from 1903 to 1906, she brought the controversy over the Scandinavian models to a head.

Somerset's replacement did not follow her predecessor's penchant for radical innovation in temperance tactics. Rosalind Carlisle was a wealthy and politically prominent aristocrat like Lady Henry, but there the similarities ended. Even though the formidable Carlisle felt constrained after 1903 to go along with high license because of the political realities, she drew the line at actual promotion of drinking, which she and other prohibitionists believed disinterested management must inevitably involve. In a commanding and electrifying speech, Carlisle threw down the gauntlet to Lady Henry at the 1905 conference. "A vicious Act had forced the B.W.T.A. into the position of advocating high license, but they would not go a step further, and they would never consent to complicity with the liquor traffic."[64] The BWTA, she told the following annual meeting in 1906, had a "great objection to enlarging the number of well-meaning persons setting their hands to try and regulate a traffic that was inevitably dangerous."[65] Carlisle carried the day overwhelmingly, and the final resolution in 1906 declared that the BWTA's "devotion" to ultimate prohibition was "unabated."[66] At last Lady Henry's grip on the BWTA was broken, and in the same year she retired from the World's presidency and returned to the Surrey countryside

Rosalind Howard, Countess of Carlisle, World's WCTU president,
1906–1921, arguably the most important leader of the WCTU after
Willard and Somerset (courtesy of the National British Women's
Total Abstinence Union)

to tend her estates and care for the alcoholic women she had gathered for rehabilitation at her Duxhurst retreat.

The demise of Somerset signaled the beginning of a shift of policy for the BWTA, and for the World's union whose policies the BWTA had so profoundly affected. The 1906 WWCTU convention in Boston came out strongly against all schemes of disinterested management and returned to the high ground of implacable opposition to anything short of prohibition.[67] The removal of Somerset's influence may have prompted the stronger stand, but also important was the location of the 1906 conference in the United States, the first held there since 1893.[68] The large majority of American delegates that geography and membership dictated may have been a factor as well. It would certainly not have been politic to have stood for anything less than total prohibition while meeting on American soil, for the results of World's WCTU conventions were reported in the major dailies. If the BWTA could take refuge in the use of the word *ultimate* to describe the prohibitionist solution, the WWCTU also condemned high license policies and so put not just Somerset's BWTA but Carlisle's as well at odds with both World's and American principles.

Carlisle tried to avoid the embarrassment by her strong advocacy of the local veto as the ultimate solution. She was able to argue that by defeating disinterested management she had served the longer-term interests of prohibitionism. Instead of reforming "public houses" to make them "more wholesome" she had opened the way to prohibition by exposing the motive of greed in the trade and by refusing to reform hotel conditions.[69] Her subsequent support for licensing legislation would be judged always by the question, "How far will it lead us to Prohibition?"[70] Yet this stand was very similar to Willard's flexible tactics in the 1890s and still recognized that circumstances faced by the WWCTU affiliates differed vastly from one country to another. The experimentation had stopped, but the BWTA still did not conform to American prohibitionist standards.

Though the BWTA had fought disinterested or public management schemes, that was not enough for some temperance women. If many drew the line at support for disinterested management, still others could not even stomach the trend to high license. The BWTA's position placed it at odds with its vigorous Scottish affiliates. These believed that north of the Tweed the people were indeed ready for local veto, and they opposed all compensation and acceptance of high license. The root of the conflict exposed the strong connection between Protestant evangelical temperance fervor and support for the moral absolutism of prohibition. In England, the BWTA had been strongest in the dissenting sects, but there was always a significant minority of Church of England supporters, who lacked the millennialist fervor of the more extreme Protestants in either Scotland or the United States. The conflict was accentuated by Somerset's reconversion to the Anglicanism of her youth, which provoked bitter comment within the BWTA by 1898. Since most BWTA members were nonconformists, they resented "the church party" taking "such a hold of Lady Henry" and spiriting her away from Methodism.[71]

The conflict with the Scots went beyond professions of prohibitionist orthodoxy. Somerset, under the influence of Anglican canon Basil Wilberforce, discouraged the passage of resolutions against Communion wine at BWTA conventions in the late 1890s, whereas the Scottish women claimed with some justice to have "stood fast to our principles."[72] The reluctance of the BWTA to pass resolutions against Communion wine was linked to the questions of moral purity and prohibitionist policies. The strong tendency toward millennialist absolutism and the anxiety over morally polluting customs at the heart of the millennialist psychology have already been explained. Mrs. Alexander Black of Glasgow summed up the Christian fervor to make the world pure: "We must vote as we pray."[73] Like prohibitionist sentiments, opposition to wine was seen as part of a pattern of correct belief through behavior that exemplified that belief.[74] But rather than this issue, it was the technicalities of licensing raised by the Peel report that brought the matter to a head and provoked the Scottish delegates to secede in 1904 to form their own Scottish Christian Union and affiliate directly with the WWCTU.[75] The Scots, who had had Sunday closing for fifty years while the English had none, feared that support for the Peel proposals would eliminate this and other advantages the Scots had or hoped to gain soon from separate treatment.[76] Tactics as much as belief signified the need to separate.

Cut loose from the BWTA, the Scottish Christian Union was able to side directly with the American prohibitionists in the battle over disinterested management. In sharp contrast to Somerset, the *Scottish Reformer*, organ of the Scottish union, attacked Sherwell and Rowntree's damaging examination of prohibition in America and used the testimony of American women who attended the 1900 World's convention in Edinburgh to make their own polemical point. "The American ladies" who praised prohibitionist successes were not, like Sherwell and Rowntree, "outsiders." They knew, "as no passing visitor can ever know, how these laws affect the home life and habits of the people." The Scottish union had not only affiliated directly with the World's union, but it had already, from the beginnings of its discontent around 1900 consistently taken a strongly internationalist and pro-American stance against all the English temperance heresies promoted by Lady Henry.[77]

The loss of the energetic Scottish unions came as a severe blow to the BWTA, and the schism may have strengthened Carlisle's resolve to defend the BWTA against further declension. She was also undoubtedly influenced by her own Christian socialist heritage of her earlier years, as a result of which she abhorred the "gain" and "greed" she found inherent in "the Trade." The bugbear of the "liquor interests" in fact enabled her to focus her radical ire on a certain form of property, which, in view of her own immense landed wealth, was not an inconsiderable psychological advantage. But Christian socialism would not carry the day in the BWTA. The Scottish defection had highlighted not only the apparent loss of power by the British women but also the discontent of the evangelical sects, even in England and certainly in Wales. Ironically it was these groups that had cemented Somerset's power and to whom she appealed in the battle with the old guard in 1892–94. Her own personal spiritual odyssey had pushed her now out of touch with these emotional, ideological, and numerical strengths of the BWTA. In contrast, Carlisle agreed to conduct the BWTA on strictly Christian principles. "Whatever my own theological opinions may be," she wrote in 1907, "I loyally hold that the White Ribbon movement must retain its present Evangelical character."[78]

The fact remains that it was Carlisle's policies on prohibition, not her religious convictions, that sealed the contest with Somerset. Carlisle was herself "an agnostic in mature years" according to Professor Fahey.[79] As a religious but honest Victorian doubter, she was an odd choice as the supreme commander of a group of "largely Methodist women."[80] What Carlisle did offer, however, was to return the BWTA to the political test of its Christian, dissenting, and Liberal heritage by abandoning Lady Henry's experiments in cultural adaptation of temperance beliefs. If this change appeared to signal the triumph of religious orthodoxy, the BWTA's continuing endorsement of the licensing strategy of the Liberals reminds us that political practice still prevailed over purely religious considerations in the shaping of BWTA policies.

The shift back to a prohibitionist stance did not take full effect until after the Liberals' temperance legislation had been shelved on the eve of the First World War. The Ulster crisis and the coming of war in 1914 deferred the temperance bills so long held up by constitutional and political strife with the Conservatives.[81] Simultaneously, the advance of prohibition in the United States gave the British prohibitionists new hope that, though they had failed to achieve even modest legislation in the context of British politics, the external example of American success would eventually carry them to victory. "Let them take heart," said Carlisle with uncanny prescience in 1914, "that over across the Atlantic there was a mighty nation that was going to stop the manufacture, importation, and sale of alcoholic beverages in six years, and let them [the British women] all put more work into their [own] movement."[82]

Carlisle's recognition of American preeminence marked a further shift in the international debate over prohibition and cultural adaptation. Prior to 1913, the issue of regulation as a viable alternative to prohibition had still been hotly debated in the World's WCTU, and until 1906 emphasis had been upon defense of prohibitionist orthodoxy against a variety of heresies. In that context, European schemes for liquor control had been of great interest in the United States as a stick with which to beat the opponents of American prohibition. After the demise of Somerset and the failure of even the pragmatic high license strategy of the BWTA, paths to prohibition in the Anglo-American temperance movement took a more orthodox turn in which American conceptions of liquor's annihilation ceased quickly to be considered utopian. The domestic (American) debate shifted to an aggressively prohibitionist stance, and interest in foreign experiments declined, except insofar as they could be assimilated to the American model pushed by the ASL and its allies. A new virulence in the strength of cultural imperialism was engendered by the closure of the debate over prohibition's alternatives, and notions of local variation disappeared from the discourse of American temperance women and their foreign supporters.

There was, for this reason, a corresponding and marked shift in the World's WCTU as the organization and its membership came decisively under American domination. The 1913 World's convention in Brooklyn roundly condemned any system of public management and explicitly named for the first time the Gothenburg experiment.[83] For the first time, too, the World's WCTU announced its ambitious declaration of unequivocal support for "world-wide prohibition."[84] World's WCTU representatives carried that assimilative message into other temperance forums as well. At the International Congresses against Alcoholism held in London in 1909 and in Milan in 1913, Agnes Slack and other Anglo-American WCTU representatives howled down the demands of German delegates who tried to point out that only the Gothenburg model would work in Europe.[85]

The newly aggressive position on prohibition was directly connected to the promise presented by recent victories in a number of American states. A concerted drive against the saloon commenced in 1907, and by 1913 nine states were under prohibition laws. These gains impressed Carlisle and gave her BWTA the courage to struggle on.[86] A further heartening factor for prohibitionists was the defeat of the statewide dispensary law in South Carolina in 1907, which took all sense of an immediate threat of municipalization of the trade from the American debate. Lillian Stevens could, for this reason, discuss the dispensary in 1912 not as a practical political alternative but as a discredited part of South Carolina history.[87]

The effect was the same elsewhere in the Anglo-Saxon world. Prior to 1914, much interest had been shown by the American WCTU in the demands made in both Australia and New Zealand for local option laws. Katharine Lent Stevenson returned from Australasia in 1910 favorably impressed with the progress of "righteousness" measured in the growing power of the local option movement.[88] New Zealand's Anderson Hughes-Drew could still command considerable publicity as late as 1912 when she appeared before the national WCTU convention in Oregon to tell "A Story of Prohibition's Progress under the Southern Cross."[89]

By 1914, however, the pattern had shifted to one of praise and adulation for the achievements of a purely American prohibition drive. Annie Carvosso of Brisbane was one of many Australian temperance women "thoroughly interested" in Lillian Stevens's "great plan" for constitutional prohibition to be achieved by 1920, which the latter announced at the 1911 national convention.[90] Australian WCTU papers like the New South Wales *White Ribbon Signal* became quite suddenly and decisively filled with American propaganda emphasizing the success of American prohibition. "Something's the Matter with Kansas," a 1913 reprint from the *Union Signal*, was typical. The "sunflower State" was said to be experiencing "unprecedented prosperity" under its prohibitory law, despite the rigors of "heat and drought" that had struck the state. The same piece, and complementary articles on prohibition in Maine and West Virginia, appeared in the *Canadian White Ribbon Tidings*.[91]

The propaganda was spewed forth in a deliberate effort to impress upon other peoples the need to follow the American trail. Much of the interest was generated quite independently of American suggestion and was dictated by local political circumstances. The *White Ribbon Signal*'s flurry of American WCTU prohibitionist "facts" was aimed specifically at "the anticipated fight for No Licence in New South Wales."[92] Later, when New South Wales, along with four of the other five Australian states, adopted drastic early closing legislation during World War I, the example of America was again trotted out. Six o'clock closing was not envisaged as an end in itself by the women's temperance forces in Australia. Along with the prohibitionists in the alliances and the other church supporters of stricter controls, early closing was seen repeatedly by WCTU representatives as a step along the American road to national prohibition.[93] This pattern was paralleled in Britain as well, where the temperance forces tried without success to emulate the total wartime prohibition instituted by the American government.[94]

This phase lasted only until 1919, when the American WCTU itself went on the global offensive once it became clear that constitutional, national prohibition would triumph. A letter from Anna Gordon to WWCTU affiliates around the world in November 1918 proclaimed the victory of world prohibition by 1925 and outlined plans for an international edition of the *Union Signal* that would chart "progress" in all parts of the world.[95]

The letter represented the culmination of the dreams of Gordon. As the close friend of Willard, she had watched and listened as her beloved chieftain had outlined her vision for a dry world in the 1880s and had established the WWCTU to carry out her grandiose plans. For a very long time the WWCTU had seemed to many an extravagance or a curiosity, but in the

Prohibition and Cultural Adaptation

hour of national victory, the WCTU turned once more to its international aspirations. True to the ambitious forecasts of Willard, Gordon's plans proposed an unprecedented effort of time and money centered around the sending out of a new corps of missionaries and lecturers who would convey the benefits of prohibition to foreign nations, just as Leavitt had introduced so many of them to total abstinence thirty-five years before. Gordon herself went with Julia Deane to Europe on a major speaking tour in 1920 that included campaigning in the Scottish no-license election of 1920. Subsequently in 1921, they undertook a tour of South America.[96]

Though this and other visits were consistent with Willard's dreams, the strength of the American commitment was simultaneously transforming the WCTU as an internationalist movement. Willard's emphasis upon the British women had been designed to prevent American dominance and to help develop a broad movement that was not simply an arm of the American WCTU. But by the 1920s, the balance had shifted. The American WCTU was, thanks to its recruitment campaigns for the defense of national prohibition, now more dominant, numerically speaking, than at any time since the early 1890s in the international women's temperance movement, and this political clout was backed by the export of American principles and methods. On the other side, the numerical strength of the British reformers had been severely affected by the war and the decline of the Liberal party, and the American WCTU could no longer rely on the BWTA as the twin pillar of the international movement, as Frances Willard had done.[97]

As a result, the discussion of international issues in the *Union Signal* became increasingly fixated on the survival of American prohibition and on foreign support for what American prohibitionists were doing. More than ever before, the World's WCTU took policy positions designed to shore up American laws despite the fact that these were frequently inappropriate for non-American conditions. Without a hint of humor or sense of the ridiculous, WCTU propagandists declared that countries not remotely interested in prohibition, like Germany, would be dry by 1930.[98] In the case of Brazil, said Julia Deane in all seriousness, the Latin republic could easily be "dry by 1922." For her this was "not such a wild prediction," more an expression of well-founded faith in WCTU principles and methods.[99] After all, the ASL's drive for national prohibition had occupied a mere decade, and only the supremely optimistic observer could have predicted wartime successes in 1907.

Much of the information channeled through the *Union Signal's* international edition was designed to show that foreigners did indeed support the American stand. One of the functions of international information therefore became the bolstering of political resolve within the United States. The WCTU sought with its new allies in the WLAA to give the impression that the whole world was watching the American experiment and hoping it would work. The many reverses suffered in the early 1920s by prohibition-ist forces attempting to emulate the American example in Sweden, Norway, Scotland, and New Zealand had to be interpreted selectively in terms palat-able to the American WCTU and the larger prohibition movement. Part of this strategy involved blaming American wet propaganda for failures abroad. As early as 1922 the American WCTU was forced repeatedly to deny what it regarded as false assertions about national prohibition copied by the foreign media from the American press. According to Mary Harris Armor, who stumped New Zealand in the 1922 national liquor plebiscite, "published misrepresentations about prohibition in America confused vot-ers" in the antipodes. "Not a cartoon or a jest flung at prohibition was ever printed in America, that it was not duplicated in New Zealand."[100] Only the fifth column of liquor sympathizers in the United States stood in the road of world victory.

A good deal of propaganda painting such a false picture of prohibitionist prospects in other countries was sent back by emissaries like Armor who toured the world in the name of the WWCTU. But they did receive support from the indigenous populations, and WCTU organizations in Australia, New Zealand, South Africa, and Canada as well as in Scotland were as readily prepared as the visiting Americans to explain embarrassing political defeats and proclaim prohibition just around the corner.[101] Even in the European WCTUs, there were women like Denmark's Dagmar Prior who threw caution aside to predict a dry Denmark by 1930.[102] To some extent, the weakness of prohibitionism in many countries outside the United States encouraged the WCTU in those places increasingly to focus on American circumstances and live vicariously the prohibition fight in the heartland of the drys.

But the exaggeration of European hopes was also based on the political reality that the period from 1914 to the mid-1920s was the high point of liquor restriction in Europe, particularly in Scandinavia. Not only had Ice-land and Finland gone dry, but Norway had adopted partial prohibition, and in 1922 prohibition was only narrowly defeated in Sweden in a hotly contested and controversial referendum. Even in Britain, the war allowed what successive British Liberal governments had been unable to achieve by effecting a historical shift to a more restrictive liquor control policy which was to last for decades. The millennialist hopes expressed by American temperance women and reinforced by their European backers were not entirely without foundation in the early 1920s. As a result of this simulta-neous affirmation of American prestige and assertion of antiliquor influ-ence in some European countries, the earlier, prewar penchant for flexible and diverse strategies of drink reform in the ranks of the WWCTU's affili-ates was lost. The conferences of the World's body became as preoccupied with legal issues as did American prohibitionists at home.[103]

Prohibition and Cultural Adaptation

An Australian view of prohibition. This cartoon, which originally appeared
in *The Grit*, a Sydney prohibitionist publication, illustrates the capitulation of non-American prohibitionists to the American model.
(*Union Signal*, 23 June 1921)

As part of the dismissal of more flexible schemes, the American WCTU
was sedulous in avoiding the advice of those who argued that American
prohibitionist standards were not applicable to European circumstances.
When Julia Deane wrote to California politician Chester Rowell in 1922 to
get information on the relationship between prohibitionist sentiment and
wine production in that state during the referendum on the Wright Law, a
stringent state prohibition enforcement law, the reply was not the encouraging one that Deane had expected. Deane had hoped Rowell would tell
her that the grape growers there accepted prohibition and were able to
adapt their vines for the production of nonalcoholic products. Deane was
especially interested in the reply because she hoped to use the information
in European campaigns, where the economic and cultural significance of
the wine industry was so great.[104]

Rowell saw some cause for optimism in the California case but did not at
all agree that the European wine industry was analogous to the Californian.

"If prohibition ever extends" to take in "the enormous crops of the wine-growing districts of Europe," Rowell advised, it would "have to be by the votes of the people outside the wine-growing districts against the will and contrary to the immediate interests of the wine growers themselves." The finest wines were produced in localities unsuitable for any other cultivation, concluded Rowell, who thought that

> the spread of prohibition throughout the world must squarely face this fact. Probably the practical answer in these parts of Europe will be with the prohibition of distilled liquors and the permission of wine . . . for at least the first generation under prohibition. . . . To restore beer and wine in America, would be to restore all the evils of the old liquor traffic. That, however, is probably not the case in the southern [European] countries, where the habits of ages have made the distinction between the two sorts of drinks, and where one is not likely to be used as a substitute for the other.[105]

Rowell's letter concluded with an open invitation for Deane to publish this more realistic analysis. She did not accept the offer, but the *Union Signal* did continue to print propaganda favoring the conversion of wine-growing regions in, for example, South Africa, to raisin production.[106] Rather than accept Rowell's advice, the *Union Signal* preferred in the early 1920s to cultivate a more euphoric temper, as its editors watched "the world mount the water wagon."[107]

Ultimately the defeat of prohibition would depend on American circumstances, though the importation of illicit supplies of alcohol from Canada, Mexico, and across the seas would not help the cause. Oddly, the WCTU was slow to acknowledge the importation of alcohol as a serious problem. Perhaps to do so would have been to deny the ability of the American government in controlling its own trading relations and to recognize popular resistance to prohibition in the United States. Only in the resolution calling on the nations and shipping companies of the world to suppress the liquor traffic "on the high seas" as a threat to "the safety" of travelers and "a menace to the peace of the world" did the World's WCTU touch upon the genuinely international dimension of the trade in alcoholic beverages in its 1922 convention.[108] By 1928, the position was different. With prohibition increasingly under threat, the importation of spirits from Europe, Canada, and Mexico became an urgent issue. Both the American WCTU and other White Ribbon affiliates, such as the Finnish, faced the problem of smuggling, and the World's conventions gave as a result much attention to the promotion of international cooperation. The 1931 convention, for example, thanked the Canadian government for refusing to clear vessels bound for United States ports carrying cargoes of liquor, and Finnish delegate Eine Salonen told the 1928 convention how smuggling in the Baltic was being cut by cooperation with the Swedish government.[109]

With prohibition now under threat in both the United States and Finland and already defeated in Iceland and Norway, the confident mood in the WWCTU evaporated, and once again the issue of alternative schemes of liquor regulation came to the fore. Especially important was the substitution of a system of government control boards in the Canadian provinces in place of wartime prohibition in the 1920s. Whereas in 1920 every province except Quebec had a prohibitory law, by 1928 only Nova Scotia and Prince Edward Island remained in the dry camp.[110] Not only was the Canadian alternative important because of geographic proximity. Governor Al Smith, Democratic candidate for president in 1928 and a prominent anti-prohibitionist, had advocated the Canadian system during the election campaign.[111]

The response to this renewed foreign threat was predictable enough yet slightly different in emphasis from the debate of the 1890s. No longer did the WCTU have to convince its own supporters of the justice or expediency of prohibition; it was merely necessary to reaffirm the applicability of prohibitionism as the correct solution anywhere and everywhere. Canada's system of governmental control was literally "unthinkable," pronounced the *Union Signal*.[112] The subsequent course of the presidential campaign reinforced this absolutism. Smith was soundly defeated, and with his political demise the alternative of government control on the Canadian model could be temporarily shelved by the World's and American WCTUs, but given the political, economic, and social pressures upon American prohibition, non-American examples were bound to be raised again.

Attention now turned to the Swedish alternative that had replaced the controversial Gothenburg system. Among the members of the Wickersham Commission, appointed by President Hoover to investigate the operation of the prohibition laws, was Col. Henry W. Anderson, who advocated the Swedish Bratt system, a strict rationing system of liquor control introduced in 1917. Bratt's scheme required possession of passbooks to obtain liquor and individually tailored permissible amounts of consumption. The WCTU's international connections enabled the organization to defend the prohibitionist stance by pointing to friendly European expertise. According to the Swedish WCTU's Maria Sandstrom, consumption of beer and wine had increased, drinking had been made respectable, and violations of the law occurred. Sandstrom did concede that the most obvious manifestations of drunkenness had decreased under Swedish law, but she attributed these improvements to the law implementing a policy of incarcerating chronic alcoholics, passed at the same time as the Bratt law. Such people no longer turned up time and time again in the statistics for drunk and disorderly conduct and so created a (false) impression that the Bratt law was working.[113]

The WCTU was happy to use Sandstrom's arguments against the hated Bratt system but selectively ignored the fact that she was, simultaneously, part of an investigative commission representing the various Swedish temperance societies that concluded in 1931 that the best course for Sweden was a return to a system of high taxation, company management, and local option that resembled the Norwegian legislation of the 1890s. Even the emphasis on using liquor revenues for social welfare and alcoholic rehabilitation was drawn from the regulationist tradition.[114] Rather than highlight Swedish acceptance of regulation and government involvement in the liquor business, the *Union Signal* in 1931 preferred to dwell on the more palatable evidence of Dr. Robert Hercod of the International Bureau against Alcoholism in Switzerland, who dismissed the significance of the Bratt system by arguing that Sweden's conditions were peculiar and its solutions inapplicable elsewhere.[115] National American WCTU president Ella Boole's conclusion from this and other "foreign" evidence was simple. "Prohibition [was still] the best policy" because "foreign nations" looked "with jealous eyes" upon its "progress" in America.[116]

The debate in 1931 over international prohibition and its meaning for the United States occurred in a political climate turning rapidly, and suddenly, against the Eighteenth Amendment. Until 1930, the negative images that have subsequently shaped our understanding of prohibition's legacy were by no means dominant. Though earlier generations of historians had lampooned prohibition, more recent and careful scrutiny has shown that prohibition was partially effective, more so than many opponents of prohibition then or now would care to admit. In particular, consumption of alcohol did decline, most of all among the working-class people whose regular labor was desired but whose cultural mores and social habits were despised by reformers and the socioeconomic elite alike.[117] More important, prohibition was politically ascendant until well after the 1928 election. The WCTU basked in the victory of Herbert Hoover, and externally prohibition also held strong in Finland throughout the 1920s. In British India, too, the stirrings of nationalism under Gandhi held out hope for a further extension of prohibitionist sentiment.[118] The defeat in Norway at the 1926 plebiscite that reversed the stand of 1921 could be explained because only liquors of more than 12 percent alcohol had been prohibited in the first place. As the *White Ribbon Signal* of New South Wales rationalized the defeat, Norway's was "the worst kind of prohibition" anyway, and hardly worthy of the name.[119]

In this climate of mutually reinforcing illusions, it was understandable for the WCTU to maintain in the 1920s the certainty of its convictions and to become preoccupied with enforcement of the Volstead Act. This focus undoubtedly did narrow the appeal of the organization internationally. Despite the fact that resolutions on women's citizenship and suffrage, peace, purity, the antiopium crusade, and so on, were still debated and passed in World's and national conventions, the WWCTU had nothing to offer should prohibition fail politically. In both Finland and the United States, the arguments against prohibition gained new force after the onset of the worldwide economic depression. But even the capitulation of the Finns to economic pressure late in 1931 did not affect the resolve of the Americans to resist. Given their monolithic commitment to prohibition, it is small wonder that the World's and American WCTUs denounced the repeal of prohibition in Finland and attributed failure to the pernicious involvement of "outside pressure on Finland" from "unprincipled interests" in the European wine-producing countries.[120] The Finnish case did not reveal the unworkable nature of the Volstead Act but rather illustrated the lengths to which antiprohibitionists would go in the service of "greed." Moreover, legalization of the trade in Finland did not appear to do away with the need to combat illegal traffic in spirits by unscrupulous dealers in defiance of Finland's new but still strict controls. For this reason, the WCTU merely felt it necessary to reemphasize the value of total and constitutional prohibition as a more effective weapon against all bootleggers.[121]

Finland *was* of course a very different case from the American. Its economy and international influence were so much smaller, and the Finnish position, like that of Iceland's prohibition law in 1921, had indeed been partially undermined by severe trade retaliation from the wine-producing countries.[122] American partisans of prohibition could still hold out hope that the same thing could never happen in the United States, an economic giant not dependent in the 1920s on European trade in a small range of vulnerable commodities. When repeal finally came to the heartland of prohibition in 1933, therefore, the blow was as crushing at home as it was for those abroad who looked to the United States for hope. New World's president Ella Boole put on a brave front at the 1934 WWCTU Stockholm convention when she argued that repeal laws in the United States, Iceland, and Finland were "simply 'skirmishes' lost," and she concluded with a plea "for world wide strengthening of the temperance movement." But her words were merely a verbal gesture of defiance that could hardly hide a now empty and vanquished policy.[123]

The defeat of American prohibition at last eclipsed the large ambitions of temperance women after nearly sixty years of agitation. During much of that time since the great crusade of 1873–74, the WCTU had sought home protection and, since the 1890s, had pushed for legal restrictions on the traffic abroad as well. Yet the whole history of the attempts to export American prohibition is a complicated and convoluted one in which the WCTU defied the simple formula of an unthinking and unchanging support for prohibition. The WCTU's desire for international influence inspired a much more flexible and pragmatic stance. Local conditions had produced notable variations from the ASL's attempts to create a prohibitionist orthodoxy. Though prohibition triumphed over cultural adaptation in the World's WCTU, it did not do so without a fight, and ironically that triumph ultimately weakened the WCTU's international standing by making life beyond prohibition practically impossible.

The shell of the World's WCTU still crusaded despite this staggering reversal. Aged organizers like Flora Strout, Christine Tinling, and Mary Campbell—all of whom had known or been inspired by Willard decades before—remained in the field in the 1930s and 1940s, and American prohibitionists took heart at their success, as measured problematically in the progress of legislation in the Indian subcontinent, and their growing membership in Japan in the 1930s. The cultural equation was now well and truly reversed, but the language was familiar. Those California WCTU convention delegates who listened in May 1948 to Mrs. J. R. Chitambar of the Indian WCTU would have had their thoughts wrenched back, if their sense of WCTU history was strong, to Mary Leavitt's Christian millennialist hopes of the 1880s and to the warning that accompanied her prospectus for the future of the "redeemer nation." Asked Chitambar: "Many Indians expect that our country will be under prohibition within five years. Will non-Christian India get ahead of Christian America?"[124]

Epilogue

Divergent Meanings of the World's WCTU

From her retirement home in Oakland, California, in the late 1930s, a frail yet still lively Katharine Bushnell looked back at her sixty-year career in the service of the Lord. Bushnell was a long-forgotten figure when she was called upon in 1939 to address the state convention of the California WCTU. There she extolled the memory of Frances Willard and retold the story of her friendship with the great English purity crusader, Josephine Butler. In the process, she recalled her own considerable efforts in the service of the World's WCTU.[1]

Forgotten were the controversies of the 1890s, the internecine conflicts over policies and personalities, the ultimate defeat of national prohibition, and the illusory dreams of an international order of peace and sobriety led by the example of Christian women. Bushnell remembered instead the more positive side of her experience. Her correspondence and speeches around this time and into the 1940s resounded with the memories of the "militant saints" who fought like Willard to show that women "could represent the cause . . . better . . . than any of the men."[2] Over the years her faith had not eroded but was rather strengthened by her reversals. "The Lord was in the W.C.T.U.," she insisted. "We did [temperance campaigning] to the best of our ability and met the best women around the world in doing the work."[3] Here the central meanings of the World's WCTU to its champions were made clear in retrospect: Christian service, women's uplift in terms intelligible to contemporaries of the late nineteenth-century Anglo-American middle class, a spirit of adventure, and the companionship of other women. These were her cherished memories, the meanings she found in her life and those of likeminded women.

Writing any history necessarily involves an element of individual judgment. There are in theory as many histories of any episode or phenomenon as historians exist who are willing to write about them. Scholars will therefore continue to find conflicting meanings in the international experience of the WCTU, but this element of flux in historical interpretation does not make all versions of its history equally valid. Any synoptic, intelligible, and historical judgment must capture the internal retrospective synthesis of

Katharine Bushnell—lost to generations of unsympathetic historians—and yet be able to convey the wider context and more contradictory ramifications of the work she and her temperance sisters and mothers undertook; only thus can we locate these women in the changing stream of history that shaped and set limits on their achievements.

The WCTU long drew its sustenance from the late nineteenth-century flowering of the American middle-class evangelical culture of domesticity and social reform and its external expansion through the missionary movement. There the organization gave expression to dreams of an "internationalism" that were in fact closely intertwined with the creation of an Anglo-American cultural aegis. Just as clearly, the historical circumstances that made the World's WCTU a potent agency of women's emancipation and cultural transmission changed rapidly in the 1920s. It is necessary for a moment to recall this context of the WCTU's demise on the international stage.

The 1920s that saw the rise and fall of international prohibition were nothing if not a contradictory decade.[4] Alongside the assertion of great wealth went enormous pockets of poverty in America and economic dislocation, technological change, and class conflict in Britain, Australia, and many other countries in which the WCTU found its strength. In the colonial world, the 1920s witnessed the visible stirrings of indigenous nationalism that would by the 1950s overthrow the entire conception of the world familiar to the temperance missionaries. While within the United States some social groups and classes, most notably immigrants and other workers, curtailed their alcohol consumption, middle-class women of the college set threw off their inhibitions and began to drink, smoke, and engage more often and more openly in premarital sexual activity. *The Great Gatsby*'s image of prosperity and indulgence rubbing shoulders with grimy poverty and its attendant social and cultural restraint is not entirely false, despite Scott Fitzgerald's rather obsessive preoccupation with American materialism.[5]

By the end of the 1920s, it was no longer possible to identify American women's opinions with those of the WCTU. In fact, the Women's Organization for National Prohibition Reform claimed more supporters than did the WCTU by 1931.[6] Among other functions the repeal association's propaganda drew upon the ire of men and women concerned not with the extension of drinking so much as the flouting of law; yet most disturbing were complementary changes going on in mass culture. New values identified with the rise of a consumer society appeared, and advertising sought to persuade Americans to spend rather than to save. The old ethics of sexual restraint seem, in retrospect, to have been eclipsed by the new technologies of radio and film, which offered Americans the images of a more cosmopolitan world of fashion, conspicuous consumption, and sexual change.[7] Sexual radicals in Britain and America proclaimed the right of women to

Epilogue

full heterosexual fulfillment, and others self-consciously adopted homosexual styles.[8] The late Victorian women's culture languished, suffering the fate of older generations at the hands of the young.[9] The cause of women's emancipation was giving way to a redefinition of feminism that was not so conducive to single-sex societies; individual achievement triumphed over sexual identification. All these and other cultural and social changes consigned the WCTU to historical oblivion by the 1930s.[10]

Ironically, the WCTU now faced stiff competition for what would once have been its own constituency. As early as 1904 the Women's Club movement had been recognized as a serious competitor, but in the 1920s such organizations proliferated on the international level. Special Women's Institutes, devoted to the improvement of country life, mushroomed in Canada and even constituted a serious competitor in parts of Britain. These joined similar societies in Australia, New Zealand, and other WCTU strongholds to form the International Country Women's Association by the 1930s. Meanwhile, another part of the WCTU's appeal was appropriated by the spread of international work in the YWCAs. These provided the opportunity for younger women to engage in Christian social service without tying that service to the program of prohibition. The older women's movement had not died, but it had fragmented, and the Do-Everything policy was one casualty of such specialization.[11]

Located as the WCTU was, through the antiliquor crusade, at the crucible of controversy in this decade of cultural upheaval, it is tempting to typecast the organization as part of the reactionary social forces that, through the cluster of prohibitionism, fundamentalism, nativism, and antiradicalism, sought to turn back the seemingly inexorable processes of economic modernization in America. This would, however, be to oversimplify the role of the WCTU at home and abroad. Through the World's WCTU and its peace efforts, temperance women were linked to the idealistic struggle for a new internationalism that produced the World Court and the Kellogg-Briand Pact. The WCTU also continued to promote issues of child welfare at home and participated in the social welfare reforms of the Women's Congressional Caucus. Abroad, moreover, the WCTU and world prohibition were seen by supporters, and even by some astute opponents, not as reactionary phenomena but as part of the process of postwar economic reorganization, linked to other "progressive" aspects of American values. The Italian Marxist Antonio Gramsci grasped the essential point that prohibition's meaning, functionally speaking, was not so much to be found in the dying gasps of an older social order. Rather, he identified prohibition as an element in the contradictory and ultimately unrealizable attempt at extending the power of corporate economic rationalization over human relations.[12]

This perspective on the WCTU illustrates the ambiguous meanings of the WCTU's achievements in such a deeply divided decade. If the 1920s saw the high point and ultimate demise of prohibition, the longer-term significance of the context of the prohibitionist struggle on the international level should not be lost. The 1920s witnessed a sharply publicized expansion of American influence. This was the context of Gramsci's remarks on "Americanism" in Europe. Though Gramsci was particularly concerned with the possibility of a new kind of ideological hegemony specifically located in the rationalization of factory production—what he called Fordism—the broader field of a new American cultural hegemony ought not to be neglected in any discussion of American influence.

Gramsci admitted the possibility of an international ideological hegemony, yet his emphasis upon Fordism and its accompanying psychology may distract us from attention to this cultural context.[13] The true field for hegemony was much more diffuse and much more akin to its processes in other periods and other societies. Here I do not use hegemony to mean, as it so often does in discussions of international relations, a material or political dominance, but rather an educative process involving class and cultural conflict. It is a commonplace in the historical literature that for American influence abroad, the 1920s witnessed an intensification of economic opportunities and business penetration. Rhetorical isolation in politics was not matched by withdrawal from economic affairs.[14] What has not been appreciated is the extent to which the 1920s also saw the preparation on a cultural level of a new offensive that was in no way subordinate to the economic. This encompassed the activities of the peace organizations, academics, missionaries, and prohibitionists as well as the voluntary service organizations like Rotary and the YMCA (which Gramsci did, to his credit, note).[15] Though these individuals and organizations by no means pushed the same uniform messages, they collectively sought to foster a new American form of internationalism that proved to be an important precursor of American efforts toward extending intellectual and cultural influence in the post-1945 world.

These exponents of internationalism in the 1920s were not concerned with preserving the privileges of the old European empires and showed little interest in acquiring a new American empire to match the European examples. Even the WCTU exhibited these changes, for the older context of Anglo-American political partnership in the civilizing of the world was in fact largely replaced by an emphasis on democratic participation and the mobilization of peoples and on an interaction with the cluster of other American-sponsored voluntary organizations, like the WLAA. American prohibitionists, like William E. "Pussyfoot" Johnson, who visited India in the early 1920s, sought to exploit the position of the nationalist movement to their own purposes at the possible expense of British rule. Though not successful, they demonstrated the ideological drift of the American voluntaristic intervention abroad.[16] Their position built upon that of the temperance missionaries before the First World War, yet it also anticipated that of Wendell Willkie in his *One World* and the verbal anticolonialism of Franklin D. Roosevelt during the Second World War.[17] That this cultural-international drive was both contentious and unrealized in the 1920s must not obscure this point.

What the internationalists of the 1920s shared with later liberals like Willkie and Roosevelt was the desire to universalize key American values. Though the 1930s saw a resurgence of isolationism and a subsequent and unprecedented governmental involvement in the spread of American culture extending into the Cold War period, the experience of the 1920s was not entirely lost.[18] For what distinguished American "imperialism" after 1945 was an attempt to persuade independent states to work together for what were defined as common interests, an approach that at the same time served preeminent American economic and ideological objectives through a system of alliances. This strategy surely depended on an identification of foreign and American democratic values and on a process in which political disagreements and cultural divergence were contained within a mutually acceptable framework. This comes close to an attempted creation on an international level of the kind of cultural hegemony Gramsci discussed.

Part of that process involved the penetration of American voluntary institutions conceived not simply as instruments of American power but as associations of a universalistic kind. The voluntaristic internationalism of the 1920s was a model for and a precursor of such a cultural and political framework. Just as surely, the WCTU, as part of this legacy of cultural influence, continued to have effects long after prohibition was dead, and the kind of women's emancipation the WCTU represented was relegated to the texts of history. It is ironic that in subsequent decades, newer technologies have supplied forms of cultural penetration that already eroded the WCTU's power at home in the United States in the 1920s, and that these have proven far more potent if unpredictable agents of "the Americanization of the world" than the moral forces W. T. Stead identified in 1902.[19]

Katharine Bushnell died in 1946, in the era of the atomic bomb. Whether she would have applauded the role in world politics the United States has taken in these times is unknown. One suspects she would not, yet her preoccupations were different. Her failing years in Oakland were dominated by two things: her search for a companionship that would offer the same sustenance that her long relationship with Elizabeth Andrew, her deceased partner, had given; and her obsession that only through a revival of true religion would emancipation for women come. The Bible had been hopelessly distorted in its 1611 King James translation to enshrine male dominance, she was convinced. Bushnell spent her last years retranslating it and holding classes to educate women in what she regarded as the true meaning of the Scriptures. The end came on 26 January 1946. Though failing fast, she saw a vision of the Lord and rose from her hospital bed with the aid of nurses to deliver her last ministry to her neighbors. Then she returned to her bed to die quietly. Her epitaph, and that of her temperance sisters, might easily have been the quip attributed to a fellow and equally aged WCTU missionary. The fierce Australasian campaigner Bessie Harrison Lee Cowie had been asked shortly before she died in Los Angeles in 1950 to rest. "Rest!" she exclaimed. "There will be all eternity to rest in."[20]

Appendix

Official Round-the-World Missionaries, 1884–1925

Missionaries listed are those whose names appeared in WWCTU convention directories. Countries of origin are shown for missionaries not from the United States.

Jessie Ackermann, c. 1857–1951
Elizabeth Andrew, 1845–1917
Helmfidor Arnadottir (Iceland)
Alvine Muriel Ayres
Susan Hammond Barney, c. 1835–1922
Mabel Beddow (England)
Ethel Beedham (England)
Helen Bullock, 1836–c. 1927
Katharine C. Bushnell, 1856–1946
Mary E. Campbell (Scotland/U.S.), 1865–1952
Bessie Harrison Lee Cowie (Australia and New Zealand), 1860–1950
Emily Cummins (Australia)
Joan Davis (India/U.S.)
Ruth Frances Davis
Jennie Ericson (Finland)
Addie Northam Fields, 1857–1920
Jennie V. Glassey (Scotland)
Elma Grace Gowen, d. 1912
Anderson Hughes-Drew (New Zealand)
Olifia Johannsdottir (Iceland)
Mary C. Leavitt, 1830–1912
Mary Lochhead (Scotland)
Ren Yin Mei (China)
Hardynia Norville, 1864–1941
Alice Palmer, b. 1856
Clara Parrish, 1865–1947
Dagmar Prior (Denmark), b. 1869
Mary B. Reese, 1832–1922
Lillian Ruth Shaffner
Kara Smart, 1870–1956
F. E. Stroud-Smith (Scotland), d. 1914
Flora Strout, c. 1864–1960
Christine Tinling (England), 1869–1938
Elizabeth Vincent (England/Australia), c. 1865–1938
Mary Allen West, 1837–1892

Women Who Made Special Round-the-World Trips for the WWCTU

Sara Crafts
Katharine Lent Stevenson, 1853–1919

Ella Hoover Thatcher

Appendix

Additional International Organizers, 1878–1928

Mary Harris Armor, b. 1863
Florence Balgarnie, b. 1871
Layyah Barakat
Frances J. Barnes, 1846–1920
Helen Barton
Mary M. Bowen
Nellie Burger
Laura Ormiston Chant, 1848–1923
Edith Smith Davis, d. 1918
Julia Deane
Carrie C. Faxon
Anna Gordon, 1853–1931
Charlotte Gray, 1844–1912
Lydia Johnson
Mary Coffin Johnson
Belle Kearney, 1863–1939
Rebecca Krikorian
Mary Livermore, 1820–1905

Deborah Knox Livingston
Ada Murcutt
Margaret E. Parker, 1828–1896
Lillian Pash
Pandita Ramabai, 1858–1922
Elizabet Selmer
Agnes Slack, 1857–1946
Emilie Jane Solomon, 1858–1939
Eliza Stewart, 1816–1908
Helen M. Stoddard
Maria C. Treadwell
Eva C. Wheeler, b. c. 1851
Frances Willard Wang (Financial
    records actually reveal she was a
    fully commissioned WWCTU
    missionary.)
Frances Willard, 1839–1898

Resident Missionaries Employed by the WWCTU

Principal country of service is shown for each missionary.

Annie C. Darley (Philippines)
Margaret B. Denning (India)
Helen Dunhill (India)
Mary Jane Farnham (China)
Sarah Boardman Goodrich (China)
Jeanette Hauser (India)
C. L. R. Hoskins (India)
Jennie V. Hughes (China)

Eliza Spencer Large (Japan)
Margaret W. Leitch (Ceylon)
May Mack (Burma)
Shih Meiyu [Mary Stone] (China)
Mary Phillips (India)
Ruth Ranney (Burma)
Ellen Stone (Bulgaria)

Additional Individuals Who Served
in the Mission Fields, 1891–1919

Individuals listed are those whose names appeared in WWCTU treasurer's
reports.

Miss S. Chandler (China)
Miss Chen (China)

Miss F. Denton (Japan)
Juana Galvin (Mexico)

Appendix

Mrs. Tsume Gauntlett (Japan)
Mrs. D. Gilmore (China)
[Miss] S. B. Goodrich (China)
Miss Hargreaves (Japan)
Miss Mier (China)
Miss Azume Moriya (Japan)

Miss Smith (Burma)
Mrs. Sugimoto (Japan)
Mrs. B. Thompson (Burma)
Isabel Vacquez (unknown)
Miss Yuen (China)
Kaji Yajima (Japan)

Others Who Received Special Mission Grants

Josephine Butler (Italy)
Miss Sevasti Callisperi (Greece)
Mrs. (Daisy) Geard (South Africa)
Mrs. Howland (Newfoundland)

Miss H. G. Ramsey (Bermuda)
F. Ricard (France)
Alli Trigg (Finland)

Notes

Abbreviations

In addition to the abbreviations found in the text, the following source abbreviations are used in the notes.

AR   *Annual Report*

BWTAU   British Women's Total Abstinence Union

NAW   James, Edward T., Janet Wilson James, and Paul S. Boyer, eds. *Notable American Women, 1607–1950: A Biographical Dictionary*. 3 vols. Cambridge, Mass.: Harvard University Press, Belknap Press, 1971.

OHS   Ohio Historical Society, Columbus, Ohio

PTD   *Permanent Temperance Documents of the American Temperance Society*. Boston: Seth Bliss, 1835.

SEAP   Cherrington, Ernest H., et al., eds. *Standard Encyclopedia of the Alcohol Problem*. 6 vols. Westerville, Ohio: American Issue Pub. Co., 1924–30.

STF Series   Scientific Temperance Federation Series

WCTU Files   Woman's Christian Temperance Union Historical Files, Woman's Christian Temperance Union Headquarters, Evanston, Ill.

WCTUHQ   Woman's Christian Temperance Union Headquarters

WCTU Series   Woman's Christian Temperance Union Series

WTPA   Woman's Temperance Publishing Association

WWCTU Files World's Woman's Christian Temperance Union Files, Woman's Christian Temperance Union Headquarters, Evanston, Ill.

Note on Citation of WCTU Material

WCTU Series, Ohio Historical Society. This refers to the microfilm edition of the Woman's Christian Temperance Union Series, prepared under the direction of Charles A. Isetts, Ohio Historical Society, as part of the Microfilm Edition of the Temperance and Prohibition Papers, a joint Michigan Historical Collections–Ohio Historical Society–Woman's Christian Temperance Union Project, described in Randall C. Jimerson, Francis X. Blouin, and Charles A. Isetts, eds., *Guide to the Microfilm Edition of Temperance and Prohibition Papers* (Ann Arbor: University of Michigan, 1977). The originals of this material are in the National WCTU Headquarters, Evanston, Illinois, but in the important case of the manuscripts of Frances Willard, these materials are not available for scholarly perusal and must be consulted and cited in the microfilm edition.

WCTU Series, 1982 Supplement, Michigan Historical Collections. Subsequent to the publication of the WCTU Series, diaries of Frances Willard and miscellaneous manuscript material relating to the WCTU were discovered and microfilmed by Michigan Historical Collections.

WCTU Files. These are the originals of miscellaneous uncataloged manuscripts not microfilmed and all scrapbooks held in the National Woman's Christian Temperance Union Headquarters, Evanston, Illinois. Some of these scrapbooks have been microfilmed under the WCTU Series, but they are cited by me as they were used, in the original form.

WWCTU Files. Held in WCTU Headquarters, Evanston, Illinois. These records have not been microfilmed and had not even been cataloged at the time of use (1981). They include correspondence, miscellaneous minutes, printed financial records, and some newspaper clippings.

Further and more extensive records of the World's WCTU are held in the Papers of Rosalind Stanley Howard, Countess of Carlisle, Howard Family Archives, Castle Howard, Yorkshire; in the Josephine Butler Papers, Fawcett Library, City of London Polytechnic; the Jessie A. Ackermann Collection, Sherrod Library, East Tennessee State University, Johnson City, Tennessee; the Hannah Whitall Smith Papers, Lilly Library, Indiana University, Bloomington, Indiana, and in the Scientific Temperance Federation Series (Microfilm Edition of the Temperance and Prohibition Papers). Others equally valuable are still held by many branches of the World's WCTU in the principal countries of its operation and are cited in the text below by existing location at the time of use.

Chapter 1

1. *Union Signal*, 25 Dec. 1884, p. 4; Frances Willard, *Glimpses of Fifty Years* (Chicago: WTPA, 1889), p. 431.

2. *White Ribbon Bulletin for Asia*, Aug. 1895, in Scrapbook 58, WCTU Files; Ernest H. Cherrington, ed., *Proceedings of the Fifteenth International Congress against Alcoholism* . . . (Washington, D.C., and Westerville, Ohio: American Issue Pub. Co., 1920), p. 130; *Report of the Eighth Convention of the World's Woman's Christian Temperance Union* . . . *1910* (n.p., 1910), p. 212; *Report of the Thirteenth Convention of the World's Woman's Christian Temperance Union* . . . *1928* (n.p., 1928), p. 22 (these reports are cited hereafter as, for example, WWCTU, *13th Conv., 1928*); *Union Signal*, 11 Aug. 1928, p. 4.

3. Cf. Ruth Bordin, *Woman and Temperance: The Quest for Power and Liberty, 1873–1900* (Philadelphia: Temple University Press, 1981), pp. 90, 156; Patricia R. Hill, *The World Their Household: The American Woman's Foreign Mission Movement and Cultural Transformation, 1870–1920* (Ann Arbor: University of Michigan Press, 1985), p. 195, takes issue with Bordin and cites the larger numbers of women involved in the foreign mission work. Hill is correct, but the vast numbers of missionary supporters were not located in a single interdenominational

society. Nor, as Hill concedes, can the more intangible questions of political influence and social impact be reduced to numbers.

4. Emily Rosenberg, *Spreading the American Dream: American Economic and Cultural Expansion, 1890–1945* (New York: Hill and Wang, 1982).

5. Francis E. Clark, *Christian Endeavor in All Lands* (Boston: United Society of Christian Endeavor, 1906), pp. 206–7.

6. See, esp., "Reassessments of 'First-Wave' Feminism," special issue of *Women's Studies International Forum* 5 (no. 6, 1982).

7. Nancy Boyd, *Emissaries: The Overseas Work of the American YWCA, 1895–1970* (New York: Woman's Press, 1986), pp. 3–6, 287–320.

8. Susan Brook, "The World League against Alcoholism: The Attempt to Export an American Experience" (M.A. thesis, University of Western Ontario, 1972), pp. 39–40, 60, 65; Ernest H. Cherrington, *The Evolution of Prohibition in the United States* (Westerville, Ohio: American Issue Pub. Co., 1920), p. 367.

9. The best treatment of the Good Templars' international activities is in David Fahey, ed., *The Collected Writings of Jessie Forsyth, 1847–1937: The Good Templars and Temperance Reform on Three Continents* (Lewiston, N.Y.: Edwin Mellen Press, 1988).

10. Rosenberg, *Spreading the American Dream*. For a sensitive analysis of the missionary aspects of this story, see Jane Hunter, *The Gospel of Gentility: American Women Missionaries in Turn-of-the-Century China* (New Haven: Yale University Press, 1984).

11. William T. Stead, *The Americanization of the World, or the Trend of the Twentieth Century* (1902; reprint, New York: Garland, 1972), p. 104.

12. The theme of cultural imperialism is prominent in Rosemary Skinner Keller, Louise L. Queen, and Hilah F. Thomas, eds., *Women in New Worlds: Historical Perspectives on the Wesleyan Tradition*, vol. 2, section 3, "Foreign Missions and Cultural Imperialism" (Nashville: Abingdon, 1982). The quotation is from Adrian A. Bennett, "Doing More Than They Intended: Southern Methodist Women in China, 1878–1898," ibid., p. 251. For critical commentary and further sources, see Patricia R. Hill, *World Their Household*, p. 199.

13. An interesting and learned example of comparative history that fails to transcend the boundaries of the nation state as the unit of analysis is Donald Meyer, *Sex and Power: The Rise of Women in America, Russia, Sweden, and Italy* (Middletown, Conn.: Wesleyan University Press, 1987). See the perceptive critiques of comparative history in the special symposium published in *Journal of Interdisciplinary History* 16 (Summer 1985): 87–116.

14. For Victoria, see Anthea Hyslop, "Temperance, Christianity, and Feminism: The Woman's Christian Temperance Union of Victoria, 1887–1897," *Historical Studies* 17 (Apr. 1976): 27–49; for New South Wales and for Australia more generally, see Ian Tyrrell, "International Aspects of the Woman's Temperance Movement in Australia: The Influence of the American WCTU, 1882–1914," *Journal of Religious History* 12 (June 1983): 284–304; for New Zealand, see Patricia Grimshaw, *Women's Suffrage in New Zealand* (Auckland: Auckland University Press, 1972); Phillida Bunkle, "The Origins of the Women's Movement in New Zealand: The Women's Christian Temperance Union, 1885–

1895," in Beryl Hughes and Phillida Bunkle, eds., *Women in New Zealand Society* (Sydney and Auckland: Allen and Unwin, 1980), pp. 52–76; for Canada, see Wendy Mitchinson, "The WCTU: For God, Home, and Native Land: A Study in Nineteenth Century Feminism," in Linda Kealey, ed., *A Not Unreasonable Claim: Women and Reform in Canada, 1880s–1920s* (Toronto: Women's Press, 1979), pp. 155–67. Britain is well served by Lilian Shiman, "'Changes Are Dangerous': Women and Temperance in Victorian England," in Gail Malmgreen, ed., *Religion in the Lives of English Women, 1760–1930* (London and Sydney: Croom Helm, 1986), pp. 193–215; and a work in progress by Olwen C. Niessen of McMaster University. See "Temperance and the Women's Movement in Late Victorian and Edwardian England" (Paper presented at the annual meeting of the Canadian Historical Association, Montreal, 1985). Only South Africa of the major affiliates is now poorly served. We are fortunate in having excellent biographies of some of the leading participants, especially J. J. G. Carson, *Emilie Solomon, 1858–1939* (Cape Town: Juto, [c.1941]), and a much better than average in-house history, *A Brief History of the Woman's Christian Temperance Union in South Africa* (Cape Town: Townshend, Taylor and Snashall, 1925).

15. Ruth Bordin, *Frances Willard: A Biography* (Chapel Hill: University of North Carolina Press, 1986), pp. 194–97.

16. Sources for this empirical study of WCTU missionary observations and cultural transformation are legion. See, especially, Randall C. Jimerson, Francis X. Blouin, Charles A. Isetts, eds., *Guide to the Microfilm Edition of the Temperance and Prohibition Papers* (Ann Arbor: University of Michigan, 1977). Among these, the most useful has been the Woman's Christian Temperance Union Series, but much use has also been made of the World League against Alcoholism Series and the Scientific Temperance Federation Series, both of which have much international material.

17. Gender conflict, Jack Blocker points out, is prominent in analyses of the WCTU, especially in the work of Ruth Bordin. See Bordin, *Woman and Temperance*; Bordin, *Willard*. Gender conflict and its effects in producing a form of proto-feminism are also stressed in Barbara Leslie Epstein, *The Politics of Domesticity: Women, Evangelism, and Temperance in Nineteenth-Century America* (Middletown, Conn.: Wesleyan University Press, 1981), which also employs class analysis to considerable effect. See, for a critique, Jack S. Blocker, Jr., *"Give to the Winds Thy Fears": The Women's Temperance Crusade, 1873–1874* (Westport, Conn.: Greenwood Press, 1985), pp. 89, 91.

18. Epstein, *Politics of Domesticity*; Bordin, *Woman and Temperance*; and Mary Earhart, *Frances Willard: From Prayers to Politics* (Chicago: University of Chicago Press, 1944) are also among those who emphasize the Willard period, to the (relative) exclusion of the Wittenmyer years and those beyond 1900. See also Susan Dye Lee, "Evangelical Domesticity: The Origins of the National Woman's Christian Temperance Union under Frances E. Willard" (Ph.D. diss., Northwestern University, 1980), pp. 363–67, 437. A broader survey is Norton Mezvinsky, "The White Ribbon Reform, 1874–1920" (Ph.D. diss., University of Wisconsin, 1959). A comprehensive bibliography, up to 1978, is available in Jacquie Jessup, "The Liquor Issue in American History: A Bibliography," in Jack S.

Blocker, Jr., ed., *Alcohol, Reform and Society: The Liquor Issue in Social Context* (Westport, Conn.: Greenwood Press, 1979), pp. 259–79.

19. The best account of the role of religion in the WCTU, Epstein, *Politics of Domesticity*, focuses on evangelicalism as an expression of a broad women's culture of domesticity.

20. They challenged male power structures at times and promoted women's equal treatment with men in both the public and the private spheres. I agree with Nancy Cott on the need to steer "clear of attributing transhistorical content to feminism." Cott, "What's in a Name?: The Limits of 'Social Feminism'; or, Expanding the Vocabulary of Women's History," *Journal of American History* 76 (1989): 826.

Chapter 2

1. Janet Giele, "Mary Clement Greenleaf Leavitt," *NAW*, 2:384.
2. *Our Union*, Oct. 1881, p. 3.
3. Ibid.
4. *PTD*, 4th Report, p. 53.
5. *Journal of Humanity*, 14 July 1831, p. 2.
6. Lois Banner, "Religious Benevolence as Social Control: A Critique of an Interpretation," *Journal of American History* 60 (June 1973): 23–41 is a convenient introduction to this theme.
7. Willard Diary, 24 Feb. 1869, book 3, p. 3, roll 3, WCTU Series, 1982 Suppl., Michigan Historical Collections, William R. Clements Library, University of Michigan, Ann Arbor; this statement is also printed (almost exactly) in Frances Willard, *Woman and Temperance, or, the Work and Workers of the Woman's Christian Temperance Union* (Hartford, Conn.: Park Pub. Co., 1883), p. 23.
8. *Union Signal*, 8 Jan. 1885, p. 10.
9. W. J. Rorabaugh, *The Alcoholic Republic: An American Tradition* (New York: Oxford University Press, 1979), p. 239.
10. Ibid., pp. 11–13.
11. *British Women's Temperance Journal*, June 1892, p. 62; BWTA, *AR*, 1903, p. 129.
12. Mary C. Leavitt, *Report of the Hon. Sec. of the World's Woman's Christian Temperance Union* (Boston: n.p., 1891), p. 55; *Union Signal*, 16 Jan. 1902, p. 1; *Second Annual Report of the Women's Christian Temperance Union of Brisbane, for 1886–87* (Brisbane, 1887), p. 24; *Our Union*, Aug. 1878, p. 1; Willard, *Woman and Temperance*, pp. 255–94.
13. *Our Union*, Oct. 1881, p. 3; *Union Signal*, 12 May 1892, p. 3.
14. Elizabeth Windschuttle, "Women, Class and Temperance: Moral Reform in Eastern Australia, 1832–1857," in *The Push from the Bush: A Bulletin of Social History*, no. 3 (1979), pp. 5–21; Ian Tyrrell, "Women and Temperance in Antebellum America, 1830–1860," *Civil War History* 28 (1982): 31. The British work is best covered in Mrs. Hinds Smith, "Pioneering Work of Temperance Women,"

in *The World's Temperance Congress, . . . of 1900 . . . Journals of the Proceedings* (London: Ideal Pub. Co., [1901]), pp. 228–35.

15. Eliza Stewart, *The Crusader in Great Britain, or, the History of the Origin and Organization of the British Women's Temperance Association* (Springfield, Ohio: New Era Co., 1893), pp. 51, xv. An excellent study of the crusade is Jack S. Blocker, Jr., *"Give to the Winds Thy Fears": The Women's Temperance Crusade, 1873–1874* (Westport, Conn.: Greenwood Press, 1985).

16. Brian Harrison, *Drink and the Victorians: The Temperance Question in England, 1815–1872* (London: Faber and Faber, 1971), p. 101.

17. American Temperance Society, *Fifth Annual Report*, p. 7, in *PTD*.

18. *New York Tribune*, 13 May 1853, 7–10 Sept. 1853; Tyrrell, "Women and Temperance," p. 147.

19. Frank Thistlethwaite, *The Anglo-American Connection in the Early Nineteenth-Century* (Philadelphia: University of Pennsylvania Press, 1959), pp. 92–96; Ian Tyrrell, *Sobering Up: From Temperance to Prohibition in Antebellum America, 1800–1860* (Westport, Conn.: Greenwood Press, 1979), pp. 152, 299; John F. Maguire, *Father Mathew: A Biography* (London: Longmans, Green, 1865); Elizabeth Malcolm, *'Ireland Sober, Ireland Free': Drink and Temperance in Nineteenth Century Ireland* (Dublin: Gill and MacMillan, 1986), chap. 3.

20. Alexis de Tocqueville, *Democracy in America*, ed. John S. Mill (New York: Shocken Books, 1961), 2:132–33.

21. Harrison, *Drink and the Victorians*, p. 196; J. K. Chapman, "The Mid-Nineteenth Century Temperance Movement in New Brunswick and Maine," *Canadian Historical Review* 35 (Mar. 1954): 43–60.

22. Donald W. Beattie, "Sons of Temperance: Pioneers in Total Abstinence and Constitutional Prohibition" (Ph.D. diss., Boston University, 1966), pp. 101, 111, 171–72, 298, 441; Jed Dannenbaum, *Drink and Disorder: Temperance Reform in Cincinnati from the Washingtonian Revival to the Woman's Christian Temperance Union* (Urbana, Ill.: University of Illinois Press, 1984), pp. 192–93.

23. St. Louis *Good Templar*, Mar. 1872, p. 109.

24. *Union Signal*, 9 July 1891, p. 5; *International Temperance Conference, Melbourne, 1880. Papers, Debates, and General Proceedings*, ed. H. G. Read and H. T. C. Coe (Melbourne: n.p., 1880), esp. p. 80.

25. Margaret Parker, *Six Happy Weeks among the Americans* (Glasgow: Hay, Hisbert, [1876]), p. 55; Eliza Stewart, *Crusader in Great Britain*, pp. xiii–xv. Margaret Bright Lucas was also a Good Templar before becoming a BWTA official (no author, *Memoir of Margaret Bright Lucas: President of the British Women's Temperance Association* [London: BWTA, c.1890], p. 14).

26. *Union Signal*, 23 June 1887, p. 10, and 7 July 1887, p. 4; NWCTU, *AR*, 1886, pp. 89, 133; Frances Willard, *Glimpses of Fifty Years* (Chicago: WTPA, 1889), p. 432.

27. David Fahey, ed., *The Collected Writings of Jessie Forsyth, 1847–1937: The Good Templars and Temperance Reform on Three Continents* (Lewiston, N.Y.: Edwin Mellen Press, 1988), p. 56; Ian Tyrrell, "International Aspects of the Woman's Temperance Movement in Australia: The Influence of the American WCTU, 1882–1914," *Journal of Religious History* 12 (June 1983): 286.

28. NWCTU, *AR*, 1883, p. 66; Willard, *Glimpses*, p. 430; Mary Earhart, *Frances Willard: From Prayers to Politics* (Chicago: University of Chicago Press, 1944), p. 340; see also Lady Henry Somerset's repetition of the mythology in *First [British] Conference of the World's Woman's Christian Temperance Union, held May 6th, 1892* (London: Hutchings, 1892), p. 50.

29. Frances Willard to Elizabeth Harbert, 21 Jan. 1876, box 8, Elizabeth Boynton Harbert Collection, Huntington Library, San Marino, Calif.

30. NWCTU, *AR*, 1880, pp. 9, 15.

31. *Union Signal*, 17 May 1883, p. 13, and 19 April 1883, p. 10.

32. Annie Wittenmyer, quoted in Eliza Stewart, *Crusader in Great Britain*, p. 83; Annie Wittenmyer to Matilda Carpenter, 15 Dec. 1874, in Jack S. Blocker, Jr., ed., "Annie Wittenmyer and the Women's Crusade," *Ohio History* 88 (Autumn 1979): 422.

33. NWCTU, *AR*, 1886, p. 88. For the convention, see *Centennial Temperance Volume. A Memorial of the International Temperance Conference, held in Philadelphia, June 1876* (New York: National Temperance Society and Publishing House, 1877), pp. 397–408.

34. NWCTU, *AR*, 1886, p. 88; Annie Wittenmyer, *History of the Woman's Temperance Crusade* (Boston: J. H. Earle, 1882), pp. 552–53; *SEAP*, 3:1401; *Our Union*, Sept. 1878, p. 2, and Oct. 1878, p. 2; W. H. Daniels, *The Temperance Reform and Its Great Reformers* (New York: Nelson and Phillips, 1878), p. 306; Willard, *Woman and Temperance*, pp. 447–48.

35. *Union Signal*, 18 July 1912, p. 3, and NWCTU, *AR*, 1885, p. 66 (Mary Willard); NWCTU, *AR*, 1884, p. cxxxiv; *Union Signal*, 23 Sept. 1883, p. 5 (Treadwell); *Our Union*, Oct. 1878, p. 3 (Quinton), and Aug. 1881, p. 5 (Livermore); NWCTU, *AR*, 1886, p. 133, and *Union Signal*, 23 June 1887, p. 10 (Gray).

36. Willard, *Glimpses*, p. 401.

37. Letitia Youmans, *Campaign Echoes: The Autobiography of Mrs. Letitia Youmans, the Pioneer of the White Ribbon Movement in Canada*, 2d ed. (Toronto: William Briggs, 1893), p. 142; Minutes, 24 Oct. 1878, in Recording Secretary's Book of Provincial Woman's Christian Temperance Union of the Province of Ontario, manuscript, Canadian WCTU Headquarters, Toronto.

38. *Our Union*, Mar. 1881, p. 7, and Jan. 1878, p. 2.

39. Tyrrell, "International Aspects," p. 296.

40. Charles Edward White, *The Beauty of Holiness: Phoebe Palmer as Theologian, Revivalist, Feminist, and Humanitarian* (Grand Rapids, Mich.: Francis Asbury Press, 1986), pp. 105–60; Charles Edwin Jones, *A Guide to the Study of the Holiness Movement* (Metuchen, N.J.: Scarecrow Press, 1974), pp. xvii–viii; Richard Carwardine, *Trans-Atlantic Revivalism: Popular Evangelicalism in Britain and America, 1790–1865* (Westport, Conn.: Greenwood Press, 1978), pp. 39, 40, 111, 143–44, 172, 182–92, 199–200; W. J. McCutcheon, "Phoebe Worrall Palmer," *NAW*, 3:12–14.

41. Frances Willard to Hannah Whitall Smith, 9 Feb. 1890, box 14, Hannah Whitall Smith Papers, Lilly Library, Indiana University, Bloomington, Ind.; Ruth Bordin, *Frances Willard: A Biography* (Chapel Hill, University of North

Carolina Press, 1986), p. 156, correctly notes that Willard's professions of holiness must be taken cautiously and that her diaries at the time of her "holiness experience" (1866) did not reflect an experience of entire sanctification; on Smith see Earl C. Kaylor, Jr., "Hannah Whitall Smith," *NAW*, 3:313–16; on Mary Woodbridge's holiness affiliation, see Willard, *Woman and Temperance*, pp. 101–7; the bibliographical entries in Charles Edwin Jones, *Guide*; and *Union Signal*, 13 Aug. 1891, p. 4. See also, for another case, John H. Bracey, Jr., "Amanda Berry Smith," *NAW*, 3:304–5.

42. Kaylor, "Smith," p. 314; Carwardine, *Trans-Atlantic Revivalism*, pp. 199–200; Charles Edwin Jones, *Guide*, p. 485.

43. Phillida Bunkle, "The Origins of the Women's Movement in New Zealand: The Women's Christian Temperance Union, 1885–1895," in Beryl Hughes and Phillida Bunkle, eds., *Women in New Zealand Society* (Sydney and Auckland: Allen and Unwin, 1980), pp. 52–76.

44. Bunkle, "Origins of the Women's Movement," pp. 52–76. Bunkle has drawn heavily upon Mary Douglas, *Purity and Danger* (London: Routledge and Kegan Paul, 1966). I have in the next few paragraphs drawn heavily on both.

45. WWCTU, *2d Conv., 1893*, p. 114; *Scottish Reformer*, 30 June 1900, p. 4; BWTA, *AR*, 1893, p. 53; see also Lady Henry Somerset, *Our Position and Our Policy: A Reply to the Charges Made against a Minority of the Executive* (Uxbridge, Eng.: Hutchings, 1893), p. 56.

46. Frances Willard, *The World's Woman's Christian Temperance Union: Aims and Objects* (Uxbridge, Eng.: Hutchings, [c.1892–93]), p. 12. On the reformist, postmillennialist tradition and the distinction discussed in the text, see George Shepperson, "The Comparative Study of Millenarian Movements," in Sylvia Thrupp, ed., *Millennial Dreams in Action: Essays in Comparative Study* (The Hague: Mouton and Co., 1962), pp. 44–45.

47. *Union Signal*, 26 Aug. 1909, p. 4.

48. BWTA, *AR*, 1892, p. 30.

49. *Union Signal*, 17 May 1883, p. 13. On the gradual and pragmatic construction of the Do-Everything policy, see Bordin, *Willard*, p. 130.

50. *White Ribbon*, Sept. 1915, p. 136.

51. Bunkle, "Origins of the Women's Movement," p. 70; on the Communion wine issue in Scotland, see WWCTU, *8th Conv., 1910*, p. 211; *Scottish Women's Temperance News*, Aug. 1904, p. 121.

52. See below, Chapters 9 and 12.

53. NWCTU, *AR*, 1886, p. 90 (italics in original).

54. Ibid., 1891, p. 195.

55. Ibid., 1892, p. 157.

56. *Woman's Herald* (London), 23 Feb. 1893, p. 9.

57. NWCTU, *AR*, 1886, p. 90; Kaylor, "Smith," pp. 313–16.

58. *Woman's Herald*, 23 Feb. 1893, p. 9.

59. Willard, *World's WCTU: Aims and Objects*, pp. 7–8.

60. Ibid., pp. 6–7; [Mary Woodbridge], *Report of the American Secretary of the World's Woman's Christian Temperance Union, 1890* (n.p., 1890), pp. 39–40; G. Evelyn Gates, ed., *The Woman's Year Book, 1923–1924*, 2d ed. (London: Women Publishers, 1924), pp. 141–42; *White Ribbon Signal*, 12 Feb. 1926, p. 4.

61. Willard, *Woman and Temperance*, esp. pp. 80, 88, 157, 321, 437, 527.

62. *Woman's Signal* (suppl.), 17 May 1894, pp. 350–51. See also Frances Willard, *Do Everything: A Handbook for the World's White Ribboners*, rev. ed. (Chicago: Ruby I. Gilbert, 1905), p. 6.

63. *British Women's Temperance Journal*, Aug. 1889, p. 85; *White Ribbon Signal*, 7 June 1899, in WCTU Album, box MLK2012, WCTU of New South Wales Records, Mitchell Library, Sydney.

64. See, for example, Letitia Youmans to Frances Willard, 20 Apr. 1893, roll 19, WCTU Series, OHS.

65. *Woman's Signal* (suppl.), 17 May 1894, pp. 350–51. See also Jack S. Blocker, Jr., *Retreat from Reform: The Prohibition Movement in the United States, 1890–1913* (Westport, Conn.: Greenwood Press, 1976), esp. pp. 56–58, for the best discussion of Willard's Populist maneuverings; and Bordin, *Willard*, chap. 11, for the broader domestic American context.

66. On the prohibition aspects of this shift in fortunes, see A. E. Dingle, *The Campaign for Prohibition in Victorian England* (London: Croom Helm, 1980), pp. 176–77; and David Fahey, "Temperance and the Liberal Party—Lord Peel's Report, 1899," *Journal of British Studies* 10 (May 1971): 132–59; and *Westminster Gazette*, 20 July 1895, Scrapbook 73, p. 53, WCTU Files. On the question of the larger women's emancipation context, the comparative assessments are sadly lacking; but see Ross Evans Paulson, *Women's Suffrage and Prohibition: A Comparative Study of Equality and Social Control* (Glenview, Ill.: Scott, Foresman, 1973); Richard Evans, *The Feminists: Women's Emancipation Movements in Europe, America and Australasia, 1840–1920* (London: Croom Helm, 1977); Donald Meyer, *Sex and Power: The Rise of Women in America, Russia, Sweden, and Italy* (Middletown, Conn.: Wesleyan University Press, 1987).

67. *Sheffield Daily Telegraph*, 6 June 1896, Scrapbook 73, p. 97, WCTU Files; *Birmingham Gazette*, 14 Sept. 1895, Scrapbook 79, p. 28, ibid.; *St. James Gazette*, 2 Aug. 1895, Scrapbook 79, no page numbers; *Boston Post*, 3 Jan. 1895, Scrapbook 73, p. 18, ibid. See also additional extensive set of clippings, Scrapbook 73, pp. 53–61, and Scrapbook 79, pp. 28–31; Frances Willard to Anna Gordon, undated, Jan.–Apr. 1893, roll 19, WCTU Series, OHS.

68. *Woman's Herald*, 8 June 1893, p. 249; see also Kathleen Fitzpatrick, *Lady Henry Somerset* (London: Jonathan Cape; Boston: Little, Brown, 1923).

69. *Woman's Signal*, 17 May 1894, pp. 350–51.

70. WWCTU, *4th Conv., 1897*, p. 52; NWCTU, *AR*, 1895, p. 129.

71. *White Ribbon*, July 1902, p. 106; *Woman's Herald*, 4 May 1893, p. 161.

72. Somerset, *Our Position and Our Policy*, p. 56. For further testimony see Catherine Impey, *Woman's Herald*, 23 Feb. 1893, p. 96.

73. NWCTU, *AR*, 1892, pp. 99–100.

74. *Woman's Herald*, 4 May 1893, p. 161.

Chapter 3

1. Katharine Anthony, *Feminism in Germany and Scandinavia* (New York: Henry Holt, 1915), pp. 3–4.

2. *Women's Studies International Forum*, 5 (no. 6, 1982), featured a special issue on "Reassessments of 'First Wave' Feminism." See, esp., Rebecca Sherrick, "Toward Universal Sisterhood," pp. 655–62. See also, for a survey of women's international organizations at this time that, like Sherrick, does not mention the WCTU, Edith Hurwitz, "The International Sisterhood," in Claudia Koonz and Renate Bridenthal, eds., *Becoming Visible: Women in European History* (Boston: Houghton Mifflin, 1977), pp. 327–45. An exception to the neglect of international women's temperance is David Fahey, ed., *The Collected Writings of Jessie Forsyth, 1847–1937: The Good Templars and Temperance Reform on Three Continents* (Lewiston, N.Y.: Edwin Mellen Press, 1988).

3. For example, *Union Signal*, 31 Dec. 1903, p. 2, and 28 July 1904, p. 1.

4. Based on a content analysis of the *Union Signal* for the month of March of every fifth year, beginning with 1885 (2 percent, 1885; 11.95 percent, 1890; 10.54 percent, 1895; 15.13 percent, 1900; 5.54 percent, 1905; 16.45 percent, 1910; 7.03 percent, 1915; 14.9 percent, 1920; 18.84 percent, 1925).

5. *Union Signal*, 14 May and 18 June 1891, p. 5. Circulation of the *Union Signal* on a regular basis was around 100,000 an issue in the early 1890s. This dropped to 25,000 after the turn of the century as the number of state (and other National) WCTU papers increased. On circulation patterns and problems, see *Union Signal*, 23 Jan. 1890, p. 1; 9 Jan. 1902, p. 8; 16 Feb. 1913, pp. 11, 13. For circulation figures, see Ruth Bordin, *Woman and Temperance: The Quest for Power and Liberty, 1873–1900* (Philadelphia: Temple University Press, 1981), p. 90; see also Jane L. McKeever, "The Woman's Temperance Publishing Association," *Library Quarterly* 55 (1985): 374, 394; NWCTU, *AR*, 1921, p. 186, and the other annual reports of the NWCTU treasurer, 1914–1929.

6. NWCTU, *AR*, 1913, p. 238.

7. Ibid., 1886, p. 88, and 1888, p. 82.

8. Ibid., 1886, pp. 30, 53, 55, 89. Meetings for the WWCTU were urged for local auxiliaries, but there was no "obligation" to pay according to the convention's resolutions.

9. *Union Signal*, 18 June 1891, p. 5, and 14 May 1891, p. 9; "Miss Willard's First Personal Appeal," [1891] clipping, Scrapbook 20, WCTU Files.

10. WWCTU, *1st Conv., 1891*, pp. 17, 79.

11. Frances Willard, *Do Everything: A Handbook for the World's White Ribboners*, rev. ed. (Chicago: Ruby I. Gilbert, 1905), p. 198.

12. K. Austin Kerr, *Organized for Prohibition: A New History of the Anti-Saloon League* (New Haven: Yale University Press, 1985), pp. 48–50; Norman Clark, *Deliver Us from Evil: An Interpretation of American Prohibition* (New York: W. W. Norton, 1976), pp. 84–88.

13. Patricia Hill, *The World Their Household: The American Woman's Foreign Mission Movement and Cultural Transformation, 1870–1920* (Ann Arbor: University of Michigan Press, 1985), pp. 150–52, 157, 159, 167–69.

14. Frances Willard, *Woman and Temperance, or, the Work and Workers of the Woman's Christian Temperance Union* (Hartford, Conn.: Park Pub. Co., 1883), pp. 362–70; Frances Willard, *The Polyglot Petition* (Chicago: WTPA, n.d. [1895]), pp. 3–5, in WCTU Organizational File, Mary Earhart Dillon Collection, Radcliffe College, Cambridge, Mass.

15. NWCTU, *AR*, 1885, pp. 65, 66; *Union Signal*, 15 Oct. 1885, p. 2.

16. NWCTU, *AR*, 1884, p. 63.

17. Willard, *Polyglot Petition*, pp. 4–5.

18. NWCTU, *AR*, 1885, p. 67.

19. Willard, *Polyglot Petition*, p. 3.

20. *Union Signal*, 14 Mar. 1895, p. 6; Gwenllian Morgan to Willard, 3 Apr. 1893, roll 19, WCTU Series, OHS.

21. Margaret Leitch to Anna Gordon, 21 Feb. 1914, WWCTU Files.

22. Paraphrased in *Union Signal*, 14 May 1891, p. 9.

23. Ibid., 13 June 1895, p. 7; NWCTU, *AR*, 1892, p. 147.

24. *British Women's Temperance Journal*, Dec. 1891, p. 144.

25. *Union Signal*, 18 Apr. 1895, p. 12.

26. Ibid., 13 June 1895, p. 7.

27. NWCTU, *AR*, 1891, p. 203; [Katharine L. Stevenson], *A Brief History of the Woman's Christian Temperance Union*, 3d ed. (Evanston, Ill.: WCTU, 1907), pp. 109–13; *Union Signal*, 14 Nov. 1891, p. 2.

28. Ruth Bordin, *Frances Willard: A Biography* (Chapel Hill: University of North Carolina Press, 1986), p. 193; Phillida Bunkle, "The Origins of the Women's Movement in New Zealand: The Women's Christian Temperance Union, 1885–1895," in Beryl Hughes and Phillida Bunkle, eds., *Women in New Zealand Society* (Sydney and Auckland: Allen and Unwin, 1980), p. 74. The breakdown of the petitions is analyzed in Willard, *Do Everything*, pp. 30–31.

29. *Union Signal*, 28 Feb. 1895, p. 8.

30. Frances Willard, *Do Everything*, pp. 29–31; Willard, typescript circular, Scrapbook 20, p. 24, WCTU Files; *Union Signal*, 6 Mar. 1890, p. 12, and 28 Feb. 1895, p. 8.

31. Morgan to Willard, 3 Apr. 1893, roll 19, WCTU Series, OHS.

32. Alice Briggs to Willard, 20 Apr. 1893, ibid.

33. WWCTU, *3d Conv., 1895*, p. 237; Willard, *Polyglot Petition*, p. 3; *Union Signal*, 14 Mar. 1895, p. 6; Josephine Butler to Fanny Forsaith, 8 Apr. 1894, Josephine Butler Papers, Fawcett Library, City of London Polytechnic.

34. NWCTU, *AR*, 1891, p. 203.

35. *Union Signal*, 4 July 1895, p. 5.

36. Willard's deathbed testimony, 10 Feb. 1898, p. 4, roll 25, WCTU Series, OHS.

37. *World's White Ribbon Bulletin*, Nov. 1919, p. 2; *Union Signal*, 1 Mar. 1923, p. 14. For the "White Ribboners as Petitioners," see *Union Signal*, 15 Dec. 1921, p. 8, and 23 May 1931, p. 2.

38. Circular in *British Women's Temperance Journal*, Jan. 1891, reprinted in Lady Henry Somerset, *Our Position and Our Policy: A Reply to the Charges Made against a Minority of the Executive* (Uxbridge, Eng.: Hutchings, 1893), p. 43.

39. Ibid.

40. Lady Henry Somerset to Willard, 26 Jan. 1891, WCTU Series, OHS; *British Women's Temperance Journal*, May 1890, p. 61.

41. WWCTU, *1st Conv., 1891*, Minutes of the Executive Committee Meetings, pp. 8–20, 25–29.

42. Ibid., pp. 20–25; *Union Signal*, 14 Nov. 1891, pp. 2–3.

43. *Union Signal*, 14 Nov. 1891, pp. 2–3; *Boston Journal*, 24 June 1894, Scrapbook 65, p. 63, WCTU Files.

44. *Union Signal*, 18 Nov. 1891, p. 1.

45. *Scottish Women's Temperance News*, July 1900, p. 102.

46. WCTU of New South Wales, *AR*, 1900, p. 34.

47. Australasian WCTU, *8th Triennial Conv., 1912*, p. 42; Ian Tyrrell, "Sara Susan Nolan," *Australian Dictionary of Biography*, 11:37; Ian Tyrrell, "International Aspects of the Woman's Temperance Movement in Australia: The Influence of the American WCTU, 1882–1914," *Journal of Religious History* 12 (June 1983): 291. North American convention arrangements can be sampled in the WWCTU Files for 1913; and *Union Signal*, 12 Feb. 1925, p. 6.

48. J. J. G. Carson, *Emilie Solomon, 1858–1939* (Cape Town and Johannesburg: Juto, [c.1941]), p. 143.

49. WWCTU, *3d Conv., 1895*, p. 87; Minutes of the Central Union, Woman's Christian Temperance Union of Queensland, 12 Dec. 1895, and 10 Mar. 1904, in Queensland WCTUHQ, Brisbane.

50. Quoted in Kathleen Fitzpatrick, *Lady Henry Somerset* (London: Jonathan Cape; Boston: Little, Brown, 1923), p. 157.

51. *Minutes of the Twenty–first Annual Convention of the Woman's Christian Temperance Union . . . Cape Colony* (Cape Town: Townshend, Taylor and Snashall, 1910), p. 6.

52. Ellen Stone to Anna Gordon, and minute to letter, 18 Oct. 1913, WWCTU Files.

53. Anna Gordon, memorandum to Frances Willard, n.d. [Sept. 1893], roll 19, WCTU Series, OHS.

54. *Twenty–first Conv., Cape Colony*, 1910, p. 6. MacKenzie was president of the South African WCTU, 1911–19. See *A Brief History of the Woman's Christian Temperance Union in South Africa* (Cape Town: Townshend, Taylor and Snashall, 1925), p. 14.

55. WCTU of New South Wales, *AR*, 1900, p. 33; WCTU of South Australia, *AR*, 1893, p. 28. See also Frances Cole to Agnes Slack, 11 May 1911, Castle Howard Archives (J23/265), Castle Howard, Yorkshire, for a New Zealand example.

56. Edward H. Todd to Elizabeth Boynton Harbert, 17 Oct. 1912, box 14, Elizabeth Boynton Harbert Collection, Huntington Library, San Marino, Calif.

57. J. H. Edwards to Frances Willard, 4 Jan. 1898, roll 25, WCTU Series, OHS.

58. Carson, *Solomon*, p. 143.

59. [J. H. More] to Anna Gordon, 4 Jan. 1898, roll 25. See also Emma Taylor to "Mother Willard," (Mary Hill Willard), 15 Nov. 1891, roll 17, WCTU Series, OHS.

60. Brisbane Central WCTU, Minutes, 21 Nov. 1895, Queensland WCTUHQ, Brisbane.

61. Margaret Suddath to Frances Willard, 2 June 1893, roll 5, WCTU Series, 1982 Suppl., Michigan Historical Collections, Bentley Library, University of Michigan, Ann Arbor.

62. [J. H. More] to Frances Willard, 4 Jan. 1898, roll 25, WCTU Series.

63. Australasian WCTU, *8th Triennial Conv., 1912*, p. 42; Brisbane Central WCTU, Minutes, 21 Nov. 1895.

64. WCTU of New South Wales, *AR*, 1895, p. 44.

65. Australasian WCTU, *8th Triennial Conv., 1912*, p. 42.

66. Amelia Pemmell to Frances Willard, 9 Dec. 1897, roll 24, WCTU Series. See also Lizzie Vincent to Frances Willard, 6 Dec. 1897, ibid.

67. *Brooklyn Enterprise*, 2 Jan. 1897, clipping in Scrapbook 76, WCTU Files.

68. Records of local auxiliaries consulted were: Minutes, Vassar (Tuscola Co., Michigan) WCTU, 1889–95, roll 47, WCTU Series, OHS; Newmarket (Ontario) WCTU Minutes, 1897–99, Canadian WCTUHQ, Toronto; Duarte, California, WCTU Papers, 1909–34, University of California, Los Angeles; Minutes of the Brisbane Central WCTU, 1894–1903, Queensland WCTUHQ, Brisbane; numerous executive and branch WCTU Minute Books, in WCTU of New South Wales Records, Mitchell Library, Sydney; Minute Books of branches of the Victorian WCTU for Geelong, Melbourne, and Bendigo, 1892–1913, WCTUHQ, Melbourne.

69. Bunkle, "Origins of Women's Movement," pp. 57–58. For a South African example, see Laura Bridgman to Jessie Ackermann, 23 July 1895, box 1, fl. 1, Jessie A. Ackermann Collection, Sherrod Library, East Tennessee State University, Johnson City, Tenn.

70. Jane Stewart, *I Have Recalled: A Pen-Panorama of a Life* (Toledo, Ohio: Chittenden Press, 1938), p. 62. For several Australian examples, see Ian Tyrrell, "International Aspects," p. 295.

71. Janet Giele, "Social Change in the Feminine Role: A Comparison of Woman's Suffrage and Woman's Temperance, 1870–1920" (Ph.D. diss., Radcliffe College, 1961), chap. 8, ignores international material in constructing an otherwise helpful content analysis of issues treated in the *Union Signal*.

72. WWCTU, *5th Conv., 1900*, p. 114; *7th Conv., 1906*, pp. 102–3; *8th Conv., 1910*, pp. 126, 127, 129; *9th Conv., 1913*, p. 162; *World's White Ribbon Bulletin*, 2, no. 2 (Indianapolis, Jan. 1897).

73. WCTU *National Educator* (Chicago: WTPA, 1896).

74. Frances Willard to the BWTA, 26 Jan. 1897, roll 1, fl. 6, STF Series, OHS; *The Temperance Record*, 9 Sept. 1897, pp. 427–28, in roll 1, fl. 11, ibid.

75. This work is extensively documented in STF Series, roll 3, fls. 29–31, OHS. The quotation is from Kara Smart to Mary H. Hunt, 29 Jan. 1904, fl. 30, ibid. See also Norton Mezvinsky, "The White Ribbon Reform, 1870–1920" (Ph.D. diss., University of Wisconsin, 1959), chap. 12; Norton Mezvinsky, "Mary Hannah Hanchett Hunt," *NAW*, 2:237–38; Marcia McGovern, "The Woman's Christian Temperance Union in Saskatchewan, 1886–1930: A Regional Perspective of the International White Ribbon Movement" (M.A. thesis, University of Regina, 1977); *SEAP*, 2:592.

76. Norman Clark, *Deliver Us from Evil*, p. 84.

77. WCTU Album, p. 37, box MLK2012, WCTU of New South Wales Records, Mitchell Library, Sydney.

78. WCTU of South Australia, *AR*, 1893, p. 33.

79. WWCTU, *8th Conv., 1910*, p. 202.

80. *The Japanese Evangelist* 4 (May 1897): 253, in Scrapbook 76, WCTU Files.

81. *White Ribbon Signal* (Sydney), 1 Oct. 1896, p. 2.

82. Mezvinsky, "Hunt," 238; Randall C. Jimerson, Francis X. Blouin, and Charles A. Isetts, eds., *Guide to the Microfilm Edition of the Temperance and Prohibition Papers* (Ann Arbor: University of Michigan, 1977), pp. 161–64. Also J. D. Crothers to Mary H. Hunt, 26 Oct. 1901; Suzannah Fry to Albert H. Plumb, 29 Aug. 1906; and Cora Stoddard to Harry Nelson, 9 July 1915, all in Mary Hannah Hanchett Hunt Papers, New York Public Library. These points are also extensively documented in roll 3, fls. 29–31, STF Series, OHS.

83. Isabel Somerset to Lillian Stevens, 20 July 1899, roll 25, WCTU Series, OHS.

84. Rosalind Carlisle to Lady Mary Murray, 1 Dec. 1906, Castle Howard Archives (J23/26); Carlisle to Lillian Stevens, 12 Jan. 1907, and Carlisle to Stevens, 31 May 1910, ibid. (J23/264). Said Carlisle in the last cited letter: "When in England, we pass from our National work & consider the World's work, there is a change of atmosphere—we come into the region . . . of not trusting the people, but of exalting the official importance of one woman, your Hon. Secretary, [Slack] who, though enthusiastic, is not equipped for so vast a responsibility." See also Charles Roberts, *The Radical Countess: The History of the Life of Rosalind, Countess of Carlisle* (Carlisle, Eng.: Steel Bros., 1962), p. 99; Hannah Whitall Smith to Mary Hunt, 5 Sept. 1904, roll 3, fl. 30, STF Series, OHS.

85. BWTA, *AR*, 1908, p. 114.

86. Emma Packe, "Federation with Australia," [dated 19 Aug. 1891] in *New Zealand Prohibitionist*, [Aug. 1891], p. 8, in New Zealand WCTU Microfiche Series, Massey University, Palmerston, New Zealand; Australasian WCTU, *5th Triennial Conv., 1903*, p. 13.

87. This point is extensively documented in the WWCTU Files. See, for example, Mary E. Sanderson to Anna Gordon, 23, 30 Dec. 1913; 28 Jan., 18 Feb., 11 Mar. 1914; *Scottish Women's Temperance News*, Sept. 1904, p. 130.

88. *World's White Ribbon Bulletin*, Oct. 1922, p. 1; WWCTU, *9th Conv., 1913*, p. 22; Anna Gordon to Rosalind Carlisle, 18 May 1914, WWCTU Files.

89. *Woman's Herald* (London), 8 June 1893, p. 249.

90. WWCTU, *4th Conv., 1897*, pp. 50–53.

91. WWCTU, *3d Conv., 1895*, p. 54; *4th Conv., 1897*, p. 52.

92. WWCTU Treasurer's Reports, 1890–94, WWCTU Files. On the case of Bidwell, a noted humanitarian and staunch supporter of the WWCTU, see the files of the John and Annie E. K. Bidwell Papers, Bancroft Library, University of California, Berkeley; *Pacific Ensign*, 20 Apr. 1893, p. 3; *California White Ribbon Ensign*, Mar. 1914, p. 2.

93. WWCTU, *4th Conv., 1897*, pp. 50–53.

94. WWCTU, *3d Conv., 1895*, pp. 50, 78.

95. Executive Minutes, 8 June 1903, WWCTU Files; *Union Signal*, 31 Dec. 1903, p. 4; *White Ribbon*, May 1903, p. 103.

96. WWCTU Treasurer's Reports, 1899–1906, WWCTU Files.

97. Australasian WCTU, *8th Triennial Conv., 1912*, p. 103; calculated from WWCTU Treasurer's Reports, WWCTU Files.

98. Calculated from Mary C. Leavitt, *Report of the Hon. Sec. of the World's Woman's Christian Temperance Union* (Boston: n.p., 1891), p. 23.

99. *Union Signal*, 21 Dec. 1893, p. 4, and 6 Aug. 1896, p. 1; *Brief History of the Woman's Christian Temperance Union in South Africa*, p. 11; WWCTU, *1st Conv., 1891*, p. 73.

100. WCTU of South Australia, *AR*, 1893, p. 35; Tyrrell, "International Aspects," p. 300. On the Temple, see Bordin, *Woman and Temperance*, esp. pp. 142, 148, 209; Norton Mezvinsky, "Matilda Bradley Carse," *NAW*, 1:292–94; Matilda Bradley Carse, "The Temperance Temple Report to the World's and National W.C.T.U. Convention," WWCTU, *1st Conv., 1891*, pp. 70–73.

101. Clara Parrish to Lillian Stevens, 2 Mar. 1897, roll 24, WCTU Series, OHS.

102. NWCTU, *AR*, 1895, p. 175; WWCTU Treasurer's Reports, 1899–1906, WWCTU Files.

103. Frances Willard and Mary Livermore, eds., *A Woman of the Century* (Buffalo: Charles Wells Mouton, 1893).

104. Frances Willard Diary, 5 Mar. 1869, book 3, p. 23, roll 3, WCTU Series, 1982 Suppl.; WWCTU, *4th Conv., 1897*, p. 48; Charles Roberts, *Radical Countess*, p. 66; [Mary Woodbridge], *Report of the American Secretary of the World's Woman's Christian Temperance Union . . . 1890* (n.p., 1890), p. 53; *Los Angeles Times*, 10 July 1937, p. 5; *White Ribbon*, Dec. 1904, p. 22; *Union Signal*, 17 Apr. 1890, p. 5; Cora Stoddard to [Mary] Lovell, 17 Aug. 1903, and *The Messenger* (Indianapolis, Ind.), Oct. 1903, no page numbers, roll 17, fl. 19, STF Series, OHS.

105. Memorandum, n.d. [1893], in roll 19, WCTU Series.

106. *Chicago Post*, 16 Nov. 1896, Scrapbook 70; *Boston Journal*, 24 June 1894, Scrapbook 65; *Baltimore American*, [20] Feb. 1895, and *Philadelphia Record*, 22 Feb. 1895, Scrapbook 73, all in WCTU Files. See also *Report of the First [British] Conference of the World's Woman's Christian Temperance Union, held May 6th, 1892* (Uxbridge, Eng.: Hutchings, 1892), p. 80; Mary S. Logan, *The Part Taken by Women in American History* (Wilmington, Del.: Perry-Nalle Pub. Co., 1912), p. 657.

107. *London Evening Dispatch*, 15 July 1895, in Scrapbook 13, WCTU Files.

108. *Chicago Daily Inter-Ocean*, 13 Sept. 1897, in Scrapbook 76, WCTU Files.

109. Aelfrida Tillyard, *Agnes E. Slack: Two Hundred Thousand Miles Travel for Temperance in Four Continents* (Cambridge, Eng.: W. Heffer and Sons, 1926), pp. 154, 131.

110. "Trouble in the W.C.T.U.," clipping in *Chicago Inter-Ocean*, 27 Oct. 1897, Scrapbook 76, WCTU Files.

111. Mary Earhart, *Frances Willard: From Prayers to Politics* (Chicago: University of Chicago Press, 1944), p. 342.

Chapter 4

1. *Report of the First [British] Conference of the World's Woman's Christian Temperance Union, held May 6th, 1892* (Uxbridge, Eng.: Hutchings, 1892), p. 80.

2. *Union Signal*, 11 Oct. 1894, p. 5; Ian Tyrrell, "International Aspects of the Woman's Temperance Movement in Australia: The Influence of the American

WCTU, 1882–1914," *Journal of Religious History* 12 (June 1983): 285.

3. NWCTU, *AR*, 1897, p. 26; *California White Ribbon Ensign*, Jan. 1940, p. 6; *Union Signal*, 30 Nov. 1922, p. 10. On the beginnings of the WCTU in Japan, see also Sho Nemoto to Jessie Ackermann, 24 Apr. 1891, and Kachi Yashima [Kaji Yajima] to Ackermann, 21 Apr. 1891, box 1, fl. 4, Jessie A. Ackermann Collection, Sherrod Library, East Tennessee State University, Johnson City, Tenn.

4. WWCTU, *8th Conv., 1910*, p. 212.

5. Cf. Lilian Shiman, " 'Changes Are Dangerous': Women and Temperance in Victorian England," in Gail Malmgreen, ed., *Religion in the Lives of English Women, 1760–1930* (London and Sydney: Croom Helm, 1986), pp. 193–215; Gail Malmgreen, Introduction to *Religion in the Lives of English Women*, p. 6. See also Olwen C. Niessen, "Temperance and the Women's Movement in Late Victorian and Edwardian Britain" (Paper presented at the annual meeting of the Canadian Historical Association, Montreal, 1985), p. 46.

6. *Union Signal*, 19 Apr. 1902, p. 1.

7. Mary C. Leavitt to Ruth Stevens, 20 July 1907, in Second Book of Records of the Woman's Christian Temperance Union of Queensland, Begun in 1910 . . . , Queensland WCTUHQ, Brisbane.

8. *Union Signal*, 24 Dec. 1891, p. 4.

9. Clipping from *Chicago Inter-Ocean*, 23 Oct. 1897, in Scrapbook 76, WCTU Files.

10. WWCTU, *8th Conv., 1910*, p. 212; *Union Signal*, 10 Mar. 1910, p. 13; WWCTU, *4th Conv., 1897*, p. 123; *5th Conv., 1900*, p. 27; Agnes Slack to Rosalind Carlisle, 30 June 1914, Castle Howard Archives (J23/265), Castle Howard, Yorkshire.

11. Steven Hause with Anne Kenney, *Women's Suffrage and Social Politics in the French Third Republic* (Princeton, N.J.: Princeton University Press, 1984), p. 258. The position was similar in Belgium. For a survey contrasting the impact of the WCTU in the antipodes with that of various European countries, including France and Belgium, see Louis Frank, *La Femme Contre L'Alcool* (Brussels: Henri Lamertin, 1897), esp. pp. 161–62, 215–21.

12. WWCTU, *4th Conv., 1897*, pp. 128–29; *8th Conv., 1910*, p. 212; *11th Conv., 1925*, p. 76.

13. Charles Roberts, *The Radical Countess: The History of the Life of Rosalind, Countess of Carlisle* (Carlisle, Eng.: Steel Bros., 1962), p. 66; *California White Ribbon Ensign*, Sept. 1913, p. 5.

14. Ottilie Hoffmann to Anna Gordon, 20 Oct. 1913, WWCTU Files; WWCTU, *6th Conv., 1903*, p. 38; Hoffmann to Mary Hannah Hunt, 20 Dec. 1904, roll 3, fl. 30, STF Series, OHS. On the German temperance movement, see James S. Roberts, *Drink, Temperance and the Working Class in Nineteenth-Century Germany* (London: Croom Helm, 1984).

15. *Union Signal*, 12 Mar. 1885, p. 9.

16. Mary C. Leavitt, *Report of the Hon. Sec. of the World's Woman's Christian Temperance Union* (Boston: n.p., 1891), pp. 53–55.

17. WWCTU, *8th Conv., 1910*, p. 25; *Union Signal*, 10 Mar. 1910, p. 13.

18. Irma Sulkunen, letter to the author, [Mar. 1984]; Irma Sulkunen, "Nais-

ten yleinen jarjestaytyminen ja naisasialiike," (The general organization of women and the feminist movement), *Eripainos Sociologia* 15 (no. 4, 1978): 204–12; Per Frånberg, letter to author, [Mar. 1984].

19. *Union Signal*, 12 Mar. 1885, p. 9; Elizabet Selmer to Jessie Ackermann, 17 June 1891, box 1, fl. 4, Ackermann Collection.

20. WWCTU, *9th Conv., 1913*, p. 79.

21. WWCTU, *8th Conv., 1910*, p. 212; *SEAP*, 5:2024. Ida Wedel–Jarlsberg to Jessie Ackermann, 5 Mar. 1897, box 2, fl. 4, Ackermann Collection.

22. Sulkunen, "Naisten," p. 209.

23. Elizabet Selmer to Jessie Ackermann, 7 Feb. 1894, box 1, fl. 4, Ackermann Collection; *SEAP*, 5:2024; NWCTU, *AR*, 1890, p. 169; Frances Willard, *Glimpses of Fifty Years* (Chicago: WTPA, 1889), pp. 306–7; *Union Signal*, 12 Mar. 1885, p. 9; Edwin A. Pratt, *Licensing and Temperance in Sweden, Norway, and Denmark* (London: John Murray, 1907), pp. 83–84.

24. The classic accounts of the sociocultural norms associated with theological cleavages in the Protestant churches and their application to the politics of prohibition include Paul Kleppner, *The Cross of Culture: A Social Analysis of Midwestern Politics, 1850–1900* (New York: The Free Press, 1969); and Richard Jensen, *The Winning of the Midwest: Social and Political Conflict, 1888–1896* (Chicago: University of Chicago Press, 1971).

25. *Union Signal*, 15 July 1909, p. 12; Sidsel Erikson, "Revival and Temperance Movement. A Contribution to the Study of Swedish and Danish Popular Culture," *Scandia: Tidskrift for historisk forskning* 2 (1988): 251–94, abstracted in *Social History of Alcohol Review*, no. 20 (1989): 6–8. For critiques of the ethnocultural method cited in the previous note, see, esp., James Green, "Behavioralism and Class Analysis: A Review Essay on Methodology and Ideology," *Labor History* 13 (1972): 89–106; and, in relation to women's temperance, Jack S. Blocker, Jr., *"Give to the Winds Thy Fears": The Women's Temperance Crusade, 1873–1874* (Westport, Conn.: Greenwood Press, 1985), pp. 87–88.

26. *Temperance in Australia: The Memorial Volume of the International Temperance Convention, Melbourne, 1888* (Melbourne: Temperance Book Depot, 1889), pp. 166–67; *Union Signal*, 30 Aug. 1888, p. 3; David Ostlund to Ernest H. Cherrington, 14 Apr. 1922, roll 26, folder 71, WLAA Series, OHS; Sulkunen letter, [1984].

27. David Fahey, ed., *The Collected Writings of Jessie Forsyth, 1847–1937: The Good Templars and Temperance Reform on Three Continents* (Lewiston, N.Y.: Edwin Mellen Press, 1988), p. 30.

28. *Union Signal*, 18 Oct. 1894, p. 5. See also Elizabet Selmer to Jessie Ackermann, 17 June 1891, box 1, fl. 4, Ackermann Collection.

29. WWCTU, *4th Conv., 1897*, p. 141; *Union Signal*, 27 Mar. 1890, p. 5.

30. Frånberg and Sulkunen letters, [1984].

31. Frånberg letter, [1984].

32. See Chapter 6; Louise Nystrom-Hamilton, *Ellen Key: Her Life and Her Work* (New York: George Putnam's Sons, 1913), pp. 98, 109.

33. Sulkunen letter, [1984]; Charlotte Gray, in *Union Signal*, 30 Aug. 1888, p. 3; *Union Signal*, 18 Oct. 1894, p. 5; WWCTU, *4th Conv., 1897*, p. 141.

34. *Union Signal*, 27 Mar. 1890, p. 5.

35. *Union Signal*, 18 Oct. 1894, p. 5; see also Elizabet Selmer to Jessie Ackermann, 17 June 1891, box 1, fl. 4, Ackermann Collection.

36. Ross Evans Paulson, *Women's Suffrage and Prohibition: A Comparative Study of Equality and Social Control* (Glenview, Ill.: Scott, Foresman, 1973), p. 109.

37. Ede Marrin to Frances Willard, 28 Apr. 1891, roll 17, WCTU Series, OHS. See also Hause with Kenney, *Women's Suffrage*, pp. 30, 37, 51, 59, 105; Bonnie Gene Smith, *Ladies of the Leisure Class: The Bourgeoises of Northern France in the Nineteenth Century* (Princeton, N.J.: Princeton University Press, 1981).

38. Harry Gene Levine, "Temperance and Women in 19th-Century United States," in O. J. Kalant, ed., *Research Advances in Alcohol and Drug Problems* (New York: Plenum Press, 1980), 5:63.

39. Ruth Bordin, *Woman and Temperance: The Quest for Power and Liberty, 1873–1900* (Philadelphia: Temple University Press, 1981), pp. 171–74; Joseph Gusfield, *Symbolic Crusade: Status Politics and the American Temperance Movement* (Urbana, Ill.: University of Illinois Press, 1963), pp. 80–81.

40. See, for example, Wendy Mitchinson, "The WCTU: 'For God, Home and Native Land': A Study in Nineteenth-Century Feminism," in Linda Kealey, ed., *A Not Unreasonable Claim: Women and Reform in Canada, 1880s–1920s* (Toronto: Women's Press, 1979), pp. 151–52, 155; Phillida Bunkle, "The Origins of the Women's Movement in New Zealand: The Women's Christian Temperance Union, 1885–1895," in Beryl Hughes and Phillida Bunkle, eds., *Women in New Zealand Society* (Sydney and Auckland: Allen and Unwin, 1980), p. 74; Anthea Hyslop, "Temperance, Christianity, and Feminism: The Woman's Christian Temperance Union of Victoria, 1887–1897," *Historical Studies* 17 (Apr. 1976): 34–35; Nancy M. Sheehan, "'Women Helping Women': The WCTU and the Foreign Population in the West, 1905–1930," *International Journal of Women's Studies* 6 (Nov.–Dec. 1983): 396. My own study of the Petersham WCTU Minute Book, 1907–1966, box MLK1983, WCTU of New South Wales Records, Mitchell Library, Sydney, bears out this research fully. Though service groups such as domestics, laborers, and tradesmen lived in close proximity in this fashionable Sydney suburb of the 1880s–1910s, the composition of the WCTU was overwhelmingly drawn from the business and professional groups.

41. James Whyte to Frances Willard, undated, 1893, roll 19, WCTU Series, OHS.

42. Paulson, *Women's Suffrage and Prohibition*, p. 148; Irma Sulkunen, "Why Did the Finnish Working Class Movement Come to Support Prohibition?" *Reports from the Social Research Institute of Alcohol Studies*, no. 151 (1981): 1–16. Also see Irma Sulkunen, *Raittius Kansalais Uskontona* (Helsinki: Societas Historica Finlandiae, 1986).

43. *Union Signal*, 15 July 1909, p. 12.

44. Per Frånberg, *Umeåsystemet: En Studie i alternativ nykterhetspolitik, 1915–1945*, Umeå Studies in the Humanities, no. 50, 1983, p. 232.

45. Irma Sulkenen, "Temperance as a 'Civic Religion': The Cultural Foundations of the Finnish Working Class Temperance Ideology" (Paper presented at the International Conference on the Social History of Alcohol, Berkeley, Calif., Jan. 1984), pp. 1–25.

46. Sara Crafts, in *Union Signal*, 9 Jan. 1902, p. 3; Josephine Butler to Fanny

Forsaith, 8 Apr. 1894, Josephine Butler Papers, Fawcett Library, City of London Polytechnic; Andrea Sharboro, *Temperance vs. Prohibition; Important Letters and Data from Our American Consuls, the Clergy and Other Eminent Men* (San Francisco: n.p., 1909), pp. 4, 11, 19.

47. WWCTU, *2d Conv., 1893*, p. 204; [Mary Woodbridge], *Report of the American Secretary of the World's Woman's Christian Temperance Union, 1890* (n.p., 1890), pp. 40–41.

48. WWCTU, *4th Conv., 1897*, p. 99; Emma Lacy to Anna Gordon, 16 Feb. 1914, WWCTU Files.

49. Frances Willard, *Woman and Temperance, or, the Work and Workers of the Woman's Christian Temperance Union* (Hartford, Conn.: Park Pub. Co., 1883), p. 111; *Sailor's Magazine and Seaman's Friend; and the Life Boat* 50 (1878): 22.

50. WWCTU, *7th Conv., 1906*, p. 67; Mary E. Massey to Ella Hoover Thatcher, 22 Oct. 1913, WWCTU Files; *Union Signal*, 7 Feb. 1895, p. 10, and 26 Feb. 1885, p. 8.

51. *Union Signal*, 1 Mar. 1917, p. 7.

52. WWCTU, *7th Conv., 1906*, p. 67; Addie Sperry to Frances Willard, 3 Jan. 1898, roll 25, WCTU Series, OHS.

53. WWCTU, *1st Conv., 1891*, p. 36.

54. *Union Signal*, 16 Feb. 1893, p. 5.

55. Muriel Ayres to *Union Signal*, 18 July 1920, in "Travel Letters of Alvine Muriel Ayres," WWCTU Files.

56. *Union Signal*, 14 Mar. 1895, p. 4.

57. WWCTU, *1st Conv., 1891*, p. 37; Leavitt, *Report, 1891*, p. 44; Scrapbook 20, p. 22, WCTU Files; *Union Signal*, 17 Dec. 1891, p. 4; Virginia Pride to Anna Gordon, 30 Sept. 1913, WWCTU Files; *Woman's Signal*, 24 May 1894, p. 365; Sylvia Vietzen, *A History of Education for European Girls in Natal, 1837–1902* (Pietermaritzburg: University of Natal Press, 1980), p. 130.

58. Laura Bridgman to Jessie Ackermann, 23 July 1895, box 1, fl. 1, Ackermann Collection; Stakesby Lewis, ed., *A Long Trek: Memories of Mary W. Tyler Gray* (Johannesburg: WCTU, [c.1938]), p. 21; *Union Signal*, 14 May 1891, p. 17.

59. J. J. G. Carson, *Emilie Solomon, 1858–1939* (Cape Town: Juto, [c.1941]), p. 78; *SEAP*, 6:2471.

60. Carson, *Solomon*, p. 12.

61. Ibid., pp. 11–12, 19–24.

62. *SEAP*, 6:2471; Carson, *Solomon*, pp. 141–43.

63. Tyrrell, "International Aspects," p. 298.

64. *White Ribbon Signal* (Melbourne), 8 Feb. 1928, pp. 19–21; Anthea Hyslop, "Marie Elizabeth Kirk," *Australian Dictionary of Biography*, 9:607–8; Amelia Pemmell to Frances Willard, 9 Dec. 1897, roll 24, WCTU Series, OHS; *Union Signal*, 7 Apr. 1898, p. 9.

65. Marie Kirk to Josephine Butler, 2 Aug. 1898, Butler Papers.

66. Marie Kirk to Jessie Fowler, 30 Dec. 1891, printed in *British Women's Temperance Journal*, Mar. 1892, p. 34.

67. Mary E. Sanderson to Anna Gordon, 15 Dec. 1913, WWCTU Files.

68. "Six Weeks of Work in the Queen's Dominions," *Union Signal*, 6 Aug. 1891, p. 4.

69. Mitchinson, "The WCTU," pp. 151–58; Marcia McGovern, "The Woman's Christian Temperance Union Movement in Saskatchewan, 1886–1930: A Regional Perspective of the International White Ribbon Movement" (M.A. thesis, University of Regina, 1977), p. 106.

70. Cheryl Walker, *The Woman's Suffrage Movement in South Africa*, Communications, no. 2 (Centre for African Studies, University of Cape Town, 1979), pp. 23, 102–3.

71. *Canadian Woman's Journal* (Ottawa), 15 May 1900, p. 10; Barbara Buchanan (Transvaal WCTU President) to Anna Gordon, 4 July 1910, Castle Howard Archives (J23/264). More generally on the South African WCTU, see *Woman's Signal*, 17 May 1894, p. 337; *A Brief History of the Woman's Christian Temperance Union in South Africa* (Cape Town: Townshend, Taylor and Snashall, 1925), p. 6. Elizabeth B. Van Heyningen, "The Social Evil in the Cape Colony, 1868–1902: Prostitution and the Contagious Diseases Acts," *Journal of Southern African Studies* 10 (1984): 187–88, stresses the international links of the WCTU in that colony.

72. *Third Bi-Ennial Convention of the Coloured and Native Women's Christian Temperance Union, South Africa* (Cape Town, 1921), esp. p. 8, roll 26, folder 4, WLAA Series, OHS; K. H. R. Stuart, "Third Tour, Seventh Letter," manuscript, 3 Aug. 1922, in ibid. See also, for the African temperance movement, Wallace Mills, "The Roots of African Nationalism in the Cape Colony: Temperance, 1866–1898," *International Journal of African Historical Studies* 13 (no. 2, 1980): 197–213.

73. WWCTU, *4th Conv., 1897*, pp. 142–44; Addie M. Sperry to Frances Willard, 3 Jan. 1898, roll 25, WCTU Series, OHS.

74. See the report by Jerome Raymond in *Union Signal*, 24 Sept. 1891, p. 10.

75. WWCTU, *8th Conv., 1910*, p. 151; see also "Across Mrs. Leavitt's Tracks in India," clipping in Scrapbook 33, p. 42, WCTU Files; *Canadian Woman's Journal* (Ottawa), Nov. 1893, p. 4; Denning to Agnes Slack, 5 Jan. 1911, Castle Howard Archives (J23/265).

76. *First Report of the National Woman's Christian Temperance Union of India* (Lucknow: Methodist Pub. House, 1893), p. 4; *Minutes and Reports of the Thirteenth National Convention of the Women's Christian Temperance Union of India . . . 1913* (Calcutta: Baptist Mission Press, 1916), pp. 2–3, 29–30, for representative reports and statistics. Others consulted are also held in WCTUHQ, Evanston, Ill.

77. WWCTU, *2d Conv., 1893*, p. 200.

78. *Union Signal*, 13 Jan. 1916, p. 3; Marinda Greenman to Jessie Ackermann, 12 July 1894, box 1, fl. 1, Ackermann Collection.

79. Sugiura to Mary F. Lovell, printed in *Union Signal*, 4 Mar. 1915, p. 10; also Sho Nemoto, in ibid., 7 Apr. 1892, p. 10.

80. Dr. Carlos Fernandez Pena to Mary Hunt, 18 Apr. 1904, roll 3, fl. 30, STF Series, OHS.

81. *Union Signal*, 14 Nov. 1891, p. 2.

82. Ibid.

83. Australasian WCTU, *8th Triennial Conv., 1912*, p. 42; WCTU of New South Wales, *AR*, 1895, p. 40; WCTU of Queensland, *AR*, 1887, pp. 13–14, 21, 24, 27, 28; Tyrrell, "International Aspects," pp. 299–300.

84. Ian Tyrrell, "Sara Susan Nolan," *Australian Dictionary of Biography*, 11:37; *SEAP*, 6:2927; Charlotte B. De Forest, *The Woman and the Leaven in Japan* (West Medford, Mass.: Central Committee on the United Study of Foreign Missions, 1923), pp. 186–87, 190.

85. Carson, *Solomon*, p. 142.

86. Willard, *Woman and Temperance*, p. 115.

87. Some historians have been more inclined to emphasize technological change. See, for example, Eleanor Flexner, quoted in Patricia R. Hill, *The World Their Household: The American Woman's Foreign Mission Movement and Cultural Transformation, 1870–1920* (Ann Arbor: University of Michigan Press, 1985), pp. 38–39; Carl Degler, *Out of Our Past: The Forces That Shaped Modern America*, 3d ed. (New York: Harper and Row, 1984), pp. 390–91; see also David Potter, "American Women and the American Character," in Barbara Welter, ed., *The Woman Question in American History* (Hinsdale, Ill.: Dryden Press, 1973), p. 122.

88. Cf. Patricia R. Hill, *World Their Household*, pp. 38–39; Parker even organized a scheme to overcome the shortage of immigrant labor. See below, Chapter 11, and Charles E. Parker, *Margaret Eleanor Parker: A Memorial* (Bolton, Eng.: Tillotson, 1906), p. 85.

89. Margaret E. Parker, *Six Happy Weeks among the Americans* (Glasgow: Hay, Hisbert, [1876]), p. 46.

90. Ibid., pp. 47, 48, 69.

91. Kathryn Sklar, *Catharine Beecher: A Study in American Domesticity* (New Haven: Yale University Press, 1973). Catharine Beecher, *A Treatise on Domestic Economy* (1841; reprint, New York: Source Book Press, 1970).

92. Frances Willard to Mary Hannah Hunt, 11 Jan. 1895, in roll 1, fl. 3, STF Series, OHS; also see Willard, *Woman and Temperance*, p. 424, on the similar case of Mary Livermore.

93. *Canadian Woman's Journal* (Ottawa), Jan. 1891, p. 3; Feb. 1891, p. 8; Mar. 1891, p. 5. For an Australian example, see *White Ribbon Signal* (Sydney), 30 Oct. 1908, p. 6.

94. Letitia Youmans, *Campaign Echoes: The Autobiography of Mrs. Letitia Youmans, the Pioneer of the White Ribbon Movement in Canada*, 2d ed. (Toronto: William Briggs, 1893), p. 82; *A Treasure Book of Friends: Biographies of Interesting Women* (Toronto: National Girls Work Board of the Religious Education Council of Canada, 1929), p. 38.

95. Willard, *Woman and Temperance*, p. 115.

96. *Report of the Third Convention of the Dominion Woman's Christian Temperance Union . . . 1890* (Toronto: Dudley and Burns, 1890), p. 63; *Report of the Fourth Convention of the Dominion Woman's Christian Temperance Union . . . 1891* (St. John, N.B.: E. J. Armstrong, 1891), p. 59; L. C. McKinney to Mary Hannah Hunt, [12] May 1908, Mary Hannah Hanchett Hunt Papers, New York Public Library.

97. *Memoir of Margaret Bright Lucas: President of the British Women's Temperance Association* (London: BWTA, 1890), pp. 14–15; Frank Thistlethwaite, *The Anglo-American Connection in the Early Nineteenth-Century* (Philadelphia: University of Pennsylvania Press, 1959).

98. Anna Gordon to Lillian Stevens, 26 June 1896, roll 24; and Hannah Whitall Smith to Frances Willard, 8 Aug. 1892, roll 18, WCTU Series, OHS.

99. Ruth Bordin, *Frances Willard: A Biography* (Chapel Hill: University of North Carolina Press, 1986), p. 202, 203. Bordin does not, however, go nearly as far as Gail Malmgreen, who erroneously concludes that "The 'do everything' faction in the [women's] temperance movement was a minority, and in the end cautious respectability prevailed." See Malmgreen, ed., *Religion in the Lives of English Women*, p. 6. See also Olwen Niessen, "Temperance and the Women's Movement in Britain," p. 46, for a similar interpretation.

100. *Scottish Reformer*, Dec. 1894, no page numbers; see also, for corroborating evidence, *United Temperance Gazette*, 2 (Mar. 1897): 117–18.

101. *Eleventh Annual Report of the Woman's Total Abstinence Union for the Year 1903–1904* (London: BWTAU, 1904), p. 66; BWTA, *AR*, 1894, pp. 2, 138–78; 1904, p. 44; 1899, p. 248; 1914, p. 102; *White Ribbon*, July 1905, p. 129; *Seventh Annual Records and Methods of Work Done by the Woman's Christian Temperance Union of Victoria . . . 1894* (Melbourne: Spectator Pub. Co., 1895), p. 20.

102. BWTA, *AR*, 1893, pp. 26–68.

103. Ibid.; *Union Signal*, 17 June 1897, p. 9; *The Churchman*, 21 May 1894, no page numbers; BWTA, *AR*, 1894, p. 2; Bordin, *Willard*, p. 181.

104. BWTA, *AR*, 1904, p. 44; *British Women's Temperance Journal*, Mar. 1889, p. 32; Kathleen Fitzpatrick, *Lady Henry Somerset* (London: Jonathan Cape; Boston: Little, Brown, 1923), pp. 167–68; BWTA, *AR*, 1914, p. 102.

105. "From Our English Sisters," *The Temperance Tribune* [Non-Partisan WCTU], 1 Mar. 1894, p. 7; Jessie Fowler to Mary Ingham, 16 Jan. 1894, in ibid.; Lady Henry Somerset to Frances Willard, 26 Jan. 1891, roll 17, WCTU Series, OHS; *British Women's Temperance Journal*, June 1890, p. 61. On Jessie Fowler (1856–1932), see also the article on her mother: John B. Blake, "Lydia Folger Fowler," *NAW*, 1:654–55.

106. Lady Biddulph, in BWTA, *AR*, 1893, p. 52; Miss Dowcra, ibid., p. 31; Mrs. Lynn, of Hollaway, ibid., p. 56; *Woman's Herald*, 23 Feb. 1893, p. 1; *United Temperance Gazette* 2 (Mar. 1897): 119. On the American Non-Partisans, see Bordin, *Woman and Temperance*, pp. 129–30. A useful case study that, however, suffers from a failure to connect local developments with larger issues of politics and ideology is Marian J. Morton, "Temperance, Benevolence, and the City: The Cleveland Non-Partisan Woman's Christian Temperance Union, 1874–1900," *Ohio History* 91 (1982): 58–73.

107. BWTA, *AR*, 1893, pp. 26–68.

108. *Woman's Herald*, 23 Feb. 1893, pp. 1, 9. Cassandra Merricton to Frances Willard, 2 Mar. 1893, and James Whyte to Frances Willard, undated, 1893, roll 19, WCTU Series, OHS; Florence Balgarnie, *"She Shall Be Called Woman"* (London: WWCTU, [c.1893]).

Chapter 5

1. *Pacific Ensign*, 13 Oct. 1892, p. 2.
2. *Union Signal*, 14 Mar. 1895, p. 9.
3. Benjamin F. Austin, ed., *The Temperance Leaders of America* (St. Thomas, Ont.: n.p., 1896), p. 55; *SEAP*, 1:46–47; undated clipping from *Banner of Gold*,

Scrapbook 13, roll 32, WCTU Series, OHS; WWCTU, *24th Conv., 1962*, pp. 24, 55; *White Ribbon Bulletin*, 23 Apr. 1900; *Los Angeles Times*, 10 July 1937, p. 5; Frances Willard and Mary Livermore, eds., *A Woman of the Century* (Buffalo: Charles Wells Mouton, 1893), pp. 4–5; death certificate, no. 51–030737, California Office of the State Registrar of Vital Statistics. I wish to thank Professor Robin Room of the Alcohol Research Group for assistance in obtaining this information. While Ackermann's death is properly documented, her birthdate and place are shrouded in mystery. After perusing the genealogical information added to the Jessie A. Ackermann Collection, Sherrod Library, East Tennessee State University, I am convinced that Ackermann's early claims that she was born in Boston on the Fourth of July are probably correct even though no official record of her birth has yet been discovered. She probably moved to Will County, Illinois, with her parents shortly afterward and was enumerated with them as a three-year-old there in the population schedule, Census of 1860. This is consistent with her deathbed claim that she was born in 1857, not 1860 or 1861 as she sometimes asserted during the years of her temperance ministry (Case File, 1987, Ackermann Collection).

4. *Woman's Herald* (London), 6 Apr. 1893, p. 112; 9 Nov. 1893, p. 599; Report of Jessie Ackermann, in WWCTU, *3d Conv., 1895*, p. 181; *Los Angeles Times*, 10 July, 1937, p. 5.

5. See Theodore L. Agnew, "Reflections on the Woman's Foreign Missionary Movement in Late 19th-Century American Methodism," *Methodist History* 6 (Oct. 1967): 3–16; Barbara Welter, "She Hath Done What She Could: Protestant Women's Missionary Careers in Nineteenth-Century America," *American Quarterly* 30 (1978): 626–38; Patricia Grimshaw, "'Christian Woman, Pious Wife, Faithful Mother, Devoted Missionary': Conflicts in Roles of American Missionary Women in Nineteenth-Century Hawaii," *Feminist Studies* 9 (1983): 489–522; Jane Hunter, *The Gospel of Gentility: American Women Missionaries in Turn-of-the-Century China* (New Haven: Yale University Press, 1984); Patricia R. Hill, *The World Their Household: The American Woman's Foreign Mission Movement and Cultural Transformation, 1870–1920* (Ann Arbor: University of Michigan Press, 1985).

6. WWCTU, *2d Conv., 1893*, p. 114.

7. Janet Giele, "Mary Clement Greenleaf Leavitt," *NAW*, 2:384.

8. See Appendix for all names.

9. NWCTU, *AR*, 1888, p. 5; WWCTU, *2d Conv., 1893*, p. 117; Willard and Livermore, *Woman of the Century*, p. 603.

10. World's Convention Reports, 1895–1925.

11. *SEAP*, 3:1406 (Mary C. Johnson); Eliza Stewart, *The Crusader in Great Britain, or, the History of the Origin and Organization of the British Women's Temperance Association* (Springfield, Ohio: New Era Co., 1893); *Union Signal*, 8 Aug. 1907, p. 4; 1 Aug. 1912, p. 3 (Gowen); *SEAP*, 5:2019 (Norville); *Union Signal*, 20 Nov. 1890, p. 4 (Bushnell); *Union Signal*, 18 June 1903, p. 5 (Fields); *Thumb-Nail Sketches of White Ribboners* (Chicago: WTPA, 1892), p. 31.

12. *Union Signal*, 3 June 1920, p. 11, and WWCTU, *10th Conv., 1920*, p. 20 (Mei); *Union Signal*, 20 Mar. 1919, p. 3; 25 Dec. 1919, p. 12; 20 July 1922, p. 6 (Wang); *Canadian Woman's Journal* (Ottawa), July 1898, p. 10, and 15 Mar. 1901, p. 6 (Large).

13. *Union Signal*, 10–17 Aug. 1921, p. 5 (Armor, Livingston, and Lydia Johnson); 14 Oct. 1920, p. 11, and Mary Alderman Garbutt, *Victories of Four Decades: A History of the Woman's Christian Temperance Union of Southern California, 1883–1924* (Los Angeles: Southern California WCTU, 1924), p. 52 (Wheeler); *Union Signal*, 21 July 1921, p. 6, and Anna Gordon, "The National WCTU, from 1914 to 1924," roll 25, WCTU Series, OHS (Deane and Gordon).

14. NWCTU, *AR*, 1883, p. 66 (Treadwell); 1886, p. 89, and *Union Signal*, 18 July 1912, p. 3 (Mary B. Willard); Charlotte Gray to Frances Willard, 22 Sept. 1892, roll 18, WCTU Series, OHS; *Union Signal*, 23 June 1887, p. 10; Frances Willard, *Glimpses of Fifty Years* (New York: WTPA, 1889), p. 432 (Gray).

15. Scrapbook 76, WCTU Files, clipping from *Nebraska State Journal*, 20 Oct. 1897 (Johannsdottir); Boston *Woman's Journal*, 1 Feb. 1900, p. 5 (Ericson); *Union Signal*, 13 Oct. 1904, p. 5 (Slack).

16. WWCTU, *3d Conv., 1895*, p. 179.

17. Welter, "She Hath Done What She Could"; Patricia R. Hill, *World Their Household*; Hunter, *Gospel of Gentility*. On the nineteenth-century women's culture and its religious dimensions, see, especially, Barbara Leslie Epstein, *The Politics of Domesticity: Women, Evangelism, and Temperance in Nineteenth-Century America* (Middletown, Conn.: Wesleyan University Press, 1981).

18. *Union Signal*, 11 Dec. 1919, p. 7, in "Travel Letters of Alvine Muriel Ayres," WWCTU Files.

19. Belle Kearney, *A Slaveholder's Daughter*, 7th ed. (New York: The Abbey Press, 1900), p. 206; Anne F. Scott, "Belle Kearney," *NAW*, 2:309–10.

20. Mary Whitney to Frances Willard, 29 Apr. 1897; Willard to "Our Temperance Brothers and Sisters the World Over," 5 Aug. 1897, roll 24, WCTU Series, OHS; Mary Logan, *The Part Taken by Women in American History* (Wilmington, Del.: Perry-Nalle Pub. Co., 1912), p. 670; Frances Willard, *Woman and Temperance, or, the Work and Workers of the Woman's Christian Temperance Union* (Hartford, Conn.: Park Pub. Co., 1883), p. 585; *Union Signal*, 7 Feb. 1895, p. 9; 13 June 1895, p. 5; WWCTU, *11th Conv., 1922*, p. 24.

21. *Union Signal*, 7 Nov. 1901, p. 3.

22. Ibid., 20 Nov. 1890, p. 4.

23. *White Ribbon*, June 1902, p. 87.

24. Ibid., Oct. 1913, p. 156; Anderson Hughes-Drew to Anna Gordon, 29 Sept. 1913, WWCTU Files, WCTU Headquarters (Drew); WWCTU, *9th Conv., 1913*, p. 102; *White Ribbon Signal* (Melbourne), 8 Feb. 1929, p. 4; Bessie Cowie, *One of Australia's Daughters*, rev. ed. (London: Richard J. James, 1924), pp. 160–66; *SEAP*, 2:724–25 (Cowie); *Union Signal*, 22 May 1913, p. 13, and 18 Nov. 1891, p. 1 (Stevenson). On Cowie, see also Patricia Grimshaw, "Bessie Harrison Lee and the Fight for Voluntary Motherhood," in Marilyn Lake and Farley Kelly, eds., *Double Time: Women in Victoria—150 Years* (Ringwood, Vic.: Penguin, 1985), pp. 139–47.

25. Joan Jacobs Brumberg, "The Case of Ann Hasseltine Judson," in Rosemary Skinner Keller, Louise L. Queen, and Hilah F. Thomas, eds., *Women in New Worlds: Historical Perspectives on the Wesleyan Tradition* (Nashville: Abingdon, 1982), 2:241.

26. Katharine Lent Stevenson, "Leaves from a Traveler's Notebook," *Union Signal*, Oct. 1909–Mar. 1910; *Union Signal*, 17 June 1920, p. 7.

27. Mary C. Leavitt, *Report of the Hon. Sec. of the World's Woman's Christian Temperance Union* (Boston: n.p., 1891), p. 25.

28. *White Ribbon*, Dec. 1901, p. 18; *Union Signal*, 25 Nov. 1909, pp. 1–2; 12 May 1910, p. 2.

29. Agnes E. Slack, *My Travels in India* (NBWTA, 1908), p. 3; *White Ribbon*, June 1914, p. 86; *Union Signal*, 13 Apr. 1905, p. 3; Christine Tinling, *Memories of the Mission Field* (London: Morgan and Scott, [c.1924]); Jessie Ackermann, *Australia: From a Woman's Point of View* (London: Cassell, 1913); Elizabeth Wheeler Andrew, "The Origin, History and Development of the World's WCTU," in May Wright Sewell, ed., *The World's Congress of Representative Women* (Chicago: Rand McNally, 1894), 2:404.

30. *White Ribbon*, June 1914, p. 86; *Union Signal*, 3 Mar. 1910, p. 1; K. L. Stevenson to Anna Shaw, 12 May 1898, Anna Howard Shaw Papers, Mary Earhart Dillon Collection, Radcliffe College, Cambridge, Mass. On antimodernism in American culture, see T. J. Jackson Lears, *No Place of Grace: Antimodernism and the Transformation of American Culture* (New York: Pantheon, 1981).

31. Page Smith, *Daughters of the Promised Land* (Boston: Little, Brown, 1970), pp. 181–89; Hunter, *Gospel of Gentility*, pp. 83–89.

32. *Union Signal*, 14 Feb. 1895, p. 3.

33. *California White Ribbon Ensign*, Mar. 1946, p. 7 (Reprint of article in *Biblical Recorder of Australasia*, Dec. 1930); Katharine Bushnell to Anne K. Martin, 7 Sept. 1943, Anne K. Martin Papers, Bancroft Library, University of California, Berkeley.

34. *Union Signal*, 6 Aug. 1896, p. 3.

35. *Our Federation* (Adelaide), 15 June 1903, p. 66.

36. Cowie, *One of Australia's Daughters*, p. 161.

37. *Woman's Herald*, 23 Nov. 1893, p. 630.

38. See *Union Signal*, 14 Feb. 1895, p. 3; *Thumb-Nail Sketches*; Willard and Livermore, *Woman of the Century*, pp. 4–5; *Union Signal*, 1 Aug. 1912, p. 3.

39. *Union Signal*, 20 Mar. 1890, pp. 4–5; 20 July 1893, pp. 5–6; *Woman's Signal*, 31 May 1894, p. 388; 12 July 1894, p. 24.

40. *Union Signal*, 22 Mar. 1906, p. 5.

41. L. C. Coombs to Anna Gordon, 28 Feb. 1914, WWCTU Files; *Union Signal*, 15 Dec. 1892, p. 9 (West), and 1 Aug. 1912, p. 3 (Gowen); "Travel Letters of Alvine Muriel Ayres," WWCTU Files; Ackermann, reported in *White Ribbon Signal* (Sydney), 1 Aug. 1895, p. 2; Leavitt, *Report, 1891*, p. 51; Mary Lochhead to Agnes Slack, 17 Apr. 1912, Castle Howard Archives (J23/265), Castle Howard, Yorkshire.

42. WWCTU, *2d Conv., 1893*, p. 185; *8th Conv., 1910*, p. 201; NWCTU, *AR*, 1923, p. 101; *Union Signal*, 24 Dec. 1927, p. 793.

43. *Union Signal*, 29 Nov. 1906, p. 4; Dorothy Staunton, *Our Goodly Heritage* (n.p., 1956), p. 73.

44. Australasian WCTU, *3d Triennial Conv., 1897*, pp. 74–75; WWCTU, *7th Conv., 1906*, p. 76; *White Ribbon Bulletin*, 23 Aug. 1903, and 8 Aug. 1904. On the

careers and motivations of Cummins and Vincent, see also Lizzie Vincent, *Broken Fetters* (Melbourne: Privately printed, 1892), esp. p. 26; *White Ribbon*, July 1908, p. 98.

45. Kearney, *A Slaveholder's Daughter*, p. 206.

46. *Union Signal*, 24 Feb. 1898, pp. 13–14; 14 May 1903, p. 12; 18 June 1903, p. 5; 24 May 1923, p. 9; Frances Willard to Mary Whitney, 14 July 1897, roll 24, WCTU Series, OHS.

47. *Union Signal*, 2 July 1891, p. 8 (Leavitt); Parrish, in WWCTU, *6th Conv., 1903*, p. 71, for Japanese language difficulties.

48. WWCTU, *3d Conv., 1895*, p. 181.

49. Australasian WCTU, *8th Triennial Conv., 1912*, p. 43.

50. *SEAP*, 5:2019; *White Ribbon Signal* (Sydney), 29 Feb. 1912, p. 7.

51. *Union Signal*, 18 June 1903, p. 5; *White Ribbon Bulletin*, 21 Aug. 1903.

52. Charlotte Gray to Frances Willard, 25 Sept. 1892, roll 18, WCTU Series, OHS; Isabella Irish, letter to *Union Signal*, 12 Mar. 1885, p. 9.

53. Australasian WCTU, *8th Triennial Conv., 1912*, p. 43; Margaret Denning to Agnes Slack, 29 Feb.–1 Mar. 1912, Castle Howard Archives (J23/265).

54. WWCTU, *3d Conv., 1895*, p. 180.

55. Executive Minutes, World's WCTU, [22?] Oct. 1897, WWCTU Files; see also Mary Earhart, *Frances Willard: From Prayers to Politics* (Chicago: University of Chicago Press, 1944), pp. 352–66.

56. Willard to Susan H. Barney, 5 Aug. 1897, roll 24, WCTU Series, OHS.

57. Mary Whitney to Frances Willard, 29 Apr. 1897, and Willard to Whitney, 14 July 1897, roll 24, WCTU Series, OHS.

58. This information was conveyed to me by a confidential source while working at the Willard Library in 1981. I was also told that a list of Willard's "enemies" was destroyed sometime in the 1960s and that both Leavitt's and Ackermann's names were on this list.

59. Rosalind Carlisle to Lillian Stevens, 12 Jan. 1907, Castle Howard Archives (J23/264); Laura Bridgman to Jessie Ackermann, 23 July 1895, and Rev. H. M. Bridgman to Ackermann, 8 July 1894, box 1, fl. 1; Frances Willard to Ackermann, 9 Feb. 1895, box 1, fl. 5, Ackermann Collection.

60. *Baltimore News*, 18 Oct. 1895, in Scrapbook 70, WCTU Files; see also Willard to Ackermann, 12 Jan. 1897, box 1, fl. 5; Anna Gordon to Ackermann, 25 Aug. 1898, box 1, fl. 1; Somerset to Ackermann, 14 Jan. 1898, box 1, fl. 6, Ackermann Collection.

61. Leavitt, *Report, 1891*, p. 62.

62. London *Times*, 23 Nov. 1897, quoting a telegram from Bushnell and Andrew to Willard, 15 June 1896.

63. *Union Signal*, 6 June 1895, p. 5; quotation from NWCTU, *AR*, 1895, p. 36; Alice Palmer to Frances Willard, 3 Feb. 1893, roll 19, WCTU Series.

64. On Vincent and Cummins, see Lizzie Vincent to Agnes Slack, 1 Jan. 1911, Castle Howard Archives (J23/265); *White Ribbon*, July 1908, p. 98, and Nov. 1909, p. 166; *World's White Ribbon Bulletin*, 18 Aug. 1904, p. 2; WWCTU, *7th Conv., 1906*, p. 76. On the health of Ackermann, Andrew, Shaffner, and other missionaries, see also Frances Willard to Jessie Ackermann, 29 May 1895, box 1, fl. 5, Ackermann Collection. *Los Angeles Times*, 10 July 1937, p. 5, and "Lincoln

Visitor . . . ," newspaper clipping, box 1, fl. 11, Ackermann Collection, document Ackermann's later career, and illustrate her falling away from "petrified creeds and dogmas." Virginia Pride to Anna Gordon, 29 Nov. 1913, WWCTU Files, is suggestive of the process of secularization and spiritual declension.

65. Dimitri D. Lazo, "The Making of a Multicultural Man: The Missionary Experiences of E. T. Williams," *Pacific Historical Review* 51 (1982): 357–83.

66. Leavitt, *Report, 1891*, p. 21.

67. NWCTU, *AR*, 1893, pp. 77–78.

68. *Union Signal* (suppl.), 9 Nov. 1893, no page numbers. On the Parliament of Religions, see Carl T. Jackson, *The Oriental Religions and American Thought: Nineteenth-Century Explorations* (Westport, Conn.: Greenwood Press, 1981), chap. 13.

69. *Union Signal*, 10 May 1894, p. 3; 18 Jan. 1894, p. 5.

70. Australasian WCTU, *2d Triennial Conv., 1894*, p. 59; "Interview with Miss Jessie Ackermann," *The China Illustrated Weekly*, 13 Jan. 1917, p. 5; "U.S. May Learn Much from China," box 1, fl. 11, Ackermann Collection.

71. *Union Signal*, 24 Mar. 1910, p. 3.

72. Ibid., 9 Jan. 1902, p. 3.

73. Ibid., 18 Dec. 1919, p. 5; WWCTU, *15th Conv., 1934*, p. 47. On Buddhist temperance, see A. P. Kannagara, "The Riots of 1915 in Sri Lanka: A Study in the Roots of Communal Violence," *Past and Present*, no. 102 (1984): 137–40. See also the case of Jeanette Hauser in India in *Canadian Woman's Journal* (Ottawa), Dec. 1893, p. 4; *World's White Ribbon Bulletin*, Dec. 1896–Jan. 1897, p. 4.

74. *Union Signal*, 21 May 1896, p. 7.

75. Ibid., 10 Aug. 1909, p. 13.

76. Ibid., 30 Nov. 1922, p. 10; 22 Mar. 1923, p. 5.

77. WWCTU, *2d Conv., 1893*, pp. 199–200.

78. *Union Signal*, 3 Dec. 1891, p. 8. See also "Lincoln Visitor."

79. *Union Signal*, 14 Mar. 1895, p. 4.

80. On Bushnell and Andrew, see Chapter 9 for an exposition of this theme.

81. Sylvia Jacobs, "Three Afro-American Women: Missionaries in Africa, 1882–1904," in Keller, Queen, and Thomas, eds., *Women in New Worlds*, 2:277–78. See also *Union Signal*, 27 Aug. 1891, pp. 8–9; John H. Bracey, Jr., "Amanda Berry Smith," *NAW*, 3:305. The cross-racial tolerance of some liberal South African whites who joined the WCTU also deserves the consideration of scholars. See, for example, *Third Bi-Ennial Convention of the Coloured and Native Women's Christian Temperance Union, South Africa* (Cape Town, 1921), in folder 4, roll 26, World League Against Alcoholism Series, OHS.

82. NWCTU, *AR*, 1892, pp. 62–63; *The Poetical Works of Reginald Heber, Lord Bishop of Calcutta* (London: John Murray, 1845), p. 90. On Pandita Ramabai, see a legion of works, including Helen S. Dyer, *Pandita Ramabai: The Story of Her Life* (n.d., n.p., [c.1900]); and her own, *The High Caste Hindu Woman*, ed. Rachel Bodley (1887; rev. ed., New York: Fleming H. Revell, 1901); *Woman's Signal*, 25 Oct. 1894, p. 264.

83. WWCTU, *1st Conv., 1891*, pp. 54–55.

84. *Union Signal*, 12 Aug. 1909, p. 3. See also, for another case, ibid., 10 Nov. 1892, p. 5.

85. Ibid., 9 Jan. 1902, p. 3.

86. WWCTU, *6th Conv., 1903*, p. 72. See also Annie Darley, quoted in *Union Signal*, 20 Apr. 1911, p. 1.

87. Ruth Bordin, *Frances Willard: A Biography* (Chapel Hill: University of North Carolina Press, 1986), pp. 158, 191–92, 231.

88. Ibid., p. 157; Jane Stewart, *I Have Recalled: A Pen-Panorama of a Life* (Toledo, Ohio: Chittenden Press, 1938), p. 165.

89. *Union Signal*, 14 May 1891, p. 11.

90. Frances Willard, *The World's Woman's Christian Temperance Union: Aims and Objects* (Uxbridge, Eng.: Hutchings, [c.1892–93]), pp. 8–9, 10–11. This point is corroborated by Willard's original diary entry. See Diary, 1 May 1870, roll 4, WCTU Series, 1982 Suppl., Michigan Historical Collections, Bentley Library, University of Michigan, Ann Arbor.

91. *Union Signal*, 20 Mar. 1890, p. 5, and 14 May 1891, p. 9; Rev. C. C. Harrah, *Jesus Christ: The Emancipator of Women* (Chicago, 1887), appeared under the imprint of the Woman's Temperance Publishing Association.

92. *White Ribbon Signal* (Sydney), 22 July 1907, p. 7; WWCTU, *2d Conv., 1893*, p. 205.

93. Willard, *World's WCTU: Aims and Objects*, p. 10.

94. *Union Signal*, 3 Dec. 1891, p. 8.

95. WWCTU, *3d Conv., 1895*, p. 48.

96. *White Ribbon Signal* (Sydney), 22 July 1907, p. 7; *Union Signal*, 10 Dec. 1885, p. 8.

97. WWCTU, *1st Conv., 1891*, p. 31; *Union Signal*, 17 Nov. 1891, p. 2.

98. Ian Tyrrell, "International Aspects of the Woman's Temperance Movement in Australia: The Influence of the American WCTU, 1882–1914," *Journal of Religious History* 12 (June 1983): 284–304.

99. WWCTU, *2d Conv., 1893*, p. 176. This also was the position in Turkey itself (p. 152).

100. WWCTU, *6th Conv., 1903*, p. 69.

101. Rosalind Carlisle to Agnes Slack, 17 June 1920, in Slack, *People I Have Met and Places I Have Seen: Some Memories of Agnes E. Slack* (Bedford, Eng.: Rush and Warwick, 1942), p. 44.

102. Rosalind Carlisle to Lillian Stevens, 12 Jan. 1907, Castle Howard Archives (J23/265); see also Charles Roberts, *The Radical Countess: The History of the Life of Rosalind, Countess of Carlisle* (Carlisle, Eng.: Steel Bros., 1962), p. 134.

103. Willard, *Glimpses*, p. 301; Willard Diary, 6 April 1870, roll 4, WCTU Series, 1982 Suppl.

104. WWCTU, *24th Conv., 1962*, pp. 39–40.

105. Leavitt, *Report, 1891*, p. 61; *Union Signal*, 24 Sept. 1891, p. 10.

106. Edward Said, *Orientalism* (New York: Vintage, 1979); Bordin, *Willard*, p. 191; Jackson, *Oriental Religions*, chap. 13; *Union Signal*, 26 Aug. 1909, p. 4; Willard, *World's WCTU: Aims and Objects*, p. 9; W. G. Carhart to Willard, 1 Jan. 1898, roll 25, WCTU Series.

107. This theme is pursued below, chap. 7, in the concrete case of the Indian response to Western temperance missionaries. See, for example, the *Official*

Report of the Third Session of the Punjab Temperance Conference . . . (Amritsar, 1919), p. 14, roll 22, folder 35, WLAA Series, OHS.

108. Leavitt, *Report, 1891*, p. 38; Jessie Ackermann in *Woman's Signal*, 12 July 1894, p. 24.

109. See, for example, Ackermann's comments in *Union Signal*, 13 Mar. 1890, pp. 4–5, and Christine Tinling's in ibid., 15 May 1924, p. 4; Margaret Denning to Agnes Slack, 29 Feb–1 Mar. 1912, Castle Howard Archives (J23/265). On Beecher, see Kathryn Sklar, *Catharine Beecher: A Study in American Domesticity* (New Haven: Yale University Press, 1973).

110. *Union Signal*, 24 Sept. 1891, p. 10.

111. Ibid., 4 Apr. 1912, p. 3.

112. Australasian WCTU, *3d Triennial Conv., 1897*, p. 59; *White Ribbon*, Feb. 1912, p. 2.

113. See Chapters 8, 9, and 12.

114. Drawn from an extensive survey of the holdings in missionary periodicals and monographs in the Library of Congress. See, esp., *Foreign Missions Conference of North America, Reports*, 1893–1916; *Missionary Review of the World*, 1903–1915; *The World-Wide Evangelization: The Urgent Business of the Church. Addresses Delivered before the Tenth International Convention of the Student Volunteer Movement for Foreign Missions* . . . (New York: Student Volunteer Movement, 1902).

115. See Chapter 3, above.

116. WWCTU, *2d Conv., 1893*, p. 53; Frances Willard, *Do Everything: A Handbook for the World's White Ribboners*, rev. ed. (Chicago: Ruby I. Gilbert, 1905), p. 14; *Union Signal*, 21 Dec. 1893, p. 4.

117. Leavitt, *Report, 1891*, p. 21.

118. *Woman's Signal*, 12 June 1894, p. 24; NWCTU, *AR*, 1893, p. 202; [Mary Woodbridge], *Report of the American Secretary of the World's Woman's Christian Temperance Union, 1890* (n.p., 1890), p. 19; *Union Signal*, 11 May 1893, p. 5.

119. *Union Signal*, 20 June 1912, p. 12.

120. Clara Parrish to Lillian Stevens, 2 Mar. 1897, roll 24, WCTU Series, OHS.

121. Leavitt, *Report, 1891*, pp. 37–38.

122. *Union Signal*, 24 Sept. 1891, p. 10.

123. Leavitt, *Report, 1891*, pp. 36–37; *Union Signal*, 22 Oct. 1891, p. 10.

124. Amelia Pemmell to Frances Willard, 23 Oct. 1897, roll 24, WCTU Series, OHS; Australasian WCTU, *8th Triennial Conv., 1912*, p. 46.

125. WWCTU, *2d Conv., 1893*, p. 114.

126. WWCTU Treasurer's Reports, 1891–1919, WWCTU Files; on Goodrich, see *Union Signal*, 11 Aug. 1910, p. 2; 2 May 1912, p. 1; 3 Oct. 1912, p. 1; Hunter, *Gospel of Gentility*, pp. 169–70; Goodrich to Agnes Slack, 4 Jan. 1911, Castle Howard Archives (J23/265); for Farnham, see *SEAP*, 3:967; for Mei, see *Union Signal*, 3 June 1920, p. 11; for other indigenous organizers, see *Union Signal*, 17 July 1923, p. 10, and 11 Aug. 1928, p. 4; for Ramabai, *High Caste Hindu Woman*; for Dunhill, Helen E. Dunhill to Jessie Ackermann, 3 Aug. 1904, box 1, fl. 1, Ackermann Collection; *Union Signal*, 29 Mar. 1900, p. 5 (quotation).

For Indian WCTU presidents, see, for example, Margaret Denning to Agnes Slack, 29 Feb.–1 Mar. 1912, Castle Howard Archives (J23/265); Jeanette Hauser in *Canadian Woman's Journal* (Ottawa), Nov. 1893, p. 4; on Mary Phillips, M. M. H. Hills to Frances Willard, 23 Dec. 1896, roll 24, WCTU Series, OHS; Mary B. Phillips, "A Plea for India," *Union Signal*, 18 Oct. 1894, pp. 4–5.

127. WWCTU Treasurer's Reports, 1891–1919, WWCTU Files; *Union Signal*, 27 Feb. 1902, p. 11; Goodrich to Carlisle, 17 Sept. 1910, Castle Howard Archives (J23/265); WWCTU, *2d Conv., 1893*, pp. 167–70; WWCTU, *8th Conv., 1910*, p. 169; N. Monelle Mansell to editor, *Union Signal*, 11 Feb. 1892, p. 4; Frances Hallowes to Rosalind Carlisle, 30 Nov. 1906, Castle Howard Archives (J23/271).

128. WWCTU, *8th Conv., 1910*, pp. 201–3; NWCTU, *AR*, 1914, p. 185.

129. *SEAP*, 2:592; similar work was done by Joan Davis in India after 1925. See *Union Signal*, 24 July 1926, p. 4.

130. *Union Signal*, 16 Dec. 1920, p. 5, and 30 Nov. 1922, p. 10.

131. Patricia R. Hill, *World Their Household*.

132. *Union Signal*, 10–17 Aug. 1921, p. 5, and 16 Sept. 1920, p. 7.

133. Based on a perusal of *Union Signal* throughout the period of national prohibition, 1919–1933, and financial reports of the WWCTU, 1919–1933, in NWCTU, *AR*, 1919–33.

134. On Campbell and the missionary-nationalism connection in the 1920s, see *Union Signal*, 30 Nov. 1922, p. 10, and 22 Mar. 1923, p. 5; *World's White Ribbon Bulletin*, Dec. 1946–Jan. 1947, p. 4. For other prominent missionaries of the 1920s, see, for example, World's WCTU, "Miss Flora E. Strout" (n.p., n.d.), pp. 1–2; WWCTU, *15th Conv., 1934*, pp. 46–47; "Christine Isobel Tinling," *SEAP*, 6:2652. On the ASL's international expansion, see Susan Brook, "The World League against Alcoholism: The Attempt to Export an American Experience" (M.A. thesis, University of Western Ontario, 1972).

135. *Los Angeles Times*, 10 July 1937, p. 5.

Chapter 6

1. "To the Christian Women of America," [Spring 1897], in Scrapbook 75, WCTU Files; NWCTU, *AR*, 1897, p. 122; "Appeal to Women," in *Calcutta White Ribbon*, 5 Sept. 1896, Scrapbook 75, p. 12, WCTU Files; Joan Jacobs Brumberg, "Zenanas and Girlless Villages: The Ethnology of American Evangelical Women, 1870–1910," *Journal of American History* 69 (1982): 347–48; Ruth Bordin, *Frances Willard: A Biography* (Chapel Hill: University of North Carolina Press, 1986), pp. 229–31.

2. "Reassessments of 'First-Wave' Feminism," *Women's Studies International Forum* 5 (no. 6, 1982), esp. pp. 647–62; Brumberg, "Zenanas," pp. 347–71; Bordin, *Willard*, pp. 191, 229–31. Some of this literature on women's culture is reviewed in the context of the new social history in Ian Tyrrell, *The Absent Marx: Class Analysis and Liberal History in Twentieth-Century America* (Westport, Conn.: Greenwood Press, 1986), pp. 156–58.

3. While it would not be true to say that what follows has been derived from secondary sources, much of my analysis has subsequently been confirmed by a reading of Lenore Davidoff and Catherine Hall, *Family Fortunes: Men and Women of the English Middle Class, 1780–1850* (London: Hutchinson, 1987). See esp. pp. 321–56. A parallel study of American family relations and ideology is desperately needed and is suggested by the evidence contained below.

4. Mary Bannister Willard to Elizabeth Boynton Harbert, [1882], box 8, Elizabeth Boynton Harbert Collection, Huntington Library, San Marino, Calif.

5. Frances Willard, *Glimpses of Fifty Years* (Chicago: WTPA, 1889), p. 592.

6. Ibid., pp. 392, 434.

7. See, esp., Nancy Cott, *The Bonds of Womanhood: Woman's Sphere in New England, 1780–1835* (New Haven: Yale University Press, 1977); Carroll Smith-Rosenberg, "The Female World of Love and Ritual: Relations between Women in Nineteenth-Century America," *Signs* 1 (1975): 1–25; Estelle B. Freedman, "Separatism as Strategy: Female Institution Building and American Feminism, 1870–1930," *Feminist Studies* 5 (1979): 512–29; Karen Blair, *The Clubwoman as Feminist: True Womanhood Redefined* (New York: Holmes and Meier, 1980).

8. Willard, *Glimpses*, p. 641.

9. Willard to Whiting, 15 Nov. 1891, ms. A.1.2. v 39, p. 143, Kate Field Collection, Boston Public Library.

10. Willard to Anna Gordon, 8, 10 May, 16 July, 5 Aug. 1891, roll 17, WCTU Series, OHS.

11. Willard to Gordon, 8 May 1891, ibid.

12. Mary Wood-Allen to "Dear Cousin," 22 Jan. 1898, roll 25, WCTU Series, OHS. Also see *White Ribbon and Wings* (London), June 1933, p. 107; Frances Willard, "Anna A. Gordon," clipping in Scrapbook 74, p. 94, WCTU Files.

13. Lizzie Vincent to Agnes Slack, 1 Jan. 1911, Castle Howard Archives (J23/265), Castle Howard, Yorkshire.

14. Katharine Bushnell to Anne K. Martin, 12 Aug., 2 Sept. 1943, 12, 22 Nov. 1943, and 26 Nov. 1944, Anne K. Martin Papers, Bancroft Library, University of California, Berkeley.

15. Amelia Truesdale to Jessie Ackermann, [c.1907], box 1, fl. 4, Jessie A. Ackermann Collection, Sherrod Library, East Tennessee State University, Johnson City, Tenn.; Helen E. Dunhill to Ackermann, 3 Aug. 1904, ibid. [filed with Mary Swaney fragment]; Gail Hamilton Waid to Ackermann, 21 June 1897, ibid.; Amelia Pemmell, "My Three Loves," fl. 9, ibid.

16. Aelfrida Tillyard, *Agnes E. Slack: Two Hundred Thousand Miles Travel for Temperance in Four Continents* (Cambridge, Eng.: W. Heffer and Sons, 1926), p. 131; Slack to Gordon, 17 Sept. 1913, WWCTU Files.

17. *Union Signal*, 29 May 1913, p. 9.

18. Jane Stewart, *I Have Recalled: A Pen-Panorama of a Life* (Toledo, Ohio: Chittenden Press, 1938), p. 180.

19. J. J. G. Carson, *Emilie Solomon, 1858–1939* (Cape Town: Juto, [c.1941]), pp. 19, 24.

20. This theme is illustrated throughout the WCTU Series, OHS. See also Mary Earhart, *Frances Willard: From Prayers to Politics* (Chicago: University of Chicago Press, 1944), opposite p. 324, for an illustration.

21. Georgia Jobson to Cora Stoddard, 1 May 1914, Mary Hannah Hanchett Hunt Papers, New York Public Library.

22. Yet another case was that of Annie Wittenmyer. See Bordin, *Willard*, p. 107. On Foster, see Frank L. Byrne, "Judith Ellen Horton Foster," *NAW*, 1:652; on Leavitt see below, Chapter 9.

23. Smith-Rosenberg, "Female World." This generalization also applies to Marilyn F. Motz, *True Sisterhood: Michigan Women and Their Kin, 1820–1920* (Albany, N.Y.: State University of New York Press, 1983).

24. Anna Gordon, *The Beautiful Life of Frances Willard* (Chicago: WTPA, 1898).

25. Letitia Youmans, *Campaign Echoes: The Autobiography of Mrs. Letitia Youmans, the Pioneer of the White Ribbon Movement in Canada*, 2d ed. (Toronto: William Briggs, 1893), p. 142.

26. Carson, *Solomon*, p. 143.

27. [J. H. More] to Anna Gordon, 4 Jan. 1898, roll 25, WCTU Series, OHS.

28. Emma Taylor to Mary Hill Willard, 15 Nov. 1891, roll 17, WCTU Series, OHS. See also Belle Kearney to Willard, 28 July 1893, roll 20, and Zerelda Wallace to Willard, 29 Jan. 1888, roll 15, ibid.

29. Mary V. G. Woolley to Willard, 16 Mar. 1893, roll 19, ibid.

30. Wallace to Willard, 29 Jan. 1888, roll 15, ibid.

31. A most sensitive and helpful review of the issue of lesbian relationships appears in Martha Vicinus, "Sexuality and Power: A Review of Current Work in the History of Sexuality," *Feminist Studies* 1 (1982): 133–56.

32. Mary Ryan, *Womanhood in America: From Colonial Times to the Present*, 3d ed. (New York: Franklin Watts, 1983), p. 208.

33. Bordin, *Willard*, pp. 44–47.

34. Mary Livermore to Thomas Wentworth Higginson, 17 Feb. 1882, ms. P.91.37.82, Kate Field Collection; WWCTU, *3d Conv., 1895*, p. 92.

35. *Union Signal*, 29 May 1913, p. 9.

36. *Thumb-Nail Sketches of White Ribboners* (Chicago: WTPA, 1892), pp. 5–6; Frances Willard to Helen Hood, 12 Dec. 1891, roll 17, WCTU Series, OHS; *Union Signal*, 10 Feb. 1898, p. 5; BWTA, *AR*, 1894, p. 2.

37. Isabella Irish to editor, in *Union Signal*, 12 Mar. 1885, p. 9; WWCTU, *6th Conv., 1903*, p. 33; *Union Signal*, 18 July 1912, p. 3, and 4 Sept. 1902, p. 1; *Thumb-Nail Sketches*, p. 22; *NAW*, 2:102–3; Barbara Strachey, *Remarkable Relations: The Story of the Pearsall Smith Women* (New York: Universe Books, 1982).

38. Annie Carvosso to Anna Gordon, 8 Dec. 1913, and Hilda Geard to Gordon, 25 July 1913, WWCTU Files.

39. Mary C. Leavitt to Ruth Stephens, 20 July 1907, in Second Book of Records of the Woman's Christian Temperance Union of Queensland, Begun in 1910 . . . , p. 11, Queensland WCTU Headquarters; Australasian WCTU, *3d Triennial Conv., 1897*, p. 34; Amelia Pemmell, "My Three Loves," box 1, fl. 9; Shylie Woolley to Ackermann, 11 June 1894, box 1, fl. 4, Ackermann Collection.

40. Anderson Hughes-Drew to Anna Gordon, 1 Oct. 1913, WWCTU Files.

41. Margaret C. Millar to Anna Gordon, 1 Oct. 1913, ibid.

42. Mary C. Leavitt to Elizabeth Brentnall [1897], and Leavitt to Ruth Stephens, 20 July 1907, in Second Book of Records, WCTU of Queensland.

43. *Union Signal*, 24 July 1913, p. 9.

44. Wilhemina Bain to Caroline Severance, 27 July 1911, box 14, Caroline Severance Papers, Huntington Library, San Marino, Calif.

45. Ian Tyrrell, "International Aspects of the Woman's Temperance Movement in Australia: The Influence of the American WCTU, 1882–1914," *Journal of Religious History* 12 (June 1983): 297.

46. *White Ribbon Signal* (Melbourne), 12 Oct. 1926, p. 3.

47. *Union Signal*, 5 July 1883, p. 4.

48. Mary C. Leavitt, *Report of the Hon. Sec. of the World's Woman's Christian Temperance Union* (Boston: n.p., 1891), p. 64.

49. Martha Vicinus, *Independent Women: Work and Community for Single Women, 1850–1920* (London: Virago, 1985), chap. 2, esp. pp. 46–47, and p. 310, n. 15.

50. K. Austin Kerr, *Organized for Prohibition: A New History of the Anti-Saloon League* (New Haven: Yale University Press, 1985), p. 48.

51. *White Ribbon*, Oct. 1898, p. 137.

52. WWCTU, *1st Conv., 1891*, p. 15.

53. *Union Signal*, 25 June 1903, p. 4.

54. Ibid., 10 Feb. 1898, p. 5, and 13 Aug. 1891, p. 4.

55. Ibid., 13 Aug. 1891, p. 4.

56. Ibid., 18 Oct. 1906, p. 3, and 19 Mar. 1917, p. 9. See also the case of Marie Sandstrom, ibid., 30 May 1931, p. 4.

57. Clipping from *Chicago Inter-Ocean*, 20 Oct. 1895, box 8, Harbert Collection.

58. Tyrrell, "International Aspects," pp. 296, 298.

59. *Union Signal*, 31 Dec. 1891, p. 4; Hannah Clark Bailey, *Reminiscences of a Christian Life* (Portland, Me.: Hoyt, Fogg and Donham, 1884), pp. 54–55; Ackermann, in *Pacific Ensign*, 13 Oct. 1892, p. 2. For the consecration to service, see Elizabeth Greenwood, Dept. of Evangelistic Work Programme for World's and National WCTU Conventions, 1897, in Scrapbook 76, WCTU Files.

60. Charles Edward White, *The Beauty of Holiness: Phoebe Palmer as Theologian, Revivalist, Feminist, and Humanitarian* (Grand Rapids, Mich.: Francis Asbury Press, 1986), pp. 128–29, 140.

61. Frances Willard's last testimony, typescript, 13 Feb. 1898, p. 5, roll 25, WCTU Series, OHS; *Union Signal*, 20 Nov. 1920, pp. 2, 8.

62. Jane Stewart, *I Have Recalled*, p. 180.

63. See, for example, Willard, *Glimpses*, pp. 641–42.

64. Clipping from 1890 Presidential Address, in Scrapbook 20, WCTU Files; WWCTU, *2d Conv., 1893*, p. 19; Frances Willard, *Do Everything: A Handbook for the World's White Ribboners*, rev. ed. (Chicago: Ruby I. Gilbert, 1905), p. 6; NWCTU, *AR*, 1890, pp. 99, 122, 139.

65. Katherine Harris, "Feminism and Temperance Reform in the Boulder WCTU," *Frontiers* 4 (1979): 20.

66. *The Japanese Evangelist*, May 1897, p. 251, in Scrapbook 76, WCTU Files.

67. Bordin, *Willard*, p. 264.

68. Frances Willard, *A Great Mother: Sketches of Madame Willard* . . . (Chicago: WTPA, 1894). The theme of maternalism in Willard has received some treatment in Nancy Hardesty, "Minister as Prophet? Or as Mother?" in Hilah F. Thomas and Rosemary Skinner Keller, eds., *Women in New Worlds: Historical Perspectives on the Wesleyan Tradition* (Nashville: Abingdon, 1981), 1:88–101, esp. pp. 96–97; NWCTU, *AR*, 1891, p. 189.

69. *Union Signal*, 3 Mar. 1892, p. 9.

70. Amelia Pemmell obituary, *White Ribbon Signal* (Sydney), 12 Jan. 1923, p. 4.

71. Bordin, *Willard*, p. 199.

72. Hannah Whitall Smith to Frances Willard, 20 Apr. 1893, roll 19, WCTU Series, OHS.

73. Hannah Clark Bailey, "Great Mothers," undated ms., roll 1, box 1, fl. 1, Hannah Clark Bailey Papers, Swarthmore College, Swarthmore, Pa.

74. *Union Signal*, 13 Feb. 1913, pp. 3, 13; Mary Slack to Lillian Stevens, 8 Dec. 1896, roll 24, WCTU Series, OHS.

75. Clipping from *Chicago Post*, 24 Sept. 1890, in Scrapbook 45, WCTU Files.

76. *Union Signal*, 23 June 1887, p. 10.

77. Addie Foster to Willard, 29 Apr. 1891, roll 17, WCTU Series, OHS; Willard, *Glimpses*, pp. 655–70.

78. Kathleen Fitzpatrick, *Lady Henry Somerset* (London: Jonathan Cape; Boston: Little, Brown, 1923), p. 92.

79. Tillyard, *Agnes E. Slack*, p. xiii.

80. Mary Slack to Lillian Stevens, 8 Dec. 1896; Belle Kearney to Stevens, 2 Dec. 1896; and Agnes Slack to Frances Willard, 25 Dec. 1897, roll 24, WCTU Series, OHS.

81. Kearney to Stevens, 2 Dec. 1896, ibid.

82. Smith-Rosenberg, "Female World," pp. 1–25.

83. An accessible if flawed introduction to this topic is Sylvia Hewlett, *A Lesser Life: The Myth of Women's Liberation in America* (New York: William Morrow, 1986). See also, for example, Cheri Register, "Motherhood at Center: Ellen Key's Social Vision," *Women's Studies International Forum* 5 (no. 6, 1982): 599–610. On the "material feminists," see Dolores Hayden, *The Grand Domestic Revolution: A History of Feminist Designs for American Homes, Neighborhoods, and Cities* (Cambridge, Mass.: MIT Press, 1981).

84. Karen Offen, "Republicanism, Nationalism, and Feminism in Fin-de-Siècle France," *American Historical Review* 89 (1984): 675–76; Register, "Motherhood at Center"; Christl Wickert, Brigitte Hamburger, and Marie Lienau, "Helene Stöcker and the Bund fuer Mutterschutz (The Society for the Protection of Motherhood)," *Women's Studies International Forum* 5 (no. 6, 1982): 611–18.

85. Ellen Key, *The Woman Movement* (New York: George Putnam's Sons, 1912), p. 26.

86. Ellen Key, *The Century of the Child* (New York: George Putnam's Sons, 1909); *Union Signal*, 9 May 1912, p. 10.

87. Willard, *Glimpses*, pp. 603, 614; Nancy Cott, *The Grounding of Modern Feminism* (New Haven: Yale University Press, 1987), pp. 46–49.

88. Cott, *Grounding of Modern Feminism*, pp. 46–49; Caroline Nelson, "Ellen

Key: A Sketch," *Birth Control Review*, 2 (May 1918): 13–14; Louise Nystrom-Hamilton, *Ellen Key: Her Life and Work* (New York: George Putnam's Sons, 1913), p. 81; Katharine Anthony, *Feminism in Germany and Scandinavia* (New York: Henry Holt, 1915), chap. 6.

89. Key, *Woman Movement*, p. 40; Register, "Motherhood at Center," pp. 599–610; Wickert, Hamburger and Lienau, "Helene Stöcker," pp. 611–18; Cf. Bordin, *Willard*, pp. 145–46; William Leach, "Looking Forward Together: Feminists and Edward Bellamy," *Democracy* 2 (Jan. 1982): 120–34.

90. NWCTU, *AR*, 1917, p. 162. International influence on maternal welfare policies in the United States from 1900 to 1930 is a neglected theme. But see, for the possibilities of such an analysis, J. Stanley Lemons, *The Woman Citizen: Social Feminism in the 1920s* (Urbana, Ill.: University of Illinois Press, 1973), pp. 154, 158, 160, 165. The WCTU did work with social feminists through the Women's Joint Congressional Committee to implement progressive programs of maternal and child welfare. See NWCTU, *AR*, 1921, p. 43, and 1925, p. 181; *Union Signal*, 20 May 1920, p. 2.

91. See Daniel Scott Smith, "Family Limitation, Sexual Control and Domestic Feminism in Victorian America," *Feminist Studies* 1 (1973): 40–57, for the American demographic data; see also Steve Hochstadt, Appendix to Patricia Robertson, *An Experience of Women: Pattern and Change in Nineteenth-Century Europe* (Philadelphia: Temple University Press, 1982), pp. 557–58; Vicinus, *Independent Women*.

92. Ruth Bordin, *Woman and Temperance: The Quest for Power and Liberty, 1873–1900* (Philadelphia: Temple University Press, 1981), p. 165, summarizes the results of these statistical studies; Erna Olafson Hellerstein, Leslie Parker Hume and Karen Offen, eds., *Victorian Women: A Documentary Account of Women's Lives in Nineteenth-Century England, France, and the United States* (Stanford, Calif.: Stanford University Press, 1985), p. 121.

93. Calculated from BWTA, *AR*, 1894, and 1904, at United Kingdom Alliance Headquarters, London.

94. *Report of the First Annual Meeting of the Woman's Christian Temperance Union of the Province of Quebec, . . . 1884* (Montreal, 1885), pp. 47–80.

95. WCTU of New South Wales, *AR*, 1893, pp. 3, 14–19; *Golden Records: Pathfinders of the Woman's Christian Temperance Union of New South Wales* (Sydney: John Sands, 1926), pp. 79-114.

96. Peter F. McDonald, *Marriage in Australia: Age at First Marriage and Proportions Marrying, 1860–1971* (Canberra: Australian National University, 1974), pp. 133–34.

97. Ian Tyrrell, "Sara Susan Nolan," *Australian Dictionary of Biography*, 11:37, discusses a typical case.

98. Bordin, *Woman and Temperance*, p. 165.

99. Hellerstein, Hume, and Offen, *Victorian Women*, p. 121.

100. Clipping, 18 Sept. 1890, in Scrapbook 20, WCTU Files.

101. Ibid.

102. *California White Ribbon Ensign*, Dec. 1939, p. 3.

103. Willard, *Glimpses*, pp. 597–99; Willard to Neal Dow, undated [1893], roll 19, WCTU Series, OHS.

104. *Union Signal*, 20 Feb. 1913, p. 3; Zerelda Wallace to Susan B. Anthony, 25 Aug. 1880, Ida Husted Harper Collection, Huntington Library, San Marino, Calif.

105. *Union Signal*, 9 May 1912, p. 9.

106. Frances Willard, *Woman and Temperance, or, the Work and Workers of the Woman's Christian Temperance Union* (Hartford, Conn.: Park Pub. Co., 1883), p. 157.

107. Frank L. Bryne, Jr., "Hannah Clark Johnston Bailey," *NAW*, 1:84; Bailey, *Reminiscences*, esp. pp. 223, 340–41.

108. Francis E. Clark, *Christian Endeavor in All Lands* (Boston: United Society of Christian Endeavor, 1906), p. 211.

109. Ibid., p. 207.

110. Willard, *Glimpses*, pp. 574, 576.

111. *Canadian Woman's Journal* (Ottawa), Dec. 1898, p. 4; *SEAP*, 3:967.

112. *Third Bi-Ennial Convention of the Coloured and Native Women's Christian Temperance Union, South Africa* (Cape Town, 1921), p. 3, in folder 4, roll 26, WLAA Series, OHS.

113. *Union Signal*, 11 May 1893, p. 3. Willard drew upon conventional Victorian middle-class conceptions of family life in developing this and similar characterizations. The idea of a chivalrous Christian gentleman had become a commonplace in late nineteenth-century Anglo-American society, particularly in the Christian socialist and reform circles with which Willard mixed. See Marc Girouard, *The Return to Camelot: Chivalry and the English Gentleman* (New Haven: Yale University Press, 1981), pp. 256, 260.

114. Willard, *Glimpses*, p. 599.

115. *Union Signal*, 11 May 1893, pp. 3–4; *Woman's Herald* (London), 29 June 1893, p. 304. On Christian brothers, see also the pertinent remarks of Lenore Davidoff and Catherine Hall, *Family Fortunes*, pp. 348–50.

116. Margaret Marsh, "From Separation to Togetherness: The Social Construction of Domestic Space in American Suburbs, 1840–1915," *Journal of American History* 76 (1989): 507, 513; cf. Barbara Epstein, *The Politics of Domesticity: Women, Evangelism, and Temperance in Nineteenth-Century America* (Middletown, Conn.: Wesleyan University Press, 1981), pp. 132–33.

117. NWCTU, *AR*, 1894, p. 118.

118. Willard, *Glimpses*, p. 613.

119. Ibid., p. 612; Frances Willard, "The Woman's Cause Is Man's," *Woman's Herald*, 21 Dec. 1893, p. 691; for another example, see *Minutes of the Queensland WCTU at the First Annual Meeting . . . 1886* (Brisbane, 1887), p. 13. Margaret Marsh, "Suburban Men and Masculine Domesticity, 1870–1915," *American Quarterly* 40 (1988): 165–86, lends weight to my interpretation on the rise of companionate marriage. For Australian material even more compatible with my thesis, see Marilyn Lake, "The Politics of Respectability: Identifying the Masculinist Context," *Historical Studies* 22 (Apr. 1986): 116–31. This is in turn challenged by Chris McConville, "Rough Women, Respectable Men and Social Reform: A Response to Lake's 'Masculinism,'" *Historical Studies* 22 (Apr. 1987): 432–40; see also the effective reply by Judith Allen, "'Mundane' Men: Historians, Masculinity and Masculinism," *Historical Studies* 22 (Oct. 1987): 627–28.

120. The actual source of Somerset's marriage breakdown is conveniently left undiscussed by her biographer, Kathleen Fitzpatrick, in *Somerset*, pp. 100–101. But see Strachey, *Remarkable Relations*, p. 108.

121. Barbara Strachey, *Remarkable Relations*, pp. 184, 312–13; Byrne, "Foster," *NAW*, 1:651; for Leavitt, see Janet Z. Giele, "Mary Clement Greenleaf Leavitt," *NAW*, 2:384.

122. David Fahey, "Rosalind (Stanley) Howard, Countess of Carlisle" (unpublished paper in Professor Fahey's possession), p. 4.

123. Willard, *Glimpses*, pp. 641–42.

124. Ibid., pp. 611, 641–42.

125. Australasian WCTU, *8th Triennial Conv., 1912*, p. 42.

126. *Temperance in Australia. The Memorial Volume of the International Temperance Convention, Melbourne, 1888* (Melbourne: Temperance Book Depot, 1889), p. 166; *Union Signal*, 18 Oct. 1894, p. 3; David Fahey, ed., *The Collected Writings of Jessie Forsyth, 1847–1937: The Good Templars and Temperance Reform on Three Continents* (Lewiston, N.Y.: Edwin Mellen Press, 1988), pp. 29–30, 55, 345.

127. Patricia Grimshaw and Graham Willett, "Family Structure in Colonial Australia," *Australia 1888*, no. 4 (May 1980): 16–17; *White Ribbon*, Mar. 1904, p. 67.

128. *White Ribbon*, Aug. 1900, p. 134.

129. See the speeches of Williams, the Rev. James Nolan, and the Hon. F. T. Brentnall in Queensland WCTU, *AR*, 1886, p. 13.

130. Cf. Grimshaw and Willett, "Family Structure," pp. 16–17; Jessie Ackermann, *Australia: From a Woman's Point of View* (London: Cassell, 1913), pp. 77–78.

131. Tyrrell, "International Aspects," p. 296.

132. On the tensions between women in family life and women's autonomy, see Carl Degler, *At Odds: Women and the Family in America from the Revolution to the Present* (New York: Oxford University Press, 1980).

133. *Union Signal*, 24 Mar. 1910, p. 3.

134. NWCTU, *AR*, 1913, pp. 380–81; Bordin, *Woman and Temperance*, pp. 152, 155; *Union Signal*, 17 Mar. 1904, p. 8.

135. Brumberg, "Zenanas," p. 361; Kinney, quoted in *Union Signal*, 1 May 1913, p. 13; Thomas G. Alexander, *Mormonism in Transition: A History of the Latter-Day Saints, 1890–1930* (Urbana, Ill.: University of Illinois Press, 1986), p. 62.

136. Brumberg, "Zenanas," p. 369; Bordin, *Woman and Temperance*, pp. 110–11. On Ramabai, see, in addition to Brumberg, Pandita Ramabai, *The High-Caste Hindu Woman*, rev. ed. (New York: Fleming H. Revell, 1901).

137. "To the Senate of the United States," 18 Jan. 1896, petition in Scrapbook 75, WCTU Files.

138. Cf. *Union Signal*, 13 Feb. 1913, p. 3, which does admit these complexities.

139. "To the Senate," 18 Jan. 1896.

140. *Chicago Post*, 26 Sept. 1896, in Scrapbook 76, WCTU Files; for a less idealized portrait of the Armenian people that recognizes the role of patriarchy, see *Woman's Work for Woman* 15 (Oct. 1885): 338; see also *Woman's Column* (Bos-

ton), 6 Jan. 1894, p. 4, reporting *Nor-Dar* [New Century].

141. Rebecca Krikorian to Anna Gordon, 28 Oct. 1913, WWCTU Files; *Union Signal*, 13 Feb. 1913, pp. 3, 13, and 16 Mar. 1897, pp. 4–5.

142. Belle Kearney to Lillian Stevens, 2 Nov. 1896, roll 24, WCTU Series, OHS; see also Ella Ives, in *Union Signal*, 13 Feb. 1913, p. 3.

143. Frederick Booth-Tucker to Frances Willard, 19 Oct. 1896, and Anna Gordon to Lillian Stevens, 18 Sept. 1896, roll 24, WCTU Series, OHS.

144. NWCTU, *AR*, 1897, p. 232.

145. Frances Willard to "Beloved Comrades," facsimile in *Union Signal*, 17 Dec. 1896, p. 1.

146. NWCTU, *AR*, 1897, p. 122.

Chapter 7

1. For a perceptive survey, see Eric Stokes, "Imperialism and the Scramble for Africa: The New View," in W. Roger Louis, *Imperialism: The Robinson and Gallagher Controversy* (New York: New Viewpoints, 1976), pp. 173–95.

2. J. A. Hobson, *Imperialism: A Study*, 3d rev. ed. (London: George Allen and Unwin, 1938), pp. 196–284.

3. Frances Willard, *The World's Woman's Christian Temperance Union: Aims and Objects* (Uxbridge, Eng.: Hutchings, [c.1892–93]), pp. 7–8.

4. NWCTU, *AR*, 1884, p. 63.

5. David Courtwright, *Dark Paradise: Opiate Addiction in America before 1940* (Cambridge, Mass.: Harvard University Press, 1986), pp. 42, 70.

6. NWCTU, *AR*, 1886, p. lxxvii.

7. Joshua Rowntree, *The Imperial Drug Trade: a Re-Statement of the Opium Question, in the Light of Recent Evidence and Developments in the East* (London: Methuen, 1905), pp. 265, 286–87; Royal Commission on Opium, vol. 6: *Final Report of the Royal Commission on Opium*, pt. 1, "The Report, with Annexures" (London: HMSO, 1895), p. 55. See *Abkari: The Journal of the Anglo-Indian Temperance Association*, July 1908, pp. 80–81, for further evidence concerning the internal opium trade; and John F. Richards, "The Indian Empire and Peasant Production of Opium in the Nineteenth Century," *Modern Asian Studies* 15 (1981): 59–82, esp. p. 69.

8. *Union Signal*, 2 Nov. 1893, pp. 8–9; WWCTU, *2d Conv., 1893*, p. 115; Jessie Ackermann, "The Situation in India," *Humanity and Health: A Household Magazine* 3 (Jan., Feb. 1894): 16, 69 (copy in Mitchell Library, Sydney).

9. London *Times*, 21 Apr. 1893, p. 3; Royal Commission on Opium, vol. 2: *Minutes of Evidence* (London: HMSO, 1895), p. 3; David E. Owen, *British Opium Policy in China and India* (New Haven: Yale University Press, 1934), chaps. 10–12.

10. BWTA, *AR*, 1904, pp. 73, 102; Virginia Berridge and Griffith Edwards, *Opium and the People: Opiate Use in Nineteenth-Century England* (London: Allen Lane, 1981), pp. 187–88.

11. *Union Signal*, 22 July 1906, p. 3; David F. Musto, *The American Disease: Origins of Narcotic Control* (New Haven: Yale University Press, 1973), pp. 25–28; Owen, *British Opium Policy*, pp. 327–28.

12. Musto, *American Disease*, pp. 24–53.

13. Mac Marshall and Leslie B. Marshall, "Holy and Unholy Spirits: The Effects of Missionization on Alcohol Use in Eastern Micronesia," *Journal of Pacific History* 11 (1976): 135, 148–49.

14. *Union Signal*, 15 Jan. 1891, p. 8.

15. W. T. Hornaday, *Free Rum on the Congo* (Chicago: Woman's Temperance Publishing Co., 1887), pp. 63–65, cited in *Cyclopedia of Temperance and Prohibition* (New York: Funk and Wagnalls, 1891), p. 14; Henry M. Stanley, *The Congo and the Founding of Its Free State: A History of Work and Exploration*, 2 vols. (London: Sampson, Low, Marston, Searle, and Rivington, 1885), 2:254.

16. *SEAP*, 4:1866; *Twentieth Annual Report of the United Committee for the Prevention of the Demoralization of the Native Races by the Liquor Traffic* (Westminster, Eng.: n.p., 1906–7), p. 7, and other reports of the same committee, 1899–1920 (copies in the Library of Congress).

17. Hornaday, *Free Rum*, pp. 7, 115; Hannah Whitall Smith, Preface to *Free Rum*, pp. i–iii; Jane L. McKeever, "The Woman's Temperance Publishing Association," *Library Quarterly* 55 (1985): 380. For further WCTU support of Hornaday's position, see *Union Signal*, 15 Jan. 1891, p. 8; *Canadian Woman's Journal* (Ottawa), Mar. 1890, p. 4; Mattie E. Phillips to Frances Willard, 19 Dec. 1891, roll 17, WCTU Series, OHS.

18. Mary C. Leavitt, *Report of the Hon. Sec. of the World's Woman's Christian Temperance Union* (Boston: n.p., 1891), pp. 26, 38, 52; *SEAP*, 4:1866; *Union Signal*, 2 July 1891, p. 8.

19. *Union Signal*, 15 May 1890, p. 5, and 11 Feb. 1892, p. 4.

20. Willard, *World's WCTU: Aims and Objects*, p. 8.

21. *Cyclopedia of Temperance*, p. 13; *Union Signal*, 14 Mar. 1895, p. 4.

22. Leavitt, *Report, 1891*, p. 22.

23. *Canadian Woman's Journal* (Ottawa), Mar. 1890, p. 4.

24. Marshall and Marshall, "Holy and Unholy Spirits," p. 161. For thoughtful studies stressing the complexity of the relationship between indigenous peoples and alcohol usage, see Thomas W. Hill, "Ethnohistory and Alcohol Studies," in *Recent Developments in Alcoholism*, ed. Marc Galanter (New York: Plenum Pub. Corp., 1984), 2:313–37; and Raymond E. Dumett, "The Social Impact of the European Liquor Trade on the Akan of Ghana (Gold Coast and Asante), 1875–1910," *Journal of Interdisciplinary History* 5 (1974): 69–101.

25. James Paton, ed., *John G. Paton, Missionary to the New Hebrides: An Autobiography*, 2 vols., 4th ed. (London: Hodder and Staughton, 1889–1890), 1:290–91; *Union Signal*, 11 Nov. 1909, p. 6; *SEAP*, 2:754; Robert L. Hardgreave, Jr., *The Nadars of Tamilnad: The Political Culture of a Community in Change* (Berkeley: University of California Press, 1969), pp. 24–26. In Portuguese Mozambique and in other parts of southern, coastal Africa, cashews were used to produce a potent brew. See Leroy Vail and Landeg White, *Capitalism and Colonialism in Mozambique: A Study of Quelimane District* (London: Heinemann, 1980),

p. 127. In China, the Dutch East Indies, and Japan, rice was distilled. WWCTU, *2d Conv., 1893*, p. 202.

26. *Union Signal*, 15 May 1890, p. 8; WWCTU, *1st Conv., 1891*, p. 30.

27. Marshall and Marshall, "Holy and Unholy Spirits," p. 148. The Marshalls' view is criticized by Char Miller, "A Temperate Note on 'Holy and Unholy Spirits,'" *Journal of Pacific History* 14 (1979): 230–32; see also the Marshalls' reply, "Some Sober Reflections on Miller's Temperate Note on 'Holy and Unholy Spirits,'"*Journal of Pacific History* 15 (1980): 232–34. The Marshalls' original article was a straightforward application of the influential work of Joseph Gusfield, *Symbolic Crusade: Status Politics and the American Temperance Movement* (Urbana, Ill.: University of Illinois Press, 1963). For criticisms of the underlying methodology, see Ian Tyrrell, "History and Sociology in *Symbolic Crusade*," *Social History of Alcohol Review*, no. 17 (Spring 1988): 31–37.

28. Petition of Cameroons missionaries in Arthur J. Brown to Elihu Root, 8 Mar. 1907, 721/15, M862, Roll 101, RG 59, Records of the Department of State, National Archives, Washington, D.C.; Marie C. Brehm and Minnie Horning (for the Illinois WCTU) to Theodore Roosevelt, 6 Oct. 1906, and attachments, 721/5, ibid.; *Ecumenical Missionary Conference, New York, 1900*, 2 vols. (New York: American Tract Society, 1900), 1:384; "America's Guilt in the Liquor Traffic," *Union Signal*, 14 Mar. 1895, p. 4; "Drink and Missions," *Canadian Woman's Journal* (Ottawa), Mar. 1890, p. 4. On the more general issue of economic and social "modernization" under missionary and temperance impulses, see also William T. Stead, *The Americanization of the World, or the Trend of the Twentieth Century* (1902; reprint, New York: Garland, 1972), p. 83; *Union Signal*, 7 Feb. 1895, p. 10. The social control version of religious benevolence has long been superseded in favor of a more particular attention to the question of religious ideologies. See Lois Banner, "Religious Benevolence as Social Control: A Critique of an Interpretation," *Journal of American History* 60 (1973): 23–41.

29. W. J. Rorabaugh, *The Alcoholic Republic: An American Tradition* (New York: Oxford University Press, 1979); Ian R. Tyrrell, *Sobering Up: From Temperance to Prohibition in Antebellum America* (Westport, Conn.: Greenwood Press, 1979); Jack S. Blocker, Jr., Introduction to Blocker, ed., *Alcohol, Reform and Society: The Liquor Issue in Social Context* (Westport, Conn.: Greenwood Press, 1979), pp. 6–8; Blocker, *"Give to the Winds Thy Fears": The Women's Temperance Crusade, 1873–1874* (Westport, Conn.: Greenwood Press, 1985), esp. chap. 4; Paton, *John G. Paton*, 1:291.

30. Paton, *John G. Paton*, 1:291.

31. Leavitt, *Report, 1891*, p. 52.

32. Craig MacAndrew and Robert Edgerton, *Drunken Comportment* (London: Nelson, 1969); Mark Lender and James Kirby Martin, *Drinking in America: A History* (New York: Free Press, 1982), pp. 23–24, and their bibliographical entries for evidence on this controversy, p. 202.

33. Charles Ambler, "Drunks, Brewers and Chiefs: The Political Economy of Prohibition in Rural Central Kenya, 1900–1939" (Paper presented at the International Conference on the Social History of Alcohol, Berkeley, Calif., Jan. 1984), pp. 6–7, 16–18.

34. WWCTU, *2d Conv., 1893*, p. 203; *Woman's Signal*, 12 July 1894, p. 24;

Dumett, "Social Impact," pp. 69–101; Frances Hallowes to Rosalind Carlisle, 21 Nov. 1907, p. 3, Castle Howard Archives (J23/271), Castle Howard, Yorkshire. See also *Abkari*, Oct. 1908, p. 134; Apr. 1908, p. 68; and July 1908, p. 95.

35. *British Women's Temperance Journal*, July 1890, p. 82; *Union Signal*, 15 Jan. 1891, p. 8, and 11 Feb. 1892, p. 4; Raymond L. Buell, *The Native Problem in Africa*, 2 vols. (New York: Macmillan, 1928), 2:946; G. P. Hunt, "Spirits of the Colonial Economy" (Paper presented at the International Conference on the Social History of Alcohol, Berkeley, Calif., Jan. 1984), pp. 43–44; Charles Van Onselen, "Randlords and Rotgut, 1886–1903," *History Workshop* 2 (Autumn 1976): 84.

36. *Canadian Woman's Journal*, Mar. 1890, p. 4; *Union Signal*, 21 May 1895, p. 4, and 11 Feb. 1892, p. 4.

37. *Report of the Prohibition Enquiry Committee, 1954–55* (New Delhi: Govt. of India Press, 1955), p. 5; Buell, *Native Problem*, 2:942; *Report of the Committee of Inquiry Regarding the Consumption of Spirits in the Gold Coast* (Accra, 1930), p. 22, in roll 22, WLAA Series, OHS; E. A. Ayandele, *The Missionary Impact on Modern Nigeria, 1842–1914: A Political and Social Analysis* (London: Longman, 1966), pp. 308–9; Dumett, "Social Impact," p. 100.

38. Vail and White, *Capitalism and Colonialism in Mozambique*, pp. 127–28.

39. *Union Signal*, 14 Mar. 1895, p. 4, and 28 Mar. 1912, p. 1.

40. Emiline Hicks to Frances Willard, 29 Nov. 1891; Mary French to Willard, 4 Dec. 1891; Laura G. Pennel to Willard, 7 Dec. 1891; Mattie Phillips to Willard, 19 Dec. 1891; Bertha A. Gerhaugh to Willard, 1 Dec. 1891, all in roll 17, WCTU Series, OHS; McKeever, "Woman's Temperance Publishing Association," p. 380; NWCTU, *AR*, 1891, p. 136.

41. Ruth Bordin, *Woman and Temperance: The Quest for Power and Liberty, 1873–1900* (Philadelphia: Temple University Press, 1981), p. 85; WWCTU, *8th Conv., 1910*, pp. 207–8; Frances Cole to Agnes Slack, 15 Feb. 1911, Castle Howard Archives (J23/265).

42. *SEAP*, 4:1866–67; Wilbur Crafts et al., *Protection of Native Races Against Intoxicants & Opium* (Chicago: Fleming H. Revell, 1900), pp. 30–51; Crafts et al., *Intoxicating Drinks and Drugs in All Lands and Times*, 10th rev. ed. (Washington, D.C.: International Reform Bureau, 1909), pp. 225–26; WWCTU, *8th Conv., 1910*, p. 209.

43. On Ellis, see *Union Signal*, 30 July 1925, p. 7.

44. Ibid., 12 Dec. 1901, p. 5.

45. Ibid., 2 Jan. 1902, p. 1. On Sara Crafts, see ibid., 3 Sept. 1896, p. 12; *White Ribbon Signal* (Sydney), 9 Aug. 1907; on Wilbur Crafts, see R. Johnson, ed., *The Twentieth Century Biographical Dictionary of Notable Americans* (Boston: The Biographical Association, 1902), 3: no page numbers. The Gillett Bill was passed into law in 1902. For a resume, with further information of the connections between Wilbur Crafts and the WCTU, see Crafts to Mary Hunt, 1 Feb. 1902, and enclosures, roll 2, fl. 13, STF Series, OHS.

46. *Union Signal*, 6 Dec. 1906, p. 9.

47. WWCTU, *9th Conv., 1913*, p. 140.

48. Anna Gordon to William Jennings Bryan, 23 Dec. 1913, WWCTU Files; J. B. Moore (Assist. Sec. State) to George W. Buckner (American Legation, Mon-

rovia), 12 Nov. 1913, Decimal File, 682.003/2, Box 6202, RG 59, Records of Dept. of State; Bryan to Buckner, 6 Dec. 1913, and Buckner to Bryan, 22 Dec. 1913, Decimal File, 882.602/3; Buckner to Bryan, 30 Dec. 1914, Decimal File, 882.602/4, Roll 29, M. 613, RG 59, ibid. See also, for earlier temperance missionary interest in Liberia, Charles H. Shepard to Mary H. Hunt, 19 Jan. 1903, Mary Hannah Hanchett Hunt Papers, New York Public Library.

49. Alvey A. Adee (Assist. Sec. of State) to Marie C. Brehm, 15 Oct. 1906, 721/5; Adee memorandum to Bureau of Trade Relations, 22 Jan. 1908, 721/25–26, attached to Mrs. Z. M. Harris to Theodore Roosevelt, 15 Jan. 1908; and quotation from Adee to Root, 5 Oct. 1906, 721/4, M 862, R 101, RG 59, Numerical and Minor Files of the Dept. of State, 1906–10.

50. *SEAP*, 3:1343–44 for summaries; WWCTU, *8th Conv., 1910*, p. 209.

51. *Union Signal*, 18 Oct. 1906, p. 3; *Alliance News*, 10 Nov. 1904, p. 765; WWCTU, *9th Conv., 1913*, pp. 138–40; Agnes E. Slack, *My Travels in India* (National British Women's Temperance Association, 1908).

52. WWCTU, *8th Conv., 1910*, p. 209.

53. Ibid.; Royal Commission on Opium, vol. 6: *Final Report*, pt. 1, p. 55; *Abkari*, Oct. 1905, pp. 62, 133; Report of the Select Committee on East India Finances . . . Great Britain, House of Commons, *Sess. Papers*, 1872, 8:506; *Cyclopedia of Temperance*, p. 242.

54. *Union Signal*, 3 Mar. 1910, p. 2.

55. *Abkari*, Jan. 1905, p. 6.

56. Slack, *My Travels in India*, p. 2; *Abkari*, July 1908, p. 95.

57. *Abkari*, Jan. 1908, p. 11.

58. A similar interpretation was offered by Lucy Carroll, "The Temperance Movement in India: Politics and Social Reform," *Modern Asian Studies* 10 (1976): 417–47. Carroll does not, however, discuss twentieth-century developments or the role of the WCTU.

59. *Union Signal*, 3 Mar. 1910, p. 2.

60. *Abkari*, Apr. 1908, p. 58.

61. The Ceylon temperance movement is extensively reported in *Abkari*. See, for example, Apr. 1905, pp. 49, 76–77; also A. P. Kannagara, "The Riots of 1915 in Sri Lanka: A Study in the Roots of Communal Violence," *Past and Present*, no. 102 (1984): 136–40; *Union Signal*, 3 Mar. 1910, pp. 1–2.

62. Frances Hallowes, *The Enemy: A Study in Heredity* (London: Headley Bros., 1908), rev. in *Abkari*, Oct. 1908, p. 134.

63. Carroll, "Temperance Movement in India."

64. D. O. Fox, "The Women's Christian Temperance Union," in *Abkari*, Apr. 1905, pp. 78–79; on Hauser, see *Canadian Woman's Journal*, Dec. 1893, p. 4; *Union Signal*, 31 Aug. 1893, p. 5, and 5 July 1923, p. 10; WWCTU, *2d Conv., 1893*, p. 165. See also *The Official Report of the 3d Session of the Punjab Temperance Association . . . 1919* (Amritsar, 1919), pp. 21–22, and Bulletin of the Representative Council of Missions, United Provinces, Dec. 1919, pp. 44–45, both in roll 22, folder 35, WLAA Series, OHS; Harris J. Stewart to Ernest H. Cherrington, 7 Nov. 1918, ibid.; Hulda Smith to Cherrington, 5 Nov. 1918, ibid.; Proceedings of the Naini Tal Temperance Conference (1922), ibid.; Mary Campbell, Report to WWCTU, *10th Conv., 1920*, p. 92.

65. *Abkari*, Jan. 1908, p. 8.

66. M. K. Gandhi et al., *Prohibition: The Dawn of a New Era* (Bombay: Prohibition Propaganda Board, 1939), pp. 5, 44. Also, Taraknath Das, "Progress of Prohibition in India"; and Herbert Anderson, "Gandhi and Excise," in Anderson, "Excise Administration in Bengal" [1921] in roll 22, folder 37, WLAA Series, pp. 32–33.

67. Gandhi, *Prohibition*, p. 44.

68. *Union Signal*, 18 Dec. 1919, p. 5.

69. Kenneth Ballhatchet, *Race, Sex and Class under the Raj: Imperial Attitudes and Policies and their Critics, 1793–1905* (London: Macmillan, 1980), pp. 111–16, expresses the missionary contradiction with admirable economy and clarity.

70. Australasian WCTU, *8th Triennial Conv., 1912*, p. 38.

71. *Abkari*, Jan. 1905, p. 6.

72. *Union Signal*, 20 May 1920, p. 7.

73. Jane Clemes to Anna Gordon, 25 May 1920, Castle Howard Archives (J23/264).

74. *Minutes and Reports . . . Sixteenth National Conv. . . . WCTU of India* (Mysore: Wesleyan Press, 1922), pp. 8–9.

75. Taraknath Das, "Progress of Prohibition in India," roll 22, folder 37, WLAA Series, OHS (originally in *Union Signal*, 29 Sept. 1921); *Union Signal*, 22 Mar. 1923, p. 5, and 23 June 1921, p. 11; *California White Ribbon Ensign*, July–Aug. 1940, p. 4, and May 1948, p. 3.

76. Clemes to Gordon, 25 May 1920, and Emma Price to Agnes Slack, 11 May 1920, Castle Howard Archives (J23/265); Carlisle to Slack, 17 June 1920, in Slack, *People I Have Met and Places I Have Seen: Some Memories of Agnes E. Slack* (Bedford, Eng.: Rush and Warwick, 1942), p. 44.

77. *Union Signal*, 1 Sept. 1928, p. 4.

78. Ibid., 1 Sept. 1928, p. 4; 30 Jan. 1932, p. 6; 20 Feb. 1932, pp. 4–5; and 3 Oct. 1931, p. 8.

79. Stead, *Americanization of the World*, p. 83; Ballhatchet, *Race, Sex and Class*, pp. 111–16; *Union Signal*, 30 Jan. 1902, p. 8.

80. Buell, *Native Problem in Africa*, 2:942; Ayandele, *Missionary Impact*, pp. 324–27; Wallace Mills, "The Roots of African Nationalism in the Cape Colony: Temperance, 1866–1898," *International Journal of African Historical Studies* 13 (1980): 197–213. "African nationalism was for Africans what the suffrage movement was for women: both were attempts to acquire equality of political, social and economic rights with those who dominated society. The role of temperance movements in the formative stages of both emancipation movements is too important to be ignored" (Mills, "Roots of African Nationalism," p. 213).

81. *SEAP*, 4:1867; Buell, *Native Problem in Africa*, 2:948–49; Alexander Blackburn, "Recent Facts Concerning the Alcohol Traffic in the Colonies," *Compte-Rendu du XVIIe Congrès Internationale Contre L'Alcoolisme . . . 1923* (Copenhagen: The Committee of the International Congress, 1924), pp. 199, 201.

82. See Buell, *Native Problem in Africa*, 2:950–53, for the text of the 1919 agreement; Arthur Burns, *History of Nigeria*, 6th ed. (London: Allen and Unwin, 1959), pp. 238–40, stresses its limitations; Blackburn, "Recent Facts," pp.

200–201; Report by Mary E. Tudor, WWCTU, *10th Conv., 1920*, pp. 137–39.

83. *White Ribbon*, June 1913, p. 81; BWTA, *AR*, 1913, p. 87.

Chapter 8

1. C. Roland Marchand, *The American Peace Movement and Social Reform, 1898–1919* (Princeton: Princeton University Press, 1972), p. 186n.

2. Hannah Clark Bailey, "Origins of the Peace Department of the W.C.T.U.," [1893], pp. 1–2, roll 1, box 1, fl. 3; Bailey, "Woman's Place in the Peace Reform," [1907], p. 5, roll 1, fl. 3; Nina Anderson to Bailey, 30 Jan. 1918, roll 1, box 1, fl. 2; *Eighth Report of the Superintendent of the Department of Peace and Arbitration for the World's WCTU* (Glasgow, 1910), pp. 2–17, roll 2, box 2, fl. 2, all in Hannah Johnston Bailey Papers, Swarthmore College, Swarthmore, Pa.

3. Frank L. Byrne, "Hannah Clark Johnston Bailey," *NAW*, 1:84.

4. Bailey, "Origins of the Peace Dept.," pp. 1–6.

5. Byrne, "Bailey," pp. 84–85.

6. See the biographical material in roll 3, box 4, fl. 1, Bailey Papers.

7. Hannah Clark Bailey, "Peace the Policy of Nations," p. 1, roll 1, box 1, fl. 3, ibid.

8. Bailey, "Woman's Place in the Peace Reform," [1907], p. 5.

9. Hannah Clark Bailey, "Woman's Power to Maintain or to Stop War," p. 8, roll 1, box 1, fl. 8, Bailey Papers.

10. Hannah Clark Bailey, "Peace and Arbitration in the WCTU," c.1902, roll 2, box 2, fl. 2, ibid.; NWCTU, *AR*, 1896, p. 401.

11. Bailey to World's WCTU Superintendents, 5 Jan. 1916, roll 1, box 1, fl. 2, Bailey Papers.

12. "Woman's Power to Maintain or to Stop War," p. 7.

13. *Union Signal*, 12 Mar. 1925, p. 7. For statements of the maternalist thesis, see also Frances Hallowes, *Mothers of Men and Militarism* (London: Headley Bros., n.d.); and Hallowes circular, c.1919, Castle Howard Archives (J23/271), Castle Howard, Yorkshire; Rebecca Sherrick, "Toward Universal Sisterhood," *Women's Studies International Forum* 5 (no. 6, 1982): 657; Jill Conway, "Stereotypes of Femininity in a Theory of Sexual Evolution," *Victorian Studies* 14 (1970): 47–62, esp. pp. 58–59; Allen F. Davis, *American Heroine: The Life and Legend of Jane Addams* (New York: Oxford University Press, 1973), pp. 232–33. Critical of this approach, particularly Conway's depiction of Jane Addams, is Linda Schott, "The Woman's Peace Party and the Moral Basis for Pacifism," *Frontiers* 8 (no. 2, 1985): 22. What follows lends indirect support to Schott's thesis but does not concern Jane Addams, who was not a WCTU supporter.

14. Bailey, "Woman's Power to Maintain or to Stop War," pp. 3, 4, 6.

15. Bailey, "Woman's Place in the Peace Reform," p. 1.

16. Frances Willard, *Glimpses of Fifty Years* (Chicago: WTPA, 1889), p. 610; on the stages theory as it applied to women in classical political economy, see Sylvana Tomaselli, "The Enlightenment Debate on Women," *History Workshop*, no. 20 (Autumn 1985): 101–24.

17. Willard, *Glimpses*, pp. 606, 610, 611, quotation from p. 612.

18. Ibid., p. 606.

19. Quoted in Calvin D. Davis, *The United States and the First Hague Peace Conference* (Ithaca: Cornell University Press, 1962), p. 12.

20. NWCTU, *AR*, 1894, p. 117.

21. Barbara Leslie Epstein, *The Politics of Domesticity: Women, Evangelism, and Temperance in Nineteenth-Century America* (Middletown, Conn.: Wesleyan University Press, 1981), pp. 116, 128.

22. Bailey to unnamed correspondent, 7 Apr. 1905, roll 1, box 1, fl. 2, Bailey Papers.

23. NWCTU, *AR*, 1912, pp. 365, 367; *The Acorn*, 1, no. 1 (July 1889): 1, and 12, no. 12 (May 1901): 1. Another paper for adults, the *Pacific Banner*, was published by Bailey between 1890 and 1895 but apparently no copies have survived, and I have followed its fortunes only in the pages of *The Acorn* in the Swarthmore College Peace Collection.

24. Benjamin F. Austin, *The Prohibition Leaders of America* (St. Thomas, Ont.: n.p., 1895), p. 55.

25. Mary F. Lovell to Frances Willard, 9 Apr. 1896, roll 24, WCTU Series, OHS. On Lovell's role in the Mercy and Peace work, see *SEAP*, 5:1609–10; Mary Earhart, *Frances Willard: From Prayers to Politics* (Chicago: University of Chicago Press, 1944), p. 345.

26. Bailey, "Woman's Place in the Peace Reform," p. 5.

27. Lucia Ames Mead to Bailey, [Sept. 1913], roll 1, box 1, fl. 2, Bailey Papers.

28. Eleanor Karsten to Bailey, 3 Feb. 1920, and Lucia Ames Mead to Bailey, 9 Sept. 1915, ibid.

29. David S. Patterson, *Toward a Warless World: The Travail of the American Peace Movement, 1887–1914* (Bloomington, Ind.: Indiana University Press, 1976), p. 26; NWCTU, *AR*, 1890, p. 384; Anna Thomas to Bailey, 22 Apr. 1889, roll 1, box 1, fl. 2, Bailey Papers.

30. Benjamin Trueblood to Bailey, 28 Dec. 1893, roll 1, box 1, fl. 2, Bailey Papers.

31. Bailey to Woodrow Wilson, c.1916; Frederick Hale to Bailey, 15, 16 Sept. 1919; undated letter to co-workers, c.1897, all in ibid.

32. Patterson, *Toward a Warless World*, p. 106.

33. Calvin Davis, *United States and the First Hague Peace Conference*, pp. 101–2, 198; Bailey to Caroline Severance, 21 Mar., 15 Apr. 1899, box 14, Caroline Severance Papers, Huntington Library, San Marino, Calif.; Frederick Hale to Bailey, 16 Sept. 1919, roll 1, box 1, fl. 2, Bailey Papers.

34. Hannah Clark Bailey, "How Woman's Ballot Can Help the Peace Department," [c.1910], p. 5, roll 1, box 1, fl. 8, Bailey Papers.

35. Ibid.

36. *Union Signal*, 12 Mar. 1925, p. 7; Alice Kercher, "Women and Peace," pp. 1–2, pamphlet in roll 1, box 1, fl. 9, Bailey Papers.

37. Patterson, *Toward a Warless World*, has the best coverage of the context of American peace agitation within which Bailey and the WCTU operated.

38. NWCTU, *AR*, 1894, p. 117; cf. Earhart, *Willard*, p. 254.

39. Draft Peace and Arbitration Report, 1909, p. 3, roll 2, box 2, fl. 1, Bailey Papers.

40. Biographical clippings in roll 3, box 4, fl. 1, Bailey Papers. That Moses

and Hannah Bailey shared this ideological stance is clear from Hannah Clark Bailey, *Reminiscences of a Christian Life* (Portland, Me.: Hoyt, Fogg and Donham, 1884), pp. 240, 243.

41. NWCTU, *AR*, 1909, p. 243.

42. Ibid.

43. Ibid.; Executive minutes, 5 Sept. 1914, p. 108, and 5 May 1915, p. 124, WCTU of Southern California, WCTU of Southern California Headquarters, Los Angeles.

44. Mary Alderman Garbutt, *Victories of Four Decades: A History of the Woman's Christian Temperance Union of Southern California, 1883–1924* (Los Angeles: Southern California WCTU, 1924), p. 105.

45. Hannah Clark Bailey, "Department of International Peace and Arbitration," Report, 1913, pp. 6–7, roll 2, box 2, fl. 2; and "The Purpose of Panama Peace Statue," pp. 1–3, roll 1, box 1, fl. 6, Bailey Papers.

46. WWCTU, *1st Conv., 1891*, pp. 55–59; "Twentieth Annual Report of the Department of Peace and Arbitration," [1907], roll 2, box 2, fl. 1, Bailey Papers.

47. "Peace and Arbitration in the WCTU," p. 4, roll 2, box 2, fl. 1, Bailey Papers; NWCTU, *AR*, 1900, p. 343.

48. "Internationalism," p. 4, roll 1, box 1, fl. 3, Bailey Papers.

49. *Union Signal*, 2 Nov. 1899, p. 8.

50. Bailey, "How Woman's Ballot Can Help the Peace Department," p. 9.

51. WWCTU, *1st Conv., 1891*, p. 58.

52. The WCTU's Indian reform activities have not been closely studied. But see Frances Willard, *Woman and Temperance, or, the Work and Workers of the Woman's Christian Temperance Union* (Hartford, Conn.: Park Pub. Co., 1883), pp. 504–10; Irene Westing, "Amelia Stone Quinton," *NAW*, 3:108.

53. *Union Signal*, 1 Dec. 1887, p. 7.

54. Bailey, "Woman's Place in the Peace Reform," pp. 1, 5; Willard, *Glimpses*, pp. 603, 608–9, 610–11; *Union Signal*, 21 Jan. 1892, p. 1; WWCTU, *4th Conv., 1897*, p. 28. For the context of this ideology, see, esp., Tomaselli, "Enlightenment Debate on Women."

55. WWCTU, *1st Conv., 1891*, p. 55.

56. Ibid., p. 59; Frances Willard, *The World's Woman's Christian Temperance Union: Aims and Objects* (Uxbridge, Eng.: Hutchings, [c.1892–93]), p. 3.

57. NWCTU, *AR*, 1896, p. 399.

58. *Union Signal*, 21 May 1896, p. 10.

59. Australasian WCTU, *8th Triennial Conv., 1912*, p. 38.

60. Hannah Whitall Smith to "My Beloved Friends and Family," letters no. 108:4 (17 Sept. 1897) and 111:4 (16 Apr. 1898), box 2, Hannah Whitall Smith Papers, Lilly Library, Indiana University, Bloomington, Ind.

61. NWCTU, *AR*, 1900, p. 342; *Canadian Woman's Journal* (Ottawa), 1 June 1900, p. 1.

62. *Canadian Woman's Journal*, 15 May 1900, p. 10, and 1 June 1900, p. 6; Barbara Buchanan to Anna Gordon, 4 July 1910, and Gordon to Rosalind Carlisle, 18 Aug. 1910, Castle Howard Archives (J23/264).

63. *Canadian Woman's Journal*, 1 June 1900, p. 6.

64. *Union Signal*, 28 Apr. 1898, p. 9.

65. Ibid., 19 Oct. 1899, p. 6.

66. "To the President of the United States," undated petition from Colorado WCTU, in roll 2, box 2, fl. 5, Bailey Papers; Luella McWhirter and Mary E. Balch to William McKinley, 189[9], box 4, Luella (Mrs. F. T.) McWhirter manuscripts, Lilly Library, Indiana University, Bloomington, Ind.

67. *Union Signal*, 8 Mar. 1900, p. 8; 20 Feb. 1902, p. 1.

68. "To the President of the United States."

69. See Chapters 7 and 9, where these issues of the antiimperial implications of purity agitation and the WCTU-nationalist connection are pursued in appropriate detail.

70. *Union Signal*, 8 Mar. 1900, p. 9. For the wider context of reform, missions, and American imperialism the best studies are Richard E. Welch, Jr., *Response to Imperialism: The United States and the Philippine-American War* (Chapel Hill: University of North Carolina Press, 1979), esp. p. 100; Kenton J. Clymer, "Religion and American Imperialism: Methodist Missionaries in the Philippine Islands, 1899–1913," *Pacific Historical Review* 49 (1980): 29–50. Neither of these studies considers the WCTU's involvement, and even the book-length version of the latter is devoid of significant material on women's perspectives on the question of imperialism. See Kenton J. Clymer, *Protestant Missionaries in the Philippines, 1898–1916: An Inquiry into the American Colonial Mentality* (Urbana, Ill.: University of Illinois Press, 1986).

71. Hannah Bailey, "Peace and Arbitration," pp. 23, 24, in draft report, c.1902, roll 1, box 1, fl. 3, Bailey Papers.

72. See Allen Davis, *American Heroine*, p. 141; Robert L. Beisner, *Twelve against Empire: The Anti-Imperialists, 1898–1900* (New York: McGraw-Hill, 1968), p. 219; Christopher Lasch, "The Anti-Imperialists, the Philippines, and the Inequality of Man," *Journal of Southern History* 24 (1958): 319–31.

73. This point is extensively documented in Scrapbook 13, WCTU Files; I have pursued the lynching question as an aspect of international influences briefly in Ian Tyrrell, "Women and Temperance in International Perspective: The World's WCTU, 1880s–1920s," (Paper presented at the International Conference on the Social History of Alcohol, Berkeley, Calif., 4 Jan. 1984), pp. 18–19. See also, Ruth Bordin, *Frances Willard: A Biography* (Chapel Hill: University of North Carolina Press, 1986), pp. 216–18, 221–22.

74. Bordin, *Willard*, pp. 216–18, 221–22; Alice May Douglas, "Lynching," roll 1, box 1, fl. 6, Bailey Papers.

75. Bailey, "Peace and Arbitration," pp. 23–24.

76. *Union Signal*, 22 May 1902, p. 8.

77. Ruth Bordin, *Woman and Temperance: The Quest for Power and Liberty, 1873–1900* (Philadelphia: Temple University Press, 1981), p. 155.

78. Elizabeth Andrew to Frances Willard, 1 Apr. 1893; Mary Kraut to Willard, 8 Apr. 1893, roll 19; and Frances Willard to Mary Whitney, 14 July 1897, roll 24, WCTU Series, OHS; *Union Signal*, 16 Feb. 1893, p. 8; see Hannah Whitall Smith to "My Beloved Friends and Family," 111:4 (16 Apr. 1898), box 2, Smith Papers, for further pro-annexationist sentiment; cf. Bordin, *Woman and Temperance*, p. 155.

79. Bailey, "Department of International Peace and Arbitration," pp. 1–2;

Union Signal, 27 Nov. 1913, pp. 6, 14; see also, *Canadian White Ribbon Tidings*, 1 July 1911, p. 1950.

80. WCTU of New South Wales, *AR*, 1916, p. 27; also see Anna Gordon to Rosalind Carlisle, 27 Aug. 1914, Castle Howard Archives (J23/264).

81. Rosalind Carlisle, in BWTA, *AR*, cited in *White Ribbon*, June 1915, p. 87.

82. Bessie Harrison Lee Cowie to Bailey, 22 Oct. 1914, roll 1, box 1, fl. 3, Bailey Papers.

83. *Union Signal*, 3 July 1902, p. 8.

84. Ibid., 30 Jan. 1902, p. 8; William T. Stead, *The Americanization of the World, or the Trend of the Twentieth Century* (1902; reprint, New York: Garland, 1972).

85. *Union Signal*, 12 Apr. 1917, p. 8.

86. Quoted in Ibid.

87. Cf. Byrne, "Bailey," p. 84.

88. WCTU of Southern California, Convention Minutes, 24 May 1917, p. 168, WCTU of Southern California manuscripts, WCTU of Southern California Headquarters.

89. *California White Ribbon Ensign*, Sept. 1934, p. 7.

90. Charles Debeneditti, "Alternative Strategies in the American Peace Movement in the 1920's," in Charles Chatfield, ed., *Peace Movements in America* (New York: Schocken Books, 1973), pp. 57–67.

91. For the international legal position and agitation, see G. Evelyn Gates, ed., *The Woman's Year Book, 1923–1924*, 2d ed. (London: Women Publishers, 1924), pp. 141–42; WWCTU, *13th Conv., 1928*, p. 51. On Australian WCTU attitudes and government policy, see *White Ribbon Signal* (Sydney), 12 Apr. 1924, p. 2; 12 Feb. 1926, p. 4; and 1 Sept. 1932, p. 166.

92. *Union Signal*, 22 Dec. 1921, p. 4, and 17 Nov. 1921, p. 2.

93. Ibid., 8 Dec. 1921, pp. 1–2.

94. NWCTU, *AR*, 1932, p. 89.

95. WCTU of South Australia, *AR*, 1916, p. 20.

Chapter 9

1. Katharine Bushnell and Elizabeth Wheeler Andrew, *A Fatal Mistake* (n.p., 1897), p. 3.

2. Ruth Rosen, *The Lost Sisterhood: Prostitution in America, 1900–1918* (Baltimore: Johns Hopkins University Press, 1982), p. 52; *Daily Transcript* (Moncton, N.B.), 4 June 1890, Scrapbook 47, WCTU Files.

3. Davis, in *Union Signal*, 30 June 1892, pp. 4–5; Frances Willard, *Glimpses of Fifty Years* (Chicago: WTPA, 1889), p. 418; Amelia Yeomans, in *Toronto Globe*, 27 Oct. 1897, in Scrapbook 76, WCTU Files.

4. NWCTU, *AR*, 1893, p. 88.

5. Phillida Bunkle, "The Origins of the Women's Movement in New Zealand: The Women's Christian Temperance Union, 1885–1895," in Beryl Hughes and Phillida Bunkle, eds., *Women in New Zealand Society* (Sydney and Auckland: Allen and Unwin, 1980), p. 74.

6. David Pivar, *Purity Crusade: Sexual Morality and Social Control, 1868–1900* (Westport, Conn.: Greenwood Press, 1973), pp. 132–35; Rosen, *Lost Sisterhood,* pp. 10, 15; Mark Connelly, *The Response to Prostitution in the Progressive Era* (Chapel Hill: University of North Carolina Press, 1980), pp. 81, 82, 86; cf. Ruth Bordin, *Woman and Temperance: The Quest for Power and Liberty, 1873–1900* (Philadelphia: Temple University Press, 1981), p. 110; Barbara Leslie Epstein, *The Politics of Domesticity: Women, Evangelism, and Temperance in Nineteenth-Century America* (Middletown, Conn.: Wesleyan University Press, 1981), p. 125.

7. Judith Walkowitz, *Prostitution and Victorian Society: Women, Class, and the State* (Cambridge, Eng.: Cambridge University Press, 1980), pp. 246–47; Pivar, *Purity Crusade,* pp. 132–33.

8. NWCTU, *AR,* 1886, p. 52.

9. Walkowitz, *Prostitution and Victorian Society,* pp. 1–9.

10. WWCTU, *2d Conv., 1893,* p. 51.

11. *Union Signal,* 17 Feb. 1887, pp. 8–9.

12. NWCTU, *AR,* 1888, pp. 141–42.

13. See, for example, for Japan, *Canadian Woman's Journal* (Ottawa), July 1899, p. 8 (Eliza Large); *Union Signal,* 21 Aug. 1924, p. 5 (Kaji Yajima); for Hawaii, see *The Shield* (London), Aug. 1901, p. 60 (Ackermann); the Philippines, *Union Signal,* 14 May 1903, p. 5 (Carrie Faxon); South African WCTU, Julia Solly to Fanny Forsaith, 15 Oct. 1894, Josephine Butler Papers, Fawcett Library, City of London Polytechnic; Hong Kong, see WWCTU, *3d Conv., 1895,* pp. 182–83.

14. Pivar, *Purity Crusade,* p. 138.

15. WWCTU, *2d Conv., 1893,* p. 51.

16. John C. Burnham, "Medical Inspection of Prostitutes in America in the Nineteenth Century: The St. Louis Experiment and Its Sequel," *Bulletin of the History of Medicine* 45 (1971): 203–18.

17. Abraham Flexner, *Prostitution in Europe* (1914; reprint, Montclair, N.J.: Patterson Smith, 1969); Connelly, *Response to Prostitution,* pp. 81–86; Willard, *Glimpses,* p. 422. Willard's own abhorrence of licensed prostitution went back as far as the time of her European tour. See Diary, 8 Feb. 1869, roll 3, WCTU Series, 1982 suppl., Michigan Historical Collections, Bentley Library, University of Michigan, Ann Arbor.

18. John C. Burnham, "The Progressive Era Revolution in American Attitudes towards Sex," *Journal of American History* 59 (1973): 885–908; Jane Lewis, *Women in England, 1870–1950: Sexual Divisions and Social Change* (Bloomington, Ind.: Indiana University Press, 1984), pp. 132–33; Connelly, *Response to Prostitution,* chap. 4, esp. p. 70; E. M. Sigsworth and T. J. Wyke, "A Study of Victorian Prostitution and Venereal Disease," in Martha Vicinus, ed., *Suffer and Be Still: Women in the Victorian Age* (Bloomington, Ind.: Indiana University Press, 1972), pp. 86–87.

19. WWCTU, *4th Conv., 1897,* p. 28; Willard, *Glimpses,* p. 422.

20. WWCTU, *4th Conv., 1897,* p. 28.

21. Clipping from *The Dawn,* p. 12, in Scrapbook 64, p. 41, WCTU Files.

22. NWCTU, *AR,* 1893, p. 76.

23. See, for example, *Union Signal*, 20 Nov. 1890, p. 4; Frances Willard and Mary Livermore, eds., *A Woman of the Century* (Buffalo: Charles Wells Mouton, 1893), p. 141; *California White Ribbon Ensign*, Mar. 1946, p. 7.

24. Elizabeth Wheeler Andrew (1845–1917) is scantily treated in the biographical sources, though her many letters appear in unpublished papers; see the brief sketch in *Thumb-Nail Sketches of White Ribboners* (Chicago: WTPA, 1892), p. 31.

25. Butler to Margaret Tanner and Mary Priestman, 9 Mar. 1891, Butler Papers.

26. Matilda Gage, *Woman, Church and State* (New York: The Truth Seeker Co., 1893), p. 184; *Some Facts, with Regard to State Regulation of Vice in India, in England, and in the Continent of Europe* (London: Friends' Association for Abolishing State Regulation of Vice, 1897), pp. 3–26; and Katharine Bushnell and Elizabeth Wheeler Andrew, *The Queen's Daughters in India*, 3d ed. (London: Morgan and Scott, 1899), for the narrative that follows; also, see Kenneth Ballhatchet, *Race, Sex and Class under the Raj: Imperial Attitudes and Policies and Their Critics, 1793–1905* (London: Macmillan, 1980), p. 58.

27. Ballhatchet, *Race, Sex and Class*, p. 62.

28. Ibid., p. 69; William T. Stead, *The Americanization of the World, or the Trend of the Twentieth Century* (1902; reprint, New York: Garland, 1972), p. 83.

29. Scrapbook 64, p. 41, WCTU Files.

30. *Union Signal*, 11 May 1893, p. 3.

31. Ibid.

32. Ibid.; Ballhatchet, *Race, Sex and Class*, p. 164.

33. Ballhatchet, *Race, Sex and Class*, p. 66. This point was taken up by Willard in her 1897 World's Presidential Address. See WWCTU, *4th Conv., 1897*, p. 29.

34. Bushnell and Andrew, *Queen's Daughters*, p. 87; Elizabeth B. Van Heyningen, "The Social Evil in the Cape Colony, 1868–1902: Prostitution and the Contagious Diseases Acts," *Journal of Southern African Studies* 10 (1984): 173.

35. Van Heyningen, "Social Evil," p. 188; *Union Signal*, 23 Mar. 1893, p. 10; "Dr. Kate C. Bushnell and Mrs. Andrew, M.A.," *New Zealand Prohibitionist*, [c. 27 Oct–10 Nov. 1892], p. 8, New Zealand WCTU Series, microfiche edition, Massey University, Palmerston, New Zealand.

36. *Union Signal*, 11 May 1893, p. 3.

37. Ibid.

38. Bushnell and Andrew, *Queen's Daughters*, p. 91; Ballhatchet, *Race, Sex and Class*, pp. 77–78.

39. Quoted in WWCTU, *3d Conv., 1895*, p. 183.

40. NWCTU, *AR*, 1893, p. 89.

41. Butler to Fanny Forsaith, 22 May 1897, and 11 July 1895, Butler Papers.

42. Butler to "Dear Friends," 2 Oct. 1893; also see Butler to Mary Priestman, 6 Nov. 1893, Butler Papers.

43. Butler to Fanny Forsaith, 8 Apr. 1894, Butler Papers.

44. E. Moberly Bell, *Josephine Butler, Flame of Fire* (London: Constable, 1962), p. 234; Butler to Fanny Forsaith, 8 Apr. 1894, Butler Papers.

45. Butler to Forsaith, 8 Apr. 1894, Butler Papers. On the European connec-

tion, see also Butler to Mary Priestman and Margaret Tanner, 27 June 1894, ibid.

46. Josephine Butler, *Sursum Corda: An Address* (London: WWCTU, 1892), pp. 6–9.

47. Frances Willard, in NWCTU, *AR*, 1897, pp. 106–7; Butler to Helen Clark, 6 May 1895, and to "Dear Friends," 4 Apr. and 3 May 1895, Butler Papers.

48. *Some Facts*, pp. 3–26.

49. Kathleen Fitzpatrick, *Lady Henry Somerset* (London: Jonathan Cape; Boston: Little, Brown, 1923), p. 177.

50. London *Times*, 21 Apr. 1897, p. 10; Ballhatchet, *Race, Sex and Class*, p. 92.

51. Bushnell and Andrew, *A Fatal Mistake*, p. 7, summarizes the Somerset proposals (copy in Scrapbook 76, WCTU Files). See also Fitzpatrick, *Somerset*, pp. 178–80.

52. London *Times*, 21 Apr. 1897, p. 10; Somerset, quoted in Fitzpatrick, *Somerset*, pp. 178–79.

53. Bushnell and Andrew, *A Fatal Mistake*, p. 8.

54. Ibid., pp. 14, 15.

55. Bushnell and Andrew, letter to WWCTU General Officers, 30 Aug. 1897, Scrapbook 76, WCTU Files; Andrew and Bushnell to Willard, 15 June 1896, in roll 1, fl. 5, STF Series, OHS.

56. Butler to Willard, 29 Nov. 1897, Butler Papers.

57. Mary C. Leavitt, "An Open Letter," 22 Sept. 1897, roll 24, WCTU Series; [repr. in *Toronto Globe*, 23 Oct. 1897, in Scrapbook 76, WCTU Files].

58. *Union Signal*, 22 Oct. 1891, p. 10.

59. Mary C. Leavitt, *Report of the Hon. Sec. of the World's Woman's Christian Temperance Union* (Boston: n.p., 1891), p. 62.

60. Josephine Butler to William Clark, 30 Nov. 1897, and to the Misses Priestman, 12 Oct. 1897, Butler Papers; Walkowitz, *Prostitution and Victorian Society*, p. 115.

61. NWCTU, *AR*, 1897, p. 107.

62. Butler to Willard, 29 Nov. 1897; also Butler to "Dear Friends," 2 Oct. 1895, Butler Papers.

63. Epstein, *Politics of Domesticity*, pp. 144–45; Bordin, *Woman and Temperance*, pp. 144–45, 208, 209; see also Mary Earhart, *Frances Willard: From Prayers to Politics* (Chicago: University of Chicago Press, 1944), p. 363, for a broader view.

64. See *Chicago Inter-Ocean*, 27 Oct. 1897, in Scrapbook 76, WCTU Files, for further evidence from Mrs. L. L. Rounds and Marion H. Dunham.

65. WWCTU, *4th Conv., 1897*, p. 90.

66. *Toronto Globe*, 27 Oct. 1897, in Scrapbook 76, WCTU Files, statement by Mrs. Amelia Yeomans. On Yeomans, see Catherine L. Cleverdon, *The Woman Suffrage Movement in Canada*, 2d ed. (Toronto: University of Toronto Press, 1974), pp. 50–52; *White Ribbon*, Aug. 1913, p. 122.

67. Clipping from *London Daily News*, 9 Sept. 1897; *Chicago Record*, 19 Oct. 1897; and *Daily Mail and Empire*, 30 Oct. 1897, all in Scrapbook 76, WCTU files; "An English Girl" to Willard, 9 Jan. 1898, roll 25, WCTU Series, OHS.

68. Hannah Whitall Smith to "My Dear Friend" [Mrs. Annie Harvey], 10 Aug. 1897, Autograph Collection, Fawcett Library, City of London Polytechnic.
69. For Canadian opposition, see "Tail of W.C.T.U. Can't Wag Dog," newspaper clipping of 4 Feb. 1898, in Scrapbook 76, WCTU Files; Mary E. Sanderson to Willard, 19 Jan. 1898, roll 25, WCTU Series, OHS; Maggie Cole to Josephine Butler, 2 Nov. 1897, Butler Papers. For New Zealand, see letters to Josephine Butler from Mrs. Emily Kelsey, 7 Sept. 1897; Mrs. S. J. Thirsk, 11 Oct. 1897; Annie E. Tucker, 12 Oct. 1897; Mrs. J. Soulsby, 14 Oct. 1897; Mary McCarthy, 21 Oct. 1897; and many others, all in the Butler Papers. For South Africa, see Janie Harvey to Butler, 28 July 1898, Butler Papers; and Julia Solly, in *The Shield*, June 1897, p. 13.
70. Jessie Rooke to Butler, 26 Aug. 1897, Butler Papers.
71. Marie Kirk to Butler, 2 Aug. 1898, ibid.
72. Letter to Josephine Butler from Australasian WCTU Executive, Sept. 1897, *The Shield*, Mar. 1898, p. 91; Elizabeth Andrew to "My Very Dear Friend" [Fanny Forsaith], 21 Dec. 1897, Butler Papers.
73. *Woman's Signal*, 17 Feb. 1898, clipping in Scrapbook 79, WCTU Files; on the impact on the continent of Europe, see Butler, "Open Letter," 30 May 1897, and Butler to Fanny Forsaith, 1 June 1897, Butler Papers; *The Shield*, Mar. 1898, pp. 91–92, and June 1898, p. 117.
74. "Tail of W.C.T.U. Can't Wag Dog"; "Confidential Relating to the Action of Lady Henry Somerset," Sept. 24, 1897, in Scrapbook 76, WCTU Files.
75. Fitzpatrick, *Somerset*, pp. 183–84.
76. Fry to Willard, 24, 26 Jan. 1898, and Lillian Stevens to Willard, 21 Jan. 1898, roll 25, WCTU Series, OHS; Fitzpatrick, *Somerset*, pp. 183–84.
77. Katharine Lent Stevenson to Willard, 27 Jan. 1898, roll 25, WCTU Series, OHS.
78. Mary Sanderson to Willard, 25 Jan. 1898, ibid.
79. Lydia F. Willson to Suzannah Fry, 31 Jan. 1898, ibid.
80. Fry to Willard, 24, 26 Jan. 1898, ibid.
81. Fitzpatrick, *Somerset*, p. 184; *The Shield*, Mar. 1898, p. 90; also, Andrew to Forsaith, 25 Feb., 1, 30 Mar., 27 June 1898; Butler to Forsaith, 16, 18 Feb., c.24 Feb. 1898; Bushnell to Butler, 22 Feb. 1898; and Bushnell to Forsaith, 21 Feb. 1898, all in Butler Papers.
82. Walkowitz, *Prostitution and Victorian Society*, pp. 251–52; see Ellen DuBois and Linda Gordon, "Seeking Ecstasy on the Battlefield: Danger and Pleasure in Nineteenth-Century Feminist Sexual Thought," *Feminist Studies* 9 (Spring 1983): 7–25, for a review of this theme; Epstein, *Politics of Domesticity*, p. 136; Rosen, *Lost Sisterhood*, pp. 1–13; Pivar, *Purity Crusade*. My argument on the contradictions of social purity is confirmed by Frank Mort, *Dangerous Sexualities: Medicomoral Politics in England since 1830* (London: Routledge and Kegan Paul, 1987). See esp. his remarks on Ellice Hopkins, who was active in the BWTA (pp. 117–26).
83. London *Times*, 26 Oct. 1897, p. 5, and 28 Oct. 1897, p. 5.
84. *The Shield*, Dec. 1897, p. 59; on Frederic, see *Woman's Signal*, 16 Dec. 1897, p. 390; Josephine Butler to James Stansfield, 24 Nov. 1897, Butler Papers; the

division in the WCTU was also exploited in the House of Lords to the benefit of the regulationist cause. See Bushnell and Andrew, *Queen's Daughters*, p. 108.

85. Ballhatchet, *Race, Sex and Class*, p. 92.

86. On Bushnell's disillusionment with the denouement of the purity crusade, see Bushnell to Anne K. Martin, 6 Jan., 2 Sept. 1943, Anne K. Martin Papers, Bancroft Library, University of California, Berkeley.

87. Ronald Hyam, "Empire and Sexual Opportunity," *Journal of Imperial and Commonwealth History* 14 (no. 2, 1986): 54; also see Pivar, *Purity Crusade*, pp. 219–26, for a perceptive discussion of the imperialism-"vice" connection.

88. Elizabeth Wheeler Andrew to Frances Willard, 1 Apr. 1893, roll 19, WCTU Series, OHS; *Union Signal*, 16 Feb. 1893, p. 8.

89. Elizabeth W. Andrew to Henry Wilson, 3 July 1900, Butler Papers.

90. Willard to Mary Whitney, 14 July 1897, roll 24, WCTU Series, OHS.

91. Reported in *The Shield*, June 1899, p. 38. See also the report on Jessie Ackermann's campaign in Hawaii in "The New Imperialism," ibid., Aug. 1901, p. 78.

92. Ibid., Aug. 1901, p. 60, Nov. 1901, p. 78.

93. This and succeeding paragraphs come, except where otherwise indicated, from "A Review of the Philippine Order," *Union Signal*, 1 May 1902, p. 6.

94. Ibid.

95. Ballhatchet, *Race, Sex and Class*, p. 160.

96. The WCTU was correct in its more general point that regulation had not, over a long period, proved efficacious from a medical perspective. See ibid., pp. 94–95, 161–62; *Union Signal*, 1 May 1902, p. 6.

97. *Union Signal*, 1 May 1902, p. 6; 28 Nov. 1902, pp. 10–11; 7 Nov. 1901, p. 3.

98. Ibid., 24 Apr. 1902, p. 8; *The Shield*, July 1902, p. 40.

99. *Union Signal*, 3 Apr. 1902, p. 5.

100. Ibid., 27 Mar. 1902, p. 9, and 10 Apr. 1902, pp. 1, 9.

101. *The Shield*, July 1902, p. 40; *Union Signal*, 1 May 1898, p. 6.

102. Margaret Ellis to Clarence Edwards, 29 Mar. 1902 (2045/27), Entry 5, RG 350, Bureau of Insular Affairs Records, National Archives.

103. George Cortelyou to Root, 21 Mar. 1902 (2045/26); Cortelyou to Root, 6 Feb. 1902 (2039/17), and 4 Apr. 1902 (2039/21); Assistant Sect. of War Cary Langer to Cortelyou, 4 Mar. 1902 (2039/22), all in ibid.

104. Clarence Edwards to Margaret Ellis, 3 Apr. 1902 (2039/18), ibid.

105. J. T. Ellis to Edwards, n.d., and clipping from the *Philadelphia Press*, [25 Mar. 1902] (2039/17), ibid.

106. Elihu Root to Acting Governor of the Philippines, 18 Feb. 1902 (2039/18½); see also David Pivar, "The Military, Prostitution, and Colonial Peoples: India and the Philippines, 1885–1917," *Journal of Sex Research* 17 (1981): 256–69, esp. p. 263.

107. On the position in India after 1898, see Frances Hallowes to Rosalind Carlisle, 30 Nov. 1906, and 31 Jan. 1908, Castle Howard Archives (J23/271), Castle Howard, Yorkshire; *Union Signal*, 29 July 1909, p. 9; Bushnell and Andrew, *Queen's Daughters*, p. 108; on the more circumspect and restrictive opera-

tion of American policy, post-1902, in the Philippines, see Col. Frank McIntyre (Bureau of Insular Affairs) to Lillian Stevens, 6 Feb. 1911 (2045/46), and Mc-Intyre to Judge Edward F. Waite, 20 Mar. 1911, Entry 5, RG 350, National Archives.

108. See Ballhatchet, *Race, Sex and Class*; and Pivar, "The Military, Prostitution, and Colonial Peoples," pp. 265–69, for useful surveys and comparisons.

109. Margaret Ellis to Clarence Edwards, 29 Mar. 1902 (2045/27), Bureau of Insular Affairs Records, National Archives.

110. *Union Signal*, 29 July 1909, p. 9.

111. Epstein, *Politics of Domesticity*, p. 145.

112. Rose Wood-Allen Chapman, *The Moral Problem of the Children* (New York: The Mary Wood-Allen Fund Committee, 1909); *Union Signal*, 21 Apr. 1910, p. 5; WWCTU, *8th Conv., 1910*, pp. 39, 168; Rose Wood-Allen Chapman to Rosalind Carlisle, 22 June 1910, and 13 Sept. 1910, Castle Howard Archives (J23/295).

113. Katharine Lent Stevenson to Anna Howard Shaw, 12 May 1898, in Anna Howard Shaw Papers, Mary Earhart Dillon Collection, Radcliffe College, Cambridge, Mass.

114. *Union Signal*, 7 Oct. 1909, p. 3. For the more general missionary process, see Kenton J. Clymer, *Protestant Missionaries in the Philippines, 1898–1916: An Inquiry into the American Colonial Mentality* (Urbana, Ill.: University of Illinois Press, 1986).

115. WWCTU, *8th Conv., 1910*, p. 40; *Union Signal*, 24 Nov. 1910, p. 6. Stevens said: "Although the traffic originated in Europe where its victims are white, it is claimed, and with reason, that the term 'white slave' does not fitly describe the heinous system, inasmuch as it involves every race and every color."

116. *Canadian Woman's Journal* (Ottawa), July 1899, p. 8; May 1899, p. 1; 15 Mar. 1901, p. 6.

117. WWCTU, *4th Conv., 1897*, p. 28.

Chapter 10

1. Ruth Bordin, *Woman and Temperance: The Quest for Power and Liberty, 1873–1900* (Philadelphia: Temple University Press, 1981), p. 61. See also Carl Degler, *At Odds: Women and the Family in America from the Revolution to the Present* (New York: Oxford University Press, 1980), pp. 318–19, 334–35, who summarizes these arguments; Steven M. Buechler, *The Transformation of the Woman Suffrage Movement: The Case of Illinois, 1850–1920* (New Brunswick, N.J.: Rutgers University Press, 1986), p. 121; Barbara Leslie Epstein, *The Politics of Domesticity: Women, Evangelism and Temperance in Nineteenth-Century America* (Middletown, Conn.: Wesleyan University Press, 1981), pp. 124–25, 128–29; Ellen Du Bois, "The Radicalism of the Woman Suffrage Movement: Notes towards the Reconstruction of Nineteenth Century Feminism," *Feminist Studies* 3 (Fall 1975): 63–71; Ross Evans Paulson, *Women's Suffrage and Prohibition: A Comparative Study of Equality and Social Control* (Glenview, Ill.: Scott, Foresman, 1973), p. 121; Paula

Baker, "The Domestication of Politics: Women and American Political Society," *American Historical Review* 89 (1984): 632, 637–38.

2. The words *expediency* and *justice*, first employed by Aileen Kraditor, have cast a deep shadow over discussions of the legacy of suffrage. Aileen S. Kraditor, *The Ideas of the Woman Suffrage Movement, 1890–1920* (New York: Columbia University Press, 1965). See also Degler, *At Odds*, chaps. 13–14; Alan P. Grimes, *The Puritan Ethic and Woman Suffrage* (New York: Oxford University Press, 1967), pp. xii, 5; William L. O'Neill, *Everyone Was Brave: A History of Feminism in America* (Chicago: Quadrangle, 1971), pp. 33–35; Buechler, *Transformation*, p. 121; Baker, "Domestication," p. 632; William H. Chafe, *The American Woman: Her Changing Social, Economic, and Political Roles, 1920–1970* (New York: Oxford University Press, 1972), pp. 15–21. A recent restatement of the Kraditor thesis is Beverly Beeton, *Women Vote in the West: The Woman Suffrage Movement, 1869–1896* (New York and London: Garland Pub. Co., 1986), esp. p. 140.

3. Nancy Cott, *The Grounding of Modern Feminism* (New Haven: Yale University Press, 1987), pp. 30, 291, n. 10, 294, n. 30; Buechler, *Transformation*, pp. 193–94.

4. Ellen Sargent to Caroline Severance, 1 Jan. 1910, box 23, Caroline Severance Papers, Huntington Library, San Marino, Calif.; Katharine Anthony, *Feminism in Germany and Scandinavia* (New York: Henry Holt, 1915), pp. 3–4; Edith F. Hurwitz, "The International Sisterhood," in Claudia Koonz and Renate Bridenthal, eds., *Becoming Visible: Women in European History* (Boston: Houghton Mifflin, 1977), pp. 333–72.

5. Degler, *At Odds*, p. 359.

6. Richard Evans, *The Feminists: Women's Emancipation Movements in Europe, America and Australasia, 1840–1920* (London: Croom Helm, 1977), p. 62. For other versions of the standard interpretation, see Raewyn Dalziel, "The Colonial Helpmeet," *New Zealand Journal of History* 11 (October 1977): 112–23; Anne Summers, *Damned Whores and God's Police: The Colonization of Women in Australia* (Ringwood, Vic.: Penguin, 1975); Wendy Mitchinson, "The WCTU: 'For God, Home and Native Land': A Study in Nineteenth-Century Feminism," in Linda Kealey, ed., *A Not Unreasonable Claim: Women and Reform in Canada, 1880s–1920s* (Toronto: Women's Press, 1979), pp. 158–59; Carol L. Bacchi, "'First Wave' Feminism in Canada: The Ideas of the English-Canadian Suffragists, 1877–1918," *Women's Studies International Forum* 5 (no. 6, 1982): 575–84; Janet Giele, "Social Change in the Feminine Role: A Comparison of Woman's Suffrage and Woman's Temperance, 1870–1920" (Ph.D. diss., Radcliffe College, 1961).

7. Hurwitz, "International Sisterhood," pp. 333–72; and Rebecca Sherrick, "Toward Universal Sisterhood," *Women's Studies International Forum* 5 (no. 6, 1982): 655–62, completely neglect the WCTU contribution to the international suffrage movement.

8. *Union Signal*, 29 Apr. 1897, p. 5.

9. On this point, see Epstein, *Politics of Domesticity*.

10. Cheryl Walker, *The Woman's Suffrage Movement in South Africa*, Communications, no. 2 (Centre for African Studies, University of Cape Town, 1979), pp. 23, 103.

11. Wilhelmina Bain to Caroline Severance, 20 Sept. 1908, and 29 Apr. 1910, box 14, Severance Papers; Patricia Grimshaw, *Women's Suffrage in New Zealand* (Auckland: Auckland University Press, 1972).

12. Grimshaw, *Women's Suffrage in New Zealand*, p. 38. Grimshaw's argument is validated by the newly available and extensive microfiche records of the New Zealand WCTU. See, esp., the clippings from the *New Zealand Prohibitionist*, special WCTU page, 1891–93, Massey University, Palmerston, New Zealand. Unfortunately and inexplicably, these filmed pages have not been dated but are filmed in order of appearance in the *Prohibitionist*.

13. Reprinted in WCTU of Western Australia, *Minutes of the Third Annual Convention . . . 1894* (Perth, 1894), pp. 33–34; see also ibid., p. 25; Helen Jones, *Nothing Seemed Impossible: Women's Education and Social Change in South Australia, 1875–1915* (St. Lucia, Queensland: University of Queensland Press, 1985), p. 146.

14. *Woman's Signal*, 14 June 1894, pp. 416, 422, and 21 June 1894, p. 432; *Woman's Herald* (London), 25 May 1893, p. 224; *Woman's Herald*, quoted in Boston *Woman's Journal*, 30 Sept. 1893, p. 308.

15. *Woman's Signal*, 21 June 1894, p. 432.

16. Kate Sheppard, *Franchise Report for 1893 of the New Zealand Women's Christian Temperance Union* (Invercargill: Ward, Wilson and Co., 1894), p. 1.

17. WCTU of Queensland, *AR*, 1894, p. 42.

18. Wilhelmina Bain to Caroline Severance, 20 Sept. 1908, and 29 Apr. 1910, box 14, Severance Papers; on Solly, see Walker, *Woman's Suffrage in South Africa*, pp. 23, 103; *Dictionary of South African Biography* (1981) 4:589; on Nicholls, see Isobel McCorkindale, ed., *Torch-Bearers: The Woman's Christian Temperance Union of South Australia, 1886–1948* (Adelaide: WCTU of South Australia, 1949), pp. 12, 17, 41; *White Ribbon Signal* (Sydney), 1 Nov. 1894, pp. 6–7, 8; Marie Mune, "Elizabeth Webb Nicholls," *Australian Dictionary of Biography*, 11:22.

19. Paul E. Fuller, *Laura Clay and the Woman's Rights Movement* (Lexington: University Press of Kentucky, 1975), pp. 177–78.

20. Catherine L. Cleverdon, *The Woman Suffrage Movement in Canada*, 2d ed. (Toronto: University of Toronto Press, 1974), p. 188.

21. Jones, *Nothing Seemed Impossible*, p. 139.

22. McCorkindale, *Torch-Bearers*, p. 7.

23. Maybanke Anderson, in *Sydney Morning Herald*, 13 May 1925, in Womanhood Suffrage Album, box MLK2012, WCTU of New South Wales Records, Mitchell Library, Sydney; Diane Scott, "Woman Suffrage: The Movement in Australia," *Journal of the Royal Australian Historical Society* 53 (Dec. 1967): 311.

24. Jones, *Nothing Seemed Impossible*, pp. 138–39.

25. Elizabeth Ward, *To the Members of the W.C.T.U. in New South Wales* (n.p., [1892]), in Womanhood Suffrage Album, box MLK2012, WCTU of New South Wales Records; *Why Should I, A Woman, Vote?* (n.p., n.d.), ibid.; Australasian WCTU, *2d Triennial Conv., 1894*, p. 97.

26. Jones, *Nothing Seemed Impossible*, p. 138.

27. Bordin, *Woman and Temperance*, pp. 120–21, 204. Bordin argues that the strategy of "home protection" in the United States was a tactical play that Willard used to move the WCTU from expediency to stress more the justice argu-

ments by the 1890s. As in Australia, this amounted to a move in the opposite direction from the drift in suffrage propaganda claimed by Kraditor and others. See above, notes 1 and 2.

28. For evidence of these comparisons, see Grimshaw, *Women's Suffrage in New Zealand*; Scott, "Woman Suffrage"; Paulson, *Women's Suffrage and Prohibition*, pp. 125–26.

29. Evans, *Feminists*, p. 60. See also Patricia Grimshaw, "Women and the Family in Australian History," in Elizabeth Windschuttle, ed., *Women, Class and History: Feminist Perspectives on Australia, 1788–1978* (Melbourne: Fontana, 1980), p. 44. The Victorian case may not be typical, as suffrage was inordinately delayed there. See Anthea Hyslop, "Temperance, Christianity, and Feminism: The Woman's Christian Temperance Union of Victoria, 1887–1897," *Historical Studies* 17 (Apr. 1976): 39–45; Ian Tyrrell, "International Aspects of the Woman's Temperance Movement in Australia: The Influence of the American WCTU, 1882–1914," *Journal of Religious History* 12 (June 1983): 294.

30. Hyslop, "Temperance, Christianity and Feminism," p. 41; *White Ribbon Signal* (Sydney), 1 Feb. 1895, p. 7.

31. *White Ribbon Signal* (Sydney), 1 Feb. 1895, p. 7; Nicholls to WCTU of New South Wales, 3 Jan. 1895, ibid.; Hyslop, "Temperance, Christianity and Feminism," p. 41; WCTU of Queensland, *AR*, 1902, p. 53.

32. Quoted in W. Sidney Smith, *Outlines of the Women's Franchise Movement in New Zealand* (Christchurch: Whitcombe and Tombs, 1905), p. iii. See also Paulson, *Women's Suffrage and Prohibition*, pp. 127–28, for a fuller account.

33. *Woman's Signal*, 14 June 1894, p. 422, and 21 June 1894, p. 432; WCTU of South Australia, *AR*, 1894, p. 29.

34. *White Ribbon Signal* (Sydney), 8 Sept. 1902, in WCTU Album, box MLK2012, WCTU of New South Wales Records.

35. Grimshaw, "Women and the Family," pp. 44–45; Evans, *Feminists*, p. 61; WCTU of New South Wales, *AR*, 1902, p. 30.

36. Agnes Williams to Rose Scott, 9 Oct. 1903, box 38/21. Scott Family Papers, Mitchell Library, Sydney; Brisbane Central WCTU, Minutes, 19 Mar. 1896, and 26 Nov. 1903, in WCTU of Queensland Records, Queensland WCTUHQ, Brisbane.

37. *Seventh Annual Records and Methods of Work Done by the Woman's Christian Temperance Union of Victoria . . . 1894* (Melbourne: Spectator Pub. Co., 1895), p. 19.

38. Wilhelmina Bain to Caroline Severance, 29 Apr. 1910, box 14, Severance Papers.

39. Jessie Ackermann, *What Women Have Done with the Vote* (New York: William B. Feakins, 1913), p. 58.

40. Tyrrell, "International Aspects," pp. 291, 298.

41. Grimshaw, *Women's Suffrage in New Zealand*, p. 37.

42. Tyrrell, "International Aspects," pp. 292, 294; WCTU of New South Wales, *AR*, 1892, p. 25; WCTU of South Australia, *AR*, 1894, p. 29; *Life of Mrs. E. J. Ward*, pp. 85, 108, clippings in Womanhood Suffrage Album; *White Ribbon Signal* (Sydney), 1 July 1896.

43. Jessie Ackermann, *Australia: From a Woman's Point of View* (London: Cas-

sell, 1913), p. 209; *Golden Records: Pathfinders of the Woman's Christian Temperance Union of New South Wales* (Sydney: John Sands, 1926), p. 50.

44. NWCTU, *AR*, 1882, p. xxxiv; *Golden Records*, p. 50; for American influence on the franchise, note the additional evidence concerning Jessie Ackermann, Catharine P. Wallace, and Elizabeth Wheeler Andrew in WCTU of Queensland, *AR*, 1889, p. 20; 1892, p. 8; 1894, p. 45.

45. *Life of Mrs. E. J. Ward*, p. 108; WCTU of New South Wales, *AR*, 1892, p. 25; Australasian WCTU, *3d Triennial Conv., 1897*, p. 38; *White Ribbon Signal* (Sydney), 1 July 1896.

46. WCTU of South Australia, *AR*, 1894, p. 29; Jones, *Nothing Seemed Impossible*, pp. 137–38.

47. *Union Signal*, 19 Jan. 1893, p. 9; 16 Feb. 1893, p. 5; 3 May 1898, p. 5.

48. Ibid., 30 July 1891, p. 10; *White Ribbon Signal* (Sydney), 1 Aug. 1895, pp. 6–7; WCTU of Queensland, *AR*, 1894, p. 45.

49. *Union Signal*, 19 Jan. 1893, p. 9; 21 Dec. 1893, p. 4; 16 Oct. 1902, p. 3; 22 Dec. 1910, p. 8; *Woman's Herald*, 21 Sept. 1893, p. 481; *White Ribbon*, Mar. 1913, p. 40; Apr. 1913, p. 53; *Woman's Signal*, 14 June 1894, pp. 416, 422, and 21 June 1894, p. 432; Hannah Whitall Smith to "My Beloved Family and Friends," no. 78:8, 19 Nov. 1893, Hannah Whitall Smith Papers, Lilly Library, Indiana University.

50. *Union Signal*, 29 Apr. 1897, p. 5.

51. Ibid., 22 Dec. 1910, p. 8. See also 16 Oct. 1902, p. 3, and 20 Dec. 1893, p. 4.

52. "Twelve Reasons Why Women Want to Vote" in Boston *Woman's Journal*, 6 May 1893, p. 142; "Sixteen Reasons for Supporting Woman's Suffrage," *New Zealand Prohibitionist* file, n.d., microfiche, Massey University, New Zealand; Jeanne M. Weimann, *The Fair Women* (Chicago: Academy Press, 1981), pp. 494, 496. The *Woman's Journal*, 18 Nov. 1893, p. 362, did reprint virtually unchanged another *New Zealand Prohibitionist* pamphlet, "Is It Right?," but significantly, this was the only example of Sheppard's arguments I have found that stressed expediency.

53. Ida Husted Harper Scrapbooks, 5:89, 93, Rare Book Room, Library of Congress. See also Anna Howard Shaw in ibid., p. 96; *The American Suffragette* 1 (no. 4, Sept.–Oct. 1909): 4, and 1 (no. 6, Dec. 1909): 4. An interesting Anglo-Australian example in the same vein is Nellie Alma Martel, *The Women's Vote in Australia: What It Has Already Accomplished* (London: Woman's Press, [c.1908]), p. 11.

54. *Union Signal*, 13 Nov. 1913, pp. 8–9; WWCTU, *9th Conv., 1913*, p. 24.

55. Anna Howard Shaw to Rebecca Chambers, 26 Aug., 9 Sept., and 8 Mar. 1904, in Anna Howard Shaw Papers, Mary Earhart Dillon Collection, Radcliffe College, Cambridge, Mass.; WWCTU, *7th Conv., 1906*, p. 21. See also Shaw to Caroline Severance, 7 Feb. 1911, and 3 Oct. 1905, box 23, Severance Papers.

56. Norman Clark, *Deliver Us from Evil: An Interpretation of American Prohibition* (New York: W. W. Norton, 1976), pp. 105–6; Paulson, *Women's Suffrage and Prohibition*, p. 140.

57. Clara Colby to Caroline Severance, 17 Sept. 1906, box 15, Severance Papers.

58. Eleanor Flexner, "Carrie Chapman Catt," *NAW*, 1:312; Mary Gray Peck, *Carrie Chapman Catt: A Biography* (New York: H. H. Wilson, 1944), pp. 122, 181–82.

59. *Union Signal*, 16 Oct. 1902, p. 3.

60. Peck, *Catt*, pp. 199–200, 205–6; Anna Gordon, *White Ribboners of Japan* (n.p., [1925]), p. 11; Charlotte B. De Forest, *The Woman and the Leaven in Japan* (West Medford, Mass.: Central Committee on the United Study of Foreign Missions, 1923), pp. 187, 190; Sharon L. Sievers, *Flowers in the Salt: The Beginnings of Feminist Consciousness in Modern Japan* (Stanford, Calif.: Stanford University Press, 1983), pp. 89–92, 143–44. On the earlier period of the Japanese women's movement, see also Sievers, "Feminist Criticism in Japanese Politics in the 1880s: The Experience of Yishida Toshiko," *Signs* 6 (1981): 602–16, esp. on the role of social purity in the women's movement.

61. House of Representatives, Committee on Woman's Suffrage, *Hearings before the Committee on Rules . . . 1913*, 63d Cong., 2d Sess., Doc. 754 (Washington, D.C., 1914), pp. 165–66 (quote), 178–89.

62. Ackermann, *What Women Have Done with the Vote*, pp. 24–25.

63. Harper, "Equal Suffrage Laws in Australia Put to the Test," *Washington Post*, 17 Jan. 1904, in Harper Scrapbooks, 5:124.

64. *Union Signal*, 25 Mar. 1909, p. 14.

65. *White Ribbon*, Apr. 1910, p. 49. See, generally, Jill Liddington and Jill Norris, *One Hand Tied behind Us: The Rise of the Women's Suffrage Movement* (London: Virago, 1978).

66. *Jus Suffragii* 10 (Feb. 1916): 66; *Votes for Women*, 16 Aug. 1912, p. 743, and 14 May 1909, p. 676.

67. Agnes Slack to Anna Gordon, 26 July 1913, WWCTU Files; National Executive Council Resolution, *White Ribbon*, Dec. 1909, p. 179.

68. See, for example, David Morgan, *Suffragists and Liberals: The Politics of Woman Suffrage in England* (Oxford: Blackwell, 1975), p. 17.

69. Ray Strachey, *Millicent Garrett Fawcett* (London: John Murray, 1931), p. 174.

70. Cott, *Grounding of Modern Feminism*, p. 60. An excellent study of suffrage propaganda that has shaped my thinking on militancy is Lisa Tickner, *The Spectacle of Women: Imagery of the Suffrage Campaign, 1907–14* (London: Chatto and Windus, 1987).

71. *White Ribbon*, June 1906, p. 123.

72. *Union Signal*, 20 Mar. 1913, p. 3.

73. Slack to Carlisle, 30 Aug., 15 Oct. 1913; and Slack to Carlisle, 28 Feb. 1920, Castle Howard Archives (J23/265), Castle Howard, Yorkshire.

74. Slack to Carlisle, 19 July 1913; Solomon to Slack, June 1913, encl. in ibid. (J23/265).

75. J. W. Holder to Slack, 9 June 1913, ibid; *Union Signal*, 20 Mar. 1913, p. 2.

76. *White Ribbon*, May 1907, p. 71, and Aug. 1910, p. 19; *The National British Women's Temperance Association: Its Origins and Progress: A Jubilee Sketch* (London: NBWTAU, 1926), pp. 35–37; Tickner, *Spectacle of Women*, p. 74.

77. *White Ribbon*, Sept. 1912, p. 131.

78. BWTA, *AR*, 1906, p. 97.

79. Sandra Holton, "Feminism and Democracy: The Women's Suffrage Movement in Britain, with Particular Reference to the National Union of Women's Suffrage Societies, 1897–1918" (Ph.D. diss., University of Stirling, 1980), pp. 102, 105, 91, 96–97. See also Sandra Holton, *Feminism and Democracy: Women's Suffrage and Reform Politics in Britain, 1900–1918* (Cambridge: Cambridge University Press, 1986), pp. 42, 109; Holton to author, 19 June 1987.

80. *White Ribbon*, Feb. 1898, p. 43; *Union Signal*, 7 Apr. 1910, p. 13. See also the recent study by David Rubenstein, *Before the Suffragettes: Women's Emancipation in the 1890s* (Brighton, Eng.: Harvester Press, 1986), chap. 10. On the broader context of women in local government, see the fine new book by Patricia Hollis, *Ladies Elect: Women in English Local Government, 1865–1914* (Oxford: Clarendon Press, 1987). Hollis gives some attention to the role of the BWTA, but there is much more to be written about this.

81. BWTA, *AR*, 1903, p. 110.

82. *White Ribbon*, June 1906, p. 122. For the chronology of these institutional arrangements, see *Union Signal*, 7 Apr. 1910, p. 13; on Mason, see Bertha Mason, *The Story of Suffrage* (London: Sherratt and Hughes, 1912); *White Ribbon*, Aug. 1912, p. 128; *Women's Franchise*, 26 Mar. 1908, p. 451.

83. *White Ribbon*, Feb. 1907, p. 26; Rubenstein, *Before the Suffragettes*, chap. 10; *Union Signal*, 7 Apr. 1910, p. 13.

84. *White Ribbon*, June 1906, p. 122.

85. Ibid., Aug. 1913, p. 117. See also Leslie Parker Hume, *The National Union of Women's Suffrage Societies, 1897–1914* (New York: Garland, 1982), pp. 17, 74, 86, 88; Mason, *Story of Suffrage*.

86. Sandra Holton to author, 19 June 1987; Holton, *Feminism and Democracy*, pp. 72–73, 116–17.

Chapter 11

1. Ruth Bordin, *Woman and Temperance: The Quest for Power and Liberty, 1873–1900* (Philadelphia: Temple University Press, 1981), pp. 107–8; Bordin, *Frances Willard: A Biography* (Chapel Hill: University of North Carolina Press, 1986), pp. 145–49; Barbara Leslie Epstein, *The Politics of Domesticity: Women, Evangelism and Temperance in Nineteenth-Century America* (Middletown, Conn.: Wesleyan University Press, 1981), pp. 142–44.

2. Bordin, *Woman and Temperance*, p. 85.

3. Epstein, *Politics of Domesticity*, p. 142.

4. Charles Roberts, *The Radical Countess: The History of the Life of Rosalind, Countess of Carlisle* (Carlisle, Eng.: Steel Bros., 1962); WWCTU, *5th Conv., 1900*, Directory of Officials, no page numbers; Charles E. Parker, *Margaret Eleanor Parker: A Memorial* (Bolton, Eng.: Tillotson, 1906), pp. 61–62; Hannah Whitall Smith, in *Union Signal*, 21 Dec. 1893, p. 4; Hannah Whitall Smith circular letter, no. 91:4, 15 Apr. 1895, Hannah Whitall Smith Papers, Lilly Library, Indiana University, Bloomington, Ind.

5. William Leach, "Looking Forward Together: Feminists and Edward Bella-

my," *Democracy* 2 (Jan. 1982): 126; Bordin, *Willard*, pp. 145–49; Epstein, *Politics of Domesticity*, p. 142; Mary Earhart, *Frances Willard: From Prayers to Politics* (Chicago: University of Chicago Press, 1944), pp. 245–59.

6. NWCTU, *AR*, 1893, pp. 104–5. Willard's commitment to socialism as illustrated in her Buffalo National Convention address in 1897 was widely publicized and frequently reprinted. Mary Garbutt to Caroline Severance, 17 Jan. 1909, and [Nov. 1912], box 17, Caroline Severance Papers, Huntington Library, San Marino, Calif.; "Frances Willard on Socialism," Socialist Party of America, *Collected Pamphlets*, 2:60; *Zion's Herald*, 21 Apr. 1937, p. 495, roll 55, National American Woman Suffrage Association Papers, Library of Congress.

7. *Union Signal*, 14 Oct. 1909, p. 5.

8. Ibid., 24 Nov. 1910, p. 8; cf. Bordin, *Woman and Temperance*, p. 155.

9. *Union Signal*, 24 Mar. 1904, p. 9.

10. NWCTU, *AR*, 1892, p. 123; 1893, p. 296; 1894, p. 479.

11. *Union Signal*, 11 Nov. 1909, p. 6. The best treatment of socialism in the WCTU is Mary Jo Buhle, *Women and American Socialism* (Urbana, Ill.: University of Illinois Press, 1981), pp. 60–66.

12. *Woman's Herald* (London), 23 Feb. 1893, p. 5, and 30 Mar. 1893, p. 90; *Woman's Signal*, 31 May 1894, p. 373; newspaper clipping [on Florence Balgarnie], [1902], 38/65, item 4, Scott Family Papers, Mitchell Library, Sydney.

13. *Southern California White Ribbon*, Sept. 1910, p. 5.

14. Mary Alderman Garbutt, *Victories of Four Decades: A History of the Woman's Christian Temperance Union of Southern California, 1883–1924* (Los Angeles: Southern California WCTU, 1924); Garbutt to Severance, [Nov. 1912], box 17, Severance Papers.

15. Frances Willard, *A New Calling for Women* (London: WWCTU, 1893), p. 5.

16. Ibid., p. 11.

17. Ibid., pp. 9, 13, 14.

18. Bernard Semmell, *Imperialism and Social Reform* (London: Allen and Unwin, 1960), is the standard account but sadly neglects women. See also, Edward H. McKinley, *Marching to Glory: The History of the Salvation Army in the United States of America* (San Francisco: Harper and Row, 1980), p. 56. On the "socialist" connection, see Gareth Stedman Jones, *Outcast London: A Study in the Relationship between Classes in Victorian Society* (Oxford: Clarendon Press, 1971), pp. 308–14.

19. WWCTU, *4th Conv., 1897*, pp. 66–67.

20. Clipping from *Woman's Signal*, 4 June 1896, in Scrapbook 73, p. 93, WCTU Files.

21. *White Ribbon*, July 1902, p. 106.

22. *A Brief History of the Woman's Christian Temperance Union in South Africa* (Cape Town: Townshend, Taylor and Snashall, 1925), p. 11.

23. Charles Parker, *Margaret Parker*, p. 85.

24. Anna Davin, "Imperialism and Motherhood," *History Workshop*, no. 5 (Spring 1978): 39; *White Ribbon*, Apr. 1911, p. 48; *Union Signal*, 5 Feb. 1903, p. 6.

25. Frances Willard, "The Handicap of England," *American Federationist* 1 (May 1894): 44–45; Samuel Gompers to Henry Demarest Lloyd, 13 Mar., 5

Apr. 1894, and Willard to Lloyd, 13 Mar. 1894, Henry Demarest Lloyd Papers, State Historical Society of Wisconsin (roll 4, microfilm, copy in Library of Congress); Earhart, *Willard*, p. 258.

26. Frances Willard, "My Observations of English Traits," correspondence, undated [Jan.–Apr. 1893], roll 19, WCTU Series, OHS.

27. Epstein, *Politics of Domesticity*, p. 142.

28. David Brundage, "The Producing Classes and the Saloon: Denver in the 1880s," *Labor History* 26 (1985): 29–52. This is confirmed for the case of Redlands, Calif., in Mrs. J. Stanley Brown to Caroline Severance, 2 Sept. 1901, box 14, Severance Papers.

29. Katharine Lent Stevenson to Anna Howard Shaw, 12 May 1898, in Anna Howard Shaw Papers, Mary Earhart Dillon Collection, Radcliffe College, Cambridge, Mass.

30. *Union Signal*, 25 Nov. 1909, pp. 1–2.

31. Ibid., 9 July 1891, pp. 4–5; see also Charles Parker, *Margaret Parker*, pp. 61–62, for another case.

32. Specifically Ackermann worked for the Australian Women's National League. Lady M. E. Forrest to Jessie Ackermann, 22 Dec. 1911, box 1, fl. 1, Jessie A. Ackermann Collection, Sherrod Library, East Tennessee State University, Johnson City, Tenn.; Mamie Swanton Press Book clipping, [c.1911], in Kay Daniels and Mary Murnane, eds., *Uphill All the Way: A Documentary History of Women in Australia* (St. Lucia: University of Queensland Press, 1980), p. 248.

33. J. D. Bollen, "The Temperance Movement and the Liberal Party in New South Wales Politics, 1900–1904," *Journal of Religious History* 1 (1960): 175, 178, 180, 182; A. R. Grigg, "Prohibition, the Church and Labour: A Programme for Social Reform, 1890–1914," *New Zealand Journal of History* 15 (1981): 153–54.

34. Anderson Hughes (Drew) to Rosalind Carlisle, 12 June 1912, Castle Howard Archives (J23/266), Castle Howard, Yorkshire. The then Australian WCTU president, Lady J. W. Holder, also strongly criticized the "socialistic" bias in recent Australian legislation after three years of a Federal Labor government (Holder to Carlisle, 9 June 1913, ibid. [J23/265]).

35. Agnes Slack to Rosalind Carlisle, 10 Apr. 1915, Castle Howard Archives (J23/265); for further evidence see *White Ribbon*, July 1914, pp. 99–100.

36. Anna Gordon, in NWCTU, *AR*, 1915, p. 115; see, on the industrial commission, Graham Adams, Jr., *Age of Industrial Violence, 1910–1915: The Activities and Findings of the United States Commission on Industrial Relations* (New York: Columbia University Press, 1966). The WCTU in the United States remained interested in the conditions of women's factory work. See *Union Signal*, 27 July 1922, p. 6.

37. Cf. Epstein, *Politics of Domesticity*, p. 143.

38. *White Ribbon*, Nov. 1899, p. 10.

39. See, for example, Agnes Slack, *People I Have Met and Places I Have Seen: Some Memories of Agnes E. Slack* (Bedford, Eng.: Rush and Warwick, 1942), p. 67.

40. *White Ribbon*, July 1902, p. 106.

41. Bordin, *Willard*, pp. 145–49; Leach, "Looking Forward Together"; on the conservative and "statist" contribution to "socialism," see Gareth Stedman Jones, *Outcast London*, pp. 308–14.

42. See "Busy Working Woman," *White Ribbon Signal* (Sydney), 30 Oct. 1908, p. 6; Jack S. Blocker, Jr., *Retreat from Reform: The Prohibition Movement in the United States, 1890–1913* (Westport, Conn.: Greenwood Press, 1976), p. 60.

43. Australasian WCTU, *2d Triennial Conv., 1894*, p. 44.

44. Frances Willard, *Glimpses of Fifty Years* (Chicago: WTPA, 1889), pp. 612–14.

45. Willard, *A New Calling*, p. 6.

46. Cf. Epstein, *Politics of Domesticity*, p. 136.

Chapter 12

1. *Union Signal*, 18 Nov. 1920, p. 9; 16 Dec. 1920, p. 1; 20 May 1920, p. 1.

2. Ibid., 18 Nov. 1920, p. 9.

3. Andrew Sinclair, *Prohibition: The Era of Excess* (Boston: Little, Brown, 1962), p. 53.

4. *Union Signal*, 20 May 1920, p. 1.

5. Ibid., 25 Nov. 1920, p. 2.

6. Ibid.

7. Ibid., 27 Mar. 1902, p. 3; 30 Sept. 1909, p. 16; *SEAP*, 6:2572, 2563. On the Gothenburg system, see, in addition to these sources, Per Frånberg, "An Economic Interpretation of Swedish Alcohol Policies in the 19th Century" (Paper delivered at History Research Institute, Seminar on The Social History of Alcohol, University of Florida, Gainesville, 1987), esp. pp. 6–10.

8. Arthur Sherwell and Joseph Rowntree, *Public Control of the Liquor Traffic: Being a Review of the Scandinavian Experiments in the Light of Recent Experience* (London: Grant Richards, 1903), pp. 146, 161–68, 249–50; Sherwell and Rowntree, *The Temperance Problem and Social Reform* (London: Hodder and Staughton, 1898), pp. 310–28.

9. *Documents Printed by Order of the House of Representatives of the Commonwealth of Massachusetts during the Session of the General Court 1894*, House Document no. 192 (Boston: Wright and Potter, 1894); *Fifth Special Report of the Commissioner of Labor: The Gothenburg System* (Washington, D.C.: Government Printing Office, 1893); on Gould, see *Elgin Ralston Lovell Gould: A Memorial* (New York: Privately printed, 1916).

10. Suggestive on the controversy among prohibitionists over government regulation is Jack S. Blocker, Jr., *Retreat from Reform: The Prohibition Movement in the United States, 1890–1913* (Westport, Conn.: Greenwood Press, 1976), pp. 52, 71–72.

11. Harry Gene Levine, "The Committee of Fifty and the Origins of Alcohol Control," *Journal of Drug Issues* 13 (Winter 1983): 95–116; Raymond Calkins, *Substitutes for the Saloon* (1901; reprint, Boston: Houghton Mifflin, 1919).

12. I am indebted for information on the ASL and the rise of national prohibition throughout this chapter to K. Austin Kerr, *Organized For Prohibition: A New History of the Anti-Saloon League* (New Haven: Yale University Press, 1985). For a different perspective, stressing the role of big capital in pushing anti-democratic reform of workers' drinking habits, see John J. Rumbarger, *Profits,*

Power, and Prohibition: Alcohol Reform and the Industrializing of America, 1800–1930 (Albany: State University of New York Press, 1989). Neither of these useful studies, however, deals with the threat of European schemes of regulation that brought convulsions to the Anglo-American temperance world in the 1890s. For these, see Blocker, *Retreat from Reform*, pp. 52, 71–72, and the text below.

13. Ernest H. Cherrington, *The Evolution of Prohibition in the United States* (Westerville, Ohio: American Issue Pub. Co., 1920), pp. 250–51.

14. There were indeed similarities in the two schemes as Raymond Calkins noted in *Substitutes for the Saloon*, p. 33, yet the differences were, he also pointed out, vast. Standard histories do not deal with the dispensary system. On its local politics, see John Evans Eubanks, *Ben Tillman's Baby: The Dispensary System of South Carolina, 1892–1915* (Augusta, Ga.: Tidwell Printing Co., 1950), pp. 208–10. Norman Clark, *Deliver Us from Evil: An Interpretation of American Prohibition* (New York: W. W. Norton, 1976), pp. 136–39, has an interesting discussion of international prohibition parallels.

15. Based on the annual reports of the ASL of Ohio and the National ASL reports after 1895; and James L. Ewin, *The Birth of the Anti-Saloon League* (Washington, D.C.: n.p., 1913); copies in the Library of Congress. See also the voluminous material in roll 1 of the Anti-Saloon League of America Series, OHS.

16. *The National Temperance Almanac and Teetotaler's Year-Book for 1897* (New York: National Temperance Society, 1896), pp. 46–49; *American Prohibition Year Book for 1905* (Chicago: United Prohibition Press, 1905), pp. 58–59; William E. Johnson, *The Gothenburg System of Liquor Selling* (Chicago: New Voice, 1903), esp. p. 8.

17. *SEAP*, 6:2563; *Union Signal*, 18 Oct. 1894, p. 4.

18. Sherwell and Rowntree, *Public Control of the Liquor Traffic*, chap. 4, has a good critical discussion of these attacks.

19. *Union Signal*, 27 Mar. 1902, p. 3.

20. Ibid., 2 Nov. 1893, p. 10.

21. Ibid., 13 July 1893, p. 8, and 26 Apr. 1894, p. 8; Eubanks, *Tillman's Baby*, p. 70.

22. *Documents Printed, Mass., 1894*, House Doc. no. 192, p. 2; John Graham Brooks, "Brandy and Socialism: The Gothenburg System," *Forum* 14 (Dec. 1892): 512–26; James E. Mooney, *John Graham Brooks: Prophet of Social Justice: A Career Story* (Worcester: Privately printed, 1968), p. 21.

23. *Union Signal*, 2 Aug. 1894, p. 8; 25 Oct. 1894, pp. 2–3; 21 June 1894, pp. 2–3.

24. Ibid., 9 Aug. 1894, p. 8.

25. NWCTU, *AR*, 1884, p. 63.

26. Mary C. Leavitt, *Report of the Hon. Sec. of the World's Woman's Christian Temperance Union* (Boston: n.p., 1891), pp. 21–22.

27. Ibid., p. 55. See above, chap. 4.

28. Sherwell and Rowntree, *Temperance Problem*, pp. 310–27; NWCTU, *AR*, 1897, p. 106.

29. Elizabet Espenak to Sara Nolan, 7 Oct. 1898, printed in *White Ribbon Signal*, 7 Dec. 1898, WCTU Album, box MLK2012, Mitchell Library, Sydney.

30. NWCTU, *AR*, 1897, pp. 106–8.

31. *New York Commercial Advertiser*, 18 Apr. 1896, in Scrapbook 72, WCTU Files.

32. Elizabeth Wheeler Andrew and Katharine Bushnell to the General Officers of the WWCTU, 30 Aug. 1897, in Scrapbook 76, WCTU Files.

33. On the Raines Law, see Frederick Wines and John Koren, *The Liquor Problem in Its Legislative Aspects*, 2d ed. (Boston: Houghton Mifflin, 1900), esp. pp. 364–69.

34. London *Times*, 23 Nov. 1897, p. 4.

35. *Rochester Democrat*, 3 Apr. 1896, in Scrapbook 72, WCTU Files.

36. *New York Commercial Advertiser*, 18 Apr. 1896, in Scrapbook 72, WCTU Files; Elizabeth Wheeler Andrew and Katharine Bushnell to Frances Willard, 15 June 1896, roll 1, fl. 5, STF Series, OHS.

37. *Woman's Signal*, 18 June 1896, p. 393; clipping from *The Corner Stone* (Wheeling, W. Va.), in Scrapbook 73, p. 104, WCTU Files.

38. Andrew and Bushnell to General Officers of the WWCTU, 30 Aug. 1897, in Scrapbook 76, WCTU Files.

39. *White Ribbon*, July 1898, p. 97.

40. Theodore Stanton and Harriot Stanton Blatch, *Elizabeth Cady Stanton as Revealed in Her Letters, Diary, and Reminiscences*, 2 vols. (1922; reprint, New York: Arno Press, 1969), 2:277–78. See also David Fahey, "Rosalind (Stanley) Howard, Countess of Carlisle" (unpublished paper in possession of Professor Fahey).

41. Royal Commission on Liquor Licensing Laws, Vol. 3, *Minutes of Evidence* . . . (London: HMSO, 1897), pp. 177, 184; Kathleen Fitzpatrick, *Lady Henry Somerset* (London: Jonathan Cape; Boston: Little, Brown, 1923), p. 186.

42. Fitzpatrick, *Somerset*, p. 185.

43. *Union Signal*, 2 June 1898, p. 8, quoted in *White Ribbon*, July 1898, p. 97.

44. See especially, for the standard account, A. E. Dingle, *The Campaign for Prohibition in Victorian England* (London: Croom Helm, 1980), chap. 10.

45. David Fahey, "Temperance and the Liberal Party—Lord Peel's Report, 1899," *Journal of British Studies* 10 (May 1971): 132–59, for an exemplary account.

46. Ibid., p. 138; Royal Commission on Liquor Licensing Laws, *Final Report of Her Majesty's Commissioners* . . . (London: HMSO, 1899), pp. 64, 280, 289.

47. Fahey, "Temperance and the Liberal Party," p. 144.

48. *White Ribbon*, 31 Oct. 1899, p. 21.

49. *Alliance News*, 5 July 1900, p. 420.

50. Scrapbook 73, p. 104, WCTU Files.

51. Josephine Butler to Fanny Forsaith, 16 Feb. 1898, Josephine Butler Papers, Fawcett Library, City of London Polytechnic.

52. *White Ribbon*, Nov. 1904, p. 8.

53. Ibid., July 1905, p. 56.

54. *Alliance News*, 10 Nov. 1904, p. 765.

55. On the BWTA/Women's Liberal Federation connection, see Scrapbook 73, p. 108, WCTU Files; Louisa Martindale to Frances Willard, 13 Feb. 1893, roll 19, WCTU Series, OHS; *Woman's Herald* (London), 8 June 1893, p. 249.

56. *White Ribbon*, Oct. 1909, p. 152.

57. *Union Signal*, 29 Mar. 1900, p. 8.

58. WWCTU, *4th Conv., 1897*, p. 90; *5th Conv., 1900*, p. 20; *6th Conv., 1903*, p. 15.

59. Sherwell and Rowntree, *Temperance Problem.*

60. BWTA, *AR*, 1899, p. 90.

61. *Canadian Woman's Journal* (Ottawa), 15 June 1899, p. 6; NWCTU, *AR*, 1897, p. 107. See also, more generally, Edwin A. Pratt, *Licensing and Temperance in Sweden, Norway, and Denmark* (London: John Murray, 1907), pp. 83–84.

62. BWTA, *AR*, 1903, p. 112.

63. See, esp., *Sir Wilfred Lawson on "Disinterested Management" of the Liquor Traffic. A Letter by the Countess of Carlisle. 16 Aug. 1906.* Copy in Pamphlet Collection, United Kingdom Alliance, London; Rosalind Carlisle to Mrs. William (Annie) Harvey, 17 Jan. 1904; Hannah Whitall Smith to Harvey, 30 Jan. 1904; Lady Henry Somerset to Harvey, 29 Oct. 1906, Autograph Collection, Fawcett Library, City of London Polytechnic; Joseph Rowntree and Arthur Sherwell, *British "Gothenburg" Experiments and Public House Trusts* (London: Hodder and Staughton, 1901).

64. *White Ribbon*, July 1905, p. 129.

65. Ibid., June 1906, pp. 120–21.

66. Ibid.

67. *Union Signal*, 29 Nov. 1906, p. 11.

68. This point is strongly suggested by Agnes Slack to Rosalind Carlisle, 30 Aug. 1913, Castle Howard Archives (J23/265), Castle Howard, Yorkshire.

69. *White Ribbon*, Nov. 1906, p. 193.

70. "How Far Will It Lead Us to Prohibition?" in WCTU of South Australia, *AR*, 1908, p. 22.

71. Alice Cameron to Frances Willard, 10 Jan. 1898, roll 25, WCTU Series, OHS.

72. *Scottish Women's Temperance News*, Aug. 1904, p. 121.

73. *Scottish Reformer*, 29 Oct. 1904, p. 10.

74. Phillida Bunkle, "The Origins of the Women's Movement in New Zealand: The Women's Christian Temperance Union, 1885–1895," in Beryl Hughes and Phillida Bunkle, eds., *Women in New Zealand Society* (Sydney and Auckland: Allen and Unwin, 1980), pp. 67–72.

75. *Scottish Reformer*, 19 Nov. 1904, p. 11.

76. Ibid., 31 Dec. 1904, p. 5.

77. Ibid., 30 June 1900, p. 4; *Scottish Women's Temperance News*, Sept. 1904, p. 130.

78. Rosalind Carlisle to Lillian Stevens, 12 Jan. 1907, Castle Howard Archives (J23/264); *White Ribbon*, Aug. 1904, p. 149; Charles Roberts, *The Radical Countess: The History of the Life of Rosalind, Countess of Carlisle* (Carlisle, Eng.: Steel Bros., 1962), p. 134.

79. Hannah Whitall Smith to Mrs. William (Annie) Harvey, 30 Jan. 1904, Autograph Collection; Fahey, "Carlisle," p. 11.

80. Charles Roberts, *Radical Countess*, p. 134.

81. The classic account of the crisis is George Dangerfield, *The Strange Death of Liberal England* (1935; reprint, London: MacGibbon and Kee, 1966).

82. Quoted in WCTU of South Australia, *AR*, 1914, p. 22; see also *White Ribbon*, June 1915, p. 91.

83. WWCTU, *9th Conv., 1913*, p. 32.

84. Ibid.; Agnes Slack to Rosalind Carlisle, 30 Aug. 1913, Castle Howard Archives (J23/265).

85. Aelfrida Tillyard, *Agnes E. Slack: Two Hundred Thousand Miles Travel for Temperance in Four Continents* (Cambridge: W. Heffer and Sons, 1926), p. 22; *Compte-Rendu du XIV Congrès International Contre L'Alcoolism . . .* (Milan: A. Bari, 1921); *The Proceedings of the Twelfth International Congress on Alcoholism* (London, 1909), p. 40.

86. Cherrington, *Evolution*, pp. 319–20.

87. *Union Signal*, 15 Feb. 1912, p. 3. On the decline of the dispensary, see Eubanks, *Tillman's Baby*, chap. 8.

88. WWCTU, *8th Conv., 1910*, p. 182.

89. *Union Signal*, 21 Nov. 1912, p. 5; see also *White Ribbon*, May 1913, p. 40.

90. Annie Carvosso to Anna Gordon, 8 Jan. 1914, WWCTU Files.

91. *White Ribbon Signal* (Sydney), 1 Nov. 1913; *Canadian White Ribbon Tidings*, 1 Dec. 1913, p. 271; *Union Signal*, 18 Sept. 1913, p. 2.

92. *White Ribbon Signal* (Sydney), 31 Mar. 1913, p. 9.

93. WCTU of South Australia, *AR*, 1916, p. 20; *AR*, 1919, p. 22; WCTU of New South Wales, *AR*, 1916, p. 28. On Six O'Clock Closing, see Walter Phillips, "'Six O'Clock Swill,' The Introduction of Early Closing of Hotel Bars in Australia," *Historical Studies* 19 (Oct. 1980): 250–66.

94. *White Ribbon*, June 1915, p. 87.

95. *White Ribbon Signal* (Sydney), 1 Feb. 1919, p. 5.

96. *Union Signal*, 17 June 1920, pp. 4–5; 7 July 1921, p. 2.

97. BWTA, *AR*, 1918, p. 27.

98. *Union Signal*, 7 Dec. 1922, p. 10.

99. Ibid., 21 July 1921, p. 6; this euphoria is well displayed in Hardynia Norville, *A Sober South America: Prohibition for Our Twin Continent* (Evanston, Ill.: NWCTU, 1920).

100. *Union Signal*, 15 Feb. 1923, p. 4.

101. Ibid., 20 July 1922, p. 6.

102. Ibid., 25 Jan. 1923, p. 5; 30 Nov. 1922, p. 7.

103. Ibid., 30 July 1925, p. 10; 30 Nov. 1922, p. 7. On Britain, see G.P. Williams and George T. Brake, *Drink in Great Britain, 1900–1979* (London: Edsall, 1980); on Sweden, see Frånberg, "Economic Interpretation," p. 22; M. Marrus, "The Liquor Control System in Sweden," in Raymond G. McCarthy, *Drinking and Intoxication: Selected Readings in Social Attitudes and Controls* (Glencoe, Ill.: Free Press, 1959), pp. 347–55; and the extensive correspondence, roll 26, folders 71–73, WLAA Series, OHS; on Norway, see Karen Larsen, *A History of Norway* (Princeton: Princeton University Press, 1950), pp. 520–21; *SEAP*, 5:2027–31; on Finland, see Sakari Sariola, "Prohibition in Finland," in McCarthy, *Drinking and Intoxication*, pp. 356–63.

104. Julia Deane to Chester Rowell, 12 Dec. 1922, Chester Harvey Rowell Correspondence, Bancroft Library, University of California, Berkeley.

105. Rowell to Deane, 22 Dec. 1922, ibid.

106. *Union Signal*, 20 Aug. 1925, p. 4; and, more generally, ibid., 1 Sept. 1928, p. 4.

107. Ibid., 25 Jan. 1923, p. 5.

108. Ibid., 30 Nov. 1922, p. 7.

109. Ibid., 27 June 1931, p. 10; 30 June 1928, p. 4; 29 Sept. 1928, p. 3.

110. Ibid., 8 Sept. 1928, p. 4.

111. Ibid., p. 8.

112. Ibid.

113. Ibid., 25 Apr. 1931, p. 5.

114. Ibid., 4 July 1931, p. 7; "Outlines of a New Swedish Liquor Legislation," pp. 1–6, box 26, folder 73, WLAA Series, OHS.

115. *Union Signal*, 8 Sept. 1928, p. 4; 27 June 1931, p. 10. For Hercod's arguments, see *Union Signal*, 25 Apr. 1931, p. 6.

116. *Union Signal*, 25 Apr. 1931, p. 6, and 4 July 1931, p. 7.

117. See John C. Burnham, "New Perspectives on the Prohibition 'Experiment' of the 1920s," *Journal of Social History* 2 (1968): 51–68; K. Austin Kerr, *Organized for Prohibition*, pp. 276–77.

118. *Union Signal*, 1 Sept. 1928, p. 4.

119. *White Ribbon Signal* (Sydney), 12 June 1927, p. 6; *SEAP*, 5:2031; Larsen, *History of Norway*, p. 521; *Union Signal*, 15 May 1926, p. 5.

120. *Union Signal*, 23 Jan. 1932, p. 8.

121. NWCTU, *AR*, 1932, p. 78.

122. Jorma Kallenautio, "Finnish Prohibition as an Economic Policy Issue," *Scandinavian Economic History Review* 29 (1981): 203–25; Ann Pinson, "Temperance, Prohibition, and Politics in Nineteenth Century Iceland" (Paper presented at the International Conference on the Social History of Alcohol, Berkeley, Calif., Jan. 1984).

123. *California White Ribbon Ensign*, Aug. 1934, p. 8.

124. Ibid., Jan. 1940, p. 6; July–Aug. 1940, p. 4; May 1948, p. 3.

Epilogue

1. *California White Ribbon Ensign*, Dec. 1939, p. 3.

2. Ibid.

3. Ibid.

4. Works on the 1920s are legion. See, especially, Henry May, "Shifting Perspectives on the 1920s," *Mississippi Valley Historical Review* 43 (1956): 405–27; Burl Noggle, "The Twenties: A New Historiographical Frontier," *Journal of American History* 53 (1966): 299–314; Paul Carter, *Another Part of the Twenties* (New York: Columbia University Press, 1977).

5. F. Scott Fitzgerald, *The Great Gatsby* (New York: Scribner's, 1925); Paula Fass, *The Damned and the Beautiful* (New York: Oxford University Press, 1977); John C. Burnham, "New Perspectives on the Prohibition 'Experiment' of the

1920s," *Journal of Social History* 2 (1968): 51–68. It was, of course, established long ago that many of these changes had begun before 1914. See James R. McGovern, "The American Woman's Pre–World War I Freedom in Manners and Morals," *Journal of American History* 55 (1968): 315–33.

6. David Kyvig, "Women against Prohibition," *American Quarterly* 28 (1976): 465–82.

7. Stuart Ewen, *Captains of Consciousness* (New York: McGraw-Hill, 1977). See, on the cinema, Lary May, *Screening Out the Past* (New York: Oxford University Press, 1980); and Robert Sklar, *Movie-Made America* (New York: Random House, 1975). However, these issues are in fact better articulated in a recent study of American cinema penetration abroad (Diane Collins, *Hollywood Down Under* [Sydney: Angus and Robertson, 1987]).

8. Lucy Bland, "Purity, Motherhood, Pleasure or Threat? Definitions of Female Sexuality 1900–1970s," in Sue Cartledge and Joanna Ryan, eds., *Sex and Love: New Thoughts on Old Contradictions* (London: Women's Press, 1983), pp. 8–29.

9. On American women in the 1920s, see Estelle B. Freedman, "The New Woman: Changing Views of Women in the 1920s," *Journal of American History* 61 (1974): 372–93; William H. Chafe, *The American Woman: Her Changing Social, Economic, and Political Roles, 1920–1970* (New York: Oxford University Press, 1972); Nancy Cott, *The Grounding of Modern Feminism* (New Haven: Yale University Press, 1987); Leila Rupp, "Reflections on Twentieth Century American Women's History," *Reviews in American History* 9 (1981): 275–84.

10. Cott, *Grounding of Modern Feminism.*

11. On the competition from clubwomen, see Virginia Pride to Anna Gordon, 29 Nov. 1913, WWCTU Files; Mary Livermore in *White Ribbon*, Oct. 1904, p. 164; Karen Blair, *The Clubwoman as Feminist: True Womanhood Redefined* (New York: Holmes and Meier, 1980). Blair notes (p. 37) that the international dimensions of this work were very weakly developed prior to 1914 at least. She does not, however, look at the 1920s in this study. On the country women's movement and the Women's Institutes, see Neve Scarborough, *History of the Associated Country Women of the World* (London: Associated Country Women of the World, 1953); Carol Bacchi, "Divided Allegiances: The Response of Farm and Labour Women to Suffrage," in Linda Kealey, ed., *A Not Unreasonable Claim: Women and Reform in Canada, 1880s–1920s* (Toronto: Women's Press, 1979), pp. 103–4; R. Erikson, B. Gibbins, and L. Higgins, *Her Name Is Woman* (Perth: Country Women's Association of Western Australia, 1974), pp. 97–102; *The National British Women's Temperance Association: Its Origins and Progress: A Jubilee Sketch* (London: NBWTA, 1926), p. 57; I am indebted to Professor John Weaver of McMaster University for suggestions on the role of the Women's Institutes. On the YWCA, see Nancy Boyd, *Emissaries: The Overseas Work of the American YWCA, 1895–1970* (New York: Woman's Press, 1986).

12. Antonio Gramsci, *Selections from the Prison Notebooks*, ed. Quentin Hoare and Geoffrey Nowell Smith (New York: International Publishers, 1971), pp. 302–5. Among supporters abroad, typical of progressive sentiments is Robert B. S. Hammond, *With One Voice: A Study in Prohibition in U.S.A.* (Sydney: New South Wales Alliance, [c.1920]).

13. Gramsci, *Prison Notebooks*, p. 350; James Joll, *Gramsci* (London: Fontana-/Collins, 1977), pp. 108–9.

14. William Appleman Williams, "The Legend of Isolationism in the 1920's," *Science and Society* 18 (1954): 1–20, touched off this long and important debate.

15. Gramsci, *Prison Notebooks*, p. 286.

16. See, for example, William E. "Pussyfoot" Johnson to Ernest H. Cherrington, 2 Oct. 1920, roll 22, folder 36, WLAA Series, OHS. See also clipping from *American Issue*, 28 May 1921, ibid.; Taraknath Das, "Progress of Prohibition in India," roll 22, folder 37, ibid. See also, on the broader American sympathies for the nationalists, Gary Hess, *America Encounters India, 1941–1947* (Baltimore: Johns Hopkins University Press, 1971), chap. 1.

17. Wendell Willkie, *One World* (New York: Simon and Schuster, 1943); William Roger Louis, *Imperialism at Bay, 1941–1945* (Oxford: Oxford University Press, 1977), pp. 7–10.

18. Emily Rosenberg, *Spreading the American Dream: American Economic and Cultural Expansion, 1890–1945* (New York: Hill and Wang, 1982), chap. 6; Frank Ninkovich, *The Diplomacy of Ideas: United States Foreign Policy and Cultural Relations, 1938–1950* (Cambridge: Cambridge University Press, 1981), esp. chap. 1.

19. William T. Stead, *The Americanization of the World, or the Trend of the Twentieth Century* (1902; reprint, New York: Garland, 1972).

20. *California White Ribbon Ensign*, Mar. 1946, p. 3; Apr. 1946, p. 2; Katharine Bushnell to Anne K. Martin, 12 Aug., 2 Sept., 7 Sept. 1943, Anne K. Martin Papers, Bancroft Library, University of California, Berkeley; *World's WCTU White Ribbon Bulletin*, Oct.–Nov. 1950.

Index

of, 198, 199–200; revenues of, 162–63, 168–69; social, 247–48, 252; technology and, 27; theories of, 146; Willard favors, 27, 186. *See also* Alcohol exports to colonial world; Cultural imperialism; "Native races"

India: alcohol and imperial rule in, 163–64; Bengal crusade, 22–23; contagious diseases acts in, attacked, 197, 198, 199–201; diversity of, 106; Eurasians in, 199; example of used in Philippines, 214, 217; foreign drinking in, 70; indigenous drinks in, 154; inspection system returns in, 203–4, 211–12; liquor imports, 158; liquor revenues in, 162–63, 166; missionary strategy in, 85; nationalism in, 164–68; opium in, 147, 149, 150, 162; temperate population of, 157; WCTU support in, 74, 164; WWCTU work in, 109–10, 112

International Bureau against Alcoholism, 282

International Camp Meetings, 22

International Congress against Alcoholism: in 1885, 41; in 1890, 152–53; in 1897 and 1903, 51; in 1909 and 1913, 275

International Council of Women, 20, 115

International Country Women's Association, 287

Internationalism, 3–9, 11–34 passim, 35–37, 54–55; and American expansionism, 288–89; changing nature of, 277; impact of World War I on, 186–88; in 1920s, 287; and peace, 179–81, 184–85; prohibition stimulates, 255–56; socialist sympathies and, 242–43, 251; suffrage issue and, 221–22, 234–35; women and, 35–36, 115, 140. *See also* Cultural hegemony

International Reform Bureau, 160, 161

International Temperance Convention (Melbourne), 19

International Woman's Christian Temperance Union, 20, 243

International Woman Suffrage Alliance, 3, 20, 221, 234–35

Ireland, 22, 65

Irish, Isabella, 64, 65, 66

Islam, 100, 103, 105, 141, 255

Italy, 70, 75, 102, 202–3

Ives, Ella Gilbert, 117, 120–21

Jackson, Kate, 103, 116

Japan: American impact on, 74–75; compared with China, 106; geisha issue in, 110, 219–20, 235; peace issue in, 171, 189; scientific temperance instruction in, 51; WCTU growth in, 62–63; WWCTU strategy in, 52, 85

Jarlsberg, Countess Ida, 203

Jobson, Georgia M., 118

Johannsdottir, Olifia, 48, 85, 87

Johnson, Eli T., 23

Johnson, Lydia, 86

Johnson, Mary Coffin, 20–22, 23, 85

Johnson, William E., 260, 288

Jones, Helen, 225

Journal of Humanity, 13

Judson, Adoniram, 89

Judson, Ann, 89

Kearney, Belle, 87–88, 90, 94, 128, 143

Kellogg-Briand Pact, 287

Kenney, Anne, 64

Kenya, 154, 156–57

Kercher, Alice, 177

Kerr, K. Austin, 38

Key, Ellen, 67, 129–30

Khama (king of Bechuanaland), 158

Kirk, Marie, 49, 57, 73, 208

Knights of Labor, 242

Koren, John, 262

Kraditor, Aileen, 350–51 (n. 27)

Krikorian, Rebecca, 143

Krishna, Sir Bhalchandra, 165

alism, 33; and prohibition, 273; and purity, 192–93, 195, 196
Polyglot Petition, 39–43, 45, 54, 202, 221
Populists (People's party), 30, 259
Powderly, Terence, 133
Price, Emma S., 166–67, 168
Pride, Virginia, 72
Primrose League, 79
Prior, Dagmar, 278
Prohibition: in Africa, 161, 255, 257; American drive for, 275; and attitudes toward labor, 251; Carlisle advocates, 270, 272, 274; and cultural expansionism, 255–57, 288; and direct veto in Britain, 266; effectiveness of, 282; 1890s crisis in, 258–60; Europe and, 262, 279–80; Gandhi on, 167–68; impact of U.S. enactment of on other countries, 274, 275–76, 278; international complications of for WCTU, 261, 262–63; international decline of, 281–82; isolation of United States on issue of, 282, 283; liquor imports threaten, 280; and military canteen, 184; political ascendancy of in 1920s, 282; and Polyglot, 43; repeal of, 283; shift to support for as orthodoxy in WWCTU, 274–75; and suffrage, 234; temperance opponents of, in Britain, 265, 269–70; wine industry and, 279–80; WCTU peace work eclipsed by, 189–90. *See also* Liquor control
Prohibition party, 30, 252, 259
Prostitution, licensed: in India, 198–99, 201, 203–5, 212, 217; international comparisons, 195, 196–97; in Philippines, 213–17; U.S. versions of, 195–96. *See also* Contagious diseases acts; Purity, social
Puerto Rico, 185
Pugh, Ester, 52
Purity, social: and Butler's abolitionism, 194, 203, 210–11; crusade for

begins in United States, 193, 194; and imperialism, 212–18; importance of in WCTU, 191–92; international aspects of, 28, 191, 193–94, 197, 198, 206–7, 210; issue of in India, 198–202; and moral pollution, 192–93, 195, 196, 197; and peace issue, 171, 184; pragmatism and, 193; split over, 202–10; WWCTU campaign for launched, 194–95, 197. *See also* Prostitution, licensed
Purlington, Louise, 25, 37, 106, 110, 117, 120–21

Quakers, 172, 176
Quebec, 131
Queensland, 138, 225, 228
Quinton, Amelia Stone, 22

Racism: WCTU and, 101–2, 185, 199–200, 219, 321 (n. 81)
Raines Law, 264, 267
Ramabai, Pandita, 102, 110, 141
Ranney, Ruth, 40, 103, 109
Raymond, Jerome H., 109
Rechabites, Independent Order of, 18
Reed, Lodie, 51
Reeves, W. Pember: *State Experiments in Australia and New Zealand*, 228
Roberts, Lord, 31, 201
Robertson, Christine, 124, 161, 162
Rooke, Jessie, 208
Roosevelt, Franklin D., 289
Roosevelt, Theodore, 151, 155, 162, 216
Root, Elihu, 162, 216
Rorabaugh, W. J., 14
Rotary, 288
Rowell, Chester, 279–80
Rowntree, Joseph, 270, 273; *The Temperance Problem and Social Reform*, 269
Royal Commission on Liquor Licensing Laws, 265, 266–67

Index

Index